The New Middle Ea

The New Middle East is one of the first comprehensive books written by prominent scholars of the region and of comparative politics to critically examine the Arab popular uprisings of 2010–2012. While these uprisings prompted a number of cursory publications, this volume contains meticulous and thoughtful reflections on the causes, drivers and effects of these seminal events on the internal, regional and international politics of the Middle East and North Africa. Although specific conditions in individual countries that have experienced large-scale popular mobilizations are investigated, they are neither treated in isolation nor separated from broader developments in the region. Instead, the authors highlight connections between individual case studies and systemic conditions throughout the Arab arena. These include the crisis of political authority, the failure of economic development and new genres of mobilization and activism, especially communication technology and youth movements. The careful analysis and reflection on the prospects for democratic change in the region ensures the book will have an immediate and enduring appeal.

Fawaz A. Gerges is a Professor of International Relations at the London School of Economics and Political Science, where he directs the Middle East Centre. Gerges is the author of several acclaimed books, including *Obama and the Middle East: The End of America's Moment?*; *The Rise and Fall of Al-Qaeda* and *The Far Enemy: Why Jihad Went Global*. He has written extensively on Arab politics and the international relations of the Middle East. His articles have appeared in *Foreign Affairs, Foreign Policy, Newsweek*, the *New York Times*, the *Washington Post*, the *Guardian* and the *Independent*.

The New Middle East

Protest and Revolution in the Arab World

Edited by
FAWAZ A. GERGES
Middle East Centre, London School of Economics and Political Science

CAMBRIDGE
UNIVERSITY PRESS

CAMBRIDGE
UNIVERSITY PRESS

32 Avenue of the Americas, New York, NY 10013-2473, USA

Cambridge University Press is part of the University of Cambridge.

It furthers the University's mission by disseminating knowledge in the pursuit of education, learning and research at the highest international levels of excellence.

www.cambridge.org
Information on this title: www.cambridge.org/9781107616882

© Cambridge University Press 2014

First published 2014

A catalog record for this publication is available from the British Library.

Library of Congress Cataloging in Publication data
Gerges, Fawaz A., 1958–
The new Middle East : protest and revolution in the Arab World / Fawaz A. Gerges.
London School of Economics.
pages   cm.
Includes bibliographical references and index.
ISBN 978-1-107-02863-0 (hardback) – ISBN 978-1-107-61688-2 (paperback)
1. Arab Spring, 2010–   2. Protest movements – Middle East – History – 21st century.
3. Protest movements – Arab countries – History – 21st century.   4. Middle East –
Economic conditions – 21st century.   5. Arab countries – Economic conditions – 21st
century.   6. Revolutions – Middle East – History – 21st century.   7. Revolutions – Arab
countries – History – 21st century.   I. Title.
JQ1850.A91G374   2013
909'.097492708312–dc23   2013018643

ISBN 978-1-107-02863-0 Hardback
ISBN 978-1-107-61688-2 Paperback

Contents

List of Figures and Tables

Figures

Tables

Contributors

Sadik Al-Azm is Professor Emeritus of Modern European Philosophy at the University of Damascus and is currently a Fellow at the Käte Hamburger Institute at the University of Bonn. He was a Visiting Professor at Princeton University until 2008. His area of specialisation is the philosophy of Immanuel Kant with a more current emphasis on the Islamic world and its relationship to the West. He has also contributed to the discourse on Orientalism. The most recent of his long list of publications is an English translation of *Al-Naqd al-dati ba'd al-hazimah* (*Self-Criticism after the Defeat*) (2011).

Madawi Al-Rasheed is Professor of Anthropology of Religion at King's College, London. She has worked on Saudi history, society, politics and religion, Arab migration to Britain, Christian minorities in the Arab world, the Islamist movement and Gulf transnational connections. Her most recent publications include *Contesting the Saudi State: Islamic Voices from a New Generation* (2007); *Kingdom without Borders: Saudi Arabia's Political, Religious and Media Frontiers* (2008); *A History of Saudi Arabia* (2010); *Demystifying the Caliphate: Historical Memory and Contemporary Contexts* (with Carool Kersten and Marat Shterin) (2012); and *A Most Masculine State: Gender, Religion and Politics in Saudi Arabia* (2013).

Atiaf Alwazir is a researcher and development consultant working with civil society organizations in the Middle East and North Africa on programmes related to social justice. She also blogs at 'womanfromyemen', providing analysis on the situation in Yemen. She is currently working on several assignments in research and her work has been featured in several outlets including the Arab Reform Initiative, *Jadaliyya*, *Foreign Policy*, Project on Middle East Democracy, *Al-Akhbar* and the *Guardian*.

Lisa Anderson was appointed president of The American University in Cairo in January 2011. A specialist on politics in the Middle East and North Africa, Anderson served as the university's provost from 2008 to 2010. Anderson has served as the James T. Shotwell Professor of International Relations at Columbia University and is the former dean of the School of International and Public Affairs at Columbia. Her publications include *Pursuing Truth, Exercising Power: Social Science and Public Policy in the Twenty-First Century* (2003) and *The State and Social Transformation in Tunisia and Libya, 1830–1980* (1986). Anderson is past president of the Middle East Studies Association and past chair of the board of the Social Science Research Council.

Mohammed Ayoob is University Distinguished Professor of International Relations at Michigan State University. He is the author of *The Many Faces of Political Islam* (2008). His edited volume, *Assessing the War on Terror*, is forthcoming. He is currently working on a book *Will the Middle East Implode?* scheduled for publication in early 2014.

Federica Bicchi is Lecturer in the International Relations of Europe in the Department of International Relations at the London School of Economics and Political Science, where she teaches European Foreign Policy, with a special emphasis on the Middle East and Arab-Israeli relations. She holds a PhD in Political Science from the European University Institute in Florence. Her research interests focus on EU foreign policy towards its southern neighbourhood, on which she has published, inter alia, *European Foreign Policy Making towards the Mediterranean* (2007), as well as on the role of information exchanges within the EU foreign policy system.

Valerie Bunce is Professor of Government and the Aaron Binenkorb Chair of International Studies at Cornell University. She received her doctorate in Political Science from the University of Michigan and taught at Northwestern University and the University of Zagreb. She is the co-author, most recently, of *Defeating Authoritarian Leaders in Postcommunist Countries* (2011). She is a former president of the Slavic, East European and Eurasian Studies Association and Vice President of the American Political Science Association. In 2010, she was elected to the American Academy of Arts and Sciences.

John Chalcraft is a Reader in the History and Politics of Empire/Imperialism at the London School of Economics and Political Science. Previous posts include a Lectureship at the University of Edinburgh and a Research Fellowship at Gonville and Caius College, Cambridge. His research focuses on history from below in the Middle East. He is the author of *The Striking Cabbies of Cairo and Other Stories: Crafts and Guilds in Egypt, 1863–1914* (2004) and *The Invisible Cage: Syrian Migrant Workers in Lebanon* (2009). He is currently writing a book on transnational popular politics and protest movements in the making of the modern Arab world, focusing on how hegemony is made and unmade 'from below'.

Kristian Coates Ulrichsen is the Baker Institute Fellow for Kuwait and an Associate Fellow of Chatham House. He was formerly a Research Fellow in the Department of Government at the London School of Economics and Political Science. His research focuses on the changing international relations and international political economy of the Gulf states, on political and economic reformulation and on the rise of new security threats and challenges. He is the author of *Insecure Gulf: The End of Certainty and the Transition to the Post-Oil Era* (2011) and the editor of *The Transformation of the Gulf: Politics, Economics and the Global Order* (2011) and *The Political Economy of Arab Gulf States* (2012).

Juan Cole is the Richard P. Mitchell Collegiate Professor of History at the University of Michigan and Director of its Center for Middle Eastern and North African Studies. He is the author of numerous articles and books on the Middle East and South Asia. His most recent are *Napoleon's Egypt* (2007) and *Engaging the Muslim World* (2009). Cole is a public intellectual and a frequent guest on television and radio, and he maintains the blog *Informed Comment*.

Philippe Droz-Vincent is an Assistant Professor of Political Science in International Relations and Comparative Politics. He is the author of *The Middle East: Authoritarian Regimes and Stalled Societies* (2004) and numerous articles, including 'Authoritarianism, revolutions, armies and Arab regime transitions' (*The International Spectator*, June 2011) and 'A return of armies to the forefront of Arab politics?' (Working Paper 11/21, Istituto Affari Internazionali, Rome, 2011.)

Anne Gough is a Researcher on food sovereignty, farming systems and landscapes. She is currently based in Beirut. After working on small farms in the United States, she became dedicated to issues of food justice and agrarian livelihoods. With Dr Rami Zurayk, she has co-authored a monograph on the use of food as a tool of control, which is currently being prepared for publication.

Ali Kadri is a Senior Research Fellow at the National University of Singapore. Kadri was a visiting Fellow in the Department of International Development at the London School of Economics and Political Science and Head of the Economic Analysis Section at the United Nations regional office for Western Asia. He is currently conducting research on the political economy of the Arab world.

Karim Mezran is a Senior Fellow at the Atlantic Council's Rafik Hariri Center for the Middle East and Adjunct Professor at the School of Advanced International Studies, Johns Hopkins University. He was an assistant professor of political science at the John Cabot University and acted as a visiting professor at the Libera Università per gli Studi Sociali in Rome. His most recent publications are (with Alice Alunni) 'Power shifts in the Arab spring: A work in progress' (*Bologna Center Journal of International Affairs*, 2012), *Libia: Fine o rinascita di una nazione?* (ed. with Arturo Varvelli 2012) and 'Libya's wars' (*The American Interest*, September/October 2011).

Roger Owen is A.J. Meyer Professor of Middle East History at Harvard University. His main research interests are the economic and political history of the Middle East since 1800 and theories of imperialism, including military occupations. Professor Owen's publications include *Lord Cromer: Victorian Imperialist: Edwardian Proconsul* (2004); *State, Power and Politics in the Making of the Modern Middle East* revised version (2004); and, with Şevket Pamuk, *A History of the Middle East Economies in the 20th Century* (1999).

William B. Quandt holds the Edward R. Stettinius Chair in the Department of Politics at the University of Virginia where he teaches courses on the Middle East and American foreign policy. He has been a Senior Fellow in the Foreign Policy Studies Program at the Brookings Institution and served as a staff member on the National Security Council (1972–1974, 1977–1979). Dr Quandt has also worked at the University of Pennsylvania, the Rand Corporation, UCLA and MIT. His publications include *Peace Process: American Diplomacy and the Arab-Israeli Conflict Since 1967*, third edition (2005); *Between Ballots and Bullets: Algeria's Transition from Authoritarianism* (1998) and *The United States and Egypt: An Essay on Policy for the 1990s* (1990).

Avi Shlaim is a Fellow of the British Academy and an Emeritus Professor of International Relations at the University of Oxford. He is the author of *The Iron Wall: Israel and the Arab World* (2000); *Lion of Jordan: King Hussein's Life in War and Peace* (2007) and *Israel and Palestine: Reappraisals, Revisions, Refutations* (2009).

John T. Sidel is the Sir Patrick Gillam Professor of Comparative and International Politics at the London School of Economics and Political Science. He is the author of *Capital, Coercion, and Crime: Bossism in the Philippines* (1999); *Philippine Politics and Society in the Twentieth Century: Colonial Legacies, Post-Colonial Trajectories* (with Eva-Lotta Hedman 2000); *Riots, Pogroms, Jihad: Religious Violence in Indonesia* (2006) and *The Islamist Threat in Southeast Asia: A Reassessment* (2007).

Charles Tripp is Professor of Politics with reference to the Middle East at the School of Oriental and African Studies, University of London, and a Fellow of the British Academy. He is the author of *Islam and the Moral Economy: The Challenge of Capitalism* (2006) and *A History of Iraq* (2007) and co-author of *Iran and Iraq at War* (1988). His most recent book is *The Power and the People: Paths of Resistance in the Middle East* (2013).

Gabriele vom Bruck is a Senior Lecturer in Anthropology at the School of Oriental and African Studies, University of London. She has conducted extensive research in Yemen and published on elites, religious movements, consumption, gender and photography. She is the author of *Islam, Memory and Morality in Yemen* (2005) and co-editor of *The Anthropology of Names and Naming* (2006).

Benjamin Wiacek is a freelance journalist based in Sana'a since September 2010. He has more than five years of experience working in the Middle East and North Africa with publications in numerous newspapers including *Liberation*, *Egypt Independent* and the *Yemen Times*, in addition to contributions to academic books. Benjamin co-founded the first news web site in French about Yemen, La Voix du Yémen. He also reports on television and radio for various outlets including France 24, RFI, TV5 Monde, BBC and CBC/Radio Canada.

Sami Zubaida is Emeritus Professor of Politics and Sociology at Birkbeck College, University of London, and Research Associate of the London Middle East Institute at the School of Oriental and African Studies (SOAS). He has held visiting positions in Cairo, Istanbul, Beirut, Aix-en-Provence, Paris and Berkeley and at NYU, and he has written and lectured widely on themes of religion, culture, law and politics in the Middle East, with particular attention to Egypt, Iran, Iraq and Turkey. His other work is on food history and culture, and he is Professorial Research Associate of the Food Studies Centre at SOAS. His books include *Islam, the People and the State: Political Ideas and Movements in the Middle East*, 3rd edition (2009); *A Taste of Thyme: Culinary Cultures of the Middle East*, 2nd edition (edited, with R Tapper, 2000); *Law and Power in the Islamic World* (2003) and *Beyond Islam: A New Understanding of the Middle East* (2011).

Rami Zurayk is Professor in the Faculty of Agricultural and Food Sciences and the Director of the Interfaculty Graduate Environmental Sciences Program at the American University of Beirut. A soil scientist by training, he has worked in rural development in several countries of the Arab world. He publishes a weekly column on food, farming and environment in the Arabic daily *Al Akhbar*. He has authored several books and hundreds of articles. His latest book, *Food, Farming and Freedom: Sowing the Arab Spring*, was published in 2011.

Acknowledgments

The book is the first major publication of the Middle East Centre (MEC) at LSE. Established in late 2010, the Centre promotes innovative interdisciplinary research on the societies, economies, polities and international relations of the region. This book could not have seen the light of the day without the intellectual and material support of many colleagues and friends. First and foremost, I want to thank all the contributors, some of whom travelled from afar, who critically reflected on key questions raised by the popular uprisings. The book is the fruit of their collective insights. Next, the team at the MEC organized participants' individual lectures and the subsequent workshop. Their tireless labours facilitated the production of this book. In particular, I owe special thanks to Robert Lowe who copyedited all the chapters and organized the notes and editorial changes. He went beyond the call of duty in his assistance and his professional touch improved the quality of the book. I am also appreciative of the support that Dania Akkad and Ribale Sleiman Haidar provided throughout the book's conception and birth, and in sourcing the cover image. I hope that my family forgives me for spending countless hours away while working on the book.

Finally, as always, edited books are challenging projects to both editor and contributors. I have spent considerable time and energy putting the book together, treating the project as edited books were once regarded in British academic circles – assembling leading specialists in a field to critically examine the topic of the century or the hour. I hope that the result shows the benefits of joint scholarly minds critically reflecting on the momentous events shaping the destiny of the modern Middle East.

Fawaz A. Gerges
London School of Economics and Political Science
June 2013

Introduction

A Rupture

Fawaz A. Gerges[*]

A psychological and epistemological rupture has occurred in the Arab Middle East that has shaken the authoritarian order to its very foundation and introduced a new language and a new era of contentious politics and revolutions. A revolutionary moment of political emancipation and self-determination challenges conventional ways and dominant thinking about the region, such as the durability and resilience of authoritarianism and the ability of autocratic rulers to police the status quo. There is a reinvigorated academic interest in bottom-up politics, workers, ordinary people, social movements, public space and resistance, the decay of hegemony, the crisis of authority and the role of agency in general – a refreshing departure from the past fixation with top-down politics and the elite.[1]

---

[*] I would like to thank several colleagues who critically read this essay and provided me with their feedback: Charles Tripp, Robert Lowe, John Chalcraft, John Sidel, Tariq Tell, and Mohamed Ayoob. Of course, whatever shortcomings remain, they are mine and mine alone.
[1] Charles Tripp, *The Power and the People: Paths of Resistance in the Middle East* (New York: Cambridge University Press, 2013); Karima Khalil, *Messages from Tahrir* (Cairo: American University in Cairo Press, 2011); Salwa Ismail, 'The Syrian uprising: Imagining and performing the nation , *Studies in Ethnicity and Nationalism*, 11/3 (2011); Asef Bayat, *Life as Politics: How Ordinary People Change the Middle East* (Stanford: Stanford University Press, 2010); Joel Beinin and Frédéric Vairel eds., *Social Movements, Mobilization, and Contestation in the Middle East and North Africa* (Stanford: Stanford University Press, 2011); N. Marzouki, 'From people to citizens in Tunisia', *Middle East Report*, 259/41 (Summer 2011); and John Chalcraft, 'Horizontalism in the Egyptian revolutionary process', *Middle East Report* 262 (Spring 2012).

Far from over, this revolutionary moment is still unfolding before our eyes, an open-ended struggle that will play out in the coming years. If history serves as a guide, revolutionary moments – as opposed to revolutions that swiftly overturn a society's social, economic and political structure, all within a relatively short time frame – will take time and space to produce a revolutionary outcome. In the process, they might be aborted, hijacked, co-opted, institutionalized, or face setbacks. Therefore, it is critical to distinguish between two processes: (1) reconstructing the conditions and settings that led to the overthrow of the Zine El Abidine Ben Ali regime in Tunisia and of the Hosni Mubarak regime in Egypt; and (2) examining transition from political authoritarianism in various countries and the prospects of sustaining the cohesiveness and unity of the masses of protesters as the struggle turns to building a governing coalition, a new system for allocating power.

The shift from a revolutionary moment to a constitutional moment is fraught with uncertainties, tensions, and differing conceptions of the political. In Tunisia, Egypt, perhaps in Libya, and maybe even eventually in Syria, one might dare to hope, we might be seeing transitions from authoritarian regimes to democracy – in other words, 'regime transitions' along the lines familiar to scholars of Southern Europe in the 1970s, Latin America and parts of Asia in the 1980s, and Eastern Europe and other parts of Asia and Africa in the 1990s and 2000s, rather than revolutions per se.

Despite uncertainties and risks about democratic change, what has transpired in the Arab world is a watershed comparable to transformative historical developments like the French Revolution and the uprisings in Eastern Europe and Indonesia – and to a lesser extent in Latin America – in the 1980s and the 1990s. What happened in all these cases is that the agenda of political and economic possibilities suddenly expanded. It is critical to recognize the significance of this revolutionary chapter in the modern history of the Middle East and the creative conceptions and articulations of resistance that shattered the system of domination, particularly the popular roots of these uprisings amongst the urban and rural poor. Regardless of what the outcome(s) will be, this revolutionary moment has turned the wheels of history in a direction of progress. Given the fragility of institutions in the Arab arena and the structural socio-economic and political crisis there, the social and political turmoil that has engulfed the region after the Arab uprisings is natural and to be expected - part of the painful birth pangs of a new world.

Signposts and Worldviews

It is worth capturing the heartbeat of this revolutionary moment. Bread, freedom, social justice, and human dignity (*al-karama*) were the rallying cries that echoed from *mayadeen al-tahrir* (liberation squares) in Tunisia, Egypt, Libya, Yemen, Bahrain, Syria, and elsewhere. Millions of Arabs revolted against *al-istibdad* (repression), defying fear and bullets and daring to call for effective citizenship and more representative and egalitarian political and economic systems. Arabs across national boundaries united in their opposition to injustice and political authoritarianism. Taking ownership of public space, symbols of liberation from colonial rule, Arabs from different ideological persuasions, imaginations, and sensibilities 'performed the nation' as united citizens, in a quest for political emancipation and civil and economic empowerment. The will of the people and electoral legitimacy echoed as a call for action, a marked departure from previous waves of social protests and discontent in Arab states.[2] Amidst this effervescence, new stories are told and new narratives of resistance, hope and determination are articulated. Decades of political authoritarianism and repression, coupled with a development failure, neither extinguished the flame of resistance nor enforced authoritarian rule. The public reclaimed effective agency and regained its voice, which had been stifled and muffled by the elite.

The authoritarian order was far from durable, as the dominant narrative had it. Instead, it crumbled under the blows of popular resistance and cleavages within ruling coalitions, particularly forming around the military institutions. In Egypt and Tunisia, popular mobilization has been enabled if not impelled by splits within the regimes, especially in the context of ongoing succession struggles if not crises, and has been championed or in due course quarterbacked by the urban middle class and business elements, in a pattern familiar from other transitions elsewhere. In Tunisia and Egypt, as the public revolt gained momentum, senior echelons of the military sacrificed Ben Ali and Mubarak, respectively, in favour

---

[2] Al-Ghad Al-Ordoniya, 'Slogans of the Arab Spring Confirmed the Unity of the Arabs' [in Arabic], *Al-Ma'had Al-Arabi*, 21 April 2012, http://www.airss.net/site/2012/04/21/; Wa'i Al-Talabah, 'Youth of Arabic Spring Spread Slogans of Arab Revolutions in Rap Songs' [in Arabic], *Al-Talabah*, 15 February 2012, http://www.altalabah.com/index.php/ 2010–06–17–23–59–23/2010–06–18–01–31–53/4226–2012–02–15–15–23–42.html; El-Nashra, 'Hassan Mneimneh: The Civil State is the Arab Spring Slogan' [in Arabic], *El-Nashra*, 31 March 2012, http://www.elnashra.com/news/show/457357/. See also Juan Cole's contribution (Chapter 3) to this volume.

of their institutional and economic interests. In Libya and Yemen, the situation was more complex because the armies splintered along opposition and regime lines. In contrast, the security apparatus in Syria, including the core of the armed forces, has remained loyal to President Bashar al-Assad, thus prolonging the ferocious battle between the opposition and the regime. Saudi Arabia and the United Arab Emirates intervened militarily in neighbouring Bahrain to assist in crushing the uprising and rescuing the royal family.[3]

Despite important differences and specificities of the various uprisings, a unifying thread runs through all of them: a call for dignity, empowerment, political citizenship, social justice, and taking back the state from presidents-for-life, as well as from their families and crony capitalists who hijacked it. This has been a call for representative government and social equity and justice. From Tunisia to Egypt, from Libya to Yemen, Bahrain and Syria, the slogans, songs and street art of protesters testify to their collective psychology and worldview, one anchored in freedom from want and oppression and desire for equality. *Silmiya* (peaceful), not *Islamiya* (Islamic state), was a common theme of the uprisings even when the regimes unleashed their thugs to terrorize protesters. In Libya and Syria, respectively, force deployed by the Qaddafi and Assad regimes transformed largely peaceful revolts into armed struggles.[4]

On the whole, demonstrators behaved in a dignified manner, displaying a sense of solidarity with one another, a commitment to principled action and unity of purpose and ranks. While authoritarian rulers sought to drive a wedge between various communities and fragment the public, for the most part protesters performed the nation and exhibited a sense

---

3 Political scientists have surprisingly little to offer when addressing the issue of who defects and when: Djazairess, 'The Egyptian Army Abandons Mubarak and Declares Legitimacy of People's Demands' [in Arabic], *Djazairess.com*, 1 February 2011, http://www.djazairess.com/ouarsenis/1697; Dunia Al-Watan, 'The Hidden Military Coup: The Tunisian Army Chose between Ben Ali Leaving or to Overthrow and Kill' [in Arabic], *Al-Watan Voice*, 19 January 2011, http://www.alwatanvoice.com/arabic/news/2011/01/19/166463.html.

4 Adil Latifeh, 'The Arabic Spring between Peaceful Transition and Decisive Bloody Destruction', *Al-Jazeera*, 4 September 2012, http://www.aljazeera.net/analysis/pages/da49d1da-84cb-47f9-a7e5-9ac2f9ffc024; Dia' Al-Issa, 'The Peacefulness of the Arab Spring Revolutions' [in Arabic], *Akhbar al-Yom*, 12 September 2012, http://www.akhbaralyom.net/articles.php?lng=arabic&id=69298; Jadaliyya, 'Syria Is Witnessing a Peaceful Popular Revolt for Freedom and Dignity' [in Arabic], *Jadaliyya Reports*, 8 July 2011, http://www.jadaliyya.com/pages/index/2090/; Al-Jazeera, 'Continuing of Peaceful Demonstrations in Syria' [in Arabic], *Al-Jazeera*, 14 September 2012, http://www.aljazeera.net/programs/pages/5cb4881c-7b5b-48d2-9953-a23e8405d8e3.

of maturity and cosmopolitanism that defied segmentation and common stereotypes. In Egypt and, to a lesser extent, Tunisia, a rainbow coalition – of men and women, Muslims and Christians, young revolutionaries, the poor, embattled lower and middle classes, Islamists, leftists, nationalists, and secularists – joined the protests and forced entrenched authoritarian incumbents from power.[5]

In Egypt, Muslims and Christians fraternized together and guarded each other while they prayed – a symbolic act of toleration and refutation of a clever 'regime-craft' of divide and rule.[6] To maintain backing by the Western powers, particularly the United States, Arab rulers portrayed themselves as protectors of women and Christians; the latter would suffer discrimination and persecution if the opposition, painted as Islamist and extremist, gained the upper hand. In fact, Mubarak's last years in power witnessed an escalation of religious tensions between Muslims and Christian Copts, as well as armed skirmishes. Many Egyptians believed these were orchestrated by the internal security services to divert attention from Mubarak's crisis of authority and grooming of his son, Gamal, to inherit the presidency. Based on conversations with Egyptians of all political colours in the last decade, there existed a consensus about the use and abuse of the 'religious card' as part of Mubarak's regime-craft to divide and rule, as well as to impress on its superpower patron one of the significant functions it performed at home.[7]

In a rebuff to autocratic rulers who cleverly manipulated minority issues, women played a prominent role in all the uprisings, showing how the public constituted itself in a drive to overthrow the existing order.[8] Resistance by women undermined a key aspect of regime-craft that targeted progressives and leftists at home and Westerners abroad. For example, both Ben Ali and Mubarak touted progressive legislation empowering women, contrasting their enlightened rule with their reactionary Islamist rivals. As protests gained momentum in Yemen, President Ali Abdullah Saleh tried to fragment and discredit the protestors by arguing that *ikhtilat*, the mixing of men and women, was un-Islamic. In

---

[5] Wael Ghonim, *Revolution 2.0: The power of the people is greater than the people in power* (London: Harper Collins, 2012); Nadia Idle and Alex Nunns, *Tweets from Tahrir* (New York: OR Books, 2011).

[6] Atfih Halawan, 'Mass Demonstrations Warns of Chaos and Confirms the Extent of Relationship between Muslims and Christians', [in Arabic], *Al-Ahram*, 12 March 2011, http://www.ahram.org.eg/The%20First/News/66924.aspx.

[7] Author's interviews, 2002– present.

[8] See Chapters 6 and 9 by Charles Tripp and Sami Zubaida, respectively, in this volume.

response, protestors planned a co-ed march to oppose Saleh's discrimination and divide-and-rule tactics.[9]

Although subsequently the ruling generals in Egypt seemed to have unleashed thugs who attacked women protesters, the attempt to humiliate women and divide dissidents produced opposite results; it reinforced the solidarity of the newly constituted public and caused a backlash against the perpetrators and elements of the old regimes.[10]

The newly constituted public included ideologically rival groups, such as Islamists, leftists, and nationalists, a rivalry fuelled and encouraged by the old regime. In particular, authoritarian rulers had co-opted an important segment of the Arab left and deployed it as an effective weapon against their Islamist nemeses. Before the 2011 uprisings, Arab leftists – and, to a lesser extent, nationalists – frequently expressed hostile attitudes towards Islamists, including mainstream religious-based organizations like the Muslim Brotherhood, and justified their cooperation with autocratic rulers as the lesser of the two evils.[11] Nevertheless, both camps briefly suspended their differences and joined ranks to oust the autocratic incumbents.

What distinguished the large-scale popular uprisings in 2011 from past small-scale protests was the active participation by urban and rural workers and the poor in general. That was a tipping point overlooked by the old regimes and their security apparatus, surprising even the young revolutionaries who had been agitating to mobilize the public. In Tunisia, Egypt, Yemen, and Syria, the sources of discontent lie as much in abject rural poverty, neglect and discrimination as in urban poverty belts. For the first time, the rural and urban poor turned out in large numbers and

---

9 See Chapter 13 by vom Bruck et al. in this volume. Also, Gabriele vom Bruck, 'When will Yemen's night really end? *Le Monde Diplomatique*, July 2011, http://mondediplo .com/blogs/when-will-yemen-s-night-really-end.

10 See Chapter 9 by Sami Zubaida and Chapter 13 by vom Bruck et al. Also, 'Egyptian women protestors sexually assaulted in Tahrir Square', *The Guardian*, 9 June 2012, http://www.guardian.co.uk/world/2012/jun/09/egyptian-women-protesters-sexually-assaulted; Masress, 'Colonel Al-Sisi: "Virginity Tests" were done to protect the army from possible accusations of rape', [in Arabic], *Masress.com*, 27 June 2011, http://www .masress.com/moheet/18380; Masress, 'Female Protestors confirm that they were forced to undergo virginity tests by army soldiers', [in Arabic], *Masress.com*, 29 June 2011, http://www.masress.com/gn4me/3929587; Yumna Mokhtar, 'Izza that tried to help the blue bra girl: "I shall take the soldier to court"', [in Arabic], *almasryalyoum.com*, 1 January 2012.

11 Author's interviews with leftists in various countries including Rifaat Al-Said, then chairman of Hizb al-Tajammu (National Progressive Unionist Party).

played a key role, a development that hastened the removal of Ben Ali, Mubarak, and Saleh.[12]

The various constituencies of the public came together and discovered one another after decades of segmentation and political apathy. Villagers and college students mingled together with urban workers, human rights activists, professionals, and the unemployed. Mothers, fathers, and children filled public squares, creating a festive atmosphere, with poetry and music performed live by artists and food donated by citizens who could hardly afford to feed their own families.[13] The nations were on display in all their glory, diversity, hope, and wretchedness. This was testament to the creative vitality of the peoples and their courage to overcome fear, mistrust, and apathy. Half a century of political authoritarianism has neither devoured civil society nor broken its will to resist.

The uprisings were not all united and harmonious. There also existed a struggle of domination inside the public squares within the protests, most notably between religious conservatives and liberal-leaning groups. In Yemen, independent protesters were beaten and incarcerated by Islamist hard-liners of the Islah party and their allies who share business interests and clan ties with the ruling elite. A few months after the outbreak of the uprising against President Saleh, hierarchies were established amongst demonstrators, which the youth activists resented. Thus, the protest movement was manipulated and taken advantage of by powerful players who had been looking for an opportunity to get at Saleh and settle scores with him. In this regard, activist and Nobel Peace Prize winner Tawakkul Karman admitted recently that the general secretary of Islah, Abdulwahab al-Anisi, had told her early in the uprising that she should not shout the slogan 'the people want to oust the regime', but focus only against Saleh. Islah and its allies were personalising the revolution. They were not opposed to the authoritarian regime itself, but rather wanted to get rid of Saleh and gain power themselves.[14]

---

[12] See chapters in this volume by Rami Zurayk and Anne Gough (Chapter 5), Ali Kadri (Chapter 4), John Chalcraft (Chapter 7), vom Bruck et al. (Chapter 13) and Roger Owen (Chapter 11).

[13] Samir Assayyid, Mohamed Hijab, and Abir al-Morsi, 'Unity of the people and army sees victory in the Second Friday of Anger', [in Arabic], *Al-Ahram*, 28 May 2011, http://digital.ahram.org.eg/articles.aspx?Serial=520706&eid=2265

[14] Mareb Press, 'Tawakkul Karman: Secretary General of Reform can reject slogan "People want downfall of regime"', [in Arabic], *Mareb Press*, 14 August 2012, http://marebpress.net/news_details.php?sid=46550&lng=arabic; Stacey Philbrick Yadav, 'Opposition to Yemen's opposition', *Foreign Policy*, 14 July 2011; Laura Kasinoff, 'Yemeni Official Puts Uprising's Toll at "Over 2,000 Martyrs"', *The New York Times*, 19 March 2012.

In Tunisia, Salafis intimidated and attacked secular-oriented activists. Similarly, in Egypt, women and young revolutionaries faced intimidation and assault by extremists of the Salafi variety and elements of the old regime.[15]

With presidents Ben Ali, Mubarak, Gaddafi, and Saleh out, the struggle within has intensified. Peoples react differently to the new emerging order and struggle over the distribution of power. More importantly, there exists a fierce conflict over the identity of the state between religious-based activists and secular-leaning ones, a clash that has deepened the divide and exacerbated social tensions and contradictions. Egypt and Tunisia are cases in point. In the Arab revolts – like others in the past – dormant power struggles have come to the fore and self-interested factions have acted as spoilers.

But the power struggle is not surprising because the institutionalization of diversity and the 'parliamentarization' of politics will take time. Trust amongst political actors is in short supply, and the old regimes went to great lengths to deepen the divide and mistrust between political groups. The performance of the nation by the protesters included people with different ideas and conceptions of the political and the social – a diverse coalition whose members may also deeply mistrust each other. Diversity cannot be wished away. The challenge facing the post-authoritarian order is to institutionalize diversity, establish a broad electoral coalition and rebuild political trust – a prolonged and complex task fraught with risks. In the meantime, we should not be blinded by the dust of political turmoil bursting out in the aftermath of the revolts. We should not confuse the revolutionary moment with the unfolding outcomes and the fierce social and political struggles. Instead of proclaiming the end of the so-called Arab Spring, analysts should focus on understanding the sources of vulnerabilities facing the transition in separate Arab societies and the drivers behind the political-ideological struggles among dominant groups. Not unlike Southern Europe, Eastern Europe, Latin America, and Indonesia, contentious politics in the Arab world will be accompanied by political storms, unstable coalitions, and street protests until the

15 Turess, 'The Salafists in Tunisia . . . What do they believe in . . . and what do they want?' [in Arabic], *Turess.com*, 5 December 2011, http://www.turess.com/alchourouk/516960; Turess, 'The Salafists in Tunisia: A Minority that scares women and the press', [in Arabic], *Turess.com*, 6 December 2011, http://www.turess.com/alhiwar/23509; Walid Balhadi, 'The Salafist Movement in Tunisia: The citizen is scared . . . the secularists and modernists reject them . . . and the government has not been resolved yet', [in Arabic], *Turess.com*, 27 February 2012, http://www.turess.com/almasdar/8802.

dust settles and institution-building is consolidated. One should not be surprised by inter-ethnic and inter-religious turmoil following the dictators' departure because they had relied on divide and rule and exclusion of critical segments of the population.

The Drivers

There is no single cause that explains the social eruptions that have shaken the Arab political system to its foundation. In the social sciences, neatly delineated single causes, though appealing, rarely capture society's nuances and complexities. Analysts focus on either political variables or economic vulnerabilities as the drivers behind the uprisings. Focussing on one without the other is a simplification of a more complex reality. Freedom, bread and social justice – a slogan repeatedly chanted by protesters – sums up the sociopolitical and socioeconomic drivers behind the Arab uprisings. *Al-Karama* (dignity and pride), the demonstrators' most popular rallying cry, reflects the economic and political disfranchisement suffered by most citizens and their humiliation at the hands of the regimes' *mukhabarat* and the repressive police.

Tunisians, Egyptians, Yemenis, Libyans, Bahrainis, and Syrians revolted because of dismal economic conditions and living standards, abject poverty, lack of hope, as well as blockage in the political system that failed to renew itself with new blood and integrate rising new social groups, particularly the youth, into the process. Equally important, the revolts were driven by a widespread belief that chronic systemic corruption by autocratic rulers and their families and associates turned the state into a family-based *uzba* (fiefdom) in which the state no longer belonged to the people but became the property of crony capitalists and their foreign allies. While the nouveau riche, a tiny class, flaunted their wealth and put their decadence on public display, half of the population languished in poverty and misery.

A few statistics are in order, even though the numbers do not portray the gravity of the social crisis in Arab lands and economic development failure in general. In stark contrast to the image of rich Arabs that dominates the Western imagination, about 50 per cent of the population live in poverty, surviving on less than $2 a day and spending more than half of their income on basic food necessities.[16] Although there are wealthy

[16] David Rosenberg, 'Food and the Arab Spring', *Gloria Center*, 27 October 2011. http://www.gloria-center.org/2011/10/food-and-the-arab-spring/#_edn37; 'Arab World Initiative for Financing Food Security', *Region MIDDLE EAST AND NORTH AFRICA*,

individuals in the Arab world, particularly the ruling elite and the crony private sector, the majority of working Arabs are poor. According to the Texas Income Inequality Database, the Arab world exhibits the highest income inequality of all regions in the world and one of the lowest and poorest quality per capita growth rates of all regions in the last three decades.[17]

Neither the steady increase in export revenues – mainly oil-related, by an average of 2 per cent annually since 1985 – nor the improvement in macroeconomic indicators and external account balances across the Arab world had 'trickled down' to national populations. In fact, GINI coefficients – which measure wealth inequalities – had remained static and even slightly worsened, and the proportions of national wealth held by the top 10 per cent of the populations had, in general, increased significantly.[18]

There is increasing evidence that economic restructuring under the Washington Consensus (opening economies to international competition and investment), which had been the dominant economic approach since the 1980s, has produced the opposite results from its intended consequences. Neoliberal reform policies adopted since the 1980s led to the enrichment of a small section of the population and the pauperization of the majority. Economists note that while the real GDP per capita for the region grew at a respectable rate in the 1970s (an average of 5 per cent), it declined in the 1980s to an annual rate of 3.43 per cent and increased at a low rate of 0.34 percent in the 1990s, and when it picked up again in early 2000, it was hollow and inequitable growth. Misguided macroeconomic policies, particularly declining investment rates in productive sectors coupled with inequitable distributional arrangements, caused a chronically

---

Report No. AB6559 (21 April 2011), http://www-wds.worldbank.org/external/default/ WDSContentServer/WDSP/IB/2011/05/27/000001843_20110601143246/Rendered/ PDF/P126506000AWIFS000PID000ConceptoStage.pdf; League of Arab States, Ataqrir al-Arabi Almouwahad, various years.

17 Ali Kadri, 'A Depressive Pre-Arab Spring Economic Performance'. According to the Survey of economic and social development in Western Asia 2005–2006: 'According to the University of Texas Inequality Project (UTIP), every ESCWA member country, with the exception of Yemen, ranks above the fiftieth percentile in the inequality scale among 140 countries. Some in the GCC, namely, Kuwait, Oman and Qatar, rank above the ninetieth percentile', http://utip.gov.utexas.edu/data.html

18 George Joffe, 'As Spring Moves Towards Autumn: The Arab Intifada in Perspective', *POLIS*, University of Cambridge (working paper, 2013); Joffe, 'The Arab Spring in North Africa: Origins and Prospects', *POLIS*, University of Cambridge (working paper, 2011).

high rate of double-digit unemployment and a generalized developmental failure.[19]

Deteriorating living standards, coupled with Arab states' declining social functions in the last decade, exacted a heavy toll on the urban and rural poor and working families and the youth, a huge constituency: 60 per cent of the population are below the age of thirty. In particular, youth unemployment reached a staggering average rate of 40 per cent. A youthful population requires massive investment in social infrastructure, including medication, education, and employment, taxing the capacity of states in the Arab world to cope with a deepening and widening societal crisis. It is difficult to portray the scale and gravity of the socio-economic conditions prevailing in non-oil-producing Arab countries and how they influenced the collective psychology and worldview of the population. In the case of Yemen, the poorest Arab state, the country is running out of oil – its key source of income – and water, a source of life.[20] Compounding the crisis, since the uprising, the economic situation has worsened, with many Yemenis laid off, putting an additional strain on an already impoverished population. A year of political turmoil has caused severe shortages of basic commodities, aggravated already high poverty and unemployment rates, and brought economic activity to a virtual halt. Yemen is frequently plagued by power shortage, fuel penury, and water cuts.[21]

Anyone who has spent time in Arab capitals' poverty belts knows well the inhumane and squalid conditions under which millions of impoverished Arabs live. One has to navigate mountains of trash and raw sewage running in the streets. Haphazardly constructed informal dwellings in

---

[19] See Kadri, 'A Depressive Pre-Arab Spring Economic Performance'; Joffe, 'As Spring Moves Towards Autumn: The Arab Intifada in Perspective'; ILO's KILM, and in this compilation the Arab world fares the worst, see http://www.ilo.org/empelm/pubs/WCMS_114060/lang-en/index.htm; Ali Kadri, 'Unemployment in the post-revolutionary Arab world', Middle East Institute, National University of Singapore, http://www.paecon.net/PAEReview/issue59/Kadri59.pdf. See the excellent paper by Christian Houle, 'Inequality and Democracy: Why Inequality Harms Consolidation but Does Not Affect Democratization', *World Politics*, 61/ 4 (2009): 589–622.

[20] According to Sarah Phillips, 'The most serious structural threats facing Yemen are the decline of its most important natural resources: water and oil. Yemen is one of the most water-scarce countries in the world and it is believed that the capital city Sana'a could run out of fresh water within 15 years'. Sarah Phillips, 'Yemen and the politics of permanent crisis', *IISS* (2011).

[21] International Crisis Group, 'Yemen: Enduring Conflicts, Threatened Transition', *Middle East Report* 1253 (July 2012); 'Friday's Protest of Imminent Victory in Yemen', *Yemen Post Staff*, 9 September 2011.

these large sprawling slums lack rudimentary living requirements like clean water and adequate sanitation, and health clinics in these areas are few, if any. For example, Greater Cairo, a mega-city of nearly 16 million people, has one of the largest slum populations in the world. Almost 50 per cent of the inhabitants, including both rural and urban dwellers, live in informal slums called *ashwa'iyyat* (disorderedly), such as Manshiet Nasser settlement and its Garbage City, Kum Ghurab, Dar al-Salaam, Imbaba, and Madinat al-Salam. Ironically, a *luxury city* (upscale suburban gated communities with multimillion-dollar houses owned by a small elite) lies adjacent to the slum city, exposing a pronounced social divide between the haves (a minority) and the have-nots (a vast majority).[22]

As most poverty in the Arab world is rural, the agrarian roots of the Arab uprisings are also very important. Increases in population and unemployment and a consistent pattern of political, economic, and ecological marginalization and exploitation have pushed rural agrarians into extreme poverty. The statistics are striking: in Egypt, more than 40 per cent of rural dwellers live in poverty; 62 per cent of poor people in Syria live in rural areas, 77 per cent of whom are landless; and in Yemen, 80 per cent of those who are poor live in rural areas. This marginalization also threatens the rural poor's ability to feed themselves. Taken collectively, Arab countries are the most food insecure in the world and also suffer from the highest land inequality, a structural crisis that alienated agrarians and turned them against the ruling elite. For example, Egypt is the largest grain importer in the world while Yemen imports 90 per cent of its wheat, its most important staple food. Countries in the (historically fertile) Fertile Crescent suffer similar problems.[23]

---

[22] Sarah Sabry, 'How poverty is underestimated in Greater Cairo, Egypt', *Environment and Urbanization* 22 (October 2010); Hala S. Mekawy and Ahmed M. Yousry, 'Cairo: The Predicament of a Fragmented Metropolis' (working paper: Faculty of Urban and Regional Planning, Cairo University, 2011); Diane Singerman, ed., *Cairo Contested: Governance, Urban Space, and Global Modernity* (Cairo: The American University in Cairo Press, 2009); Mike Davis, *Planet of Slums* (London: Verso, 2010).

[23] See Chapter 5 in this volume by Rami Zurayk and Anne Gough. Also, M. Elmeshad, 'Rural Egyptians Suffer most from Increasing Poverty', *Egyptian Independent* (28 September 2011), http://www.egyptindependent.com/node/199833; International Fund for Agricultural Development (IFAD), 'Rural Poverty Portal: Syria', http://www.ruralpovertyportal.org/web/guest/country/home/tags/syria (accessed January 2013); World Bank Indicators, http://data.worldbank.org/country/tunisia#cp_wdi (accessed January 2013); WFP, *The State of Food Security and Nutrition in Yemen* (2012); World Bank, FAO, and IFAD, *Improving Food Security in Arab Countries* (2006). For a critical study, see Habib Ayeb, 'The marginalization of the small peasantry: Egypt and

The rise in food energy prices at the end of 2010 had devastating effects on the poor. In December 2010, food prices rose to their highest level since records began to be kept in 1990. The cost of a barrel of oil reached $100 compared with $71 a barrel five months previously, and many of the fuel subsidies were removed. These sudden and massive increases hurt millions deeply and laid the dry kindling for social unrest. The spark that ignited the Arab fires was the self-immolation of Mohammed Bouazizi in the Tunisian town of Sidi Bou Zid in response to the abuse he received by the local authorities after his fruit-and-vegetable stall was seized, ostensibly because he did not have the appropriate municipal license.[24]

The death of Bouazizi resonated with millions of impoverished Arabs, including Egyptians, Libyans, Yemenis, and Syrians, who related to his desperation, humiliation, and pride, as well as his humble background. In Egypt, the rural and urban poor came out in full force in Cairo, Alexandria, Suez, and other towns, surprising and overwhelming the police and security services. The Syrian uprising began in Dara'a, a rural, agricultural area that used to be part of Assad's social support base. A convergence of factors turned agricultural areas like Dara'a, Deir al-Zor, and al-Rastan from being supportive of the Assad regime to hostile. These include Assad's neoliberal policies since 2000, which opened Syrian markets to cheaper agricultural imports, as well as a drought since 2005 that left rural agrarians dependent on foreign food aid as Damascus kept withholding infrastructural investment because the areas were not seen as important to the central power structure.[25] Similarly, rural-urban migrants, including unemployed youth, in Yemen were present at the creation of the protest movement and were a permanent fixture of the uprising.[26]

The activation and involvement of new social groups, particularly rural and urban migrants, fuelled the large-scale protests that removed autocratic incumbents from power. This variable – the unruly collective action

Tunisia' in Ray Bush and Habib Ayeb, eds., *Marginality and Exclusion in Egypt* (London: Zed Books, 2012). See also Saker el Nour, 'National geographical targeting of poverty in Upper Egypt' in Bush and Ayeb (London: Zed Books, 2012)]. See Mohammad Pournik's article, *Pour une croissance inclusive dans la région arabe*, at http://www.afkar-ideas.com/fr/2012/04/por-un-crecimiento-inclusivo-en-la-region-arabe/

[24] George Joffe, 'As Spring Moves towards Autumn: The Arab Intifada in Perspective', (working paper: POLIS, University of Cambridge 2012).

[25] See Khaled Yacoub Oweis, 'Assad's Aleppo focus allows rebel gains in Syria's east', *Reuters* (14 August 2012).

[26] See vom Bruck et al., Chapter 13 in this volume.

of the poor – caught the authoritarian regimes offguard because they had thought that Islamist rivals would spearhead any potential resistance. 'The explosion of the poor' was a strategic surprise that cost Ben Ali, Mubarak, Qaddafi, and Saleh their thrones. Indeed, active participation by the poor transformed the protests into a cross-national wave of popular mobilization, a social movement that took almost everyone by surprise, including the regimes, the opposition, and outside observers.[27]

Although it is difficult to precisely measure the weight of the social forces that tipped the balance of power against authoritarian rulers, the role of the rural-urban migrants appears to have been pivotal, a testament to the significance of abject poverty in Arab societies. In the past decade, the gravity of socio-economic conditions in Arab societies, particularly the lack of jobs and lack of hope, has been illustrated by young Arab men risking their lives and liberty in their efforts to reach Europe and find employment. The flight of educated young Arab men overseas is a barometer of the health of the nations and the psychology of the youth in particular. These young men are desperate to feed their families and to feel a sense of worthiness and respect.[28]

The plight of the urban-rural poor and the unemployed was a critical cause of the uprisings, and will most likely be a constant factor in contentious Arab politics for many years to come, as the cases of Tunisia, Egypt, Yemen, and Libya clearly show. Post-authoritarian governments will come and go depending on their ability to provide employment, hope, and a measure of fairness and justice; they neglect the social and economic public goods at their peril.

Time and again, young men and women say that *al-fasad wal istibdad* (corruption and tyranny) have fuelled their opposition and resistance to authoritarian rulers. Ordinary people see a close link between their abject poverty and the systemic corruption and political repression they have suffered. The grooming of the presidents' sons to replace their fathers, together with police brutality, is as important as the enrichment of the few and the impoverishment of the many. The protestors' slogans reflected their intertwined and interlinked socio-economic and

[27] See John Chalcraft's Chapter 7 in this volume. Also, Alaa Al Aswany, *On the State of Egypt: What Caused the Revolution*, [in Arabic], translated by Jonathan Wright (New York: Vintage, 2011).
[28] For example, in Egypt sexual impotency is a widespread phenomenon that has escaped attention, a direct casualty of the deep socio-economic crisis has wrecked the well-being of millions of Arabs. Author's interviews with scores of political activists, including Islamists and nationalists, July/August/September 2007.

sociopolitical grievances; so did the composition of the rainbow coalitions that removed authoritarian incumbents from power.

Conditions were ripe for the 2011 popular mobilizations against autocratic rulers. The question is not why the uprisings took place, but why had they not occurred earlier given the dismal state of the Arab world and the Arab regimes' deepening crisis of authority? And why did we fail to predict when and where they would erupt? Autocratic Arab rulers had been running on empty – a life of domination without hegemony. In the 1990s and first decade of the twenty-first century, Arab activists and observers believed their authoritarian rulers were illegitimate; that it was a matter of when and how – not if – they would be forced out.

Egypt as a Case Study

The first decade of the twenty-first century witnessed a systemic pattern of resistance to the Mubarak regime, a pattern that culminated in the large-scale 2011 uprising. The 'Arab Spring' revolt was not an immediate, sudden reaction to a specific development. Many causal elements had been building over a much longer period and dissidents and activists had developed the art of social mobilization against the Mubarak authorities by trial and error. Revolutions are built on the sweat, toil, and blood of activists who sow the seeds, yet they often do not reap the rewards. Egypt clearly shows there is not a single cause or an event that caused the revolutionary upheaval in 2011. Throughout the first decade of the twenty-first century, the revolutionary momentum steadily gathered strength. In 2000, a prominent Egyptian jurist, Tariq al-Bishri, observed that Mubarak, together with other Arab dictators, was much more vulnerable than commonly assumed, and that Egyptians would ultimately rise up against his dictatorship. Four years later, al-Bishri, who is highly respected, called on Egyptians to resist by civil disobedience Mubarak's plans to be a president-for-life and to turn Egypt into a hereditary state – installing his son, Gamal, as his successor.

Other highly respected civil-society leaders and public intellectuals, such as Jamil Mattar and Wahid Abd al-Majid, passed a similar indictment on Arab authoritarian rulers and cautioned against taking their durability for granted. As the first decade of the twenty-first century neared its end, even mainstream politicians like Amr Moussa and Mohammed Heikal went public with their opposition to Mubarak's desire to make his son his successor. They cautioned Mubarak's men that Egypt was losing its compass and that the country had reached a

tipping point of no return. Heikal, doyen of Egypt's journalists, repeatedly warned that Egypt was seething with rage against Mubarak and was
ready for a big explosion.[29] Equally importantly, jurists were vocal in
their denunciation of the regime's subversion of the judicial process and
the rule of law. Opposition and resistance spread across social classes
and groups, including professional organizations, bloggers, human rights
activists, elements of the labour movement, nationalists, and Islamists.[30]

The Mubarak regime used fear and segmentation to prevent dissent
from tuning into large-scale popular mobilization and to weaken the most
influential opposition movement, the Muslim Brotherhood, by frequently
arresting its officials and hindering its operations. In particular, it used
the fear of the Islamists to sow divisions amongst its opponents and
co-opt leftists. The regime also convinced its superpower patron that
there was no other political alternative. As its hegemony became frayed,
the Mubarak security apparatus relied more and more on domination
and brutality to prolong its existence and pave the way for Gamal's
succession. It routinely practised systematic torture and even the rape
of leading (male) opposition figures to terrorize dissidents. The beating
to death of Khaled Mohamed Said by security agents in Alexandria in
June 2010 reflected a criminal mindset designed to silence the population,
although it ultimately had the opposite result of rallying more Egyptians
against the police state.[31]

---

[29] Author's interview with Mohammed Heikal, December 2007.
[30] Tarek Osman, *Egypt on the Brink: From the Rise of Nasser to the Fall of Mubarak* (New
Haven: Yale University Press, 2011); Samer Soliman, *Autumn of Dictatorship: Fiscal
Crisis and Political Change in Egypt under Mubarak* (Stanford: Stanford University
Press, 2011); Salwa Ismail, *Political Life in Cairo's New Quarters: Encountering the
Everyday State* (Minneapolis: University of Minnesota Press, 2006); Nadia Oweidat,
Cheryl Benard, Dale Stahl, Walid Kildani, Edward O'Connel, and Audra K. Grant, *The
Kefaya Movement: A Case Study of a Grassroots Reform Initiative* (Santa Monica, CA:
Rand Corporation, 2008); Manar Shorbagy, 'The Egyptian Movement for Change –
Kefaya: Redefining Politics in Egypt', *Public Culture* 19/ 1 (Winter 2007); Rabab El-
Mahdi and Phil Marfleet, eds., *Egypt: The Moment of Change* (London: Zed Books,
2009); Rabab El-Mahdi, 'Enough! Egypt's Quest for Democracy', *Comparative Political
Studies* 42/ 8 (August 2009).
[31] Mohammed Zahid, *The Muslim Brotherhood and Egypt's Succession Crisis: The Politics
of Liberalization and Reform in the Middle East* (London: I. B. Tauris, 2010); Bruce K.
Rutherford, *Egypt After Mubarak: Liberalism, Islam, and Democracy in the Arab World*
(Princeton, NJ: Princeton University Press, 2008); Motaz Nadi, '"We are all Khalid
Saeed" launches "national agreement document" to achieve the goals of the revolution',
[in Arabic], *Al Masry Al Youm* (31 May 2012); IzzaMaghazi, Safa Surour, and Motaz
Nadi, 'Second Anniversary of Khalid Saeed's Death . . . Torture continues', [in Arabic],
Al Masry Al Youm (5 June 2012), http://www.almasryalyoum.com/node/896586.

The regime's scare tactics dissuaded many Egyptians from joining the small protest movements, such as Kefiya ('Enough!') and the April 6 Movement, which were made up mainly of urban middle-class activists, students, and professionals. Many activists and dissidents bemoaned the absence of the masses in their protests and accused the government of scaring off the public. From the late 1990s until 2010, this author often observed protests at the attorneys' and journalists' syndicates in Cairo at which the numbers of police and security personnel exceeded those of protestors. At al-Azhar mosque, scores of police vans blocked the exit to prevent demonstrators from spilling into the streets. Anyone who dared jump the security barricade was mercilessly beaten and officers in civilian clothes often snatched protestors away to be interrogated, battered, and dumped in the desert.

Another reason for the weakness of the protests was the failure of the agenda of the liberal-leaning dissidents to resonate with the poor and the Islamists. As long as the labour movement and the Muslim Brotherhood were not activated, fragmentation of the opposition allowed the Mubarak regime to easily control dissidents. The security services kept a close watch on the two social movements and treated the rest as a nuisance. After the ouster of Ben Ali, the April 6 Movement planned a demonstration in Tahrir Square on 25 January 2011. The police and security services were caught napping, having naively thought that this demonstration would flop like its predecessors.[32]

As the protests gathered steam, Mubarak's men held to misperceptions and misconceptions about the rising opposition, convincing themselves that the Muslim Brothers were the instigators and trying to use the menace of the Brotherhood to warn the United States of what lay ahead if Mubarak should go. As the political crisis reached a climax at the end of January, Barack Obama telephoned Mubarak and tried to find a way for him to leave the scene gracefully. A White House official summarized the response: 'Muslim Brotherhood, Muslim Brotherhood, Muslim Brotherhood.' The Americans did not bite and concluded that Mubarak was no longer an asset but a liability, communicating their concerns to Egyptian generals and impressing on them the need not to fire at the protestors.[33]

---

[32] Jeannie Sowers and Chris Toensing, eds., *The Journey to Tahrir: Revolution, Protest, and Social Change in Egypt* (London: Verso, 2012).

[33] Ryan Lizza, 'The Consequentialist: How the Arab Spring Remade Obama's Foreign Policy', *New Yorker* (2 May 2011); Fawaz A. Gerges, *Obama and the Middle East: The End of America's Moment?* (New York: Palgrave and MacMillan, 2012); Helene

The Mubarak regime not only lacked accurate information about the weight of social forces arrayed against it, but also overestimated the solidity and cohesiveness of its allies – the generals who served as the power brokers and guardians of the political system. As the crisis escalated and the Americans finally withheld their support, the military pushed Mubarak out and sacrificed him on the altar of its institutional and financial interests. As the most powerful institution in society, the military's priority was to maintain its privileges and prerogatives and shape the making of the new order. The goal was to arrest the march of the revolutionary process and keep the structure intact. Fissures within the Mubarak ruling elite accelerated his ouster.

Unthinkable Revolutions?

Like its authoritarian neighbours, the Egyptian regime overlooked its structural vulnerabilities and the strengths of the opposition. Academics were not immune to this error of judgment, a conceptual deficit in understanding and making sense of Arab politics. A most pressing question is why did political scientists and policymakers overestimate the durability of autocratic Arab rulers and underestimate their vulnerabilities and the role of agency? Social scientists do not have a good record of forecasting social revolutions or great popular mobilizations. They predicted neither the social revolution in Iran in the late 1970s that removed the Pahlavi dynasty nor the collapse of the Soviet Union and the uprisings in Eastern Europe in the late 1980s and early 1990s. That is not surprising given that socioeconomic and sociopolitical systems are 'grounded in complexity, interdependence and unpredictability'.[34]

In this regard, in his book, *Iran: The Unthinkable Revolution*, Charles Kuzman deals extensively with the problems of 'retroactive prediction'. His argument is that hindsight is always 20/20 and even with perfect information, one cannot predict. Conventional modes of explanation are therefore redundant – he aims for what he calls an 'anti-explanation'.[35] Kurzman highlights the fluid and unpredictable nature of the social conditions in which revolutionary movements occur. Rather than looking for

Cooper and Mark Landler, 'White House and Egypt Discuss Plan for Mubarak's Exit', *The New York Times* (3 February 2011).

34 Nassim Taleb and Mark Blyth, 'The Black Swan of Cairo: How suppressing volatility makes the world less predictable and more dangerous', *Foreign Affairs* (May–June 2011).

35 Charles Kurzman, *The Unthinkable Revolution in Iran* (Cambridge, MA: Harvard University Press, 2004).

static, immutable conditions or recurrent patterns, an 'anti-explanation' gives due attention to the shifting nature of conditions and perceptions in moments of revolutionary turmoil. When thinking about what causes people to decide to join a revolutionary movement, Kurzman notes that "people make such judgments in real time, during moments of confusion, and that these judgments can be self-fulfilling".[36]

Similarly, Timur Kuran's research on preference falsification and his expansion of the idea to look at the spread of revolutions like 'prairie fires' is relevant. Preference falsification is precisely what disables the opinion polling that is, of course, the favoured tool of the generalists who theorize about the Middle East. Kuran argues that the key reason why huge popular revolutions can come seemingly out of the blue is 'preference falsification' – the difference between peoples' private political preferences and the allegiance they profess in public. In revolutionary situations this can mean that few people are willing to support opposition to a seemingly unshakeable regime publicly, but do so in private. Therefore, as soon as the opposition movement starts to look stronger, or the ruling regime starts to look vulnerable, a huge swell of support for the opposition can develop very quickly, and ruling regimes can fall very suddenly.

A secondary factor is that even those who do not privately support the opposition may well switch allegiances once it becomes clear that the regime has no chance of survival. This explains why a small spark can start a huge uprising – even a small growth in support for the opposition can prompt a flood of hidden support to make itself visible. There can, therefore, be extremely strong social factors that in hindsight make revolution almost inevitable. But these factors remain hidden, as the building support for revolution that results from them also remains hidden. Whereas in hindsight a revolution seems inevitable, it is only after the event that these causes are revealed. There is a tendency to project what we know in hindsight onto the past, and therefore, it may seem that a revolution was inevitable and thus should have been predicted, when in fact it is only with hindsight that it can be seen as inevitable.[37]

---

[36] By this, Kuzman means that people may judge that a revolution is going to be successful, and therefore that it is worth the risk of joining the protests. Whatever these perceptions are based on, if enough people share them and join, they will strengthen the movement and make it more likely to succeed. John Foran, 'Review of *Iran: The Unthinkable Revolution*', *Social Forces* 83/4 (2005: 1774–1776), http://muse.jhu.edu/journals/social_forces/vo83/83.4foran.html.

[37] Timur Kuran, 'Sparks and Prairie Fires: A Theory of Unanticipated Political Revolution', *Public Choice* (April 1989), http://econ.duke.edu/uploads/assets/People/Kuran/Sparks%20and%20prairie%20fires.pdf

After the Arab uprisings, Nassim Taleb and Mark Blyth argued that
it is impossible to predict the shape of future social and economic structures. The past may not be used to predict the future because of the enormous impact of 'black swans' – rare, random, and therefore completely
unpredictable events. Previous 'black swans' do not help provide a guide
because of the nearly infinite complexity and randomness of contributing factors involved. Taleb and Blyth further contend that attempting to
explain the past is like trying to describe the shape of an ice cube from
knowledge only of the water left after it has melted. If the past cannot be
'explained', then using it to predict the future is foolhardy.[38]

Beyond the challenge of prediction, the Arab uprisings have shattered
two myths about the Arab region: the durability of authoritarian Arab
regimes since the 1970s and the powerlessness of agency, both taken as an
article of faith at face value and invested with theoretical and ideological
currency by political scientists and policymakers alike.[39] Arab autocratic
regimes were seen as powerfully capable of maintaining the status quo
and stifling dissent. It is ironic that so many specialists, some of them
inclined towards game-theoretic arguments, were so blind to the possible
power of agency effects in dictatorships. Agency was fine for the leader,
but for no one else. The problem with rational choice is that it can only
cope with sovereign, autonomous agents (by definition) and therefore
cannot theorize or explicate heteronomy – and by extension, issues of
subalternity, violence, and structural power, and probably the entire field
of imperialism.

A second related misconception is that fear and fragmentation neutralized efforts by activists to mobilize the public against the existing order.
There existed an implicit assumption about the inability of agency in the
Arab world to spearhead change from below, as well as the paucity of
democrats in the region. In this context, the rise and popularity of Islamist
groups convinced many Western social scientists, who had a secular bias,
that the political opposition in the Arab-Islamic world was incapable of
advancing democratization.[40]

---

[38] Ibid.
[39] For a representative sample, see Eva Bellin, 'The Robustness of Authoritarianism in
the Middle East', *Comparative Politics* 36/2 (January 2004); Stephen King, *The New
Authoritarianism in the Middle East and North Africa* (Bloomington and Indianapolis:
Indiana University Press, 2009); Marsha Pripstein Posuney, 'Enduring Authoritarianism: Middle East Lessons for Comparative Theory', *Comparative Politics* 36/2 (January
2004); Steven Heydemann, 'Authoritarian Upgrading in the Arab World', *Brookings*
(2007).
[40] Samuel P. Huntington, 'Will Countries Become More Democratic? *'Political Science
Quarterly* 99 (Summer 1984); John Waterbury, 'Democracy without Democrats? The

The democracy deficit in the Middle East has distorted the lens through which many political scientists study the region. Instead of examining the root causes of the democracy deficit and many sources of discontent, a highly complex and laborious exercise, political scientists shifted focus to the topic of the durability of political authoritarianism. Coinciding with the rising popularity of rational choice approaches to the study of politics, Valerie Bunce argues persuasively that this shift of focus was particularly well-represented amongst students of authoritarianism who had the luxury, in contrast to their counterparts working on more pluralist orders, of restricting their focus to a handful of political leaders and carrying out their studies without the complications introduced by having a wealth of information about politics on the ground and within the palace.[41]

The result was to overemphasize high politics and downplay low politics and the role of independent action, as well as overlook the vulnerabilities and weaknesses of political authoritarianism. Despite increasing evidence that Arab rulers faced a deepening and widening crisis of authority and legitimacy in the first decade of the twenty-first century, that crisis was not seen as detrimental to the survival of Arab autocratic rulers because of a two-pronged widespread belief: 1) the ability of Arab leaders to engage in exceptionally clever 'regime-craft', including the establishment of a new political system – 'liberalized autocracy' – that combines guided pluralism, controlled elections, and selective repression; and 2) the ability to mount effective popular challenges to these rulers would have to have stringent requirements, such as large-scale mobilization and organization.[42]

The durability of political authoritarianism in the Arab Middle East acquired the trappings of a scientific topic, which was barely vivisected or challenged. Political scientists shared a kind of a group-think tendency, one that viewed authoritarianism in the region as enduring and viable. Moreover, there existed a group of observers who based their analysis on a "political culture approach to Middle Eastern politics" and who

potential for political liberalization in the Middle East', in Ghassan Salame ed., *Democracy without Democrats: The Renewal of Politics in the Muslim World* (New York: I. B. Tauris, 1994); Bernard Lewis, 'The Roots of Muslim Rage', *Atlantic Monthly* 266 (September 1990); Bernard Lewis, 'Islam and Liberal Democracy', *Atlantic Monthly* 271 (February 1993); and Giovanni Sartori, 'Rethinking Democracy: Bad Polity and Bad Politics', *International Social Science Journal*, 43 (August 1991).

[41] See Chapter 21 in this volume.
[42] Daniel Brumberg, 'The trap of liberalized autocracy', *Journal of Democracy* 13/4 (October 2002).

attributed the democracy deficit and the prevalence of despotism to Arab exceptionalism and the legacy of Islam. The late Elie Kedourie argued that 'the idea of democracy is quite alien to the mind-set of Islam',[43] while Bernard Lewis maintained that the

political history of Islam is one of almost unrelieved autocracy. There are no parliaments or representative assemblies of any kind, no councils or communes, no chambers of nobility or estates, no municipalities in the history of Islam; nothing but the sovereign power, to which the subject owed complete and unwavering obedience as a religious duty imposed by the Holy Law.... For the last thousand years, the political thinking of Islam has been dominated by such maxims as 'tyranny is better than anarchy' and 'whose power is established, obedience to him is incumbent.[44]

Influential scholars such as Ernest Gellner and Samuel Huntington advanced similar arguments.[45]

Although conceptually and epistemologically different, the two viewpoints reinforced the idea that authoritarianism was deeply entrenched and that there was little space for independent action. Many of these scholars have in practice been exponents of Middle East (or more accurately Arab) exceptionalism with regard to the "Third Wave" of democratization. Although it is also the case that a critical segment of this school has distanced itself from the 'political culture approach to Middle Eastern politics', its protagonists have also expended much ink making the case for the durability of the region's authoritarianisms (not least on the pages of the journal *Comparative Politics* less than a decade ago). Even though it is clear that it was the elite-based approach that dominated 'transitology' to produce this bias, and led political scientists to miss the precursors of the Arab upheavals in 2011, the more interesting question is whether

---

43 Elie Kedourie, *Democracy and Arab Political Culture*, 2nd edition (Portland: Frank Cass, 1994).
44 Bernard Lewis, 'Communism and Islam', in Walter Z. Laqueur, ed., *The Middle East in Transition* (New York: Frederick A. Praeger, 1958).
45 Ernest Gellner, *Conditions of Liberty: Civil Society and its Rivals* (New York: Penguin, 1996); Samuel Huntington, *The Clash of Civilizations and the Remarking of World Order* (New York: Simon and Schuster, 1996). Indeed, MENA studies produced some strange bedfellows! That was also true in communist studies – the right wing émigré academic crowd expected these regimes to fall any minute whereas the behavioralists (the young rebels who came to the regional study in the 1970s and 1980s) thought the same. This is the interesting puzzle for the two area studies. Specialists chronicled in enormous detail all the problems with these regimes. But problems are one thing and collapse is quite another.

the top-down focus is a result of the enduring influence of modernization theory and its distrust of mass politics, particularly in the United States.

There existed grounds for political scientists' pessimism. For forty years, autocratic Arab rulers weathered many storms and insulated themselves with layers of protection. Many groomed their sons to inherit the thrones. This is a long period of time in terms of explaining political outcomes and the persistence of authoritarian trends. Although the Arab uprisings force scholars to re-examine Middle East politics, this does not mean that previous research explaining the persistence of authoritarianism was wrong.[46] The question lies in political scientists underestimating increasing sources of discontent, as well as devoting minor analytical effort to examining the Arab regimes' sources of instability as opposed to their durability. Low-level fissures were inevitably missed by the *generalist* comparativists, the rational choice theorists and quantifiers, who are not deeply immersed in local society and politics.

Only prolonged immersion in the region could generate the local knowledge needed to discern and then tease out the significance of low-level rumblings in the nooks and crannies of the ancien régime. In a way, this contributed volume is deeply immersed in the region's rich history and society and informed by historical sociology and global-political economy. The contributors pay close attention to the 'micro-politics' of social struggles and contentious politics – the 'quiet encroachment' and the everyday strategies of resistance and 'low key politics', the hidden movements and 'non-movements', that shaped actors and their strategies as they poured into *mayadeen al-tahrir*.

Far from underestimating the crisis of authority of autocratic rulers, students of the region repeatedly warned of a gathering storm in the Arab world, although they failed to predict when and where and how lightning would strike. Their warnings did not anticipate large-scale popular mobilizations along the 2010–2012 lines. Western policymakers, in particular, convinced themselves that despite the lack of legitimacy and loss of hegemony of their Arab-ruling clients, the latter relied on domination and coercion for survival. With the exception of the Islamists who were suppressed, the opposition was not seen as capable of spearheading an effective challenge to pro-Western Arab rulers. Instead, a more plausible scenario – widely discussed by security-trained specialists – focussed on reforms instituted from within the ruling coalition, a gradual and

---

[46] Joshua Stacher, *Adaptable Autocrats: Regime Power in Egypt and Syria* (Stanford: Stanford University Press, 2012).

controlled process from the top down.[47] Agency had hardly any role to play in bringing about change, a prerogative and domain of elite politics.[48]

The Parliamentarization of Politics

Why dwell on the conceptual deficit in the study and practice of Arab politics? First, the exercise throws further lights on the distorted lenses through which many political scientists viewed the Arab region. More importantly, taking stock is crucial to avoid falling into a similar conceptual trap when examining the prospects of transition from authoritarianism to democracy. A chorus of voices has already declared that the Arab Spring is either over or has already turned to a darkening winter and that the region has long seemed like 'infertile soil for democracy', with the military (the most powerful institution) and the Islamists (the most influentially organized force) hijacking the uprisings.[49] It is argued that both the military and Islamists, illiberal and undemocratic, have a vested interest in perpetuating the autocratic status quo with minor modifications. Evidence is marshalled to show how the remnants of the old regimes and the Islamists stifle dissent and debate and oppose an overhaul of the political and economic structures that sustain authoritarianism and socioeconomic hierarchies. The post-Mubarak dichotomy between the military and the Muslim Brotherhood confirmed the worst stereotypes about Arab politics. The choice was between two forms of authoritarianism with a weak secular and liberal segment caught in the middle. Arab politics was therefore caught in a vicious cycle of despotism, according to this interpretation, and the prospects for democracy were bleak.[50]

---

[47] For more information on this, see Marina Ottaway and Michele Dunne, 'Incumbent Regimes and the "King's Dilemma" in the Arab World: Promise and Threat of Managed Reform', *Carnegie Papers*, 88 (2007).

[48] It is worth mentioning that democracy is a lot easier to predict when the collapse of authoritarianism can lead to a return to democracy, rather than the invention of it.

[49] See for example, Thomas Friedman, 'The Arab Quarter Century', *New York Times* (9 April 2013), http://www.nytimes.com/2013/04/10/opinion/friedman-the-arab-quarter-century.html/ref=thomaslfriedman&_r=0.

[50] Bret Stephens, 'Who Lost Egypt?' *Wall Street Journal* (25 June 2012); Martin Kramer, 'Worst-case scenario in Egypt', *Sandbox* (26 June 2012), http://www.martinkramer.org/sandbox/2012/06/worst-case-scenario-comes-true/; Sohrab Ahmari, 'The Failure of Arab Liberals', *Commentary Magazine* (May 2012), http://www.commentarymagazine.com/article/the-failure-of-arab-liberals/; Daniel Byman, 'After the hope of the Arab Spring, the chill of an Arab Winter', *Washington Post* (2 December 2011), http://www.washingtonpost.com/opinions/after-the-hope-of-the-arab-spring-the-chill-of-an-arab-winter/2011/11/28/gIQABGqHIO_story.html.

Israeli Prime Minister Benjamin Netanyahu was perhaps the single most vocal prime minister or president to speak against the Arab uprisings. He called Western leaders, and especially U.S. President Obama, 'naïve' for taking risks on democratic change in the region and pushing Mubarak to resign from power. Netanyahu said, 'In February, when millions of Egyptians thronged to the streets in Cairo, commentators and quite a few Israeli members of the opposition said that we're facing a new era of liberalism and progress... They said I was trying to scare the public and was on the wrong side of history and don't see where things are heading'. But time has proved him right, he added. His forecast that the Arab Spring uprisings would turn into an 'Islamic, anti-Western, anti-liberal, anti-Israeli and anti-democratic wave' turned out to be true, he concluded'.[51]

Others caution that overcoming the authoritarian inheritance is not easy because of the robustness of deeply entrenched interests, and this can be proven by the internal variation in regime collapse and survival observed in the Arab world thus far.[52] There is a real tension and difference between the more agency-centred, voluntaristic accounts of transitions from authoritarian rule (or revolution) which this contributed volume pursues, on the one hand, and the more structuralist, institutionalist, or class-based analysis on the other hand.[53] In some ways, this more

---

[51] Barak Ravid, 'Netanyahu: Arab Spring pushing Mideast backward, not forward', *Haaretz* (24 November 2011), http://www.haaretz.com/news/netanyahu-arab-spring-pushing-mideast-backward-not-forward-1.397353.

[52] Eva Bellin, 'Reconsidering the Robustness of Authoritarianism in the Middle East: Lessons of the Arab Spring', *Comparative Politics* 44/ 2 (January 2012): 127–149.

[53] In light of Middle East analysts' failure to predict the Arab uprisings, do we need to reconsider previous theoretical analysis of the region? Eva Bellin reassesses her previous article, *The Robustness of Authoritarianism in the Middle East*, after the fall of the Tunisian and Egyptian regimes. The original article argued that authoritarian regimes in the region have been so robust owing not to a lack of conditions for democracy, but because of the prevalence of the structural conditions for authoritarianism. She outlines four main conditions, two of which are particular to the Middle East: the fiscal health of the regime (access to oil and other rents) and high levels of international support for ME authoritarian regimes, sustained in the post-cold war era. These factors determine the regime's *ability* to repress democracy. Its *will* to repress is determined by two other factors: the level of institutionalization of the state's coercive apparatus (e.g., how professional/patrimonial the army or security elite is) and the level of political mobilization against the regime. Bellin argues that ultimately the question of whether individual regimes would fall as a result of the uprisings or not rested on whether the army would shoot protestors (and this in turn was determined not only by how closely tied the army was to the regime, but also to the level of popular mobilization). She concludes that, while political phenomena such as protest, revolution, and transition to democracy are near impossible to predict, we can still analyse causes in hindsight.

structuralist analysis is deeply pessimistic about the prospects of political change in the Arab region. By the end of this essay, I acknowledge a set of concerns that are in some ways similar to the same ones as these structuralists stress, namely economic inequality and social injustice and fragile institutions, as opposed to the 'identity' and 'Islamist' bogeymen that are so strongly emphasized in the mainstream literature and in public commentary as well.

One qualification is in order. What has transpired in the Arab world since 2010 does not mean the end of history or the immediate dawn of a new democratic and egalitarian era. It is a revolutionary moment; the start of a process towards a democratic transition, not the conclusion of democratic consolidation. The ravages of decades of political despotism and its corrosive effects on the political culture of the Arab-Islamic world cannot be undone overnight. The political turmoil accompanying the transition is bound to last for years, and even a couple of decades. The Arab uprisings are more like the colour revolutions in the sense that they focussed on stage one – removing the authoritarian leader from power (which can be a goal for a variety of reasons, only one of which is regime change). Stage two – introducing a new leader and perhaps a new regime – was a much more difficult proposition, although it becomes one only when stage one has been completed. The events of 1989 were extraordinarily unusual because stage one was so quickly followed by stage two in so many (but not a majority of) cases.

Although the protestors forced authoritarian incumbents from power, they did not press their advantage by swiftly installing their people at the top of provisional authorities and developing a revolutionary road map for transforming the political and social order. It is doubtful if the rainbow coalition would have held, as there was not a unified vision amongst various social constituencies about a future political architecture(s) beyond the ouster of autocratic rulers.

Distancing itself from Ben Ali and Mubarak by refusing to fire on the demonstrators, the military swiftly filled the vacuum and endeared itself to the public. In the aftermath, however, the senior echelons of the Egyptian army schemed to slow down transition to a new civilian order and control it, fuelling a fierce struggle. There is no doubt that civil-military relations are a major hurdle in the institutionalization and parliamentarization of Arab politics. After more than half a century of direct rule, the military

She also concludes that her previous analysis of structural conditions is still useful in ascertaining why certain regimes fell and others did not.

has established a vast financial and economic empire and its top brass are fighting tooth and nail to preserve it. They are reluctant to relinquish power to an elected civilian authority. In contrast to Tunisia with a small army that retreated to barracks after the ouster of Ben Ali, Egypt's top generals exercised legislative and executive powers through the Supreme Council of the Armed Forces convened in the last dying days of the Mubarak administration. They used every craft in the profession and acted as a 'shadow custodian' of the nascent political system with a veto power over decisions affecting their institution.[54]

Fortunately for Egyptians, the ruling generals proved to be incompetent and amateurish, alienating a large segment of the public and making themselves politically vulnerable. Despite the gloom and doom about the ruling military council hijacking the revolution, the newly elected President Mohammed Morsi of the Muslim Brotherhood surprised the army's power brokers by retiring dozens of generals and officers, including the key figures Field Marshall General Hussein Tantawi and Chief of Staff Sami Annan. Morsi could not have pulled off this stroke without driving a wedge between the old guard of the Tantawi variety and younger officers who recognize the harm done to their institution because of the Supreme Council of the Armed Forces (SCAF)'s expanding political appetite and organizational incompetence.[55] Although younger officers, like their senior counterparts, want to safeguard their institutional prerogatives, this does not mean that the military will not attempt to exercise influence or surrender its autonomy; instead, it will do so indirectly. For instance, the final draft of the Egyptian constitution institutionalized the military's autonomy over its budget and other matters. Abdel-Fattah el-Sissi the military's ouster of Morsi – July 2013 is another case – point. Although General Abdel-Fattah el-Sissi, Defence Minister, was the driver behind the coup, he has gone to great length to stress the organic unity between the people and he armed forces and that he and his commander

---

[54] On Egyptian military's political role, see Chapter 8 by Philippe Droz-Vincent in this volume. See also Yezid Sayigh, 'Above the State: The Officer's Republic in Egypt', *Carnegie Paper* (August 2012), http://carnegie-mec.org/publications/?fa=48972&lang=en); John T. Sidel, 'The Fate of Nationalism in the New States: Southeast Asia in Comparative Historical Perspective', *Comparative Studies in Society and History* 54:1 (2012): 114–144.

[55] 'Crowds in Cairo praise Morsi's army overhaul', *Al Jazeera* (13 August 2012), http://www.aljazeera.com/news/middleeast/2012/08/20128121551142445.html; Wael Al-Lithi, 'The World Comments on Morsi's Surprises', [in Arabic], *Al-Ahram* (14 August 2012), http://www.ahram.org.eg/Print.aspx?ID=165608.

protect the interim civilian authority. He knows that Egyptians no longer accept a direct military rule.

Nevertheless, there is a real change that the deep cleavages and clashes between the Islamists and the secular-leaning opposition could trigger a return of the military into politics under the pretext of protecting the national interest. The old regime (power and knowledge) has given way to a new language of politics, new modes of thinking, new collective psychology – a new era of politics that requires reconsideration of our ideas and the ways we study the region.[56] Despite social turmoil, the institutionalization and 'parlimentarization' of politics is slowly proceeding with differing social and political constituencies struggling over the new identity of the state and the distribution of power.

Others countries that have revolted (such as Yemen, Libya, Bahrain, and Syria) face severe challenges in trying to wean the military-security apparatus away from politics and institutionalize civil-military relations. In the Libyan case, the task is to build a national army from the bottom up after Qaddafi systemically dismantled it. In Yemen, there is an urgent need to institute structural reforms in the army and unify its ranks and turn it from a 'personalistic' and 'primordial' to a professional institution, a complex and risky process.[57] The very survival of the Syrian state depends on its ability to overhaul its political system and restructure and institutionalize civil-military relations, an unlikely development as the embattled regime there continues to mete out maximum violence against an uprising that became an armed struggle.

In addition to fears about the military, observers warn that the Islamists, or religio-political forces that only belatedly joined the protestors, are poised to hijack the revolts and take ownership of the seats of power in the Arab heartland. They accuse the Islamists of paying lip service to democracy, while plotting to Islamize state and society. Liberal and conservative suspicions of the Islamists increased considerably as the latter won majorities of parliamentary seats in a number of countries, including Tunisia, Egypt, and Morocco, and proceeded to impose its political agenda against the objections of the revolutionary and

56 Hamid Dabashi, *The Arab Spring: The End of Postcolonialism* (London and New York: Zed Books, 2012); Charles Tripp, *The Power and the People: Paths of Resistance in the Middle East* (New York: Cambridge University Press, 2013); John Chalcraft, 'Horizontalism in the Egyptian Revolutionary Process', *Middle East Report* 262.42 (Spring 2012): 6–11.
57 See Chapter 8 by Droz-Vincent in this volume.

liberal-leaning groups.[58] Taking the argument to the extreme, conservatives in the United States claim that the Arab uprisings and the victory of Islamist groups is a replay of the 1979 Revolution in Iran. The fear is that in the same way that Khomeini came to power initially on a democratic agenda, Arab Islamists will ride the wave of democracy to obtain political power and then they will implement authoritarian and illiberal policies.[59]

Regardless of what one thinks of the Islamists' social agenda, which is reactionary, fears of a takeover along the Iranian model are misplaced. The overwhelming majority of Arab Islamists look to Turkey, not Iran, as an example; a fact that shows how far they have travelled. Although Islamists did not trigger the Arab uprisings, their decades-long resistance to autocratic rulers turned them into shadow governments in the peoples' eyes. In the last four decades, centrist or modernist Islamists, such as the Muslim Brothers and Ennahda, skilfully positioned themselves as the alternative to the failed secular authoritarian order. They invested considerable capital in building social networks on the national and local levels, including non-government professional civil society associations, welfare organizations, and family ties. In contrast to their secular-minded opponents, Islamists have mastered the art of local politics and built a formidable political machine that delivers the vote. Islamists' recent parliamentary victory was not surprising because they had paid their dues and earned popular credibility and the trust of voters. They are cashing in on social investments that they made in their local communities. A vote for the Islamists implied a clean break with the failed past and a belief (to be tested) that they can deliver the local public goods – jobs, economic stability, and transparency. Thus, the political fortunes of Islamists will ultimately depend on whether they live up to their promises and meet the rising expectations the Arab publics (the evidence is not reassuring so far, as the Egyptian and tunisian cases show). The new forces that have emerged in recent times, voices that represent millions of people, are not institutionalized or organized as Islamist groups. It is therefore the case that, in the next two rounds of elections, it is to be expected that social

---

58 Byman, 'After the hope of the Arab Spring, the chill of an Arab Winter'; Aaron David Miller, 'The Stalled Arab Spring', *The National Interest*, 6 June 2012, http://national interest.org/commentary/the-stalled-arab-spring-7014http://www.rferl.org/content/human-rights-us-state-department-country-reports/24592058.html; Isobel Coleman, 'Women's Rights in the New Islamist States', *Council on Foreign Relations* (June 2012), http://www.cfr.org/north-africa/womens-rights-new-islamist-states/p28860.

59 For a sample, see Lee Smith, 'Arab Winter', *The Weekly Standard* (9 August 2012), http://www.weeklystandard.com/blogs/arab_649650.html.

movements such as the Muslim Brotherhood and Ennahda dominate the parliamentarization process.

It is too early to offer a definite judgment on how centrist Islamists will govern, and if they will show toleration towards others, although signs from Tunisia are more encouraging than Egypt. There is a big debate taking place in Egypt and Tunisia about Islamists' intolerance of free speech and the treatment of journalists who criticise Islamist figures in power, as well as their authoritarian ways.[60] However, in the last three decades, a pattern has emerged that allows scholars of religious activists to advance working hypotheses regarding the broad contours of Islamists' governance. To begin with, increasing evidence shows that the balance of social forces amongst Islamists has shifted towards pragmatists. It is a generational shift that favours open-minded and reformist technocrats and professionals such as engineers, dentists, doctors, attorneys, and teachers who are less obsessed with dogmas, identity, and culture wars and more willing to build governing coalitions with ideological opponents who are non-Muslim and liberal. For example, Ennahda in Tunisia prefers to form alliances with liberals and leftists, not with the ultraconservative Salafis. The Muslim Brothers have recently endeavoured to differentiate themselves from the Salafis and show moderation, although the struggle over the constitution exposed a rift between the Salafis and the Muslim Brothers, on the one hand, and liberal-leaning groups on the other hand. The Muslim Brothers aligned themselves with the Salafis and rammed a contentious constitution through, thus alienating a significant segment of Egyptians. The big point to stress is the direction depends not just on the structural shifts in alliances, but also on the outcomes of collective political struggles. More than two years after the Arab uprisings, Egypt, together with other post-Spring countries, continues to witness waves of protests by both the Islamists and the secular-leaning opposition, a testament to the durability of contentious politics and collective action. In other words, things could go in different directions as the Islamists have recently discovered Egypt on the first anniversary of Morsi's Presidency, millions of protesters, some of whom had voted for the Muslim Brotherhood, filled the streets demanding his resignation and called on the military to force him out.

---

[60] Kareem Fahm, 'Egyptian President's Move Ends Detention of Critic', *The New York Times* (23 August 2012), http://www.nytimes.com/2012/08/24/world/middleeast/morsi-move-ends-detention-of-a-critic.html?_r=1&ref=middleeast.

Nevertheless, as I have argued elsewhere, Islamist parties are slowly moving away from their traditional agenda of establishing an authoritarian Islamic state and imposing Islamic law while moving towards a new focus that is centred on creating a 'civil Islam' that permeates society and accepts political pluralism. Unlike the mullahs in Iran, centrist Islamist parties like Ennahda in Tunisia and the Muslim Brotherhood in Egypt are travelling down a similar path towards pluralism and parliamentarianism already traversed by the Nahdlatul Ulama and the Muhammadiyah in Indonesia and the AK Party and the Gulen Movement in Turkey.[61]

Next, Islamist parties are increasingly becoming 'service' parties concerned mainly with the provision of social services and local public goods. This constituent-oriented party is an acknowledgement that political legitimacy and the likelihood of re-election rests on the ability to supply public goods (particularly jobs), economic growth, and demonstrate transparency. This factor introduces a huge degree of pragmatism in their policies. The example of Turkey, especially its economic success, has had a major impact on Arab Islamists, many of whom would like to emulate the Turkish model. The Arab Islamists have, in other words, understood that 'It is the economy, stupid!' The Turkish model, with the religiously observant provincial bourgeoisie as its kingpin and a pattern of linkage with the business classes and market liberalism, also acts as a reminder that Islam and capitalism are mutually reinforcing and compatible.

Finally, despite their rhetoric, centrist Islamists continue to compromise in the arena of foreign policy and have shown a willingness to work with Western powers when their interests converge. This includes their posture towards Israel. The Islamists' commitment to Palestine, rooted in popular pressure from their constituencies, will mean that, while they will not renege on existing peace treaties, their relationship with Israel will remain frozen in the absence of a just solution to the Israel-Palestine conflict that is endorsed by Hamas.

Like their Eastern European, Latin American, and Indonesian counterparts, the Arabs' parlimentarization journey will be rocky, messy, uneven, and prolonged, as the Egyptian case shows. There is no assurance of success, and there will undoubtedly be setbacks. Spearheaded by elements of the old regime and their conservative regional backers,

---

[61] Fawaz A. Gerges, 'The Islamist Moment: From an Islamic State to Civil Islam', (forthcoming: *Political Science Quarterly*); Asef Bayat, 'What is Post-Islamism?' *ISIM Review* (Autumn 2005); Bayat, 'The Post-Islamist Revolutions', *Foreignaffairs.com* (26 April 2011); Bayat, 'Egypt and the Post-Islamist Middle East', *Jadaliyya.com* (10 February 2011).

counter-revolutionary forces have putup stiff resistance in a concerted effort to abort the nascent political process and keep the lid on further liberalization and reformation. The solidarity of the public during the protests has given way to diverse and even fragmented publics. Political mistrust and suspicion have replaced hope and solidarity, well displayed during the uprisings. Secular-leaning groups accuse the Islamists of replicating the authoritarian state by suppressing freedom of press and monopolizing the decision-making process. Some of them have even thought the unthinkable and invested their hopes in the military as a counterweight to the Islamists. The Islamist-Nationalist fault line that emerged the mid-1950s still exists and the culture wars are still raging with the toppling of the first Islamist elected president, the ideological rivalry between Islamists and Nationalists has been invested with cultural overtones. In Tunisia and Egypt, no consensus has emerged amongst leading groups on the identity of the state and its political economy. Intense struggles are raging on the streets and elsewhere, a dramatic shift from the era of political authoritarianism and state-sanctioned repression.[62]

Although Tunisia and Egypt are making modest progress rebuilding their fragile institutions, Libya lags far behind, lacking rudimentary institutions and a strong memory of a centralized state. Qaddafi's mafia state has left the country in ruins without a functioning civil society. Despite great odds, including local, tribal, and regional cleavages, Libya has passed its first test in summer 2012 and successfully held parliamentary elections for a National Assembly that subsequently named a new government. Libya is still a work in progress, but public enthusiasm and morale remain very high and this may rescue the country from descending into warring fiefdoms.[63] Similarly, Yemen has not recovered its equilibrium after the removal of Saleh and is weighed down by infighting within

[62] Turess, '100 injured during violence in Tunisian capital and arrests of Salafist members', [in Arabic], *Turess* (12 June 2012), http://www.turess.com/alwasat/23215; Turess, 'Tunisia begins crackdown against Salafists and calls for calm', [in Arabic], *Turess*, (16 September 2012), http://www.turess.com/alwasat/23741; Turess, 'Al Ghanouchi calls for "tighter security measures" on Salafists in Tunisia', [in Arabic], *Turess*, (21 September 2012), http://www.turess.com/almasdar/11969; Mohammed Hassan and Jamal Abu Aladhab, 'Christian Brotherhood are like the Muslim Brotherhood... Salafists welcome, Copts reject, and Liberal[s] warn', [in Arabic] *Ahram* (8 July 2012), http://www.ahram.org.eg/Al-Ahram%20Files/News/159198.aspx; Makram Mohamed Ahmed, 'The Salafist and Brotherhood Race!' [in Arabic], *Ahram* (8 July 2012), http://digital.ahram.org.eg/articles.aspx?Serial=954834&eid=786.

[63] One, however, cannot forget the recent attacks against the U.S. Embassy and the kind of debates engendered in it. For details, see David D. Kirkpatrick and Steven Myers, 'Libya Attack Brings Challenges for U.S.', *The New York Times* (12 September

the ruling elite and insurgencies in the north and south, including a costly fight against a local extremist faction called al-Qaeda in the Arabian Peninsula (AQAP). For now, the uprising in Bahrain has been aborted, although at the cost of the 'empowerment of radical voices across the political spectrum and the marginalization of Bahrain's political middle ground'.[64] Sadly, Syria has already plunged into a prolonged armed conflict, a regional and international war-by-proxy, a bleeding struggle of unknown duration and consequences.[65]

The challenges that endanger parliamentarization and democratic change in Arab countries should not be used as evidence to reinforce the dominant narrative about the resilience of authoritarianism in the Arab region, as well as 'under-predict' the rise of democratic experiments there. A comparative perspective is useful. As a scholar of communism and Eastern Europe, Valerie Bunce cautions specialists in the Middle East and North Africa against making similar mistakes to students of communism who tended, once the regimes they knew so well collapsed, to under-predict the growth of democratic experiments and their ability to endure. For example, in his influential book, *The Third Wave*, American political scientist Samuel Huntington contended that neither the Soviet Union nor Eastern Europe would join the democratic wave because these regimes had succeeded in combining ideology and organization and were thus able to avoid the problem, as argued in his previous work, that participation would be in a position to outpace institutionalization.[66]

Debunking the notion of exceptionalism, Bunce points out that many former Communist countries that became democratic after 1989 (immediately or within fifteen years) lacked any democratic tradition and faced at the same time the daunting tasks of building a capitalist economy while constructing democracy and a new state. Not unlike their Arab counterparts, some of these countries had experienced significant ethnic conflict, a fact that did not hinder democratic change.[67]

2012), http://www.nytimes.com/2012/09/13/world/middleeast/us-envoy-to-libya-is-reported-killed.html?pagewanted=all.

[64] See Kristian Coates Ulrichsen's Chapter 15 in this volume.

[65] See the most recent report on Syria by the International Crisis Group at http://www.crisisgroup.org/en/regions/middle-east-north-africa/egypt-syria-lebanon/syria.aspx.

[66] Samuel Huntington, *The Third Wave: Democratization in the Late Twentieth Century* (Norman: University of Oklahoma Press, 1992). See also Valerie Bunce's Chapter 21 in this volume.

[67] See Bunce's Chapter 21 in this volume.

The situation is grim in Syria and very worrying in Yemen, Bahrain, and Libya. However, Tunisia and Egypt have begun to institute important democratic reform. It is worth stressing specificity when measuring the extent of political change and its durability in the MENA region because there is no single model that applies across the spectrum. Like other regions that have experienced democratic change, the MENA region will likely go through a complex and lengthy process of democratic transition. There are no shortcuts to the birth pains. The challenge for students of the Arab world is not to be blinded by the dust generated by political turmoil and bickering. Political contestation and mobilization will be a dominant feature of Arab political life for many years to come. The return of contentious politics signals the end of an era and the beginning of another, one fuelled by a new collective psychology of empowerment and engagement. It should be celebrated, not feared. The fear is not a return to the old, discredited political regime but only tinkering with the socio-economic structures that pauperized the public, as opposed to implementing structural economic reforms. In this sense, there will be no closure, no end, in the foreseeable future to the revolutionary moment that has shaken the political system to its foundation.

Structure and Scope of the Book

Indeed, one era has ended and another one has started. An underlying thread that runs through the various chapters in this book is that a rupture has taken place in the Arab world and that there is no return to the old ways. Popular mobilization and hegemonic contestation will affect the practice and conduct of politics. The contributors, well-established political scientists, political economists, social anthropologists, and historians who have worked in the region for a long time, call for rethinking the study of the region and refinement of traditional political science concepts and approaches that analyze political change and democratization. The lens through which we view sociological and political dynamics must be adjusted to take in a panoramic view of the new Middle East.

The underlying perspectives in this volume put the large-scale popular upheavals in historical, political, and sociological contexts and reflect on the prospects for democratic change in individual states and the region as a whole. The importance of the book lies in offering a set of both micro and 'big picture' perspectives on the uprisings. While specific conditions in individual countries that have experienced large-scale popular mobilizations are investigated, they are neither treated in isolation nor separated from broader developments in the MENA. The authors highlight links and connections between individual case studies and systemic conditions throughout the region such as a deepening crisis of political authority, general failure of economic development, and new genres of mobilization, activism, freedom, and hope that are especially fuelled by new mass communication technology and the rise of youth movements. Contributors to this volume also consider the role of the poor, the smashing of the stereotype about authoritarian persistence, and the inadequacies of Orientalist and/or rational choice approaches. Additionally, the authors discuss the need to attend to contentious politics, re-evaluate the role of structure, and understand the orientation of Islamists to democratic forms of politics as well as the importance of the variable roles of the military.

Moving away from a binary model of politics, the book does not depend on a sometimes artificial distinction between monarchies and republics, or strong and weak states – political constructs that can overlook underlying conditions and causes. When such binary opposites (stable monarchies versus volatile republics) are invoked, they often tend to be grounded in either wishful thinking or normative assumptions. Equally important, the authors avoid the pitfalls of determinism and structuralism – setting up a series of structures and causations, such rural pressure or increases in food prices – that mechanically lead to the revolts. Instead, most focus on the dialectical interplay between social movements and contentious politics and changing conditions on the ground in order to make sense of the large-scale popular uprisings. Eschewing a focus on traditional top-down politics, contributors concentrate on bottom-up activism and contentious politics.

The book is divided into four parts. Part I examines the context and causes of the Arab popular uprisings. In Chapter 2 ('Authoritarian Legacies and Regime Change'), Lisa Anderson revisits the political science of authoritarianism in light of the Arab revolts and suggests new perspectives on the nature of political change and the modern study of politics. Shedding further light on the 2011 uprising that removed Mubarak from power, Juan Cole (Chapter 3) provides context by comparing and contrasting the big social and political movements that produced rapid political change in Egypt since the late 1880s. Economist Ali Kadri (Chapter 4) investigates the dismal economic performance of the Arab world in the last three decades and concludes that the popular uprisings are deeply rooted in a failure of development and in a failure of the state. In their discussion on the agrarian roots of the uprisings, Rami Zurayk and Anne

Gough (Chapter 5) establish direct linkages between these seminal events and social and economic policies of the Arab states, particularly the atomization of rural society and the disconnect between people, land, and food. Although the analysis of the material conditions of the Arab landscape as it entered the neoliberal economic scene draws our attention to serious deterioration, the authors allow a serious consideration for non-material conditions that are explored in Part II.

Part II investigates thematic and comparative aspects of the revolts. Looking at the uprisings as acts of mass resistance against the appropriation of public resources and public spaces, Charles Tripp notes in Chapter 6 that the protests were against the absolute power that for decades denigrated the public and denied it its citizens' rights. Zeroing in on hegemonic contestation and the explosion of the poor in Egypt, John Chalcraft (Chapter 7) reminds readers that politics is not just about foreign meddling, elite politics, institutional power, and the security forces. Instead, contentious and unruly politics, the popular political imagination, and highly-motivated collective action also play key roles in shaping the political field in Egypt. Philippe Droz-Vincent (Chapter 8) assesses the military's responses to the popular uprisings in various Arab countries, as well as the pivotal role that the military plays in the transition process. Sami Zubaida assesses the effects of the electoral success of Islamic parties regarding policy and legislation on women and family in Chapter 9. His conclusion is that the more robust civil society in Tunisia, including women's organizations, is better placed to resist religious pressures than that of Egypt, which has been Islamized from the bottom-up. John Sidel (Chapter 10) illuminates the ongoing transition from authoritarianism to democracy in Egypt since 2011 through a paired comparison with Indonesia since 1998. He identifies crucial commonalities between the two countries and reaches thought-provoking conclusions about the prospects of political change in Egypt.

Part III focusses on specific countries, including Egypt, Tunisia, Syria, Yemen, Libya, Bahrain, and Saudi Arabia. Roger Owen (Chapter 11) analyses the revolutionary situation in Tunisia and Egypt that needed only a 'spark' to ignite it, before examining the complexities of the post-revolutionary transition to constitutionalism and parliamentarianism. Sadik Al-Azm (Chapter 12) situates the raging struggle in Syria within the context of the revolutionary momentum sweeping the Arab lands, as well as the failure of the two dominant ideologies in the postcolonial Arab order: pan-Arab nationalism and pan-Islamism. Gabriele vom Bruck, Atiaf Alwazir, and Benjamin Wiacek title Chapter 13,

'Yemen: Revolution Suspended?'– a testament to the fact that the old regime endures in another guise, although the authors note that the new President 'Abd-Rabbu Mansur Hadi has begun to dismantle some of its pillars. In Chapter 14 ('Libya in Transition'), Karim Mezran analyzes the drivers behind the Libyan revolution, the role played by regional and Western powers, and the prospects for a successful political transition and pluralistic transformation. Kristian Coates Ulrichsen (Chapter 15) explores the domestic, regional, and international implications of the uprising in Bahrain. Although Coates Ulrichsen situates the 2011 revolutionary protests as part of a longer pattern of recurrent opposition to the ruling Al-Khalifa family, he shows how the uprising that began at the Pearl Roundabout was distinct from previous waves of protest both by its size and its initial cross-sectarian mobilization.

Part IV analyzes the regional and international implications of the popular uprisings. In her analysis of Saudi Arabia's internal and regional responses to the uprisings, Madawi Al-Rasheed (Chapter 16) argues that the kingdom has not engaged in serious political reform or encouraged open debate about these developments at home. She lists three strategies that Saudi leaders deployed towards the uprisings in neighbouring countries: containment in Tunisia, Egypt, and Libya; counter-revolution in Bahrain and Yemen; and support for revolution in Syria. Avi Shlaim (Chapter 17) examines the negative reaction of the Israeli political-military elite to the Arab revolts. Two factors account for this. The first has to do with the politics of Israel's identity as a Western, not a Middle Eastern, state and the second factor is the fear that political change in Israel's neighbourhood will generate instability and undermine its security. Mohammed Ayoob (Chapter 18) examines the regional balance of power and concludes that in the short to medium term, Turkey and Iran will be the key players, as the post-uprising Arab countries will be preoccupied with rebuilding their institutions and economies. The regional players that are now taking the lead in influencing the fate of the Arab uprisings, especially in Syria, point to the Arab region as a weak landscape that may be held hostage to the national interest of other powerful regional players. Taking stock of the response by the Obama administration, William Quandt notes in Chapter 19 that no grand strategy emerged and Obama acted in a cautious and pragmatic way, being attentive to the currents of domestic public opinion at home. Federica Bicchi (Chapter 20) argues that Europe's response(s) to the Arab uprisings has been limited and inspired by a conservative, rather than progressive, attitude to Euro-Mediterranean relations. She concludes that Europe's slow and reactionary approach confirms to a historical pattern of European foreign policy towards its Southern neighbours over the last five decades.

In the conclusion (Chapter 21), Valerie Bunce compares three waves of large-scale popular mobilizations against authoritarian rule – the collapse of communism in the Soviet Union and Eastern Europe, the colour revolutions in post-communist Europe and Eurasia, and the Arab revolts. Bunce develops lines of explanation about the difficulty of predictions in the social sciences and lessons learned about challenges and prospects of democratic transformation and consolidation.

PART I

CONTEXT AND CAUSES

2

Authoritarian Legacies and Regime Change

*Towards Understanding Political Transition in the Arab World** *

Lisa Anderson

Abstract

Juxtaposing the political science of authoritarianism with the dynamics of the Arab Spring, this chapter suggests often unseen lacunae in the modern study of politics and proposes new perspectives on the nature of political change. A close examination of how political science theory defines authoritarian political regimes indicates that the uprisings of the Arab world may permit or even demand refinement in our understanding of autocracy. The skill of incumbent rulers, the character and quality of the previous authoritarian regime and the resilience of the contemporary state itself all inform patterns of political change in the Arab world – and they do so in predictable ways. Both the theory and the practice of the transition from authoritarianism are complex, contentious and still unresolved, and as such they reflect important and ambitious commitments to enhancing both our conception and our conduct of politics.

* This essay is less a conventional research article than a reflection on the state of the art in political science, focused on and informed by the upheavals of the Arab popular uprisings. Hence, the absence of most of the conventional scholarly apparatus – apologies and thanks to all of those whose work I draw on, but do not cite and whose ideas I borrow, but do not acknowledge. I hope all of those who debated these notions with me over the years recognize themselves in these pages, and realize how grateful I am for both their wit and their indulgence. An earlier version was delivered as a lecture sponsored by the Middle East Centre of the London School of Economics in July 2011, and some of the discussion of corruption and the secular public sphere was rehearsed at the 18th Annual Conference of the Economic Research Forum (ERF) on Corruption and Development, Cairo, Egypt, 25–27 March 2012.

For decades – certainly, since the fall of the Berlin Wall, and perhaps since the wave of democratization in Latin America and southern Europe in the 1970s – political scientists, area specialists, and policymakers have been puzzled by what became known as the persistence of authoritarianism in the Arab world.[1] The uprisings of 2011 that toppled a number of Arab dictators surprised nearly everyone, within the region and beyond, and provoked renewed interest among political scientists and political activists alike in the historical experience of the transition to democracy.[2]

The costs of the region's remarkable resistance to the global movement to freer, more transparent, and more accountable government in the latter decades of the twentieth century were borne principally by several generations of citizens whose prospects were thwarted by government policymaking that was opaque, unresponsive, demeaning, and increasingly aimed at little more than the perpetuation of the regime itself. Far less important, but nonetheless deeply troublesome for the advancement of social science and political analysis, was the isolation and marginalization of the region in conventional political science. The study of politics as we know it today in the United States and Europe reflects its origins in efforts in the late nineteenth century to understand, promote, and protect democratic government. In the United States, where the study of American politics sets the standard for political science, this has been particularly marked. Even in Europe, however, at least since the collapse of the Weimar Republic in Germany, the study of politics has been shaped by the desire to prevent the breakdown of democracy and to ensure its speedy restoration in the event that it fails. In many respects, the ideological struggle of the Cold War reinforced this democracy-centric science because it discouraged taking seriously alternative regime types except in the search for their flaws and vulnerabilities.

As a democrat, I am profoundly sympathetic with the normative biases of political science; as a scientist, however, I have been frustrated by our inability – nay, unwillingness – to take authoritarianism seriously. The vast majority of human history has been organized in what we would now call authoritarian, or at least "non-democratic," regimes – tribes,

---

[1] Two excellent collections illustrate this literature: Marsha Pripstein Posusney and Michelle Angrist, eds., *Authoritarianism in the Middle East: Regimes and Resistance* (Boulder, Colo.: Lynne Rienner, 2005); Oliver Schlumberger, ed., *Debating Arab Authoritarianism: Dynamics and Durability in Nondemocratic Regimes* (Stanford: Stanford University Press, 2007).

[2] F. Gregory Gause, "Why Middle East Studies Missed the Arab Spring: The Myth of Authoritarian Stability," *Foreign Affairs* July/August 2011.

kingships, monarchies, empires, oligarchic city-states, slave republics. Scattered across the landscape of Egypt alone is evidence of millennia of remarkably powerful polities whose rulers were not even mere mortals, but the children of gods. Nevertheless, these are all treated by political science as endearing (or sometimes grotesque) anachronisms belonging to the realm of disciplines like history and anthropology, but not the responsibility of a science of politics.

Now that the Arab world seems to be shrugging off the shackles of anachronistic authoritarianism, the temptation to view democracy as the measuring rod for politics is even stronger. The dramatic popular uprisings against the regimes of the Arab world – so contagious, so sudden, and simultaneous – seems to suggest that these autocracies were all of a piece – aging leaders; corrupt and ineffectual governments; educated, unemployed, and disaffected youth – and are all common elements in a repeated story of popular revolt and regime change. Moreover, the uprisings themselves were animated at least in part by a desire for accountable and transparent government and hence, they themselves rejected the anachronisms of autocracy. So, it would seem that political scientists could safely ignore where these countries had been and focus their attention on where they aspired to be. Yet, the authority these young rebels confronted – the knowledge they acquired and the problems they tackled in the aftermath of the uprisings – were very different from country to country; the varied legacies of different kinds of authoritarianism shaped the opportunities and challenges of change in dramatic ways.[3] In many ways, for those of us who study the region, and for those of us who live there, understanding authoritarianism may be even more important than ever.

Charles Tilly argued that there are a number of reasons why we may actually need to know whether a country is democratic.[4] Democracies behave differently, he said: in the international arena, they make alliances and break commitments, accept loans, offer credit, and declare war in ways different from other kinds of regimes. So, too, the quality of life in a democracy is different, and the nature of political change is distinctive. This seems quite plausible and, indeed, I would suggest that on all these dimensions – understanding how they behave internationally, how they treat their own citizens, and how they evolve – being able to

---

[3] See Lisa Anderson, "Demystifying the Arab Spring: Parsing the Differences Between Tunisia, Egypt, and Libya," *Foreign Affairs*, May/June 2011.

[4] Charles Tilly, *Democracy* (Cambridge: Cambridge University Press, 2007).

characterize not just democracies, but all kinds of regimes would be enormously valuable to scientists and policymakers alike.

The Arab uprising of 2011 gives us both an opportunity to celebrate the first genuine efforts at democratization in the Arab world and an occasion to examine exactly why and how knowing more about the varied nature of authoritarian regimes may be useful to understanding political change. Common causes – widespread protests – very quickly produced varied effects in government responses and regime resilience; we should be able to say why and identify what consequence these differences might have on how these countries will operate internationally, how they will interact with their own citizens, and how they will change in time.

Thus, in this essay I examine the political science of authoritarianism from the perspective of the Arab uprisings: what do they reveal about each other? How does political science theory shed light on the practice of transition in the region, and how do the regime changes of the Arab world permit or perhaps even demand refinement in our understanding of autocracy? In fact, both the theory and the practice of transition from authoritarianism are complex, contentious, and still unresolved, and as such they reflect important and ambitious commitments to enhancing both our conception and our conduct of politics.

Defining Regimes and States

In order to develop any hypotheses about the features of autocratic regimes that may be important in shaping the trajectories and outcomes of transitions, I must make a brief digression into the technicalities of typologizing. As it is typically used in political science, a *regime* is the set of rules, or cultural or social norms that regulate the relations between ruled and rulers, including how laws are made and administered and how the rulers themselves are selected. A regime may be a monarchy whose king is selected by divine right and whose laws are applied by his feudal retainers, for example, or a democracy in which the president is selected by popular vote and whose laws are made and administered by legislators and civil servants. The *government* itself comprises those incumbents and the policies associated with them. (In the United States, we refer to what most Europeans – and most political scientists – call the "government" as the "administration," as in the "Obama administration.")

As is evident, the relations between rulers and the ruled can be quite varied: rulers can own the ruled as property, as in slave republics and some kinds of serfdom; rulers can be deemed divinities to be worshipped by the ruled; rulers can be viewed as representative of a popular will. Each theory of rule will be reflected in a particular kind of regime. All of the regimes about which we are concerned are devices designed to produce and regulate the government of a modern *state*, as opposed, for example, to a family domain or a religious community.

A political unit is, to borrow Max Weber's well-known definition, a state, "if and insofar as its administrative staff successfully upholds a claim on the *monopoly* of the *legitimate* use of violence in the enforcement of its order within a given territory."[5] Its existence is associated with, and indeed reflected in, the existence of a secular public sphere. For most of human history, there were no modern states and little or no such secular public sphere. Social, political, and economic transactions took place between individuals and groups defined by personal and property relations – that is, by ties of kinship, patrimonialism, slaveholding, clientelism, feudalism, and the like – and these relations afforded little room for a "public sphere" or "public interest," except in the imagined communities of religious faith.

Typically, these three layers of political organization – the government, regime, and state – are distinguishable. Morocco, for example, has been a relatively stable state for centuries, recognized, if sometimes grudgingly, by those who live there for its monopoly of the legitimate use of force. Its regime is a more or less absolutist monarchy and its government is selected by the king, largely these days from an elected parliament. Sometimes, the distinction is less clear. Saudi Arabia, for example, is a polity defined – as you can tell by its name – by a family, and whether it is the family or a separable state that claims the legitimate use of force is not altogether clear. That family provides the principal incumbents of government through the mechanism of a quasi-monarchical regime. The regimes of both Morocco and Saudi Arabia rely heavily on the adherence of their subjects to religious identities that provide a rationale for popular acquiescence and support for the ruler. In republican regimes, such as those of Egypt and Tunisia, not only is the state clearly separable from the private domain of the ruler – even, or perhaps especially, when he

---

[5] Weber, Max. *The Theory of Social and Economic Organization* (New York: The Free Press of Glencoe; 1966), 154. Also see Margaret Levi, "The State of the Study of the State," in Ira Katznelson and Helen Milner, eds., *Political Science: The State of the Discipline* (New York: W. W. Norton, 2002).

oversteps the boundary – but a secular public sphere supplements and to some extent supplants identity based on personal ties and religious communities.

Most discussions of democracy as a regime type are predicated on the assumption that the state is not a matter of contention – and in North America and Europe, that is by and large a reasonable assumption. In the Arab world, however, as the Saudi instance suggests, the state as the organizing principle of politics is not uncontested – and certainly the states currently arrayed across the map do not necessarily all enjoy recognition as legitimate sources of law and order. The Syrian Ba'ath Party's continuing rhetorical attachment to Arab nationalism, the ongoing ambiguity of the status of Palestine (and hence of the states in which large numbers of Palestinians live), and the refusal of the former Libyan ruler, Muammar Qaddafi, to acknowledge his status as a head of state – he was, as he insisted, the leader of a revolution – all illustrate in various ways the continuing debate about the state and its exemplars in the region. This suggests that rather than assume the stability and legitimacy of the state, political scientists of the Middle East must treat it as a variable: the state is stronger, more widely accepted, and better institutionalized in some places than others or, conversely, it is more hotly contested, routinely ignored, or otherwise weaker in some places than others.[6] The strength of the state shapes the extent and character of regimes available for any given polity. However, we have not taken at all seriously the implications of various attachments to, or measures of the strength of, states in our efforts to understand or even categorize various types of regimes.

What kinds of regimes are there? What is the available repertoire of regime types? Indeed, how do we define different kinds of regimes? In 1975, in his magisterial synthesis, *Totalitarian and Authoritarian Regimes*,[7] Juan J. Linz attempted to develop a typology of regimes and it remains the standard for such efforts to this day. He began his synthetic essay with the observation that

one of the easiest ways to define a concept is to say what it is not. To do this obviously assumes that we know what something else is, so that we can say that our concept is not the same. Here we shall start from the assumption that we

---

[6] A point I made many years ago in "The State in the Middle East and North Africa," *Comparative Politics*, October 1987.

[7] Lynne Rienner Publishers, 2000; originally published in Fred Greenstein and Nelson Polsby, eds., *Handbook of Political Science* (Reading, Mass.: Addison-Wesley Educational Publishers, 1975).

know what democracy is and center our attention on all the political systems that do not fit our definition of democracy . . . we shall deal here with nondemocratic systems.[8]

The preoccupation with democracy as the standard and measure – the "norm" of politics – is not difficult to discern, as is the absence of attention to the character of the state for which the regimes are expected to produce a government. In fact, Linz seems to believe that the existence of a stable and coherent state can be assumed or held constant, at least for his "modern" states. It is the regimes that are thought to vary from one state-based polity to another, not states themselves.

For Linz, a totalitarian regime is like democracy in that "citizen participation in and active mobilization for political and collective social tasks are encouraged, demanded, rewarded . . . " but in other respects, totalitarianism is the *opposite* of democracy – it is institutionally and structurally monistic rather than pluralistic, and, far from the free-wheeling marketplace of ideas that characterized democratic competition, "there is an exclusive, autonomous . . . ideology. . . . "[9] In other words, totalitarianism is democracy turned on its head, almost mocking the American commitment to what Philippe Schmitter called, in another influential typology, the "multiple, voluntary, competitive, nonhierarchically ordered and self-determined categories" of pluralist participation.[10]

If totalitarianism was democracy's perverse antithesis, the two regimes shared one important feature: they were both "modern" – that is, based in states. Not all regimes are, of course, and even Linz felt constrained to briefly acknowledge "traditional authority and personal rulership" in his essay. These, he said, were the residue of "the small and diminishing number of Third World traditional political systems. . . . "[11] In other words, politics without state institutions can be relegated to the past.

Having distinguished the distinctly modern from the purely historical, and shown totalitarianism to be the modern perversion of democracy, Linz was left with everything else – all the other regimes in the world that fit into none of these categories – and these he called "authoritarian." In Linz's schema – as for nearly all subsequent political science – authoritarianism is, in fact, a residual category, defined almost completely by what

---

[8] *Ibid.*, p. 51.

[9] *Ibid.*, p. 70.

[10] "Still the Century of Corporatism?" F. B. Pike and T. Stritch, eds., *The New Corporatism* (South Bend, IN: Notre Dame University Press, 1974), 96.

[11] Linz, *op. cit*, p. 145.

was missing: "political systems with *limited, not* responsible, political pluralism, *without* elaborate and guiding ideology ... *without* intensive nor extensive political mobilization except at some points in the development, and in which a leader or occasionally a small group exercises power within formally *ill-defined* limits but actually quite predictable ones."[12]

The hope that there is something "actually quite predictable" in regimes that were "ill-defined," "non-ideological," "neither intensive nor extensive," and indeed, even "occasional," led Linz to attempt to develop a typology of this subset of regimes itself. He distinguished "bureaucratic-military authoritarianism," "organic statism," "postdemocratic," "postindependence mobilizational authoritarianism," "post-totalitarian authoritarianism," "racial and ethnic 'democracies,'" and a variety of other "'defective' and 'pretotalitarian' political situations and regimes." This list was less a typology than an inventory, and in some important respects it was an admission of failure.

Dimensions of Autocracy

In fact, there do seem to be common features of authoritarian rule, or non-democratic policy settings, and they seem to reflect the fragility or instability of the state, and the contested character of the secular public sphere.

> *Information Scarcity.* In general, information is scarce and what is available is unreliable. Hence, the proliferation of rumor, innuendo, conspiracy theory – there are few ways to verify claims. Neither rulers nor their subjects have reliable access to, or even accepted definitions of, the kind of data that permits effective policymaking or citizen participation. The collection and dissemination of reliable data and statistics – provoked by rulers' needs for sustained and reliable military conscription and tax collection in early state formation – is an essential feature of the modern state, and is missing in many countries where autocracy thrives.
>
> *Private Authority and Manifold Identities.* Citizenship – an identity created and sustained by modern states – competes for political salience with other identities, such as kinship, religion, region, and ideology, and partly as a result, recognized political action in authoritarian contexts is restricted to authorized vehicles, groups, and institutions. This, combined with the lack of widely disseminated

[12] *Ibid.*, p. 159. Emphases mine.

information, has several predictable consequences. The definition and reach of the public interest is relatively shallow, and thus the opportunities for policy debate are reduced and corruption amplified. Policy decisions are shaped by proximity to power rather than public deliberation.

Political Subservience. Rulers are typically portrayed as protecting rather than serving the populace, a posture that invites distinctions based on reciprocal obligation and patronage and breeds subservience in the general population. The relative fragility of citizenship, in which distinctions are based on the exercise of civic responsibilities, and the strength of alternative identities mean that compliance is not born of rights-based acknowledgment of government authority but of personal relations, including intimidation, fear, and resignation.

Ambiguous Accountability and Political Irresponsibility. Because discussion and debate are typically restricted and reliable information is limited, political actors often make outrageous claims, knowing they cannot be held accountable, even if they wish to be. Hence, the Muslim Brotherhood can claim that "Islam is the solution;" the Egyptian National Democratic Party can call itself "democratic;" the "Leader of the Libyan Revolution" can describe himself thusly (and characterize his opponents as "cockroaches"), with little fear of a public test, much less contradiction. The quality of public discourse is shaped by rhetorical grandiosity and very modest attention is given to substantive policy debate.

Tribute and Favoritism. In part because the reach of the secular public sphere is not coterminous with the polity, the realm of the polity outside or beyond that public sphere impinge on its operation. The formal economy and the official institutions are shaped, and often distorted, by values and priorities inconsistent with their ostensible purposes. The privy purse of the ruler is rarely fully distinct from the public treasury, and state income is often co-mingled with the personal resources of the rulers and their retainers. This creates the conditions for political corruption, which is often a reflection of behavior at the metaphorical edges of an expanding public sphere, where the existence or legitimacy of this public domain is incomplete, misunderstood, or disputed. In these circumstances, public resources will be deployed to reward the ruler's loyalists and punish his opponents, and to provide leverage to state employees whose formal statuses do not otherwise afford them access to sufficient resources or authority.

In essence, to borrow from John Adams, authoritarian regimes are "governments of men and not of laws."[13] But perhaps because they resist law-like features, for all their similarities, political science has made little progress in identifying the crucial regularities of authoritarian regimes. There is no systematic, scientific typology, no universally accepted dimensions on the world's regimes are arrayed – there is only democracy, its perversion, and its absence – and the recent enthusiasm for "hybrid" regimes merely carries this ambiguity into the twenty-first century.[14] Political science continues to be marked by its pre-Copernican conviction that democracy is the center of the political universe. Normative commitments have distorted scientific standards.

Dimensions of Resistance and Rebellion

Perhaps, as is so often the case, we are better served by literature and in this instance, by Tolstoy's famous observation that in fact, "Happy families are all alike; every unhappy family is unhappy in its own way."[15] Our authoritarian regimes – or at least the bulk of their citizens – may all be unhappy, but in very different ways and, as I hope to show, exactly how will matter a great deal for the outcome of the processes of political change we witness today in the Arab world.

Let us examine this change in more detail. Starting in mid-December 2010, when the Tunisian vegetable vendor, Mohammad Bouazizi, set himself on fire in a display of helpless, hopeless frustration at government harassment, almost every country in the Arab world saw protests. Bouazizi's act was copied in Algeria, Jordan, and Egypt; peaceful demonstrations, marches, and rallies – starting with protests against corruption, police brutality, and high food prices – escalated to calls for changes of policies in Saudi Arabia and Oman, of governments in Jordan, Morocco, and Bahrain and ultimately of regimes in Tunisia, Egypt, Libya, Yemen, and Syria – virtually no country was exempt, and no government unscathed. By mid-June, the governments of Algeria and Saudi Arabia

---

13 In 1774, John Adams recommended 'a government of laws, and not of men,' See Charles Francis Adams, ed., 'The Works of John Adams', vol. 4, p. 106 (Boston: Little, Brown and Co., 1856).

14 Steven Levitsky and Lucan Way, *Competitive Authoritarianism: Hybrid Regimes after the Cold War* (Cambridge: Cambridge University Press, 2010) illustrates the democracy-centric character of this literature, although their concluding general observations about "organizational power, regime transitions and democracy," are not inconsistent with the arguments made here. See pp. 354–358.

15 *Anna Karenina*, any edition, p. 1.

had announced major infusions of money, including across-the-board wage increases; the cabinets in Jordan and Morocco had been sacked; the regimes in Egypt and Tunisia had fallen; Libya had slid into civil war; Yemen was in limbo after the evacuation of the president for medical treatment after he was injured in a bombing; and Syria was confronting a brutal crackdown by its government.

There were certainly common themes in all of these developments, and they reflect the common dimensions of authoritarianism.

Information-rich Politics. The new information and communication technologies, especially the social media, were important in fuelling and disseminating the protests. In obvious ways, they permitted relatively unimpeded access to information about the way people live elsewhere in the world as well as the depredations of the regimes themselves, and they permitted organization and communication among and across protesters within and beyond the borders of each country.[16]

Imagined Communities and Distributed Authority. Perhaps more subtly, the new technologies – especially the social media of the early twenty-first century – empowered a generation who had become accustomed early in their lives to being more tech-savvy and hence, in modest but significant ways, more knowledgeable and authoritative than their elders. The young people of the Arab world are not only a large proportion of the population, as we know – this is, after all, the "youth bulge" – but their experience of growing up is qualitatively different from that of their parents. This generational cohort actually developed and disseminated these technologies and in doing so assumed a kind of social responsibility that their parents had not borne at their age Before the development of mobile telephony, as anyone who visited the country will remember, the inadequacy of the telephone network was a regular staple of the fabled Egyptian humor. By the turn of the millennium, however, there were a million mobile phones and by 2012, in a country of 85 million people, there were 95 million mobile phones. Egypt was said to have the highest per capita number of bloggers in the world. Their impatience and frustration at being unable to deploy the information they accessed, the knowledge they acquired, and the responsibility they shouldered

---

[16] See, among many other testimonies, Wael Ghonim, *Revolution 2.0* (New York: Houghton Mifflin Harcourt, 2012).

in the public sphere goes a long way to explain why millions of young people continue to militate for more open, transparent, and accountable government.[17]

Personal Dignity and Political Citizenship. Although in many places economic grievances played an important role in early mobilizations, by and large these were liberal, participatory, deliberative revolts, reminiscent of the "liberal, democratic revolutions" of nineteenth-century Europe.[18] That is, they were about demands for citizenship. The nearly universally complacent, unresponsive, and often contemptuous policies and positions of the governments produced a nearly universal response: demands for effective citizenship, personal agency, and government accountability. Hence, the remarkable accent on dignity.

Accountability and Responsibility. In this area, many of the aspiring citizens surprised even themselves. The community watches that sprang up in the wake of the still mysterious but, as it turned out, very valuable and instructive withdrawal of the police in Egypt during the January 25th revolution not only demonstrated that Egypt was not on the brink of chaos, as the government had argued, but that ordinary citizens across the country – not just the protestors in Tahrir Square, Suez, and Alexandria – would be able to take responsibility for, and indeed wanted to take control of, their own neighborhoods, and by extension, their own country. This desire to participate, to be useful and productive members of society, was apparent throughout the country in those, young and old, who staffed the overnight community-watch committees and manned the spontaneous roadblocks set up to protect residents from prisoners released when the police vanished. For the first time, neighbors of all social classes "lost their fear" and came out of their politically imposed isolation and learned about each other, while the young people at the barricades enjoyed the acknowledgment, respect, and gratitude of

[17] For more on the Information and Communication Technology (ICT) developments in Egypt before the revolution, see Sherif Kamel, "Information and Communication Technology for Development: Building the Knowledge Society in Egypt," in *Access to Knowledge in Egypt: New Research on Intellectual Property, Innovation and Development*, edited by Nagla Rizk and Lea Shaver (London: Bloomsbury Academic, 2010) 174–204.

[18] On the parallels with Europe, and on pessimistic conclusions, see, for example, Jonathan Steinberg, "1848 and 2011: Bringing Down the Old Order is Easy; Building A New One is Tough," *Foreign Affairs*, 28 September 2011. http://www.foreignaffairs.com/articles/68306/jonathan-steinberg/1848-and-2011?page=show

those whose streets they policed.[19] This experience of new networks of trust among not just families and co-religionists, but citizens as well, is still new and perhaps fragile, but there is reason to think that it marks a qualitative and permanent change in the conception and experience of political efficacy.

Taxes, Equality, and Transparency. Among the most vociferous of the claims against the authoritarian regimes were accusations of the diversion of public resources for private gain – that is, corruption. The universal condemnation of the failure of the old regimes to clearly and consistently distinguish between the public treasury and the privy purse or private household of the rulers, their tolerance of bribery and tax evasion, and their extension of special privileges to government favorites reflected not only moral revulsion, but a principled embrace of the equality of citizenship and a new awareness of the value and opportunities in the rule of law.

There were common elements in the Arab uprisings – not least a desire for a government of laws and not of men – but there have also been very different trajectories and, already, very different outcomes of the Arab uprisings. Why?

Responses to Rebellions and Transitions from Authoritarianism

Here, we return to the "unhappy families" of authoritarianism. Although they are all unhappy in their own way, there appear to be predictable patterns. For example, two, possibly three, characteristics seem to bode well for regime survival.

1. Governments that control large revenue streams that are independent of local labor are able to diffuse or control opposition. That is, rentier governments, such as in the large oil and gas exporting countries of the region, may distribute resources so as to both bolster acquiescence and strengthen coercion, thereby surviving political protest. Where there is no taxation, enhanced distribution appears to deflect calls for greater political representation and reinforce relations of political subservience and political irresponsibility. The availability of non-tax income appears to militate against

---

[19] Fred Brooks and Tatiana Jaunzems, "Community Organizing in Egypt During and After the Revolution," *Social Policy*, 2011, http://www.socialpolicy.org/index.php/about-us/511-community-organizing-in-egypt-during-and-after-the-revolution

democracy, reinforcing relations based on patronage-based distribution of state resources as personal largesse, but in other respects,
the putative character of the regime is of little consequence for stability in these circumstances: more or less, "democracy" would not
alter the government's capacity to survive, as the apparent stability
of regimes as otherwise diverse as Saudi Arabia, Algeria, and Oman
illustrates. Obviously, however, Libya's counter-example suggests
that ample rents cannot be the only factor in regime survival.

2. Timing is important, and quick decisive responses to protestors'
demands enhanced the prospect for regime survival. In all cases of
authoritarian rule, the relatively low levels of institutionalization –
the primacy of individuals over laws – makes time an important
variable. Whereas parliamentary debates and judicial processes are
known to be unavoidably measured and deliberate, authoritarian
rulers control the timing of their policy process, and decisions can
be virtually instantaneous. Hence, unhurried reactions to popular
demands may appear to be (and may actually be) dismissive and
uncaring. And, in fact, one of the striking features of events in
Tunisia, Egypt, Yemen, and Libya was how slowly and maladroitly
the rulers responded to the initial protests. Had they made the
concessions they eventually made even a week or so earlier, all of
these presidents would probably have survived. By contrast, the
relative alacrity of the responses of the kings of Jordan, Morocco,
and Oman in sacking their cabinets and promising further reforms
seemed to have staved off, and possibly diffused altogether, more
serious calls for the downfall of the regime.

3. Monarchy may be a useful device by which rulers can distance
themselves from the failings of their policies, salvaging the regime
by dismissing the government. In emphasizing the dependency of
the government on the monarch, such repudiation serves both to
respond to popular complaints and reinforce the personal authority
of the king. This hypothesis was widely cited to explain the ability of the kings of Morocco, Jordan, Saudi Arabia, and Oman to
weather protests that seems to have capsized presidents elsewhere,
although the first two factors – the availability of resources to the
governments and the agility of the ruler – confound this correlation
to some extent, as Algeria suggests. In principle, however, in any
regime that is separable from its government, it should be possible
to sacrifice personnel to salvage the system; the extent to which this
occurs in highly personalized regimes may depend turn on the skill
of the individual whose regime is under siege.

And what of those regimes that fell, or seemed to be collapsing? We have also to account for the relative ease with which the Egyptians and Tunisians were able to slip out from under their governments to begin building new regimes, while the Libyans and Yemenis fought long and bruising civil wars, and Syria's citizens faced a brutal onslaught from their own rulers. This leads us to another set of hypotheses, which link the regime not simply to its revenues and rulers, but with the state over which it presides.

4. In countries where affiliation to the state is widespread and participation in the public sphere relatively extensive and clear cut, discarding the regime is relatively unthreatening – few Egyptians or Tunisians worried that his right to live in his country would be challenged should the president resign and the constitution be rewritten. Like the civilian administrations, although more so in Tunisia than in Egypt, the militaries were relatively strong, coherent, and well-disciplined, and they saw themselves more as protectors of the nation and defenders of the state than as components of the regime. When pressed, the Tunisian military was prepared to sacrifice the regime for the sake of the state. Rather like the responsive monarchies, the Egyptian military jettisoned the government for the sake of a regime in which it was more clearly implicated – and struggled with whether it would be forced to acquiesce in genuine regime change for the sake of the state itself.

5. In countries where the state is weak – where it does not enjoy a monopoly on violence or where the legitimacy of the monopoly claimed by the government is widely contested – and there is no genuine public sphere, regime change entails state collapse. Few Libyans felt any affinity or loyalty with the Socialist Libyan Arab People's Jamahiriyyah, in which their ruler had insisted they live. Thus, the breakdown of the regime triggered a collapse of the state apparatus, civilian and military alike, which in turn provoked political opportunism and demanded local-level alliance building, as previously unrelated networks of family and region worked to knit together a Libyan identity and build a Libyan state. Similarly, in Yemen, where the authority of tribal leaders routinely trumped that of the central government, the prospect of the fall of the regime threatened to remove the device by which the tribes had negotiated their relations.

6. In countries where the project of the regime *is* state building, the identity of the regime is so closely tied to that of the state that

efforts to dislodge the regime are interpreted as challenges to the state itself. Here, the regime and its allies are better equipped than their weak state counterparts, since they have built at least some of the elements of a modern state – a strong standing army, for example, and a public bureaucracy – and they enjoy support among a significant proportion of the population. Unlike the regimes in strong states, however, the relatively strong military and civilian administration is a reflection and extension of the regime and its ambitions; these state-building regimes and their supporters have everything to lose should the regime fall and the state-building project be reversed. Hence, the military behaves not as the guardian of the still nascent state, but as the instrument of a strong and determined regime and they are quite brutal in suppressing opposition – as we see in Syria. This regime as state builder is quite commonly associated with sectarian or regional identities – the Prussian role in the unification of Germany comes to mind – but it can also represent social formations forged as ideological vanguards, such as the Fascists in Spain. The Alawis in Syria represent the first type and the *Front de Libération Nationale* [FLN] revolutionary elite in Algeria the second; the predominately Sunni Ba'ath Party in Iraq may have reflected both impulses.

Thus, it appears that the nature of the government, the regime and the state, and the resulting lineaments of various types and kinds of authoritarian rule, do in fact matter as we try to understand, explain, or perhaps even predict what happens in regime change. To put it simply, among the dimensions that we should examine in accounting for the persistence and downfall of autocracies are these:

Skill. Authoritarian regimes, in their relatively low premium on institutions for consultation, deliberation, and accountability amplify the importance of the ruler: the distribution of political agility and skill is always an important component of political change, but never more so than in autocracies under duress.

Resources. So too, regimes of all kinds dispose of different kinds of revenue bases, and these can be crucial in determining the ability of governments to respond to popular demands. Any government or regime – autocratic or democratic – is more vulnerable in straightened circumstances and all regimes that have access to non-tax rents have more room for maneuver. That said, autocracies may distribute revenues as domestic patrons in ways that exhibit flexibility and responsiveness that democratic institutions rarely afford.

Institutional Design. Rulers who can plausibly distance themselves from their governments – as is often the case of monarchs and may sometimes be the case of militaries, such as in post-Ataturk Turkey – may have opportunities to respond to popular demands for change that facilitate regime survival. Sacrificing a government to save a regime is only possible when they are distinguishable, but when they are, it can be an effective strategy.

State Strength. A strong state means that regime change is not an existential threat to the polity, permitting it to take place relatively peacefully and efficiently.

State Weakness. Weak states collapse as their regimes fall.

State Formation. Threats to regimes in states-in-formation pose existential threats to governments that have relatively high levels of popular support and control over military and bureaucratic resources, and so the prospect of regime change provokes a particularly brutal response.

What does all this mean for the Arab uprisings of 2011? There is ample reason for optimism in Egypt and Tunisia. Strong states, populations with relatively robust identities as citizens, and increasingly experienced and agile political actors bode well for transitions that are ultimately successful – if contentious – and the building of sustainable institutions of more open, transparent, and accountable governments. The amplified importance of individual skill in circumstances of weak institutions does heighten the contingent quality of some of the specific outcomes: the skills of the members of the government, the military leadership, the protest organizers, and public intellectuals shape some of the process, including its speed and its institutional results. Nonetheless, these are transitions that have every reason to work.

For the countries facing state collapse, such as Libya, reconstruction is rendered difficult as already strong non-state identities are reinforced in battle, whereas civic relationships may erode in wartime. Tribal and regional networks shift and shrink, political opportunism is reinforced as a survival strategy, and mistrust grows – not only between government supporters and opponents, but among and within a population accustomed to a secular public sphere. The crucial supporting role of international military assistance in the prosecution of the Libyan rebellion revealed the porous and uncertain boundaries of these kinds of polities, which in turn suggests the likelihood of continued reliance on international institutions for both military and civilian reconstruction in the transition. Even with their ample financial resources – and in some respects because of their ample financial resources, which will permit difficult choices to be postponed and popular support secured on the basis of personal rather than public interests – building of the state apparatus in Libya, and the construction of a regime that can take responsibility for its functioning, will be arduous and lengthy.

For the regimes that are constructing states – and this includes not only Syria, but also Algeria and Iraq, which all saw ample violence in the last twenty years – the international community is confronted far more starkly with the challenge of taking seriously their rhetorical commitment to a "responsibility to protect" populations at risk from their own governments. As Charles Tilly reminded us, state formation in Europe was a brutal affair, privileging the fortunate and destroying the unlucky and ill-fated. "European states built up their military apparatuses through sustained struggles with their subject populations and by means of selective extension of protection for the different classes within those populations."[20] Why should state formation in the Arab world be different?

Thus, to return to our initial questions about how the previous regimes mold politics in transitions, there are good reasons to think that the nature of the authoritarian regime, and particularly how it is related to the project of state formation, will shape how states operate internationally, what the quality of life in the polity is like, and how political change takes place.

On all these dimensions, understanding how the Arab uprisings evolve requires that we differentiate among various forms of authoritarian and autocratic legacies. These forms reflect the quality and character of the state in a part of the world in which there is still considerable contention about the strength, stability, and legitimacy of the state – and the states – of the region. On the international level, the speed of dissemination of ideas, contagion of practices, demands for intervention, and suspicions about interference reflect the specific nature of each state and the broad character of the complex and multi-layered state system in the

---

[20] Charles Tilly, "War Making and State Making as Organized Crime," in *Bringing the State Back In*, Peter Evans, Dietrich Rueschemeyer, and Theda Skocpol, eds. (Cambridge: Cambridge University Press, 1985), 185–186.

Arab world. The quality of life in these polities, before and during the uprisings, has reflected the novel public spheres born in the encounter of established private authorities and sanctioned patterns of political subservience with anti-authoritarian communities of the information-rich and socially-networked demanding social justice and personal dignity. The velocity, stability and direction of change will reflect the skill and timing of political actors navigating competing public spheres of religious faith and public interest, contending community values of virtue and citizenship, and clashing institutional domains of discretion and law.

Democracy may be the model of politics and the standard of political science, but everywhere it exists it has been built from something else, and everywhere it will flourish, it will have been constructed on the foundations and with the materials of what went before. If we are to promote democracy effectively, we need to understand how politics and political change are shaped by the inheritance of authoritarian regimes; if we are to be genuine political scientists, we need to comprehend the vastness and variety of our universe. To do any of this, we must better understand the nature and legacies of autocracy.

3

Egypt's Modern Revolutions and the Fall of Mubarak

Juan Cole

Abstract

This chapter compares and contrasts the four big social and political movements that produced rapid political change in modern Egyptian history. These include the 1881–1882 'Urabi Revolt, the 1919 Egyptian Revolution, the 1952 Cairo fire and Young Officers' Coup, and the upheaval of 2011–2012. It is argued that all of these events involved a 'rapid and systematic political change' that is 'brought about by a social movement.' In turn, social movements involve organized campaigns to achieve their goals by using techniques such as rallies, vigils, strikes, public speaking, and pamphleteering to influence their audience. The chapter discusses the goals and the forms of popular mobilization deployed in each of these revolutionary moments, and compares and contrasts them to one another.

The Egyptian revolt of 2011 was the fourth such mass movement for political and social change in the country's history since the late nineteenth century. Each of these revolutionary moments was characterized by a political agenda and by a social dimension, usually a protest about the comportment of economic elites and the form of the country's political economy. These political and social movements have clearly and powerfully shaped the evolution of the modern Egyptian nation. In order to understand the events of 2011–2012, it will be helpful to place them in this historical context. Some themes are common across the movements whereas others are unique to the twenty-first century.

The first large-scale political movement in modern Egyptian history was the 'Urabi revolt of 1881–1882, an attempt at the establishment of a parliamentary government led in part by military officers and in part by a new class of modern intellectuals, and aimed at curbing the absolute prerogatives of the Ottoman viceroy, who was in turn seen as subservient to foreign interests. Egypt was not yet a nation state at this point, but rather a vassal state of the Ottoman Empire reigned over by Sultan Abdulhamid II from Istanbul. The popular movement was nipped in the bud by a British invasion and occupation. The second mass movement was that of 1919–1922 against British rule and against the economic stringencies of the wartime years. As in the 'Urabi revolt, greater independence was among the goals of 1919, as Egypt moved toward constitutional monarchy, although it did not escape strong British influence. Both in the British colonial period (1882–1922) and in the Liberal age (1922–1952), Egypt increasingly suffered from big landlordism, cotton monoculture, and peasant immiseration.

The third popular mobilization was around the Young Officers' Coup of 1952, against the corruption of the Wafd parliament and of the playboy king, Faruq. The Revolutionary Command Council made Egypt a Republic and pursued a significant land reform programme that largely liquidated the old hacienda elite and created a rural middle class. Unlike 1882 and 1919, parliamentary governance was not part of the popular agenda in the 1950s, that form of government having been given a bad name by the way it was dominated by the big landlords and manipulated by the British. Egypt was a military dictatorship until 2012, although in the last decades of the First Republic, a rubber-stamp parliament was allowed to function and carefully controlled elections were held. The revolution of 2011 rejected dictatorship and the corruption that accompanied it, and renewed a demand for civilian, parliamentary governance, as well as generally attacking the predatory business classes that had grown up as clients of the dictatorship. The themes of the place of the army in national life, of the degree of foreign influence over politics, of social equity, and of popular input into governance all characterized in varying degrees these four revolutionary moments in modern Egypt. Of course, the way these issues were conceived and articulated changed enormously over time, but their continued salience points to continuities in Egyptian nation-making in the modern era.

Social Movements and Revolutions

A great deal of ink could be spent on what a revolution is and whether any of the four upheavals in modern Egypt fits the definition. At a basic level, a revolution is a rapid and systemic political change brought about by a social movement. A social movement in turn, as defined by Charles Tilly, involves an organized *campaign* for the achievement of specified goals through influencing a target audience; the deployment of *repertoires of social action* such as rallies, vigils, strikes, public statements, and pamphleteering; and *displays* of worthiness, unity, numbers, and commitment.[1]

Some observers attempt to tie essential attributes to such movements, that is, they would like to distinguish between backward-looking and forward-looking political upheavals, with only the latter being revolutions. This romantic approach to definition founders when one looks at concrete cases. The transition in Spain from fascist dictator Francisco Franco to constitutional monarchy, after all, involved a restoration of the authority of the Bourbon throne. Was that reactionary or progressive, traditional or modern? Political scientist George Lawson argued that revolutions are best seen as a variegated set of phenomena. They can be led by peasants or business classes, and can result in all sorts of new political and economic systems. He wrote:

In this way, revolutions can be seen as: the rapid, mass, forceful, systemic transformation of a society's principal institutions and organisations. Revolutions are systemic in the sense that they are processes in which the major institutions and organisations in a society are transformed. Ways of doing business and competing politically must change alongside shifts in values and attitudes if an example of radical change is truly to warrant the name revolution... Revolutions seek to overturn a society's social, economic and political structures, and recast its international relations, all within a relatively short time-frame. This differentiates revolutions from evolutionary change that is comprehensive but takes place over the long-term, reform programmes that take place in the short-term but do not engender fundamental change, and transitions which see only a partial modification of a society's main institutions and organisations, and take place over a medium-term time-frame. In other words, revolutions can be differentiated from other processes of social change primarily by their scope, depth and effect.[2]

As Lawson notes, some social scientists distinguish between structural alterations and mere 'personnel wars' (in which the ruler is changed out). When pundits ask if the Arab uprisings really consisted of revolutions,

---

[1]   Charles Tilly, *Social Movements, 1768–2004* (Boulder, Colorado: Paradigm Publishers, 2004), p. 53–54.
[2]   George Lawson, 'Negotiated Revolutions: The Prospects for Radical Change in Contemporary World Politics', *Review of International Studies*, Vol. 31, No. 3 (July 2005), pp. 473–493, this quote on p. 479.

they are inquiring as to whether they were simply personnel wars or whether something more fundamental changed. Sociologist Theda Skocpol made a distinction between political revolutions and social revolutions.[3] In a political revolution, there is a change in the ruler-ship but not necessarily in the social structure. In a social revolution, as she defines it, at least 5 per cent of property has to change hands, and typically the laws governing property are changed.

Another question is the difference between a coup and a revolution, that is, of change at the top conducted by a small number of conspirators as opposed to a mass movement. The 'Urabi revolt was traditionally seen as a coup, but it had more the character of a social movement, and was in fact (through urban guild tax protests and through land invasions by peasants of the estates of the Ottoman notability) turning toward social revolution when the British invasion cut it short. The 1952 'revolution' was more clearly a coup, although it had, and developed, a set of supporting crowd repertoires of social action. Such typological issues are less useful than social science definitions that are generative rather than classificatory. That is, a definition of a revolution as involving a widespread popular demand for systemic change, accompanied by a repertoire of mass social action, such as Tilly and Lawson proposed, seems more useful than a typology.

The 'Urabi Revolt

The 1882 'Urabi Revolution was provoked in some large part by an economic and fiscal crisis.[4] Egypt under Khedive Isma'il (r. 1863–1879) experienced a boom and a bust, as the American Civil War drove a cotton boom in the 1860s that caused growers to vastly expand cultivation around the world, which in turn caused a price plunge in the late 1860s and the 1870s. Khedive Isma'il fancied himself a Western monarch, declaring that Egypt had seceded from Africa and acceded to Europe. In 1866, he convened a Chamber of Deputies, elected mainly by rural village headmen and mayors, initially intended as a mere debating society and façade of governmental modernity. The Egyptian government borrowed a great deal of money from European banks and bondholders,

---

[3] Theda Skocpol, *States and Social Revolutions: A Comparative Analysis of France, Russia and China* (Cambridge: Cambridge University Press, 1979).

[4] Juan Cole, *Colonialism and Revolution in the Middle East: Social and Cultural Origins of Egypt's 'Urabi Movement* (Princeton, NJ: Princeton University Press, 1993).

on the expectation of continued high cotton income, and then found it increasingly impossible to meet debt servicing obligations or to repay the bondholders. The government sold the recently-built Suez Canal for a song to the British, who then stationed troops there for decades. The European powers insisted on inserting a French and a British representative into the Egyptian cabinet to forestall against fiscal irresponsibility (although, in fact, most of the money borrowed had been spent on infrastructure and other sound projects). The Egyptian populace by 1876 was the most indebted in the world on a per capita basis. At the same time, the implementation of European-style property law allowed the repossession of peasant-held lands for debt payment arrears or arrears in taxes, in contrast to the more lenient Ottoman policy. Land was becoming a capitalist commodity, and the phenomenon of the landless peasant was growing.

The viceregal or khedivial state took a number of drastic measures to deal with the debt crisis. It slashed the army, and made it increasingly difficult for an Egyptian to advance into the officer corps, which was dominated by Ottoman notables. It raised taxes to unconscionable levels, having recalcitrant peasants all over the country whipped and mulcted for arrears. The increased state demands for resources from the peasantry came at the worst possible time, as they faced bad weather and successive failures of the Nile to rise sufficiently to fertilize farmland, along with continued high population growth, so that food insecurity became widespread and some peasants formed militant bands to confront the tax collectors. Urban guilds were also taxed at ever higher rates. In 1879, the Europeans, having lost confidence in Khedive Isma'il, installed his son, Tawfiq, in his place, an action signed off on by the nominal ruler of Egypt, Ottoman Sultan Abdulhamid. The Chamber of Deputies, which had evolved into a much more lively body than its founder had intended, was prorogued.

By 1881, popular discontents had multiplied. Young Arabic-speaking Egyptian officers protested in spring of that year. In September 1881, a demonstration was held before the Khedive's palace led by Colonel Ahmad 'Urabi, demanding that elections be held for the Chamber of Deputies, that an organic law or constitution be drafted, that the size of the army be restored to 18,000 men, that military promotion opportunities for Sons of the Nile be opened up, and that the upper-class ethnicities (the Ottoman-Egyptians) be less dominant. Already that summer, pro-reform intellectuals distributed printed petitions in the countryside asking that the Chamber of Deputies be convened. Rural notables came to Cairo with 1,500 signatures from village headmen (*'umdahs*) asking that a just, consultative government be established, free from tyranny and corruption. 'For this reason,' they proclaimed, 'assemblies of people's representatives had been created in the civilized kingdoms to protect the rights of the community against its government and as a means of carrying out the just orders of this government.'[5] Khedive Tawfiq gave in and held the elections in mid-November. The resulting parliament was dominated by rural large landholders, but despite their conservatism, they demanded that the parliament be a legislative body and that it have control over the part of the budget not already devoted to servicing the debts to Europe. The European consuls in Alexandria, who served as a sort of senate for Egypt in this period, worried that the Chamber of Deputies might overspend its part of the budget, leaving too little for the debt servicing. Ultimately, they demanded that 'Urabi and the reform cabinet on which he served be dismissed, implicitly threatening a naval action against Alexandria in late May 1882.

Tawfiq acquiesced in the European demand and dissolved the cabinet. A massive outcry from the Egyptian public, however, impelled him to reinstate 'Urabi as minister of defence shortly thereafter. The Alexandria population, inflamed at naked European interference in Egyptian affairs, mounted big demonstrations on 11 June and fighting left 50 Europeans and 250 Egyptians dead, an event seen by the British press as a 'massacre' of Europeans.[6] On 11 July, the British navy bombarded Alexandria and landed troops, so that the khedive (who was summering in that city) became their captive.

In late July, 'Urabi, having again been dismissed and branded a rebel, called a national congress of 400 Egyptian notables and intellectuals in Cairo, which decided to depose Tawfiq. Some 13 per cent of signatories of the revolutionary declaration were village headmen, 22 per cent were Muslim and Christian clergymen, and 22 per cent were urban merchants. Some 18 per cent were pashas, beys, and other high Ottoman notables. Ottoman Turkish was the language used in the opening proceedings, but the delegates clamored that they be held in Arabic, pointing to an

---

[5] Alexander Scholch, *Egypt for the Egyptians! The Socio-political Crisis in Egypt, 1878–1882* (London: Ithaca Press, 1981), p. 170; John Chalcraft, 'Engaging the State: Peasants and Petitions in Egypt on the Eve of Colonial Rule', *International Journal of Middle East Studies*, Vol. 37, No. 3 (August 2005), pp. 303–325.

[6] Juan Cole, 'Of Crowds and Empires: Afro-Asian Riots and European Expansion, 1857–1882', *Comparative Studies in Society and History*, Vol. 31, No. 1 (January 1989), pp. 106–133.

Arabic-speaking nativism. Some Muslim clergyman declared Tawfiq an apostate for going over to the Europeans. The Copts, alarmed, announced that if the fight against the Europeans was religious (i.e., Muslim), they would leave, but if it was national (*watani*), then they would gladly join in.[7] Urban crowds in areas not under British control often supported the rebel government. 'The shoemakers, coffee servers, and tailors swarmed the streets, shouting "O God, destroy the army of the infidels."'[8] The coal heavers of Port Said declared a strike, paralyzing shipping. In the countryside, peasants began invading the estates of fleeing Ottoman landlords. The revolutionary state was snuffed out by a British invasion in September, foreclosing the question of how Egypt might have developed if it had been allowed in the 1880s to have a successful revolution dedicated to consultative and parliamentary governance and at a fairer distribution of wealth.

The Revolution of 1919

The British installed a veiled protectorate over Egypt, appointing a viceroy who subordinated the khedives and their appointed cabinets. They eventually allowed an appointed Chamber of Deputies, which, however, was little more than a debating society. Far more democracy was allowed in British India than in Egypt. The British adopted policies of austerity for Egypt in 1882–1922, insisting on paying down the debt to foreign banks and bondholders. They built few schools, did nothing to promote industry, and their censorship policies harmed printing business and culture. In essence, they kept Egypt as a huge cotton plantation and whether they intended it or not, their property laws allowed the continued growth of enormous estates or haciendas (*'izbah*) and a vast increase in the number of peasants with too little land to farm. As of the early twentieth century, some 13,000 landowners owned 40 per cent of all cultivated land. Between one and two million Egyptians were landless labourers. The poorer 80 per cent of the population owned less than 20 per cent of the privately held land.[9]

---

[7] Egyptian National Archives, 'Urabi Revolution Dossiers, Dossier 19, Folder 140, 'Taqrir 'Ali Mubarak Pasha', 12 October 1882.

[8] Mikha'il Sharubim, *Al-Kafi fi ta'rikhmisr al-qadimwa al-hadith*, 4 vols. (Bulaq: al-Matba'ah al-Kubra al-Amiriyyah, 1898–1900), 4:332.

[9] Gabriel Baer, *Studies in the Social History of Modern Egypt*, (Chicago: University of Chicago Press, 1969), pp. 136, 215; Peter Mansfield, *The British in Egypt* (London: Weidenfeld and Nicolson, 1971), p. 111.

During the First World War, many Egyptians suffered hardships because of fluctuating cotton prices; diversion of food, men, and livestock to the Palestine front; high inflation; and other wartime hardships. It seems likely that the ways in which the British 'veiled protectorate' threw off its face covering and asserted control over key sectors of the economy – for instance, the price and marketing of cash crops such as cotton – made colonial rule ever less acceptable.[10] When the war came to an end, the disposition of former Ottoman territories was to be decided at the Versailles peace conference and its satellite conferences, such as that at San Remo. President Woodrow Wilson supported self-determination for former possessions of the defeated Austrian Empire, but his principles were formulated generally. Activists among the Egyptian political elite, many of them French-trained attorneys, took a deep interest in Wilson's principles and wanted to make an argument at Versailles for Egypt's transition to independence, along the lines of Hungary or Czechoslovakia. This group was led by Saad Zaghlul, a politician who had served in the Egyptian cabinet and as vice president of the toothless legislative assembly. Zaghlul and his colleagues promoted a grassroots organization to mobilize both urban and rural populations in support of their demand that a delegation or 'Wafd' be allowed to make the case for Egyptian independence at the peace conference. The British authorities, alarmed, exiled Zaghlul and other activists to Malta, arresting him on 8 March 1919.

The response of the Egyptian people to this high-handed act of repression was to mount large demonstrations in Cairo, Alexandria, and other cities, as well as to engage in rural acts of defiance and sabotage against British facilities.[11] In the initial stages of the protests, students at Cairo University and the al-Azhar (Sunni Muslim) seminary played a leading role. On 15 March, some 10,000 of them marched. The protests came to encompass virtually all social classes over time. On 16 March, the wives of the exiled nationalist leaders organized a march of thousands of women. Coptic Christians joined in the national struggle, and crowds held up banners with the cross and the crescent. Attempts were made to breach the divide between Egyptian and European quarters, with demonstrators reaching Shepheard's Hotel in Cairo's posh Garden City.

[10] Robert L. Tignor, 'Egyptian Revolution of 1919: New Directions in the Egyptian Economy', *Middle Eastern Studies*, Vol. 12, No. 3 (October 1976), pp. 41–67.
[11] W. J. Berridge, 'Object Lessons in Violence: The rationalities and irrationalities of urban struggle during the Egyptian Revolution of 1919', *Journal of Colonialism and Colonial History*, Volume 12, Number 3 (Winter 2011).

Alongside relatively peaceful protests, some Wafdists secretly waged a campaign of assassination against British officials. Through April, a general strike increasingly paralyzed the country. Tramway workers joined in, refusing to operate a major means of public transportation.[12] As with the 'Urabi revolution of twenty-seven years before, the countryside joined enthusiastically in the protests, joining the Wafd political party in huge numbers and seeking leadership from it.[13] Peasants disrupted the rails and reclaimed resources that had been requisitioned by the British during the war. Thousands of Egyptians were killed and wounded in the consequent British military attempt at repression. But by late April, London relented and agreed to allow Zaghlul and his allies to go to Paris in order to plead their case with the victors of the Great War. Their arguments fell on deaf ears there, but the mass mobilization of the Egyptian public pushed the British to seek a bilateral settlement of the crisis. In December 1919, Lord Alfred Milner arrived in Egypt on a fact-finding mission. He was greeted with a fresh outbreak of demonstrations and acts of civil disobedience. In March, he penned a recommendation that Egyptians be given their independence. As late as May 1921, a major anti-British riot broke out in Alexandria, which may have had more influence on subsequent British willingness to negotiate with the nationalists than is generally realized.[14]

The British managed to retain a large influence in Egypt, despite granting it nominal independence in 1922. The Egyptian army would be led by a Briton, a base would be leased to the Royal Air Force, and Egypt would buy arms only from Britain. British troops would garrison the Suez Canal, which remained British property. Until the 1950s, high Egyptian politics would henceforth be a three-cornered game among the monarch (the scions of the Ottoman viceroys or khedives began styling themselves kings from the 1920s), the British ambassador, and the prime minister and his party supporters (mostly, big landlords). Zaghlul became Egypt's first elected prime minister in 1924, inaugurating three decades of

---

[12] Zachary Lockman, 'The Social Roots of Nationalism: Workers and the National Movement in Egypt, 1908–19', *Middle Eastern Studies*, Vol. 24, No. 4 (October 1988), pp. 445–459.

[13] Ellis Goldberg, 'Peasants in Revolt – Egypt 1919', *International Journal of Middle East Studies*, Vol. 24, No. 2 (May 1992), pp. 261–280.

[14] Great Britain, Army, Egyptian Expeditionary Force, Court of Enquiry on the Alexandria Riots, 'Minutes of proceedings and Report of the Military court of enquiry into the Alexandria riots', May 1921 (Google Ebook at http://books.google.com/books?id=spQxAQAAMAAJ&q).

'Liberal' constitutional monarchy in which big landlordism and economic stagnation increasingly characterized the society.

The revolution of 1919–1922 displayed many similarities with the 'Urabi revolution, but ended very differently. In 1882, the British Empire was powerful enough simply to invade, defeat 'Urabi's army, and restore the khedive to the throne. In the aftermath of World War I, having lost nearly a million men on the battlefield and over a million and a half wounded, with its economy badly hurt, the British public had little stomach for more interventions in the colonies. Faced with the high degree of popular mobilization that the Wafd achieved in Egypt, British officials decided that the costs of repression were too high. Therefore, they instead strategized how to retain British interests, in the Suez Canal, and in the Egyptian economy via neocolonial technologies of control. They were forced into abandoning their geostrategically central protectorate by the actions of students, peasants, bootblacks, tramway workers, artisans, and society ladies, both Muslim and Coptic Christian. The combination of youth revolts and economic discontent with new forms of political and media mobilization typified the building tradition of modern Egyptian mass revolt.

1952: Cairo Fire or Cairo Revolution?

Although 1952, after decades of British informal dominance and big landlord politics, witnessed a military coup in Egypt that inaugurated the first republic and profoundly altered Egyptian society, the coup was in important ways the outcome of a popular explosion. Two large social and political contradictions drove Egyptian politics by 1951. The extreme concentration of wealth in the hands of landlords was provoking peasant unrest. The rise of a small industrial sector and lack of legal protections for workers likewise was provoking strikes and labour activism in the cities. Alongside this sharpening of domestic-class contradictions, the nation confronted continued British control of the Suez Canal, on which a newly assertive post-war Egypt was increasingly making claims.

On 9 October 1951, the nationalist Wafd government withdrew from the Suez Canal treaty, at which the country had long chafed. Protracted negotiations with the British had not proved fruitful. It was increasingly clear that a wide spectrum of Egyptians sought to nationalize the Suez Canal, where British troops were based, as a last vestige of British colonialism. From October 1951, student and other groups, including the Muslim Brotherhood, began forming informal guerrilla brigades to infiltrate the Canal Zone and harass British troops. These efforts received support from Wafdist Interior Minister Fouad Serag Eldin, who also organized police auxiliaries to make claims on the Canal Zone and confront British troops. From 13 January 1952, fighting in Ismailia between the auxiliary police and British troops escalated. As British casualties mounted, on 25 January the British riposted forcefully, deploying a Centurion tank and taking a warehouse where the police/guerrillas were based. Over the weeks, some forty British soldiers died in the Ismailia violence. Fifty Egyptians were killed in the fighting and about 100 wounded. The British took the headquarters of the auxiliary police and captured some 1,000 police, along with their commander.[15]

The battle of Ismailia inflamed passions in the capital. The next morning, 26 January, security police staged a demonstration, asking to be sent to support their comrades in the Canal Zone, and were joined by al-Azhar seminary and university students along with railway workers. The chants turned against the king himself, who was involved in a sumptuous celebration of the birth of his heir, and he ordered that the demonstrators be fired on. The protesters began setting fires. Initially, the targets were associated with the king or with foreigners. British icons were burned, from exclusive clubs to the offices of the Thomas Cook travel agency, Barclays Bank, Shepheard's Hotel, and British Overseas Airways. Later in the day, the anti-imperial crowd actions became a class riot, in which people attacked department stores, tourist hotels, bars and cabarets, and cinemas. Reflecting unhappiness over the loss of the 1948 war with Israel and the reduction of most Palestinians to refugee status, some Arab nationalists attacked Jewish establishments. The Muslim Brotherhood supporters appear to have concentrated on puritan rioting against licentious establishments, although many of them were foreign or had their roots in the British occupation and the servicing of British troops during the war. Much of the vandalism and arson was politically driven, but with the breakdown in law and order, some of the crowd turned to looting.

[15] Christopher Weeks, 'Egypt's Canal Zone Guerrillas: The "Liberation Battalions" and Auxiliary Police, 1951–1954', *Military History Online*, 19 February 2011 at http://www. militaryhistoryonline.com/20thcentury/articles/egyptcanalguerrillas.aspx; John 'Jock' Marrs, 'The Ismailia Riots: "The Lancs & the Tanks go into Action"', *Britain's Small Wars, 1945–2005*, 1999, at http://www.britains-smallwars.com/Canal/ISMAILIA-RIOTS.htm; Michael Mason, 'Killing Time: The British Army and its Antagonists in Egypt, 1945–1954', *War & Society*, Vol. 12, No. 2 (October 1994), pp. 103–126; Michael Mason, 'The "Decisive Volley" – The Battle of Ismailia and the Decline of British Influence in Egypt, January–July 1952', *Journal of Imperial and Commonwealth History*, Vol. 19, No. 1 (January 1991), pp. 45–64.

The Wafd government did not intervene until late in the day, by which time some 40 buildings had been reduced to ash or rubble and more than 700 commercial establishments had been destroyed. The death toll stood at twenty-six, comprising both foreigners and Egyptians. The property damage was 15 million Egyptian pounds, about a third belonging to British investors. Between 15,000 and 30,000 shop employees, clerks, artisans, and other lower-middle-class employees were left without jobs. Some historians are suspicious that British intelligence played a role in encouraging agent provocateurs to delegitimize the protests. Wafd Prime Minister Mustafa al-Nahhas declared martial law late in the day. It was, however, too late. King Faruq, who had never liked the Wafd (with its populist and anti-imperial rhetoric), dismissed the government. During the following six months, he experimented with three different prime ministers, none of them enjoying the same kind of majority support in parliament as the Wafd. The constant labour unrest, the peasant uprisings, the great Cairo riot, and the derailing of the Wafd government arguably gave an opening to impatient young officers to make their coup of July 1952.[16]

The 'Cairo Fire' was not an irrational outburst of mob destruction, but a set of repertoires in a social movement, and it not only served as background to, but was organically linked to, the policies of the later revolutionary government. The targets of the wrath of the crowds in the Cairo upheaval included the king, who had long been resented for the failure of the Egyptian army in the 1948 war, for his complaisance towards continued British influence, and for his image as an opulent playboy. Big international capital was another target, as manifest in the upscale stores and offices of the European quarter and the downtown. One downside of consumerism is that it often displays and promotes merchandise that is beyond the means of most targets of its advertising, and so can excite resentment as well as desire. But in addition to the international dimension, the attack on high-end retail was also a protest against the extremes

---

[16] Nancy Y. Reynolds, *A City Consumed: Urban Commerce, the Cairo Fire, and the Politics of Decolonization in Egypt* (Stanford: Stanford University Press, 2012), chapter 6: 'The Cairo Fire and Postcolonial Consumption;' Joel Gordon, 'The Myth of the Savior: Egypt's "Just Tyrants" on the Eve of Revolution, January–July 1952', *Journal of the American Research Center in Egypt*, Vol. 26 (1989), pp. 223–237; Joel Gordon, *Nasser's Blessed Movement: Egypt's Free Officers and the July Revolution* (Oxford: Oxford University Press, 1992); Fayza Hassan, 'Burning down the house', *Al-Ahram Weekly Online*, No. 57c, (24–30 January 2002) at http://weekly.ahram.org.eg/2002/570/sc3.htm

in Egypt's wealth distribution. The big absentee landlords and rentiers – the pinnacle of Egyptian high society – found themselves hunted in their cabarets and fancy hotels. The Muslim Brotherhood attacked symbols of the libertine lifestyle, in which the king himself was a trendsetter, and which they associated also with the moral corruption and cultural arrogance of the imperial West. British commercial establishments also provoked the ire of the protesters, as icons of continued British military occupation of the Canal Zone, held at the cost of dozens of Egyptian dead, and as symbols of the British policy of having implanted Israel in the midst of the Arab world and displaced hundreds of thousands of Palestinians.

Many of the policies of the Revolutionary Command Council that came to power in the July after the riots came as implicit answers to these discontents. They deposed the playboy king and sent him into exile. They initiated extensive land reform, liquidating the landlord class that had entrenched itself in the course of the twentieth century. They national-ized industries and ultimately even much of the retail sector, putting the country's productive energies and even consumer items at the service of a socialist nation. Colonel Gamal Abdel Nasser, who from 1954 became the leader of the ruling officers, nationalized the Suez Canal and stood up to the subsequent British, French, and Israeli onslaught. By 1957, Egypt was an independent country with the prospect of new rural and urban middle classes, in which the old monarchy and its corrupt hacienda-owner courtiers were history. The officers went on to vastly expand the educa-tional system, a key element of modern society deliberately neglected in the period of British colonial rule. Between 1960 and 1970, the average wage of the typical worker doubled, under the impact of Abdel Nasser's policies of import substitution and state-led industrialization.

At the same time, the military government that began in 1952 rejected parliamentary democracy and the rule of law. Unlike in the 'Urabi revolt and the 1919 revolution, a constitution and elected national legislature were not the cynosure of republican Egypt. In part, the evolution of Egypt as an authoritarian dictatorship and then effectively a one-party system was made possible by the ways in which the big landlord politicians of the Liberal era had shown themselves corrupt, easily bought by the imperial power, arrogant, and servants of their own narrow class interests. Many Egyptians of the 1950s were in search of a new model of governance more suited to an anti-imperial republic, and the military – coded as servant of the nation and defender against imperial and Israeli aggression – seemed suitable. Although the authoritarian state engaged in a good deal of uplift under Abdel Nasser to 1970, in the long run (under Anwar El Sadat and

Hosni Mubarak), it was susceptible of becoming itself the vehicle of corruption and nepotism of a sort that would have made the hacienda-owning gentlemen of the 1930s and 1940s blush.

The Tahrir Revolt of 2011

From 1970, Anwar El Sadat took Egypt in a new direction, opening up the economy and openly siding with the new multi-millionaire contracting class. It in turn was eager for European and American investment. With the Camp David Peace Treaty, which ended the state of war with Israel in 1979, Egypt made what has widely been seen in the region as a separate peace. Over time, this insouciance towards Israel's treatment of the Palestinians and Lebanese grated on the nerves of many Egyptian nationalists.

On the economic front, from 1970–2000, there was no real development in the country. Health, education, and standard-of-living statistics showed stagnation for an entire lost generation.[17] The government did not encourage a private market in contraception, and could never grow fast enough to increase the per capita income significantly, given rapid population growth. The ever-increasing population also increasingly crowded into the cities, although 40 per cent ended up in the marginal economy (e.g., selling matches). The social structure did change, despite the stagnation in key sectors. Nearly half the country is now urban, and even many villages have become 'suburbs' of vast metropolises.

The rural middle class, while still important, was no longer such a weighty support for the regime as it had been in the Abdel Nasser and Sadat periods, after land reform. A successful government needed to have ever-increasing numbers of urban people on its side. But there, the neoliberal policies pressed on Hosni Mubarak by the United States since 1981 were unhelpful. Samer Soliman has argued that the Egyptian state of the 1980s – Mubarak's first decade – was oriented towards providing salaries and perquisites to the large class of government employees and those dependent on government expenditures. From the 1990s, the state suffered substantial declines in external rents that limited its ability to satisfy this salaried class.[18] The state was thus increasingly seen to be a state for the few. Its old base in the rural middle classes was rapidly declining

---

[17] Richard H. Adams, 'Evaluating the Process of Development in Egypt, 1980–97', *International Journal of Middle East Studies*, Vol. 32, No. 2 (May 2000), pp. 255–275.

[18] Samer Soliman, *The Autumn of Dictatorship: Fiscal Crisis and Political Change in Egypt under Mubarak* (Palo Alto, CA: Stanford University Press, 2011).

as young people moved to the cities. An ostentatious state business class emerged, deeply dependent on government contracts and state goodwill, and meeting in the fancy tourist hotels. Workers attempting to strike over declining wages and working conditions were repressed.[19]

The failure of the regime to connect with the rapidly growing new urban working and middle classes, and its inability to provide jobs to the masses of college graduates it was creating, set the stage for the January–February 2011 upheaval. Also galling to the activists was the Mubarak government's seemingly unlimited appetite for obsequiousness towards Washington, including its willingness to torture suspected Muslim militants rendered by the Central Intelligence Agency, its treatment of the Palestinians (for example, helping with the blockade of Gaza), its willingness to sell natural gas to Israel at far-below-market prices, and the surreptitious help it gave the United States in the Iraq War (including over-flight rights). Even though the economy has been growing 5 and 6 per cent in the past decade, what government impetus there was to this development remained relatively hidden – unlike its role in the land reform of the 1950s and 1960s. Moreover, the income gained from increased trade largely went to a small class of investors. The Mubarak government took steps in recent decades towards neoliberal policies of privatization and a smaller public sector under pressure from Washington and allied institutions – and the process was often corrupt. The ruling families used their prior knowledge of important economic-policy initiatives to engage in a kind of insider trading, advantaging their relatives and buddies. Indeed, in 2012 Gamal and Alaa Mubarak, the sons of the deposed president, were formally charged with insider trading. From 1991, the government sold 150 of 314 state factories it put on the block, but the benefit of the sales went to a narrow sliver of people.[20] Because the Mubaraks rigged the elections so that the National Democratic Party always won, and the party officials favoured by the president prospered, Egypt was ruled by a closed elite.

Among the groups that made the revolutions demanding more democracy in Egypt were workers, women, and youth. Although university-educated new middle classes played a key role in organizing the protests and mobilizing youths, they are typically tightly connected with labour

---

[19] Ann Lesch, 'Egypt's Spring: Causes of the Revolution', *Middle East Policy*, Vol. 18, No. 3 (Fall 2011): 35–48. Some of what follows is a reworking of my essay, 'The Great Arab Revolt', *The Nation*, 17 February 2011.

[20] Michael Slackman, 'Egypt Concedes to Resistance on Privatization Push', *New York Times*, 27 June 2010.

syndicates and blue-collar workers, whether urban or rural. Many of the key demands of the movement had to do with pay equity and living conditions for the working poor and the unemployed. High food prices for the poor also created severe discontent that aided in mobilizing them. The educated youth, office workers, and factory workers spearheaded the revolution, having the organizational and material resources to do so.[21]

Among the actions supporting the crowds were effective labour strikes that closed factories and offices, freeing workers to demonstrate. Thus, in the midst of the uproar at Cairo's downtown Tahrir ('Liberation') Square in January–February 2011, a new umbrella labour organization was formed – the Federation of Egyptian Trade Unions – and welcomed by the American Federation of Labour-Congress of Industrial Organizations. It unites white-collar and blue-collar workers on the need for reform of the Egyptian state, and seeks to supplant the state-controlled Federation of Trade Unions.

The unrest in Egypt in some ways can be traced to the attempt of workers at the state-run textile factories of al-Mahalla al-Kubra just outside Cairo to launch a major strike on 6 April 2008.[22] Although the regime had some success in forestalling a successful outcome that time, an 'April 6 Committee' of youths and labour activists was formed and continued to plan and agitate. They were among the major forces calling for the big demonstration on 25 January at Tahrir Square that brought down the Egyptian Cabinet and placed a question mark over the government's future. There have been more than 3,000 labour actions since 2004 in Egypt, where manufacturing now accounts for about a quarter of the economy. Recent years have given workers reason to be unhappy. The 2008–2009 banking crisis in the West hurt North Africa and the Middle East by slowing trade and tourism.[23] Some 20 per cent of Egyptians already lived below the poverty line, and another fifth lived just above that line and were vulnerable to going under.

---

[21] Some of these thoughts first appeared in a different form in Juan Cole, 'Labor movement drives Egypt, Tunisia protests', *The Detroit News*, 10 February 2011. See also Joel Beinin, 'Egypt's Workers Rise Up', *The Nation*, 7–14 March 2011 and Chapter 7 by John Chalcraft in this volume.

[22] Manar Shorbagy, 'Understanding Kefaya: The New Politics in Egypt', *Arab Studies Quarterly*, Vol. 29 no. 1 (Winter 2007): 39–60; 'The April 6 Youth Movement', *Frontline* (22 February 2011) at http://www.pbs.org/wgbh/pages/frontline/revolution-in-cairo/inside-april6-movement/

[23] Arnie Klau, 'Impact of the Economic Crisis on Trade, Foreign Investment, and Employment in Egypt', ILO SRO Cairo Working Paper Series (February 2010) at http://www.unglobalpulse.org/sites/default/files/reports

The techniques used to open up politics in the Arab uprisings have been the flashmob, the cascade, and blackmailing the elite. Youth movements and office and factory workers used social media such as Facebook and Twitter to call for demonstrations at particular times and places, creating enormous spontaneous gatherings of physical crowds impelled by a spontaneous Internet call to assemble.[24] The flashmob technique eluded many procedures of the security police because of their unpredictability and dependence on non-transparent networks. In addition, the size of the resultant crowds was enormous and unpredictable. The more people in the street, the less likely it was that any particular person would be in danger. And, a tipping point was reached that produced a cascade. That is, 30,000 people in the street might not inspire the masses to join, but 40,000 might. Crucial to reaching the tipping point is that demonstrators create a perception that change is possible and perhaps even inevitable.[25]

The overthrow of Zine El Abidine Ben Ali in Tunisia on 14 January 2011 may have contributed to the success of the Egyptian movement. Previous demonstrations never reached the tipping point and so never produced a cascade. When the movement showed itself able to consistently put tens and even hundreds of thousands of people in the streets, and in many cities around the country, it was able to paralyze the economy and so threaten elite interests. The crowds gave the elite a choice between having the army fire on them or pushing out the narrow mafia-like families and networks of cronies that dominated the upper echelons of the power structure. In Egypt, where the vast majority of troops were conscripts for three years, using the military against the crowds was politically undesirable. The United States also had some influence with the Egyptian officer corps and appears to have pressured the corps to avoid a bloodbath.

The crowds more or less provoked a coup by other members of the elite against the president for life and his family and associates. The 23-member Supreme Council of the Armed Forces (SCAF) functioned as the executive branch of government until the presidential election in June 2012. The groups that made the uprising typically demanded a transition to liberal, parliamentary democracy in the aftermath. Whereas

---

[24] Walid El Hamamsy, 'BB = BlackBerry or Big Brother: Digital media and the Egyptian revolution', *Journal of Postcolonial Writing*, Vol. 47, No. 4 (2011), pp. 454–466.

[25] Timur Kuran and Cass R. Sunstein, 'Cascades and Risk Regulation', *Stanford Law Review*, Vol. 51, No. 4 (April 1999), pp. 683–768.

the movement of 25 January 2011 had as its immediate political effect a military coup, the political mobilization of so many Egyptians cannot be denied, and the transitional phase developed as a struggle between the military and civilian networks and organizations, such as the leftist youth groups, the revitalized labour movement, and the Muslim Brotherhood. The struggle played out with continued demonstrations throughout the country, labour strikes, and villager protests involving blocking major roads with felled trees, as well as in electoral contests for parliament and president. In the first two years of the transition, at least, the military typically retained the upper hand, but it could not be said to have ruled without opposition or never to have been forced to compromise.

Conclusion

In the context of Egypt's history of social upheavals, the Arab uprisings bear many resemblances to their predecessors. The filling of the streets with protesters and general strikes by workers and shopkeepers were deployed in the 'Urabi revolt, the 1919 revolution, and the Cairo revolt of 1952. However, the 2011 uprising resembled the 1919 revolution most of all, being that it was nationwide, rocking the country from Alexandria to Aswan. In every case, young people and students played an important role, alongside workers and peasants. The new media of the time were deployed by organizers – the telegraph and the newspaper in 1882 and 1919, the landline telephone in 1952, and Facebook and Twitter in 2011. In all of them, word of mouth was probably as effective as other sorts of media on a local level, although the other means of communication were important in allowing a national movement. As in 1952, many crowds in Egypt in 2011 set fire to official buildings (the headquarters of the National Democratic Party [NDP], which loomed over the downtown, was reduced to a burned-out hulk, and NDP headquarters in provincial cities were often also torched). Unlike in earlier episodes, the national police themselves were targeted, with police buildings often attacked and burned in the provinces. But whereas the 'Urabi revolt and those of 1919 and 1952 were all revolts to some extent against foreign domination, 2011 was primarily directed against an indigenous ruling cartel and its agents, the secret police, and even the ordinary police. Anti-imperialist themes played a role but were muted.

The upheaval of 2011–2012 differed from the three earlier instances of Egyptian mass mobilization by being much less concerned, on the whole, with imperial or neo-imperial Western domination than with poor indigenous governance. In field work in Tahrir Square in 2011, this author found it remarkable how few placards, banners, or graffiti slogans made reference to the United States, Europe, or Israel. In part, this downplaying of such issues may have been a response to the attempts by the Mubarak state to divert attention away from issues in local corruption and the inadequacies of its rule by diverting the gaze of the public towards the Palestinian-Israeli conflict. The Egyptian public seemed determined to keep its focus on the corruption and malfeasance of the National Democratic Party. The previous big social and political movements also critiqued governing elites, of course. But in 1882, the Khedive Tawfiq was called a 'traitor' by revolutionaries for his decision to side with the Europeans against General Ahmad 'Urabi, and in 1952, rioting crowds blamed King Faruq for allying himself culturally with the British occupiers and for not responding forcefully to what they saw as the British affront at Ismailia. The upheaval of 2011–2012 differed from 1952 insofar as it did not succeed in displacing or neutering the old elite, save at the very top of the political and economic hierarchy. No ban was placed on political activity by the former National Democratic Party politicians. In the presidential election of June 2012, a representative of the old regime, Ahmad Shafiq, was narrowly defeated by the Muslim Brotherhood candidate. No liquidation of the former regime's social base seems envisioned, in contrast to Abdel Nasser's land reform. There seems likely to be more social and economic continuity from the first Egyptian republic to the second than was the case between the monarchy and the first republic.

Many among the demonstrators in the Arab world during the Arab uprisings, whether union organizers, villagers, or college graduates, seem to have believed that once the lead log in the logjam is removed – that is, once the narrow, mafia-like elites at the top are removed – the economy would return to normal and opportunities for advancement would open up to all. Once the ruling family was gone, the interim government promptly froze the accounts of regime cronies and in many instances initiated legal proceedings against them. Seeing the writing on the wall, the ambitious resigned en masse from the now notorious former ruling party. They put their hopes in free and fair parliamentary elections. In this regard, they were echoing the demands of 'Urabi for a modern constitution and an effective legislature, and of Saad Zaghlul, for an independent Egypt with its own Westminster-style system of government. Today, they continue to turn against the implicit Leninism of the Nasser period, which set aside representative government as overly open to penetration by anti-nationalist forces and by class enemies. Thus, the Middle East may be swinging back to a new liberal period, formally resembling that of the 1930s and 1940s. The success or failure of this new liberal age will heavily depend on whether the new governments can achieve economic and social development, and whether they can overcome the legacy of corruption and cronyism.

4

A Depressive Pre–Arab Uprisings
Economic Performance

Ali Kadri[*]

This chapter examines the economic vulnerabilities behind the Arab uprisings. The analysis shows that per capita income in the Arab world has
stagnated since the early 1980s. The core reasons for this retrogression
are successive Arab military defeats, compradorial ruling elites and an
imperialist oil grab. Arab states lost autonomy over policy which instead
became dictated by the demands of global capital. Economic growth
became more heavily dependent on oil rather than on productive investment while conflict and a failure of the state have caused a failure of
development and hindered long-term investment. The business cycle in
the Arab world is mainly driven by exogenous pressures and represents
a case of an 'imperialistically determined cycle'. Development will continue to fail unless post-uprising governments adopt radical measures that
deliver redistribution and land reform.

    This essay investigates the determinants of the business cycle in the
Arab world (AW) prior to the Arab popular uprisings. As is the case
after a military rout, several defeats against Israel and the United States
stripped Arab countries of sovereignty and autonomy over policy and
subjected the working population to the terms of surrender dictated by
the World Bank and International Monetary Fund (WB-IMF) policy at
the behest of global capital. The social products and assets of the Arab
world, including no less the human component, were taken in a manner

[*] I am grateful to my colleagues from the UN, Dr. Yasuhisa Yamamoto and Dr. Linda
Matar, for their research support and comments. All shortcomings are, however, my own
responsibility.

reminiscent of colonial patterns of capital accumulation. In particular, pursuant to the Camp David accords, which splintered the Arab world, the pattern of economic growth has come to depend more heavily on oil and geopolitical rents, as opposed to the systemic component associated with productive investment. The inverse relationship between political instability and developmental growth became more pronounced with the progress of time. Uncertainty over the time horizon associated with conflict and potential state collapse hampered long-term investment and capital accumulation. This essay contends that the business cycle in the AW is determined by a quasi-colonial relationship underpinned by oil control, and propelled almost in its entirety by political considerations relating to imperialist hegemony.

In accounting terms, for developmental growth to take hold in the AW, oil prices/revenues should more than cover the political instability premium and the state should be representative, as distinct from corporatist, of working-class interests. In other words, it is hypothetically possible to grow under stable conditions with low oil prices because the peace or 'defused tensions' dividend in a state that promotes the rights of labour could be channelled into the social infrastructure and productive activity; realistically, however, the opposite of this desirable path materialised. The regressive developmental process leading to the Arab uprisings, which permitted the transfer of resources abroad at 'cheapened' prices, was reinforced at every stage by WB-IMF proposed pro-cyclical policies that accentuated the many negative shocks to which the AW was subjected. These shocks were doubly potent because the vacillation of oil prices intertwined with a precarious political environment to deepen the troughs in the cycle. As conflicts arose, oil prices also rose on account of the risk element. Increasing oil revenue, however, was squandered in regime security spending and capital flight. In Arab countries, the ruling-class commitment to the WB-IMF neoliberal framework created a whole set of macro prices (exchange and interest rates) that ensured anti-developmental outcomes by lowering national prices to levels insufficient to maintain decent standards of living. Prices, to be sure, are not deus ex machina. Prices were reproduced across time by a quasi-colonial power relationship in which Arab resources – human or otherwise – get undervalued and transferred abroad in money form.

In the state of defeat of social ideology, the WB-IMF and the local ruling autocracies, at the behest of global capital, elevated private sector development from a reasoned position with drawbacks and failings into a system of belief. The obfuscation reached its zenith in the immediate years prior to the Arab uprisings as the WB-IMF spewed out a litany of literature recommending good governance to Arab despots. Advising absolute monarchs or despots of the type of Hosni Mubarak of Egypt or Ali Abdullah Saleh of Yemen to govern in 'good' ways was not haphazard, it was purposeful and calculated. Asking for the impossible was the manner by which the unreal is transmuted into the real by the power of ideology. These Arab regimes did not codify a whole number of power relations that render their functioning possible; they confiscated all power.[1] Hence, alluding that good governance and reform were possible under these regimes was the ideological means by which capital bamboozled working people into accepting the logic of existing polity.[2] The WB-IMF consortium prolonged and endorsed Arab despotism.

In addition to the uncertainty related to political tensions/conflicts, which acquire the semblance of force majeure, the interface between private sector based macro policy and outcome generated disastrous results leading up to the Arab uprisings. Privatisation, trade, capital-account openness, and deregulation seized resources at prices below value. The incomes earned by the working population were insufficient to better their lot in life and, circuitously, power-brokered prices did little to support developmental growth.[3] Prior to the uprisings, the forces weighing negatively on the business cycle grew to the point where, as evidenced by poor productivity and technological progress contributed little to economic growth. In short, the AW's economy grew from without and by the impact of oil prices and by the impact of regional uncertainties

---

[1] M. Foucault, *Power/Knowledge* (New York and Toronto: Pantheon Books, 1980).

[2] Eugene Dili Lio, 'The Neoliberal-Developmental State: Singapore as Case-Study', *Critical Sociology*, Vol. 38, No. 2, (2011), 241–264. http://crs.sagepub.com/content/early/2011/09/21/0896920511419900

[3] Developmental growth is regarded as a process of economic growth, with expanding output and employment, institutional transformation, and technological progress of a country that steadily improves the well-being of all people. When that well-being is regarded as the fulfilment of human rights and fundamental freedoms that enhance the capabilities of the people to realize their full potential, the process of development that leads to the improvement of that well-being can be claimed as a human right. The realization of the right to development is seen as the fulfilment of a set of claims by people, principally on their State but also on the society at large, including the international community, to a process that enables them to realize the rights and freedoms set forth in the International Bill of Human Rights. Economic and Social Council, COMMISSION ON HUMAN RIGHTS (Working Group on the Right to Development, Geneva, 11–20 February 2004).

and tensions – and the policy framework, which was structured by the WB-IMF – ensured that the damages wrought from external shocks were steeper and the benefits were lost.

Pre-analytic

Although Arab countries are broadly diverse, the recent history of economic growth in the AW can be characterised by three distinct periods: a period of high growth driven by comparatively heavy government intervention beginning in the early 1960s and ending in the early 1980s; a period of low growth typified by collapsing oil prices, free market reforms, and gradual structural adjustments, ranging from the early 1980s until early 2000; and a period of high oil prices and highly inequitable growth beginning in early 2000. If anything, vulnerability to external shocks in the AW was and is decisive to the growth process. In an environment fraught with uncertainty, contagion and boom/bust cycles, economic shocks were further compounded by the liberalisation of the financial market, a freer trade regime, and a particular type of public sector, which became increasingly privately owned by the ruling autocracies. At first sight, ensuring equitable and developmental growth while insulating the regional economy from negative shocks earmarks a policy imperative par excellence for the post-uprising Arab regimes. To date, however, the new regimes, elected or otherwise, still shy away from radical reform and pursue the same path as that of their predecessors.

Empirical research on the Arab growth performance using the method of growth accounting finds that the knowledge-based sector or internally developed technologies are either absent or yield a net negative impact on economic growth on account of fiscal leakage.[4] AW growth is driven principally by its extensive components or net additions to capital and labour without the scale-enhancing effect of the knowledge economy or what is referred to as the intensive component. Furthermore, searching for the contribution of capital and labour to output in rent-based economies generally falls victim to a fallacious specification – namely, the lag between investment demand and the subsequent

---

[4] X. Sala-I-Martin and E. V. Artadi, *Economic Growth and Investment in the Arab World* (Working Paper; Departament d'Economica i Empresa, Universidad Pompeu Fabra 2002); M. A. El-Erian, A. Bisat, and T. Helbling, *Growth, Investment, and Saving in the Arab Economies*, International Monetary Fund (IMF) (2000).

incremental build-up of capital stock. Investments enter national accounts as investment demand and, at later stages, they register as the relevant component of growth, which is the incremental rise in capital stock. In the case of Arab rent economies, however, the high rate of leakages in assets and capital flight distinguishes the background relationship that underlies the allocation of resources as an anomaly, not only different from the developed countries, but also from the majority of developing countries. Much of investment in Arab rent economies pours into areas that are of little or no relevance to productivity growth. The bigger share of investment is lodged in short gestation-period capital, low capital-output ratio areas, and what is known as FIRE economies (Finance, Insurance, and Real Estate). Value added is created on account of high imports and a significant part of the financial assets fly abroad – a greater part of consumption is composed of imported goods and capital flight, which, in the case of Saudi Arabia, can represent about a quarter of Gross Domestic Product (GDP).[5] Without the ploughing-back effect of rents into the social infrastructure and plant and equipment, the mobilization of national resources proceeds at rates below what is necessary to absorb population growth effectively in decent employment. Regulating exchange and interest rates to stem the outflow of resources at prices set way below value by a coalition of national and international capital has been a policy of immediate post-independence and up to the early 1980s. In the neoliberal age, macro prices, wages, interest, and exchange rates were deregulated to restrict the expansion of the social and physical capital stock. The point is that variations in growth rates have to be interpreted, not only in terms of the share of oil in total product, but also subject to waste (mislaid investment), high levels of imports, and a considerable leakage in assets.

That oil prices or oil revenues matter to the economies of the AW appears somewhat self-evident. On the policy side, however, what should be brought under investigation is the macroeconomic environment that may make oil revenues contribute to equitable growth and development. In a region beset by conflict and one that allocates at least twice the world's rate to defence spending,[6] defining the attributes of such an environment or the threshold at which oil rents would seep into development

---

5 UN Survey of Economic and Social Conditions in Western Asia, 2007–2008.
6 Source: SIPRI and WDI (World Bank) Database, various years.

is by no means self-evident. A priori, what matters for regional development is not so much the level of oil prices or revenues per se, it is rather the level that offsets the costs of uncertainty and begins to trickle into productive investment activity. All other things considered, a higher level of political instability fed by working-class insecurity and imperialist policies, would necessarily imply that for regional development to take root, oil revenues must more than offset the need to cover defence spending, smooth government consumption, act as a propeller of public investment, and an insurance premium for private investment. With persistently high levels of political tensions in the Middle East, that may be too much to ask from oil exports – one of the most volatile export commodities in world trade.[7]

Moving away from oil dependency to diversification ('kicking the oil habit') is unlikely. Persistent dependence on oil is not haphazard; it is defined and reproduced in consortium between Arab regimes and U.S.-led powers. No country can escape this gridlock given the implications of Arab development to the reigning balance of forces that thrive on accumulation by encroachment and militarism; that is, if development were potentially to occur. The forces that tie down development supersede Arab national boundaries and represent a cross-border alliance of Arab comprador elites and Western capital. With this class configuration in place, the business cycle of the AW remains principally an externally driven cycle, the share of oil relative to national output is at more than half of national income, and the contribution of technology and/or the knowledge-based sector to the economy is minimal. These are closely intertwined manifestations of one and the same social relationship, bred by a cross-border class alliance that encumbers the path of development. Ultimately, Western elites in cahoots with the ruling Arab autocracy and, in their quest to stake oil, deny the working population in the AW their sovereignty over their national resources, which is also a human right.[8]

---

[7] In a ranking of commodity export revenues by degree of volatility, oil revenues assumed one of the highest values of instability amongst globally traded commodities. J. Mayer, A. Butkevicius, and A. Kacri, 'Dynamic products in world exports' (Discussion Paper No. 159, United Nations Conference on Trade and Development [UNCTAD], May 2002).

[8] 'Articulation by the barrel of a gun', lecture by S. Avramidis, Historical Materialism, (SOAS) School of Oriental and African Studies, 2006. http://mercury.soas.ac.uk/hm/pdf/2006confpapers/papers/Avramidis.pdf

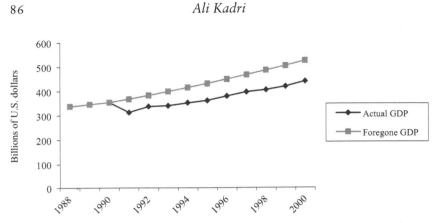

FIGURE 4.1. Actual and foregone GDP in the AW as a result of the Gulf War (*Billions of United States dollars*). *Source:* Author's computation based on data from Word Development Indicators (WDI).

The Impact of Conflicts

Conflicts and the persistent threats thereof, which continue to dampen long-term investment, exact a heavy toll on the AW. In 1991, there was a 14 per cent loss in AW output (GDP) in the immediate aftermath of the first Gulf War. This was equivalent to about US$50 billion in 1990 prices. Had the war not occurred and had the growth rate in the region continued to rise at the modest growth rate of 3 per cent since 1990, the cumulative losses in constant 1990 prices from 1990 to 2002 are estimated at around US$600 billion (see Figure 4.1). The recovery from the war was lethargic and inadequate. It took about five years for output to regain its pre-1990 levels. These are hypothetical calculations of value added, the real human and economic losses were portentous. Although difficult to assess, the foregone losses in employment possibilities were potentially between six and seven million positions in the 1990s alone. Directly, or through their destabilising threats, the calamity of war imposes a heavy and unrelenting burden on the regional economy. The spectre of war also circularly justifies the security apparatus that sustains Arab autocracies and, by implication, shifts resources from productive investment to stabilisation efforts (see Table 4.1).

In the past 50 years, the Middle East witnessed more wars than any other region in the world (see Table 4.2). Despite the significantly negative impact of wars on human development, there are surprisingly few studies that try to assess the effects of militarized conflicts on growth. Mainstream literature on that subject is limited to the link between militarized conflicts and trade, and assesses the direction of the causality between trade and

TABLE 4.1. *Military Spending as a Percentage of GDP for Selected Arab Countries, 1988–2005*

	1988	1989	1990	1991	1992	1993	1994	1995	1996	1997	1998	1999	2000	2001	2002	2003	2004	2005
Bahrain	5	5.1	5.1	5.4	5.2	5	4.6	4.7	4.7	4.6	4.8	4.9	4	4.2	4	4.9	4.4	3.6
UAE	8.6	7.8	6.2	6.3	6.1	6.1	5.9	5.5	[5.1]	4.8	5.1	4.3	3.4	3.4	3.3	2.8	2.3	2
Oman	18.3	16.7	16.5	14.8	16.2	15.4	15.7	14.6	12.5	12.5	12.5	11.4	10.6	12.2	12.3	12.1	12	11.9
KSA	15.2	13.4	14	12.5	11.3	12.5	10.6	9.3	8.5	11	14.3	11.4	10.6	11.5	9.8	8.7	8.4	8.2
Kuwait	8.2	8.5	48.5	117	31.8	12.4	13.3	13.6	10.3	8.1	8.8	7.6	7.2	7.7	7.4	6.5	5.9	4.8
Egypt	6.9	5.8	4.7	4.6	4.5	4.3	4.2	3.9	3.5	3.3	3.3	3.2	3.2	3.3	3.4	3.3	3	2.8
Jordan	8.3	8	6.9	8.9	6.1	6.2	5.9	5.8	5.4	6.3	5.6	5.6	5.5	5.2	6	6.7	5.7	5.3
Lebanon	1.2	-	7.6	5.2	8	6	7	6.7	5.7	4.3	4.1	4.9	4.4	5.6	4.9	4.6	4.4	4.5
Syrian Arab Republic	6.9	7	6	9.1	7.9	6.4	6.5	6.2	5.2	5	5.1	4.8	5.5	5	4.7	5.6	6.4	5.1

Source: Stockholm International Peace Research Institute [SIPRI] Database

TABLE 4.2. *List of Selected Conflicts and Wars in the Arab World*

Year	Countries	Description
1948	Israel-Iraq-Egypt-Jordan-Lebanon-Syria	Arab-Israeli War
1956	Israel-Egypt-France-UK	Suez War
1958	Lebanon	Civil War
1962–1967	Yemen	North Yemen Civil War
1967	Israel-Egypt-Jordan-Syria	Arab-Israeli War
1973	Israel-Egypt-Syria	Arab-Israeli War
1975–1990 .	Lebanon	Civil War
1982–2000	Israel-Lebanon	Invasion
1980–1988	Iran-Iraq	War
1990	Iraq-Kuwait	Invasion
1990–1991	International Coalition-Iraq	Gulf War I
1994	Yemen	Civil War
2003-Now	United States-UK-Iraq	Gulf War II
2006	Israel-Lebanon	War

Notes: This list excludes the ongoing Israeli-Palestinian conflict, the U.S. embargo on Iraq in the 1990s, and the various waves of domestic violence such as within Jordan in 1970, Syria in 1982, and Iraq in 1988.
Sources: Various sources.

war. However, a broader perspective needs to underscore the negative effects of wars on withering a considerable part of the human and physical infrastructure. Lebanon and Iraq never fully replaced their past losses. Wars affect long-term growth, particularly in the light of irreversible weakening of capacity and, in an Arab context, the tailoring of policy to the implicit or explicit terms of surrender. Destruction ensures that the balance of forces is further tilted in favour of imperialist powers that have a direct interest in cheapening and grabbing Arab as well as other Third World resources. Imperialism is a relationship in which undervaluing and seizing resources by more advanced countries contributes to boosting profit rates alongside the sale and exchange of commodities on the market.

War may be costly in terms of increasing public debts and tax burdens or of distortions to industrial production through the disproportionate expansion of militarized manufacture and imports; however, this is not why the lingering impact of war in the Arab region appears to be permanent. In the AW, there are few taxes, the public domain is privately owned, and most weapons are imported; hence, the regular baggage of war is not so relevant to economic performance. In an oil targeted-for-control region, the class alliance with Western capital ensures the

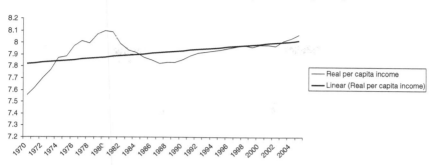

FIGURE 4.2. Long-run average per capita growth rate. *Source*: Author's computation based on data from WDI and World Bank database.

reproduction of war and the exaggerated image of world dependence on oil, time, and again, to the disadvantage of the working population – not only to the Arab world, but across the globe. Pauperising the workforce and subjecting it to the misery of war serves by the demonstration effect to prop up an ideology of ultranationalism in the Western hemisphere. The class alliance in charge of development disempowers working people, stripping them of the right to organize and their sovereignty over national resources. War remains part and parcel of global accumulation and a neo-colonial agenda of resource grab, or the process by which developed formations garner the resources of the Third World under highly inequitable terms imposed by outright military power.

Past Performance of the Arab World

Based on a forty-year average, the AW has been characterised by one of the lowest real average per capita growth rates in the world (the average yearly real per capita GDP growth is .35 percent, see Figure 4.2). That the AW is rich in capital is a false dictum that dominates the development discourse. Development is about the mobilization of real resources and not money capital. The skewed distribution of resources and the extent to which autocracies have relinquished sovereignty of oil to the United States make the Arab countries poor in overall resources, including their oil. Arab regimes, by virtue of their shared security and sovereignty with the United States, are only custodians of an oil resource, which is not theirs. Arab private financial resources abroad are personal and private resources and, as such, they remain unrequited transfers and practically unavailable for regional development.

Thus, insofar as the image of rich Arabs persists, the broader picture –
one in which around 50 per cent of the population survive on less than
US$2 a day and spends more than half of its income on basic foods
prior to the uprisings – is likely to continue to be purposefully concealed
and/or overlooked.[9] As of early 2000, Arab poverty worsened with a
growth performance in which distribution was carried out within a state
that is mainly at the disposal of foreign powers – directly as U.S. satellites or indirectly by conceding to WB-IMF policy – through U.S.- and
Arab-ruling autocracies. It may be relevant at this juncture to dispel the
image of 'rich Arabs' and to state things as they are: within the strict
confines of economic wealth there are rich individuals in the Arab world,
but the majority of working Arabs are in fact pauperised. According to
Texas Income Inequality Database, the AW exhibits one of the highest
income inequalities of all regions.[10] Despite the formal change in elites
in some 'Arab Spring' countries, which occurred without any redistribu-
tional measures, the divide between the private and the social aspects of
wealth continues to grow, which only aggravates the past conditions. For
the time being, the Arab uprising is a revolution without redistribution.

Upon a closer examination of the per-capita income performance (see
Table 4.3), the broader picture tends to conceal some very diverse patterns, the most visible of which is that since about the early 1980s, the
more diversified economies (less dependent on oil) have consistently out-
performed big oil exporting economies. These more diverse economies
have proven to have a more stable growth path and, consequently, were
less exposed to disturbances caused by external shocks – falling oil prices
(see Figure 4.3). Although the putative view holds that low oil prices
were the culprits behind this poor-growth performance, a more serious
analysis finds that this may only represent a partial assessment of events.
Driven by higher output levels, export revenues – principally composed of
oil revenues – rose at an average yearly rate of 2 per cent since 1985. The
chief issue remains, however, that this revenue did not bolster the investment rate or the principal component in the growth mechanism because
by the early 1980s, the accent shifted to private sector-led investment.
The investment rate, dependent on risk considerations and uncertainties,

---

[9] All the computations I carried out for this research were conducted while at the
United Nations on the UN database or the World Bank's WDI database. Also see
national accounts database, League of Arab States, Ataqrir al Arabi Almouwahad.
(various years), and the World Bank, http://www-wds.worldbank.org/external/default/
WDSContentServer/WDSP/IB/2011/05/27/000001843_20110601143246/Rendered/
PDF/P126506000AWIFS000PID000ConceptoStage.pdf

[10] http://utip.gov.utexas.edu/data.html

TABLE 4.3. *Growth in Real GDP Per Capita in the Arab World*

	1971–1980	1980–1990	1990–2000	1971–2000
Bahrain	9.25	(3.51)	0.97	0.48
Kuwait	(8.60)	(4.81)	9.43	(3.36)
Oman	1.05	2.81	0.83	2.07
Qatar	(4.75)	(5.22)	4.33	(2.61)
Saudi Arabia	3.69	(9.44)	(1.11)	(3.37)
United Arab Emirates	16.93	(8.29)	0.07	(0.10)
Gulf Cooperation Council countries	1.85	(7.67)	0.50	(2.78)
Egypt	3.81	3.26	2.52	2.73
Iraq	7.84	(1.87)	(5.23)	(4.95)
Jordan	2.84	(1.27)	0.00	0.88
Lebanon	(4.63)	(8.39)	3.41	(2.45)
Syrian Arab Republic	6.16	(2.96)	2.92	1.27
Yemen	3.96	12.23	0.70	7.87
More Diversified Economies	5.87	(0.16)	0.35	0.02
TOTAL AW	4.99	(3.43)	0.34	(0.85)

Note: () indicates negative growth.
Source: United Nations Statistics database.

which are chiefly non-quantifiable risks, decreased on average by about two percentage points over the 1990s. In contrast to this, in the 1970s, export earnings increased at a much higher rate of 8 per cent with proportionately more resources spilling over into economic investment activity and, hence, a much higher investment and growth rate.

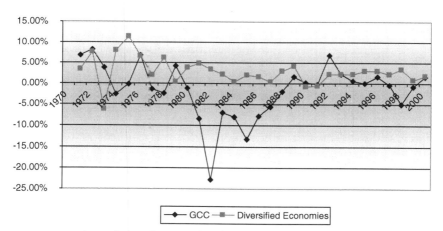

FIGURE 4.3. Annual growth rates of real GDP per capita. *Source*: Author's computation based on data from WDI and World Bank database.

Higher oil prices in the 1970s, conditioned by etatism, meant that more resources were available for investment in spite of the perennial state of tensions plaguing the region. National security and development concerns ran parallel to each other in the post-independence period. Although spending on defence and other security considerations bit off a comparatively considerable chunk of total investment, the remaining resources propped up productive capital intended for civilian usage. The stylized relationship between economic growth and investment was such that for every one percentage point of growth, there needed to be three percentage points of investment.[11] When the macro context became liberalised at a later stage beginning in the early 1980s, this relationship changed considerably. It then required around 5 per cent of growth in investment to register 1 per cent of economic growth. Under etatism and regulated markets, the growth rate responded favourably to the channelling of public savings into an investment/growth nexus.

A continued state of instability along with a laissez-faire framework (introduced gradually since the early 1980s) meant that the investment rate remained low and indeed fell. Investment was to be placed on ephemeral, low-capital output-ratio activity. It may be difficult to pin down the threshold level of risk at which regional oil rents would flow into productive investment and the share of development in growth, which is determined by the rapport de force of social classes, but had the region only furnished the average world rate on defence spending, it may be safe to say that, roughly estimated, because of instability alone, the AW loses on average about two percentage points of growth every year since 1980. This estimate is hypothetical and only a potential assessment of losses. The real losses of instability associated conflicts, however, would be commensurate with the losses in human and capital assets, which were immense.

Pattern of Growth

A high variance and an overall poor yearly average growth rate characterise the Arab business cycle. In the AW, it is possible to grow under stable conditions with low oil prices because the peace dividend could be channelled into infrastructure and productive activity, but the opposite of this pattern occurred. The national rent-grab intertwined imperialist control motives, pre-empted social investment in labour, and recirculated capital away from the national formation. Also note that because most economic activity is based on import-led consumption and a commercial

---

[11] These calculations are based on the WDI database.

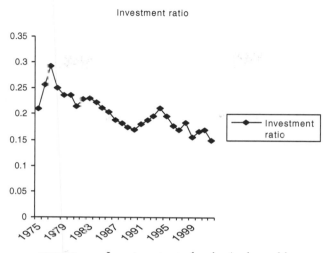

FIGURE 4.4. Investment rate for the Arab world.

circuit of capital as opposed to an industrial one, it is partly unnecessary for the ruling autocracies to invest socially in labour; social investment in labour, including the education of women, forms part of the regime stabilisation strategy. It so follows that under persistent tensions and a policy interface facilitating the transfer of resources abroad, the AW exhibited one of the lowest and poorest quality per capita growth rates of all regions over the last three decades (See Figure 4.2 – based on calculations from the World Development Indicators [WDI] database). A poor-quality growth performance is more pronounced in 'adjusting' countries, which were touted as model WB-IMF students such as Tunisia and Egypt. In both countries, income inequality was eroding the income of working people at a faster rate than the high rate of growth in GDP (WDI). In analytical point form, three anti-developmental processes and one outstanding impediment underpin the path of growth in the AW:

(a) The volatility and dependence of growth on oil price fluctuations in oil-exporting economies and geopolitical flows disturbances in the case of the more diversified economies;

(b) An overall poor trade integration in the regional and global economy (principally oil exports) – continued heavy reliance on oil exports and a marked lack of competitiveness;

(c) A lower investment rate relative to the 1970s/ early 1980s that yielded lower growth rates in the 1980s–1990s. Investment rates fell from 30 per cent in 1980 to around 18 per cent in 2010 (see Figure 4.4);

(d) The relatively minor contribution of technology and other knowledge-based activities to growth.

Although, in part, a slower rate of growth in oil revenues can explain the decline in investment since the early 1980s, the accent on promoting private investment and trade openness that were carried out under the auspices of the Breton-Woods institutions, irrespective of the speed or degree to which they were implemented, resulted in poor investment and trade performances. The investment rate dipped at an average of around −2 per cent annually and basic sectors, such as agriculture or industry, declined as shares of output. Manufacturing decreased at a rate of about 1.5 per cent since 1990 and agriculture declined to 8 per cent of GDP.[12]

Neoliberal reform policies were implemented piecemeal which pauperized the working population and by controlling resources at prices cheaper than value from the AW. These policies are an indirect restitution of colonialism insofar as the control of national resources by an outside power and the below-value resource transfer are concerned. Insecure Arab states are partly constituted by a foreign military (mainly the U.S. military) and capital component. Further, despite most Arab countries' adherence to the terms of World Trade Organization (WTO), market access problems persisted for the areas in which the region displayed a comparative advantage, namely textiles and agriculture. More importantly, on the investment side where the decline has been substantial, the risks were considerable given the small domestic market, capital-biased institutions, poor regional integration and, ultimately, precarious and uncertain political cycles/state instability. Thus, for instance, when 'one-stop shops' that reduce red tape and facilitate domestic and foreign investment were set up, very little investment flowed into Arab economies and, more pertinently, the type of investment that arrived from abroad was resource seeking and domestic investment sought a quick recovery of the initial outlay of capital.

Investors' confidence remained low on account of stability concerns. This begs the question as to whether the stark absence of the sort of non-economic losses insurance scheme that offsets the risks to long-term investment was not considered because of the very risks it poses to the regional geopolitical security. Developmental investment would have unleashed a sort of tabooed economic growth, one with expanding

---

[12] Ataqrir Al-Arabi Al-Mouwahad, national accounts database, League of Arab States. Various years.

output and employment, institutional transformation, and technological progress that might steadily improve the well-being of working people; these different layers of a holistic process, which is developmental, would imply popular sovereignty or the right of peoples to design and implement policies that conform to their social needs. In view of the fact that the AW is integrated with global capital via the militaristic and encroachment side, no effort could be spared by the cross-border class alliance in snuffing any policy moving in the way of empowering people socially and economically. The extraction of value at fire-sale prices from the Arab world contributes to lowering the costs of inputs required for global accumulation and to raising the rate of profits for financial capital. War and neoliberalism worked together to ensure the deterioration of social conditions in the AW and, by implication, its knock-on ideological effect on working people everywhere. Yet, the mainstream position went on advocating liberalisation in social formations where the institution was reduced to the rule of a small clique supported by Western, principally U.S., security coverage at the behest of global capital.

The Mainstream View

Mainstream investigations of economic growth can be summarized as an effort to find a stable relationship between aggregate output and the stocks of physical inputs and technical knowledge. Supposing such a relationship exists, the growth rate of an economy depends on the rate of accumulation of primary production factors (often named as 'labour' and 'capital', but which enter as symbols in an equation) and the speed of technological progress. It is natural to envisage a wide variety of economic and social issues that affect the growth of an economy. The purpose of growth investigations is to provide a framework to examine how these economic and social issues can be counted on in the accumulation of primary production factors and the speed of technological progress, and ultimately their impact on economic growth.

Various manipulations to growth research since its reignition in neoclassical growth theory by Nobel Laureate Robert Solow have been introduced.[13] The standard neoclassical growth function produced poor empirical results because of its assumption of diminishing returns to factors of production. Real growth was exponential, whilst any measurement

[13] R. M. Solow, 'A contribution to the theory of economic growth', *Quarterly Journal of Economics* Vol. 70, No. 1 (1956), pp. 65–94.

of growth using this class of models tends to produce an image of reality where growth falls with diminishing returns. The stylized facts of steady growth were not adequately covered by the rate of accumulation of primary production factors in traditional neoclassical growth theory. Economic growth was assumed to be dominated by the global speed of technological progress and this very exogenous determinant of long-term economic growth provides insufficient answers to policy questions regarding the path of accumulation. But exogenous impetus implies that state policies and extra-economic measures are necessary to sustain growth.

Once we reject Say's Law and recognize that capitalism is prone to deficiency in aggregate demand, we have to accept that sustained growth in this system requires exogenous stimuli. By exogenous stimuli, I mean a set of factors that raise aggregate demand but are not themselves dependent on the fact that growth has been occurring in the system; that is, they operate irrespective of whether or not growth has been occurring in the system. Moreover, they raise aggregate demand by a magnitude that increases with the size of the economy, for instance with the size of the capital stock. They are, in other words, different from 'erratic shocks' on the one hand, and 'endogenous stimuli', such as the multiplier-accelerator mechanism, on the other: the latter can perpetuate or accelerate growth only if it has been occurring anyway. 'Erratic shocks' can explain the persistence of business.[14]

For the free marketeers, the notion that government and social policy are necessary for long-term growth ran counter to their belief in self-adjusting markets. That their models always stumble on a steady state was not a desirable outcome. Further mainstream investigations of growth uncovered a class of endogenous growth models, which emphasise behavioural mechanisms and technological conditions through which the accumulation of production factors themselves can be a source of exponential economic growth. With this class of models, some factors (knowledge-related ones) enhance predictions of long-term growth. The rate of growth becomes determined endogenously by the economy's dynamic decisions to internalise human or technological capital. The crucial assumption that underlies this class of models is that the dynamic decisions for investment are not wholly subject to diminishing returns. This assumption is intuitively appealing because it emphasises 'learning effects', research and development activities by firms, the role of

---

[14] 'Finance and Growth under Capitalism', Prabhat Patnaik, 11 December 2012. http://networkideas.org/ideasact/dec11/pdf/Prabhat_Patnaik.pdf

economic institutions, as well as social and political ones as direct sources of long-term economic growth.

Endogenous growth theory showed that a theoretical prediction of long-term economic growth is partly sustainable with aggregate scale economies in which knowledge is endogenised as a factor of production.[15] A litany of related research followed and included: a discussion of the role of human capital;[16] the role of innovation and international trade;[17] the role of politics in economic growth, or how income distribution policy affects economic growth.[18] These developments aimed at providing an analytical framework for the behavioural mechanisms underlying the growth process. They furnished a wide range of insights into interpreting the results underlined not only with rigid economic factors, but also with the role of social policy and institutions. However, in all these cases, historical conditions were confined to the 'rigour' of mathematical modelling. A multifaceted reality determined by the actions of politically organized social groups, which are at loggerheads with each other, was reduced to a manageable system of individual agents enjoying level playing fields and reaching a contract that satisfies an equilibrium condition. Reality was perverted for the sake of mathematics and, worse yet, equilibriums of any sort imply that models lead to steady states. This new class of growth models seems to tweak the symbols of the growth equation to delay the inevitability of declining marginal returns to factors of production. However, once more analysis succumbs to tautology, the variables that are explaining growth are themselves explained by growth:

By their very nature, since they are conditioned by the fact of growth itself, they cease to operate when the system is in a stationary state; they cannot be adduced as an explanation for the system experiencing a positive trend. Such an explanation can only be based on the operation of exogenous stimuli, that is, of stimuli which are not themselves dependent upon the fact of growth taking place.[19]

In spite of its narrow scope, mainstream growth theory generated much-needed empirical literature using cross-country data samples that analyse

---

[15] P. M. Romer, 'Increasing returns and long-run growth', *Journal of Political Economy* Vol. 94, No. 5 (1986), pp. 1002–1037.
[16] R. E. Lucas, 'On the mechanics of economic development', *Journal of Monetary Economics* Vol. 22, No. 1 (1988), pp. 3–42.
[17] G. M. Grossman and E. Helpman, 'Comparative advantage and long-run growth', *American Economic Review* Vol. 30, No. 4 (1990), pp. 796–815.
[18] A. Alesina and D. Rodrik, 'Distributive politics and economic growth', *Quarterly Journal of Economics* Vol. 109, No. 2 (1994), pp. 465–490.
[19] Op. cit., Prabhat Patnaik.

growth and the possibility of poorer countries catching up with the richer ones. Although cross-country studies may show empirical evidence on sources of economic growth, criticism has been raised that these studies may miss the thresholds on development by grouping together countries of different stages of development. This represents a serious shortcoming when constructing or examining growth models in the AW region. The historically more advanced Arab economies succumbed to the inflow of geopolitically determined petro dollars and the result was a slow process of deindustrialisation. At a later stage, the dependence of the region on exports of oil and oil-related products was reinforced by the permanent state of political instability and conflict, and the process of development has come to differ from either developed or developing economies. The mainstream policy message based on cross-country empirical studies was that economic development depends primarily on the creation of an enabling environment for the private sector, including free markets, and free flows of trade and finance. Given these conditions and the absurdity of good governance under Arab despotism, presumably, economies will naturally grow. Instability and uncertainty hamper the drive for investment by the private sector. In this region, regional growth has been pinned almost entirely on oil. The recent growth episode beginning in 2002, much like its predecessor, which started in the early 1970s, occurred concomitantly with rising oil prices. In between high oil price periods, the growth rate slowed down considerably. In light of the variability in oil price and in the presence of comprador capital-biased institutions and policies, which have an inbuilt tendency to dislocate huge sections of the population, the recent growth experience (beginning 2002) was highly inequitable, both within countries and across the region.

In a nutshell, empirical assessment of growth performance of the AW shows that the capital they build generates relatively less output than other regions, or, there are weak positive effects of capital formation on GDP growth in the AW region.[20] Conflicts, by their corrosive nature, nullify the contribution of physical capital formation. Moreover, the Arab region lacks the capacity to absorb smooth technical spill over from

---

[20] Mustapha K. Nabli, 'Long term economic development challenges and prospects for the Arab countries' (Paper presented at the Conference of the Institut du Monde Arabe, World Bank, Paris, 12 February 2004); Aamer S. Abu-Qarn and Suleiman Abu-Bader, 'Sources of Growth Revisited: Evidence from Selected MENA Countries', *World Development* Vol. 35, No. 5(2007), pp. 752–771.

the outside.[21] Trade openness provided no extra inputs to long-term growth.[22] The arrival of new technology has no statistically significant effects on the growth of labour productivity in the AW region.[23] Empirically, apart from the element of political instability, all other economic variables would result in statistically insignificant outcomes.[24] It is not unusual to witness these results in a region who e average growth rates were nearly on par with its population growth rates. If anything, by the natural growth rate approach, this implies that labour productivity experiences no relevant expansions.

These anomalies highlight the poor intermediation between financial capital and real resources. Unlike many other developing countries, the AW enjoys an abundance of financial capital, yet it fails to mobilize real resources. Both real factors, capital and labour, are subject to a schismatic relationship, which is WB-IMF sponsored on account of exercising austerity in a capacity-wanting context, meaning while labour naturally grows, governments cap the expansion of capital. This is not a case where capital and labour are incongruous in terms of skills (e.g., one needs engineers but we are producing economists), but a case in which the policy on hand created too much labour vis-à-vis a lowering of the rate of expansion in productive capital. Unless some coordination or an expansion of capital is carried out, unemployment grows in absolute terms. High unemployment in the region is structurally rooted in this lopsided accumulation process and could only mean a rise in social instability.

A Critique of the Mainstream

Mainstream theory is not intended to be a mantra of growth; 'its aim is to supply an element in an eventual understanding of certain important elements of growth and to provide a way to organize one's thoughts on these matters'.[25] Yet, invariably, in the literature propounded on the AW, the policy design for development rests on the basis of complete liberalisation, without due regard to the history and the particularity of

---

[21] S. Krogstrup and L. Matar 'Foreign Direct Investment, Absorptive Capacity and Growth in the Arab World' (The Graduate Institute of International Studies Working Paper No. 2, 2005).

[22] Op. cit., Xavier Sala-i-Martin.

[23] Op. cit., Krogstrup and Matar.

[24] UN Survey, 2004.

[25] This description of neoclassical growth theory is taken from *The New Palgrave Dictionary of Economics* (Macmillan Press, 1998).

a specific accumulation process under uncertainty. In one determining aspect of this accumulation process, Arab autocracies are more allied to Western elites than they are to their own working people. Much national wealth can be converted into dollars and sent abroad. No matter how complacent one is, liberalising in a state practically owned by few auto-crats whose vested interests lie in extra-national territory will mean that national resources will be stifled. There is little chance that the Western-governed WB-IMF consortium was unaware of this fact. The 'market', even in the neoclassical sense, is not the unquestionable control of few persons over allocation; it is a whole set of institutions guaranteeing intermediation and welfare under more or less equal power platforms. The usual sermon-like policy of the WB-IMF is to liberalise, increase the effectiveness of labour, and improve technology: '[r]estoring growth will require raising private investment . . . and improving the efficiency of investment through greater integration with the global economy'.[26]

Given the unrealistic assumptions, these policy measures are, in one sense or another, tantamount to a form of obfuscation. Raising growth is not a matter of simple additions to the arguments of growth – namely, capital, labour, and technology – in an equation. Growth represents a numeric benchmark for capital accumulation. Capital accumulation is a socio-historical process decided by organized power groups and not something that can be traced to a neoplatonic argument. Thirty years of reforms aimed at expanding and enhancing the efficiency of the private sector bear witness to no substantive expansion in investment capable of dodging an inequitable growth path. Should this not beg the question as to whether a neoclassical growth framework can release reasonable grounds on which a policy for capital accumulation can be formulated? Indeed, it should, and the alternative approach has to be traced in terms of the history of social classes reconstituting institutional change in the region, which would allow savings to be re-ploughed back into scaled augmenting-investment activity.

The continuing poor quality growth in the AW region represents, sui generis, a measure of how stagnant is the rate of expansion in the exist-ing productive capacity, institutional and distributional arrangements. The persistence of these low rates for more than three decades points to a much deeper problem with the intermediation between financial and

---

[26] J. Page, 'From Boom to Bust - and Back? The Crisis of Growth in the Middle East and North Africa', in N. Shafik, ed., *Prospects for Middle Eastern and North African Economies – From Boom to Bust and Back?* (London: Macmillan Press, 1998) 133–158.

physical capital – one that would not allow for successive and vigorous redeployment of savings in high-output capital building projects. Simply, cash is not being transferred into productive physical assets at an adequate rate. Without a fundamental change in the distributional structure that underpins the process by which resources are re-funnelled back into the region and one that provides for long-term security via regional integration – or that enhances the performance of public investment, even at high oil prices or revenues as occurred since early 2002 – the languid path of capital accumulation may remain unchanged. To date, the elected post-uprising governments have neither clamped down on resource transfers by tightening trade and capital controls nor redistributed resources. Fundamentally, nothing has changed.

Apart from investment, which is deterred by uncertainty and small markets, the region experiences a significant resource and/or affluent consumption leakage, hence reducing effective private or public savings; by effective, I mean, nationally retained savings. Capital inflows (rent or otherwise) are channelled into raising consumption either directly or through shifting resources currently earmarked for investment. Consequently, public savings fell with falling tax receipts (under adjustment) or by the impending change in the composition of government expenditure carried out under structural reforms. In any case, oil rents – in the oil-producing economies or geopolitical rent injections stabilising the more diversified economies – lowered domestic savings altogether. It is worth mentioning that although capital flight is prone to calculation errors, the growing cleavage between the share of oil revenues and investments tends to corroborate the immense impact that these capital movements have on the retention of resources in this region. Additionally, rising foreign imports reduced savings by stimulating the consumption of both importable and exportable components of the regional economy. The biggest crunch on domestic savings, however, remains that of insecurity, the compradorial nature of elites, and, less substantively, the underdeveloped state of the financial market.

The argument of neoliberal reforms pinned development on steady growth in the share of private investment and subsequent economic growth. The role of development policy was primarily one of maintaining public accounts with much spending centred on building political capital and stability to an order that marginalizes many. Promoting fiscal stability at the expense of investment in social infrastructure and relying heavily on indirect taxation in contrast to more socially responsible progressive and capital gains taxation (usually in the context of open capital accounts of the balance of payments) was perceived to contribute to development mainly through the transfer of the mechanisms and processes of resource allocation from governments to the private sector. Induced private investment growth, however, hinges on prospective returns and the degree of risks. But, in the AW, it is more an issue of context rather than an individual response to market signals. The risks to investment in the AW are unquantifiable because neither the external political threats nor the internal political and social stability factors can be thought to be of minimal import when transitions peak. Keynes differentiated between unquantifiable uncertainty and quantifiable risks. The regional risk function in question here is not of the usual smooth and continuous type, nor is it quantifiable – that is, one that is associated with price volatilities arising from market failures, ease of entry into market, or the development of new cost-cutting technology; rather, it is one where the bulk of institutions and capital assets could be wiped out overnight in some act of war. When uncertainties associated with complete collapse exist, the inducement to invest private capital is nearly null and void.

The Missing Discourse in the Arab Uprisings

Relative to its wealth, the AW has been performing a long way below potential. Although the real GDP per capita (for the region as a whole) was growing annually at a respectable rate during the 1970s (at an average of 5 per cent), it declined during the 1980s at the annual rate of −3.43 per cent, and grew at the low rate of 0.34 per cent during the 1990s. When it picked up again in early 2000, it achieved hollow and inequitable growth. Inequitable distributional arrangements (demand side) and declining investment rates, especially investment rates in plant and equipment, which are usually associated with long-term stability and sizeable markets, represent the principal cause behind the poor economic performance. Investment rates in the Arab region were on average four percentage points below the developing world rate (WDI-based calculations). This prolonged contraction in economic activities was associated with a chronically high rate of unemployment as a result of a shift in the structure and sources of growth, wherein the technology employed in the oil sector was labour saving and that of the private sector relied heavily on imported labour services.

The current uprising represents a welcome occurrence that could, under an egalitarian distributional setup, entrench the welfare gains of high growth. However, these transitions come with rising regional tensions and a trumpeted larger role for a private sector under Islamic finance. The Arab private sector is deeply rooted in commercial activity as opposed to industry. It chiefly buys imports for local consumption. On the flip side, industrial capital would have a long-term stake in the region. It may be too early to substantiate with data, however, so far, no policy is seen in terms of boosting public investment in the physical and social infrastructure, and of promoting state-sponsored industrial projects. There definitely was no redistribution of wealth and a sort of divine fatwa is now being used to protect grabbed property under the previous dictatorships. Working people may soon come to terms that an Islamic economy is no different than its predecessor.

Even though the region's dependency on oil and aspects of its negative externalities exist, they cannot explain or be the cause of underdevelopment. Rather, the explanation lies in a peculiar dependent process whereby the agency (the comprador class) of development recirculates the region's capital and labour outside the region as opposed to within. The agency is the ruling autocracy, their Western allies and the policy designer is the WB-IMF. Indeed, regimes lacking legitimacy also lack the political will to carry out an integrative regional development policy. For the autocrats and the elected regimes, there appears to be more to gain in the short term from shifting the region's resources abroad than there is in reinvesting over the long term in the region. These are not misguided macroeconomic policies. The elected Islamic governments also exhibit blind faith in free-market operations. They are purposeful ones ensuring that the abundance of the oil resource is responsible for weak macroeconomic performance when seen against the backdrop of the dollar-peg and free-capital accounts.

In the 1960s and 1970s, the resource boom offered the improvement of the AW balance of payments. This improvement enabled the AW economies to command additional resources in the world economy, including imports, investments abroad, and remittances to other parts of the world, at no immediate or apparent cost to itself. In addition to this, additional spending in domestic currency became possible when part of the new foreign currency inflows were internalised and exchanged for local currency. Through these diverse channels, the extraordinary currency inflows tend to induce a higher level of activity in the domestic economy. They also tend, in turn, to trigger, in some cases, the real appreciation of the currency. This appreciation can become a source of difficulty for the economy if it hinders industrialisation and export diversification or erodes the competitiveness of traditional areas of activity. This may increase the structural fragility of the balance of payments, or

reduce the ability of the economy to cope with adverse shifts in resource
inflows. However, in the 1960s and 1970s and in view of the populism
of the regimes and their alliance with working people, capital accounts
were controlled, interest and exchange rates were construed and monitored to arrest leakages and internalise accumulation and knowledge
processes. Later in the 1980s, in view of the shift in the class alliance of
Arab regimes, neither the rich oil countries with small populations nor
the poorer and relatively more populated non-oil countries as a result of
openness have been able to internalise the complex chains of economic
activities that might have permitted their sustained and autonomous economic development. In addition to this, the lessening of social cohesion
and the concentration of income and wealth tend to favour predatory
accumulation strategies, in which the export gains are mostly retained by
a small section of the population (the autocratic cohort) and, later, transferred abroad either directly or through the state. In this case, resource
revenues were used for regime stabilisation and to alleviate pent-up social
tensions, while a large part of the net resource inflows was misallocated,
financing and distorting socially desirable policies.

A cycle that began in the early 1980s with low oil prices, followed by
poor investment performance, reduced and lowered the quality of growth
altogether. Private investment-promotion policies were not sufficiently
adequate to raise growth because, although they allegedly provided the
partial institutional framework and guarantees to varying degrees, they
did not deal with the real risk and market-size issues, which are the potentially failed states themselves. Moreover, these policies were built on the
implicit understanding that the private and the public sectors compete
for the same resources. In developing countries, performing way below
potential and with immense slack in resources, they do not. Indeed, there
is plenty of slack in the economy for both sectors to use in a complementary fashion. Instead of a Marshall plan and an initial capital injection
that is required so that public and private investments rise simultaneously
and set the economy on a new growth footing, the AW got a Morgen-
thau plan (this was the plan offered initially to Germany after the Second
World War with the aim of limiting German industrialisation). The WB
recommended a retrenchment of anything public whilst the risk to private investments in relation to market size and geopolitical tensions were
significant. Whereas in the immediate post-independence period, private
investment was underwritten by the state in a 'non-economic losses' insurance scheme (the private sector piggybacked on the public sector), still
the WB-IMF promoted private investment as a panacea when no rational

private investor could possibly invest over the long term in the uncertain AW.

Specialisations in the export of primary products and 'unearned' incomes have come to typify the Arab world. In this case, slow and inequitable growth rates and institutional distortions may be construed (implicitly) as natural outcomes. The long-term growth consequences of primary resource dependence is said to create 'rich countries or regions with poor people', which in the case of the AW, has actually happened.[27] Nonetheless, this interpretation needs not be the case.[28] The macroeconomic impact of resource earnings depends on circumstances of time and place, and on the economic policies adopted by the state. It is not possible to conclude whether resource earnings are likely to lead to the so-called overvaluation of currency and devaluation, inflation, or to precarious economic growth. Empirical evidence also shows that an adverse impact from resource earnings on the exchange rate may be associated with export growth and the expansion of capacity rather than deindustrialisation, and that they can support improvements in welfare provision rather than corruption and sloth (Norway is a case in point).[29] The outcomes are likely to depend heavily on the policy mix implemented by the government, their choice of priorities, and the government's capacity to implement consistent policies. It depends on the capacity of the government to retain social values and recirculate them within the national economy.

What matters to resolve the political debacle are the socially, politically, and historically specific *mediations* between capital and labour insofar as the political rapport addresses the policy outcome. WB-IMF literature has purposefully overlooked the obvious, which is the autocratic/comprador Arab context. Autocrats do not take advice to pursue good governance. At one point, the WB implicitly suggested that some countries may be better off ignoring potential sources of oil wealth. Oil can represent a source of funds for continuing economic growth and improvements in social and welfare standards; however, if that were to be so, and welfare improvement empowered Arab working folk, then the imperial grip on oil would be loosened by the degree of popular sovereignty attained by peoples in the Arab world. Poor performance

---

[27] J. Stiglitz, 'We Can Now Cure Dutch Disease', *The Guardian*, 18 August 2004.

[28] G. Wright and J. Czelusta, 'Why Economies Slow: The Myth of the Resource Curse', *Challenge*, Vol. 47, No. 2) 2004, pp. 6–38; A. Rossser 'The Political Economy of the Resource Curse: A Literature Survey' (IDS Working Paper No. 268, 2006).

[29] See, for example, Gupta et al. (2005).

associated with imperialist hegemony is not related to oil per se; it is a much broader phenomenon wherever primary material exists.

Conclusion

Until 1977, real per-capita income in the AW grew at about the same rate as that of East Asia. However, since then, East Asia's per-capita income grew at a rate that allowed its per-capita income to triple by 1996, while on average, per-capita income in the Arab world stagnated (as of the early 1980s). The decline could not be fully attributable to oil prices or revenues because the latter declined once and started to rise again as of the mid-1980s. Successive Arab defeats, compradorial ruling elites, and an imperialist oil grab altogether represent the context and the agent of development and the core reason for Arab retrogression. The state was gradually stripped of sovereignty whose substance is working-class security, hence losing autonomy over policy. This eroded sovereignty and failure of the state constituted a failure of development. Swings in the regional business cycle could be attributed to pressures arising from external forces, and not to forces generated *causa sui* by the economy's internal mechanism. The business cycle of the AW, therefore, represents a case of an 'imperialistically determined cycle' or one mainly driven by exogenous pressures. Oil prices and revenues are relevant to development only insofar as they exceed the costs of political tensions in a state that mediates the interests of the working class; otherwise, they simply act as stabilisation measures. Unless post-Arab uprising measures go to empower the working population by direct redistribution and land reform, development will continue to be a case of de-development.

5

Bread and Olive Oil

The Agrarian Roots of the Arab Uprisings

Rami Zurayk and Anne Gough

Abstract

The Arab world is the most food-insecure region of the world. As a group, the Arab countries also suffer from sweeping inequality in the distribution of wealth and resources among social classes. We argue in this chapter that there are direct linkages between the Arab uprisings and social and economic policies of the Arab states, which have resulted in the atomization of rural society and in the creation of a disconnect between people, land, food and the state.

From this central thesis, four primary corollaries emerge. First, social discontent in the Arab world is rooted in the rapid economic transformation from an agriculture-based economy in the mid-twentieth century to service-, trade- and real-estate-based economies catalyzed by oil rent. Second, the demise of the farm sector was accelerated by the accumulation of land, ecological resources and state facilities in the hands of a few beneficiaries of the various regimes. Third, this demise was caused by, and led to the flourishing of, trade-based food regimes where low-quality food is available cheaply and good-quality food is a luxury. Lastly, successive Arab governments since decolonization have practiced a double level of rural development policies.

We provide a cursory analysis and discussion of salient features of selected agricultural policies in Egypt, Tunisia, Yemen and Syria. Tunisia's uprising began in rural areas like Sidi Bouzid, yet the post-uprising government has done little to address the needs of rural people. Egypt's case is characterized by the liberalization of land rents in 1992, a process that forced thousands of smallholder farmers off their land and into city slums. Yemen is different in that it is in the midst of a food crisis, with the number of people suffering from food insecurity doubling since 2009, with many of them rural agrarians. In Syria, the farming sector has been hit by curtailed state subsidies and cheap imports since 2000. We conclude that understanding the agrarian roots of social protest and dissent is vital to understanding the Arab uprisings.

Whenever food is mentioned in the context of the Arab uprisings, it is usually for the purpose of attributing direct causality between the rise in world food prices and the protests.[1] This chapter examines the links between food production and the Arab uprisings. At the outset, it is important to note that what brought people out onto the streets was a complex set of social, economic, and political causes, including: profound discontent with authoritarian modes of governance shored up by oppressive security apparatuses and by subservience to external political agendas, failed economic regimes that promoted social injustice, the absence of a social contract between citizen and state, the breakdown of the communal moral economy, widespread corruption, and crony capitalism. These are the direct and deeply profound causes of Arab despair as they were crystallized in the popular slogan: *Aish, Horreya, Adala Egtema'eya* ('Bread, freedom, social justice').

However, food and farming remain extremely important issues for Arabs.[2] The Arab countries are, as a group, the largest importers of food in the world, and cereal grains form the major part of these imports. The Arab region is the most food-insecure part of the world. It imports 50 per cent of the calories it consumes, and local food production is hindered by serious ecological and structural conditions.[3] Egypt is the largest grain importer in the world. Other countries of the historical Fertile Crescent (parts of present-day Iraq, Lebanon, Syria, and Palestine) suffer from the same predicament.

Yet, it is in these countries that wheat was first domesticated, that settled farming began, and that agriculture provided sufficient surplus to build empires and civilizations. Even though biophysical limitations

---

[1] Y. Bar-Yam et al. 2012. *Economics of Food Prices and Crises* (New England Complex Systems Institute); J. Harrigan, 'Did Food Prices Plant the Seeds of the Arab Awakening?' Presentation at IFPRI Conference *Food Secure Arab World*, Beirut, Lebanon, February 2012.

[2] By Arabs we mean the Arabic-speaking countries of the League of Arab States. In 2010, the population of these 22 countries was 320 million.

[3] World Bank, FAO, and IFAD. 2006. *Improving Food Security in Arab Countries*.

to food production are severe, especially with periodic and recurrent droughts that are worsened by climatic fluctuations, they do not fully explain the lamentable state of Arab food production. The interrelated issues of climate change, drought, water availability and use, and food production have been adequately addressed by a plethora of researchers.[4]

This chapter will examine the political causes underlying the massive breakdown of farming that most Arab states have witnessed since their liberation from direct colonialism in the mid-twentieth century. It will analyze the agrarian roots of the Arab uprisings whereby the term 'agrarian' is used both as a noun and as an adjective. Agrarians are those people who are directly involved in the cultivation of land for the production of food and fibre within the context of a rural society based with a collective sense of belonging. As an adjective, we use the term to describe an ideological position (as in agrarian reform) that advocates the redistribution of landed property.[5]

We argue that among the driving forces of the Arab uprisings are a combination of external and internal pressures that have resulted in the atomization of rural society, increased unemployment, rampant poverty, and the creation of a disconnect between people and state, people and land, and people and food. This state of affairs signals profound dissatisfaction that accumulates and is dissipated through intense episodic reactions once a breaking point is attained. The Arab uprisings constituted a space for the articulation of one such episode by the rural disenfranchised.

From this central thesis, four primary corollaries emerge: First, at the root of the Arab uprisings lies a profound discontent based in the rapid social-geographical transformations associated with the 'laissez-faire' shift from rural to urban. This was characterized by the rapid economic transformation from an agriculture-based economy in the mid-twentieth century to service, trade, and real estate-based economies catalyzed by oil rent.

Second, the demise of the farm sector was accelerated by the accumulation of land and associated ecological resources as well as state facilities,

---

[4] F. Hole. 11 May 2007. 'Agricultural Sustainability in the semi-arid Near East', *Climate of the Past* 3, pp. 193–203; L. Brown. May / June 2011. 'The New Geopolitics of Food', *Foreign Policy*. http://www.foreignpolicy.com/articles/2011/c4/25/the_new_geopolitics_of_food

[5] Based on the definition of the noun in *New Oxford American Dictionary*, 2nd edition (Oxford: Oxford University Press, 2005).

such as support subsidies, in the hands of a few beneficiaries and cronies of the various regimes. This created a new agrarian question[6] in the Arab world, one expressed on the human and natural landscapes. Hundreds of thousands of farm workers were uprooted from their land through a process of legislated immiseration and are working on other people's land in other regions.

Third, the demise of local food systems was caused by, and led to, the flourishing of trade-based food regimes. The Arab countries are now uncomfortably incorporated into a global food regime[7] where low-quality food is available cheaply and good-quality food is a luxury.

The fourth corollary is that successive Arab governments since decolonization have practiced a double level of rural development policies. Following the prevalent entrepreneurial practice, states keep two policy ledgers – a fictitious one for public consumption and a real one to map out the strategies that serve the interests of the ruling groups. This political *taqiyya*[8] confuses the issues of rural development.

A logical inference is that tangible changes in the structure of the food and farming system can only be made through radical transformations in those agrarian policies that were at the root of Arab discontent. These agrarian policies are in turn dependent on a set of statewide political, economic, and social policies. It is the ability to influence these policies that constitutes the litmus test of the success or failure of the Arab uprisings and the conditions for transformation of popular action from protest to revolution.

---

[6] The agrarian question began with the writings of Karl Katusky in 1899. He asked: what are the political and economic consequences of capitalist agriculture for landscapes and societies? The topic has since been debated and analyzed throughout the years. Paul McLaughlin (1998) addressed the agrarian question in the light of the (limited) survival of the family farm. He attributed the resilience of smallholder agriculture, inter alia, to the specific nature of agriculture and the peculiarities of land as a factor of production and to state intervention. See P. McLaughlin, 'Rethinking the Agrarian Question: The Limits of Essentialism and the Promise of Evolutionism', *Human Ecology Review*, 5:2, (1998): pp. 25–39. Also see: P. McMichael. 1997. 'Rethinking Globalization: The Agrarian Question Revisited', *Review of International Political Economy*, 4:4, pp. 630–662.

[7] 'Global food regime' is the name given to the political economy of the food system. As a theory it states that the study of food and agriculture offers insight into global power structures, an understanding of 'capital accumulation', and the function of food and land in spatial politics. P. McMichael. 2009. 'A food regime genealogy', *Journal of Peasant Studies*, 36:1, pp. 139–169.

[8] *Taqiyya* refers to the concealment of one's beliefs. Commonly associated with religious practices; it is used here to address the practice of disguising the true consequences of agricultural policies.

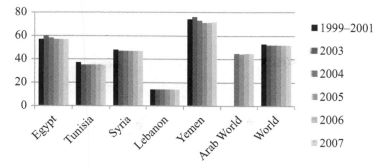

FIGURE 5.1. Proportion of Rural Population in Selected Arab Countries.[9]

This chapter analyzes the current state of rural areas in Arab countries, and then examines the policy decisions that have caused de-development in rural areas. Each section draws on examples from Tunisia, Egypt, Yemen, and Syria. It will conclude with an inquiry into the future of agrarian lives and farming systems in the Arab region.

To Be Rural in an Urban World

The Arab area is one of the most rapidly urbanizing regions of the world. Currently, 56 per cent of the population is considered to be urban; in 1980, it was 44.9 per cent and it is projected to be 66 per cent by 2020.[10] As of 2010, the urban population of Egypt was 42.8 per cent, that of Tunisia, 67.3 per cent and that of Syria 54.9 per cent.[11] The region's largest cities have sprawled over thousands of hectares of arable land.[12]

Although the total rural population is declining in relative figures, the absolute figure for rural people is increasing in most countries (see Figure 5.1). This is in spite of the constant stream of migration from rural areas. In Syria, for instance (see Figure 5.2), the rural population growth rate has increased between 1995 and 2008. Unemployment in Syria has also

---

[9] Authors' compilation based on data from Arab Organization for Agricultural Development (AOAD). 2009. *Arab Agricultural Statistics Yearbook 29* and *FAO Statistical Yearbook 2010*.

[10] UN. (2010). 'World Urbanization Prospects: The 2009 Revision', Department of Economic and Social Affairs, United Nations (UN). http://esa.un.org/unpd/wup/index.htm

[11] Ibid.

[12] UN-Habitat. 2012. *The State of Arab Cities 2012: The Challenges of Urban Transformation*, 16.

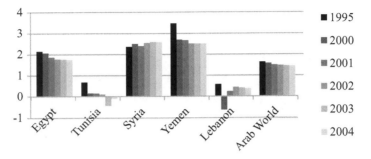

FIGURE 5.2. Annual Percentage of Rural Population Growth in Selected Arab Countries.[13]

increased annually since the 1980s.[14] The percentage of the economically active labour force employed in agriculture decreased from 24 per cent in 2001 to 20 per cent in 2010 (see Figure 5.3). Rural, agricultural areas like Dara'a were once the strongholds of the Syrian regime, but it is in rural areas like these that the Syrian uprising began in 2011.[15] This shift in loyalty is owing to the convergence of a number of factors. Bashar Al-Assad's government cut support for agricultural inputs after 2000 and opened Syrian markets to cheaper agricultural imports. As a result, rural areas were increasingly unable to depend on agriculture as a source of stable livelihoods. The erosion of state support for rural areas led people to organize against the regime.

Poverty in the Arab region mostly exists in rural areas and is increasing alongside growth in population and unemployment (see Figures 5.4 and 5.5). In Egypt, poverty levels in rural areas are at 43.7 per cent and recent reports have found this number increasing.[16] Syria's rural poverty rate in 2007 was 15 per cent, but 62 per cent of poor people in Syria live in rural areas. Of the poor in rural Syria, 77 per cent are landless.[17] Yemen has 40 per cent rural poverty and 80 per cent of those who are poor live in rural Yemen. Tunisia's poverty rate is commonly listed as 3.8 per cent.[18]

[13] Authors Compilation based on data from UNDP Arabstats.
[14] J. Yazigi. 24 May 2012. 'Syria's Growing Economic Challenge' *Bitter Lemons* 10: 18. http://www.bitterlemons-international.org/previous.php?opt= 1&id=380#1544
[15] Ibid.
[16] M. Elmeshad. 28 September 2011. 'Rural Egyptians Suffer Most from Increasing Poverty', *Egyptian Independent*. http://www.egyptindependent.com/node/199833
[17] International Fund for Agricultural Development (IFAD),'Rural Poverty Portal: Syria', http://www.ruralpovertyportal.org/web/guest/country/home/tags/syria
[18] World Bank Indicators, http://data.worldbank.org/country/tunisia#cp_wdi

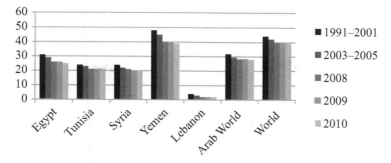

FIGURE 5.3. Share of Agricultural Population as Percentage of Total Population Considered Economically Active in Selected Arab Countries.[19]

However, rural poverty in Tunisia is measured at 13.9 per cent.[20] Such disparities between rural and urban poverty indicates unequal access to resource entitlements and to development opportunities.

In spite of these limitations, the rural Arabs account for a significant share of economic activity, with the exception of Lebanon. In Yemen, the majority of the labour force is employed in agriculture and herding.[21] Agriculture is an important source of livelihood, yet many Arab countries are trapped under the double-edged sword of labour efficiency.[22] Pursuit of labour efficiency in agriculture means fewer jobs for fewer rural people, yet as unemployment in rural area increases, so does the lack of job opportunities. In many countries, rural livelihoods are already diversified, and agricultural income is only a share of the total income.

Access to adequate land resources remains one of the challenging hurdles facing Arab small farmers, who are the backbone of local food systems.[23] In many Arab countries, the fertile land endowment is limited by natural conditions, a mixture of terrain and water availability. In Egypt, the farmland area per capita is just 1/25 of a hectare ('ha'). Those

[19] Authors Compilation based on data from FAO 2010.

[20] IFAD. 2011. Tunisia fact sheet.

[21] WFP. 2012. *The State of Food Security and Nutrition in Yemen*, 12.

[22] 'Labour efficiency' refers to the number of labour hours needed in production. The rate is often measured as the amount of time allocated versus the amount of time actually required and used for each unit of production. Although improving labour efficiency may be desirable for reducing labour costs and enhancing competitiveness, it also reduces the net number of persons employed in agriculture and therefore increases unemployment.

[23] H. Ayeb and R. Saad. 2012. 'Gender, Poverty and Biodiversity Conservation in Rural Egypt and Tunisia' (Essay presented to workshop on 'Agriculture & Food Production in the Shadow of the Arab Oil Economy', Amman, Jordan).

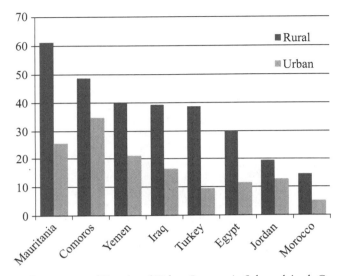

FIGURE 5.4. Percentage of Rural and Urban Poverty in Selected Arab Countries.[24]
Source: International Fund for Agricultural Development (IFAD).

in power hold much of this land. In Arab countries, the Gini coefficient (Gini being a measure of the inequality in distribution in which 0 is equal distribution and 100 is most unequal) for land (see Figure 5.6), is among the highest in the world. In Egypt it is 69, in Jordan it is 81, in Lebanon it is 69, in Morocco 62, Tunisia 69, and in Algeria 65. Figures for Yemen, Syria, Libya, Bahrain, and other Gulf countries are unavailable. Few areas in the world show higher land inequality figures as a group.

A direct outcome of the profound land inequality is the phenomenon identified by Manus Midlarsky (as the 'bifurcation in the patterns of land-holdings') whereby the amount of land accessible to small and medium-sized farmers is increasingly subdivided into smaller parcels, primarily because of inheritance.[25] Conversely, the property of the rich remains relatively intact. Midlarsky proposes this phenomenon as one of the causes of political violence in the Middle East. This is apparent in Tunisia where 62 per cent of landowners own less than 10 ha, while 8 per cent of the

[24] International Fund for Agricultural Development.
[25] M. I. Midlarsky. 1988. 'Rulers and the Ruled: Patterned Inequality and the Onset of Mass Political Violence', *The American Political Science Review* 82:2, pp. 491–509. http://www.jstor.org/discover/10.2307/1957397?uid=3738432&uid=2&uid=4&sid=21100839192271

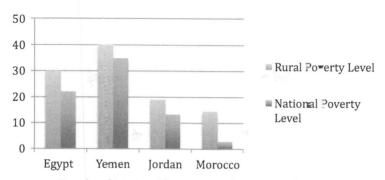

FIGURE 5.5. Rural and National Poverty Levels in Selected Arab Countries.[26]

farmers own more than 50 per cent of the land area.[27] Tunisia's central and southern rural areas have long been marginalized. The majority of farmers, 54 per cent, own smallholdings of 0–5 ha,[28] while 25 per cent of the rural population is landless.[29]

In Egypt, land inequality was formalized under the Mubarak regime in 1992 through an infamous piece of economic legislation, Law 96. The law 'liberated' land rents, which had been held at affordable levels for many smallholder farmers since a series of land reforms instituted and led by the government of Gamal Abdel Nasser between 1952 and 1960.[30] It is estimated that between 1 and 5 million small farmers have stopped farming across Egypt in the last twenty years since the enactment of Law 96.[31] At the time of the law, tenant farmers and their families constituted around 10 per cent of the Egyptian population.[32] During the parliamentary debate on Law 96, tenant farmers were called 'lazy' and undeserving of low rents, revealing the class prejudices behind the legislation.[33] Farmer and leftist groups protested against Law 96 in Cairo

[26] Authors Compilation based on data from IFAD.

[27] IFAD. 2005.

[28] AUC–ECA–AFDB Consortium. 2010. *Land Policy in Africa: North Africa Regional Assessment.*

[29] IFAD. 2005.

[30] R. Bush. 2007. 'Politics, Power and Poverty: Twenty Years of Agricultural Reform and Market Liberalisation in Egypt', *Third World Quarterly* 28: 8, pp.1599–1550.

[31] S. Tolan and C. Buchen. 22 December 2011. 'Egypt: Food for a Revolution', *Al Jazeera English*. http://www.aljazeera.com/indepth/opinion/2011/12/2011121974454601107.html

[32] Ibid.

[33] R. Saad. 2002. 'Egyptian Politics and the Tenancy Law' in R. Bush, ed., *Counter Revolution in the Egyptian Countryside* (London: Zed Books).

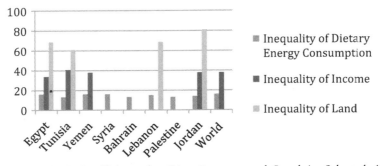

FIGURE 5.6. Gini Coefficients for Diet, Income, and Land in Selected Arab Countries.[34]

and Dakhalia.[35] A petition of 350,000 signatures was delivered to the Ministry of Agriculture who dismissed it, refusing to believe that so many could object to the law.[36]

The law was passed under Mubarak, but the groundwork was laid by Anwar Sadat who began an economic process that he called *infitah* ('opening'). Under Sadat, agriculture was marginalized and he began to reverse Nasser's landmark reforms.[37] After *infitah*, Egypt's external debt level increased from 5 billion in 1970 to 30 billion in 1981.[38] Mubarak further instituted *infitah* after he inherited the dictatorship from Sadat. By 1991, he had accepted the package of Structural Adjustment Policies proffered by the World Bank and IMF. In a clear admonition of ideology, the US Agency for International Development (USAID) blamed Nasser's land reforms for the lack of agricultural productivity in the 1980s, rather than Sadat's policies of neglecting the rural sector.[39] Such ideological dictates obfuscate the context for the current status of rural people in Egypt.

In the aftermath of Law 96, landowning classes reaped the benefits as land rents rose in some places by 400 per cent while the cost to purchase

34 Authors Compilation based on data from FAO 2010, represented as Years Diet/Income/Land. Egypt: 1981/2004/2000. Tunisia: 1990/2000/1995. Yemen: 1998/2005. Syria: 1961. Bahrain: 2003. Lebanon: 1997. Palestine: 2003. Jordan: 1986/2006/1997. World: 1998/2005.
35 R. Bush, 2007.
36 Ibid.
37 Ibid.
38 Ibid.
39 Ibid.

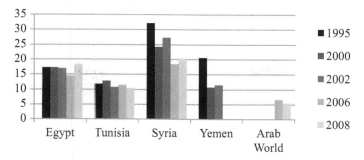

FIGURE 5.7. Agriculture, Value Added (Percentage of GDP) for Selected Arab Countries.[40]

agricultural land grew five times over a decade.[41] To paraphrase Saskia Sassan, land in Egypt became more valuable than the lives of its food producers.[42] Many poor farmers had paid taxes towards the goal of eventual ownership on the parcels of land they had been leasing prior to the law; those tax payments were ignored after the passage of the law, although some farmers are still struggling to gain state recognition of their payments and claim to the land.[43]

In summary, rural Arabs are poor and marginalized. Their economic contribution, although significant (see Figures 5.7 and 5.8), is grossly unrecognized. As shown in Figure 5.8, the share of the agricultural budget in the Arab world is 2.4 per cent. For Egypt, it is 3 per cent, a decrease from 5 per cent in 1995. For Tunisia, it is 6 per cent and for Syria it is 5.6 per cent, down from 10 per cent in 1995. Agriculture makes up nearly 20 per cent of the Yemeni GDP and yet the Yemeni state only spends 1 per cent of allocated public expenditure on agriculture. The state of the services in rural areas is deplorable, and governmental neglect is the norm. Meanwhile, dependency on food imports continues to rise, making these nations increasingly vulnerable to market volatility. Yemen imports 90 per cent of its wheat – the most heavily consumed staple food in the

[40] Authors Compilation based on Data from UNDP Arab States. Arab world data from AOAD 2009.
[41] Ibid.
[42] S. Sassan. 2010. 'A Savage Sorting of Winners and Losers: Contemporary Versions of Primitive Accumulation', *Globalizations* 7:1, pp. 23–50.
[43] Y. Moataz Ahmed. 6 March 2012. 'Farmers stand up to former Mubarak regime stalwart', *Egypt Independent*. http://www.egyptindependent.com/news/farmers-stand-former-mubarak-regime-stalwart

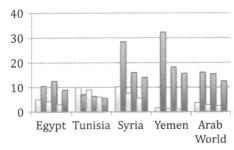

FIGURE 5.8. Share of Government Expenditure in Agriculture and Defence (Percentage of Total Expenditure) for Selected Arab Countries in 1995, 2003, 2007.[44]

country.[45] Egypt imported 10 million tonnes of wheat in 2010–2011.[46] To fully understand the implications of this imbroglio, one must delve further into the entrails of Arab policymaking.

Policing the Policy Space

Arab agriculture has become a capital investment sector in which agrarian people are incidental, and often bothersome. It is thought by decision-makers to be best managed through an industrialized, business-driven approach based on comparative advantages and economies of scale. State support is deviated towards such investments as they are seen to bring in hard currencies and contribute to economic growth. Investors and high-level politicians are usually connected through blood or money ties. In this perspective, the agrarian is a nuisance; all lands should be placed under intensive large-scale modern farming and farmers should be converted into farmworkers earning daily wages. Labour efficiency in this economic model is generally described as 'low' and could be improved, using the menace of the market, whose invisible hand grips the poor by the throat. This plan cannot be publicly disclosed lest it fuels or causes protest. So a 'formal' policymaking process is allowed, sometimes to satisfy individual political ambitions. Underneath it, a second-level policy process, unwritten but far more powerful, shapes the farming sector and

---

[44] Authors compilation based on S. Malaiyandi. July 2010. *A Quick Reference and Statistical Appendix for Statistics of Public Expenditure for Economic Development (SPEED)*, IFPRI.

[45] WFP, 2012.

[46] Food and Agriculture Organization (FAO). 12 April 2012. 'GIEWS Country Briefs: Egypt' http://www.fao.org/giews/countrybrief/country.jsp?code=EGY

controls the lives of agrarians. The people directly concerned: farmers, consumers, and citizens, have no say in this process.

The root of the current situation, in which small farmers are forced to choose between immiseration in rural areas or urban slums, is the result of misguided political economic policies. The application of policies integrating Arab countries and their farming systems into the global food regime has held damaging consequences for agrarian livelihoods and food security.[47] As Habib Ayeb astutely states, the hallmarks of neoliberalism, 'liberalism, privatization, investment aid, integration into world markets, marginalization of subsistence agriculture and the peasantry, overconsumption of resources and unequal competition over resources',[48] form the basis of the global food regime. Agriculture's role is to contribute to the nation state's trade balance, rather than to provide food and agrarian livelihoods. The status of agriculture within the trade balance has become the way to measure food security. Food security is diluted to mean the ability of a country to purchase food on the international market. Arab countries, like others, are encouraged to embrace their comparative advantage for the year-round production of fruits and flowers; using state resources to prop up export-oriented production of perishable high-value farm products.[49]

Organic herbs and strawberries destined for export have been extolled as a path to economic stability by development agencies and governments, even though a plethora of reports indicate that small farmers do not benefit from this type of agriculture.[50] For example, Tunisia exports cut flowers, at a time when its domestic food production is decreasing and small farmers are leaving rural areas.[51] Countries are expected to export their shrinking water and other natural resources for short-term returns. International development organizations like USAID are involved in promoting this luxury farming for the delicate palates of northern

---

[47] Food security, according to the accepted definition by the Food and Agriculture Organization (FAO, 1996) '. . . exists when all people, at all times, have physical and economic access to sufficient, safe and nutritious food that meets their dietary needs and food preferences for an active and healthy life'. See FAO. June 2006. *FAO Food Security Brief.*

[48] H. Ayeb. 4 June 2012. 'L'Afrique du Nord entre dépendance alimentaire et marginalisation sociale', *Kapitalis.* http://www.kapitalis.com/afkar/68-tribune/10235-lafrique-du-nord-entre-dependance-alimentaire-et-marginalisation-sociale.html

[49] H. Ayeb. 4 June 2012.

[50] L. Sarant 3 April 2012. 'Limits to development: Q & A with Habib Ayeb, co-director of "Green Mirages"', *Egypt Independent.* http://www.egyptindependent.com/node/75044

[51] H. Ayeb. 4 June 2012.

consumers.[52] In Egypt, this has meant that organically grown herbs and fruits, irrigated by the Nile waters, are easier to find in Europe than in Egyptian markets.[53]

Ayeb elucidates the connections between the policy to intensify irrigated agriculture, food security, and agrarian impoverishment.[54] His particularly salient point is that economic liberalization was one of the drivers and even the goal of the extensive irrigation systems installed by a mixture of state governments and international financial institutions in Arab countries. Yet, this has not helped Tunisia, Egypt, Morocco, or other Arab countries achieve food security or food sovereignty.[55] The food protests of 2008 revealed deep inequities between social classes and geographical locations in terms of access to entitlements like food, water, and land. The countries that were the hardest hit by the food crises in 2008 also depend on the world market for food. This includes the entire Arab region.

The marginalization of Tunisian labouring classes, combined with the global financial crises, led to organized protests against the Ben Ali dictatorship in 2008. While labelled a 'food protest', the 2008 protests were in fact about the class divisions and denial of entitlements under the neoliberal regime. The 2008 protests consolidated around labour exploitation at a large phosphate company (one of Tunisia's most valuable natural resources).[56] Ben Ali's security forces rounded up hundreds of union members and two of the leaders were sentenced to eight years in prison. The motivation, organization, and strategies of the 2008 protests were precursors to the 2011 uprising.

Similarly, in Egypt in 2008, commodity foodstuff prices increased by 30 per cent in local markets. Wheat and rice disappeared from shelves and were sold at even higher prices on the black market.[57] The government subsidized bread upon which many poor Egyptians depend also disappeared. People were left without options for food. After three weeks of protests, strikes, and the death of fifteen people in clashes with the police

[52] Tolan and Buchen. 2011.

[53] S. Cox. 10 March 2012. 'The Politics of Bread in Egypt', *Al Jazeera English*.http://www.aljazeera.com/indepth/opinion/2012/03/201237104725536741.html

[54] H. Ayeb. 4 June 2012.

[55] Food sovereignty is essentially the 'right of peoples to define their own food and agriculture'. See M. Windfuhr and J. Jonsén. 2005. *Food Sovereignty: Towards Democracy in Localized Food Systems* (Warwickshire, UK: FIAN ITDG Publishing).

[56] R. Bush. 2011. 'Food Riots: Poverty, Power and Protest', *Journal of Agrarian Change* 10:1, pp. 119–129.

[57] H. Ayeb. 4 June 2012.

and the army, the government finally addressed the crisis by increasing wages and controlling food prices.[58]

There is a sizeable and sometimes violent disconnection between subsistence–sustainable agriculture and capital investors or policymakers. These decision-makers often do not understand the importance of agriculture in providing livelihoods and economic safety nets for agrarian communities. Farmers are rarely involved or consulted in creating policy, although their lives and landscapes are frequently the most altered by policy changes. The rupture of this divide manifested itself in several precursors to the 2011 uprisings. Egypt is one example, since the passing of Law 96, around 119 people have died and over 800 have been injured in violence related to this law.[59] The absence of government support for agrarian livelihoods has pushed Egyptian farmers into high levels of indebtedness. Often, farmers are in debt to the same banks that sell fertilizers on the black market to encourage reports of scarcity and increase prices.[60]

Yemen is another telling example. Spurred by the World Bank, the Yemeni government unilaterally cut subsidies for fuel and other basic necessities in 2005, despite the fact that about half the Yemeni population lives under the poverty line and the majority of the population spends 60 per cent of their income on food.[61] Such a measure avoided any necessary voting or passage of legislation in the Parliament. People in Yemen depended on the subsidies for cooking fuel, industry, and agriculture. Protests organized in response to the measure were met with violence from police and the army.[62] According to news reports, thirty-six people died during the protests.[63] At the time of these protests, Yemen was lauded for real GDP growth and decreasing inflation.[64] However, other indicators revealed that people did not have sufficient access to entitlements. Yemen is in the midst of a severe crisis; the number of food-insecure households

[58] R. Bush. 2007.
[59] Land Centre for Human Rights, quoted in S. Tolan and C. Buchen. 21 December 2011. 'Egypt: Food for a Revolution', *Al Jazeera English*. http://www.aljazeera.com/indepth/opinion/2011/12/2011121914345460110 7.html (22 December 2011).
[60] Y. Moataz Ahmed. 31 January 2012. 'Ganzouri's old projects back to haunt farmers', *Egypt Independent*. http://www.egyptindependent.com/node/629611
[61] A. Kadri. 8 Februay 2012. 'The World Bank in Yemen prior to the Arab Spring', *Triple Crisis*. http://triplecrisis.com/the-world-bank-in-yemen/
[62] Ibid.
[63] B. Whitaker. 23 July 2005. '36 die in riots after Yemen fuel price hikes', *The Guardian*. http://www.guardian.co.uk/world/2005/jul/23/yemen.brianwhitaker
[64] A. Kadri. 8 February 2012.

has doubled between 2009 and 2011 and child malnutrition is at almost 50 per cent.[65] In addition, only a quarter of farming households own the land they farm, leaving 75 per cent dependent on tenant farming.[66] Landless agrarians are more likely to be agricultural wage labourers, which in Yemen means they are currently more likely to suffer from higher levels of food insecurity.[67]

Who Benefits?

If agricultural sector policies have not benefited farmers and farm workers, who has benefitted? The answer is embedded in the system utilized by various regimes to maintain power and distribute profits to those in their inner circles. One such example is the Egyptian enterprise Dina Farms. Founded in the late 1980s by the conglomerate Osman Group, an investment company that according to Adam Hanieh was one of those that 'benefited from the privatization process' of the IMF's structural adjustments and Mubarak's private circle.[68] Dina Farms uses 10,000 acres for vegetable, dairy, and cow production, most of which they export.

Profits from exports line the pockets of the large landowners and are cycled back to policymakers in order to ensure their support. Smallholder farms lack the access to power and capital necessary to make the favourable deals for subsidized water, fuel, and marketing that larger landowners and industry are willing to cultivate.[69] A two-tiered agricultural system is created in which cut flowers and herbs are exported while many people, urban and rural, cannot afford to grow or purchase staples like legumes. In Yemen, rural households currently purchase 28 per cent of their food on credit.[70]

The Syrian example illustrates the effect of embracing neoliberal policies. While it was claimed that adopting privatization plans and opening Syrian markets to new imports would result in economic development for the entire country, in reality the policies held negative consequences for rural areas. When Bashar Assad came to power in 2000, the neoliberal

[65] WFP. 2012.
[66] Ibid.
[67] Ibid.
[68] A. Hanieh. 14 February 2011. 'Egypt's Uprising: Not Just a Question of 'Transition', *MR Zine*. http://mrzine.monthlyreview.org/2011/hanieh140211.html
[69] S. Tolan and C. Buchen. 22 December 2011.
[70] WFP. 2012.

process accelerated. The real estate market was deregulated and private-property protections instituted, which meant farmers faced increasing land rents and higher prices for agricultural inputs.[71] Assad signed free-trade deals in the mid-2000s, leading to the dumping of cheaper agricultural and manufactured products into the Syrian market.[72] In Syria, around 9 million people live in rural places. Agriculture is the main activity in these areas, employing 55 per cent of the labour force. The sector accounted for more than a quarter of GDP and total employment in 2004.[73] Neoliberal policies have hurt these people. The policies have worsened standards of living, unemployment is higher than 30 per cent, and poverty level estimates are between 11 and 30 per cent.[74] Although agriculture still contributes a sizeable amount to the Syrian GDP, its figure dropped ten points between 1995 and 2008.[75]

Whereas these neoliberal policies impoverished the original supporters of the Ba'ath party, Assad's government received many accolades for its economic liberalization, in particular for the deregulation of the banking sector, from which Lebanese banks have profited.[76] *The Economist* praised the new cars and consumerism on the streets of Damascus as signs of new 'life' resonating from foreign direct investment and the cutting of state subsidies. Financial analysts linked this market transition to Assad's diplomatic and leadership role in the region. One of the reasons cited for this new power was that Syria's economy had not been heavily affected by the 2008 financial and food crises because of its low levels of foreign debt, ranked ninth out of thirteen Arab countries.[77] Yet, the reasons for the low debt, the formerly centralized economy, and its likely reversal under Assad's authoritarian capitalism were ignored.[78]

Prolonged drought, increase in costs of agricultural inputs, and government cuts to agricultural subsidies have compounded the situation

[71] A Kadri. 2012.
[72] J. Yazigi. 24 May 2012.
[73] IFAD. 2007.
[74] O. S. Dahi and Y. Munif. 16 October 2011. 'Revolts in Syria: Tracking the Convergence between Authoritarianism and Neoliberalism', *Sanhati*. http://sanhati.com/excerpted/4249/
[75] J. Yazigi. 24 May 2012.
[76] *The Economist*. 'Syria: Has it Won?' 26 November 2009, http://www.economist.com/node/14984967?story_id=14984967
[77] J. Al Tamimi. 30 March 2010. 'Syria: An economy in transition', *Gulf News*. http://gulfnews.com/business/features/syria-an-economy-in-transition-1.604982
[78] O.S. Dahi and Y. Munif. 2011.

for rural Syrians.[79] Smallholder farming is ever more untenable. The UN reported that 200,000–300,000 families from the rural north and eastern parts of Syria have moved to cities in search of work.[80] In addition to rural and urban migration, the crony capitalism at play has forced many farmers to seek work as farm labourers in other countries. Lebanon's potato fields and wine industry depend on Syrian workers.[81] Many of the workers are women and come from smallholder farming families in Syria. Neoliberal policies have transformed them from farmers to displaced wage labourers, susceptible to exploitation and a myriad of health problems.[82]

Rural de-development in Syria has been linked to the causes of the Syrian uprising.[83] Dera'a, Dariya, al-Moadamiya, Doma, Harasta, al-Tell, Saqba, al-Rastan, and Talbisa are all areas that depended on agriculture before the liberalization of the sector. Recent violence has worsened the situation and led to fuel and fertilizer shortages. As a result, 70 per cent of land in Dera'a has not been planted and farming activities have halted in Idlib and Ghoota.[84]

In a recent assessment, the Food and Agriculture Organization (FAO) reports that 4 million of Syria's 22 million people are estimated to be food insecure and 6.8 million in need of 'humanitarian' assistance.[85] It is estimated that Syria's farm sector lost 1.8 billion dollars since the violence began; this includes losses to crops like wheat, barley, olives, and cherries as well as the destruction of irrigation systems and other infrastructure.[86] The 'modernisation' and liberalisation of farming and the lack of investment in family farming has led to the reduction in the

[79] 'Syria: Over a Million People Affected by Drought', *IRIN*, 17 February 2010. http://www.irinnews.org/Report.aspx?ReportId=88139

[80] Ibid.

[81] L. Garçon and R. Zurayk. November 2010. 'Lebanon's Bitter Garden', *Le Monde diplomatique*. http://mondediplo.com/2010/11/14lebannon

[82] R. Habib, 'Health of Farm Workers: A Social Justice Framework' (Paper presented to workshop on 'Agriculture & Food Production in the Shadow of the Arab Oil Economy', Amman, Jordan, January 2012).

[83] Ibid.

[84] P. Sands. 19 March 2012. 'Syria's Food Crisis: "The fuel goes to army tanks, not to tractors"', *The National*. http://www.thenational.ae/news/world/middle-east/syrias-food-crisis-the-fuel-goes-to-army-tanks-not-farm-tractors

[85] FAO Media Center. 2 August 2012. 'Three million Syrians need food, crops and livestock assistance'. http://www.fao.org/news/story/en/item/153731/icode/ and FAO in Emergencies. 'Syria needs to produce food: Agriculture cannot be an afterthought'. http://www.fao.org/emergencies/crisis/syria/en/

[86] Ibid.

resilience of the food and farming systems in Syria. Those people that are most vulnerable to food and nutrition insecurity in Syria tend to depend on agriculture and raising livestock for livelihoods and food.[87] Farmers fleeing Syria for Lebanon often try to bring their livestock with them as it is their only economic asset, this has led to feed shortages in Lebanon and impacted Lebanon's limited grazing areas.[88] According to the FAO, 30 per cent of rural Syria is at risk for food insecurity and 1.5 million people are in need of 'immediate food aid'.[89] Food aid has been distributed since October 2011.[90] Currently, FAO is raising funds to support cereal planting this fall.[91] A plan for both an emergency and a long-term, rural-farming food policy is imperative in order to avoid over-reliance on food aid, which in the case of Iraq, resulted in the annihilation of the local farming systems.[92]

In summary, current economic and political policies stand as obstacles to social justice, to food security, and food sovereignty. They create dependency on the globalized economic regime while linkages between the ruling elites and powerful exporting nations are fostered and enriched. Evidence for this is plentiful, such as the Wikileaks revelation that the U.S. ambassador to Tunisia pleaded with Sakher el Materi, Ben Ali's son-in-law, to support the introduction of the McDonalds fast-food chain to Tunisia.[93] Diplomatic relations are also used as a tool to achieve signatures on bilateral trade agreements and for accession to the World Trade Organization (WTO), of which Tunisia and Egypt are already members. Dual policies strengthen the influence and role of international finance institutions, such as the World Bank and the IMF, both of which expressed admiration for Ben Ali's and Mubarak's economic liberalization before turning against them after the uprisings.

There are, in all these countries (except in Syria which lacks a formally organized civil society), attempts by civil society actors to influence

---

[87] AFP. 2 August 2012. 'Three million Syrians need food and farming aid'. http://www.yourmiddleeast.com/news/three-million-syrians-need-food-and-farming-aid_8551

[88] Food and Agricultural Organization (FAO) in Emergencies. 10 June 2013. 'FAO calls for immediate support to farmers affected by Syrian crisis'. http://www.fao.org/emergencies/fao-in-action/stories/stories-detail/en/c/177702/

[89] Ibid.

[90] Ibid.

[91] FAO Media Center. August 2012, *op. cit.*

[92] G. Hassan. 12 December 2005. 'Biopiracy and GMOs: the Fate of Iraq's Agriculture'. http://www.globalresearch.ca/index.php?context=va&aid=1447

[93] Wikileaks Cable, '09TUNIS516: TUNISIA: DINNER WITH SAKHER EL MATERI'. http://213.251.145.96/cable/2009/07/09TUNIS516.html

policies in favour of the agrarians. The Arab NGO Network for Development has produced a number of documents warning against accession to the WTO and predicting the further demise of small farming under unfair trade rules.[94] Other pan-Arab civil society movements, such as the Arab Group for the Protection of Nature campaign for food sovereignty, are very active in international fora. There are also smaller groups of farmers and food producers in Tunisia and Egypt and a number of Arab countries. They remain, however, disorganized, marginal, and unable to influence the real policy process.

Agrarian Futures

Despite the differences, all of the uprisings in the Arab world have articulated a desire to change the current relationship between citizen and state. People want a state that benefits all the people in the country, not simply a chosen few. Those who participated in the uprisings also seek to affirm the idea that they create the state, rather than living at the mercy of the elite and powerful.

Years after the revolutionary events in Tunisia and Egypt, the uprisings appear to be far from over. Former regime stalwarts are still clinging to power in Tunisia and Egypt while the United States and other international interests are not interested in seeing true democratic participation in the region.[95]

Tunisia after Ben Ali

Tunisian farmers are demanding renewed investment in small-scale agriculture and conservation agricultural practices that improve yield.[96] However, they need investment from the state for these efforts to be successful.

---

[94] K. Mohamadieh. et al. 22 October 2007. *The Arab Region and Trade Liberalization Policies,* The Arab NGO Network for Development (ANND).

[95] For regional examples, see Wikileaks cable 09STATE34688 regarding Secretary Clinton's April 7, 2009 meeting, 'Secretary Clinton encouraged military intervention in Lebanon's elections'. https://wikileaks.org/cable/2009/04/09STATE34688.html; *Al Akhbar English.* 24 May 2012. 'Jeffrey Feltman Leaks Again'. http://english.al-akhbar.com/node/7635; *Al Sumaria.* 1 December 2010. 'Wikileaks: Mubarak Advises U.S. to find "fair dictator" to Iraq'. http://new.alsumaria.tv/news/34778/wikileaks-mubarak-advises-us-to-find-fair-dictator/en

[96] C. Lamboley. 16 March 2012. 'Tunisia: Farmers Call for Renewed Support of Conservation Agriculture', *Tunisialive.* http://allafrica.com/stories/201203190202.html

The elections in Tunisia, similar to those in Egypt, have shifted control to the parties identified as 'Islamist'. Reports on the future direction of Tunisian policies are mixed. Some commentators have pointed to the diverse makeup of the parties as a sign of progress; more women have been elected to the Tunisian parliament than serve in many European countries.[97] The Ennahda Party has rhetorically opposed unfettered free-market policies and says it will operate according to 'social justice' principles.[98] After their election, they came to a tentative agreement with the Tunisian Federation of Trade Unions (UGTT).[99] However, as the UGTT helped workers organize more strikes and protest actions against exploitative labour practices, Ennahda has advocated a crackdown on the union.[100] One politician went so far as to call any strikers 'enemies of god'.[101] After the uprisings, workers in Tunisia and Egypt continue to face exploitative environments, with little option for recourse.[102]

Post Mubarak: What Is in Store for Egypt?

It is unknown how Egypt's political economy will develop after the revolution. One example of continued state neglect in rural areas is the case of new government-owned chemical factories in Fayoum. Egypt's military council opened the factories after the removal of Mubarak.[103] Farmers have linked pollution from the factories to their deteriorating olive and palm tree productions, their major exports from the 15,000 feddans of agricultural land in the area.[104] Livestock has also suffered, which directly affects the food security of farming households as much of the

---

[97] I. Kherigi, 28 November 2011.'Tunisia: the calm after the storm', *Al Jazeera English*. http://www.aljazeera.com/indepth/opinion/2011/11/201111289415287735 1.html

[98] K. Bouarrouj. 22 September 2011. 'The Arab Revolts: Neoliberalism not Primary Target', *Al Akhbar English*. http://english.al-akhbar.com/content/arab-revolts-neoliberalism-not-primary-target

[99] Ibid.

[100] Committee for Workers International. 24 February 2012. 'Hands off the UGTT Trade Union', *Socialist World*. http://www.socialistworld.net/doc/5599

[101] Committee for Workers International, 2012. Wikileaks cable, '09TUNIS516: TUNISIA: DINNER WITH SAKHER EL MATERI'. http://213.251.145.96/cable/2009/07/09TUNIS516.html

[102] Associated Foreign Press (AFP). 31 May 2013. 'Food giant violating workers rights Egypt, Tunisia: unions', *Al Akhbar English*. http://english.al-akhbar.com/node/15970

[103] A. Z. Osman. 21 December 2011. 'Military-owned factories threaten farmers' livelihoods in Fayoum', *Egypt Independent*.

[104] Ibid.

dairy and meat consumed by farmers originates from their own livestock. However, a popular movement has recently emerged in the countryside, where 18 million farmers live. Farmers are organizing independent unions in Egypt. Building on a thirty-year movement, this is the first time such efforts have been successful.[105]

After the uprisings toppled Mubarak and after the brief rule of the Supreme Council of the Armed Forces (SCAF), the Muslim Brotherhood is the party in the strongest political position to change Egypt's economy. Although the Muslim Brotherhood said they would not alter any of the current economic policies, it is also the party with the strongest ties to rural areas.[106] This marks a contradiction between its rhetoric of social justice and its liberal economic policies. The Muslim Brotherhood and other similar parties receive a great deal of their funding from Gulf Cooperation Council (GCC) countries, leading many to speculate that they are advancing a GCC agenda (in cooperation with the United States).[107] This agenda includes a pliant regime in Egypt that maintains an active U.S. presence in the region and neighbouring Palestine.

Under Egyptian president Mohamed Morsi, the Muslim Brotherhood is leading the Egyptian government for the first time. Reportedly, Egypt is now facing the worst economic crisis since the 1930s.[108] Imported food prices are increasing in parallel with farming inputs needed for domestic food production.[109] The World Food Programme reports an increase in food insecurity, though they found the roots of the insecurity to be in a "succession of crises since 2005".[110] Urban poor cannot purchase food due to inflation and poor rural farmers are unable to sell their products for a profit. At the same time, the Egyptian government is under pressure to cut urban and rural diesel subsidies. Meanwhile diplomacy between Egypt and Ethiopia over sharing access to the Nile River water resources

[105] J. Charbel. 23 June 2011. 'Egypt's farmers ready for independent organizing', *Egypt Independent*. http://www.egyptindependent.com/node/470802

[106] F. Sulehria. 3 February 2012. 'Adam Hanieh: "The Arab revolutions are not over"', *International Journal of Socialist Renewal*.

[107] Ibid.

[108] P. Kingsley. 16 May 2013. 'Egypt "suffering worse economic crisis since 1930s"', *The Guardian*. http://www.guardian.co.uk/world/2013/may/16/egypt-worst-economic-crisis-1930s

[109] Ibid.

[110] L. Loveluck. 6 June 2013. 'Egypt's gathering economic gloom leaves millions facing food shortages', *The Guardian*. http://www.guardian.co.uk/global-development/2013/jun/06/egypt-economic-gloom-food-shortages

is failing.[111] Increased pressure on water is certain to make Egyptian food security more precarious.

Both the Muslim Brotherhood in Egypt and Ennahda in Tunisia have taken great pains to assure the United States and Europe that they will continue to embrace free market capitalism. In a forthcoming essay Political Science Quarterly, Fawaz A. Gerges notes that Khairat Al Shater, the director of the Muslim Brotherhood's economic platform, has met with the IMF in order to sign Egypt up for a new 3.2 billion-dollar loan. As Gerges has stated, in Egypt and Tunisia, they want to send a clear message: 'Islam – is – good – for – business'.[112]

Conclusion

It is clear that the consistent political, economic, and ecological marginalization and exploitation of rural areas in the Arab region have pushed rural people into poverty and food insecurity. Without access to resources and decision-making abilities, rural agrarians have little choice but to organize and protest against state regimes that continually abandon agrarian livelihoods to the mercy of the free market. The free market has not functioned equitably; rather, it is skewed through political connections towards favouring influential elites. To solve unemployment, food insecurity, and issues of food access, heterodox ideas must be explored. Support for smallholder farmers should not be seen only in terms of reducing poverty. Nations invest heavily in armies to protect their 'national security'; why not invest in smallholder farmers? Those who are on the front lines of the struggle for food security are also actively protecting the sovereignty of the state.

Public investment in agriculture by a functioning state is crucial in reversing decades of neglect and marginalization. Support for agriculture, as well as health and education, in rural areas would also expand opportunities for more people. As Mohammad Pournik recently wrote, 'All economic reform programs (in the Arab region should give priority to agricultural and rural development'.[113] The uprisings in the Arab

---

[111] Reuters. 13 June 2013. 'Ethiopia dismisses Egypt's "psychological warfare" on dam', *Egypt Independent*. http://www.egyptindependent.com/news/ethiopia-dismisses-egypt-s-psychological-warfare-cam

[112] F. Gerges, forthcoming in Political Science Quarterly (sept. 2013) (PSQ).

[113] M. Pournik. April 2012. 'Por un crecimiento inclusivo en la region arabe', *Afkar*. http://www.afkar-ideas.com/fr/2012/04/por-un-crecimiento-inclusivo-en-la-region-arabe/

region have yet to lead to any equitable redistribution of accumulated resources and capital.[114]

To make this public investment possible, a new Arab integration is called for. Oil revenues, as Ali Kadri writes in Chapter 4 in this volume, could fund domestic development opportunities instead of being used by elite classes for foreign investments. In terms of agriculture, oil profits could feasibly be invested in farmers from Sudan to Syria, rather than diverted to foreign investments like ports. The heart of the problem is that oil resources in the region are viewed as 'American oil under Arab sands'.[115] This relationship signifies the denial of sovereignty over resources, which are signs of de-development and the abandonment of functioning states by autocratic rulers in the Arab world.

One possible basis for such integration is, unexpectedly, the Arab Organization for Agricultural Development's (AOAD) food security definition. With its focus on regional cooperation, a 'recognition of the importance of the agricultural sector within the Arab economy' and local production and healthy sustainability to all 'citizens of the Arab nation', the AOAD comes closer to food sovereignty than many other definitions of food security.[116] Food sovereignty is a 'precondition'[117] of food security and is essentially the right to make decisions about development based on the needs of people and the specific context of their farming systems, something too long denied to the majority of people in the Arab world.

An equitable Arab integration must also address the sizeable food import bill. Even with revalorization of agriculture, Arab countries will not be self-sufficient. In all likelihood they will continue to import a large amount of commodity food products. However, the Arab region has never used its food import bill as a tool to demand favourable price structures on the world market. Although the Arab world may be dependent on food imports, the global food regime is also dependent on the sizeable Arab market for profits.

The Arab uprisings were always about more than food prices and jobs. Rural poverty, however, is a significant factor in understanding the

---

[114] See Chapter 4 by Ali Kadri in this volume.

[115] See note 100 to this chapter.

[116] The AOAD definition also refers to the following: 'At the national level, AOAD is to assist member countries in developing and enhancing their respective agricultural sectors. At the regional level, AOAD is to facilitate coordination amongst member states in the agricultural sector, with the aim of achieving a fully integrated Arab economy union, and food self-sufficiency'. http://www.aoad.org/about_en.htm

[117] Via Campesina. 11–17 November 1996. *Food Sovereignty: A Future without Hunger.*

causes. The Arab agrarian question links the issues of natural resource management, economic livelihoods, and food security. Rural people have long struggled for recognition of these issues; their struggles have played an important role throughout history as well as in the recent protests and sociopolitical mobilization and organization in the Arab region. The disconnect between policymakers and people continues to expand, the uprisings are far from over and the necessity of food sovereignty is increasingly urgent. Understanding the agrarian roots of social protest and dissent is vital to understanding the current Arab uprisings and unfolding contentious politics in the region.

.

PART II

THEMATIC AND COMPARATIVE ASPECTS

6

The Politics of Resistance and the Arab Uprisings

Charles Tripp

Abstract

This chapter looks at the uprisings of 2011 as acts of mass resistance to the appropriation of public resources and public spaces. They were protests against the power that had been used for decades to denigrate and exclude the public, those who were formally citizens of these states but who were also effectively denied citizens' rights. It therefore emphasises the centrality of public space and the way in which the method of its occupation brought the public into being as a mobilised political force. In the enactment of these multiple projects of resistance across the region, two features stood out. The first was the performative aspect of this politics. The second was the way in which resistance followed the capillary forms of power itself, confounding the state authorities. Of course, coming together to express a common demand that the regime should fall did not imply uniformity of opinion about what should replace it. In some countries, this is when fracture lines began to appear, because some found it difficult to accept the plurality of the activist public. Similarly, the need to institutionalise the public to ensure genuine empowerment of those involved has sometimes proved contentious. Neither problem is insuperable, but the preservation of spaces – physical, institutional and imaginative – that are genuinely public and open to all will determine whether or not the Arab uprisings have set in motion processes that will genuinely transform politics in the region for a generation.

Introduction

Perhaps the most striking feature of the uprisings in 2011 was the sight and sound of hundreds of thousands of people gathered in towns and cities across the Middle East, calling for the overthrow of the regimes that had ruled them for so long. It was this that gave such encouragement to their fellow citizens and to the citizens of neighbouring countries. By the same token, it struck fear into the heart of the regimes, causing panic and disconcerting their foreign backers. In some respects, these mass uprisings could be said to have been the most visible sign of the evaporation of *haibat al-dawla* (awe of the state) that had been cultivated for so long by those who had seized and retained power in the postcolonial Middle East. More importantly, these mass demonstrations spectacularly confirmed the power of a mobilized public against the threadbare authority of the authoritarian regimes. It would not be too much of an exaggeration to say that the spectacle itself helped to generate *haibat al-sha'b* (awe of the people).

It is for this reason that it is worth reflecting on the uprisings in the Arab world in the context of a politics of resistance. This takes the analysis beyond the focus on dissent or contestation of specific policies, although this did feed into the larger resistance movements. More importantly, such a framework broadens and deepens our understanding of the processes at work in 2011. The mobilization of hundreds of thousands of people across the region took place in the specific contexts of each state where uprisings developed, following paths that differed from each other as much as the dynamics of power differ from one country to the next. However, across the Middle East, there was a common impulse to resist the many abuses of power by unrepresentative coteries of ruthless individuals and their systematic exclusion of the bulk of the population.

The uprisings of 2011 therefore were acts of mass resistance to the appropriation of public resources and public spaces, as well as protests against the power that had been used so ferociously to defend this denigration and exclusion of the public. The systematic brutalities and contempt displayed by the police and security forces as they routinely violated citizens' rights and dignity were both catalyst and target of the uprisings. People fought against systems that had long exposed them to this violence, trapping them in petty rules and regulations, the better to subordinate and exploit them. The very arbitrary nature of the enforcement of these rules had been part of the system of power itself. Thus, people were not simply rising up against the humiliations of daily life, but against regimes of power of which these bruising and humiliating encounters were an integral part. In doing so, they were also rejecting the overarching myths of patriarchal benevolence that had long been used to justify these blatantly unequal systems of power. Phrased in slightly different idioms, depending on the country concerned, these myths were much alike, portraying the head of state as the sole guarantor of stability and the foremost embodiment of the state and of the nation. In some respects, this was the ultimate act of appropriation: the leader had taken the whole community into his person, revealing the hegemonic project at the heart of power.

It was this that unravelled so spectacularly in 2011 – but the ground had long been prepared. Indeed, a politics of resistance had been underway for many years prior to the unseating first of Zine El Abidine Ben Ali in Tunisia and then of leaders in Egypt, Libya, and Yemen. The scale of the uprisings in 2011, their intensity and sustained power, as well as their dramatic outcomes were, of course, unprecedented, but they had been preceded by years of quiet encroachment and not so quiet resistance. Sometimes, as in the riots that swept across North Africa in the 1980s, or the strikes and sit-ins that had become so frequent in Egypt in the first decade of the twenty-first century, these had taken forms that re-emerged in 2011 on a larger scale. The repertoire was known and established. In some cases, the same people were involved, bringing with them memories of defiance and the forms it could take. The very fact that the earlier uprisings struck such a powerful chord in the popular imagination across the region would suggest that much preparatory work had already taken place.[1]

This was not the organized and coordinated conspiratorial preparation alleged by the beleaguered regimes. On the contrary, and ironically, the regimes themselves had been responsible for creating the conditions of their own demise, behaving over the years in such a way that they had already been displaced in the imagination of many. Their hold on power was no longer sustained by even a modicum of authority as far as most of the population was concerned. Instead, the nature of their domination was exposed for what it was: *haibat al-dawla* had given way over the years to *khawf al-nizam* (fear of the regime). The relationship between

---

[1] See, for instance, the prescient article on the movement to reclaim Cairo's public spaces that had been taking place since the early twenty-first century: Wael Salah Fahmi, '"Bloggers" street movement and the right to the city. (Re)claiming Cairo's real and virtual "spaces of freedom"'. *Environment and Urbanization* 21/1 (April 2009): 89–107.

ruler and people had become mechanical, instrumental, and effectively external. It was no longer internalised by the subject population and thus no longer hegemonic, as it might once have been. When the cry went up, 'There is no fear! There is no fear! After today there is no fear!',[2] the game was up – or at least it left governments with the choice between making concessions, and using massive violence in the hope of re-establishing at least a regime of fear. In this sense, the uprisings were a manifestation of a longer-running politics of resistance. It was resistance against what the state had become over the years, in terms of its coercive power, its appropriation of public goods for the benefit of the few, and its exclusion of the many under the guise of a 'popular' or 'national' image wholly at odds with the reality that millions of citizens knew so intimately.

Framing a Politics of Resistance

Within the frame of resistance politics, a number of features of the 2011 uprisings stand out. They had been part of the symbolic and enforced order of the incumbent regimes, but were deftly transformed by the actions of hundreds of thousands of citizens into a force of startling power. In particular, across different countries, in various towns and cities, two related factors emerged to challenge and eventually – at least in Tunisia, Egypt, Libya, and Yemen – displace autocratic rule. The first of these was the centrality of public space, dramatically visible in the demonstrations and occupations of the Avenue Bourguiba in Tunis, Qaid Ibrahim Square in Alexandria, Tahrir Square in Cairo, Arbaeen Square in Suez, Sahat al-Taghyir in Sana'a, or the Pearl Roundabout in Manama. These spaces were physically and symbolically central to the organization of resistance to the power confronting the citizens of these countries. Space in this sense was not simply an arena where power plays itself out. Rather, it was a key component in the exercise of power. Physically, this can be seen in the often coercive disciplining of the body and comportment of the subject. Imaginatively, it resides in its use to shape the ways in which power is viewed.[3] By the same token, however, it could – and did

---

[2] Lina Sinjab, 'Middle East unrest – silence broken in Syria', Dara'a, Syria, 19 March 2011. http://www.bbc.co.uk/news/mobile/world-middle-east-12794882 (accessed 7 February 2012).

[3] Henri Lefèbvre, *The Production of Space* (trans. D. Nicolson-Smith) (Oxford: Blackwell Publishers, 2000); Ash Amin, 'Collective Culture and Urban Public Space', *City* 12/1 (2008): 5–16.

during 2011 – become central to the organized and determined resistance of those who were challenging regimes across the region.

It was they who were able to transform these spaces from sites of order into places of apparent disorder. They negated the hierarchies that had been sustained by and helped to support the dictatorships. However, in Tahrir Square, as in the Pearl Roundabout and in Taghyir Square in Sana'a, this was not the disorder of the destructive riot that the security forces had been geared to suppress. On the contrary, to the consternation of those in power, this was a disordering that produced different kinds of order, suggesting both other ways of organizing the world, and other visions for society and for political relations, negating the certainties of the patrimonial, autocratic state. This was owing in large part to the imagination and vision of the people who took part in these occupations and manifestations. They brought with them their individual ideas, their voices, and their aspirations and found common cause with fellow demonstrators, echoing the concerns of others and providing the spaces in which artistic, educational, and political alternatives could be debated.[4]

More than that, through their individual actions and their determination to come together, driven by different visions but united in common purpose against the dictators, these people were bringing the public into being, not simply as an idea, but as a mobilized political force.[5] Long misused as a term and abused as a body of citizens, the public was now reconstituting itself in a way that clearly escaped the grip of the so-called 'public' authorities. It was the latter who now looked increasingly beleaguered, identified as the autocrats or, as one debunking piece of street art by Ganzeer in Cairo had it, *habayib al-ra'is* (sweethearts of the president).[6] Having for so long claimed the right to dictate and to use their power to shape and to restrict access to public space, they were now confronted by a public that had reconstituted itself and had begun to assert its own claims.

---

4 Karima Khalil, *Messages from Tahrir* (Cairo: American University in Cairo Press, 2011); film *Laisa li-l-karama jadran* (Karama has no walls) directed by Sara Ishaq (2011). http://karamahasnowalls.com/ (accessed 15 February 2012).
5 Dan Hind, *The Return of the Public* (London: Verso, 2010), pp. 44–47, 201–203.
6 This was in a powerful mural in Zamalek by Ganzeer under the heading, '*Al-Sha'b yurid isqat habayib al-ra'is*' the people want the fall of the sweethearts of the president), showing Ahmad Ezz (a steel magnate and NDP hierarch), Field Marshal Tantawi (head of SCAF), and Safwat Sharif (former Speaker of the Shura Council) clustered around former President Mubarak, with little hearts floating in the air between them. http://ganzeer.blogspot.co.uk/2011/03/mubarak-posse-love.html (accessed 2 February 2012).

Thus, the politics of resistance in the Arab uprisings had taken the form of an activist public, re-appropriating public space – the second factor of significance. This had happened in a number of countries where such a political force had little or no substance up to that point, no space in which to develop and little imaginative resonance amongst much of the population. However, with the uprisings of 2011, more and more people became personally involved in a variety of collective acts against the dominant regimes. They came together to work with others they may not have known in order to dislodge an apparatus of power, not merely an autocrat. They were thereby disproving the rationale used by power throughout the region (and beyond) that the regime knew best the nation's true interests and was rightfully in possession of the power to defend and realize them. By coming together and acting in concert, for the same political end, the population became citizens and, as citizens, asserted their individual rights and the collective rights of the public to the freedoms and the resources that had so long been denied them.[7]

In doing so, two features became clear that made resistance so effective. The first was the performative aspect of politics and the second was the way in which resistance followed the capillary forms of power itself, countering the flow of command and using these same channels to confound the state authorities. The running battles for space and the visible denial of an imposed order were intended as performances for multiple audiences. The sites, the open defiance, the slogans, chants, and placards – as well as the numbers involved – were meant to impress upon their compatriots the scale of the protests now developing, encouraging them to join and to mobilize under the same banners.

They were also, of course, meant to impress upon the president and the inner circle of the regime, the power of a mobilized public and the fruitless efforts of the security forces to suppress, prevent, or break the momentum. In Tunisia, Egypt, Yemen, and Libya, this had the desired effect of shaking the confidence of the inner circles, leading to cracks within the state apparatus and the eventual fall of the autocrats. But in mounting such public performances, there was also an external audience, both in the region and among the great powers that had for so long been the mainstay of the autocrats, often against their own people. As the Yemeni and the

---

[7] Clive Barnett and Murray Low, eds., *Spaces of Democracy: Geographical perspectives on citizenship, participation and representation* (London: Sage Publications, 2004).

Syrian examples showed, the timing and the outcomes were very different, but the performances of resistance were unmistakeable.

Equally relevant was the constitutive aspect of a politics of performance. This goes further than simply staging performances, however powerful they may be, as a form of political communication. It concerns the role of performance in self-constitution.[8] Effectively, this was happening across the towns and cities of the Middle East during 2011: in the hundreds of thousands, people were discovering the novelty and the power of acting as a public. They were paying attention to the ways in which diverse individuals and groups could come together to constitute themselves into a body that had power, but also rights, using this power and this self-discovery to re-appropriate the authority that had for so long been claimed by the rulers of the state alone. By performing the public over the days, weeks, and months of the uprisings, ordinary Tunisians, Egyptians, Libyans, Yemenis, and Bahrainis were establishing a counter-system to that maintained by the autocrats. The citizens were using public space to assert their own power and their own authority. The performative opportunities of resistance had therefore been both symptom and catalyst of a new kind of political actor, challenging the old order and holding out the promise of a new dispensation of power.[9]

In doing so, resistance was made all the more effective through the participants' intimate knowledge of the ways in which power operated, flowing along the capillary channels that brought it – and the order it represented – into the everyday lives of the people, making them who they were and in theory producing the disciplined subjects congruent with the order of the state.[10] With the disordering performances associated with the uprisings of 2011 came the opportunity to reverse the nature of the relationship. Disorder of the kind witnessed in streets, public squares, factories, and places of education became a way of engaging with and of disorienting the very nerves of the system of power itself. This was more than simply the technological mastery of countermeasures that made state surveillance and communication far less effective than the crowd-sourced messaging, imaging, and texting that was now possible in the

---

[8] Judith Butler, 'Bodies in alliance and the politics of the street' (Lecture in Venice, 7 September 2011, European Institute for Progressive Cultural Policies). http://www.eipcp.net/transversal/1011/butler/en (accessed 24 May 2012).

[9] Elzbieta Matynia, *Performative Democracy* (Boulder, CO: Paradigm Publishers, 2009).

[10] Michel Foucault, *Discipline and Punish: The birth of the prison* (London: Penguin, 1991); C. Fred Alford, 'What would it matter if everything Foucault said about prison were wrong?' *Theory and Society* 29/1 (2000): 138–142.

twenty-first century. It came, rather, from the very constitution of the disciplined subject and the ways in which, through a politics of resistance sustained over time, the system that had been intended to manufacture docility became the basis of a common register of resistance.

In this respect, therefore, the performances made sense to people – common antagonism to humiliating power had served to produce the resistant subject. This was made manifest not only in the immediacy and speed with which slogans, songs, and chants used in one country could travel and have equal resonance and power in another, but also in the now famously 'leaderless' nature of these uprisings. From Tunisia to Yemen, a characteristic feature of the uprisings of 2011 was that they were not so much led as coordinated by loose alliances of individuals, associations, and informal groupings. More established political parties and organizations joined in later as the uprisings developed, but even then they never managed to achieve the kind of primacy that might have been expected in more conventional revolts against established power. On the contrary, it was as if the very capillary channels that had carried the flow of power and discipline had gone into reverse, bringing defiance, disorder, and resistance from all extremities of the body politic to its heart. The public had been brought into existence and this had been made possible not only by the immediate performances of resistance, but by the underlying, gradual reversal of the flow of capillary power itself that had been going on for years.

Public Space and its Significance: A Key to the Political Fabric

Nowhere was the reversal of this flow more evident than in the ways in which public space was reclaimed and made into a space for the imagination and performance of counter-hegemonic projects of resistance. It is this aspect that will be the focus of the remainder of the chapter. In the Middle East, as elsewhere, there is often a marked gap between the representation of power and the location of those whose privileged access to resources and to position gives them power over others. Myths are developed to disguise the true beneficiaries and the terms on which they enjoy these privileges. Sometimes, this is cynically done, but it can also be an outgrowth of the very nature of the structures and discourses that have marked the history of a state, becoming accepted even by those who are excluded as the way things are and always have been. This gap is therefore related to the nature of the state and the social formations with which it, and the power vested in it, are intertwined.

It is a gap that has been characterised as that between the public state and the shadow state, where the former is made up of the visible institutions of the state, its administrative and coercive apparatus, its representative and judicial institutions, as well as the educational and welfare provision that shape its citizens' lives. The shadow state, by contrast, is hidden from public scrutiny, although by no means insubstantial. It comprises the networks of association, favour, and influence that shadow, penetrate, and ultimately control all state agencies. It is in these networks, unacknowledged in the public discourse of the regime, that real power lies. It is also here that the regime may use violence to maintain the gap between the public institutions and their shadows.[11] Violence is also used to crush anyone who dares to strip away the myths that are meant to sustain the authority of the public state. In doing so, it ensures that people will see what the government wants them to see. This, at least, is the theory and the intent, but as the exploration of the capillary paths of counter-hegemony suggests – and as the events of 2011 bear witness – this is not something any government can guarantee.

It is here that the battle for and the reconstitution of public space play key parts, as was evident in the uprisings of 2011 across the Arab world. The public spaces – streets, squares, and roundabouts – of the cities and towns had long been the sites for the exercise and display of state power. They were the sites of surveillance, of public humiliations to reinforce respect or fear of the ruling order, and of numerous encounters that underlined the subordinate status of the rest of the population.[12] They were the parade grounds where the powerful would produce the disciplined subjects they craved, organizing sponsored manifestations or simply enforcing the kind of public conduct that suggested compliance. This demanded docility in the face of state authority, assembly only on terms and in the numbers allowed by the regime, and performances that acknowledged the superiority of the established order. These were the mechanisms for enforcing the dominant order and these were the prime sites for that enforcement, and thus for the instruction of the population at large. Looming over these public spaces was the image of the supreme leader, the autocrat who was the heart and driving force

[11] Charles Tripp, *A History of Iraq* (Cambridge: Cambridge University Press, 2007), pp. 259–267.

[12] Salwa Ismail, *Political Life in Cairo's New Quarters: Encountering the everyday state* (Minneapolis, MN: Minnesota University Press, 2006), pp. 146–147; see the section of the film, 'The Egyptian Revolution 2011' entitled 'The Reasons'. http://www.youtube.com/watch?v=DaxepUuCFFM (accessed 24 February 2011).

of the shadow state, but who was represented as a national hero in the vast portraits and posters that dominated public space. Symbolically, as well as materially, this was an assertion of his power and of his right to control all spaces in the state.

For this very reason, these became sites of effective resistance in 2011, as they had been at various times in the past when they had witnessed anti-colonial and other forms of protest. The very features of these spaces that had made them so much a part of the fabric of authoritarian power made them also powerful sites of resistance. Their very visibility – enhanced by television, mobile phone images, and social media made them amplifiers of mass defiance, resonating with chants and slogans denigrating the rulers. They became the places in which to demonstrate before the world the solidarity of the excluded, given common cause by having been shut out of the preserves of the powerful. Mass occupation turned these spaces into truly public spaces where a protesting public could be mobilized and be seen to be mobilized, driven by common concerns and complaints.[13] Physically, the hundreds of thousands of ordinary citizens of Tunisia, Egypt, Yemen, Bahrain, and Libya who converged on these spaces quite simply overwhelmed and negated the power of the agents of the regime.

These citizens fought hard to seize back the space and in some cases, as in Green Square in Tripoli in the spring of 2011 or the Pearl Round-about in Manama they succeeded in doing so through the use of over-whelming violence. However, when the body was used as a weapon in a sustained campaign of non-violent resistance, where the mere physical presence of bodies negated the power of government and refuted official claims to speak for the public, the effect could be dramatic, as the cases of Tunisia, Egypt, and indeed Yemen demonstrated. The massive violence used by the Syrian regime against peaceful demonstrators showed just how threatening such bodily defiance could be. The ferocity of the rattled Syrian security forces' attempt to dismember this collective body through the dismemberment and destruction of individual bodies testified to the potency of this non-violent 'weapon'.[14] Mass occupation of public

---

[13] Neil Smith and Setha Low, 'Introduction: The Imperative of Public Space' in Setha Low and Neil Smith (eds.) *The Politics of Public Space* (London: Routledge, 2006), pp. 3–8.

[14] International Crisis Group, *Popular Protest in the Middle East and North Africa (VI): The Syrian People's Slow-motion Revolution* (MENA Report 108, 6 July 2011); International Crisis Group, *Popular Protest in the Middle East and North Africa (VII): The Syrian Regime's Slow-motion Suicide* (MENA Report 109, 13 July 2011). http://www.crisisgroup.org/en/regions/middle-east-north-africa/egypt-syria-lebanon/syria.aspx (accessed 12 September 2011).

space relayed a message to the state authorities and to their foreign backers through the mere sight of hundreds of thousands of defiant citizens, orderly and peaceful but adamant in their demands for the removal of the regimes. The very scale of such assemblies also countered and subverted the electronic surveillance capacities of the regimes. Mobile phones above all, but also computer networks, had placed into citizens' hands means of communication and information that far outpaced the authorities' abilities to monitor them, amplifying the message of defiance and countering the state's surveillance networks.

The occupation and the claiming of public space were not confined only to demonstrations in streets and squares. Nominally, public buildings also became targets. These housed institutions associated with an unrealised public voice and interest, that had been appropriated, one might say 'privatised', for the benefit of the interests that controlled the shadow state. Thus, institutions associated with citizens' rights and their protection, as well as with the public interest more generally, became the focus of mass demonstrations. In Benghazi it was the Court House that attracted the first, initially modest demonstrations in February 2011. In Tunis, the parliament and the law courts had been targeted in January 2011 and in Cairo, there were similar gatherings, sit-ins, and assemblies in front of the parliament, the law courts, as well as the journalists' union in January and February 2011. In Sana'a, it was the university campus that became the major draw, leading to the establishment of the permanent site of public protest in Sahat al-Taghyir (Change Square). In all of these places, the choice of venue was by no means arbitrary. They had significance precisely because of the feeling of many citizens that these institutions and the spaces around them, as well as what they represented, needed to be reclaimed from those who had seized them from the public.[15]

Similarly, those buildings associated with the production over the years of the manufactured, counterfeit public became the targets of demonstration and sometimes of arson. Ruling-party buildings, such as those of the RCD (Rassemblement constitutionnel démocratique) in Tunis, or the NDP (National Democratic Party) headquarters in Cairo and Suez, as well as the local Ba'thist offices in Dara'a and elsewhere in Syria, were set on fire. The demonstrators were venting their rage against these organizations that had monopolised political life but had claimed to be ruling 'in the name of the people'. The same fate befell state television and

[15] Samia Mehrez (ed.) *Translating Egypt's Revolution* (Cairo: American University in Cairo Press, 2012).

broadcasting buildings in the Syrian town of Dara'a, whilst in Cairo the state television building was placed under siege because of its misleading stream of reports about the nature of the uprisings. In January, this became the scene of a tense stand-off between the state security forces and the demonstrators. In October 2011, it witnessed the darker side of enduring power when twenty-eight people, mostly Coptic Egyptians, demonstrating against the lies that continued to be broadcast by the state television networks were killed by army units ordered to disperse them.[16]

The massive demonstrations of 2011 therefore precipitated political change. Persistent, physical acts of defiance by so many citizens could, in some places, defeat the security forces sent to crush them, or cause significant splits in those forces, fracturing the coercive power of those who controlled the state. The mass occupation of city centres, the associated strikes, and the paralysis of national economies – as well as the open disobedience and refusal to be cowed – forced compromises, as well as violent reaction, – on the part of governments and made Tunisia, Egypt, Libya, and Yemen ungovernable by those who had enjoyed unrivalled power for decades. Equally important were the symbolic aspects of the occupation of public space. These, too, played a part in the ordering and disordering of power. They helped to undermine authority and to project a new kind of public speaking for itself, rather than awaiting the barked commands of the regime.

In the first place, the hundreds of thousands of demonstrators exposed the fraudulent nature of governments' claims to speak for the public. Although still a fraction of the population as a whole, those encamped in the public squares had come together to form a new collective political actor and could plausibly claim to represent a growing, activist public far more convincingly than anything the government could muster.[17] The importance of this battle for symbolic terrain was underlined not only by the mass protests, but also by the counterdemonstrations organized by governments across the region. Thus, throughout 2011, Bashar al-Assad summoned thousands onto the streets to pledge their loyalty to himself and to the Ba'th party as the true representatives of the Syrian people.

---

[16] Sarah Carr, 'A firsthand account: Marching from Shubra to death at Maspero', *Egypt Independent* 10 October 2011. http://www.egyptindependent.com/node/503496 (accessed 7 February 2012).

[17] This was reminiscent of the 'Monday protests' that began in Leipzig in October 1989 with their repeated slogan: '*Wir sind das Volk*' (*We* are the people). They helped to precipitate the collapse of the German Democratic Republic and only ended in March 1990 with the first truly representative, multiparty elections.

It was noticeable, however, that although impressive displays could be mounted in the capital, it was far harder to organize counterdemonstrations of any note in the streets and squares of Syria's provincial cities.

Similarly, in the first weeks of the uprising in Yemen, Ali Abdullah Saleh and his supporters organized large counterdemonstrations in Sana'a. In Libya, having chased the demonstrators out of Tripoli's public spaces by force, Muammar Qadhafi's well-orchestrated displays of public support occupied Green Square and other spaces in the capital. In Cairo, more modest demonstrations were organized in the aftermath of the fall of President Mubarak in Midan Abbasiya and also Mustafa Mahmud in Muhandisin, to remind people that the dominant narrative of the uprising was contested by other Egyptians, using the same idiom.[18]

Counterdemonstrations of this kind were tolerated, even encouraged by the security forces. Thus, in Bahrain, counterdemonstrations organized by the regime took on a markedly sectarian character protected by the police. Meanwhile, extreme violence was used against those who defied the authorities and had dared to occupy public spaces, as well as against those who had tried to protect and help them, as the medical staff at the Salmaniyya Medical Complex discovered at their cost.[19] Backed by forces from Saudi Arabia and the United Arab Emirates (UAE), the Bahraini authorities dispersed the demonstrators and demolished the monument in the middle of Pearl Roundabout, which served as the epicentre and symbol of the uprising. They presumably hoped that by removing the focus of the protests, the resistance would be broken. In Algeria, with its own long history of urban protest that had triggered such dramatic changes in the 1980s, the security forces moved in rapidly, flooding the streets of Algiers and other cities with tens of thousands of riot police, deployed very precisely to prevent any significantly large gathering of people in any one place. In all of the countries where regimes faced mass occupations and demonstrations, violence was the initial response, escalating, as in Egypt, Yemen and Libya when it seemed that initial efforts at crowd control had failed to work. In Syria, the escalation was so widespread and so protracted that government forces laid waste to large sections of

[18] Naira Antoun, 'The Battle for Public Space: Squares and Streets of the Egyptian Revolution', *Ahramonline* 23 January 2012. http://english.ahram.org.eg/NewsContent/1/114/32336/Egypt/-January-Revolution-continues/The-battle-for-public-space-Squares-and-streets-of.aspx (accessed 9 February 2012).

[19] Human Rights Watch, 'Bahrain: Systematic attacks on medical providers', 18 July 2011. http://www.hrw.org/news/2011/07/18/bahrain-systematic-attacks-medical-providers (accessed 17 September 2011).

those cities that had risen in revolt and effectively provoked an armed uprising that engulfed the country in a civil war. Such was the power of symbolic politics.

Forming a Public

There was an added dimension to the symbolic struggle between the regimes and those who were resisting them that went beyond the question of space and revolved around the question of the public itself. This emerging collective actor was to be the subject of ferocious contestation between the ruling elites and the newly assertive public; an actor feeling its strength, stating its identity, and claiming its rights.[20] It was this determination to represent and to enact a new public, as much as the physical occupation of public space, that was to be so striking a feature of the uprisings of 2011. Across the region – in the squares of Tunis, Cairo, Alexandria, and Ismailiyya; of Manama, Benghazi, and of cities the length and breadth of Syria – people congregated, coming together not only in their determination to see the downfall of the regimes that ruled over them, but united also in their determination to assert their collective and common political identity as citizens. This went beyond vast groupings and demonstrations of individuals. Acting as individuals, they were nevertheless joining with others, with whom they may have had ideological differences, as well as differences of class, gender, sect, and ethnicity, to establish common purposes revolving around the realisation of the rights of the public.[21]

This led to many striking performances of social diversity united by a common purpose. Thus, Tahrir Square provided a gigantic stage on which the unity of Egyptians could be played out: Christians guarded Muslims at prayer and Muslims returned the favour when the time came for Christian prayers; men linked arms with women to defy the security forces; women and men prayed together as equals. In Syria, fully aware of the communal and sectarian differences amongst the population and the possible reverberations of an uprising against a regime that was not only

---

[20] Bruce D'Arcus, 'Dissent, public space and the politics of citizenship: Riots and the "outside agitator"', *Space and Polity* 8/3 (2004): 358–361; Fawwaz Traboulsi, 'Public spheres and urban space: A critical comparative approach' in Seteney Shami (ed.) *Publics, politics and participation – locating the public sphere in the Middle East and North Africa* (New York: Social Science Research Council, 2009), pp. 45–63.

[21] Salwa Ismail, 'The Syrian uprising: Imagining and performing the nation', *Studies in Ethnicity and Nationalism* 11/3 (2011), pp. 538–549.

oppressive, but also associated with the Alawi minority, a common slogan of demonstrators in Homs, Banias, Aleppo, and elsewhere was 'One, one, Syrians are one!' Furthermore, the practice of the Syrian resistance in giving distinct names to the Fridays on which mass demonstrations were to be held throughout 2011 took account of Syria's diversity by associating them with the Kurdish (*Jum'at al-Azadi* (Freedom Friday) or the Christian minorities (*Jum'at al-Azimeh* (Great Friday – for the Friday before Easter).[22]

In their efforts to prevent the coming together of a mobilized public demanding common rights and asserting a forceful presence as a political actor, regimes across the region tried to disrupt this unity with all the resources at their disposal. In Bahrain, the uprisings were blamed on the sectarian prejudices of the demonstrators, portrayed as serving an agenda that was fundamentally Shia and dictated by Iran. The Sunni ruling house of the Al Khalifa had long practised sectarian discrimination against the Shia citizens of Bahrain and was now seeking to mobilize Sunni Bahrainis around the defence of the state. Indeed, one concern of the regime in the early weeks of the uprising was that the protestors came from both Sunni and Shia communities, although the latter, like the population at large, outnumbered the former in the constitution of a *Bahraini* public.

Similar themes were used during the long months of the Syrian uprising by a regime that wants to fragment the idea and the reality of a *Syrian* public, the better to dominate the fragments, persuading them that they have more to fear from their fellow citizens than from the regime itself. Thus, the uprising was portrayed as the work of al-Qaida-affiliated *salafi* extremists, pursuing a sectarian agenda under the cover of general unrest. Reinforcing this in its own way, the regime deployed its sinister and violent *Shabbiha* militia, largely recruited from Alawi communities of the coastal mountains, to terrorise neighbourhoods and villages that had dared to protest – and leaving them in no doubt about the sectarian identity of their attackers. Clearly, of concern to those Syrians trying to hold the public together in opposition to the violence and divisiveness of the regime, after months of suppression, bombardment, and murder, there were reports of sectarian slogans being shouted by protestors, as well as of graffiti that was both anti-regime and sectarian in its messages. Some alleged that these were the work of *agents provocateurs* working

---

[22] Khalil Habash, 'Syria One Year after the Beginning of the Revolution. Part 2: a Sectarian Movement?' *Uruknet info* 21 March 2012. http://www.uruknet.info/?p=86712 (accessed 31 March 2012).

for the regime.[23] Nevertheless, the violence of the regime did its work over the course of two years. By early 2013, some 60,000 Syrians were estimated to have lost their lives, creating conditions that generated and provided opportunity for violent resistance that did indeed identify itself in sectarian terms in some parts of the country.

In other countries, different idioms were used to divide the public. In Yemen, former President Ali Abdullah Saleh proclaimed that demonstrating in public space was 'improper conduct for women'. Women had, of course, been to the fore in many of the open protests in Sana'a and Ta'iz, calling for the overthrow of the regime and vividly demonstrating that gender difference mattered little when the cause was that of reclaiming the rights of the public as a whole. So unsuccessful was this effort to split the public along gender lines that not only did women remain enthusiastic and committed members of the mobilized public, but one of their numbers, the journalist and activist Tawakkul Karman, was awarded the Nobel Peace Prize in 2011 for her sustained advocacy of human rights and press freedoms over the years. A similar tactic was tried by the ruling Supreme Council of the Armed Forces in Egypt following the removal of President Mubarak. As the demonstrations in Tahrir Square continued, calling the Supreme Council of the Armed Forces (SCAF) to account, the army-backed security forces found ways to humiliate and intimidate women. These included the notorious virginity tests and the very public stripping and beating of a female demonstrator in December 2011.[24] These efforts spectacularly backfired, with women taking the security forces to court in one case and organizing massive protest demonstrations in Tahrir Square that called for the overthrow of the military government and proclaimed that 'The women of Egypt are the country's red line' (*nisa' masr khatt ahmar*).

Of course, there always exists the possibility of the fragmentation of a mobilized, yet plural public. Coming together to express solidarity and a common demand that the regime should fall, did not imply uniformity of

[23] Aljazeera, 'Nir Rosen on Syrian sectarianism', 18 February 2012. http://www.aljazeera .com/indepth/features/2012/02/20122218165546393720.html (accessed 22 February 2012); Bassel Oudat, 'Not sectarianism' *Al-Ahram Weekly* (28 July – 3 August 2011). http://weekly.ahram.org.eg/2011/1058/re91.htm (accessed 15 July 2012).

[24] Riazat Butt and Abdel-Rahman Hussein, '"Virginity tests" on women protestors are illegal, says judge', *The Guardian* online 27 December 2011. http://www.guardian.co.uk/ world/2011/dec/27/virginity-tests-egypt-protesters-illegal (accessed 7 February 2012); Maggie Michael and Sarah El Deeb, 'Egypt military uses heavy hand in crushing protest', *The Daily News Egypt* online 18 December 2011. http://www.thedailynewsegypt.com/ human-a-civil-rights/egypt-military-uses-heavy-hand-in-crushing-protest-dp2.html (accessed 7 February 2012).

opinion about what should replace it. On the contrary, it is the ability of people of diverse origins and opinions to constitute a sovereign people, acting in a space where difference can be debated, that is the key to the constitution of a public with shared rights.[25] Unlike the old top-down construction of 'the people', this does not demand unanimity of opinion, but rather a common respect for difference to be expressed. It takes popular sovereignty seriously, relocating it from the sovereign command of the few to that of the many. It was this that the regimes were so intent on disrupting.

However, there were signs during 2011 that, even without regime encouragement, fracture lines were emerging. This was not surprising, given the diversity of backgrounds of those who were coming together to voice their open defiance. The political public is, after all, neither uniform nor unanimous. It is a political actor diverse in nature that embodies the rights of citizens to express differences and to engage in civil debate of those differences. Even as people experienced the heady power of collective action, the plurality of the public was not easy for all to accept. In some places, this showed itself in sharp differences of opinion about the suitability and propriety of some of the public performances.[26] In other places, it was reflected in reluctance to accord equal political rights to fellow citizens who differed in social background, gender, sexual orientation, communal origins, or ideological choice.

In Egypt, for instance, this has been apparent in the widening gap that has developed between the Islamists – Muslim Brotherhood and *salafi* – and their secular and liberal critics over the drafting of the new constitution. This is an argument about the fundamental orientation of the polity, the arena that will frame the very existence of the public in the future. Sometimes, the differences were sharpened by the transformation of the uprisings into open armed rebellions, as in Libya and in Syria. In both countries, the dangers and violence of armed conflict fuelled passions for revenge – for attacks on known and even suspected collaborators that could follow already existing social fault lines, especially where particular communities or locations were associated with the ruling regime.[27]

---

[25] Dan Hind, *The Return of the Public* (London: Verso, 2010), pp. 201–203; Jürgen Habermas, *Between Facts and Norms* (trans. William Rehg) (Cambridge, MA: MIT Press, 1996).

[26] See Chapter 13 in this volume by Gabriele vom Bruck, Atif Alwazir, and Benjamin Wiaceck, 'Yemen: Revolution Suspended?'

[27] Amnesty International, 'Libya: "out of control" militias commit widespread abuses, a year on from uprising', 15 February 2012. http://www.amnesty.org/en/news/

Conclusions: When Does Resistance End?

The incidence of armed conflict sharpened the question of the fragmentation of the public and the shattering of the solidarities of resistance, whether during the uprising or, as in Libya and in Yemen, after the dictator had been overthrown. This, however, was an extreme example of a more general problem facing those who had succeeded in overturning regimes across the region. They were now facing the challenge of transforming resistance into a new ordering of power: how to institutionalize the public space that had been so hard won, at the cost of so many lives, and how to empower the people, the mobilized public that had achieved so much in such a short space of time?

The reclaiming of public space and, equally importantly, the reclaiming of public institutions as sites that would serve for deliberation and decisions relating to the public good, were achievements of the uprisings. However, institutionalizing the public was a different matter to performing it on the streets and squares of the cities, creating new conditions and requiring different skills. On the one hand, there was the question of how best to harness the enthusiasm of the risky, yet exciting, days of defiance while retaining the engagement of the newly mobilized public in the more mundane tasks of registering, voting, and making one's voice heard through representation.

This was a challenge that was met ingeniously by a group of Tunisians concerned about the onset of public apathy in the months that followed the ousting of Ben Ali. In an effort to rekindle the flame of resistance, to remind people what the struggle had been about, and to urge them to go out and vote, they hit upon the tactic of draping a massive poster of the fallen dictator on one of the walls of old Tunis. So startled were people to see Ben Ali's face, once so ubiquitous, return to their neighbourhood that they gathered round, becoming more and more enraged until some of them finally acted in concert and tore down the poster – only to reveal an equally large poster behind it that stated in huge letters: 'Beware! Dictatorship can return. On 23 October go and vote'. It was said that the voter turnout in this district, anticipated to be only 55 per cent, rose to an impressive 88 per cent.[28]

---

libya-out-control-militias-commit-widespread-abuses-year-uprising-2012-02-15   (accessed 14 March 2012).

[28] Engagement Citoyen, 'Tunisie – retour de Ben Ali à la Goulette', 17 October 2011. http://www.youtube.com/watch?annotation_id=annotation_789191&feature=iv&src_vid=TXNu2z_zmog&v=yxWvgASA_Q4 (accessed 18 February 2012).

In addition, the very act of institutionalizing the public through systematic public accountability and voice, although no longer symbolic, was prey to many of the features of institutional life – the division of labour, the necessary obscurity of functions, the tendency towards elite formation – that had helped to remove nominally public institutions from public control under the old regimes and that had therefore created so much mistrust of the procedures associated with them. The election of representatives who would act for different sections of the public was clearly a key first step, but it was a necessary rather than a sufficient condition to ensure that the public no longer remained symbolic and that the power of the public therefore became a reality.

As always, there were forces both within the public at large and within the surviving state institutions that were keen to dilute the reality of public power, to ensure that it should remain either unable to coalesce around key demands, or incapable of standing in the way of specific political and ideological direction. In addition, there were forces at work that wished effectively to exclude significant sections of the public, limiting their rights and their ability to have their voices heard. Those who had come together at a certain moment in history to bring the public into being through performance did not always like what they saw in the aftermath when they looked around at their fellow performers. This became abundantly clear during the long, drawn-out process of electoral competition, demonstration, and counterdemonstration in Egypt in 2012 and 2013. The troubled relations between the revolutionary youth that had brought about the uprising and the Muslim Brotherhood that seemed to have emerged as its principal beneficiary erupted into periodic violence on the streets of Egyptian cities under Muhammad Morsi's presidency. Whether the potential for 'agonistic pluralism' exists in such a situation and can produce democratic outcomes has yet to be seen.[29] Much will depend on whether the idea of the public as a body with common rights but plural voices can survive. Equally, the leaderless nature of some of the uprisings that was part of their strength became more troublesome in the aftermath of the overthrow of the dictator – as in Libya, where armed militias each asserted their own rights to a share in the new dispensation of power, based on their revolutionary credentials and on their capacity for violence.

---

[29] Edward C. Wingenbach, *Institutionalising agonistic democracy* (Farnham, UK: Ashgate Publishing, 2011), pp. 105–156.

Thus, the same features of a politics of resistance that had been so effective in undermining the dominant order complicated the transition to a more institutionalized public order where the locus of power would be diffuse, rather than concentrated in the hands of the few.[30] Indeed, there were concerns in Egypt during the course of 2012 and 2013 that a prolongation and extension of the open protests and occupations of public spaces that had been so much a feature of the unravelling of the president's power might reinforce those who represented the enduring presence of the regime, the senior command of the armed forces. Disorder and civil disobedience were still thought of by many as key strategies in holding power to account, thereby pursuing the unfinished part of the slogan of the uprisings: 'The people want the fall of the *regime*!'. This was a double-edged weapon since public disorder could become an asset for those seeking to close down the debate, to narrow the options, and to transform the plural public into the 'one', as the scarcely veiled warnings by Egypt's Minister of Defence and Chief of the General Staff, General Abd al-Fattah al-Sisi, made clear in January 2013.[31]

Beyond that, many in Tunisia – as well as in Egypt and in Libya – have discovered that the mobilization of a public to resist autocracy and regimes based on violence may well have been more straightforward than trying to mobilize resistance against new iterations of hegemonic power. Enduring forms of privilege and exclusivity persist, clothing themselves in a language of civility, of national sovereignty, and of religiosity. Against this dispensation of power, new strategies would be needed. Nevertheless, difficult as the path might be, the reclaiming of public space, the reconstitution of a mobilized public, and the breaking of the spell of dictatorship opened up a space in which distance can be achieved and criticism voiced. It is the preservation of such space that will determine whether or not exclusive power can re-establish itself or whether the politics of resistance in the Arab uprisings of 2011 will have set in motion processes that will genuinely transform politics in the region for a generation.

[30] See Chapter 7 by John Chalcraft in this volume.
[31] Amirah Ibrahim, 'Army Deployed', *Al-Ahram Weekly* 30 January 2013. http://weekly.ahram.org.eg/News/1247/17/-Army-deployed.aspx (accessed 31 January 2013).

7

Egypt's 25 January Uprising, Hegemonic Contestation, and the Explosion of the Poor

John Chalcraft

Abstract

While Middle East history and politics is often studied in top-down ways, the uprising of 25 January 2011 in Egypt is a reminder that politics is not just about foreign meddling, elite decision making, institutional power, the security forces, and vested interests. Contentious and unruly politics, non-state actors, the popular political imagination, the appropriation of ideas across borders, and highly motivated collective action also play an important role in shaping the political field. This chapter offers a preliminary assessment of the role of this popular politics in Egypt's uprising and the removal of President Hosni Mubarak from power on 11 February 2011. My aim is to develop our relatively weak conceptual and empirical grasp of this popular politics. The premise is a rejection of culturally essentialist and exceptionalist (neo-)Orientalism on the one hand and that of materialist and Eurocentric modernism on the other. Unruly contestation is situated not in 'Arab culture' or in a modernist progression, but within a context of hegemonic contestation. This chapter argues that the educated youth, the labour movement, and the Muslim Brotherhood have attracted more than their fair share of scholarly attention, and that we must therefore assess the vital role played by the urban poor in the uprising, as well as the limitations of their forms of spontaneous mobilization. I argue that the riot police could not have been broken down without the defensive physical force provided by the urban poor, and that the army itself was heavily influenced by the demonstration of the popular will extant in the appearance of millions of ordinary Egyptians on the streets. Nonetheless, most ordinary Egyptians were ready to give the army a chance, at the very least, after the seizure of power by the Supreme Council of the Armed Forces on 11 February, a factor that was also vital in shaping the medium-term outcome of the uprising.

Introduction

The uprisings in the Arab world have drawn scholarly and public attention towards history and politics 'from below'. Highly visible and disruptive dynamics and initiatives emanate, at least in the immediate and observable sense, not from established authorities or power-holders, but from unexpected quarters – from low-status, poor, or subordinated persons, and non-routine, unauthorized, or new political actors and groups. This scholarly interest should not be a surprise, given the protests involving millions of people, the battles fought against police and security forces, the toppling of entrenched dictators in Tunisia, Egypt, and Libya, and the extraordinary tenacity for more than a year of Syrian protestors suffering intensive levels of repression.

However, in keeping with recent top-down emphases in Middle East Studies, many continue to focus on how elites have reacted to social protest – leaving the latter under-studied. Many of the chapters in this volume are no exception to this: they focus on coercion, vested interests, and institutional power. This chapter will instead look at another key aspect of the political field – the struggles, movements, and political principles that play important roles in shaping the political order. It will investigate the nature of the contentious politics that played such a role in toppling President Hosni Mubarak on 11 February 2011.

This chapter offers a brief, critical evaluation of some of the preliminary assessments already given, and lays out a broadly chronological and analytical account of Egypt's contentious politics from the 1990s to 2011. More research is needed to substantiate properly the argument, but the aim is to indicate in outline form the important but nonetheless rather occluded role in the uprising played by the relatively spontaneous and mass uprising of the urban poor. The analysis will not be made in relation to the exceptionalism and essentialism of Orientalism, or in terms of the abstractions and hydraulics of capitalism, modernization, and globalization, but will instead aim to root the account in dynamics of hegemonic contestation.

Usual and Unusual Suspects: Facebook, Islam, and Workers

While extensive empirical research has not yet been carried out, some preliminary answers have been given as to the 'who' and the 'how' of the contentious politics that fuelled Egypt's uprising. Many academics rightly deny that this was a 'Facebook revolution'. But, few serious researchers have actually claimed that it was. The idea of a Facebook revolution is, in fact, 'a swear-word, by which nobody is swearing' as Raymond Williams once remarked of positivism (Williams 1983: 239). Even Wael Ghonim, the administrator of the well-known Facebook page '*Kullina Khaled Said / We Are All Khaled Said*', plays down the idea of a Facebook revolution. Ghonim's main emphasis is on the idea of a 'leaderless revolution'. He argues that Facebook played a vital role in the mobilization in the run-up to 25 January, but after that, the action was mostly offline and on the streets.[1] In like manner, the anarchist and autonomist philosophers Michael Hardt and Antonio Negri avoid Internet puffery by being careful to specify that social media are 'symptoms, not causes, of this [networked] organizational structure. These [Facebook, YouTube, and Twitter] are the modes of expression of an intelligent population capable of using the instruments at hand to organize autonomously' (Hardt and Negri 2011).

Indeed, the source of simplistic and overreaching claims as to a Facebook revolution appears to be journalists, rather than any extended academic analysis. Beyond the 'twitterati', most scholars have taken a cautious (but not usually an entirely dismissive) attitude toward social media in the uprising (e.g., Filiu 2011: 56). Many seem to accept the idea that social media, along with satellite and private media, helped break down the old state media monopoly in Egypt and beyond. This development, which emerged in the late 1990s, played a role in exposing the population to ideas and information that eroded the legitimacy of existing regimes in the Arab world and prepared the ground for mass protest. Social media, likewise, is said to have played a certain role in coordination and communication during the protest itself. Critics, nonetheless, need to probe the extent to which these ideas are bound up with

---

[1] Ghonim, pp. 292–294. Nadia Idle and Alex Nunns write, 'The Egyptian uprising has been described as a "Twitter Revolution". It was not. Revolutions do not come out of thin air, or even cyberspace. But the internet provided a tool that helped shape the form of the uprising, and it gave us some of the most riveting real-time coverage ever recorded'. See *Tweets from Tahrir*, p. 19.

technological determinism, and with a modernization theory that accords too much agency to educated middle classes (with whom Wael Ghonim [2012: 293] certainly identifies), or with any simplistic or teleological idea about how globalization erodes the legitimacy and sovereignty of existing states.

Those who have emphasized the role of the Muslim Brotherhood and Salafism since 11 February 2011, or argued that the uprising paved the way for Islamism, have not argued that the Muslim Brotherhood (let alone Salafism) was responsible for toppling the dictator in the first place (Rosefsky-Wickham 2011). Detailed accounts of the role of the Muslim Brotherhood in the uprising are lacking. Numerous commentators have plausibly pointed to the importance of the Muslim Brotherhood youth in urging the older leadership to announce its support for the uprising on 27 and 28 January, the infrastructure that the organization brought to Tahrir, and its role in defending the square against the regime thugs that were unleashed during the first week of February. Here, critics will be alert to the ways in which any overemphasis on Islamism betrays Orientalist or essentialist assumptions about how Islam determines in some transcendent and exceptionalist sense the politics of Muslim-majority countries. Islamist observers themselves were more likely to lament the lack of a serious political programme among the revolutionaries than to find Islamism lurking in their midst.

Another group of scholars, working with the analytics of capitalism and class, have started to explore the idea that workers or even the working class played a decisive role in the toppling of the dictator. The start point here is the fact that 'from 1998 to 2009 over two million workers participated in more than 3,300 factory occupations, strikes, demonstrations or other collective actions' (Beinin 2011: 189). This was a fashion-bucking 'class struggle' against cutbacks, privatization, and deteriorating wages – privations in turn linked to International Monetary Fund-imposed and corruptly administered neoliberalism (Beinin 2009; Beinin and Hamalawy 2007). These protests bore fruit in the form of specific concessions and the founding of independent trade unions outside of the state-run corporatist structure by the late 2000s. When up to 300,000 workers came out on strike in the last three of the eighteen days of protests, this delivered the decisive blow to the regime by threatening the extensive economic interests of the military, paralysing the economy and the regime's control over it (Alexander 2011). The new militancy, and the proliferation of independent trade unions that have accompanied it, is believed to herald a return to the development of independent labour struggle, a growing class consciousness, and forms of socialist politics on the Egyptian scene (De Smet 2012). Critics will need to probe these accounts carefully, not only for their empirical and causal validity, but also for the problems of materialism, determinism, teleology, and Eurocentrism that have loomed so large in the Marxist tradition (Chalcraft 2005; Lockman 1994; Sewell 1993).

Hegemonic Contestation

The framework adopted here is heavily informed by an acute, postcolonial sensitivity to problems associated with the cultural essentialism and exceptionalism (associated with Orientalism) on the one hand, and materialism and determinism (associated with Modernism) on the other hand. The assumption made here – against the former position (and against some forms of discursive determinism) – is that culture is made, not found; that it is constructed, syncretic, and in some measure, creative. Against the latter position, the assumption here is that social subjects interpret the world around them, often in political ways, and can (and regularly do) act on these interpretations, sometimes in a disruptive, transgressive, and collective fashion (cf. Chalcraft and Noorani 2007: 1–19). In a given political community, usually linked to a given state, power-holders at the centre offer – or are offered – justifications for the exercise of sovereign, coercive, fiscal, regulative, and allocative power in order to win consent for key institutions and undertakings. Such justifications are fought over in a political field that is 'understood both as a field of forces and as a field of struggles aimed at transforming the relation of forces which confers on this field its structure at any given moment' (Bourdieu 1993: 171).

These struggles always involve incomplete and often competing projects of moral, political, and intellectual leadership – or attempts to achieve hegemony – defined as the attempt to link power and right, interest and principle, abstraction and immediacy – at the level of the political community as a whole. Projects of leadership engage, perforce, the popular political imagination – even if only to win passive acquiescence from most people, most of the time. Hegemony can be relatively thick or thin (Knight 2007: 24), and is never complete because it has definite exclusions and gaps, spheres of official and unofficial group or individual autonomy, and is continuously contested because it has many fissures, tensions, forms of selectivity, and contradictions. Contentious movements in the political field, which owe a good deal to popular mobilization, make a vital impact on the political order and its particular shape and structure at a given moment – a shape that is by no means determined in advance by a cultural essentialism (such as Muslim culture) or a grand process (such as capitalism). An account of Egypt's uprising premised on these assumptions is given below.

Weakness on the Regional Stage

The failure* of the Egyptian government to offer a meaningful national response to the outbreak of the second *intifada* in Palestine in September 2000 – just as older currents of resistance were defeated – meant a blow to the authority of the regime and inaugurated a slow-burning crisis of its authority, which formed an enabling condition for new forms of popular collective action in Egypt in the 2000s.

In the 1970s and 1980s, Sadat's *infitah* (open door policy), and his assault from above on the economic and social terms of the Nasserist hegemony, had provoked secular and often Leftist student, worker, popular (and even police) protests in defensive modes that sought to restore the achievements and social protection of Nasserism (Beinin 1994; Chalcraft 2011; Posusney 1993; Walton and Seddon 1994). These protests made modest achievements in slowing the pace of neoliberal restructuring and winning concessions on subsidies, pay, and conditions at least until the 1990s. But the Leftist generation that had come of age in the wake of the 1967 defeat and played such a prominent role in these collective actions (Abdallah 2009) perhaps experienced their high-water mark with the sit-in and violent repression at the Helwan Iron and Steel Plant in 1989, for it was mostly defeated and demobilized by the late 1990s (Duboc 2011).

When Sadat, in the eyes of many, betrayed the Arab and Islamic cause in 1979 by signing with the historic enemy (Israel) a peace agreement selling out the Palestinians, a new militant, Islamist current splintered from the reformist and mainstream Muslim Brotherhood. The latter, energized by a 'New Guard' comprising coming-of-age students in the mid-1970s who then entered the professional syndicates in the 1980s, organized intensively on reformist and mostly charitable lines, running for elections and building grassroots support for a more Islamic society, making gains especially where the state retreated from social and economic provision (Rosefsky-Wickham 2002; Zahid and Medley 2006) and embraced Western economic packages and consumption patterns.

Small groups of militants, however, in sharp contrast, declared that *jihad* was a 'neglected obligation' – and should be waged against an infidel regime in the name of Islam (Faraj 1980). These groups assassinated Sadat and then led a failed uprising in Asyut. They were only defeated after a bitter, militant struggle with the regime in the 1990s – a struggle that flared up especially after Mubarak joined the U.S.-led coalition of Arab states that ousted Iraq from Kuwait. These militants stood little chance of achieving their maximalist goals, however, especially when ordinary Egyptians were not convinced of their political programme, and were hit by their attacks on the tourist trade (Rubin 2002). Most of these militants undertook an *ijtihad* renouncing the use of armed struggle from prison between 1997 and 1999, simultaneously announcing their support for crucial aspects of the regime's neoliberal programme (Murib 2010). An important legacy of their militancy was the para-militarization of sections of the police and security forces (Gunning 2012).

It was at the moment, therefore, when the major Leftist and Islamist currents of disruptive opposition to the regime were defeated that the second *intifada* arose in Palestine in the wake of the definitive collapse of the Oslo process. This uprising had no negative impact on the institutional and coercive powers of the Mubarak regime, but it vivified a policy of national submission on the regional stage, which cost the regime in terms of its ability to stand for ideas commanding compromise and consent. For the first time, formerly sharply opposed ideological currents (Islamists, liberals, secular Left, and Nasserists) started to organize together (Mahdi 2009) in support of the Palestinians – an innovation even if these alliances were hardly complete or unproblematic (Abdel-rahman 2009). After September 2000, protestors started to identify the regime (rather than Israel, the West, or capitalism) as the major problem. This meant that the usual 'safety valve' effect, in which domestic regimes were let off the hook amidst the criticism of Israel, or of larger abstractions, ceased to operate. Open criticism of the president – initially compared to the then recently discredited and corrupt Suharto in Indonesia – was voiced in demonstrations and in secular terms for the first time.[2]

Protest was reactivated with Mubarak's policy of submission on the U.S.-led invasion of Iraq in 2003; the Israeli assault on Lebanon in August 2006; the trade and gas treaties with Israel, which stimulated criticism of

---

[2] See Chapter 10 by John Sidel in this volume.

regime corruption; and later the more punishing inertia of Egypt and even active support for Israel over the latter's bombardment and massacre of trapped Palestinian civilians in Gaza in 2008 and 2009. None of these events was like the catastrophic defeat inflicted by Israel in 1967. Nor did any of them provoke a crisis of authority like the dispossession of the Palestinians in 1948 or a debt crisis like that of 1876, which impacted the institutional and coercive capacity of the government. Indeed, the regime's key institutions were unaffected and for the regime and its supporters, these regional happenings were best seen as non-events in regard to which it was unrealistic to expect anything else from Egypt, especially during the War on Terror. Mubarak had made throughout his time in office only few and modest promises – certainly compared to a Nasser or a Khomeini – regarding the regional stage. There was less scope, therefore, for criticism of Mubarak's stated goals, which were usually cautious: more soporific than demagogic.

Nevertheless, Egypt's submission mattered in varying degrees to any Egyptian or Arab patriot, and was heavily underlined on new satellite television stations, foremost among them, Al-Jazeera. Egypt's inaction in the face of (literally) the screams of Palestinian women and children, aired on satellite television, increased the immediacy of the reportage, underlined a craven regime weakness before Israel and capitulation to the United States in what, after all, was supposed to be the Umm al-Dunya ('mother of the world') and a leader among the Arab states. The arrival of press titles independent of the old state monopoly (*al-Misry al-Yawm*, *Al-Dustur*, *Al-Shuruq inter alia*) during the 2000s, as part of the logic of economic restructuring, was also an important site for the airing of views critical of the regime.

And on the Domestic: The Succession and Neoliberalism

Weakness abroad was only one feature of this slow-burning crisis of authority, with its concomitant increases in unruly collective action. There were two others. The first was what became known as 'the succession' (*tawrith*): the attempt by Hosni Mubarak to install his widely disliked son Gamal as as the next president, and thus effectively change the constitutional basis on which Egypt was ruled. This was the direct inspiration for the *Kifaya!* (Enough!) Movement. It declared that the proposed transformation of the republic into a hereditary dynasty was constitutionally and legally unacceptable, and exposed the hollowness of the claim that Egypt was on the road towards political liberalization. This movement – which involved the more or less active participation of several thousand people signing petitions, attending meetings, and some demonstrations – was a creature of mainly urban (chiefly Cairean), educated, secular, and relatively high-status youth. Most within the movement were new to political action of any kind, many being students or recent graduates (El Mahdi 2009) and the offspring (in the literal sense) of the now demobilized Leftist generation of the 1970s. *Kifaya!* did not bequeath a continuous organization: it was a more networked form of activism without a clear centre. This made it weak and insignificant in the eyes of the security forces, but in fact gave it a certain strength, as there was no vanguard to imprison, headquarters to ransack, newspaper to close, bank account to seize, or chain of command to disrupt. In fact, this network was significant for bringing new and more secular and human rights-oriented groups into political activism for the first time – and for raising demands that resonated with many, even if the movement lost momentum by 2007.

The second – and probably more significant – feature of this crisis was the more intensive assault on the social protections and forms of statism bequeathed by Nasserism. This assault 'from above' had a history dating back to 1974, but intensified in the guise of privatization in the late 1990s and early 2000s, and even more so after July 2004 with the installation of a businessman's government – itself part of the so-called *fikr jadid* (new thinking) of Gamal Mubarak and his clique. State-owned factories and businesses were increasingly sold off to Egyptian, Saudi, and other financial interests, and cutbacks, job insecurity, redundancies, and deteriorating wages and conditions were the result. In addition, a long-term decline in the wages and conditions of public servants of all kinds – from teachers to tax-collectors, along with cuts to subsidies and the rising prices of basic commodities hitting every poor household – had stemmed from Washington consensus-style policies more generally. A whole generation had acquired wealth and status through permanent, skilled work in Nasser's state employment and nationalized industry (Makram-Ebeid 2010). Their sons and daughters, however, came of age in the 2000s in a completely changed environment – one in which the stable employment and upward mobility afforded their parents (and sometimes grandparents) were things of the past.

Many sought collectively and visibly to defend their livelihoods and recuperate a place in a comprehensive national plan for industrial development (Bassiouni 2007). They joined tenacious forms of collective action – strikes, sit-ins, demonstrations of all kinds – in the hundreds of thousands. The reports of the Land Centre for Human Rights indicate that collective actions by workers were already becoming more frequent in the early 2000s, with more than 100 incidents per year. During 2004–2006, more than 200 actions per year were recorded. During 2007, there were 'a staggering 614' collective actions (Beinin 2009: 77), and then 608 during 2008 (Alexander, 2009). Involving more than 1.2 million people, here was the most widely joined popular movement in Egypt's history since 1952 (Beinin 2009: 77). These movements were strong enough to break out of the statist trade union framework for the first time – the real estate tax collectors managing to establish Egypt's first independent trade union in 2007–2008. Until protest fatigue amongst journalists set in, many of these protests were reported in the new print press – and thus transmitted in various forms to a wide audience.

The reformist (but banned) Muslim Brotherhood, meanwhile, with its main cadres drawn from pious, urban, professional strata and 'light' business enterprise and services, sometimes with connections to business in Saudi and the Gulf, did not stand against neoliberalism in any significant measure, although there were gestures here and there (Naguib 2009). Instead, the Muslim Brotherhood, still led by an 'Old Guard' (Zahid and Medley 2006) that had known Hasan al-Banna in the 1940s and spent up to twenty years in prison after 1954, contested elections, won seats, and suffered major repression, especially after the electoral victories of 2005 and in the context of the War on Terror. Here, the para-militarization of police and security continued – and human rights abuses multiplied.

There was an attempt to articulate the new currents of opposition in spring 2008, when elements of the *Kifaya!* movement called a 'general strike' in which workers were meant to stay at home in solidarity with the strikers at Mahalla al-Kubra, who planned a strike on 6 April 2008. The Mahalla strike, however, was broken up, and the 'general strike' had little visible impact. Calls for a 'Day of Anger' by similar networks in April 2009 largely fizzled (Alexander 2009). The virtual was not here capable of mobilizing the real and the organizational and even ideational basis for coordination and solidarity between industrial workers and urban youth was largely lacking. Apart from anything else, the idea of staying at home (designed to avoid confrontation and repression) had little appeal amongst industrial workers loyal to the idea of national productivity. But these events had a legacy in a new form of activism. Educated, secular groups (including the 6 April Youth Movement) now not only watched satellite television and read the newly independent print press, but started to re-appropriate social media (Facebook, blogs, Twitter, *inter alia*) for new ends. Instead of consumption, dating, and celebrity gossip, social media sites were appropriated for a completely different task. Hundreds worked, in the relative safety that the anonymity of the web afforded, to expose the human rights abuses of the regime on the Internet, including those meted out on Islamists during the War on Terror. These bloggers and groups attracted followers and readers in their tens of thousands amongst the new generation – born mostly in the 1980s.

Domination without Hegemony

By 2010, Egypt presented a case of what Ranajit Guha has called (in a different context) dominance without hegemony – a situation in which coercion outweighed consent in the political order at large (Guha 1998). Professional and business classes linked to the Muslim Brotherhood were suffering wide repression and abuse – and the elections of 2010 were so completely rigged as to deliver a major blow to their electoral strategy. Educated youth and militant bloggers – even those connected to wealth and power by family – had been frustrated in their liberal, constitutional, and human rights-based calls for change – even as human rights organizations developed their organizational capacity in the country. Civil servants and industrial workers had won individual concessions in particular work places, but had failed to secure their livelihoods more generally by changing the overall project of Washington consensus economics – under which the urban poor continued to suffer rising prices and a lack of employment. The national and pan-Arab achievements and social and economic protections of the Nasser years were a distant memory – but the regime had not replaced them with either democracy or prosperity. Only Gamal and his clique, an ever-lengthening list of corrupt ministers, officials, and businessmen, who increasingly cared less to cover their tracks, and a tiny minority of the ostentatiously wealthy, appeared to be prospering. As commentators such as Alaa al-Aswany perceived, Egypt was living a moment of acute humiliation, abuse, and poverty (Al-Aswany 2010).

Meanwhile, the regime read this scene as a victory over its opponents, and a sign of its own omnipotence. Their mantra ran as follows: the masses of the population were far too busy struggling to get by to rise up. The Islamists were under lock and key – and who wanted Egypt to become another Iran? The educated youth were 'not serious'. The workers had been 'dealt with' – especially by 'magnanimous' interventions by this or that minister making small concessions in particular cases. There were no real socialists in Egypt in any case. Indeed, foreign agitators, enemy governments (from Sudan to Israel to Iran) and alien ideologies – the usual suspects in the eyes of security apparatuses – had little traction in the country. No one was offering an alternative to Mubarak and the security he offered in a tough neighbourhood where sectarianism and Islamic 'fundamentalism' were always a threat. In any case, quietist and authoritarian Salafi currents were positive allies of the Mubarak regime. The security forces and the army were extraordinarily well-provided for at the top via U.S. strategic rents – with hospitals, clubs, leisure facilities, and perks such as drivers, housing, and consumer goods. Meanwhile, the United States lauded Egypt as a beacon of stability and a cautious liberalizer, and the IMF heaped praise on its economic model and GDP growth. Some serious commentators may have marvelled at the absence of a revolution in Egypt, but no one explained exactly how a revolution might unfold. (Where they attempted to do so, they usually got actual mechanisms quite wrong.) Egypt, like Syria, would just have to absorb the succession. As long as Egypt gave Gaza to Israel, the Americans would not complain about Gamal becoming president – and they would allow Interior Minister Habib Al-Adly to do what he wanted with elections and Islamists. Additionally, Saudi Arabia, erstwhile rival to Nasser, was now a friend to Mubarak. Therefore, the status quo, even if imperfect, would survive. Egypt, after all, was the land of the Pharaohs. The people were subservient and would never rise against their rulers.

It is too easy to rubbish these attitudes in hindsight. The coming uprising was so difficult to predict in part because although Egypt was suffering from a slow-burn crisis of authority – an acute hegemonic weakness – its institutions of coercion and patronage, along with its superpower backing, were intact. These conditions bear remarkable comparison, in this precise sense, to Iran in 1978 – where the Shah's foreign backing, structures of patronage, institutional and coercive power all seemed to be intact – making the revolution famously hard to predict (cf Beinin and Vairel 2011: ix). The problem is partly to do with the very intangibility of authority, hegemony, and the popular political imagination that are necessary accompaniments. These political attitudes register hardly at all in statistics enumerating the coercive capacities of institutions, the performance of the economy, or in static approaches to the delineation of sociological structure. As a political imaginary rooted in the thoughts and feelings of low-status, poor, and disenfranchised groups, it is also easy to dismiss (because those who imagine are not close to power, or are stigmatized, or do not have access to the means of communication), and hard to track because it is insufficiently or inadequately researched.

Nevertheless, the popular political imagination, linked to structures of authority and hegemony, shows up in sentiments, feelings, and attitudes. Some of those who paid a lot of attention to subjective elements in the social appeared to have a better grasp of the future than those who did not (Mossallam 2012) – even if while claiming that *something* was happening, they did not specify *what* was happening – in concrete terms. This author visited Egypt on fieldwork in June 2010 – in the week following the regime's murder of blogger Khaled Said in Alexandria – and found an atmosphere that was crackling. Compared to the 1990s, there was an enormous sense of new energy and initiative, a clear sense that Egyptians were holding the regime responsible for their problems, but a heavy and oppressive security presence crushing the relatively small street protests that did occur.

The bombing, supposedly by Islamists, of a Coptic church in Alexandria at the dawn of 2011 was the most inauspicious and even depressing start to the new decade possible, playing into regime mantras of security, sectarianism, and the threat of Islamic 'fundamentalism'. It appeared to illustrate how little had been achieved over a decade of 'rich' and 'unexpected' activism (Beinin and Vairel 2011: 1), or 'post-Islamism' (Bayat 2007), involving new kinds of alliances, worker and liberal activism, new forms of Islamic 'feminism' and so on. In some respects, this bombing, and the thinly attended candlelit vigil in downtown Cairo that followed, presented a double scene: an intimation of a rising curve of activism from the previous decade, but also the failure of a decade of activism to bear fruit.

Ghonim, for his part, perceived a certain loss of energy already in the autumn of 2010 (Ghonim 2012: 113–114). For all but the most ebullient, frustration and fear jostled for pole position. The Muslim Brotherhood braced itself for more arrests. The Old Left muttered 'same old, same old'. Workers looked to their own economic conditions. Regime supporters looked to a strong president. On his popular website, 'We Are All Khaled Said', Wael Ghonim denounced sectarianism with some confidence, but chose not to cover the Tunisian protests for fear that their likely repression and failure would create 'frustration and helplessness' (Ghonim 2012: 122). The murders of Khaled Said and of Sayyed Bilal by the security forces had both aroused revulsion in the blogosphere, but they were just as much symbolic of regime ferocity and the impotence of opposition as they were sparks that would somehow ignite a major, popular uprising. Human rights abuses were nothing new in Egypt. For all the impressive confidence and energy of the educated youth and the militant bloggers, they – along with other oppositional groups – did not have much to show for their efforts in early 2011 apart from a tremendous and important sense of stifled aspiration. The structures of state power – coercion, police, and so on – were as solid as ever and the wall of fear – 'fear and the culture of fear that continuous monitoring, surveillance, humiliation and abuse have created' (Ismail 2006: 165) – was yet to be broken.

Pirating the Tunisian Model

Onto this terrain of impasse and aspiration, frustration and energy, defeat and mobilization, came the news from Tunisia. Although there were some tactical discussions amongst a small number of Egyptian and Tunisian online activists, no guns or money flowed from Tunisia to Egypt. No Tunisian diplomacy backed an uprising in Egypt or stood against Mubarak. No Western or Arab League initiative was launched. Instead, even in an age of the globalization of people and resources, it was simply the power of an idea that was appropriated across borders, and power-holders largely looked on. The events in Tunisia involved an extraordinarily potent demonstration effect as to how to break the impasse and to generate change in Egypt. The tactical lessons were simple: popular and unarmed street protest could work. The political model was clear: a Western-backed Arab dictator could and should be thrown from office.

In this context, regimes around the region looked to secure their borders, insisting that every country was different, and that there would be no 'contagion' from Tunisia. In fact, no security apparatus could stop the appropriation of an idea, in a real historical, not romantic, sense. Egypt's system of repression had little defence against an idea that took wing through sites of communication and the ways they were being actively used. There was no patent on the Tunisian model; in a tense situation of domination without hegemony, however specific in national, historical, social, economic, or political terms, the Tunisian model was available for pirating and appropriation (cf Anderson 2006: 4, 228) on a dramatic scale by those ready to take matters into their own hands and contest the political field amidst an existing crisis of authority and frustrated activism.

The Educated Youth

The energies of the militant bloggers were immediately engaged. The April 6 Youth Movement and others amongst the educated youth started to plan for a popular, non-violent uprising in Egypt on the Tunisian model. Popular web pages such as 'We Are All Khaled Said' – with hundreds of thousands of readers by this time – devoted themselves to coverage of Tunisia (Ghonim 2012: 131–160). National Police Day (25 January) was chosen for a mass uprising (*thawra*) – a word, usually translated as revolution, which suddenly gained wide currency. The idea was that a number of demonstrations would converge on Tahrir and force change on the regime. Special attention was paid less to goals and ideology and more to tactics of peaceful protest: how to deal with tear gas, how to gather a crowd in the side streets before bursting onto the main avenues, how to bring in supporters, and how to induce the police to lay down their batons and join the revolution. Much of this coordination and communication happened online, but some of the crucial meetings amongst the 6 April Youth required more secrecy and took place in private houses.

The activism of the educated youth played an important role. The Egyptian uprising, unlike that of Tunisia, was indeed in some measure planned because Tunisia had proposed a political model and tactics to go with it. The youth had already developed tactical expertise and savvy for more than a decade. They had maintained a space for street protests against heavy repression. They had appropriated new sites of mobilization and communication in social media – that had facilitated anonymity and kept the regime flat-footed. They had brought news of regime human rights abuses to thousands in Egypt. They cleverly picked the day of the uprising – National Police Day – for this would activate a very wide range of grievances against the hated police by large numbers. Their insistence on non-violence was a crucial element in maintaining the neutrality of the army. A mode of mobilization that started in the backstreets and moved to the squares proved effective.

Their mobilization caught the regime by surprise – especially because it was not rooted in an ideological programme, or linked to oppositional political parties or the Muslim Brotherhood, or to 'foreign subversives'. This may explain why Wael Ghonim was released in the midst of the uprising: the regime could find nothing in him but a sincere patriot, without a threatening ideology or 'political connections' who could presumably be co-opted with some warm words from Hossam Badrawi on the cuddly end of the National Democratic Party (NDP). But here the regime underestimated their opponents. Ghonim's appearance on national television immediately after this release – the very picture of a true son of the nation, distressed at the violence he had 'caused' – was a powerful message to those who wavered in support of 'noisy' protestors inviting chaos and 'foreign agenda'.

It is important to note that the educated youth had no way of knowing a mass uprising would actually take place. Fear and uncertainty is clearly revealed in their communications prior to 25 January, just as their delight and surprise is revealed in their communications during and immediately after the eighteen days. *Tweets from Tahrir* (Idle and Nunns 2011) also reveals the extent to which the militant youth were *present at*, and *caught up in* the street protests, but were not leading them in any ideational or organizational sense. So many of the tweets involve communicating what the crowds were doing – and much fewer of them reported initiatives to lead crowds to particular places or direct them to do or say particular things (e.g. pp. 31–45).

The tweets and other evidence reveal the existence of highly unexpected, unruly, and participatory initiatives that seemed to flood from all directions. Much of the action of the eighteen days was thus relatively spontaneous – and had a 'horizontalist' and decentralized form (Chalcraft 2012). One would be mistaken to attribute to it the character of a highly organized or vanguard-ist uprising where centrally controlled cadres mobilized their constituencies. Online activism had not yet succeeded in bringing out the crowds – and had often failed to do so. On the contrary, the militant youth were quite unable to *keep* the crowds in Tahrir *after* Mubarak had stepped down – in spite of what was in many of their eyes the clearly unfinished business of the 'revolution', the ambition of which was not to install a military junta. The militant bloggers had very little in the way of organizational roots amongst the popular strata anywhere in the country – a lack that had been cruelly exposed in April 2008 – not to mention since February 2011. It was also not clear whether a human-rights frame would resonate with wider strata, or whether ordinary people would respond when educated youth started to talk more about social justice and dignity when these groups did not have a track record in these areas and whose attire, consumption, leisure habits, sexual mores, and social class did not seem to suit them to the role of being the authentic bearers of Egyptian cultural identity or economic and social grievances.

Moreover, the 'silent stands' advocated by Wael Ghonim in 2010 and the candlelit vigil in early January 2011 were very different tactics to a mass uprising that could sustain a confrontation with the police and security forces. Some of the online activism, indeed, had been about developing tactics that avoided seemingly pointless confrontations with repression – hence, the stay-at-home general strike, the anonymity of the web, the silent stands, and so on. A mass uprising would involve a major confrontation with the state coercion – and for this, the activists proposed that demonstrators should try to win over the police with flowers and non-violence. Events were to take a very different course, insofar as the police would have to be degraded and even defeated in pitched battles. The educated youth neither prepared nor planned for this. There is no evidence that prior to 25 January anyone believed that the regime's police forces could be defeated in a physical confrontation. The insistence on non-violence pointed to non-compliance, but in no way to physical confrontation.

The Explosion of the Poor

The educated youth were joined on the streets (at east by 28 January) by those other elements who had already been mobilizing during the previous decade (and sometimes before). The Muslim Brotherhood, urged on by their youth, went on to play such an important role in defending Tahrir Square against attacks by thugs in the first week of February. Workers and civil servants, hit by the regime's neoliberalism, also joined the crowds up and down the country. At first, they did so in an individual capacity. But over time, some of the independent unions came out in favour of the uprising or strike action, and from 8–11 February, strikes were joined by around 300,000 workers according to some (cited in Alexander 2011), contributing to the institutional paralysis of the regime and the threat felt by the military to the businesses that they owned or from which they profited.

The crowds were also made up of many who had never demonstrated or signed a petition. Indeed, a vital aspect of the uprising was the sudden politicization and hopeful activation of those taking matters into their own hands for the first time. The protest of the eighteen days was 1,000 times more numerous than the typical street protests (as opposed to strikes) of the 2000s. Whereas demonstrations had attracted hundreds, and, on rare occasions, thousands of participants, the uprising attracted hundreds of thousands and even millions of protestors – although exact numbers await further research. The statistics are reflected in the reports of experienced activists, who professed astonishment in the first days of the uprising to see all these people who were completely unknown to them directly participating and taking initiatives in the demonstrations. Alaa Al Aswany called it a 'miracle' (Al Aswany 2011: viii). Moreover, the sub-national demonstration effect of initiatives in Suez, which some insist caused the youth to stop leaving Tahrir and return to consolidate the crucial tactic of its occupation on the evening of 25 January, came from well beyond the sphere of influence or impact of the militant bloggers.

In some respects, what was decisive in the dynamics of the situation was precisely the unruly collective action of those who moved for the first time. Here, the language of explosion – deployed by protagonists, observers, and intelligence officials alike – captures something important. One former high-ranking intelligence official described the revolution as an 'explosion of the poor'. He said that in 2010 everyone imagined something would happen. But, he added, 'If anyone tells you they predicted an explosion of the poor, he is a liar!'[3]

Arguably, indeed, the 'neophyte' crowds of the eighteen days not only provided the numbers, but also the tactics that were able to degrade significantly the coercive capacity of the police, and, by a huge demonstration of the popular will, to win the neutrality of the army. The sheer unexpectedness of this 'explosion of the poor' – especially in the eyes of those in the regime who had expected them to keep their heads down while murmuring '*that amrak ya sidi*' ('whatever you say, boss') and carrying on trying to make a living – was an important factor in throwing regime figures off balance and contributing to the strategic blunders that they made, especially in regard to withdrawing the police force in the evening of 28 January. The way the crowds fraternized with the army – hugging officers and demonstrating friendship, but also swarming tanks, dealing forcefully with elements in the army that went on the offensive, and insisting that 'our brothers and fathers' in the army defend Egypt's people against a corrupt regime – was an important dynamic in securing the neutrality of the army (Ketchley, forthcoming).

One important and less discussed set of persons who made up a key element in the ranks of those acting for the first time was the increasingly desperate sons and daughters of parents who came of age during Sadat's *infitah*. This generation, which came of age in the 2000s, were petty vendors and small retailers, self-employed service providers, small producers, and those working on their own account (Elyachar 2005) or in survivalist (as opposed to profit-making) small business involved in labour squeezing and self-exploitation. Many of these persons were poor and low-status; they were often rural-urban migrants, and the older ones had worked for a spell abroad at one time or another. They sought marriage, decent housing, and respectable work. Many lived in 'informal areas' in

---

[3] Interview with senior Egyptian Intelligence Official, 13 June 2011.

substandard or overcrowded housing without state-provided utilities. They worked outside government employment, large firms, the professions, or agriculture. They had little recent tradition of political activism almost anywhere in the region – preferring what Asef Bayat has called 'the quiet encroachment of the ordinary' – making a living, and making small and patient gains by acquiring a space to live (squatting), to work (via negotiation and contestation with the police), and acquiring goods and services by one means or another (Bayat 1997). They have kept their protests hidden – and have tended to adopt 'everyday modes of resistance'. Where they have engaged in protest, it has been fleeting and discontinuous.

Indeed, rather than being linked to those who challenged the status quo, these groups had been championed by neoliberal theorists and 'reformers' in Egypt since the 1970s. The informal sector and small business enterprise, as they were known in this discourse, were lauded as providers of employment and boosters of growth amidst the crisis of old-fashioned statism (Elyachar 2005). And if one is to judge by the fieldwork of Diane Singerman, conducted in the 1980s, or even that of Bayat more generally, these forms of work, as well as the informal networks they sustain, were clearly capable of aggregating goods and delivering incomes and new levels of consumption to an important section of the population, especially at a time when out-migration to the Arabian peninsula was common and hundreds of millions of dollars in remittances were fed into the 'informal sector' from this source (Singerman 1995; Bayat 2010).

However, these groups found themselves entangled, in spite of their best efforts, in an 'invisible cage' (Chalcraft 2009) and in what Elyachar has analysed as 'markets of dispossession' (Elyachar 2005). Since the 1980s, migration opportunities have diminished or become less remunerative, prices in housing and basic commodities have risen, subsidies have been cut back, incomes have been hit by inflation, and businesses have been taxed by the bribery and corruption of police and the authorities. These groups have been particularly offended by the corruption that enabled wealthy businessmen to get ahead while they themselves were subjected to police abuse and the indifference or hostility of the authorities. The new generation, born in the 1980s and growing up in this milieu, and sometimes unemployed to boot, have found precious little of the upward mobility that some of their parents enjoyed – and they have encountered an increasingly securitized and corrupt police, with which they have done battle (Ismail 2006).

These battles with police, and the elements of contentious politics they involved, left a legacy that would become useful. Young men became adept in how to fight, taunt, outwit, and neutralize the police. Their concerns in the mid-2000s were very far from those of the wealthy, liberal *Kifaya!* movement or industrial workers facing cut backs. But developments through the decade altered this situation. One of these was the higher levels of confrontation on the football terraces between the young men of the popular quarters and the police. This was partly a result of the fact that fans were also better able to respond to police violence from the mid-2000s as they got organized into close-knit and loyal groups of those who were most committed to supporting their teams – the Ultras – on the model of similar groups in North Africa and Europe (Bashir 2011). The Ultras brought together, in the name of an intense devotion to football, the wealthy and even the politically minded, with the young men of Mit Ghamr and other slum quarters drawn from the ranks of the new poor. The football fans were adept at sloganeering and coordinating in street battles. And by late 2010, according to a 'White Knight' Ultra (Zamalek), their fight with the police was increasingly directed at the Interior Ministry and Habib Al-Adly, who was rightly seen as having a major responsibility for how games were policed.[4] The effect of this was to focus the ire of football fans on the heart of the regime.

If heightened themes of masculinity were enacted in the stadiums, in the world of breadwinning and households, male social honour amongst the poor was under crushing pressure with rising prices and police corruption. The kind of desperation involved was illustrated dramatically in Tunisia by Mohamed Bouazizi's act of self-immolation: here was a man to whom many ordinary people in Egypt could relate – especially those inhabiting the world of invisible hard labour amongst survivalist small business and slums. Instead of dying in the obscurity to which Sidi Bouzid seemed to condemn him, Bouazizi became the hero of a revolutionary Tunisia in a matter of weeks. Although some in Egypt 'made their lack of voice be heard' with similar acts of self-immolation, others found that Mohamed Bouazizi turned their hitherto unsung plight of survivalism, inflation, stifled aspirations, male honour, police violence, and official corruption and indifference into the basis for, and origin of, a major political and historical change. Bouazizi was one of the people who had brought Ben Ali down, and they, the Egyptian people (*sha'b*), could do the same in Egypt. We do not know who first chanted '*Irhal Irhal*' in Egypt, or indeed, *Al-Sha'b Yurid Isqat al-Nizam* (The People Demand/The Fall of the Regime), but both these phrases came straight from Tunisia – the words

---

[4] Interview with senior member of Ultras White Knights (Zamalek), 17 March 2012.

not even being altered to fit Egyptian colloquial. It would be a foolhardy analyst who ascribed these phrases exclusively to educated sectors in Egypt when they were taken up with such gusto by those from all walks of life.

Strengths and Weaknesses

The explosion of the poor – the unruly collective action of large masses of ordinary Egyptians, many of whom were working in survivalist small businesses between town and country and who were not previously involved in activism of any visible kind – deserves an important analytic place in our understanding of the uprising in part because it is difficult to see how the barrier of fear could have been broken, the police degraded, and the army neutralized without it. When the crowds met the police on 25 January, something new happened. Previously, protestors were out-numbered, surrounded, and plucked away 'like chickens' as described by a despairing student activist in June 2010.[5] This time, however, far from offering flowers as the educated youth had prescribed, the crowds fought back, using unarmed defensive force, occupying territory, and actually scoring victories in the pitched battles that followed. Armoured cars were torched, tear gas was thrown back at the police by gloved 'fish-ermen' (*sayyadin*), Molotov cocktails were used to break police lines at bottlenecks, and more than eighty police stations and the headquarters of the National Democratic Party were destroyed by fire. Transcripts of police communications later published in Egypt's press, gave a glimpse of the force of this unprecedented activism. These transcripts show how police felt when they did not have the training to deal with these intensely motivated crowds or the men coming at them who 'did not care if they lived or died'.[6] The police ran out of tear gas and supplies and suffered from the tear gas themselves. The burning of police stations crippled their functionality and by 28 January, the police were exhausted and many walked off the job.

What was new in this situation was that suddenly it appeared that even the regime's instruments of domination – as opposed to its long-defunct forms of hegemony – were now vulnerable. This helped account for the exhilaration and determination that coursed through

---

[5] Interview with student enrolled at Ain Shams University, 10 June 2010.
[6] Jailan Halawi, 'Conspiracy, Treason or corruption?' *Al-Ahram Weekly*, 10–16 February 2011, p. 8.

the crowd as it chanted for what had until days before seemed a foolish pipedream – the fall of the regime and the toppling of Mubarak
from power. Moreover, while the insistence of the educated youth on
'*silmiyya!*/peaceful [protest]' mattered in maintaining the neutrality of
the army, the tremendous demonstration of the united popular will that
the explosion of the poor conveyed, with its clear and singular demand
for the regime to go, also made it that much harder for the military to
shoot upon the crowds insofar as the generals feared disunity in the ranks
and the rebellion of junior officers. The army was also reluctant to defend
a regime that was weak in national and Arab credentials, determined to
install a much-disliked Gamal as president, and prepared to sell off the
country to Gamal's clique. Indeed, the complex ideational tissues of hegemony that form a basis for compromise amongst elites were threadbare
in Egypt in early 2011, as they had been for some time. Crucially, the
actions of the crowd were precise enough to exploit these divisions at
the top and the immediate outcome was an army neutralized – neither
supporting the regime, nor the uprising.

At this point (by the weekend of 29–30 January), with the army neutral and the police in tatters, the president was surely finished, as the
intelligence services were not trained for crowd control. The apparatus
of domination – the only thing maintaining the regime in power – was
effectively broken, aside from units of the presidential guard positioned
at the state TV station and the presidential palace.

In the mini-city that Tahrir Square became, the strengths of spontaneity
and this creative, non-doctrinal, leaderless – or indeed, 'leaderful' – revolutionary uprising, were now vividly on display. Everyone participated.
Pharmacists brought medicines, cooks prepared food, doctors treated
wounds, skilled workers wired the square for electricity, surgeons operated, bakers distributed bread, rich kids from Zamalek bought armour
for the lads from the popular quarters, football fans fought, worker-poets
invented songs and chants, students set up tents, manual labourers broke
pavement slabs for use against regime thugs, shopkeepers fetched cell
phone chargers, and so on. Tahrir became a direct, popular democracy
of a kind rarely seen before or since. In the words of a line of graffiti
visible in Tahrir in the week following 11 February 2011, 'Here I spent
the best days of my life in freedom, dignity and revolution'. The Egyptian
people were demanding the fall of a corrupt regime and thus mobilized
and unified, they were irresistible. The thugs were repelled in disarray
and now symbolized the bankruptcy and desperation of the regime.

But, one must also mark the strategic weaknesses (as opposed to inspirational strengths) of such a spontaneous (if coordinated) uprising. This was not an uprising with a clear strategic leadership, an organized vanguard, a specific ideology, or a strong, grassroots organizational basis. There was not, nor could there be, a coordinating body or a leadership ready to take over the state television, the Interior Ministry or the presidential palace – whether by a mass crowd action or an armed confrontation (possibly with the support of a renegade group from within the army). A crowd that assembled spontaneously, even a crowd of millions, could also disperse relatively rapidly. At the moment when it was clear that the regime was defenceless – the initiative came not from the crowd, which was outflanked for the first time, but from the Supreme Council of the Armed Forces, who deposed the president and took the reins of power for themselves, riding on the immense popularity that their neutral stance had won them.

Conclusion

This chapter has offered an account of Egypt's uprising premised on a set of assumptions about the political field and the dynamics of hegemonic contestation. The idea has been to avoid the forms of essentialism and determinism associated with Orientalism and Modernism alike. It has been argued that a foreign policy of submission on the regional stage, the succession attempt and the assault on Nasserist statism and social protection together with the corruption, the 'markets of dispossession', and aggressive policing all worked to break up the hegemonic tissues of ideational compromise and consent so important in shaping political order in Egypt. These were enabling conditions for new and unruly initiatives from sometimes unexpected quarters during the 2000s, especially the *Kifaya!* movement, the protests of workers and civil servants, and the new energies of the youth of the Muslim Brotherhood. But these new movements were unable to articulate in any thoroughgoing fashion before 2011, and although they opened a space for new connections and forms of activism, they were short on concrete successes at the beginning of 2011. Nonetheless, it was partly their achievement, in addition to the failures of the regime, that contributed to a situation of domination without hegemony by the beginning of the new decade. These movements exposed the violence of the regime, but this very violence hindered them in the achievement of their goals.

In early 2011, the fall of Ben Ali in Tunisia suddenly demonstrated a new model for action that brought new groups onto the streets and united millions of diverse origins under the banners of a patriotic and popular uprising aimed at overthrowing a corrupt and oppressive regime. In particular, the celebrated martyrdom of Mohamed Bouazizi helped to inspire an important section of the urban poor to move, a group that had been uninvolved in the visible contentious politics of the 2000s. This group, under conditions of inflation, poverty, and predation, had reached a point of intense dissatisfaction with the status quo and the regime that was held responsible. It exploded on 25 January and thereafter.

The urban poor moved as much because of the failures and inattention of the activists of the 2000s as because of their successes. Activist successes opened a space for the poor, but their failures obliged the poor to take matters into their own hands. The Muslim Brotherhood threw their hat in the ring partly because of the dead-end of their own electoral strategy. Satellite TV, the new independent press, and social media all played important roles in communication, coordination, and mobilization – which were done in distinctively spontaneous and horizontalist ways. The explosion of the poor – their numbers, commitment, and unity – allowed the uprising to be understood as a battle between a patriotic people and a corrupt and discredited regime. This way of comprehending the situation would not, arguably, have been possible without such a mass mobilization, or were the situation to have been solely a matter of the 'Facebook Youth', the workers, and/or the Muslim Brotherhood. These groups acting together or alone would have been seen as either disunited or merely bringing sectoral demands. Moreover, the direct actions of the crowds, their use of defensive force, and their tactics of occupation neutralized or degraded the crucial coercive institutions of the state in a way that made the continued tenure of the regime impossible.

It was the activism of the poor, above all, who physically degraded the state's capacity for violence – which, in the absence of a broad-based authority – was the existing basis of the regime's continued existence. At the last moment, however, the Supreme Council of the Armed Forces took the initiative and assumed power. The crowds melted away from Egypt's squares and streets, ready to give what was perceived as a patriotic, honourable, and brotherly military a chance, and ceding the political field to more organized political forces. The basic dynamics of the Egyptian political field now entered a new phase.

This analysis clearly brings to the fore the importance of mass, noisy, disruptive, overt, collective action or popular mobilization in the political field. Top-down analysis is clearly not enough. Unruly collective action – here in relatively spontaneous and horizontalist modes, while unfashionable as a topic in Middle East studies in recent years – has an impact and needs to be better understood. Bottom-up dynamics are clearly not exhausted by the notion of 'weapons of the weak'. Neither are discursive forms of power all-determining; subalterns are not merely ghostly presences, the playthings of elite discourse.

The account offered here suggests (against materialism and determinism) that we cannot understand the actions of the millions who came on to the streets without taking seriously the popular political imagination. The poor may not have been engaged in activism during the 2000s, but they were paying a great deal of attention to what authorities were doing, had already defined 'the regime' as the problem and not the solution, and responded with extraordinary rapidity to the message from Tunisia that mass protest might be able to overthrow that regime. These political constructions were crucial to political mobilization – and they did not march lockstep with capitalist exploitation or the forces unleashed by modernizing or globalizing technology. Indeed, the idea amongst the poor that seems to have become more widespread since the 25 January uprising is that the revolution itself is disrupting the economy, eliminating jobs and income, and causing criminality and insecurity on the streets; it has been a potent solvent of revolutionary commitment and unity and hence of popular mobilization in its name.

Popular mobilization and demobilization has mattered for revolution and counter-revolution alike. Twitter, Facebook, and forms of exploitation still exist, but popular mobilization must be situated in a political and imaginative terrain if it is to be adequately understood. However, the forms of imagination at stake are by no means defined by the stereotypes of neo-Orientalism. At no point in the analysis do supposedly essential, timeless, and exceptional features of Oriental, Muslim, or Arab cultures (authoritarianism, violence, terrorism, fanaticism, factionalism, submissiveness, and chaos) play a discernible role. Instead, the search for freedom, bread, dignity, defensive and peaceful protest, commitment to principled action, unity at key moments, coordination amidst spontaneity, assertion, and bravery are the more obvious themes that one could easily explore in more depth if one took the flimsy charges to which they respond more seriously

8

The Military amidst Uprisings and Transitions in the Arab World

Philippe Droz-Vincent[*]

Abstract

The Arab world is in the midst of a process of change whose main engine are mobilized societies against authoritarian rule. Yet, the military has played a decisive role in the course of uprisings, easing transitions (Egypt, Tunisia), imploding (Libya), repressing (Bahrain), or fracturing (Yemen, presumably Syria). This is no surprise as the military was an essential, but very specific, part of Arab authoritarian regimes. In the 1950s–1960s, the military acted as modernizers with a nationalist vision. In 2011–2012, the military was unwilling to take power. The military has been propelled into politics, either remaining the only institution or as an instrument of repression. I assess the military's reactions to the mass uprisings and the regime's call for heavy repression. After regime change, the nature and course of transition is once again heavily dependent on the actions of the various militaries or their remnants when they have fractured.

Massive societal uprisings (*thawra*) against authoritarian rule in 2011 came as a surprise to regimes as well as outside observers in the 'quiet landscape' of persistent authoritarian rule in the Middle East (dubbed 'the Arab exception'). The strength of active and young societies and their ability to present their demands in forceful mobilizations calling for dignity (*karama*), humanity (*insaniyya*), and liberty (*huriyya*) while pouring into symbolic public spaces was the crux of the Arab uprisings. Nevertheless,

---

[*] I thank Fawaz Gerges very much for his essential help in completing this chapter.

armies have played the role of midwife for transitions in Tunisia and Egypt where the military refused to shoot at protesters, thereby easing the end of both regimes. The army was involved in repression in Bahrain, Syria, and Yemen. In Libya, the army imploded in the first 'days of anger', and then became engaged in a civil war. In addition to the essential role of autonomous societal mobilizations, the role of the military is absolutely critical in all cases.

Two variables are crucial to understanding the militaries' reactions. Firstly, the military is an essential component of Arab authoritarian regimes, although its role is different from the military's direct interference in politics (coup d'états, military juntas) that occurred up until the early 1970s. For enduring authoritarian regimes suffering from a lack of legitimacy and whose civilian institutions are fragile (regimes enfeeble them for the sake of protecting their own networks of power), the military is an essential pillar behind the scenes, a reserve of power to back up the status quo. This is the essential military dimension in modern Middle Eastern politics, even if regimes have seemingly assumed a civilian character more than ever before: the military is mostly kept under control within the barracks, with regimes having reached agreements with the top brass that allow for the maintenance of their status quo. Some regimes have gone beyond the expansion of their control networks within the military and have been engaged in a thorough 'social engineering' inside the officers' corps: they have promoted officers with direct links (such as blood, sect, ethnicity, community, village, region) to those in supreme power positions, and have then organized a kind of 'primordialization' of the military with loyal, selectively recruited praetorian units acting as 'the army of the regime'.

Secondly, such an authoritarian equilibrium was severely tested in 2011 by 'the element of surprise' – massive mobilizations in public spaces utilizing civil resistance. Repression then turns on the question of the will of the military to put its full lethal might behind the regime's survival. In the face of heightened dilemmas at a time of massive and resilient social protests, the military has preferred to opt out, while the praetorian units entered the fray. The further key question is whether the military under stress can retain its coherence and autonomy from the regime, and then ease into transition, as happened in Tunisia and Egypt but not in Libya. When the military takes part in repression, this comes at a high cost for its image, prestige, and even morale and discipline: the more thoroughly and the longer it is engaged in forceful repression, as in Yemen and Syria but not in Bahrain, the more it fractures.

Following the overthrow of established regimes, the military is then engaged in transitions, especially in states where it is large, such as Egypt, Yemen, and Syria, but not Tunisia. Conversely, the lack of a rebuilt military apparatus is an essential problem weighing on the transition in Libya. The nature and course of transitions in the Arab states is once again heavily dependent on the responses and actions of the various militaries or their remnants. This chapter will analyse three models of transitions in motion in the Arab world in 2012: a return to re-institutionalization with the military acting as a crucial stakeholder and a shadow custodian; a lack of institutions and hence of a monopoly on force; and a stalemate in the struggle, veering towards civil war and fragmentation into militias.

The Puzzle of the Militaries' Reactions to the Uprisings

In all regimes shaken by the wave of protests in 2011, regime survival ultimately turned on whether the military would shoot at protesters. The regimes were caught offguard by mass mobilizations that gathered momentum in public spaces. This was a dramatic contrast to what the regime saw as quiescent societies and moribund oppositions of previous decades. The regimes had been able to 'contain' scattered mobilizations through harsh repression and minimal concessions, to defeat armed uprisings led by Islamists in the 1980s and 1990s, and to fragment their societies in order to manage them. But in 2011, autocratic regimes did not know how to respond to mass civil mobilizations. The regimes' durability did not mean they possessed strength or stability and the weakness of the authoritarian institutions was quickly revealed.[1]

In Tunisia and Egypt, the ruling parties, the Constitutional Democratic Rally (RCD) and the National Democratic Party (NDP) were forums designed to co-opt elites into the regime and to provide a means for the regime to distribute the fruits of corruption. Once demonstrations began, these parties immediately collapsed and the regimes preferred to rely on the security apparatus. In Syria, the regime's political solution to the crisis was to pursue reforms within limits [the so-called *al-khutut al-hamra*, ('red lines') that include untouchable topics such as the Assad family's exclusive hold on power]. Yet, this political response was accompanied by

---

[1] In Egypt, documents smuggled out of the State Security Investigation (*Mabaheth Amn Al-Dawla*) reveal the extent to which the regime knew how vulnerable it really was. A trove of documents can be found at http://www.facebook.com/SSLeaks.

a strategy of severe repression, hence signalling for most of the opposition the futility of all negotiations with the regime.

The regimes' method of governing their societies by both the fear of, and actual, repression did not stand up to the determined and massive mobilizations in 2011. While protesters were engaged in peaceful civil resistance, regimes unleashed the full violent power of their security forces. A clear distinction should be made between security forces (police, paramilitaries, political polices, and intelligence services) whose primary function is to shield the regime from any societal protests in public spaces and the military that intervenes when the regime is threatened. As exemplified by the management of protests in 2011, the regimes do not initially choose to rely on the military as this would be a departure from the routine of 'quiet authoritarianism' and lead towards full-scale and open bloodbaths. The regimes prefer to contain protests with the police apparatus and the fear its operation creates. However, in Tunisia, Egypt, Libya, Yemen, Syria, and Bahrain, the significant strength of the police in terms of manpower and equipment and its brutality did not translate into impact on the ground when faced with determined mass demonstrations utilizing civil resistance and the power of numbers in prominent limited spaces. The violent response of the regimes simply hardened the determination of protesters. When the security forces failed to contain the popular mobilizations, the regimes quickly called on the militaries to exert their full panoply of repressive methods.

The militaries then became the critical factor in the fate of the regimes. This level of analysis offers a first typology of Arab armies' immediate reactions to the uprisings, with armies called by regimes to open fire on protesters either siding with revolutionaries (Tunisia, Egypt), fragmenting (Yemen), exploding (Libya), or remaining loyal and enabling incumbent rulers to fight back (Syria 2011–13, Bahrain).[2]

However, such an analysis should be refined. Firstly, to put Tunisia and Egypt in the same category reflects the choice made by their militaries not to shoot at protesters and hence to ease transitions. But the different political trajectories of the countries following the uprisings should be recognised: in Tunisia the military has displayed a strictly legalist posture and returned to barracks; in Egypt it has taken power (from February 2011 to August 2012) and operates as the most powerful stakeholder in a protracted transition process. Tunisia remains a very specific case and risks producing a bias by creating a group of cases with very

---

[2] Sayigh, 2011; Barany, 2011; Droz-Vincent, 2011b.

divergent properties. The state was built up by civilian elites from the Neo Destour Party[3] rather than by military elites as in other republics. Huge interventionist military establishments have been characteristic of Arab states, but President Habib Bourguiba made a concerted effort to keep the army out of domestic politics.[4] The tiny Tunisian military, with a very low budget compared with other militaries in the region, did play a controversial role in repressing protests in the late 1970s and mid-1980s, but its role was then limited to external defence. The Ben Ali regime relied heavily on the police, the *sûreté générale* (the political police), and the national guard that fell under the purview of the Interior Ministry, along with some militia linked to the Constitutional Democratic Rally (RCD).[5]

Secondly, such a view is too static. General statements about military behaviour that seem plausible in the abstract break down once applied across various countries. The Yemeni military was increasingly involved in repressive tasks: the Saleh regime called in more and more military units with the massive turn of societal mobilizations across the country and the ensuing loss of control of whole neighbourhoods or cities to the demonstrators. As a result, a kind of 'overstretching' of the military took place and defections began, culminating in a split within the army. Several top commanders, including General Ali Mohsen, the head of the Northwestern military zone and an essential pillar of the Saleh's regime, along with militia related to the Ahmar family, Salafi units, and tribal elements (such as the Hashed confederation) that had been more or less integrated into the regular military after operating as adjunct forces during the 1994 civil war, would protect demonstrators. Those under the command of members of the Saleh family (the military police, the security wing of the air force, the paramilitary Central Security Forces, the Republican Guard, and the brigades of the army headed by Saleh's nephews) were taking part in repression. Rival military factions began to fight near the capital in April 2011, then fighting intensified in October–November 2011, pitting the regime and the opposition against each other as two equal armed blocks.

---

[3] *Destour* means 'constitution' in Arabic.
[4] Ware, 1985 for Tunisia. In the Gulf monarchies, armies have been systematically 'underdeveloped', that is, undersized in comparison to the scale of potential threats, both because strong armies have been viewed as a threat and because, in an emergency, regimes could rely on the United States, whose fifth fleet is headquartered in Bahrain. The small size of the military has been a guarantee against military coups.
[5] Camau and Geisser, 2003; Bellin, 2002.

A similar process took place in Syria after the summer of 2011. When the popular uprising began to spread across the country, elite units were insufficient in number to contain it and the regime cautiously used regular units staffed with conscripts. Defections, although not of the scale seen in Yemen or Libya, increased, giving the Syrian uprising a very distinctive character with a process of militarization; and the unravelling of the Syrian regular army became the centrepiece of the Syrian uprising. In the second half of 2012, the Syrian opposition and international actors began to openly bet on the gradual dismemberment of the regular army as an essential way to move out of the mutually painful stalemate between a mobilized opposition and a resilient regime.

The military's reaction is a relational property: it has to be related to the characteristics of the regimes (e.g., enduring authoritarian rule) to which the military belonged (the element of 'path dependence') and the radical newness of the setting in 2011 ('the element of surprise').

The Military Dimension in Modern Middle Eastern Politics

The military dimension in Middle Eastern politics was a classic feature of the 1950s and 1960s, when armies were loci of socialization and politicization for 'new middle classes', as exemplified by the occurrence of military coups d'état and the place of the military within the whole process of state and nation building.[6] This historical legacy is resonant for the old generations of the contemporary officers' corps in Syria and Egypt, but the whole setting has dramatically changed since the 1970s.

Coups d'état in the Arab world have waned and have given way to 'authoritarian stability', or more precisely, authoritarian durability, for decades. This is testimony to the efficacy of new strategies of control and management. Arab regimes have developed structures around networks, processes and institutions outside the military that have shifted the centre of gravity of regimes away from the military.[7] Even in countries where rulers have hailed from the military, there has been a creeping 'civilianization' or 'demilitarization' of the political system and the core of

---

[6] The dimensions of military politics in the Middle East in the 1960s were the following: army officers were able to seize power and build new regimes (republics); they engineered a process of modernization and social change (with side effects on traditional monarchies); the influence of military rulers tended to spill over borders into the politics of neighbouring states; this Middle Eastern military politics was related to great superpowers because it was also based on arms races. Halpern, 1963, Hurewitz, 1969.

[7] Pripstein Posusney and Angrist, 2005; Schlumberger, 2007; Guazzone and Pioppi, 2009.

authoritarian rule has become less rooted in the military establishment, shifting the locus of power. The crux of authoritarian rule has been the control of the state apparatus by a few networks of family members, high bureaucrats, party apparatchiks, advisers, political elites, crony capitalists, and high officers linked to the president or the king, rather than representing the army as a corps. The interior ministries, the police, and the secret services (the *mukhabarat*) have played an essential role as the administrative arm of the state and have often been the ultimate arbiter in daily politics and social life. Authoritarian Arab regimes are better described as 'securitocracies', *mukhabarat* states, than military regimes in the strict sense, with the general staff ruling the country.[8] The 'authoritarian equilibrium' (or status quo) has not been based primarily on the military's direct role in politics, but rather on the 'wall of fear' erected by the interior ministries, the role of power networks linked to the executives, the co-optation of key constituencies, patrimonialism in the public sector, and the delivery of selective incentives to new clients (for instance, with privatizations in the economic sector or openings in the media).

Arab regimes have also developed various 'coup-proofing' and control devices within the military, favouring loyalists and those seen as the regime's natural social base, such as rural inhabitants of the 'Sunni triangle' in Iraq under Saddam Hussein, Alawis or rural Sunnis in Syria, Northerners in Yemen, rural East Bankers in Jordan, and Nejdis in Saudi Arabia. The regimes have closely watched promotions in the officers' corps, maintained rapid promotions in command positions, and favoured a compartmentalized internal force structure to prevent coups by coordinated units. The military intelligence apparatus has also been developed with agencies gathering information against potential threats and counterbalancing the regular military command hierarchy, as exemplified by the role of Omar Suleiman in Egypt with the General Intelligence Organization from 1993 to 2011. Authoritarian regimes 'tamed the beast' by developing a system in which authoritarian control of the armed forces ensured the military was kept within barracks.

At the same time, however, the military has remained a pivotal constituency for authoritarian regimes. Despite the eclipse of its direct influence, the military has remained the primary repository of force. In

---

[8] For example, whereas the four Egyptian presidents preceding Mohammed Morsi were military men, until the overthrow of Hosni Mubarak, it was a virtual certainty that the next president would be from the ruling party (with the essential approval of the military's top brass), although there was strong reticence to the accession of Gamal Mubarak.

Egypt, the first line of repression after the police has been the paramilitary Central Protection Forces (CPF) from the Interior Ministry, but these have always been considered a second-rate force lacking equipment, badly motivated, and staffed by rural illiterate conscripts who failed to meet criteria for acceptance in regular armed forces. Hence, the military has remained the ultimate guarantor of the regime. In 1986, when 20,000 CPF members rioted over low pay, the Egyptian army deployed one-quarter of its forces to suppress the rebellion. In 1997, at the peak of the offensive by armed Islamists against the Egyptian state and its sources of revenue, some army units supported the police in Upper Egypt – but the CPF was the frontline force in the battle against Islamists. The CPF again took the lead role in 2011–12, during and even after the revolution, allowing the Egyptian military to maintain its professional ethos.[9]

In Jordan, riots in Kerak in 1996 and Maan in 1998 were dealt with by military deployments. In Saudi Arabia, the military has been deployed on numerous occasions in the oil-rich Shi'a eastern province to support the police and the paramilitary National Guard. The Syrian army more than doubled in size between 1978 and 1984. This was not just the product of a Syrian resolve to establish 'strategic parity' with Israel, but was related to the Assad regime's internal challenges in the 1980s, chiefly the insurgency led by the Muslim Brothers.

But military interventions have acted more as exceptions than general rules. In most cases, the day-to-day actions of the Interior Ministry were sufficient to control dissent, and the army was a supporting pillar of the regime, acting as a deterrent to opposition. Every time regimes resorted to military intervention to quell protests or to buttress their political moves, the political stature of the military increased, and reshufflings and retirements followed, as illustrated by the removal of Marshal Abu Ghazala in the 1980s in Egypt, or the reshuffling of the Syrian officers' corps in the late 1990s as Hafez al-Assad organized the meteoric rise of his son Bashar, after the death of his presumed successor, Basel.

The militaries have adapted to the authoritarian control of the armed forces, as regimes have tried to tie the militaries to their survival and remove them from active political decision-making. Two elements are pivotal:

Firstly, besides its proclaimed role in external defence, the army has positioned itself as a symbol of the state, carefully cultivating the image of

---

[9] Some parts of the Egyptian army (and its military police) were involved in controversial military tribunals to try terrorism suspects.

an actor at the service of the country, while generally abstaining from the dirty task of policing society. As a result, armies have retained some legitimacy without threatening regimes and have been far less delegitimized than other state institutions such as interior ministries. Hence, the recurring slogan in the 2011 demonstrations across the Arab world: 'the people and the army are one hand' (*al-jaish wa al-shaab ayad wahda*). This was a call from protesters to the army to side with them against the hated police and paramilitary forces. Such a stance requires that the military defines itself in terms of professionalism as separate (to some degree) from the regime, and can therefore keep some form of autonomous legitimacy, but far from any autonomous political clout that will threaten the regime. For regimes, such professionalism is useful in enhancing the performance of the institution upon which their rule depends, while maintaining strict control over it.

Although often taken as a point of comparison (especially in Egypt), the Turkish case is very different. It entails much more autonomy for the military from the regime's dynamics. Military autonomy under the guise of professionalism has been buttressed with broad civilian elite political support, military involvement in managing politics (with civilian aides), and legitimacy through the encompassing ideology of Kemalism. The Turkish military's autonomy has been institutionalized through the role of the General Staff in the National Security Council since 1983.[10] In Egypt, by contrast, a fine but essential line has been drawn between the military's roles in the political regime and the military as an integral institution of the state. The military is integrated in the political regime and some officers play crucial roles in the corridors of power. Civilianization has not altered the fusion of roles by those in the highest echelons of power. The military corps also keeps some distance from day-to-day politics, especially in conducting repression, a defining feature of authoritarianism. Hence, in 2011, the military that closely stuck with the Mubarak regime was able, under very exceptional circumstances, to define its own interests separately from the regime. By comparison, the Syrian army has been much more 'organic' to the regime, as preparation for war and militarization have been essential ideological

---

[10] The Egyptian military academy, unlike its Turkish counterpart, does not devote much attention to ideological indoctrination (although cadets are carefully screened to prevent Islamist infiltration or the recruitment of those with 'bad' familial background, for instance, whose grandfathers opposed the Free Officers in the early 1950s).

features – 'the strategic parity' with Israel and 'resistance' to 'American-Israeli projects' – for the Assad regime.[11] And the Syrian army has had less institutional capabilities within the structure of power to separate its destiny from the Assad regime.

Secondly, the military has built itself, in most cases, as a strong corporatist group with its own economic interests as a relatively privileged actor within the public sector, with powerful patronage networks. Regimes have taken care of the corporate requirements of their militaries through large budgets, modernization programmes, freedom from external oversight, formation trips in the United States (Egypt) or rotations in well-paid positions in Gulf armies as officers (Jordan). Militaries have also gained from the purchase of high-prestige weapons systems and access to U.S. military aid (Egypt, Jordan). Regimes have provided support for the private interests of officers both while in service and following retirement. In Jordan, Egypt, Sudan, Algeria, Yemen, Syria, and Saudi Arabia, social welfare for military officers and their families, such as access to military-only facilities, cheap housing, easy access to low-interest credits, access to scarce consumer goods at cheap prices, and better medical care have been maintained and even enhanced.[12] In Egypt, the military has also invested in large and profitable economic ventures, including tourism in Sinai and reclaimed coastal lands. This has created a very specific inroad by the military into the economy, called by Egyptians 'the military economy'.

The expressions 'military economy' or 'military interests' may be misleading as they imply a big rationale. The economic activities of the Egyptian military are a reflection of the military's role in the Egyptian system as a foundational pillar with large prerogatives within strict limits. The Egyptian military has defended its privileges and increased its encroachment into the economy in the 1990s–2000s, through a complex mixture of the Mubarak regime closing its eyes, the military asserting itself at a time of aggressive privatizations by the government of Ahmed Nazif (2004–11), and with the army taking shares in enterprises including shipyards, maritime companies, and petrochemicals. That very complex network of military interests, allegiances, and dependence of officers from military networks also explains why the Egyptian military has retained

---

[11] Heydemann, 2000.

[12] In Egypt, generals earn the same as young engineering or commerce graduates from good private universities; symptomatically, generals' wives have increasingly been driven into the workforce to cover family expenses including the rising costs of education for their children.

its coherence during and after the regime-shaking mobilizations in 2011. In Syria, the arrangements are less organized. In the 1990s, the Syrian army had neither the institutional capability, nor the necessary autonomy, nor sufficient resources (at a time of declining Russian aid and of budget battles in the Syrian system around scarce resources) to follow the path of its Egyptian counterpart and enter into economic ventures. The military economy in Syria is not an autonomous sector; rather, high officers serve as essential brokers in economic openings (*infitah*) between the state and society, in a kind of 'military-*munfatihun*' lobby,[13] veering towards the plundering of scarce state resources by well-connected high officers. Additionally, until 2005, officers deployed in Lebanon benefited from the administration of smuggling networks. In all cases, the military has enjoyed a kind of impunity (within limits) to defend its own corporate interests.

All in all, the military has been a closed and secretive sector, close to regimes but maintained at a distance through economic benefits. Militaries have displayed complex bureaucratic structures adverse to change, with aspirations to modernization and investment in new military technologies provided by the state. Both these elements have combined to create a 'quietist' military institutionalized within the regimes.[14] Armies are usually painted, somewhat exaggeratedly, as powerful actors with a strong sense of corporatism and self-interest who act forcefully as a corps. The current military is also the product of thirty years of complex relations with the authoritarian regime, not just of the indigenous dynamics of a (self-) isolated sector. Authoritarianism has a propensity to produce its own creatures amongst the high officers' corps, characterized by a mix of unwavering loyalty, caution, and reluctance to change. These people keep the military loyal and prevent it becoming imbued with a sense of national mission as in the 1950s–60s. There have been regular purges, and conversely, some high military leaders have been entrenched at the summit for years to ensure loyalty (as Mustafa Tlass, Hikmat Shehabi, and Ali Duba under Hafez al-Assad or Hussein Tantawi from 1991–2012 in Egypt). Arab regimes are geared towards the progressive institutionalization of the military apparatus into the authoritarian state. This entails a mixture of professionalism based on performance, corporate identity, enduring cronyism and patrimonialism, preferential treatment of some

---

13 *Munfatihun* (lit. 'those who are receptive to openings') refers to those who have taken advantage of economic openings. Picard, 1993.
14 Droz-Vincent, 2007.

high officers close to regimes and passivity for other colourless and non-threatening individuals who comply with political directives.

'The Element of Surprise': Authoritarian Coercion in the Face of Mass Mobilizations

The regimes' call for harsh repression against mass societal mobilizations in 2011 was stressful for the militaries. Using lethal force against disarmed and pacific civilians is problematic – and when the number of protesters is large, repression will amount to a bloodbath – because it undermines the image of the military and more importantly, it threatens its internal cohesion and discipline. Junior officers and the rank and file are called to open fire on their social equals with whom they may identify. Furthermore, mass opposition, especially when it manifests itself in open defiance of political authority and of its police-based 'apparatus of fear', also tests the loyalties of the military personnel who might themselves be disenchanted with the regime's policies. Although military training is designed to secure the complete loyalty of the army to the regime, these stressful factors that undermine morale and discipline are exacerbated by the increased public display of exactions by the regime's police against civilians, women and children included, with videos posted on the Internet and news spread by familial networks.

Armies' decisions to participate in repression depend on their relationship with the regimes, but also on the distance they keep from the societies. The military is never completely cutoff from societal trends or changes, despite its closed and secretive image.[15] There was no open dissidence in the Egyptian military – the military's top brass perceived change as an anathema, while other officers avoided divisions and supported the regime's status quo.[16] However, some rumblings were increasingly heard in mid-2010 in circles usually close to the Mubarak regime. With the advances of neoliberal policies, officers have suffered from relative deprivation through stagnating salaries, while the cost of living has skyrocketed

---

[15] While active officers may take a quietist stance, retired officers, with links to active officers through officers clubs or living in the same neighbourhoods, have been increasingly vocal in Egypt about dynastic succession (with letters circulated within the Egyptian elite in August 2010) or in Jordan about the 'ethnic' identity of the country (with open letters circulated on the Internet in April 2010).

[16] Following their takeover of power in 2011, Egyptian military spokesmen now trumpet the armed forces' opposition to Gamal Mubarak's rise and to the corruption of the regime's cronies. This posture has been adopted after the event.

and the crony capitalists associated with Gamal Mubarak have become ostentatiously wealthy.

In the 2000s in Syria, the so-called social-market economy, or modernization within limits, under Bashar al-Assad has created a situation where public provision has remained important, but the value of welfare benefits for those depending on the state has severely deteriorated. In the Syrian army, thousands of regular soldiers and conscripts have seen extensive corruption and abuse of power by high officers linked to the regime and hence might identify with protesters. As violence has grown with the use of the military in repression after March 2011, defections within the army, the rank and file, and then increasingly amongst officers have been on the rise; and from the beginning, soldiers or officers who disobeyed orders to open fire on disarmed civilians have been executed by security services and loyalist militia. In all cases, the decision to shoot unarmed protestors is problematic for the military.

The key question is not just whether the military will defect or repress, but how it can do either and keep some coherence. The counter example is Libya. Colonel Gaddafi strongly distrusted the army after his takeover in 1969 and systematically weakened the military as well as the whole state apparatus. The regular military as an institution was counterbalanced by the upgrading of special units and militias within and outside the army that were better equipped and trained than the regular army. These units fell under the direct control of Gaddafi's sons, members of the Gadhafa tribe, or close tribal allies such as Warfalla and Magarha. The regime gave far more priority to the revolutionary credentials and loyalty of high officers than to their qualifications. Gaddafi's geographic areas of control dwindled dramatically in the first two weeks following the 17 February (2011) uprising, with entire army units defecting and providing the Benghazi-Zintan-Misrata 'rebels' with a nascent military force, while the loyalists regrouped along with the 'mercenaries' called in by the regime. Civil war ensued until external intervention by NATO forced the end of the Gaddafi regime.

In other cases, militaries under stress have managed to keep some coherence. This has been based on the military ability to emphasize its professionalism, expertise, responsibility, and corporatism. When the Ben Ali regime threatened severe repression in Tunisia in January 2011, the chief of staff, General Ammar, is reported to have refused orders to open fire at protesters. The army supported Ammar, respected its rules of engagement (to the letter), and strove to maintain stability as the regime collapsed (by securing public buildings). This meant that the army had to fight the presidential guard and members of the police who were shooting at demonstrators. Hence, the military quickly forced Ben Ali out and ended with power falling into its hands.[17]

In authoritarian settings, when it plays on its professionalism to resist being drawn into repression, the military has to balance the comforts of 'quietism', its corporate interests, and shadow political influence with the consequences of its response to the regime's requests to re-establish order. In Egypt, the military leaned towards the incumbent regime as long as it could avoid being fully driven into repression. It kept a neutral position between protesters and the regime's thugs, such as armed camel drivers on the bloody day of 2 February 2011. The military rank and file, especially in Tahrir Square, became more sympathetic to the demonstrators, but the military leadership to whom President Mubarak belonged seemed to want to give the president every opportunity before asking him to step down. The question of keeping cohesion was at the core of the decision of the Supreme Council of the Armed Forces (SCAF). The SCAF, a body of twenty-four most senior officers that theoretically could not meet in the absence of the president, did so on 10 February 2011 and forced him to formally hand over power to it. The Egyptian military, under the SCAF's guidance, abandoned its lingering 'quietism' to protect itself.

However, as the debate on professionalism and praetorianization between Huntington and Perlmutter shows,[18] professionalism under strict authoritarian control can be unbalanced by the regime's long-term engineering in the officers' corps. Quite differently from a professional military that might define to some extent its interests separately from the regime, within the limits of political non-involvement, a military can be submitted to a thorough 'social engineering': a regime can resort to the preferential recruitment of minorities or familial/regional/tribal groups in the officers' corps. These groups will have self-interested reasons for protecting the regime or difficulties separating their destiny from the regime if they are implicated in repression. Some regimes have even developed full-blown dual militaries to counter their regular military, such as the National Guard in Saudi Arabia, special anti-terrorist forces in Yemen, or the Republican Guard (4th armoured division) in Syria. There has been a kind of 'primordialization' of parts of the military, a blurring of distinctions in the security apparatus between police, paramilitaries, and

---

[17] Interviews in Tunis with high officers, October 2011. See also the detailed report in 'La véritable histoire du 14 janvier', *Jeune Afrique*, no. 2662, 15–21, January 2012.

[18] Huntington, 1957 and Perlmutter, 1977.

regular armed forces and shadow or dual command and oversight structures. This part of the military that is 'organically' linked to the regime through bonds of family, sect, ethnicity, community, and regional ties, is more likely to be deeply invested in the regime's survival.

In Yemen, the regime manipulated the state and its main institution of state-building, the army, and tribes, to build a very personalised army without much coherence, except the cohesion given by the network built around President Saleh.[19] Strategic units, which are estimated to number 15 to 20 per cent of the whole army, were led directly by members of President Saleh's immediate family.[20] In Syria, Hafez al-Assad carried out extensive 'organic' engineering in the officers' corps, establishing the unwritten rule that every combat unit would be under the command of an Alawi officer related to him by blood or bonds of allegiance. There were also many Sunni officers, especially hailing from rural areas. Hafez al-Assad imposed a division of labour in his armed forces that emphasized political loyalties and clannish links in units charged with regime defence. These praetorian units, which were stationed around big cities, especially Damascus, were mostly staffed by Alawis and formed up to 25 per cent of the overall military. In the 1980s, they acted as 'the army of the regime', committed widespread massacres, and were at the forefront of the shock strategy used by the regime in 1982 to crack down on Hama (with approximately 10,000–30,000 dead). Professional competence and strict discipline were emphasized in the larger regular army in which Sunnis comprise up to 70 per cent of the rank and file because of demographic reasons. This division of labour has been inherited by Bashar al-Assad.

In Bahrain, the key to understanding the army's reaction to the 2011 protests is the strong Sunni bias in its social/confessional composition. The Sunni Khalifa regime responded to the demonstrations in Pearl Square by declaring a state of national safety and ordering the Bahrain Defence Forces to crush the unrest. The massive civic mobilizations were presented by the regime as Shi'a demonstrations linked to a foreign conspiracy devised in Shi'a Iran. The Bahrain Defence Force and the Interior

---

[19] Videos posted on the Internet show how disparate units from the Yemen military are, in terms of age, training, equipment, or just uniforms, a very clear indicator.

[20] The president's survival hinged almost entirely on the loyalty of the Special Forces led by his son Ahmed; the Republican Guard (encircling Sanaa) led by his nephew, Tariq; the air force, led by Saleh's stepbrother; the domestic intelligence (with its own armed forces) led by another nephew, Ammar; and the riot police and the (U.S.-funded) counterterrorism units led by his nephew, Yahia.

Ministry forces are also staffed with a number of foreigners. These include Pakistanis, Jordanians, and others, either as individuals or as units embedded in the national military according to planned rotations. All of these foreigners are Sunnis and this is another way to tip the sectarian balance in a country where probably 70 per cent of the population is Shi'a. In March 2011, the Bahraini security apparatus was further strengthened by 1,000 'lightly armed' Saudi troops and an unspecified number of troops from the United Arab Emirates. The military crackdown on demonstrators was short in time (so as not to submit the military to the stress of enduring repression), with the military supporting the police, to whom it gave the upper hand in its less visible, but still ruthless, repression.

Yet, the primordialization of the army does not guarantee an open hand for repression. Even where the regime has been engaged in close engineering of its army, it has preferred to deploy praetorian units and use the regular army only for support. In Syria, special divisions directed by the president's brother Maher al-Assad have been at the forefront of the repression. However, as the uprising has spread to more and more cities and as the repression has endured, the regime has relied on a broader swath of the military, and defections by Sunni officers or by the rank and file have started and formed the nucleus of the Free Syrian Army (FSA). The context of repression is different in 2011–13 from the 1980s. The regime faces a full-scale revolution, not an armed insurrection by Islamist militants, as between 1975 and 1982,[21] and the constant flow of video footage means there is much greater awareness of its actions. The Syrian case shows that the military's involvement in repression should not be taken for granted even when regimes have carried out 'engineering' in their officers' corps. Enduring repression will increase the stress felt within the military.

Civil-military Models in Transitional Political Systems: The Re-Institutionalization of Politics

There are three models of transitions in motion in the Arab world and each one involves the military in some capacity. To begin with, there is the

---

[21] In 2012–13, the main strategy of the Syrian regime was to push the opposition towards militarization and violence to justify its own 'war effort' (to borrow the regime's justification). In 2013, it tried to replay the 1980s with a regime offering, according to its rationale, the prospect of stability to its society (those parts it still controls; but at the same time, it bombs its own society) in a fight against an Islamist-tainted insurrection whose Sunni sectarianism is growing as jihadists and Salafis play a greater role.

model of the re-institutionalization of politics, with important variations across the cases. In Tunisia, the military has played a crucial logistical role in securing electoral processes, notably the landmark elections of 23 October 2011, but has refrained from political meddling, maintaining an apolitical and legalistic role under the guidance of the chief of staff. The military has let Tunisian civil society – activists, jurists, trade unionists, human rights activists, university teachers, and journalists – and the state bureaucracy (which had been corrupted, but not annihilated by authoritarian practices) channel the transition through constitutional processes. Yet, the Nahda-led government has not lifted the state of emergency under which Tunisia has remained since the revolution (extended from 14 June 2011 until 4 July 2013, at the time of writing, by periods of one or three months): the army has kept a 'complementary and secondary role' to that of the Interior Ministry (to quote the terms of the law) in securing public spaces with tanks and soldiers, in combating Salafist jihadist groups in the mountainous border with Algeria (in 2013) and in protecting borders, especially with Libya. This leaves the army in a complex and awkward posture at a time of increased disturbances, with social grievances in the south interacting with riots led by Salafis because of the ambiguity of Nahda towards Salafis protesting over an art exhibition in June 2012 and violent protests against an inflammatory film trailer in September 2012.

In Egypt, the military was in transitional power until a civilian political system emerged. It then retained essential powers as the rebuilt political scene has remained truncated, until elected president Morsi reasserted the powers of the presidency in a dramatic fashion in August 2012. While the military did not want to rule, it also did not want to be sidelined and has acted in a very controlling way to prevent a civilian political system from emerging. The military had acted in a shadowy way behind the doors of the Mubarak regime; after February 2011, it was propelled into politics in the exceptional circumstances of regime change. Egypt's political transition has become extended and is not helped by the inherent contradiction of the May–June 2012 presidential elections taking place before constitutional reform is completed. From February 2011–August 2012, the SCAF has acted behind the scene to retain and even upgrade its position. It has displayed procrastination strategies resisting change and has shifted the road map for transition. The SCAF has also reacted forcefully and even violently when it feels threatened, but it has always given way when popular mobilization presents a united front. This results in a very chaotic transition process with regular and dangerous showdowns between various groups. On one side is the military with a heavily centralized command structure that retains coherence and some legitimacy, but is strongly criticized for its day-to-day governance of the country from February 2011–August 2012 – there have even been rumblings of dissatisfaction amongst the low and mid-level officers.[22] Other groups are the revolutionary forces and liberals who instigated and led the revolutionary movement, but who lost parliamentary elections in November 2011–January 2012 and presidential elections in May–June 2012. They retain a veto power with, for example, the potential to mobilize people in a country whose socio-economic problems have not been addressed by the provisional government and its military backers. The other main group is the Muslim Brothers, who gained a strong hand in the parliament until its dissolution through rivalry with the Salafis, and who won the presidential election and have striven to preserve their new institutional power gained through electoral processes.

The reconfiguration of the military's role is undertaken in this very shaky context, away from the initial authoritarian framework and in a transitional setting with some democratic attributes (e.g., free and fair elections, an assertive civilian president) and societal awakening. The Egyptian military proactively asserted its posture from February 2011–August 2012. The Egyptian military does not want to establish a blunt military dictatorship, with the SCAF taking direct decisions daily to manage Egypt. And, as Egypt's transition continues, it is unlikely that the military will become a political actor similar to the General Staff in Turkey in the years before the demilitarization of Turkish politics began in 2005. The Egyptian military has neither the appetite nor the ability to do so, and it does not seem to have acquired a taste for politics while in power from February 2011– August 2012. The Egyptian military has an inflated vision of itself, as the protector of stability against the whims of incapable politicians, ungrateful revolutionaries (whom it sees as not representative of Egypt), the Muslim Brothers (whom it sees as their main contender and the only organized political force), and alleged unidentified foreign plots against Egypt to weaken the country (as exemplified by the NGOs' trials in February 2012). With a self-inflated sense of their own historical worth reinforced by feelings of professional superiority, Latin American, Algerian, and Turkish militaries have been very interventionist in their respective political systems. But, they have developed institutions or at

---

[22] 'Egyptian army officer's diary of military life in a revolution', *The Guardian*, 28 December 2011.

least shadow cabinets to govern and have developed ideologies – internal security and development in Latin America, Kemalism in Turkey, the heritage of the war of independence in Algeria – to sustain their role. The Egyptian military does not seem to have such institutional capabilities and no ideological pretence. It does not see itself as the saviour of the country which must rescue the nation from the ineptitude of politicians (as in 1952), but rather as a shadow custodian, a guardian of the people.

Nevertheless, the SCAF wanted to forcefully maintain its prerogatives in the very different context opened up by the end of the Mubarak regime. The SCAF handed over legislative power when the Parliament was elected in June 2012, then recovered it, after the democratically elected parliament was dissolved by a ruling of the Supreme Constitutional Court (a group of unelected judges stacked in its favour, who ruled that the parliament was elected on an unconstitutional law). The SCAF handed over executive power to the civilian-elected president (for the fist time in Egypt since 1952) Mohammed Morsi on 30 June 2012; however, the SCAF issued a few days before a 'complementary constitutional declaration', that stated that the president will not be able to declare war without first seeking permission from the SCAF, that the president will not control what is going on in the military corps, that the military will have a huge say in the writing of the future constitution (and that any objection between the military and other actors on the constitution will be decided by the Supreme Constitutional Court), thereby denying Morsi most of his executive powers. Then, on 12 August 2012, President Morsi struck back and issued his own supra-constitutional declaration superseding that of the SCAF; he appointed a civilian vice president (a very important departure from president Mubarak, who had resisted for thirty years filling such a post, either with a civilian or a military figure); he sacked Defence Minister Tantawi and his influential deputy, Chief of Staff Enan, making them presidential advisors (in face-saving positions); and he reshuffled the high military hierarchy and groomed a new generation of officers.

The SCAF tried to preserve the military's privileged position in the Egyptian system in a very awkward manner from February 2011–August 2012, trying to translate its lingering power under Mubarak into a right to shape the 'rules of the game' in the new post-revolutionary system. It tried to talk to political forces, to exhaust them and benefit from their extreme divisions, and to enforce a political narrative that confirmed the military as a shadow veto holder. Generals from the SCAF were able to impose their narrative by playing on the desire for stability amongst Egyptians and shaped some political outcomes in the aftermath of the uprising (the March 2011 referendum, the mobilization of liberals against the Islamist-dominated first constitutional committee, the disqualification of some of the main candidates for the presidential election in May 2012). Yet, the SCAF's manipulative role was not without clear limits: in November 2011, the SCAF circulated 'supra-constitutional principles' to guide the future constitution-making process, with provisions to cordon off the military from civilian oversight. This provoked uproars and ensuing demonstrations made the SCAF backtrack. In June 2012, the SCAF helped spread an atmosphere of uncertainty (or 'diffuse fear', but quite different from fear under the Mubarak regime) via the official media, also capitalizing on the sense of dissatisfaction amongst ordinary Egyptians more than one year after the uprising and its many unmet demands. This was a manipulative move to try to legitimize its enduring political encroachments into the political realm with a 'complementary constitutional declaration' issued a few days before Morsi's election. The manipulative role of the SCAF acting as a shadow cabinet pushed the SCAF towards a clash with elected President Morsi immediately after his election.

The SCAF was increasingly driven in the second half of 2012 in a kind of prisoner's dilemma: it was stressing its strong desire to quit power, but it was unable, and perhaps unwilling, to go back to barracks, and its enduring rule was weakening its position, displaying a kind of prisoners' dilemma for the military's high hierarchy. This stalemate was also the product of the real nature of a military institution that came out of the Mubarak era as a powerful stakeholder, but was not particularly geared to direct rule. The ease with which President Morsi managed to unfasten the SCAF's lock on the Egyptian polity (with the replacement of the high hierarchy of the military) in August 2012 was certainly a blow designed to subordinate the military to civilian control; but it can also be better interpreted as an amiable solution to a stalemate. It was done with the approval of the military's middle and high ranks – and the Muslim Brothers astutely played those officers who understand that there is a new order in Egypt against the minority of old-generation officers. It was also a safe exit for the most exposed military leaders, especially Field Marshal Tantawi who increasingly bore the costly weight of military mismanagement. Slogans such as, '*al-shaab yourid isqat al-marshal*'/'the people want the removal of Marshal [Tantawi]', were increasingly heard in Tahrir Square.

The military is likely to retain a strong influence in a new Egyptian system quite different from its role under the Mubarak regime or its role as a shadow ruler following Mubarak's fall. The military wants to retain some veto power on essential decisions in three essential domains: firstly, foreign policy, especially relations with Israel (the peace treaty) and the United States (military aid); secondly, internal security matters, formerly the preserve of the Interior Ministry (from February 2011–August 2012, the SCAF resisted any reform of the police that might do away with the practices of the police state in Egypt); and thirdly, questions related to the whole economic structure of the Egyptian economy of which it is a part.[23] The military wants to cordon off the essential decisions in these domains away from the purviews of party and electoral games and hence from democratic choices. It will try to preserve its economic assets and continue to manage military matters in complete autonomy from the political system. This also means that any structural economic reform will have to gain the approval of the military. In institutional terms, with the enfeeblement of the reviled Interior Ministry and the taking over of some of its command structures by military officers, the military is now much more involved in internal security matters. Finally, it might try to go beyond strictly defined functional requirements to keep some institutional prerogatives or some veto power on key ministers, while avoiding the pitfalls of direct power and maintaining good standing with the public. All in all, the military is trying to retain some 'structural power' in the Egyptian polity.

The military remains a powerful stakeholder. Yet, it has to negotiate with other political forces in a way quite different to its behind-the-doors lobbying in the Mubarak era. Despite its incompetent stewardship of the transition, the military has been able to keep a resilient popularity as the most credible institution in Egypt. During the writing of the constitution after the summer of 2012, the military made its voice heard through its representatives in the constituent assembly. In the Egyptian constitution adopted by referendum in December 2012, very symptomatically, the role of the military appears very early in the text of the Constitution (principle 8). This is a marked difference from the 1971 Constitution. And the generals have worked successfully to secure their own interests: there will be no parliamentary oversight over the military budget, which will be the preserve of a National Defence Council (article 197); the National Defence Council will be dominated by the military (and amongst the civilian

---

[23] Not all economic topics, but those with structural effects on the Egyptian economy. For instance, the aggressive and (for the first time) real privatizations launched by the Nazif government in 2004 with the blessings of the NDP's young guard and Gamal Mubarak had such structural effects to transform the Egyptian economy.

'representatives', only three will be elected); the armed forces will preserve their right to try civilians (article 198); the 'black box' represented by the Egyptian military economy will not be open; and the defence minister will be appointed from amongst officers (article 195). However, democracy and an awakened society prevents the military guardianship from being too visible, and there are strong countervailing forces – including the mobilizations in Tahrir Square and Egyptian society – that will not accept anything overtly detrimental to democratic accountability in a newly open political field that is now closely monitored from below. The military also faces a strong and organized political actor, the Muslim Brotherhood that waited for the right moment – the discrediting of the military's high hierarchy owing to their mishandling of an Islamist raid in Sinai in August 2012 – to move against the SCAF's 'diktats'.

Civil-Military Models in Transitional Political Systems: The Lack of a State Monopoly of Force

Another model is the Libyan case, where the lack of a genuine state monopoly of force is a major problem. The crux of the matter is related to the way the Gaddafi regime was toppled, with a 'military logic' buttressed by an international intervention. The National Transition Council (NTC) was an important focal point for the 17 February uprising in terms of fundraising and international legitimacy, but it never acted as a government or a unified political wing. Hence, the 'military logic' prevailed: towns and cities, and tribes or their remnants, created revolutionary brigades on a local basis, most of them with a local agenda. A few were recruited amongst people close to the Libyan Islamic Fighting Group of the 1990s, such as Abdel Hakim Belhadj in Tripoli who emerged as a key military player with Qatar's support. Revolutionary brigades operated independently from the NTC. The end result was a fragmentation of the security field with 125,000–150,000 young revolutionary Libyans in arms and scores of militias operating in the country in a process of dissolution and reconsolidation based on local dynamics. Some fighting occurred, especially in Tripoli and the risks of civil war were raised by senior Libyan officials in the first half of 2012.

The challenge for the new Libyan authorities is to regain a genuine monopoly of force through rebuilding the central military and police units. Until March 2012, the Defence Ministry had no funding to rebuild a nucleus of armed forces, owing to the transitional authorities' lack of decision-making and to internal rivalries (between the chief of staff, a general who retired from Qaddafi's army before the uprising, and the defence minister, who is the former head of the influential Zintan military council). Thus, transitional authorities were forced to strike deals with local militias to maintain order locally.

Furthermore, there remains strong distrust amongst the new Libyan elites towards the military. Eastern brigades quickly defected in February 2011, whereas Western units remained loyal to the Qaddafi regime for some time. Another solution or compromise (quite different from a rebuilt national military) seems to have been chosen in 2012 by the new Libyan elites, with the National Transitional Council calling local communities to set up their own local self-defence brigades and granting them permission to operate as 'revolutionary brigades' nominally under the authority of the Defence Ministry (and Interior Ministry). The most powerful (and 'historic' – namely, those involved in the uprising) brigades from Zintan and Misrata, along with the Military Council of Tripoli set up a coalition and received official sanction in April 2012 to build the Libyan Shield Force (*Quwwa Dira' Libya*); a kind of parallel army to compensate for the national military's deficiencies. This force has intervened in the South and in restive areas.

The Libyan setting is unstable, but it is different from Somalia and Sierra Leone where the state is destroyed by plundering militias because there are countervailing societal forces in Libya to the destructive potential of the 'military logic': this is exemplified by the numerous local demonstrations against militias' rule (and exactions) in the second half of 2012 and this is also highlighted by citizens' mobilizations in Benghazi ousting jihadist militias after the assassination of the highly regarded American ambassador in Libya in September 2012. There is a desire amongst young generations to rebuild the country and demand responsibility based on the idea that ordinary people can rebuild their country from scratch, with the essential milestone of legislative elections in July 2012. The Libyan militias are also made up of educated young people quite different from the uneducated and uncontrolled fighters in Somalia or Sierra Leone: there is a crucial difference between uncontrolled actors plundering their country out of a sense of 'rage against the machine' (namely the state) and actors in transitional settings trying to keep a stake in what is going on in terms of institutional rebuilding. There is another difference between the militias on the urban Mediterranean shore of Libya and the militias in the undeveloped southern part of the country that are closer to the former model. Successful overall state rebuilding with the revamping of security forces will be the essential determinant of the new Libyan rulers' recovery of a Weberian monopoly of force.

Civil-Military Models in Transitional Political Systems: Enduring Stalemate

The third model of transition is stalemate. The popular, mainly peaceful, uprising against authoritarian rule gives way to a mutually painful stalemate between a mobilized society that keeps demonstrating in the streets and a resilient regime that benefits from army units' loyalty to exert repression. In such settings, the military holds a central stake and the opposition must gain defections from the security apparatus to fragment the coercive power of the regime. The 'military logic' can become predominant and there is then a risk of civil war.

The Yemeni army fractured, easing the enfeeblement and then the transition of Ali Abdullah Saleh's rule. In an authoritarian system relying on various familial networks in the state apparatus and society, there is a moment when members of the regime's military elite will accept fewer favours to preserve their position and hope for the best for the ones who will split the military and be the heroes of the revolution: more ambitious non-family members such as General Ali Mohsen sided with demonstrators when members of the Saleh family stuck with Ali Abdallah Saleh. Hence, the military's coherence in repression was split and the Saleh regime enfeebled, especially after the assassination attempt against Saleh sidelined him for medical treatment in Saudi Arabia. The Yemeni tradition of negotiation in a fragmented country and regional mediation by the GCC supported by Western embassies helped chart a course away from civil war through the departure of President Saleh. However, the restoration of the fractured army remains a daunting challenge and one of the most controversial issues in post-Saleh Yemen – Saleh spent thirty-four years building his networks and playing the tribes and the state in the army apparatus – in a pressing context of lawlessness where Al Qaeda in the Arabian Peninsula (AQAP) has gained some footholds in the South.

In 2012–13, the transitional government tried to remove checkpoints and an armed presence in the cities, especially Sanaa and Taez, and to reunify the army by recombining units and rotating high commanders. Those efforts were hampered by the risks of 'warlord politics' that might be played by those forces loyal to President Saleh (and his sons and nephews), the allies of General Ali Mohsen, and Islah-associated tribal troops, using their fire power to carve out political positions in transitional Yemen. External pressures help, as exemplified by the threats of sanctions by UN Security Council Resolution 2051 (12 January 2012) against those obstructing presidential decrees concerning military and civilian appointments in the state.

In Syria, there is no regional or international alternative to the increasing militarization of the popular uprising, as Russian and Chinese opposition blocked a replication of the Libyan scenario and as the regional issues of Shi'as versus Sunnis and Iranian assertiveness fuel the Syrian conflict rather than offer a negotiated way out from war as in Yemen. The Annan plan of March 2012 was less antagonistic to Russian and Chinese views and was approved by Russia to allow breathing space for Damascus, but it did not stop the conflict. The Brahimi mediation in September 2012 did not begin well, at a time of heightened violence. A new development of the Syrian uprising from October 2011 was attacks on military convoys or bases and ambushes of the security forces. In the first half of 2012, the Free Syrian Army's military operations became much more lethal and militarily efficient, avoiding direct confrontation with larger forces. The FSA also received huge external funding and deliveries of arms from Qatar and Saudi Arabia and foreign training in Turkey. The protest movement was sustained – in Aleppo, which had previously been quiet, protests began in April 2012 – reinforcing coordination inside and cutting its teeth in the difficult process of building a viable although divided opposition. However, the militarization of the uprising, to some extent, overshadowed its basic nature – namely, peaceful demonstrations against authoritarian rule: in the first half of 2012, the numerous FSA brigades staffed with Sunnis soldiers and officers from rural backgrounds, who are socially different from urban Sunnis, increasingly sidelined the civilians (the new generations hailing from urban middle classes, old elites in the Syrian National Council, and the Muslim Brothers) who were at the forefront of the uprising in 2011.

The FSA launched audacious attacks in June and July 2012, even in the centre of Damascus, the preserve of the regime. In August 2012, rebel brigades launched the battle for Aleppo, a strategic city close to Turkey that might act as a liberated area. The FSA became more assertive in military terms, taking over control of large parts of the Syrian countryside and conducting audacious operations against security forces and their infrastructures. It became the centrepiece of the Syrian uprising in 2012. But, quite contrary to its expectations, in 2012 it did not take over the symbolic big cities, especially Aleppo and Damascus. Conversely, the

Assad regime accelerated military repression with the use of heavy weapons against the most restive regions, including, from the summer of 2012, Scud missiles, military helicopters and planes, especially within civilian-populated neighbourhoods in big cities, then chemical weapons whose "limited" use (as compared with Iraq's Anfal campaign) was attested in mid-2013, but it was not able to restore 'authoritarian normality' in Syria. Hence, conflict endures. If the regime loses its capacity for coercion through the security apparatus and its territorial control through force, it will unravel and lose many of its 'quietist' supporters.

Yet, the 'military logic' is fraught with acute dangers. Militarization feeds fragmentation, with the proliferation of very thinly organized and coordinated armed groups operating under the FSA, but in fact with little command and control and not under the authority of a civilian political wing. Violence in a mosaic country such as Syria breeds sectarian fears and then sectarian violence, which in 2012 unleashed a cycle of attacks and reprisals along with provocations by the regime's thugs. In such a context, the military's unravelling and the upgrading of the capabilities of the FSA raise the spectre of sectarian civil war. Additionally, in 2012–13, the Syrian regime struggles against the clock and fights back by playing on the sectarian card, which utilized the minorities' (Alawis and other minorities, especially Christians) fear of violence to coalesce them around the embattled Assad regime.[24] It benefits from the loyalty of Alawis in regular units or militia recruited on a confessional basis (called the 'ghosts' or *shabiha*) who fully cast their lot with the regime. The FSA is essentially staffed with Sunni Muslims and has gained a free hand in numerous Syrian villages or quarters. Finally, an enduring military stalemate feeds despair among combatants and drives young generations into jihadist armed brigades loosely controlled by the FSA, along with foreign Salafi jihadists (10–20 per cent of the combatants) flooding into northern Syria from southern Turkey, northern Lebanon, or al-Anbar province in Iraq. In the second half of 2012 and in 2013, with a military stalemate on the ground and no prospect of international intervention to tip the balance of power, jihadists of all stripes became more influential in military units (especially with the rise of Jabhat al-Nusra li Ahrar al Sham, an al Qaeda-affiliated group), fuelling more suspicion than support towards the armed rebellion from Western circles.

---

[24] Alawis in Homs or around Damascus have felt the threat of Sunni resentment against them; they migrated to cities and settled on lands often confiscated to Sunni merchants in the 1980s and have worked in the state apparatus or the army.

Conclusion

In all cases and whatever the divergent trajectories of transitions or of authoritarian resilience, the military plays a pivotal role. In cases of transition, the focus has shifted from the previous concern about armies in authoritarian settings to discussions about armies and civilians in Arab transitions. In Tunisia, the military has signalled and negotiated a complete return to barracks. In other cases, the rebuilding of the military is an essential milestone, either from scratch, as in Libya, or through building a unified and professional army under a professional command, as in Yemen. In Egypt, beyond the ebb and flow of political scuffles and deals between the military's hierarchy and the Muslim Brotherhood-led government, the problem is, in the process of transition, the redefinition of the role of the military in a new Egyptian political system. A whole new setting has to emerge for new political systems in transition to stabilize. The conundrum is that military dynamics are not the only intervening variable: the emergence of a solid and functioning civilian leadership is also a crucial factor in the negotiation of new civilian-military relations.

We might hazard a few speculations about future trends. What is at stake is a redefinition of the role of the military in the Arab world. From the 1970s–2011, an intimate nexus between the state and the military was at the core of Arab authoritarian regimes. In such military-backed authoritarian regimes, power was structured exclusively from the executive, in a model of a unanimous system. That unanimity was broken by sudden revolutions in 2011. Yet, quite differently from previous textbook revolutions that installed a new revolutionary elite in power, the Arab uprisings of 2011 broke down unanimous powers and replaced them with an equilibrium between different forces – in Egypt, the military, the Muslim Brotherhood, the revolutionaries, and the remnants of the old regime; in Libya, a very fragmented political scene with armed revolutionary groups and regional differences; in Yemen, tribes, a fragmented state, regional autonomies, and secessionist movements, along with Al Qaeda in the Arabian Peninsula's inroads – with no group gaining a decisive hegemony on the others.

The military is no longer in a position, and harbours no will, to openly take power. In all Arab countries in transition, what is at stake is the rebuilding of political systems on this equilibrium and perhaps the building of 'a democratic equilibrium' and the rebuilding of new civil-military relations. Tunisia acts as a special case with a very apolitical/legalistic and tiny military. In cases where the military is much more important in terms of manpower (hence, as a potential stakeholder), either it acts with some coherence, as in Egypt, or it comes out fragmented (in Yemen, presumably in Syria when the regime falls) or imploded (in Libya). In Egypt, the military, however powerful, cannot merely act as a behind-the-scenes shadow ruler because it enfeebles itself, as exemplified by its calamitous rule from February 2011–August 2012. The military must negotiate its place. In such a context of reawakened new political groups and forces enters the issue of the prospects for (democratic) control of the armed forces. A whole literature of theoretical reflections and lessons based on the empirical experiences of transitions in Latin America in the 1980s, Spain and Portugal in the 1980s, and Eastern Europe after the fall of Communism in 1989 can be invoked.[25] According to lessons learned, during transitions, civilian leaders should try to establish some degree of civilian control, in essence to remove as far as possible the military's ability to play a direct role in determining the course of events. These were the very processes at stake in Egypt in the second half of 2012 in the debates to write the constitution that was then adopted in December 2012.

In other cases, such as Libya and Yemen, and presumably Syria, the fragmentation of the military or its implosion is a liability (to reinstate the Weberian monopoly on force), but also an asset when compared with the Egyptian case, namely a potent military acting as a stakeholder. The danger lies in the immediate short term with militia intervening in the political space and then with the difficult rebuilding of a military apparatus after a phase of fragmentation. As exemplified by the case of Iraq after 2003, the rebuilding of the Iraqi armed forces from scratch offers a window of opportunity to reinstate real civilian control; yet the emerging political games can dangerously interfere with this process, especially in cases of fragmented polities: in Iraq, emerging political forces control militias that are 'a life insurance' for them in ensuring a reasonable share of the 'political pie'. The new Iraqi political system is based on an equilibrium of political parties backed by militias now integrated in the security forces and the military, with brigades and units cohesively recruited from a given political party. For instance, Prime Minister Nouri al-Maliki built a network of close associates circumventing the formal

---

[25] See Valerie Bunce's Chapter 21 in this volume.

institutional structure of the Defence Ministry. This is at the core of his power base and complements his fragile (democratic) political coalition. Such Iraqi lessons should be carefully watched in fragmented polities whose transition was eased out with the militarization of uprisings or where 'the military logic' has become prevalent as in Syria.

9

Women, Democracy and Dictatorship in the Context of the Arab Uprisings

Sami Zubaida

Abstract

The electoral success of Islamic parties in Arab countries of recent transition has raised questions about policy and legislation on women and family. Pragmatic leaders make reassuring noises, which are challenged by vocal constituencies proclaiming the reinstatement of Sharia provisions and the moralisation of public space. The history of policy on women and families since the early twentieth century indicates that it was dictators, such as Ataturk, Reza Shah and later Nasser and Saddam, who took partial steps for family reforms and female emancipation, often against opposition from religious and patriarchal authorities supported by popular constituencies. Dictatorial and dynastic regimes had largely suppressed the citizen politics of civil society and associational life, benefitting religious and communal networks, which, though politically suppressed, maintained their socio-economic powers as survival units for the popular classes. The emergence of electoral democracy and free elections in the absence or weakness of political institutions and organisations had favoured the populist religious parties. Iraq was the prime and extreme example, where elections brought in fragmented sectarian parties, giving free reign to religious authority over personal-status issues and exposing women to coercion and intimidation. The leadership of the Muslim Brotherhood in Egypt and of Ennahda in Tunisia has so far maintained ambiguity on these issues, caught between the pragmatic exigencies for a liberal and inclusive appearance and the clamour of popular conservative and salafist constituencies for Islamic law and morality. The more robust civil society in Tunisia, including women's organisations, is better placed to resist the religious pressures than their Egyptian counterparts faced with a more thoroughly Islamised society.

The electoral success of Islamic parties in Egypt, Tunisia, and Morocco, has raised worries about policy and legislation on family and gender issues, this despite reassuring noises from leading figures. Earlier electoral successes of Islamists in Iraq brought about a disorderly mix of family policies and rules of disparate religious authorities, accompanied by much constraint and intimidation. This may be a good time to reflect on the record of various Middle Eastern countries on these issues over the course of the twentieth and twenty-first centuries and their relations to political regimes, and what that history may augur for the current transformations.

The uprisings in Egypt, Tunisia, and elsewhere were initiated by groups, mostly of urban young people, demanding an end to repressive regimes and for liberty, dignity, and social justice. They were distinct from the dominant nationalist and religious preoccupations of previous oppositions and demonstrations. Women were at the forefront of these events, sharing the space of protest and demand with their male counterparts. In Egypt, these were the Tahrir crowd, later dubbed 'Tahriris'. In the course of the Egyptian 'revolution', these crowds were subjected to attacks and violence from police and military forces, as well as the informal *baltagiya*, the regime thugs. Women in the crowd were specially targeted with sexual violence and verbal denunciation. Conservative and religious pronouncements denounced protesting women for mixing with strange men in common spaces: Islamist women demonstrators, when they did come out to support their parties, were covered and segregated.

The Tahriris and their equivalents did not prevail in the political arrangements that followed the fall of the regimes. Electoral democracy brought into prominence Islamist parties, primarily challenged by elements of the previous regime and the 'deep state'. These were the forces with established constituencies and networks of following and patronage with organization and finance. The citizens who initiated the revolution were sidelined. The Islamic leaders elected to office have been pragmatic and ambiguous regarding the Islamism of their programmes. Although always referring to the Sharia, they at the same time make liberal noises about a 'civil state' and basic rights, including the status of women. Yet, their followers and constituencies are much more vocal about restoring the Sharia provisions on family and morality. After all, the Sharia is largely irrelevant to most issues of policy and administration under modern conditions: its real domain is the family, women, public morality, and the control of cultural production, backed by a reformed education system. This chapter delves into the modern history of these issues with the aim of illuminating the current situation.

Women, Dictatorship, and Democracy in the Middle East: A Historical Perspective

In the early and middle decades of the twentieth century, it was always dictators who embarked on policy and legislation that took steps to liberate women in both family and society. Mustafa Kemal Ataturk started the process in Turkey, followed partially by Reza Shah in Iran, a model followed less boldly by some Arab leaders in later decades. It is important to note that these measures were introduced by native dictators in the two countries that did not come under direct Western colonial rule. British and French colonial regimes avoided, for the most part, challenge and confrontation with native custom, law, and religion, insofar as they did not threaten order and control. They, and the Dutch in Indonesia, worked to formalise and codify religious and customary provisions of their domains, including Islamic law with regard to social life and personal status, often reinforcing and rigidifying patriarchal rules and practices.

The nationalist struggles for independence often included the ideologies of native cultural authenticity that reconstructed religious and customary practices against the colonial models, including the rules on family, sexuality, and women. This was a particularly important issue in Algeria, where French settler society and the attempts to make the country part of French domains led to an emphasis on Islam as national authenticity in the independence struggle. Women played an important part in the war of independence, but once independence was achieved, women were driven back into the family sphere ruled by reconstituted religion and custom. Later decades saw women's movements and organizations challenging religious law and practice, but with little success on legal reform in the face of populist Islam and then violent jihadism. This was at odds with the actual progress of women in social and economic spheres, and remains an issue to the present day. Algeria may have been a polar case, but elements of this anti-colonial authenticity in nationalist anti-colonial ideology were present in other countries.[1]

Turkey and Iran, while similar in not having undergone colonial rule, were the products of very different histories. Turkey was much more

---

[1] For an overview of this history, see Keddie 2007, pp. 75–100.

exposed to the forces of modernity and capitalism, with a long history
of reforms and transformations than the more backward Iran. Ataturk
emerged as a national hero from a liberation struggle and had the legitimacy to dictate to a society devastated and destabilised by war and
occupation. Ataturk, at the head of a national political movement, was
able to subordinate religious institutions and personnel: Sharia was ban-
ished and banned, while Sunni Islam continued to be an implicit essential
component of national identity. Reza Shah subordinated the clergy and
removed them from judicial power, but compromising on the personal-
status law and the position of women was a cheap price to pay in avoiding
further confrontation. He did, however, decree the compulsory unveiling
of women, a step with profound symbolic significance, just as the compulsory veiling under the Islamic Republic became a public symbol of the
power of the clergy: both use women's bodies as symbolic manifestations
of their power.[2]

But what did these modernists and reformers mean by 'liberation'? It
was not sexual liberation: the modern liberated woman was above all
virtuous and modest, maybe unveiled, but well covered. Sexuality was
a taboo subject within the discourse of liberation. Whereas traditional
scholars and jurists discoursed on sexuality in detail, regarding the licit
and the forbidden, purity and danger, the modernists avoided the subject.
The advocacy was for women to be unveiled and to come out in public
space, and to be educated. Advocates differed or did not specify the categories of work or public participation in which women were to engage,
or whether they can compete with men on equal footing. The question of
whether they should have the vote or political or judicial office were also
not issues of consensus, and many demurred.[3] On family relations and
personal-status law, the point of general agreement was disapproval of
polygamy. This, like the widespread practice of pederasty, was part of the
complex of backwardness and degeneracy to be eradicated by progress.
The modernists and reformists had internalised the European 'gaze' that
found this libidinous decadence to be integral to Oriental or Muslim
countries.[4] The liberated, educated woman was to have a domestic role
that was at once a national duty: to run an efficient and hygienic home

---

[2] On Turkey, see Kandiyoti 1991; on Iran, Najmabadi 1991; for a general analytical history
on Iran, see Afary 2009, 109–173.

[3] A survey of reformist advocacy in the different countries can be found in Keddie (2007),
75–101.

[4] Afary (2009), 79–108; Zubaida (2011), 17–23.

as a wife and mother, and thus breed a healthy and strong generation to lead the national renaissance.

A common pattern for nationalist and leftist parties, but also for modernising dictators, is to sacrifice advocacy and policy regarding women and the family for populist considerations: why antagonise religious and conservative constituencies who could provide useful support. Reza Shah for all his fierce repression of religious opposition drew the line at family law reform. The Tudeh (communist) party, as well as their Iraqi equivalent, were ever sensitive to charges of atheism and immorality from their conservative opponents, and refrained from confrontations on issues of family and sexuality.[5] Reformist and revolutionary nationalists acted similarly. Gamal Abdul Nasser, while firmly controlling the religious institutions, and effectively nationalising al-Azhar, trod carefully on family law reforms and women's rights, granting women the vote (for what it was worth) and participation in public life, but did little on family law. It was his successor, Sadat, who, while displaying his piety as the 'believing president' and promoting conservative Islam, nevertheless instituted the most far-reaching reforms of family law. Reforms favouring women were and continue to be hostage to calculations of political advantage and popular support.

We should bear in mind that policy and legislation were constrained by structured social and cultural processes associated with modernity: the transformation and individualisation of many spheres of work and labour; social and geographical mobility and urbanisation; the rise of education, literacy, the arts, and media. All these had inputs into objective conditions and subjectivities that exerted various degrees of pressure towards liberalisation. Capitalism and consumption added to pressures for liberation in new 'economies of desire'. Equally, they raised anxieties in conservative and patriarchal quarters about loss of control over women and the young. It is interesting to note that Saudi Arabia is the one country that was most successful in resisting these pressures for the longest time: not only was it the most socially and culturally backward, but its bonanza of oil revenues and their distribution exempted its rulers from the pressures for change in other parts of the region. 'Islamic' Iran enjoyed no such luxury.

Some elements of the historical Sharia provisions on family law remained in the reformed systems of all Middle Eastern countries bar

[5] Najmabadi, 1991; Afary, 2009, 234–262.

Turkey.[6] Ataturk abolished all Sharia provisions and made the advocacy of Sharia an offence. At the other extreme, Saudi Arabia maintained the full force of the historical Sharia in family and gender provisions. Most other countries instituted legal reforms that retained some elements of Sharia provisions. Issues affected included restrictions on the rights of a man to multiple marriages and unilateral divorce at will, as well as giving the wife some rights regarding divorce and custody of children. Liberties of the wife to work outside the home and to travel abroad without the husband's or male guardian's permission have remained thorny issues in many countries.

It was in the 1950s that many of the 'mainstream' countries such as Egypt, Syria, Iraq, and Morocco abolished the separate Sharia courts and integrated family law into the regular civil courts, but ruling in accordance with reformed, codified, Sharia provisions.[7] This step was enacted by military dictators, against the stifled displeasure of religious and conservative circles. This was most notable in Iraq under Abdul-Karim Qasim, who came to power at the head of a military coup in 1958 and enacted some of the most liberal family provisions in 1959. These reforms, which abolished Sharia courts and gave women enhanced rights in marriage, divorce, and inheritance, delighted the strong leftist-secularist current of the time, and angered religious conservatives.[8] A mocking rhyme chanted in the streets was: *tali al-shahar maku mahar, wul-qadi nthebba bil-nahar*, 'come the end of the month there will no longer be dowries, and we shall chuck the qadi in the river'. Sections of the communists and the left, feeling strong, lost their populist inhibitions regarding religious sentiment and gave full voice to their secularist positions. The bloody, Central Intelligence Agency (CIA)-assisted Ba'athist coup in 1963 put an end to the relatively benevolent Qasim dictatorship and brought in the rule of a pan-Arabist and sectarian Sunni regime under the backward Arif brothers. Sure enough, a delegation of venerable clerics, Sunni and Shia, prevailed on Arif to reverse all Qasim's reforms.

The second Ba'ath coup in 1968 ultimately brought Saddam Hussein to dominance in the 1970s, the 'golden age' of prosperity and cultural revival funded by the multiplication of oil revenues, which also reinforced the security state and bloody repression. This regime pursued secularism

---

[6] Zubaida (2003), 147–157; 171–181; Keddie (2007), 102–165.
[7] Zubaida 2003, 121–157.
[8] Tripp, 2007, 143–185.

quite seriously, aimed, in part, at weakening religious and patriarchal loyalties in favour of the regime and party.[9] The 1970s and 1980s saw great strides in the empowerment of women in family and society and the curbing of religious authority over family law, albeit within the limits of the totalitarian security regime that integrated all women's organizations within the Ba'ath Party and the state.

All this came to an end in the following decades of destructive wars: against Iran in the 1980s, then the 1990 invasion of Kuwait and the subsequent pulverisation of Iraqi economy and infrastructure by American and allied bombardment followed by disastrous UN sanctions. An increasingly weakened regime resorted to tribalism and religion to shore up social controls, easily bypassing its own reforms to return to patriarchy, 'honour' violence, and all kinds of impositions on women. By that time the class of people who would 'chuck the qadi in the river' had been all but eliminated. The violent repression of all politics and civil autonomies had been highly successful in killing, imprisoning, and exiling the 'citizen' middle classes; the Ba'ath Party itself had been transformed from an ideological campaign to a passive vehicle of allegiance to the ruling dynasty.

Most important, individuals had been driven by the violence and collapse of the economy to seek safety and livelihood in family, clan, patron bosses, and religious networks. The only political opposition facing the regime became the Shia parties, tied to those patrimonial networks and Iran. The fragmented electoral 'democracy' imposed by the Americans after the invasion inaugurated chaotic sets of legal and religious practices on family law, largely restoring the religious and patriarchal authorities' powers over family and women. The dictators liberated women in the good days, but retreated under pressure, and it was the populists ushered in by 'democracy' who oppressed women.[10]

Tunisia is generally reckoned to be the most liberal of Arab states on family law and women's rights. It is, for instance, the only Arab country to ban polygamy outright, while most of the others could only introduce restrictions of the man's right to multiple wives. These measures were part of the modernising project of another dictator, Habib Bourguiba. We should add, however, that Tunisia was the Arab country with the

---

[9] For a historical account of the Qasim regime then the Ba'ath, see Tripp 2007, 143–185; 197–202. Nadje Al-Ali (2007), *Iraqi Women: Untold stories from 1948 to the present* gives vivid accounts of these events as experienced by informants: on the Qasim regime, 56–108; on the Ba'ath , 109–146.

[10] Ghanim, 2011, 40–49.

most vibrant civil society and associational life, which chimed in with Bourguiba's reforms. The Nahdha Islamists, brought to power by elections that followed the 'revolution' have promised not to reverse these reforms, but will they resist the voices from below clamouring for a more vigorous Islamic project?

This pattern is repeated in Morocco, where liberalisation of the family code was instituted in steps in the 1990s and 2000s, first by King Hassan, then King Muhammad, culminating in the most liberal code in 2004, against stiff religious opposition backed by populist agitation. Now, an Islamic party has a parliamentary majority and forms the government, but under royal control.[11] Kuwait is another example of cautious measures by the ruler, including enfranchising women and allowing them to stand for office, strongly denounced by Islamists in parliament. Their latest move was to demand that women members wear the veil.

In Egypt, the most significant reforms of the twentieth century were promulgated by Anwar Sadat in 1979, known as the 'Jihan law', after Sadat's wife who was believed to be the instigator. This law was promulgated by presidential decree, under emergency powers, bypassing parliament that was not sitting at the time. This was to prove its later undoing in 1985. These laws gave further rights to women within the family, imposing conditions on polygamy, requiring divorces to be subject to judicial procedures, giving more rights to wives in divorce and custody, enabling married women to work and travel, and giving them a right in the matrimonial home. Sadat cobbled together a committee of ulama who rubber stamped the reforms, but some of whom reneged later, after Sadat's death.

These reforms were at odds with Sadat's general tenor of appeasing Islamists, and his amendments to the constitution to declare the principles of the Sharia as *the* source for all legislation. These contradictions gave rise to much controversy and litigation after Sadat's assassination (by jihadists) in 1981. Islamist lawyers petitioned the Supreme Constitutional court, which ruled in 1985 that the law was unconstitutional, not because it did not conform to the Sharia, as the litigants demanded, but because it was passed by presidential decree. Many of those provisions, however, were re-enacted, some in diluted form, by parliament soon after, amidst much controversy and resistance by Islamists. In 2000, further controversy surrounded another decree giving wives the option of initiating divorce if they renounce any financial or property rights. This

[11] Keddie 2007, 144–148.

was based on an obscure and controversial provision in the Islamic canon called *khul'*.[12]

Sadat's reforms of family law, and the prominent role attributed to his wife in this process, is a common pattern in other, mostly monarchical and pro-Western regimes, such as Jordan, Morocco, and Tunisia. Liberal measures on women's issues score points in international public relations, demonstrating the liberalism and modernism of rulers, distracting attention from their otherwise repressive regimes. The participation of prominent and modern rulers' wives in this process is another public relations plus. By the same token, the reforms can be denounced by Islamists as Western inspired and arbitrary measures carried out by repressive rulers and their wives, against the piety of the populace. Calling Sadat's reforms 'Jihan's law' sums up these denunciations. The Muslim Brotherhood leaders and deputies in the present legislature, flanked by more conservative salafis, include many of the activists that resisted and challenged the previous legal reforms and are not likely to have changed.

Women's Activism and the Transitions

The early advocates of reform were men, such as Muhammad Abduh and Qasim Amin. From the early decades of the twentieth century, women, understandably from the upper classes, took up the banner of reform. The pioneer in Egypt was Huda Sha'rawi who founded the Egyptian Feminist Union (EFU) in 1923. After returning from an international congress on women's suffrage in Rome, she famously removed her veil at the train station and was applauded and followed by other women in the welcoming party. This event was the culmination of a course of activism, including Sha'rawi's heading a women's demonstration in the nationalist struggle against the British occupation in 1919.[13] Women's activism in many countries in the region, including Turkey, started as participation in nationalist struggles, and was often subordinated to that goal. The EFU was a significant step in a chain of events and organizations involving women. The Wafd, the main nationalist party, soon founded its own women's organization, as did other nationalist and leftist parties. Women's organizations had different aims and natures, between political demands and philanthropic activities, with girls' education and domestic instruction as key elements. What Beth Baron called 'scientific

[12] Zubaida 2003, 165–176.
[13] Baron 1994; Badran 1995.

domesticity' was a key element: instruction in domestic management, hygiene, diet, and childcare. Although this can be seen as a conservative move tying women to domesticity, it is thought to have had a positive effect in education and awareness.[14] The Muslim Brotherhood, founded in 1928, had many female adherents, and Zaynab al-Ghazzali, a close associate of Hassan al-Banna, the founder, played an important part in the ideology and organization, and the movement always had a considerable following amongst women. These women were, of course, conservative and pious, but this did bring women into political awareness and activism.

In the course of the twentieth century, Egypt and many countries in the region underwent social and economic developments and ever greater integration into world systems, generating many avenues for women's participation. Wars, revolutions and political struggles inevitably involved women and their organizations. Nationalist and leftist parties included women's organizations. Nationalist 'revolutions', usually military coup d'états, transformed many countries, notably through Nasserism in Egypt and the Ba'ath in Iraq and Syria. Those repressive and authoritarian regimes may have promoted women's rights and participation, although not much in family reforms, but they suppressed women's autonomous organizations, alongside any other political party and civil society associations, only authorising state-controlled bodies. Women were prominently involved in all the events, protests, and revolutions in the region. They played a major part in the events leading to the Iranian Revolution in 1979, both as Islamists and as secular leftists. They are prominent participants in all the events of the current Arab transformations. The outcome of those revolutions and transformations, however, are often far from favourable to women's rights, welfare, and liberty.

The wave of Islamisation and piety that engulfed many countries in the region since the 1970s had a dramatic effect on women's visibility and comportment in public spaces. Many have remarked on the transformation of the images of female students at, say, Cairo University from the 1970s when they appeared uniformly without hijab, often with sleeveless blouses and short skirts, to later decades in which they are almost uniformly veiled with the conventional headscarf. Women with the black niqab also became more common images, extending from the Salafi depths of Arabia to Egypt and the Mediterranean. This sartorial

---

[14] Baron 1994.

transformation was part of a greater moralisation of public space, with more instances of gender segregation and censorship of cultural production and entertainment, with special attention to the iconic restrictions on alcohol and its venues. Yet, while some restrictions were imposed on women, they continued, veiled or not, to participate in work, education, the professions, and in political campaigning, on both the Islamic and the secular fronts. This activism was dramatically apparent in the recent transformations. Asmaa Mahfouz, a young, veiled activist is credited with helping to spark the 'revolution' in January 2011, in a video-recorded speech denouncing the regime and issuing a call to action that inspired the demonstrations and activities.[15]

The ideological trajectory of women's issues in the twentieth and twenty-first centuries is well illustrated by the example of Iran. The era of the constitution and then of Reza Shah saw the reformists advocating women's liberation confronting conservative and religious resistance, some of which was overcome by Reza Shah's repression. From the 1950s and until the 1979 revolution, women made considerable strides into public space – in work and politics, as well as the emergence of the 'modern' woman, in fashionable modes and make-up – amongst the urban prosperous and educated classes, headed by the royal family and court notables.[16] The whole project of modernity and power under the Shah elicited a new kind of nativist reaction, distinct from the traditional conservative religion. It was a modern, cultural, and nationalist revolt against Western modernity and capitalism, in favour of a cultural authenticity that included various versions of Islam, often in combination with leftist ideologies and strands of Marxism, as many of the protagonists started from leftist affiliations

The root ideologue of this trend was Jalal al-e Ahmad; his essay on 'Westoxification' (*Gharbzadegi*) was not entirely coherent, but full of slogans and motifs that found a ready echo amongst oppositional forces: leftist, nationalist, and religious.[17] The ideology relating to women was, perhaps, best expressed in the works of Ali Shari'ati, a hybrid of Fanonism (referring to Franz Fanon's advocacy of cultural authenticity against imperialist hegemony) and romanticised Shiism. In his essay 'Fatima is Fatima', he held the Prophet's daughter and the mother of martyrs as the

---

[15] www.youtube.com/watch?v=SgligMdsEuk.
[16] The history of these transformations are well covered in Afary (2009), 263–291.
[17] Gheissari, 1998, 74–108.

ideal of Muslim womanhood: devout, modest, yet active in the struggle for righteousness and justice.[18] This was contrasted to the modern woman: a product and victim of Western consumerist capitalism, an exploited sex object, and consumer of fashion and make-up. Secular women and leftists subscribed to elements of this ideology: women in the Maoist Fedayin faction dressed in shapeless Mao jackets and refused all ornament and make-up.

These ideas played into the initial support for Khomeini amongst leftists and secularists, anti-imperialist and anti-Western, seeking political and cultural authenticity and liberation. Of course, they soon discovered what the clerics had in store for them. But, while opposing the Islamic regime, many secularist and women's groups continued to seek this authenticity. The campaigns for women's rights and law reform have included women of diverse ideologies, with prominent presence of various forms of Muslim or national 'feminism' as distinct from the West. This trend is based on a rereading of the canonical sources to discover the elements in 'real' and 'original' Islam that favour equality and public participation. Needless to say, they have uniformly failed to convince the 'real' Muslims in authority or their populist following.

Arab feminist ideology has followed a similar trajectory. A pioneer in the critical·rereading of the Quran and the Hadith was the Moroccan Fatima al-Mernisi, who found in the Quran and the *sira* (conduct) of the Prophet strong support for equality and public participation. She challenged the misogynistic passages in the Hadith collections as specious later additions with political motives.[19] This kind of reasoning has become a common trend amongst liberal Islamists and secularists throughout the region and in other Muslim majority countries, but without much practical policy outcomes.[20] Women's advocacy in recent times throughout the region has ranged between outright secular positions, through various culturalist qualifications, to various forms of Islamic feminism, including those who see liberation in the veil. Women's campaigns that appeal to a rereading of Islamic sources had a prominent voice in Iran under the reformist presidency of Khatami 1997–2005, but went under on the election of the hard line Ahmadinejad, the 2013 incumbent. Even at its height, it achieved little of practical consequence.

---

[18] Afary 2009, 242–244; Zubaida, 2009, 20–32; Shari'ati, n.d.
[19] Mernisi 1991.
[20] Ziba Mir-Husseini is a leading advocate and analyst of this approach: see Mir-Husseini 1999 and 2000.

Native feminism retains a powerful attraction, not just for women in the region but also for anti-imperialist, postcolonial, Third World-ist ideologies in the West. Official denunciation of women's oppression, in Afghanistan and elsewhere, is presented as a hypocritical stance of 'white men liberating brown women' and a pretext for imperialist adventures.

Women in the 'Revolution'

The events of the transformation in Egypt and Tunisia featured women as leading participants in the demonstrations and the protests. The slogans and demands of the movements were remarkable for their universalism in emphasising liberty, social justice, dignity, jobs, and an end to corruption. This was a departure from the nationalist slogans of earlier demonstrations. Women shared this universalism with little in the way of cultural hang-ups.

In Egypt, women's participation also generated occasions of considerable violence and harassment, not only from soldiers and *baltagiyya*, but also from male bystanders or participants in the demonstrations. Islamic voices were often deprecatory of women's participation: women should not march or protest because it was more 'dignified' to let their husbands and brothers demonstrate for them. This did not stop the Salafists from parading their women, fully wrapped in black, to demonstrate their cause, but totally segregated from any male proximity. And this was the crucial factor in the objections by Islamist, conservative, and government opinions to women's participation: they shared the spaces with male colleagues, even when camping overnight in Tahrir. No decent, modest woman, it was argued, would mix so closely with unrelated males. This was also one of the pretexts advanced for the episode of the virginity tests. To quote Amnesty International's report on the episode:

On 9 March 2011, when army officers violently cleared Tahrir square of protesters, they took at least 18 women into military detention. Seventeen of those women were detained for four days. Some of them told Amnesty International that during that time male soldiers beat them, gave them electric shocks and subjected them to strip searches. They were then forced to undergo 'virginity tests', and threatened with prostitution charges. Before they were released, the women were brought before a military court and received one-year suspended sentences for a variety of confected charges.[21]

[21] Amnesty International, 2012.

There were various justifications advanced by official spokesmen for this transgression, one of which was to guard against accusations of rape by the army! But one official assured the public that these were not decent women like your sisters or wives, but loose types, associating with unrelated men in common demonstrations and even camping with them overnight. The virginity tests, then, were to check on their virtue. The complaint of some of the women led to a trial of the military doctor involved, who was exonerated by a military court in March 2012. There were many other episodes of soldiers, police, and their thugs attacking demonstrating women, including the widely publicized image of a veiled young woman being dragged along the road by soldiers, the upper part of her garments having slipped exposing her brassier. But was it only soldiers and thugs who engaged in such conduct?

Mona El-Tahawy, a U.S.-based Egyptian journalist who participated in the Tahrir uprising, wrote a highly provocative article in a special issue of *Foreign Policy* on women and sexuality entitled 'Why do they hate us?', detailing examples of misogyny of Arab males and their institutions.[22] Predictably, the article elicited a storm of protests from women and men in the region, which apart from pointing out the many contexts in which men loved women, were defensive culturalist arguments, with the usual accusations of 'orientalism' of both the author and the journal. Aside from the merits of the article, one of its allegations, widely supported by other reports, is that it was not only the soldiers and thugs who harassed women protestors, but normal civilian Egyptian men. The harassment of women in public places, especially, but not only when not veiled, is a regular and long-standing complaint. The prominent public presence and action of women in the demonstrations made them particular targets. Female journalists, Egyptian and foreign, were similarly targeted. A different sort of harassment comes from bearded men and women in niqab haranguing uncovered women and urging them to cover up in obedience to Islam. There are many reports of the intensification of this directive preaching in more recent days, deriving confidence and authority from the electoral success of Islamist parties.

Elections and Constitutions

At the time of writing, both Egypt and Tunisia are in process of writing constitutions in divided Constituent Assemblies, where Islamists have a

---

[22] El-Tahawy, 2012.

majority. The divisions in the Egyptian Constituent Assembly (with still unclear status) are not just Islamist and liberals, but also within Islamist, between the Muslim Brotherhood and the Salafists. A central issue is the wording of the clause authorizing the Sharia, first inserted by Sadat's amendment of 1980, which states that the 'principles' (*mabadi'*) of Sharia are the source of all legislation. The Salafists want to omit 'principles' or substitute 'rules', so that there is no room for interpretation. The Brotherhood is non-committal, wanting to play it pragmatically. There is also the question of what authority al-Azhar should have in legislation and legal interpretation regarding conformity to the Sharia in relation to the Supreme Constitutional Court and parliament. The reformist wing of the Brotherhood wants al-Azhar authority to be consultative and not binding, as against the conservatives and Salafists who demand a more directive authority. The Salafists are not likely to succeed, but this is an example of the constant pressure, with populist support, for the extension of Islamic principles.[23]

The main targets, as usual, are women, family, and sexuality, as well as the control and moralization of public space and of cultural production, at the expense of existing personal liberties and freedom of expression. Azza al-Garf, elected to parliament on the Freedom and Justice Party ticket (one of only nine women elected), and head of the Muslim Brotherhood's women's committee, proclaims her support for women's political activism, but maintains the classic conservative Sharia stances on all social and family issues, advocating revision of the reformed family laws into conformity with the Sharia, denouncing divorce as a disaster, but not, apparently, for the husband's right to unilateral renunciation. She also advocated the repeal of the law banning female circumcision.[24] In any case, within the Muslim Brotherhood, women are still excluded from leadership or policymaking positions. These views are widely shared amongst Muslim parliamentarians and their popular constituencies, both Brotherhood and Salafist.

Ennahda – the majority party in the Tunisian parliament – at first calmed secular and liberal fears by declaring that it did not intend to go back on the 1956 personal-status code. However, like other pragmatic Islamic parties, it is subject to considerable pressure from its conservative constituencies. In August 2012, its representatives in the Constituent Assembly introduced an article to the draft constitution stating

[23] Scott, 2012.
[24] Topol, 2012.

that women were 'complimentary' to men, altering the 1956 statement that women were equal. This draft was passed by their majority on the Assembly, but raised a storm of protests and demonstrations.[25] Tunisian civil society and women's organizations have strong roots and influence, and the battle for the 1956 provisions and their extension is likely to continue against the conservatives and the Salafists. It is not clear how their Egyptian equivalents will fare against a more pious hinterland.

Conclusion

This chapter has sketched the various stages and steps of the treatment of women, family, and sexuality in the different stages and contexts of the modern Middle East, ending with the culmination of these issues in the current transitions. In the early stages of modernization and reform, intellectuals and some dictators favoured the emancipation of women in a restricted sense: to get women out of seclusion and the veil into the public space of education and work. Family law reform in this perspective was limited, mostly to limiting or hindering polygamy. None followed Ataturk's radical abolition of Sharia provisions, and few made serious inroads into patriarchal family arrangements. These were to be eroded, slowly and unevenly, in some countries by reformers and social movements, including women's organizations, aided by the socio-economic transformation of these countries and the ever greater participation of women in public space and the occupational realm.

Reformers faced constant opposition from conservative and religious quarters, often backed by considerable popular sentiment. In most countries, populations continued to be divided between the citizens of civil society; urban, educated middle classes (including both secularists and Islamic activists); and the communitarian, conservative, and religious hinterlands. Electoral politics, when free elections become possible, work strongly in favour of conservative advocacy. The leaders of the newly elected Islamic majorities in Egypt, Tunisia, Morocco, and Kuwait are trying to balance between the more secular and liberal sectors of the citizens of civil society and the vociferous demands of their conservative and Salafist constituencies. The commitment to Islamic law and a religious identity typical of the platforms of Islamic parties sit uneasily with the reassuring noises from their 'moderate' leaders that all will be well with women's issues and civil liberties.

[25] *The Guardian*, 14 August 2012.

The Arab world and the Middle East are not exceptional in the tension between electoral democracy and a culture of citizenship and human rights. India, Russia, and Turkey are amongst the countries featuring these issues. Vladimir Putin's authoritarian rule in Russia is opposed by activists, mostly in Moscow and the major cities, campaigning for human rights and the rule of law, liberty, and social justice: they are the citizens of civil society, motivated and organized by ideological programmes. They do not, however, constitute the main body of the electorate in the vast hinterlands of the Russian federation, whose votes are mobilized according to local patterns of power and patronage, striking bargains with political bosses. Putin also enjoys the cult of the powerful leader and national champion. He is always trying to portray his critics as agents of foreign powers, a recurrent theme in all authoritarian regimes, especially in the Middle East. Indian politics, different in major ways from Russia, but sharing this pattern of urban, educated middle classes, is ever more assertive in political organization and campaigning, but facing a popular electorate voting according to bargains and deals of local bosses with a hierarchical chain of party agents.[26] Social conservatism and communal authoritarianism are common features of these instrumental voters, and the issues of women and family are prominent in their ideology and practice.

To repeat, the Shar.a is largely irrelevant to most important issues of policy and administration. Its historical and symbolic locus is on family and sexuality: patriarchal rights, segregation of the sexes, enforced female modesty. Civil rights of free expression and cultural creativity are also subject to religious censorship, especially if ulama are given the authority of interpretation over these issues. The other iconic mark of Islamism is the banning of alcohol. which is confronted in most countries with the exigency of the lucrative tourist trade, making for uneasy compromises.

The developments of these societies over the course of modernity, from the turn of the twentieth century, have provided the conditions for social presence and activism of civil-society citizens of both sexes: trends that can only be put back with intense repression, as we see in the case of the Islamic Republic of Iran. The increasing displays of piety and the veiling of women in Egypt and elsewhere have not held back many of those veiled women from public participation and vociferous advocacy. The political fields and social spaces of many countries in the region have been opened, however chaotically in many cases: there are battles still to come.

---

[26] Chatterjee, 2001.

10

Dangers and Demon(izer)s of Democratization in Egypt

Through an Indonesian Glass, Darkly

John T. Sidel

Abstract

This chapter illuminates the ongoing transition from authoritarian rule since 2011 and prospects for democratization in Egypt in the years ahead through a comparison with Indonesia since 1998. The chapter identifies crucial commonalities between Egypt and Indonesia, including the political transformations leading up through the fall of Suharto in 1998 and Mubarak in 2011, suggesting that the situation in Egypt as of late 2012 mirrors the.early post-Suharto interlude of 1998–1999. Political trends in Indonesia since that time, it is argued, suggest that the current political strength of Islamist forces in Egypt may be both more exaggerated and more ephemeral than is commonly understood. But both the similarities and the differences between the two countries also suggest the likely staying power of conservative forces associated with the *ancien régime* – the military establishment, the entrenched business oligarchy, and local political bosses – impeding the continuing struggle for democratization in Egypt.

As of January 2013, the ongoing transition from authoritarian rule in Egypt had unfolded through a series of developments that seemed to defy the expectations of most Egyptians and the predictions of most expert observers of Egyptian politics. In a few short weeks in early 2011, sustained popular protests in the squares and streets of Cairo produced the surprisingly swift forced resignation of President Hosni Mubarak, who had remained in power for thirty years without encountering any previous such serious challenges to his authoritarian rule. Over subsequent months, however, the sense of élan and optimism generated by this

'People Power' moment faded in the face of rising criminality and episodes of inter-religious violence, on the one hand, and the entrenchment of the Supreme Council of the Armed Forces (SCAF) as a ruling military junta, on the other hand. Parliamentary elections in late 2011, moreover, produced yet another set of unanticipated political changes, with the Muslim Brotherhood exceeding expectations to claim 37.5 per cent of the vote and 45 per cent of parliamentary seats, and the 'dark-horse' Salafi Islamist Al-Nour Party winning more than 27 per cent of the vote and a quarter of the seats in the People's Assembly.

The year 2012 produced similarly unexpected and ambiguous developments. The Muslim Brotherhood's candidate, Mohamed Morsi, won the presidency after a tightly contested two-stage election, even as the Supreme Constitutional Court invalidated the 2011 parliamentary elections and dissolved the elected parliament. Following his election in June 2012, moreover, President Morsi defied expectations of civilian weakness vis-à-vis the military establishment, first by recruiting diverse representatives of Egyptian society to his cabinet, and then, in mid-August, by removing and replacing military officers and revoking the decree that had vested effective executive and legislative powers in the hands of the SCAF. In November 2012, Morsi issued a set of decrees strengthening the powers and prerogatives of the presidency vis-à-vis the judiciary, even as the allegedly Islamist-dominated Constituent Assembly finalized the drafting of a new Constitution. These moves provoked widespread protests in the streets of Cairo and other major Egyptian cities amidst accusations that Morsi and the Muslim Brotherhood had assumed dictatorial powers and hijacked Egypt's transition to democracy. In December 2012, the new Constitution was approved in a popular referendum, with preparations for a new round of parliamentary elections mandated for the months to come. But as of January 2013, ongoing protests against the Morsi administration, Morsi's imposition of a state of emergency in several cities, calls by opposition party leaders for their inclusion in a national unity government, ambiguities about new regulations for parliamentary elections, and expressions of concern by senior military officers all pointed to continuing anxieties and uncertainties with regard to the prospects for democratization in Egypt.

Against the backdrop of these unexpected events, ambiguous developments, and abiding uncertainties, how can we understand, explain, and predict the course of democratization in Egypt today? One recent study has approached this question by comparing autocratic entrenchment and 'adaptation' in Egypt and Syria, where Bashar Al-Assad's regime has persisted in power to the time of this writing in the face of mounting popular mobilization and internal regime defections.[1] Another obvious point of comparison is nearby Tunisia, where popular protests in early 2011 similarly forced out long-time president Zine El Abidine Ben Ali, and where elections later the same year saw a similarly strong showing for the *Nahda* party, Tunisia's counterpart to the Muslim Brotherhood's Freedom and Justice Party in Egypt. A close comparative analysis of the similarities and differences between the processes of democratization in Egypt and Tunisia to date would be highly illuminating and instructive.[2] Yet, insofar as the transition from authoritarian rule remains an ongoing process and consolidation of democracy has yet to be achieved in either Egypt or Tunisia, it is necessary to look beyond these two cases – and beyond the Middle East – for points of comparison that might help us to understand Egypt's experience of democratization to date as well as the prospects for democratization in the years to come.

Here, the case of Indonesia suggests itself as especially useful as a point of comparison and a prism for the analysis of democratization in Egypt. If the fall of long-time Egyptian President Hosni Mubarak in February 2011 recalls the forced resignation of long-time Indonesian President Suharto in May 1998, and if the ambiguities, anxieties, and uncertainties haunting Egypt over 2011–2013 are reminiscent of Indonesia in 1998–2001, then perhaps democratization in Indonesia over the past thirteen to fourteen years might shed some light on the prospects for Egyptian democracy in, say, 2025. Such is the premise – and the promise – of what follows in this chapter. On the one hand, insofar as this paired comparison reveals similarities between the two countries' experience of transition from authoritarian rule, it demonstrates that the processes and outcomes coming into view in Egypt are less contingent and more structurally determined than would otherwise be understood to be the case. On the other hand, insofar as the comparison spotlights the differences between Indonesia and Egypt and specifies the peculiarities of Egypt's experience of democratization to date, it may help to offer explanations for provisional outcomes and ongoing processes in Egypt to date and help to identify pathways, if not predictions, for democratization in Egypt in the months and years ahead.[3]

---

[1] Joshua Stacher, *Adaptable Autocrats: Regime Power in Egypt and Syria* (Stanford, CA: Stanford University Press, 2012).

[2] See also the very insightful and interesting Chapter 11 by Roger Owen in this volume.

[3] On the possibilities and limitations of paired comparisons, see: Sidney Tarrow, 'The Strategy of Paired Comparison: Toward a Theory of Practice', *Comparative Political Studies*, Volume 43, Number 2 (February 2010), pp. 230–59.

Egypt and Indonesia: Historical Parallels

Although Egypt and Indonesia are different in many obvious and important ways, there are also a number of striking similarities and shared features of the two countries in broader regional and global contexts and in historical and sociological terms that render a paired comparison between them not only plausible but potentially illuminating. Both countries, after all, are regional giants: Indonesia's population of more than 240 million makes it the largest country in Southeast Asia, whereas Egypt, with its 80 million, is the biggest in the Arab world. Yet both countries were first incorporated into the world capitalist economy under various forms of European colonial rule as producers of agricultural commodities and have remained dependent on foreign capital and capital goods for their economic development and limited industrialization. Both countries, moreover, are heavily reliant not only on Western imports and investment, but also on wealthy neighbouring countries – Saudi Arabia and the other Gulf states in the case of Egypt, Singapore and Malaysia in the case of Indonesia – as sources of financial intermediation, on the one hand, and sites for large-scale labour migration and remittances, on the other. Egypt and Indonesia are giants, in other words, but poor and weak giants nonetheless.

Alongside their parallel positions within regional and global economic contexts, Egypt and Indonesia are also homes to societies that share a set of important distinguishing features. Both countries are predominantly Muslim and boast long traditions of Islamic scholarship and social activism. Cairo's Al-Azhar is recognized as the Muslim world's most enduring and important 'mosque university', even as the Java-based *Nadhlatul Ulama* stands as the single largest independent association of 'traditionalist' Islamic schools in the world. Self-consciously modernist Islamic education, associational activity, and political organizing in Indonesia dates back to the 1910s with the rise of the school networks of *Muhammadiyah*, *Al-Irsyad*, and *Persatuan Islam*, and the unprecedented mass mobilization of the *Sarekat Islam*, while the Muslim Brotherhood (*Al Ikhwān Al-Muslimūn*) and other Islamic networks in Egypt have enjoyed tremendous growth and influence in Egyptian society since the first half of the twentieth century. Thus, both countries have long boasted rich and varied forms of independent Islamic associational life and political activism in the name of the faith.

At the same time, both Egypt and Indonesia are countries whose national identities are not exclusively grounded in Islam. In both countries, the infrastructure of a modern national bureaucratic state and the circuitries of a national economy emerged under the auspices of Western imperialism and colonial rule, with 'modernization' and 'progress' associated with Western capital and 'secular' education and 'scientific' knowledge. The rise of nationalist consciousness and nationalist mobilization in both countries unfolded not only as a reaction to European colonial encroachment and domination, but also through the emergence of new nationalist imaginings and 'reinvented traditions' harking back to pre-Islamic eras of cultural formation. Both countries, moreover, have long played home to important non-Muslim minorities who played prominent – and in some ways, problematic – roles in European colonial rule and early capitalist development. Here, the disproportionately high representation of Indonesians of immigrant Chinese ancestry and Christian faith, and of Egyptian Copts, in the professional classes and in the business world is still very noticeable in the two countries today.

Against the backdrop of these historical and sociological commonalities, Egypt and Indonesia have, in broad terms, experienced markedly similar political trajectories over the past sixty-odd years. In the 1950s and 1960s, both countries were led by populist nationalist leaders – Soekarno in Indonesia, Nasser in Egypt – who championed "Third World" independence, economic nationalism, and 'socialism'. The two countries engaged in parallel conflicts with former colonial powers, pro-Western, 'neo-colonial' neighbours, and U.S. 'imperialism': Egypt's Suez War with the UK, France, and Israel in 1956, and Indonesia's nationalization of Dutch businesses in 1957; Egypt's proxy war with Saudi Arabia in Yemen in the mid-late 1960s and its brief armed conflicts with Israel in 1967 and 1973, and Indonesia's mobilization against continuing Dutch rule in West Papua and *Konfrontasi* with the United Kingdom and Malaysia in the early to mid-1960s. Under Nasser and Soekarno, both Egypt and Indonesia were positioned as prominent members of the Non-Aligned Movement. Both experienced tensions and conflicts with the United States while exploring various forms of linkage with Khrushchev's USSR and Mao's PRC over the course of the late 1950s and early 1960s.

But over the course of the late 1960s, popular nationalism in both countries met with defeat and disillusionment, as seen in the decline, demise, and death of Nasser and Soekarno by 1970. By the early-mid 1970s, both Egypt and Indonesia had experienced the emergence and entrenchment of more conservative military rulers – Sadat in Egypt, Suharto in Indonesia – who moved to seek accommodation with their neighbours, embraced the United States, and opened their economies to flows of international finance, investment, and trade. This rightward shift in domestic and foreign policy was accompanied and enabled by tightening repression of leftist forces and drastic narrowing of the permissible political spectrum in both countries. Over subsequent years, economic liberalization, privatization, and deregulation allowed for widening social inequalities and the withdrawal of many of the subsidies and other forms of support for the poor promised in the preceding eras of Nasserist and Soekarnoist 'socialism'.

Against the backdrop of the dramatic rightward shifts of the late 1960s and early-mid 1970s, both countries experienced three decades of authoritarian rule under a single military strongman: Indonesia under Suharto (1966–98), Egypt under Mubarak (1981–2011). In both Egypt and Indonesia, the powers and prerogatives of the military establishment were greatly enhanced, expanded, and insulated from civilian control, even as heavily scripted elections and closely stage-managed parliamentary bodies provided a thin veneer of democratic accountability. Over the years, both Egypt and Indonesia adjusted their economic policies in tune with the 'Washington Consensus', reducing dependence on external rents and moving from import-substitution industrialization to export-oriented manufacturing under structural adjustment programs that entailed economic liberalization, privatization, and deregulation. In both countries, these policies enabled higher economic growth and the emergence of new business classes, while increasing social inequality and leading to rising labour unrest and urban and rural land struggles. The result was greater vulnerability to regional and global economic crises, as seen in Indonesia in 1997–98 and Egypt in the 1990s and again from 2008 onwards.[4]

In both Indonesia and Egypt, thirty years of authoritarian rule under a single military strongman spawned centralized corruption, cronyism, and nepotism. Both presidents encouraged their children to emerge as major figures in the business world, as seen in the diversified conglomerates of Suharto's sons and daughters and the vast empire of Mubarak's son Gamal. Over their final years in office, moreover, both presidents began to set the stage for dynastic succession in politics, with Suharto's daughter Tutut and Mubarak's son Gamal promoted to positions of increasing prominence in both regimes' electoral machines and growing influence in the innermost circles of power in Jakarta and Cairo.[5]

---

[4] On these trends, see: Andrew Rosser, *The Politics of Economic Liberalization in Indonesia* (Richmond, Surrey: Curzon Press, 2002); Samer Soliman, *Autumn of Dictatorship: Fiscal Crisis and Political Change in Egypt under Mubarak* (Stanford, CA: Stanford University Press, 2011).

[5] Jason Brownlee, 'The Heir Apparency of Gamal Mubarak,' *Arab Studies Journal* (Fall 2007–Spring 2008), pp. 36–56.

In both Indonesia and Egypt, the final decades of military strongman rule fuelled significant social and political change. In both countries, visible signs of religious piety became more prevalent in the public sphere, and Islamic organizations began to assume more prominent positions in social and political life. In Indonesia, this trend was recognized and reinforced by the formation of the government-linked All-Indonesian Association of Islamic Intellectuals (ICMI) in 1991.[6] In Egypt, the Muslim Brotherhood increasingly asserted its presence in various professional syndicates in the 1990s and made a dramatic showing in the 2005 parliamentary elections.[7]

Meanwhile, new secular or ecumenical opposition groups also emerged to challenge the two entrenched dictatorships. Under the leadership of former president Soekarno's daughter, Megawati Soekarnoputri, the *Partai Demokrasi Indonesia* (PDI) performed strongly in the 1992 elections, whereas Egypt saw the rise of the *Kifaya!* ('Enough') movement and Ayman Nour's failed presidential bid in 2005.[8] In both countries, however, the entrenched authoritarian regimes stubbornly resisted pressures for political change. In Indonesia, Megawati was forcibly removed from the leadership of the PDI in 1996, considerably diminishing the party's popularity and paving the way for a strengthened showing by Suharto's political machine, *Golkar*, in the parliamentary elections of 1997.[9] In Egypt, heavy-handed electoral fraud, manipulation, restrictions, and vote-buying enabled the ruling National Democratic Party (NDP) and allied independent candidates to win 90 per cent of the seats in parliament, drastically reducing the representation of candidates affiliated with the Muslim Brotherhood and various opposition parties.[10]

---

[6] Robert W. Hefner, 'Islam, State, and Civil Society: ICMI and the Struggle for the Indonesian Middle Class', *Indonesia* 56 (October 1993), pp. 1–35.

[7] Mona El-Ghobashy, 'The Metamorphosis of the Egyptian Muslim Brothers,' *International Journal of Middle Eastern Studies*, Volume 37, Number 3 (August 2005), pp. 373–95; Bruce K. Rutherford, *Egypt after Mubarak: Liberalism, Islam, and Democracy in the Arab World* (Princeton, NJ: Princeton University Press, 2008), pp. 163–90.

[8] Manar Shorbagy, 'The Egyptian Movement for Change – Kefaya: Redefining Politics in Egypt', *Public Culture*, Volume 19, Number 1 (Winter 2007), pp. 175–96; Nadia Oweidat, Cheryl Benard, Dale Stahl, Walid Kildani, Edward O'Connell, and Audra K. Grant, *The Kefaya Movement: A Case Study of a Grassroots Reform Initiative* (Santa Monica, CA: Rand Corporation, 2008); Rabab El-Mahdi, 'Enough! Egypt's Quest for Democracy', *Comparative Political Studies*, Volume 42, Number 8 (August 2009), pp. 1011–39.

[9] Edward Aspinall, *Opposing Suharto: Compromise, Resistance, and Regime Change in Indonesia* (Stanford, CA: Stanford University Press, 2005).

[10] For a careful and insightful study of the significance of parliamentary elections during the Mubarak era, see: Lisa Blaydes, *Elections and Distributive Politics in Mubarak's Egypt*

In both Indonesia and Egypt, the resulting political sclerosis set the stage for eventual mobilization against authoritarian rule in 1998 and 2011, respectively. In both countries, the presidents in office had ruled in autocratic fashion for thirty years without broadening political participation or deepening political institutionalization. As Suharto reached the age of 77 in 1998 and Mubarak turned 83 in 2011, protracted succession crises were already under way, with Suharto's daughter Tutut and Mubarak's son Gamal already moved into leadership positions within the ruling *Golkar* and NDP party machines in anticipation of their ascent to the highest offices in their respective lands. As 1998 unfolded in Indonesia and 2011 opened in Egypt, the two countries were faced with the prospect of inevitable – and rapidly approaching, if not imminent – transfers of power that favoured presidential family members at the expense of broader institutional and economic interests represented within the Suharto and Mubarak regimes.[11]

It was against this backdrop that transitions from authoritarian rule began to unfold in Indonesia in early-mid 1998 and in Egypt in the first weeks of 2011. With electoral challenges foreclosed, ongoing internal succession struggles combined with international economic crises to heighten the sense of urgency and opportunity for new forms of political action. In this context, opposition to the Suharto and Mubarak regimes assumed the form of 'People Power' protests, with university students and other middle-class elements spearheading and sustaining non-violent organizing efforts, even as more disruptive forms of mobilization by the 'dangerous classes' erupted on the streets as well. Thus, April and May 1998 saw mounting student protests – and, in mid-May, mass riots – in Jakarta and other major Indonesian cities, much as January and early February 2011 witnessed growing mobilization in Tahrir Square and other key locations in Cairo and other Egyptian cities. Protesters focussed their grievances and their demands on Suharto and Mubarak, calling on these long-time authoritarian presidents to resign from office. In both Indonesia in 1998 and Egypt in 2011, the entrenched military establishment equivocated, with the Indonesian and Egyptian Armed Forces prioritizing their

---

(Cambridge: Cambridge University Press, 2010). See also: Mohamed Fahmy Menza, *Patronage Politics in Egypt: The National Democratic Party and Muslim Brotherhood in Cairo* (London: Routledge, 2013).

[11] On the succession crisis in Indonesia, see: John T. Sidel, '*Macet Total*: Logics of Circulation and Accumulation in the Demise of Indonesia's New Order', *Indonesia*, Volume 66 (October 1998), pp. 159–95. On Gamal Mubarak in Egypt, see: Alaa Alaswany, *On the State in Egypt: What Caused the Revolution* (Cairo: American University in Cairo Press, 2011), pp. 1–64.

own institutional and economic interests over the personal concerns of the president and, notably, his family. Facing mounting popular protests in the streets and diminishing support from the military establishment, President Suharto resigned in May 1998, much as Hosni Mubarak did in February 2011, with both presidents choosing early retirement under military protection over forced exile overseas. Thus, the broad historical and sociological parallels between Indonesia and Egypt over the previously noted *longue durée* were fairly matched in the specific trajectories of Indonesian and Egyptian political transformation and regime breakdown until the fall of their respective long-time dictatorships.[12]

The parallels between Indonesia and Egypt, moreover, extended into the early aftermath of the fall of Suharto and Mubarak and the uneasy interregnum that ensued. In Indonesia in mid-1998 and Egypt in early 2011, the forced resignation of the long-time dictators did not spell an immediate end to authoritarian rule, as unelected governments remained in office and the military establishments, through their commanding officers, assumed powers and prerogatives – and occupied political space – previously reserved for the nominally civilian long-time strongmen presidents. In both countries, the onset of a regime transition had destabilizing consequences in society, with ongoing and anticipated shifts in power structures undermining established patterns of business influence, criminal activity and organization, and religious structures of authority and identity. Both Indonesia in 1998–99 and Egypt in 2011 thus experienced an upsurge of gang warfare and criminality as well as episodes of inter-religious violence, as seen in Christian-Muslim pogroms in parts of Maluku and Central Sulawesi in early 1999 and attacks on Coptic Christians in Cairo in October 2011. Both Indonesia in 1998–99 and Egypt in 2011, moreover, saw the seemingly unified force of 'People Power' in the streets replaced by more diverse and fragmented forms of street politics in response to the interim governments' stalling and stage-managing of constitutional reform, institutional change, and parliamentary and presidential elections.

In both countries, this uneasy interregnum appeared to draw to a close with the holding of competitive and free elections, the convening of new parliaments, and the – direct or indirect – election of new presidents,

---

[12] On the fall of Suharto, see: Geoff Forrester and R. J. May (eds.), *The Fall of Soeharto* (London: C. Hurst, 1998). On the fall of Mubarak, see: Jeannie Sowers and Chris Toensing (eds.), *The Journey to Tahrir: Revolution, Protest, and Social Change in Egypt* (London: Verso, 2012).

a series of events that unfolded in mid-late 1999 in Indonesia and in late 2011 and early-mid 2012 in Egypt. In contrast with the praetorian 'People Power' moment that had forced the resignation of Suharto in May 1998 and Mubarak in February 2011, these processes promised the institutionalization of a democratic mechanism for political change and thus the reassuring prospect of demobilization and demilitarization, shifting politics from the streets and barracks to the realm of political opinion surveys, polling stations, parliamentary debates, and presidential policy initiatives. For the advocates of *Reformasi* in Indonesia in 1998 and the avowed supporters of *Al Thawra* (The Revolution) in Egypt in 2011, this shift to electoral politics spelled the limits of genuine political change. For businessmen and other more conservative forces in Indonesian and Egyptian society, the 'institutionalization of uncertainty' through elections was welcomed as offering a potential basis for the restoration of social order, political stability, and economic recovery and growth.

But in both Indonesia in 1999–2001 and Egypt in 2012–13, the electoralization of politics also conjured up new forms of anxiety, without resolving key ambiguities and uncertainties created by the forced resignations of Suharto and Mubarak and the messy interregnum that had ensued in their aftermath. In both countries, parliamentary and presidential elections elevated Islamic parties and politicians to positions of unprecedented prominence and power, as the infrastructure of Islamic social institutions provided unique bases for nationwide political networks in the new context of genuinely open and free electoral competition for state power. In Indonesia, Islamic parties won nearly 40 per cent of seats in parliament, a former head of the leading Islamic university student association *HMI* (and leader of the second-largest non-Islamic party) was named speaker of parliament, the head of the 'modernist' Islamic association *Muhammadiyah* was named to lead the supra-parliamentary People's Consultative Assembly (MPR), and chairman of the 'traditionalist' Islamic association *Nadhlatul Ulama*, Abdurrahman Wahid, was elevated to the presidency in October 1999. Egyptian parliamentary and presidential elections in late 2011 and early-mid 2012 followed similar lines. The Muslim Brotherhood's Freedom and Justice Party won 47 per cent of the parliamentary vote, with the Salafi-led *Al-Nour* party claiming an additional 23 per cent. One former member of the Guidance Bureau of the Muslim Brotherhood was elected as Speaker of the National Assembly, and, in June 2012, another member, Freedom and Justice Party head Mohamed Morsi, was popularly elected to the presidency.

In both countries, moreover, the ascension to the presidency of representatives of prominent Islamic associations led to increasing anxieties and uncertainties as to the prospects for the stabilization and consolidation of democracy. In Indonesia in 1999–2001, Wahid's moves to replace senior military officers and to impose reforms on the Indonesian Armed Forces ran up against considerable resentment and resistance from the military establishment. Wahid's efforts to assert presidential powers and prerogatives vis-à-vis the diverse political parties in parliament (who had supported his elevation to the presidency in October 1999), moreover, led to rising accusations of corruption and abuse of power, parliamentary censure of the president and moves to unseat him, a clumsy attempt by Wahid to seize emergency powers, and his forced resignation in July 2001, with Vice President Megawati Soekarnoputri assuming the presidency in his stead. In Egypt, Morsi's moves to assert control over the Armed Forces, his decrees arrogating special supra-judicial powers for the presidency, and his promotion of a controversial Constitution have likewise isolated his administration, galvanized the opposition, and renewed fears of military intervention in the political arena. In today's Egypt, as in Indonesia in 1999–2001, there is thus considerable anxiety and uncertainty about the role of Islam in politics, the aggregation and abuse of power by elected civilian presidents, and the continuing political prerogatives of the military establishment. Overall, as of January 2013, Egypt's past and Egypt's present were in many ways strikingly similar to those of Indonesia up through the early post-authoritarian context of 1999–2001.[13]

Democratization in Indonesia since 1998: Implications for Egypt?

If Egypt is so similar to Indonesia, and if the transition from authoritarian rule to democracy in Egypt has, so far, been so 'Indonesian', then what do the years from 1999–2012 in Indonesia portend for the future of democratization in Egypt in the years ahead? How seriously should we take all the alarmism today about the various dangers said to be threatening democratization in Egypt?

First of all, the trajectory of Indonesian politics since 1999 suggests that the putative dangers attributed to the rise of Islamic parties and politicians in Egypt today are likely to be grossly inflated and exaggerated. In

---

[13] For a detailed and well-documented chronicle of major developments and trends in early post-Suharto Indonesia, see: Kees van Dijk, *A Country in Despair: Indonesia Between 1997 and 2000* (Leiden: KITLV Press, 2001).

Indonesia, it is worth recalling, Suharto's resignation was followed by the ascension to the presidency of his Vice President B. J. Habibie, the founder and chairman of the All-Indonesia Association of Islamic Intellectuals (ICMI), an umbrella organization founded in 1991 that served as a major patronage network for Muslim politicians and a source of protection and support for diverse Islamist causes and groups in the late Suharto years. As previously noted, moreover, the 1999 parliamentary elections saw parties rooted in Islamic organizations winning nearly 35 per cent of the vote, and the new speaker of parliament, the new chairman of the supra-parliamentary MPR (*Majelis Permusyawaratan Rakyat* or People's Consultative Assembly), and the new president were all closely associated with leading Islamic associations as well. In subsequent parliamentary elections in 2004 and 2009, Islamic parties continued to claim a quarter to a third of the electorate and a roughly commensurate position in parliamentary politics. Yet, the past thirteen years have also seen these Islamic parties failing to coalesce, to grow, or (since 2001) to achieve success for Islamic candidates for the presidency. At the same time, even the most stridently Islamist of these parties have abandoned efforts to demand constitutional change in favor of Sharia law and concentrated their energies instead on coalition politics with non-Islamic politicians and parties. These diverse Islamic parties have assiduously cultivated alliances with successive presidents to win seats in Cabinet, while actively fundraising and recruiting from amongst major businessmen and machine politicians in order to strengthen their campaigns. Even the supposedly puritanical Prosperous Justice Party (*Partai Keadilan Sejahtera* or PKS) has been absorbed into and infested by 'money politics'.[14]

Thus, thirteen years of parliamentary politics has meant thirteen years of compromise, coalition building, cooptation, and corruption for Islamic parties and politicians, rather than aggressive or effective promotion of Islam. This outcome has reflected not only the limits of popular support and electoral success for parties rooted in Islamic organizations and avowedly Islamist aspirations, but also the inevitable diversity, fragmentation, and fractiousness of political parties claiming to represent Muslims in a populous country notable for pluralism of religious practices, education, and associational life. Thus, 'Islamic' parties in Indonesia have ranged from the National Awakening Party (PKB or *Partai Kebangkitan Bangsa*) with a base in the 'traditionalist' Islamic boarding

---

[14] Syahrul Hidayat, 'Managing the Impact of Moderation: The AKP in Turkey and the PKS in Indonesia' (Ph.D. Thesis, University of Exeter, 2012).

schools (*pesantren*) of *Nahdlatul Ulama* across rural Java, to the National
Mandate Party (PAN or *Partai Amanat Nasional*) with its roots in the
'modernist' *Muhammadiyah* association, to the Prosperous Justice Party
(PKS or *Partai Keadilan Sejahtera*) founded and led by more puritanical Islamic university student activists of the 1980s and 1990s, and the
United Development Party (PPP or *Partai Persatuan Pembangunan*) that
served as the sole Islamic party in the elections of the Suharto era and has
retained some of its pseudo-populist pretensions and its political machinery. But the inexorable decline if not of Islamic parties, then of Islam as
a distinctive basis for parliamentary politics in Indonesia over the past
thirteen years has also stemmed from the 'parliamentarization' of politics
itself. As parties originally rooted in Islamic organizations and oriented
towards Islamist aspirations have competed – and cooperated – with non-
Islamic parties in elections, in parliament, and in presidential cabinets in
successive administrations, they have been compelled not only to reach
compromises on matters of religious principle, but also to recalibrate
relations with their constituencies, shifting away from linkages based on
notions of religious community and structures of religious authority, and
building new linkages based on delivery of public goods and popular policies, as well as rent-seeking activities and patron-client relations instead.
The imperatives of coalition politics, of campaign financing, and of competition for constituencies, votes, and parliamentary and cabinet seats in
democratic Indonesia have produced not only what some analysts celebrate as 'moderation' of Islamic parties, but also 'regression towards the
mean' of money and machine politics as well.[15]

Second, the broader trends in Indonesian society since 1999 have likewise suggested that the more generalized fears about religious violence
and sectarian conflict in Egypt today may be considerably overblown.[16]
The localized anti-Chinese riots that took place in Indonesia in the mid-
1990s disappeared after Suharto's fall in 1998, and the Muslim-Christian
violence that erupted in Maluku and Central Sulawesi in early 1999 ran

[15] Edward Aspinall, 'Elections and the Normalization of Politics in Indonesia', *South East Asia Research*, Volume 13, Number 2 (July 2005), pp. 117–56; Kikue Hamayotsu, 'The End of Political Islam? A Comparative Analysis of Religious Parties in the Mus-lim Democracy of Indonesia', *Journal of Current Southeast Asian Affairs*, Volume 30, Number 3 (December 2011), pp. 133–59.
[16] For background on the Coptic minority in Egypt, see: Mariz Tadros, 'Vicissitudes in the Entente between the Coptic Orthodox Church and the State in Egypt (1952–2007)', *International Journal of Middle East Studies*, Volume 41, Number 2 (May 2009), pp. 269–87; and Elizabeth Iskander, *Sectarian Conflict in Egypt: Coptic Media, Identity and Representation* (London: Routledge, 2012).

its course by the end of 2001. Today, ethnic-Chinese Indonesians enjoy far greater freedom from discrimination, harassment, and persecution than ever before, and, by and large, Christians across Indonesia likewise practice their faith with few real fears or restrictions.[17] To be sure, 2002–05 saw some Islamist terrorist activity (a single bombing attack on a foreign target each year), and since 2005 some Islamist groups have waged a campaign of persecution against "deviant" Muslim sects such as the Ahmadis. The Islamic parties succeeded in passing an anti-pornography law in 2008, and some local assemblies have passed new regulations supposedly inspired by Islamic law. But all in all, Indonesian society under democracy today is more pluralistic and liberal than it ever was under authoritarian rule. Even activists fighting for the rights of gay, lesbian, and transgender Indonesians have claimed real progress over the past decade and see bright prospects for the years ahead.[18]

These trends in religious violence and conflict have reflected not only the declining organizational power and political influence of forces mobilized in the name of Islam over the past thirteen years, but also shifts in the structures of religious boundaries, identities, and hierarchies of authority accompanying the transition from authoritarian rule and the consolidation of oligarchical democracy in Indonesia. With the fall of Suharto came destabilization of the centralized structures of authority that had underpinned not only the organization of state power, but also the allocation of monopoly franchises and concessions to businessmen, the awarding of 'protection' to gangsters, and the according of recognition to leaders of various churches and Islamic associations. Without any stable centralized source of authority and recognition, those who claimed to represent Islam and Muslims in Indonesia experienced new uncertainties and anxieties as to the nature and extent of their religious authority, much as their counterparts in Protestant and (perhaps to a lesser extent) Catholic churches did at the same time. It was against this backdrop that the uneasy interregnum between the 'People Power' moment leading to Suharto's forced resignation in May 1998 and the elections of June 1999 saw the unfolding of myriad 'turf wars' between rival urban street gangs, anti-witchcraft campaigns in the remote highlands of rural Java, and rising tensions between competing networks of local businessmen, bureaucrats,

---

[17] John T. Sidel, *Indonesia: Minorities, Migrant Workers, Refugees, and the New Citizenship Law* (Geneva: United Nations High Commissioner for Refugees, March 2007).

[18] On these trends, see the various fine essays in Greg Fealy and Sally White (eds.), *Expressing Islam: Religious Life and Politics in Indonesia* (Singapore: Institute of Southeast Asian Studies, 2009).

politicians, gangsters, and retired and active military and police officers in regencies (*kabupaten*) and provinces around the country. In some localities – Ambon, the capital of Maluku and Poso, in Central Sulawesi – where these rival networks were divided along religious lines, and where Protestant and Muslim residents were in rough demographic and electoral parity, such tensions developed into full-blown inter-religious pogroms, with hundreds killed and tens of thousands forcibly displaced over the course of 1999, 2000, and 2001.[19]

But if the onset of transition from authoritarian rule enabled and impelled the irruption of inter-religious violence in Indonesia at the turn of the twenty-first century, the consolidation of democracy facilitated if not forced the demilitarization and demobilization of sectarian conflict over the course of the subsequent decade. In Jakarta, the influence of non-Muslim minorities in parliament, in the Armed Forces, and vis-à-vis the president eventually led to armed intervention and the imposition of a cessation of inter-religious hostilities. On the local level, moreover, the election of new local assemblies and of new mayors, regents (*bupati*), and governors combined with new opportunities for gerrymandering and the creation of new districts and provinces (*pemekaran*) to encourage power-sharing arrangements and the division of the spoils of local office between Protestant and Muslim political-cum-business networks, even in conflict-torn areas like Maluku and Poso.[20]

Meanwhile, successive local and national elections worked to undermine confidence in 'the Muslim vote' and in the claims of Islamic parties and politicians to represent Muslims in Indonesia in a coherent, compelling, and consistent fashion. This trend in the arena of parliamentary politics arguably opened up new possibilities for extra-electoral efforts to assert claims not to represent Indonesian Muslims, but to represent Islam in Indonesia, whether through terrorist violence as seen in 2002–05, or through vigilante-style campaigns of harassment, intimidation, and violence against the threats to Islam allegedly posed by Christian proselytization, immorality (e.g., alcohol consumption, gambling, pornography, and prostitution), and 'deviant sects' within the faith. Thus, the past several years have witnessed episodic attacks on brothels and gambling casinos, Christian churches, and Ahmadiyya mosques, along with sporadic

---

[19] John T. Sidel, *Riots, Pogroms, Jihad: Religious Violence in Indonesia* (Ithaca, NY: Cornell University Press, 2006), pp. 132–95.

[20] *Indonesia: The Search for Peace in Maluku* (Jakarta/Brussels: International Crisis Group, February 2002); *Indonesia: Managing Decentralization and Conflict in South Sulawesi* (Jakarta/Brussels: International Crisis Group, July 2003).

efforts by various actors – not all of them 'Islamist' – to impose local government regulations (*perda*) allegedly inspired by Sharia law, as well as restrictions on various forms of perceived religious deviance and immorality.[21] But overall, such much-publicized activism in the name of Islam has been waged largely as a rear-guard action in the face of the downsizing of Islamic agendas and ambitions in government, the deterioration of Islamic political parties, the declining influence of established Islamic associations and the diminishing fixity and force of any one source of religious authority in the face of democratization, decentralization, and the continuing liberalization of Indonesian economic, cultural, and social life.[22]

Third and finally, Indonesia's experience since 1999 has also demonstrated that there are more serious threats to democratic institutions and practices from other quarters than those associated with Islam. Since the overthrow of Suharto in 1998, the Indonesian military establishment has remained largely insulated from outside scrutiny. The Armed Forces has retained many of its business interests, its huge off-budget sources of finance, and its considerable freedom from external scrutiny in the procurement of weaponry and materiel. Thirteen years after the fall of Suharto, the Armed Forces still enjoys effective impunity for human rights abuses, the Army retains its territorial command structure down to the local level across the archipelago, and the military establishment as a whole commands substantial residual political influence.[23] Today, the President of Indonesia is a retired Army general – (Retired) Lieutenant General Susilo Bambang Yudhoyono (2004–14) – and many other retired military officers occupy positions of real prominence and power in Indonesian politics and society. As of this writing, the leading candidate for the Indonesian presidency in the 2014 elections is another

---

[21] *Indonesia: Implications of the Ahmadiyah Decree* (Jakarta/Brussels: International Crisis Group, July 2008); *Indonesia: 'Christianisation' and Intolerance* (Jakarta/Brussels: International Crisis Group, November 2010); Michael Buehler, 'The Rise of Shari'a By-Laws in Indonesian Districts', *South East Asia Research*, Volume 16, Number 2 (July 2008), pp. 255–85.

[22] John T. Sidel, 'The Changing Politics of Religious Knowledge in Asia: The Case of Indonesia', in Saw Swee-Hock and Danny Quah (eds.), *The Politics of Knowledge* (Singapore: Institute of Southeast Asian Studies, 2009), pp. 156–92.

[23] See: Marcus Mietzner, *Military Politics, Islam, and the State in Indonesia: From Turbulent Transition to Democratic Consolidation* (Singapore: Institute of Southeast Asian Studies, 2009), especially pp. 195–250, 360–83; Marcus Mietzner, *The Politics of Military Reform in Post-Suharto Indonesia: Elite Conflict, Nationalism, and Institutional Resistance* (Washington, DC: East-West Center, 2006).

former Army general. Overall, democratization has yet to lead to a full demilitarization of political life in the country.

Meanwhile, with the establishment of competitive elections, parliamentary rule, and a directly elected presidency, Indonesia has experienced the consolidation of a decidedly oligarchical form of democracy. On the one hand, as previously suggested, the vast agencies of the Indonesian state – most obviously its coercive apparatuses – have retained considerable autonomy from democratic control. The vestiges of the authoritarian 'deep state' include not only the Indonesian Armed Forces, but also the Indonesian Police, the State Intelligence Agency, and the court system, where a 'judicial mafia' is said to remain deeply entrenched.[24] In recent years, much publicized evidence of rampant rent-seeking within the ministries of education, health, and religious affairs has demonstrated the continuing insulation of the bureaucracy from external pressure and scrutiny, even as myriad state enterprises and state-owned landholdings still loom large in the national economy. On a local level, the remarkable success of career civil servants in winning elected executive positions as *bupati* (regent), *walikota* (mayor), and *gubernur* in *kabupaten* (regencies), cities, and provinces across the country has attested to their privileged control over state personnel and patronage, and to the relative importance of state-based resources vis-à-vis those in the private sector in the mustering of campaign funds and the mobilization of voters.[25]

On the other hand, the past thirteen years have witnessed the continuing entrenchment of an oligarchy of interlocking private business interests that have succeeded in penetrating, capturing, or otherwise exerting considerable influence over political parties, parliament, and pockets of the bureaucracy. The costs of campaign financing have encouraged all political parties – and presidential candidates – to solicit donations from businessmen, to support businessmen as candidates for local and national offices, and to engage in assiduous efforts to provide assistance and advantages to favoured business interests through the discretionary use of state power.[26] Meanwhile, the costs of purchasing entry to, and ascending within, the bureaucracy have also encouraged many civil servants,

---

[24] Edward Aspinall and Gerry van Klinken (eds.), *The State and Illegality in Indonesia* (Leiden: KITLV Press, 2011).

[25] Marcus Mietzner, 'Soldiers, Parties, and Bureaucrats: Illicit Fund-Raising in Contemporary Indonesia', *South East Asia Research*, Volume 16, Number 2 (July 2008), pp. 225–54.

[26] Marcus Mietzner, 'Party-Financing in Post-Soeharto Indonesia: Between State Subsidies and Political Corruption', *Contemporary Southeast Asia*, Volume 29, Number 2 (August 2007), pp. 238–63.

police and military officers to find businessmen 'sponsors', thus further facilitating privileged access to and influence over the myriad agents and agencies of the Indonesian state on the basis of private wealth and personal connections. Overall, the past thirteen years in Indonesia have seen the consolidation of an oligarchic form of democracy, highly corrupt and hardly responsive to growing problems of social inequality and injustice across the country.[27]

Against this backdrop of democratization and discontents in Indonesia from 1998–2012, an Indonesian future for Egyptian democracy is all too easy to envisage, both for better and for worse. Indeed, to date, Egypt has begun to follow Indonesia's trajectory, with President Mohamed Morsi working hard to extend his authority vis-à-vis the military establishment, much as 1998–2001 witnessed a protracted power struggle between presidents B. J. Habibie (1998–99) and Abdurrahman Wahid (1999–2001) and the leadership of the Indonesian Armed Forces. At the same time, as Egypt has begun to follow Indonesia's trajectory, Morsi's tenure in office has to date been marked by the president's difficulties assuaging Coptic Christian, liberal, and secular fears of Islamist ascendancy, on the one hand, and tensions and conflict with Salafi groups calling for Islamism, on the other hand, much as Abdurrahman Wahid faced during the height of inter-religious violence in Indonesia in 1999–2001. If Egypt continues to follow Indonesia's trajectory, moreover, the presidency of Mohamed Morsi will mark not only the apogee of political influence for the Muslim Brotherhood in Egypt, but also the limits of civilian success in extending democratic control over the military establishment and the Egyptian state, much as 1998–2001 served as a narrow window of opportunity for presidents Habibie and Wahid to reduce the political powers of the Indonesian Armed Forces and to implement limited democratic reforms. Meanwhile, as Egypt has begun to follow Indonesia's trajectory so far, Morsi's presidency has faced rising dissatisfaction with the limitations of political change and economic recovery, and disillusionment with the compromises and allegations of incompetence and abuse of power that have haunted his administration, much as was seen in Indonesia in 1998–2001 under the notoriously 'mercurial' Habibie and the infamously 'erratic' Wahid.

---

[27] Richard Robison and Vedi R. Hadiz, *Reorganising Power in Indonesia: The Politics of Oligarchy in an Age of Markets* (London: Routledge, 2004); Dan Slater, 'Accountability Trap: Party Cartels and Presidential Power after Democratic Transition,' *Indonesia*, Volume 78 (October 2004 , pp. 611–92; Marcus Mietzner, 'Indonesia's Democratic Stagnation: Anti-Reformist Elites and Resilient Civil Society', *Democratization*, Volume 19, Number 2 (April 2012), pp. 209–29.

In years to come, if Egypt continues to follow Indonesia's post-authoritarian trajectory, the administration of Morsi may be followed by a marked retrenchment in democratization in Egypt, much as unfolded in Indonesia after Abdurrahman Wahid's forced removal from the presidency in Indonesia in mid-2001. The enactment of a new Egyptian constitution in November 2012 sets the stage for a new round of parliamentary and presidential elections that could see fragmentation and decline in the strength of parties and presidential candidates backed by the Muslim Brotherhood and Salafi groups, and a commensurate regrouping and restrengthening of conservative political forces associated with the remnants (*feloul*) of the ancien régime, the 'deep state', and the business class, relying on money and machinery for mobilizing voters and (re)capturing parliament and the presidency. In this 'Indonesian' scenario, a second round of civilian political turnover would signal the 'consolidation' of Egyptian democracy, even as the Armed Forces would continue to enjoy informal power and prerogatives for years to come, with the military budget and economic interests, and both internal security and foreign policy, considerably insulated from civilian democratic control. In this 'Indonesian' scenario, the politics of the street (including the dimension of inter-religious conflict) would belatedly give way to what we might call the 'parliamentarization' of political life, with elections and political parties serving as the sole effective channels for popular participation and for access to state power and influence on state policy. In this 'Indonesian' scenario, Islamic parties and politicians in Egypt would remain strong, but suffer from increasing fragmentation and fractiousness, and coalition-building and corruption would inexorably erode the transformative potential of religion. Overall, the years ahead would see the entrenchment of an oligarchic democracy in Egypt, one in which money and machinery predominate in the electoral realm, business interests prevail in economic policy, and the military establishment and other fixtures of the 'deep state' would preserve their impunity and insulation from civilian democratic control and scrutiny. Perhaps in this 'Indonesian' scenario, Egypt would even see the rise to the presidency of a former Armed Forces general, much as Indonesia has seen with (Retired) Lieutenant General Susilo Bambang Yudhoyono from 2004 through the present day.

Egyptian Idiosyncrasies and Departures from the Indonesian Model?

Needless to say, however, Indonesia and Egypt also differ in important ways that suggest both predictions and explanations for Egyptian deviations from the Indonesian trajectory of democratization. By early 2013, some of these differences had already become evident insofar as Egypt departed from the Indonesian script over the two years since the fall of Mubarak. A close analysis of Egyptian deviations from the Indonesian script to date reveals the significance of differences in the institutional forms of state power under authoritarian rule and in the early phases of transition to democracy, differences that may spell further departures in Egypt's democratic trajectory in the months and years to come.

First of all, the military establishment assumed a much more prominent and problematic role in the early phase of transition from authoritarian rule to democracy in Egypt as compared with Indonesia. In Indonesia, the withdrawal of military support forced Suharto's resignation in May 1998, and under the two short-lived presidencies of B. J. Habibie (1998–99) and Abdurrahman Wahid (1999–2001), the Armed Forces enjoyed considerable success in resisting and restricting efforts to diminish its political powers and prerogatives, and to expand civilian and democratic control over the coercive apparatuses of the state. Thus, the Army retained its territorial command structure; senior Army officers moved into positions of great prominence and power in parliament, the cabinet, and, in due course, the presidency; and the military as an institution preserved many of its economic interests and much of its insulation from civilian democratic oversight. But at no point did the military as an institution occupy the position of a military as government, or effectively undo civilian-led initiatives producing political change. From Suharto's choice of vice president in March 1998 to the circumstances of his resignation in May 1998, from Habibie's ascension to the vice presidency in May 1998 to his decision to offer a referendum on independence to the people of East Timor, from the parliamentary elections of June 1999 to the elevation of Abdurrahman Wahid to the presidency in October 1999 – all the major turning points in this early post-authoritarian interregnum saw civilian initiatives encountering military ambivalence or antagonism, stimulating military foot-dragging and rear-guard sabotage, but winning military acquiescence in the end.[28]

By contrast, the military establishment in Egypt played a more coherent, decisive, and proactive role in the developments and trends from the beginning of 2011 through mid-2012, not only defending the interests of the military as an institution, but imposing the military as government

---

[28] Mietzner, *Military Politics, Islam, and the State in Indonesia*, pp. 195–250; Mietzner, *The Politics of Military Reform in Post-Suharto Indonesia*.

as well. Convened in the final weeks of the Mubarak presidency, the Supreme Council of the Armed Forces (SCAF) continued to exercise legislative and executive powers even in the aftermath of the parliamentary and presidential elections of late 2011 and early-mid 2012. Well into August 2012, SCAF's proclaimed prerogatives and perceived powers continued to loom large over newly elected president Mohamed Morsi's efforts to form a cabinet and otherwise exert his authority, and over ongoing efforts to draft a new constitution. Through SCAF's decrees, the military establishment very actively and openly moved to narrow the parameters of democratization in Egypt, far more than the Armed Forces did during the early post-Suharto years in Indonesia.

This Egyptian deviation from the aforementioned Indonesian trajectory should be understood in the light of important institutional differences between the military establishments under authoritarian rule in the two countries. Both Indonesia and in Egypt, to be sure, experienced decades of centralized authoritarian rule under the presidency of a retired senior military officer, in which the military as an institution enjoyed not only considerable impunity and insulation from external oversight, but also enormous privileges, powers, and prerogatives in the realms of business, on the one hand, and civilian administration on the other hand. In both Indonesia and Egypt, the military establishment came to own and operate a vast, diversified corporate empire and to enjoy enormous off-budget sources of finance, even as senior military officers came to occupy manifold positions of 'civilian' power as ministers, provincial governors, and directors of government agencies. But in Indonesia in the Suharto era, the military's own economic interests were increasingly dwarfed by the expansion and growth of diversified private business conglomerates, even as senior Armed Forces officers were increasingly drawn into civilian patronage networks rooted inside and outside the state. This trend was enabled and impelled by Suharto's strictly enforced retirement policies, which compelled Army generals to leave active service at the age of fifty-five and to seek higher office within the civilian realm, whether as members of parliament, cabinet ministers, heads of government agencies, ambassadors, or provincial governors, even as more junior officers sought similar 'pension schemes' at lower levels in the state hierarchy.[29] By the end of the Suharto era, this trend had taken its toll on the Armed Forces leadership, with the most senior officers known to be very intimately

---

[29] John A. MacDougall, 'Patterns of Military Control in the Indonesian Higher Bureaucracy', *Indonesia*, Volume 33 (April 1982), pp. 89–121.

affiliated with the president, members of his family, or other highly influential civilian figures in the regime.[30]

This pattern of steady, relentless circulation, rotation, promotion, and retirement in the Indonesian Armed Forces prevented the consolidation of power in the hands of a military strongman or military junta in the aftermath of the fall of Suharto in May 1998. Even in the midst of all the political turmoil of the early post-Suharto era, Armed Forces officers continued to rise through the ranks year after year, and to 'retire' into civilian positions of power, privilege, and prestige.[31] With the transformation from centralized authoritarian rule to decentralized democracy, retiring military officers thus shifted from alignments with rival factions within the regime to affiliations with rival powerbrokers and political parties in parliament. Thus, individual former senior military officers rose to prominent positions within a number of political parties, won seats in the national parliament or positions in local government, and, in a few cases, founded their own political parties and launched campaigns – in Susilo Bambang Yudhoyono's case, successfully – for the presidency. In this way, the military as an institution succeeded not in actively entrenching itself as a military government, but rather in restricting and retarding the continuing diminution of its political powers and prerogatives as democratization proceeded after 1998.

In Egypt, by contrast, the military establishment continued to preserve its economic interests and institutional autonomy far more effectively under Mubarak than the Indonesian Armed Forces had done under Suharto, thus spelling much greater cohesion, coherence, and coercive power under the Supreme Council of the Armed Forces (SCAF) in the face of the ongoing transition from authoritarian rule to democracy. The vast, diversified business empire of the Egyptian Armed Forces continued to remain effectively impervious to external scrutiny and to retain a sizable share of the country's economy as a whole even as Egypt underwent extensive economic liberalization in the 1990s and 2000s, thus preserving more of a fiscal and social basis for autonomy than the Indonesian Armed Forces could claim in the face of economic reforms in the 1980s and a private investment boom of the early-mid 1990s in Indonesia. Instead of steady turnover within the armed services and 'retirement' into

---

[30] Sidel, 'Macet Total'.

[31] Douglas Kammen and Siddharth Chandra, *A Tour of Duty: Changing Patterns of Military Politics in Indonesia in the 1990s* (Ithaca, NY: Cornell University Southeast Asia Program, 1999).

civilian-led pillars of an authoritarian regime as in Suharto's Indonesia, the Egyptian Armed Forces combined extensive business interests of its own and extensive control over key cabinet ministries, government agencies, and provincial governorships with extended service by its senior officers, as witnessed in the long tenure of Field Marshal Muhamed Hussein Tantawi as minister of defense from 1991 through the end of the Mubarak era in early 2011. Up until early-mid August 2012, SCAF was thus led by a septuagenarian (the seventy-seven-year-old Tantawi) and a set of sixty-something service commanders and other senior officers. The contrast with Indonesia in late 1999, when the supposed military 'strongman' of the early post-Suharto era, General Wiranto, gave up his posts as Armed Forces Commander and Defense Minister at the age of fifty-five, could not be more striking. Compared to the Indonesian Armed Forces, it is clear that the Egyptian military has greater cohesion and capacity as an institution to retain its economic interests, its insulation from external control and scrutiny, and to resist ongoing pressures for democratization and demilitarization. Even President Morsi's decisive, dramatic, and much-debated removal of Tantawi, reshuffle of the military leadership, and revocation of SCAF's executive and legislative authority in early-mid August 2012 represented only an initial, exploratory effort to assert civilian control over the enormous, still well insulated, and seemingly impenetrable military establishment.[32]

Additionally, the key civilian parliamentary pillar of authoritarian rule in Egypt, Mubarak's National Democratic Party (NDP), has proven far weaker than its Indonesian counterpart, Suharto's *Golkar* (*Golongan Karya* or Functional Groups), as a bulwark for continuity and conservatism in the context of a transition to democracy. The protests in Cairo in early 2011 led to the destruction of the NDP national headquarters, the party was subsequently dissolved, and former NDP politicians faced legal and other obstacles to participation in the parliamentary elections

[32] Imad Harb, 'The Egyptian Military in Politics: Disengagement or Accommodation?', *Middle East Journal*, Volume 57, Number 2 (Spring 2003), pp. 269–90; Steven A. Cook, *Ruling but not Governing: The Military and Political Development in Egypt, Algeria, and Turkey* (Baltimore: Johns Hopkins University Press, 2007); Ahmed S. Hashim, 'The Egyptian Military, Part One: From the Ottomans through Sadat', *Middle East Policy*, Volume 18, Number 3 (Fall 2011), pp. 63–78; Ahmed S. Hashim, 'The Egyptian Military, Part Two: From Mubarak Onward', *Middle East Policy*, Volume 18, Number 4 (Winter 2011), pp. 106–28; Yezid Sayigh, *Above the State: The Officers' Republic in Egypt* (Washington, DC: Carnegie Endowment for International Peace, August 2012); and Hazem Kandil, *Soldiers, Spies, and Statesmen: Egypt's Road to Revolt* (London: Verso, 2012).

later the same year, thus enabling a 'critical realignment' in Egyptian party politics. By contrast, leading Golkar politicians in Parliament belatedly called for the resignation of President Suharto in Jakarta in May 1998, embraced the ascension of Habibie (a major Golkar powerbroker) to the presidency, and endorsed his favoured candidate as the party's new chairman in June of the same year. In the parliamentary elections of 1999, Golkar captured 22 per cent of the vote, second only to the *Partai Demokrasi Indonesia – Perjuangan* (Indonesian Democractic Party of Struggle [PDIP]) with 34 per cent, thus positioning itself to play a major role in the coalition of parties electing Abdurrahman Wahid as president in October of that year and to win key cabinet seats in his administration. Subsequent parliamentary elections have seen Golkar continuing to perform as strongly in a very fragmented field of competition; its 20–22 per cent of the popular vote consistently landing it amongst the top two parties in successive elections over the years and winning the party key cabinet seats in successive administrations.[33]

For a number of reasons, the NDP has not been fated to follow Golkar in this trajectory of post-authoritarian survival and success. Although Golkar enjoyed deep institutional roots in the bureaucracy and the Armed Forces in the early Suharto era and the party opened its ranks to private businessmen and Islamic activists in the late 1980s and early-mid 1990s, the NDP remained a weakly institutionalized rubric for patronage and, over the final decade of the Mubarak era, evolved into a vehicle for the launching of Gamal Mubarak's campaign to succeed his father as president of Egypt.[34] Against this backdrop, the forced resignation of Mubarak in early 2011 left business and other conservative elements associated with the former regime without an effective nationwide political machine through which to protect and promote their interests under conditions of competitive democratic elections, such as Golkar provided in Indonesia in 1999 and beyond. Thus, even as the military establishment demonstrated far greater staying power in Cairo in 2011–12 as

---

[33] Dirk Tomsa, *Party Politics and Democratization in Indonesia: Golkar in the Post-Suharto Era* (London: Routledge, 2008).

[34] Blaydes, *Elections and Distributive Politics in Mubarak's Egypt*, pp. 125–47; Rutherford, *Egypt after Mubarak*, pp. 218–24; Stacher, *Adaptable Autocrats*, pp. 98–107; Tarek Osman, *Egypt on the Brink: From the Rise of Nasser to the Fall of Mubarak* (New Haven, CT: Yale University Press, 2011), pp. 127–57; Mohammed Zahid, *The Muslim Brotherhood and Egypt's Succession Crisis: The Politics of Liberalisation and Reform in the Middle East* (London: I. B. Tauris, 2010), pp. 129–74; Fahmy, *Patronage Politics in Egypt*; and Sophie Pommier, 'Égypte: Le Parti National Démocratique au Coeur du Dispositif de Succession', *Politique Étrangère*, Volume 1 (2007), pp. 67–78.

compared with Jakarta in 1998–99, it did so without commensurately strong representation of civilian remnants (*feloul*) of authoritarian rule in the parliamentary arena, thus associating the shift from authoritarian rule to democracy with far greater electoral realignment and effective political change in Egypt as compared with Indonesia.

Finally, the role of Islamic associations and political parties in the ongoing transition to democracy in Egypt has proven even more prominent and powerful than was the case in Indonesia after the fall of Suharto. In large measure, this difference can be attributed to diverging patterns in the evolution of dominant party organizations, on the one hand, and in the engagement with autonomous Islamic associations, on the other hand, under authoritarian rule. In Indonesia, the final decade of the Suharto era witnessed various efforts to co-opt *Nahdlatul Ulama* and *Muhammadiyah*, and to incorporate into *Golkar*, parliament, the Cabinet, and other senior echelons of the bureaucracy (including the Armed Forces), upwardly mobile Muslim businessmen, civil servants, military officers, and professionals educated under the umbrella of these major Islamic associations. These efforts were reinforced by the formation in 1991 of the All-Indonesia Association of Islamic Intellectuals (ICMI) under the chairmanship of long-time Suharto associate and Minister for Research and Technology B. J. Habibie, who used ICMI to create a vast patronage network that stretched from the cabinet, *Golkar*, the parliament, and the Armed Forces into the business world and the ranks of various Islamic organizations.[35]

This co-optation strategy, which culminated in the elevation of Habibie to the vice presidency in March 1998, had fateful consequences not only for Suharto, but also for post-Suharto Indonesia. In May 1998, Islamic organizations and activists linked to ICMI loomed large amongst the anti-Suharto protesters in the streets of Jakarta, even as Muslim politicians affiliated with Habibie were prominent amongst those submitting their cabinet resignations or calling for Suharto's resignation from the floor of the national parliament. Thus, Habibie's assumption of the presidency in late May 1998 was met with acceptance if not enthusiasm both by elements within the ancien régime and by many of the organizations and activists who had mobilized in the anti-Suharto protests

[35] Hefner, 'Islam, State, and Civil Society'; Takashi Shiraishi, 'Rewiring the Indonesian State', in Daniel S. Lev and Ruth McVey (eds.), *Making Indonesia: Essays on Modern Indonesia in Honor of George McT. Kahin* (Ithaca, NY: Cornell University Southeast Asia Program, 1996), pp. 164–79.

of the preceding weeks and months. The provisional empowerment of Islamic organizations and the partial encouragement of Islamist aspirations under Habibie's interim government also coloured the June 1999 parliamentary elections in significant ways. *Golkar* succeeded not only in winning 22 per cent of the national vote, but also in continuing to attract support from Muslim politicians and voters and from Islamic activists and organizations who under other circumstances might have been drawn to other – Islamic – parties. Together with *Golkar*, the only other two parties that had been allowed to compete in Suharto-era elections – the omnibus Islamic PPP (United Development Party) and the secular-nationalist PDIP (Indonesian Democratic Party of Struggle) – captured two-thirds of the 1999 parliamentary vote, 34 per cent for PDIP and 11 per cent for PPP. Of the myriad new parties that competed in these first post-authoritarian elections, only those associated with Indonesia's two major Islamic associations – *Nahdlatul Ulama*'s PKB (National Awakening Party) and *Muhammadiyah*'s PAN (National Mandate Party) – performed strongly, with 13 per cent and 7 per cent of the vote, respectively. Thanks to Suharto's co-optation strategy of the late 1980s and early to mid-1990s, the critical realignment accompanying the first post-authoritarian election in Indonesia was thus qualified by significant continuities in the party system and by considerable success by the *Golkar* and PPP machines in absorbing Islamist energies and attracting Muslim votes otherwise represented almost exclusively by parties affiliated with the most established Islamic associations in the country.[36]

In sharp contrast with the co-optation strategy of the late Suharto era, the continuing exclusion of the Muslim Brotherhood and other Islamic organizations from state power under Mubarak spelled a different trajectory for Islamic parties in the elections of 2011 and 2012. As previously noted, in sharp contrast with *Golkar*, the National Democratic Party (NDP) under Mubarak remained weakly institutionalized and became increasingly more narrowly associated with efforts to launch Gamal Mubarak's bid to succeed his father as president, even as the Muslim Brotherhood and other Islamic groups remained effectively excluded from its ranks and from direct access to state patronage and

---

[36] For contrasting accounts, see: Robert W. Hefner, *Civil Islam: Muslims and Democratization in Indonesia* (Princeton, NJ: Princeton University Press, 2000); and Andrée Feillard and Remy Madinier, *The End of Innocence? Indonesian Islam and the Temptations of Radicalism* (Singapore: Singapore University Press, 2011).

power.[37] Thus, the critical realignment accompanying the first post-
authoritarian elections in Egypt unfolded in the absence of an effective
vehicle to promote continuity and to protect conservative interests associated with the former regime, and without other well-established, firmly
institutionalized, nationwide political machines in place, aside from those
associated with Islamic associational life. It was in this context that the
Muslim Brotherhood-affiliated Freedom and Justice Party and the Salafi-
led *Al-Nour* Party dominated the 2011 parliamentary elections and that
the Brotherhood's candidate Mohamed Morsi won the presidency in June
2012. Thus, more than Indonesia during the presidencies of ICMI chairman Habibie (May 1998–October 1999) and *Nahdlatul Ulama* chairman Wahid (October 1999–July 2001), Egypt today is experiencing a
transition from authoritarian rule to democracy in which Islamic – and
decidedly Islamist – associations and aspirations, parties and politicians,
are playing a very prominent and powerful role, and one more problem-
atically counterposed against the continuing coercive power and institutional entrenchment of the military establishment.[38]

Conclusion: Egyptian Democratization through an Indonesian Glass, Darkly

Overall, as previously suggested, Egypt's ongoing transition from authoritarian rule to democracy in the early 2010s can be illuminated in new
ways through a paired comparison with Indonesia's experience in the
early post-Suharto years at the turn of the twenty-first century. On the
one hand, this comparison has suggested that a similar set of structural opportunities and constraints enabled and impelled the breakdown
of authoritarian rule in Indonesia and Egypt, opened and inflected the
early post-authoritarian interregnum under interim governments, and

---

37 Zahid, *The Muslim Brotherhood and Egypt's Succession Crisis*; Rutherford, *Egypt After
Mubarak*; Blaydes, *Elections and Distributive Politics in Mubarak's Egypt*, pp. 148–
70; Fahmy, *Patronage Politics in Egypt*; Tarek Masoud, 'Why Islam Wins: Electoral
Ecologies and Economies of Political Islam in Contemporary Egypt' (Ph.D. dissertation,
Yale University, 2008); and Nathan J. Brown, *When Victory is Not an Option: Islamist
Movements in Arab Politics* (Ithaca, NY: Cornell University Press, 2012).
38 See: Jonathan Brown, *Salafis and Sufis in Egypt* (Washington, DC: Carnegie Endowment
for International Peace, December 2011); Nathan J. Brown, *When Victory Becomes an
Option: Egypt's Muslim Brotherhood Confronts Success* (Washington, DC: Carnegie
Endowment for International Peace, January 2012); and Stéphane Lacroix, *Sheikhs and
Politicians: Inside the New Egyptian Salafism* (Doha: Brookings Doha Center, June
2012).

established the parameters of the possible for democratic parliamentary politics with the first set of post-authoritarian elections in the two countries. This comparative perspective thus reveals that the apparent uncertainties, anxieties, and indeterminacies of the early post-Mubarak era in Egypt have been somewhat exaggerated, and that a set of more ordered if not over-determined processes and outcomes have fallen into place, ones familiar to observers not only of Indonesian politics, but of oligarchical democracy in many other countries across the world. This comparative perspective also suggests that alarmist fears of dramatic social transformation or reconstituted authoritarianism under an early post-Mubarak, Islamist-led government in Egypt are misguided and misplaced, and that greater concern about the staying power of the military establishment and the reconstitution and re-entrenchment of Mubarak-era business interests and local bosses under oligarchical democracy is warranted instead.

On the other hand, this comparison has also cast new light on the distinctiveness of the Egyptian experience of transition from authoritarian rule to democracy and the specificity of the institutional and electoral constellations at play as of this writing. The entrenchment of the Egyptian military establishment and the electoral strength of the Muslim Brotherhood and other Islamist forces in 2011–12, it has been shown, can be understood not as persistent reflections of the inherent and eternal features of the Egyptian political landscape, but as enduring institutional legacies of the authoritarian era and contingent provisional outcomes of the peculiarly structured pathways of authoritarian regime breakdown and transition to democracy in Egypt. Indeed, the nearly victorious presidential campaign of retired Air Force commander and Mubarak-era Prime Minister Ahmed Shafiq in June 2012 signalled the enduring strength of conservative forces associated with the ancien régime, even as the strong showing of liberal, leftist, and Nasserist candidates in the May 2012 first round of the presidential elections suggested potential future bases for political alignment and opposition other than those associated with organized political Islam, as became increasingly evident on the streets of Cairo and other Egyptian cities in late 2012 and early 2013. Thus, even as the apparent inevitability of Indonesia-style oligarchical democracy looms large on the horizon, a distinctively Egyptian set of institutional obstacles, political options, and lived experiences lie ahead, laying the groundwork for a longer-term struggle for democratization for many years to come.

Against this backdrop, the comparison with Indonesia has also highlighted a set of key questions that merit further attention by political analysts and democracy activists alike in Egypt today. If, as previously suggested, the military establishment is peculiarly problematic for democratization in Egypt, then much more needs to be unveiled and understood with regard to its institutional autonomy, economic empire, political power, and relationship with the United States. If, moreover, as has also been suggested, corporate interests and other conservative remnants of the authoritarian Mubarak regime have not preserved the NDP as a *Golkar*-like vehicle to protect and promote their interests, then it is essential to examine the alternative forms of influence and intermediation linking businessmen and local bosses to the Muslim Brotherhood and the Salafi-led *Al Nour* party, and to rival politicians and parties in elections to come. Finally, if an Indonesia-style oligarchical democracy crystallizes in Egypt in the years ahead, then there will be much research to expose – and oppose – rent-seeking and corruption, local bossism and gangsterism, and the remnants of the 'deep state', much as scholars and other researchers have revealed in Indonesia over the past decade. It is only to be hoped that, in years to come, more positive developments and 'progressive' trends in Indonesia will provide new points of comparison, illumination, and inspiration as Egypt continues in its struggle for democratization.

PART III

COUNTRIES IN TURMOIL

Egypt and Tunisia

From the Revolutionary Overthrow of Dictatorships to the Struggle to Establish a New Constitutional Order

Roger Owen

Abstract

This chapter begins with an account for the presence of a revolutionary situation that needed only a 'spark' to ignite it in Tunisia and Egypt. It then goes on to examine the post-revolutionary timetable of elections in these two countries leading to the establishment of a constitutional assembly obligated to create an entirely new structure for the practice of a representative and plural politics. It underlines not only the somewhat different paths taken in Egypt and Tunisia as they progress towards the same general goal, but also the passage of lessons and political experience of both, including what appear to be obvious mistakes. While the Arab world in general made use of examples taken from a global and historical repertoire of revolutionary change going back to the influence of both the American and French revolutions of the late eighteenth century, the mutual influences exercised in the Egyptian-Tunisian case remains something extra special in their intensity and effect.

Introduction

The popular uprisings that toppled the dictatorships of Zine El Abidine Ben Ali in Tunisia and Hosni Mubarak in Egypt in early 2011 were so completely unexpected that they took everyone, including the bemused presidents themselves, by surprise. Yet, in retrospect, it is possible to observe two aspects that might have directed thinking along the right track. One was the handicap provided by the notion of 'authoritarianism', borrowed from the literature of Latin American development, which exaggerated the ability of a single source of power to manage all aspects of social, economic, and political relations in such a way that there was no space left for independent action.[1] This, we can now see, blinded observers to the significance of many sites of protest; for example: the workplace, the universities, and, in Tunisia, inland areas which, traditionally, had felt ignored by the Mediterranean-oriented central government.[2]

The second handicap was the general tendency to underestimate the impact of the many sources of discontent in the last few years. These had increased exponentially, stirred up by huge increases in the cost of living and the consequent fall in real wages. Discontent was further aggravated by the heavy-handed management of the Egyptian elections of 2010, the increase in the number of egregious human rights abuses, and the aggressive takeover of so many Tunisian firms by Leila Trebelsi, Ben Ali's wife, and her many avaricious relatives.[3] This had a particularly serious impact on the professional middle classes, making them, inter alia, more tolerant of religious movements like the Muslim Brothers whose new moderation seemed to align them more with other moderate Islamic forces like the *Adalet ve Kalkınma Partisi* (AKP) in Turkey.

This chapter will try to account for the presence of a revolutionary situation in these two countries that needed only a 'spark' to ignite it. It will then examine the process of the post-revolutionary timetable of elections leading to the establishment of a constitutional assembly obligated to create an entirely new structure for the practice of representative and plural politics. This will allow for commentary not only on the somewhat different paths taken in Egypt and Tunisia as they progress towards the same general goal, but also on the passage of lessons and political experience between them, including obvious mistakes. Whereas the Arab world in general made use of examples taken from a global and historical repertoire of revolutionary change going back to the influence of both the American and French revolutions of the late eighteenth century,

---

[1] See Guillermo A. O'Donnell, *Modernization and Bureaucratic Authoritarianism: Studies in South American Politics* (Berkley: University of California Press, 1973); Eva Bellin, 'Reconsidering the robustness of Authoritarianism in the Middle East: Lessons from the Arab Spring', *Comparative Politics*, Vol. 44, No. 2 (January 2012), 127–149. As far as 'protests' go, there were also some protests against the oppositional protests organized by the regimes themselves.

[2] See, for example, Nadia Marzouki, 'From people to citizens in Tunisia', MERIP, 259, 41/2 (Summer 2011), 18.

[3] For increasing public criticism of economic performance, see Clemens Breisinger, Olivier Ecker, and Perrihan Al-Riffai, *Economics of the Arab Awakening: From Revolution to Transformation and Food Security*, IFPRI (International Food Policy Research Institute), Brief 18 (Washington, DC, May 2011), 1–4.

the mutual influences exercised in the Egyptian-Tunisian case remains something extra-special in their intensity and effect.

The 'Spark' and Its Immediate Consequences

Lenin's notion of the 'spark' posited the existence of a revolutionary situation that simply required one small incident to ignite it, even if no observer, however prescient, could know exactly when and where this might happen. A useful elaboration of the same notion is provided by Timur Kuran in his seminal article, 'Sparks and prairie fires: A theory of unanticipated political revolution', based on a study of the French, Russian, and Iranian revolutions.[4] Here, he theorizes that in repressive regimes, people conceal their true opinions but at considerable psychological cost. In response to a slight surge in more open opposition, a rapidly increasing number of individuals is emboldened to express open political dissatisfaction until there is a major shift in 'public sentiment'.[5] This, it seems, is what happened in Tunisia following the self-immolation of the unfortunate market trader, Mohammed Bouazizi, on 17 December 2010, leading, within thirty days, to a wave of protests that caused the Ben Ali family to leave in panic, urged on, according to some reports, by the commander of the country's small army.[6] This happened again when, emboldened by the Tunisian example, a group of young Egyptians decided to use the annual National Police Day, 25 January 2011, to hold simultaneous demonstrations designed to surprise the powerful security police, the largest of which took place in Cairo's Maidan Tahrir.[7] Eighteen days later, as a result of the intervention of Egypt's military high command, combined with high-level U.S. pressure, President Mubarak stepped down as well.

The Tunisian Road to Elections and a New Constitution

Once Ben Ali fled, the main revolutionary force – a grassroots coalition of Trade Unionists, leftists, human rights groups, and Islamists – turned Tunis's central Casbah Square into a site both for intense political discussion and protests against any attempt by the members of the old

---

[4] Timur Kuran, 'Sparks and Prairie Fires: A Theory of Unanticipated Political Revolution', *Public Choice*, Vol. 61, No. 1 (April 1989), pp. 41–74.

[5] Ibid.

[6] For example, Borzou Daragahi, 'Former security chief's son says Ben Ali fled to avoid coup', *Financial Times*, 13 January 2012.

[7] Charles Levinson and Margaret Coker, 'The secret rally that sparked the uprising', *Wall Street Journal*, 11 February 2011.

regime to re-establish their control. Unlike Egypt, the small Tunisian army played little role in the process, the main driving force being a series of mass popular sit-ins untroubled by the presence of the hated police force whose members had more or less disappeared. All this was enough to force the resignation of two successive interim governments on the grounds of being too closely associated with the old regime, the resignation of the provincial governors appointed by Ben Ali, the dissolution of the old ruling party, the *Rassemblement Constitutionel Démocratique* (RCD), and the disbanding of the State Security Apparatus including the secret police. Most important of all, on 4 March, the interim Prime Minister Beji Caid Essebi gave in to the protesters' core demand and announced that national elections for a Constituent Assembly would be held on 24 July.

There were some Tunisians who then said, and many who hoped in their hearts, that the revolutionary part of the political struggle was over, an aspiration that found its symbolic outlet in a new postage stamp with a picture of Mr Bouazizi together with the tools of his trade that an over-officious police official had tried to confiscate: his barrow and his weighing scales. But this was to disregard the whole logic of a process that necessitates that the unity required for the overthrow of an old order gives way to the political divisions that a pluralist party system requires. Hence, there were the beginnings of a period of infighting and factionalism so intense that, for a while, there could be no agreement about the law needed to govern the upcoming election. This forced its postponement to 23 October, with serious campaigning able to begin just three weeks before.

Looked at in retrospect, this three-month delay, although disappointing for many at the time, had many positive benefits. It allowed a sorting out of the many parties and groups that had initially announced their participation – more than 100 – to a more manageable number of serious contenders. It was also important for the party leaders to reach as much agreement as possible on the electoral system itself, given the natural desire for each party to derive particular advantage from its provisions. In the end, the expanded Commission for Political Reform decided, sensibly, to look to France for a method of proportional representation – the 'largest remainder' list system – which, by making it very difficult to achieve an absolute majority of seats, renders coalitions more or less inevitable.[8] Further compromises were contained in a mid-September

---

[8] Asma Nouira, 'Tunisia: Elections...and then what?' *Arab Reform Brief*, 54 (January 2012), 1.

agreement to limit the term of the Constituent Assembly to just one year, with its work to be finished by October 2012.

Just as important, the fact that each party had to provide at least some rough guidelines as to their thinking about what should be in the new constitution provided an opportunity to discuss, although not necessarily to agree on, a number of contentious issues. The most important of these was that concerning the role of religion within the new order. The previously outlawed and savagely persecuted religious organization, Ennahda, under its charismatic leader, Rashid Ghannouchi, possessed sufficient nationwide support to make a strong political showing. One particular significant pointer towards future policy was provided by Ennahda's September announcement that it preferred a system in which the president had to name the prime minister from the largest party, thus paving the way for a more parliamentary system of government.

In the event Ennahda won the most seats in the election: 89 out of 217. This was a reflection of its deep popular support across the country, as well as the result of using modern electoral practices such as advertising and poll watching, learned, for example, by members of the Ghannouchi family during their long exile in London. Coming in at a distant second, with thirty seats, was the liberal and moderate CPR (Congrès Pour La République) under its leader Moncef Marzouki. Turnout was extraordinarily high with more than 90 per cent of the country's registered voters going to the polls and there were no reports of any significant infractions.[9] Also noteworthy is the fact that women candidates, many on Ennahda's own list, obtained nearly a quarter of the votes, enough for forty-nine seats in the new Assembly. Altogether, it was a remarkable achievement.

What followed might be called a Lebanese model of power-sharing in which, after 'marathon negotiating sessions', Ennahda's governing alliance with two smaller parties, the CPR and the Democratic Forum for Labour and Liberties (Ettakatol), was formally represented through an Ennahda prime minister, Hamad Jabali, balanced by an interim president from the CPR, Moncef Marzouki, and a speaker of the Constituent Assembly from Ettakatol.[10] So, too, with the committees set up to report on various aspects of government, with Ennahda generally supplying nine out of twenty-two or twenty-three members. A final agreement allowed

---

[9] Issandr El Amrani, 'Tunisia moves to the next stage', *MERIP*, 8 November 2011. Note that only half of those eligible to vote actually registered, suggesting that, for them, the overthrow of Ben Ali was enough and that they had no wish to participate in the remaking of the political system.

[10] Nouira, 'Tunisia', 6.

the three partners to go their separate ways in the coming constitutional debates so as to avoid bringing the government to a standstill.

The next task was the adoption of a provisional constitution of twenty-six clauses outlining 'the conditions and procedures to be followed by the county's executive, legislature and judiciary ... until a final constitution is agreed'.[11] Once again, there was what Al-Jazeera called a 'tumultuous debate' lasting for five days and attracting thousands of demonstrators outside the Assembly building. These people were concerned to express rival views over the role of Islam in the new document. The final vote was 141 votes in favour, with 37 against and 39 abstentions.[12]

Ennahda also took great pains to demonstrate its newfound moderation (as well as to distance itself from the Tunisian Salafis, who had made an unexpectedly strong showing in the elections) by organizing a series of debates, lectures, and discussions. Perhaps the most notable was the lecture given by Rashid Ghannouchi at the Tunisian Center for the Study of Islam and Democracy on 2 March 2012 on 'Religion and secularism' in which he argued for a principle of citizenship that encompassed all citizens 'regardless of their religion, sex or any other consideration' and their right to believe whatever they desired 'within the framework of mutual respect and observance of the law which is legislated by their representatives in parliament'.[13] The party's other pressing task was to present its ideas about economic and social development in the form of a plan presented to the Constituent Assembly at the end of March 2012.[14]

Fifteen months after the overthrow of Ben Ali, much had been done to set up a new constitutional structure, including agreement on two fundamental laws – on personal status and basic liberties – to be protected from future amendment by the establishment of a Conseil d'Etat or Constitutional Tribunal. There was also a basic understanding about the role of the Sharia with a large area of agreement that it is a man-made rather than God-given set of rules and practices, the interpretation of which can be decided by the peoples' elected representatives. Other matters of substance remained under discussion, notably the type of government itself,

[11] 'Tunisian assembly adopts provisional constitution', *Al-Jazeera English*, 11 December 2011.

[12] Ibid.

[13] 'Ghannouchi: Secularism Doesn't Conflict with Islam', *Eurasia Review*, 10 March 2012. http://www.eurasiareview.com/10032012-ghannouchi-secularism-doesnt-conflict-with-islam/

[14] *Radio Tunisienne*, 'Le gouvernement présentera un programme économique et social cohérent', 19 March 2012.

with opinion divided between a desire for a more parliamentary system under a relatively weak president, largely favoured by Ennahda, and a stronger presidency, perhaps along French lines, favoured by some of the secular parties. Meanwhile, little progress had been made in addressing a number of the basic problems the country had inherited from the old regime. For one thing, virtually no reform of the police and security services had been achieved. For another, progress was painfully slow in locating the assets of Ben Ali's family and his close cronies hidden outside the country while their assets inside Tunisia remained in the hands of various government institutions with not a single company restructured or sold off. Borzou Daraghi of the *Financial Times* blamed this state of affairs on the unwillingness of an uncertain provisional government to do anything that 'might damage the fragile economy'.[15] Meanwhile, the sad state of the economy, including the very high rate of unemployment, remained of huge concern to politicians and the public.[16]

Egypt

Although the popular protests in Tunisia were definitely the spark that ignited similar protests in Egypt, the way the process developed in Cairo had a different character owing to the central role played by the military high command, even if it led to a similar timetable concerning elections and the drawing up of a new constitution. Not only was the Egyptian army a much more powerful force and more closely integrated to the Mubarak regime, but it also possessed significant weaknesses, one of which was its susceptibility to American pressure. Hence, once the mass demonstrations in Cairo's Maidan Tahrir began, the senior generals under Marshal Mohamed Hussein Tantawi had to steer a difficult course in order to protect their own privileged position and extensive economic infrastructure, beginning with their decision to force President Mubarak's resignation on 11 February and his handover of authority to a new twenty-man body known as the Supreme Council of the Armed Forces (SCAF).

---

[15] 'No sign of missing Ben Ali funds one year after he fled uprising', *Financial Times*, 14 January 2012.

[16] At the end of 2011, the unemployment rate was 18%. Amongst university graduates, the rate was 44%. Anne Wolf and Raphael Lefevre, 'Tunisia: A revolution at risk' *The Guardian*, 18 April 2012. http://www.guardian.co.uk/commentisfree/2012/apr/18/tunisia-revolution-at-risk.

Several important factors underlay this decision. One was a concern that members of Egypt's largely conscript army would not fire on the demonstrators. Another was the series of almost daily phone calls Tantawi received from President Obama and his secretary of state, Hillary Clinton. The third was a desire not only to protect the military's own lucrative economic interests – its factories, its commercial farms, its links with the wider business community – from public scrutiny, but also what might be called its own 'guilty' secret that, for all the huge (and hidden) defence budget, its ability to put on even the smallest military exercise, let alone confront a major enemy on the battlefield, had been seriously impaired.[17]

In these circumstances, it was the SCAF itself which, by initiating both the timetable and the substance of the move towards a new constitution in an atmosphere of secrecy, hesitation, and incompetence, was responsible for much of the suspicion that surrounded its intentions and its relationship with major political forces including the newly emerged Muslim Brothers. To some extent this was because of its unwieldy composition, combining senior military figures in the army and in the security services, each with different sets of intelligence at their disposal and with different ideas about the military as well as the national interest, notably how to shield their activities from democratic scrutiny.[18]

However, much of the confusion was owing to more general factors. One was the difficulty guiding the unruly popular forces released by a revolution, including those who wanted a root-and-branch reform of the entire governmental and administrative system (including the punishment of those who ran and profited from the Mubarak state) to those who, equally unrealistically, yearned for a return to the good old days. Another factor was the inevitable intrusion of political confusion and division into the ranks of the senior officers as they sought both to understand and to guide what was going on outside their closely guarded headquarters. The military members of the Revolutionary Command Council, set up to guide the 1952 revolution, had experienced much the same thing before deciding, or being forced, to give unchallenged leadership to Gamal Abdel Nasser. But this time a combination of prudence, self-protection, and American pressure – and perhaps also Field Marshal Tantawi's venerable age – made that option unthinkable.

---

17 Zeinab Abul-Magd, 'The generals' secret: Egypt's ambivalent market', *Analysis on Arab Reform*, Carnegie Endowment for International Peace, 9 February 2012.
18 Issandr El Amrani, 'Sightings of the Deep State', *MERIP Online*, 1 January 2012.

The first step towards a new constitutional order was taken two days after Mubarak's departure, with the SCAF's somewhat contradictory decision to suspend the existing 1971 constitution while appointing a committee of eight legal experts, all but one with no political affiliation, to suggest how it might be amended. After only ten days of closed meetings, a package of eleven amendments emerged. This was then put to a national referendum on 19 March and passed with 77.2 per cent voting in favour. The majority appeared to see it as either the quickest route to return to civilian rule or, in the case of the Muslim Brothers, the best way to protect the unamended Article Two of the 1971 constitution stating that the 'principles' of the Sharia should be its main source of legislation.[19]

Next, a draft of Parties Law was issued on 26 March that also largely followed the wording of Article Two with its ban on parties founded on sectarian, geographic, or religious constituencies. The Muslim Brothers responded immediately by founding their own party, the Freedom and Justice Party, based, as they were quick to point out, on the principle of 'citizenship' rather than religion.[20] And then, only four days later, in what Tamir Moustafa describes as a complete change of course, the 'Provisional Constitutional Declaration of 30 March' appeared. This was a hybrid document of sixty-three Articles that was to serve as an interim constitution until the drafting of a new one in March and April 2012.[21] As Nathan Brown and Kristen Stilt point out, it represented a kind of 'middle ground' between scrapping the 1971 constitution entirely, as critics of the 19 March referendum desired, and using it and the previously agreed amendments to try to bridge the gap between the various political constituencies while keeping to the timetable of progress towards civilian rule.[22]

On close inspection, the Provisional Constitutional Declaration proved to be an incoherent and deeply problematic document, drafted in secrecy in consultation with some of Egypt's political leaders and on an ad hoc basis. It caused considerable confusion amongst the Egyptian population.

---

[19] Nathan J. Brown and Kristen Stilt, 'A haphazard constitutional compromise', Commentary, Carnegie Endowment for International Peace, 11 April 2011.

[20] Ibid.

[21] Here and in the paragraphs that follow, I rely very much on Tamir Mustafa's paper, 'Drafting Egypt's constitution: Can a new legal framework revive a flawed transition?' published by the Brookings Doha Center and the Centre on Democracy, Development and the Rule of Law, Stanford University.

[22] Brown and Stilt.

As Moustafa notes, some of its sixty-three Articles did not 'match' the wording of the previous amendments.[23] Others contained 'substantive' changes to the wording of the 1971 constitution itself, for example, concerning Article Five dealing with political parties, removing references to the prohibition of those founded with a 'religious frame of reference', a phrase now used by the Muslim Brothers to 'describe its own orientation'.[24] Another oddity was the decision to keep some other provisions, like the Nasser-era requirement that half the members of the National Assembly be 'workers and peasants'. Inter alia, this led many political activists to suspect that this was designed to benefit parties and groups containing members with pre-existing electoral networks based on various local constituencies, such as those belonging to Mubarak's now defunct National Democratic Party.[25]

All this speaks of a great deal of ignorance and confusion about constitutions and how they work amongst members of the SCAF who were worried how to protect their military interests from criticism. But what now seems clear is that, despite the muddled attempt, the real result was, as Kristen Stilt notes, the SCAF 'transitioned from presenting itself as a caretaker of the revolution and the constitution to taking control of the process' in a move that left it with significant powers and discretion.[26]

It was probably with some relief that the SCAF decided to hand over the business of managing further constitutional debate to a civilian cabinet, the more so as the beginning of April saw the revival of large public protests in Maidan Tahrir, triggered both by the SCAF's obvious desire to normalize the situation with a new law banning strikes and protests and by the sense that the military was backing away from the prosecution of the Mubarak family and those of its cronies. That twenty junior military officers joined the biggest of these, the so-called Day of Rage on 8 April, only added to the generals' anxiety. This was manifest in the announcement of an official investigation into Mubarak's corrupt activities including a notorious deal that delivered Egyptian natural gas to Israel at low prices and in heightened criticism of elements of the youthful

---

[23] Moustafa, 2.
[24] Brown and Stilt.
[25] Ibid.
[26] 'The end of "one hand": The Egyptian constitutional declaration and the rift between the "people" and the Supreme Council of the Armed Forces', *Yearbook of Islamic and Middle Eastern Law*, Brill (forthcoming).

revolutionaries, whom the SCAF referred to as 'dubious elements' or 'thugs' in the pay of hostile foreign forces.

It is perfectly natural that when revolutions begin seriously to threaten the interests of established conservative economic and social forces, they aim to end them. In practice, this is not easily done, as seen in the French, Russian, and Iranian revolutions. Amongst many factors, there is just too much unfinished business. In the Egyptian case, this includes the conflicts between various political agendas and the need to reconcile these within a single system of plural institutions that has yet to be properly defined.

That the process was still far from over was well-illustrated by yet another round of Tahrir protests in late May. These were once again motivated by the slow pace of reform and were exacerbated by the continued sense of an imminent deal between the military and the Muslim Brothers, itself given further credence by the Brothers' boycott of a mass rally on 27 May. This set the stage for yet another attempt to reach what a posting on the SCAF Facebook page called a 'national consensus on the political priorities of the coming stage' by way of the organization of a National Accord Conference. At issue, once again, was the issue of timing: whether to hold elections first, a procedure thought to benefit existing political parties including those close to the SCAF, or to create the constitution first, to prevent the assembly being dominated by groups with narrow sectoral interests. In the end, it was the elections-first camp that won, but these were postponed from the original June date to 28 November. According to this calendar, a portion of the elected representatives (not the whole assembly as in Tunisia) would draw up a new constitution, followed by presidential elections and, only then, the final hand over of military power.

Nevertheless, it remained a bumpy road. There were more Tahrir demonstrations – in June in memory of young Egyptians killed by the security force, and in July against the slow pace of security reforms, the increased use of military courts to try activists, and the release of the police officers accused of the June killing of activists – but these were snuffed out by the clearance of the Maidan in August, an act that more or less brought an end to this form of largely peaceful revolutionary protest. Meanwhile, various public figures came forward to try to influence future events, notably the Nobel Prize winner, Mohamed Al-Baradei, who not only announced his candidature for president, but also used his good reputation to propose a basic bill of rights concerning freedom of religious practice, the right to form political parties and equality before the law which would be written into the constitution in a way that defied amendment.[27]

The mood became more heated in October as the elections approached. Given that it seemed increasingly likely that the Muslim Brothers would win a parliamentary majority, some political groups, including members of the SCAF and the SCAF-appointed cabinet, looked again to prevent an attempt to manipulate the new constitution in such a way as to discriminate against secular or non-Muslim interest. This fear was encouraged by a nasty outbreak of anti-Coptic violence in early October. One result was the appearance of the so-called Selmi document circulated by the Deputy Prime Minister Ali Al-Selmi. This was a botched attempt to define certain 'supra-constitutional principles' that were ostensibly to guide the constitution-writing process, but it could just as easily be seen as a way of creating certain un-amendable provisions designed to provide permanent protection for the military from civilian oversight.[28] These, including the provision that only the Army High Command would know the details of the military budget and that all legislation concerning the military would need its prior approval, were enough to bring tens of thousands of demonstrators, mainly Muslim Brothers and the more fundamentalist Salafis back to Tahrir with chants of 'Down, down with military rule'.[29]

Well-intentioned though it might have been with its appeal to the notion of a 'civil' state, the Selmi document turned out to be extremely counterproductive. It was no matter that the cabinet immediately distanced itself from it while moving the date for the presidential election (the moment when it would finally hand over direct power) to June 2012. The document increased distrust of military intentions and posed a brief threat to the holding of the first round of national elections. But, in the event, there was no postponement and the three stages of the elections, involving nine of Egypt's twenty-seven provinces at a time, began smoothly with much popular enthusiasm on 28 November. According to the committee entrusted with running the elections, turnout in the first round was 62 per cent. Such was the appeal of the Muslim Brothers' Freedom and Justice Party (FJP) that when the three rounds of polling were over in January, it controlled nearly half of the 508 seats in the

[27] Heba Saleh, 'Elbaradei tries to draw Egypt together with a bill of rights', *Financial Times*, 20 June 2011.

[28] Moustafa, 4–5.

[29] Stilt, 'The end of "one hand"'; Heba Saleh, 'Protestors rally in Cairo against military rulers', *Financial Times*, 19 November 2011.

People's Assembly and nearly two-thirds of the 180 seats subject to election to the Shura or upper house, with another 90 to be appointed either by the SCAF or the newly elected president.

For some observers, this sweeping victory along with the strong showing of the Salafi 'Nour' party, constituted Egypt's real 'revolution', a revolt against the secular republican forces that had dominated Egyptian public life since 1952. But, by emphasizing the military rather than the revolutionary aspect of what took place in January 2011, such a comment overestimates the 'religious' component of the Brothers' victory while underestimating the existential change that took place in the hearts and minds of so many Egyptians inspired by the Tahrir events. What the victory in fact represented is the incorporation of one aspect of political Islam into an ongoing process of institution building and political change, a fact readily appreciated by the Brothers' leadership with its immediate stress on moderation, a civic vision, and its ability to attend immediately to the country's pressing economic and social problems. Its success in the latter will determine its future electability, just as for Ennahda in Tunisia.

Beyond this, a host of more pressing matters required attention. The most important were those connected with the necessarily hurried process of drawing up the constitution which, according to the new SCAF timetable, had to be completed before the first round of the presidential election, now brought forward to 23–24 May. What should be the powers of the first post-revolutionary president and how should these mesh with the powers of an elected parliament? Clearly, few people wanted an all-powerful presidency. But there was also a growing recognition that, with a parliament inevitably much occupied with short-term political and electoral considerations, there needed to be some institution within the system that was able to address to the longer-term problems of the economy and the pressing need to reconstruct the domestic security forces to make them fully answerable to the Assembly and the courts.

To state only the very obvious, such considerations are underpinned by their relationship to a set of enormously important conceptual problems that all essays in revolutionary constitution-making must face. Where does sovereignty lie? And, if it is assumed to lie with the people and their elected representatives, should they be free to amend the constitution as they wish, even if this does harm to the interests of either particular groups or particular republican principles such as equal citizenship for all, as well as, in this modern age, the recognition of certain universally accepted human rights?

Conclusion: Some Lessons and Observations for the Future

Writing in 2012, it is clear that neither the Tunisian nor the Egyptian revolutions have run their course. Both countries are still some way from the creation of new and permanent institutions that can protect the gains made in creating a new sense of citizenship and satisfy the general desire for open and accountable government, economic improvement, and better systems of education. Given the scope of the endeavour and the discouraging lessons from other countries in transition, perhaps Tunisian and Egyptian revolutionaries will never achieve all their goals. But one thing is sure – there can be no way of going back to the bad old days of the dictatorships they overthrew. Moreover, the two countries, near neighbours in Arab North Africa, can give each other advice and encouragement, supported on occasions by the new wave of solidarity and desire for more democratic practices sweeping the Arab world.

What can we learn from all this? First, if we look at the revolutionary timeline, we see an almost identical timetable in which protests gave way to a decision to start the rebuilding of the political system. Elections to a constituent assembly were held in October 2011 in Tunisia and in late November 2011 in Egypt, where the revolution started a month later. Moreover, it looked as though both processes, including the election of a new president and parliament, would be complete by the early summer of 2012.

Hence, there are two almost identical timetables with similar outcomes, but reached by often quite dissimilar political actors and often quite dissimilar routes. Whereas in Egypt the decisive role of shepherding the various political forces was played by the army under constant pressure both from the American administration and its own desire to get out of politics with is privileged position intact, in Tunisia it was the leaders of the various political forces who engineered the move away from provisional governments led by leftovers from the Ben Ali regime to the election of a constituent assembly that was more inclusive of the wide variety of popular sentiment regarding the reshaping of the political system.

A second significant lesson concerns the problem of drafting a new constitution that has enough popular legitimacy to withstand the test of time while addressing contentious contemporary issues of citizenship as well as, in the Egyptian case, an institutionalized independence for the armed forces. As a rule, this involves devolving the actual drafting work to constitutional lawyers and other experts somewhat removed from day-to-day popular pressure. But how can it be ensured that non-experts feel comfortable not only with the result, but with the way it might be interpreted in the light of unforeseeable future circumstances? One can imagine senior Egyptian generals, drafts on the table in front of them, trying to puzzle all this out. One can also observe the noisy and sometimes chaotic scenes outside the Tunisian Assembly in February 2012, while the members inside voted on each of the twenty-six clauses of the new constitution. Historians can write later about what Bruce Ackerman has defined as 'the constitutional moment' when, having made a revolution, the revolutionaries at large are content to let a small group of well-read men (and more occasionally women) speak in their name, as in the famous 'We the People' preamble to the United States Constitution.[30] But the actual reality is likely to prove much, much messier.

Then, third, there is the question of the return of a politicized Islam, when 'return' means the re-emergence of the once powerful Muslim Brothers in either their Egyptian or their exported Tunisian form. As it turned out, the sufferings of the persecuted brothers had been put to very good use, allowing them to use their time in prison or exile to re-think their approach to politics while avoiding any of the stigmas attached to those who had had anything to do with the hated Ben Ali and Mubarak regimes. This, together with their ability to recreate national networks while making the largest possible appeal to the post-revolutionary electorate, is probably more than enough to account for their immediate electoral success. Further, in North Africa, like almost everywhere else in the world, religious belief shades imperceptibly into a more conservative desire either to preserve or to return to what are identified as more traditional ways.

Fourth, what have we learned about the tools we need for understanding such genuinely revolutionary moments that appear so rarely in world history while exciting such strong opinions on all sides? On one level there is the question of the enthusiastic response of the young standard-bearers of the revolts who, by all accounts, seem to have experienced a type of existential personal change best approached in principle through notions of mass psychology, but given more immediate concrete reality through their slogans, their graffiti, their songs, and the sheer joie de vivre so well-captured in Wordsworth's famous lines prompted by the revolution in France, 'Bliss was it in that dawn to be alive, But to be young was very heaven'.

[30] Bruce Ackerman, *We the People. Volume I: Foundations* (Cambridge, MA: Harvard University Press, 1991).

On another, more profound level, this was a process best-described by
reference to the Hegelian notion of a 'dialectic' in which multiple forces
interact with one other in such a haphazard way that there can be no
rest, no stasis until either they have exhausted themselves or one is able to
impose itself powerfully and permanently on all the others. There is bound
to be a period in which the new freedoms are tested, when the balance
between legitimate protests and public disorder is in flux and the role of
the police is a matter for heated debate. It is also equally inevitable that
new rules for political behaviour have to develop and that new boundaries
between what is the proper area of party competition and what is not
need to be delineated and confirmed. Such is the dynamism released by
the destruction of a despised dictatorial order and the passionate desire
to create something more representative of popular need.

Why this should have been so in the particular cases of Egypt and
Tunisia must remain an open matter for further research and debate.
But there is a great deal to be learned from Khalid Elgindy's analysis
of the contradictory role played by Egypt's military, the self-proclaimed
'guardian' of the revolution and, clearly, the most powerful and largely
coherent agency around. As he wisely notes, 'the sudden shift from a
depoliticized to a hyper-politicized public sphere was bound to have a
destabilizing effect on the country in the short run' – the more so because –
'by holding the transition hostage to the emergence of new political institutions such as parliament and a new constitution, the ruling military
council denied itself the very stability it had always sought and helped
sustain the protest movement it so desperately sought to quell'.[31]

Given the sheer power and comprehensiveness of such nationwide
processes, it seems pointless to imagine other scenarios and other outcomes. Once the Tunisian demonstrators both felt, and manifested, their
own sense of power, and once this same sense of popular empowerment
spread to Egypt, it is difficult to conceive of any other path forward.
Perhaps future historians will find arguments to suggest that with a bit
of foresight and a greater willingness to use state power, Ben Ali and
Mubarak might have survived, as Bashar Al-Assad is fighting to do in
Syria. But caught up in the daily drama of such enormous upheavals it is
difficult, probably impossible, to find a vantage point from which to even
begin to think through possible alternatives.

---

[31] 'Egypt's troubled transition: Elections without democracy', *Washington Quarterly*
(Spring 2012), 93.

Arab Nationalism, Islamism and the Arab Uprisings

Sadik Al-Azm

Abstract

When considering the Arab uprisings, it is necessary to examine two ingrained and regressive tendencies in Arab political life: the absence of meaningful change and the persistence of the *ancien regime*. Comparisons of the uprisings in Syria and Egypt reveal connections to classical European revolutionary politics. The Syrian revolution is also reminiscent of Arab revolutionary politics of the 1950s and 1960s. Traditional Arab nationalism is absent in the current uprisings, but there are commonalities in the uprisings and the regime reactions across the various states. The remarkably charismatic nature of the uprisings is a new and important development: Islamism has 'returned' to the debate, and the definition of Islam is fiercely contested between the religious/state establishment, middle-class commercial Islam and militant insurrectionary Islam. The middle-class model is the AKP in Turkey, while militant jihadist groups can be compared to European armed factions in the 1970s. Even if only partially successful, the uprisings will usher in a new era in Arab politics.

Introduction

We are speaking of a new era of politics inaugurated by the unfolding of the Arab Spring (if, in fact, we Arabs are on the verge of a new era of politics). It is necessary to draw the attention of the newly emerging forces of the Arab Spring to two highly related, deeply ingrained, and highly regressive tendencies in Arab political life in general.

The first tendency, as past experience has shown, is for Arab political changes and shifts to proceed, in spite of inflated rhetoric and hyperbolic discourses, on the basis of the famous French maxim that says: 'plus ça change, plus c'est la même chose'. The second tendency is that the ancien régime will persist, no matter what, even after the revolution has worked itself out. We can already see the persistence of the ancien régime asserting itself in Egypt and also the opposition to it in Cairo's Tahrir Square. In a certain sense, this is also the paradigm for all the other Tahrir Squares of the Arab world during this recent period.

It is clear that the military ancien régime in Egypt sacrificed part of itself in order to save the rest. Another means of persistence is for the ancien régime to make a tactical withdrawal to barracks and leave the front stage to civil society, civil politicians, political parties, and electoral politics, while still wielding power behind the scenes. In other words, we may very well have in Egypt a situation similar to the one that prevailed in Turkey before the Justice and Development Party won power.

That is, without the utmost careful attention to these two regressive engrained tendencies in Arab political life, the inauguration of a new era of Arab politics (where various Arab peoples may have finally found their voice and are in the process of affirming it), will be hindered, distorted, and even reversed. The worst and most damaging form of the persistence of the ancien régime is when it persists in the very lives, behaviour, habits, and decisions of the revolutionaries themselves. This has been a very common and prevalent Arab failure, as we all ought to know from experiences with past Arab revolutions, or so-called revolutions, and past Arab revolutionaries.

The unfolding of the Arab Spring can be connected to classical European revolutionary politics and the intellectual energies expended on the theorisation of these politics. The Tahrir Square experiences seem to come nearest to the venerable European debates, theories, and practices of the general strike.[1] The revolution in Syria has no Tahrir Square as yet. The Syrian revolutionary experience now seems to come closest to the theory and practice of the revolutionary 'foco', especially as first expounded by Régis Debray in his early work 'Revolution in the Revolution'. Here the revolution takes the form of a large number of exploding points and

---

[1] A workers' strike that completely interrupts production in the whole country and stops communication, particularly for the ruling classes, all for a time long enough to totally disrupt and disorganize the existing state of society, economy, and polity.

centres distributed all over the country, instead of being concentrated in one major and highly visible spot such as Tahrir Square in Cairo. This tactic compels the forces of the regime to spread themselves very thinly over the entire Syria territory at one and the same time.

Again, the revolution in Syria is often criticized for being spontaneous, leaderless, and lacking in strategy, but then is there not in all this an echo of classical European revolutionary politics, debates, and controversies over the role of the organized vanguard party as against the natural spontaneity of the revolution? Do not the formation and the rise of the Syrian *tansiqiyat* – the local coordinating committees – sound familiar to European minds as these are similar to the venerable idea of local revolutionary councils that operate regardless of what the traditional political organizations, opposition groups, and personalities say or do?

In Syria today, these *tansiqiyat* lead and energise the street power of the revolution and were responsible for sustaining the largely non-violent early character of the intifada against military rule, martial law, and the police state that Syria has suffered for the last half century. Despite the spontaneity of these *tansiqiyat*, they have been able to knit themselves into a national network continually in touch with similar activists in Syria and the Arab world, as well as the wider world beyond. Using modern communications to further their revolutionary agenda, they have been able to frustrate the military regime's efforts to suppress the flow of information. They have achieved this by sustaining a steady flow of real-time images and vital pieces of information concerning what is actually taking place on the ground, all around the country, and practically all around the clock.

One last reflection concerning these kinds of comparisons: The revolution in Syria is very reminiscent of the Arab revolutionary politics of the 1950s and 1960s, particularly in Egypt and Syria. Remember that at that time, Egypt and Syria formed a short-lived union called the United Arab Republic. The major enemy of the revolutionaries, activists, and progressives in those days was called *tahalof al iqtaa wal bourgeoiusiyya* – the alliance of the feudal lords with the high bourgeoisie. This alliance dominated the politics, power, and wealth of those countries to the detriment of everyone else. Today's revolution in Syria is again directed against a similar alliance of new military feudal lords with a state-formed high bourgeoisie that arrogantly, vainly, haughtily, and insolently dominates the politics, power, and wealth of the country to the detriment of everyone else. In its earlier stages, the alliance that still rules Syria could be called the 'merchant-military complex'. The activists and commentators of a younger generation today have refined this to *al mourakkab al siyasi al amni al mali* – the political-security-financial complex.

Popular Charisma Replaces Old Arab Nationalism

Conspiciously absent from the Arab uprisings and from its Tahrir Squares and its revolutionary 'foco' in Syria are the traditional cries, slogans, demands, and banners of good old Arab nationalism, especially as we have known it in the nationalist-populist period of the last century. Its heyday was the early post-colonial era in Egypt and Syria. No banner was raised anywhere from Tunis to Cairo to Tripoli, Sana'a to Manama to Homs, saying 'Islam is the solution'. Similarly, no banner was in sight saying 'Arab unity is the solution'. Actually, it is remarkable that what was on display through the Arab revolts were more interesting and more sublimated expressions of a different kind of Arab unity than have been seen before. First, the Arab regimes being put to the test by the intifadas of their peoples showed a peculiar kind of official Arab unity after years of vociferous rhetoric about the basic unity of *Al Umma Al Arabiyya* – the Arab nation – and about its unifying historical commonalities such as language, religion, ethnicity, culture, shared destiny, and all the rest. These same Arab regimes seemed united in going on a rhetorical binge emphasising Arab particularities, peculiarities, uniquenesses, singularities, and so on.

So, all of a sudden, instead of the traditional Arab nationalist discourse and rhetoric, we hear the tumultuous Arab governmental claims that Egypt is not Tunisia and that Libya is neither Egypt nor Tunisia and that Syria is neither Tunisia nor Egypt nor Libya and so on. This occurs at a time when Egypt was never more similar officially to Tunisia, Bahrain, and Libya than in these revolutionary days. So just as the revolting Bahraini citizen wants reform that provides a constitutional monarchy and a prime minister that is not appointed by the royal place, but produced by the actual political arena and its balance of forces, similarly the revolting Egyptian and Syrian citizens want reform that provides a genuine constitutional president of the republic and a prime minister not appointed by presidential fiat, but actually produced by the democratic political arena of the country. Thus, for a relatively long time, the Arabs did not feel the closeness, similitude, and unity of the Arab countries as to their challenges, blockages, tyrannies, social movements, and possible solutions as the Arabs now feel them. The unity of the Arab states as police states and their similarities as tyrannical regimes were never as manifest as during the Arab Spring. The Arab unity in despotic rule and in the realities of oppression was certainly on display as never before.

The regimes rushed with extreme anxiety and unmistakable panic to take refuge in mega-conspiracy theories to explain away what in the end they brought on themselves. All this after the incessant efforts and the coercion that the regimes of tyranny and the states they run had worked hard to present themselves as the centre and locus of the most rational, enlightened inclusive, patriotic, and civilized tendencies in Arab societies. Societies that are still, they say, plagued by vertical sectarian, ethnic, tribal, and regional divisions, which cause the fragmentation of the peoples and act to reinforce their backwardness and anachronism.

We saw those very Arab regimes united in clinging mechanically, repetitively, and neurotically to the fables of conspiracy explanations and interpretations and persisting at any rate with the Kafkaesque absurdities of their delirious logic. It is certainly significant that it was not the Tahrir Square revolting masses that resorted to conspiratorial justifications, although many have accused those same masses of following those theories at times to the point of dementia. The Arab unity of the top dogs showed itself best in such united policies as official, wilful blindness, arrogance, and denial and in devising a security solution for each protest, demand, and demonstration and in treating popular demands as nothing more than subversion, rebellion, treachery, and betrayal. This is why the unity of the Arab states as police states and their similarities as tyrannical regimes were never as manifest as during this Arab Spring. The Arab Spring showed as well the emergence of another type of Arab unity, welling up from below this time. This kind of popular Arab unity was never more evident than in the resounding shout reverberating from Tunisia to Egypt to Libya to Yemen to Syria: '*Al shaab youridou iskat al nizam*' – 'The people want to overthrow the regime'. Since when had words such as 'the people want' meant anything at all in the Arab world?

Another important manifestation of Arab unity from below – that is from the world of the underdogs, not the top dogs – is to be found in the fact that the charisma of the revolutionary moment shifted from the usual concentration on a single and unrivalled leader to the flow and diffusion of the assembled masses in the many Arab Tahrir Squares, making the congregation itself the true charismatic moment of the revolution and of change. This important development is certainly new for us Arabs and for our modern, social, and political history.

For this reason, the Tahrir Squares in Tunis, Cairo, Manama, Sana'a, and Benghazi were unified, for example, by immense civil participation of women and the visible presence of children (boys and girls) – this in extremely conservative societies and prudish cities. In addition, they were unified by various forms of art, innovative forms of expression, music performances, songs, plays, dances, balloons, prayers, satirical cartoons, sarcastic comments, and critical graffiti. Generally, all this was done with relatively happy faces. This was in spite of the wholesale use of aggressive thugs, deadly militias, indiscriminate repression, and live ammunition. There was something of a carnivalesque spirit and practice in all these packed squares and I use 'carnivalesque' here in the Bakhtinian sense of carnival mocking and deflating the pretensions of high power and oppression. This is something that is certainly unheard of in the history of modern Arab political demonstrations and forms of mass political protest.

The charismatic moment of the Arab Spring showed a high degree of maturity trying to transcend the alarmist scenarios promoted, reinforced, and put into practice for a long time by the top dogs of the regimes. These scenarios put our societies before drastic, harsh, and inescapable choices such as, either the continuation of despotic regimes, their marshal law, permanent state of emergency and their security apparatuses in place or the inevitable vertical disintegration of our societies along religious, sectarian, ethnic, regional, and tribal lines with what all this means in terms of social fragmentation.

The 'Return' of Islamism and its Contested Forms

If Arab nationalism and the usual ideas about Arab unity were conspicuously absent from the Arab Spring, it remains undeniable that political Islam proved to be conspicuously present and the talk is all about Islam, Islamism, the Muslim Brothers, Salafis, Salafism, fundamentalism, and the spontaneous religiosity of the masses of the Tahrir Squares everywhere. A good way to start the discussion on this issue is Bernard Lewis's essay of the 1970s, 'The return of Islam'.[2] The most important question that Lewis fails to address in his essay is where had Islam been? Let me clarify that for Lewis, Islam neither really goes nor returns, but it simply reverts to type. In other words, Islam here is presented as an expressive

---

[2] Bernard Lewis, 'The return of Islam', *Commentary Magazine*, January 1976, pp. 39–49.

totality with a constant core that manifests itself and infuses every bit, piece, and part of that totality.

The movements, processes, drifts, tugs, and pulls of history may temporarily affect the surface of that expressive totality and introduce abnormalities and distortions in it such as nationalism, socialism, populism, modernism, Marxism, secularism, reform, and so on. But in the end, the totality reverts to type and remains faithful to its transcendental core, eventually shaking off all these foreign distortions and abnormalities in the process. So, *homo islamicus* remains *homo islamicus* no matter what. And Lewis's concept of the return of Islam turns out to be no more than a static euphemism for Islam simply reverting to type as usual. There were also grand Arab debates and controversies of the 1960s and 1970s on such issues as *al-asala wal mouaasara* (authenticity versus contemporaneity), *al tourath wal hadatha* (heritage versus modernity), *al Islam wal tajdid* (Islam and renewal) in which very prominent public intellectuals and thinkers were involved including Tayyib Tizini in Damascus, Adonis the famous Syrian poet and public intellectual, Muhammad Abid al Jabiri, Hussein Mrowa, Mohammed Arkoun, and others. These debates were certainly not innocent at all from similar Lewisian assumptions and premises. A more empirical and realistic approach is required, instead of Lewis's of Islam reverting to type. No one can compare, say, Egypt under Nasser and during the nationalist-populist phase of Arab socialism to the Egypt of Hosni Mubarak without being struck by the fact that there is a return of Islam in some primary manifest sense, and by the presence of new Islamic symbolic reference points for communal and inter-communal identification, and for differentiation, conflict, and strife. If there is then such an obvious empirical sense of the return of Islam, still the question remains: where did Islam go in the first place?

Here is an answer: during the nationalist-populist phase in the postcolonial life of key Arab countries – especially Egypt, Syria and Iraq – Islam's primacy over the public, institutional, economic, social, legal, and cultural life of Arab society had eroded unmistakably. Thus, it was strikingly clear that hardly anything in the society, economy, politics, culture, and law of those key countries was run according to Islamic precepts, administered along the lines of Sharia Law or functioning in conformity with the theological doctrine and/or teachings of Islam, except in family law. In those countries, the modern secular nationalist calendar with its new holidays, symbols, monuments, historical sites, battles, heroes, ceremonies, and memorial days had come to fill the public space, relegating the old religious calendar and its landmarks to the margins of public life. Nasser himself never justified his own regime by appealing to religion or Islam, for example. To give an idea of the mood prevalent during that phase, it is useful to quote Adonis's manifesto directed to the revolutionary Arabs of the times:

As revolutionary Arabs, what we aspire to and work for is laying the foundations for a new age for the Arabs. We know that instituting a new age presupposes from the very beginning a complete break with the past. We also know that the starting point of this founding break is criticism, the criticism of all that is inherited, prevalent and common. The role of criticism here is not limited to exposing and laying bare whatever prevents the establishment of a new age but extends to its destruction. Our past is a world of lostness in a variety of religious, political, cultural and economic forms. It is a realm of the unseen and the illusory, which continues and extends. It is a realm that not only hinders the Arab from finding himself but also prevents him from making himself. And since the structure of prevalent Arab life and culture is based on religion, we understand very well the dimensions of Marx's statement to the effect that the criticism of religion is the condition for all other criticism. If we keep in mind also that criticism for Karl Marx is neither mental nor abstract, but practical and revolutionary, then we can say that the revolutionary criticism of the Arab heritage is the condition for any revolutionary Arab action.[3]

To press the point more seriously, a similar declaration was also made by a prominent Syrian theoretician and activist of those days, Yassin Al Hafez. This reflects the same prevalent mood and spirit, especially concerning religion – this is where Islam went:

A critique of all aspects of actually existing Arab society and its traditions, a strict scientific and secular critique plus a deep and penetrating analysis is one of the fundamental obligations of the revolutionary socialist Arab vanguard in the Arab homeland. Such a critique alone is capable of readying the conditions that would permit the uprooting of all the negative, inhibiting and disabling aspects of our social heritage. Exploding the traditional frames of Arab society will lead precisely to the acceleration of the rate of work on the construction of a completely modern Arab society. Without this act of exploding, the possibility of a systematic, speedy and revolutionary development of the traditional intellectual and social structures of the Arab people becomes questionable if not impossible. At the same time, this will in its turn cast its negative and disabling shadows on serious and swift Arab economic growth.[4]

The concept of the return of Islam will start making historical and soci-ological sense in contrast and in comparison with what was prevalent during the nationalist-populist phase of Arab political social and cultural

---

[3] *Mawaqif*, Beirut, No. 6, Autumn 1969, p. 2.
[4] Yassin Al-Hafez, *The Complete Works*, Centre for Arab Unity Studies, Beirut, p. 231.

life. Given the Arab Spring and its forces now, what is the present situation and distribution of forces of this returned Islam, especially in its ideological form known as Islamism? The stakes are very high in the fierce struggle over the definition of Islam and over the control of the meaning of Islam. This is the case in the Middle East in general and in the Arab world in particular – of course, the Arab world being the heartland of Islam. It is instructive to classify the main contending parties in this battle over the definition of Islam and over the control of the meaning of Islam as the Arab Spring is unfolding.

First, there are governments, state apparatuses, established clerical elites, and hierarchies that formulate, propagate, and defend what may be conveniently called 'Official State Islam'. The most prominent form of this kind of Islam at present is the petro-Islam of countries like Saudi Arabia and Iran, funded and supported all over the world by abundant petro-dollars. The official doctrine of Iranian petro-Islam is that of the rule of the jurist (*Velayat-e Faqih*), while the official doctrine of Saudi Islam says 'the Quran is our constitution.' In other words, there is no need for a constitution of any kind for the kingdom and absolute monarchy is best for true Islam. Every state in the Islamic world certainly has by now developed its own version of official state Islam to help serve its vital interests and check those of competing states. Even the secular Kemalist Turkish state has found for itself a benign, elastic, and tolerant version of Islam to toy with as necessary for a while.

On the whole, Sunni official Islam proved to be an indispensable ally for the West throughout the Cold War and particularly in its most literal scripturalist and rigorous readings, forms, and applications. Thus, this Islam and the West know each other very well, understand each other very well, and know how to operate together very well. This is why the bombastic complaints each makes about the other in public should be taken with a grain of salt. We know also that official Shia Islam in Iraq has come around by now to align itself as well with the United States and with Western politics and policies in the Middle East. Official state Islam in Iran has gone a long way in liquidating all the autonomous, independent, dissenting, and marginal forms and varieties of Shia Islam that flourished throughout the history of Shi'ism by slowly but surely bringing them all under the sway and control of the Iranian state and by absorbing them into official state Islam. For Sunni Islam, this process was completed long ago by the Ottoman sultans. This process of subjugation and absorption partially explains the eruption of the vigorous protest movements in Iran after the presidential elections of 2009, as well as the participation of many mullahs and ayatollahs in the protest movement, who wanted to maintain their autonomy and independence.

On the other extreme side of official state Islam, there is militant insurrectionary Islam, with a plethora of fractions, factions, and groupings that resort to spectacular terroristic violence both locally and on a world scale under the banner of resurrecting Islam's forgotten imperative of jihad (*al farida al ghaiba*) against all infidels to further their agendas. It is this version of Islam that occupied the holy shrine in Mecca, the Kaaba, in 1979, shaking the Saudi Arabian kingdom to its foundations; assassinated president Anwar Sadat in Egypt in 1981 in the hope of sparking an Islamist revolution in Egypt; conducted a losing but bloody battle against the Syrian, Egyptian, and Algerian regimes; and carried out the assaults of 9/11 inside the United States. Its doctrine of jihad apostatises (*takfir*) all the ruling regimes in the Islamic world as well as all the Muslims who serve those regimes, regarding them as no more than nominally Muslim entities and governments that require urgent re-Islamisation.

The practitioners of this type of Islam summarize their approach in two words: *takfir wa tafjir*, 'apostasise and explode'. The logic of *takfiri* Islam is simple and far reaching and can be formulated rigorously in the shape of what may be called the '*takfir* syllogism', using the Muslim Brothers in Egypt as an example and using Sayid Qutb as a basis. Premise 1): The Muslim Brothers were persecuted and tortured in Egypt during Nasser's time, when all they were saying was 'God is our Lord', 'Islam our way', and the 'Quran our constitution'. All they were doing was working for Islam in supposedly a Muslim country and society. Premise 2): Those who carried out the persecution of the Muslim Brothers and inflicted such pain and suffering on them cannot be really Muslims and must be Kafirs (apostates). This is now the first level of generalized *takfir*. Premise 3): If these agents of persecution and practitioners of torture are Kafirs, then the authorities who appointed and commanded them must be more Kafirs than those Kafirs, which is the third level of *takfir*. Premise 4): All the elites, who do not acknowledge that those authorities are Kafirs, are themselves Kafirs as well. Therefore, the popular masses that obey, applaud, and follow these Kafir authorities and their Kafir elites become Kafirs themselves because any approval of *kufr* (unbelief) is itself a *kufr*. This is then the *takfir* of the entire society.[5]

---

[5] See Sayyed Qutb, *Milestones*, Chicago: Kazi Publications, First Edition (English), January 1993. Also Muhammad Qutb, *The Jahilliyya of the 20th Century* (Arabic), Cairo, Dar al-Shuruq, 1965.

A cautionary remark is in order. Although Lebanon's Hezbollah and Palestine's Hamas carry some family resemblances to this kind of Islam, they are not to be reduced to it. Both organizations are, up to a point, reminiscent of old twentieth-century national liberation movements with an Islamist mobilizing ideology concentrating mainly on liberating occupied territories. They conduct their struggles and fights locally, attack only the occupying country, and have a carefully defined and achievable goal. They are, in principle, ready to negotiate a deal with the enemy and have strong and highly supportive popular constituencies. However, because Hezbollah is a purely Shia organization and Hamas is a purely Sunni movement, neither of them can qualify for the honorific title of a national liberation movement.

This kind of jihadi Islam declared unambiguously its distinction from any other method of furthering its vital goals and programmes through the direct and immediate attack on the internal and external enemy as violently, extravagantly, spectacularly, and destructively as possible, heedless of the longer-term chances of success of such attacks, contemptuous of their self-destructive consequences, and dismissive of their social, political, and economic fallout even on Islam and Islamism itself. In fact, the general outlook and tactics of this kind of Islam bear resemblances to the outlook and tactics of Europe's left-wing armed insurrectionary factions of the 1970s, such as the Action Directe in France, the Baader-Meinhof Gang in Germany, and the Italian Red Brigades. In other words, this is a kind of Action Directe Islam, opting for blind, spectacular, and violent forms of jihad. Obviously, these two sorts of jihad, the European and the Muslim, share a preference for shortcut solutions such as assassinations, hostage taking, kidnappings, and suicide bombings over long-term political work and the patient elaboration of credible alternatives and programs to the status quo. The American equivalent for that period would be the Action Directe of the Weathermen, Jerry Rubin's manifesto of 1970 'DO IT!' and the resulting cries of the Watts riots of 1965, 'Burn baby Burn'.

The third main contender in the fierce struggle for the definition and control of the meaning of Islam is middle-class commercial Islam, represented primarily by the bourgeoisies of various Muslim and Arab countries and led by an assortment of agencies such as the chambers of commerce, industry, agriculture, multiple forms of Islamic banking, investment houses, venture capital, and so on. In so far as these middle classes form the backbone of civil society in their respective Middle Eastern countries, their Islam becomes the Islam of civil society in general. It is an Islam that is moderate, conservative, good for business, and certainly not to be confused with either the Islam that aspires to absolute power or with the other form of Islam that promotes violent eruptions without a cause. It abhors the salvific projects of the radical secular left, no less than the similar projects of the radical Islamic right. Generally speaking, this Islam organizes itself around the notion of civil society and its empowerment and around an emerging quasi-consensus calling for some respect of human rights, a measure of democratic rule, an independent judiciary, the end of martial law, and the end of the state of siege imposed on any one of its countries.

A model of the hegemony of this kind of Islam is to be found today in Turkey under the rule of the Justice and Development Party. The lure of the Turkish example is already being powerfully and widely felt in the Arab world. Politically, this Islam is of decisive importance at present because Turkey now is the only Muslim country with a developed and explicit secular ideology, tradition, and practice and also the only Muslim society to produce a seemingly democratic political party, something like Europe's Christian democratic parties (they certainly present themselves that way), capable of ascending to power electorally and peacefully without a catastrophe befalling the whole polity, as happened elsewhere. This novel achievement of middle-class, good-for-business Islam showed itself capable of bringing the Turkish military establishment finally under democratic civilian control. Arab Islamic Justice and Development political parties are already mushrooming in various Arab countries and states. Therefore, my own anticipation is that when currently turbulent Arab states and societies stabilise, and to some extent democratize, it will be some version of a middle-class, good-for-business Islam that will float to the surface.

Conclusion

All in all, the Arab Spring revolutions, revolts, and intifadas represent the finest hour of our civil societies that are still in the making. They signify major epistemological, ideological, and political breaks with a generally despotic, stagnant, and arbitrary postcolonial political condition. Even if only thirty to forty per cent of the features and innovations of this charismatic moment are eventually incorporated into Arab social and political life, then we can speak seriously of the inauguration of a new era in Arab politics.

13

Yemen

Revolution Suspended?

Gabriele vom Bruck, Atiaf Alwazir and Benjamin Wiacek

Abstract

Against the backdrop of a UN-brokered transition agreement, in February 2012, the Yemeni President 'Ali 'Abdullah Saleh relinquished power to his deputy, who formed a new government which included the opposition. Unlike uprisings in other Arab countries, in Yemen, elite rivalries revealed themselves in the uprising of 2011 and shaped its trajectory. Saleh's rivals joined the protest movement and took control of it, establishing hierarchical relations among the protesters and thus enabling themselves to exercise censorship. In certain respects, the old regime has endured in another guise, but the new president, 'Abd-Rabbu Mansur Hadi, has begun to dismantle some of its pillars. In the light of a collapsed economy, a humanitarian crisis, unresolved conflicts in several parts of the country, political instability and greater U.S. involvement, he faces extraordinary challenges.

> 'Our people will remain present in every institution. Two months have passed since the creation of this weak government. It won't be able to build a thing or put one brick on top of another'. Former President 'Ali 'Abdullah Saleh, March 2012.[1]

Following several months of protests against his rule, in November 2011 the Yemeni President 'Ali 'Abdullah Saleh agreed to sign a transition agreement obliging him to transfer power to his deputy. In spite

---

[1] Associated Press, 15 March 2012.

of declaring the deal a 'coup' and the uprising a 'charade'[2] – after all, he had won the presidential election of 2006 – he insisted he had given up power voluntarily in order to spare the 'blood of Yemenis'.[3] Indeed, as the protest movement beginning in January 2011 grew stronger, Yemen's long-serving president, who prides himself on having unified the country in 1990 was confronted with two choices: 1) crush the uprising causing the death of hundreds of people and facing an uncertain future thereafter, or 2) accept a deal that guaranteed him immunity from prosecution. By not following in the footsteps of his counterparts in Tunisia and Egypt, nor Libya and Syria, and by announcing that he would remain leader of the party he had founded in 1982, the General People's Congress (GPC), he had chosen a 'third way'. He had bowed to the inevitable, but departed with his head unbowed.

Prior to Mubarak's forced resignation in February 2011, the Yemeni political elite's belief in its ability to maintain power was unshaken (Phillips 2011: 21). Saleh had weathered the storms of three decades. For example, because of his shrewd manipulation of jihadis, they never posed a real threat to his rule.[4] Anti-regime demonstrations in northern and southern Yemen since 2003 were met with extreme force, and for almost a decade failed to escalate into nationwide protests. In spite of being the first ruler on the Arabian Peninsula to have introduced an embryonic democratic system, Saleh's government retained key features of Arab military regimes such as unaccountable security agencies. Saleh preferred 'closed-door patrimonial bargaining over inclusive participatory politics' (Phillips 2011: 12).[5] His 'divide and rule' strategies served to maintain a level of disorder paradoxically conducive to ensuring regime survival rather than state building (Wedeen 2008: 51, 179).[6]

The botched unification of the Yemen Arab Republic (YAR) and the People's Democratic Republic of Yemen (PDRY) ended in the latter's defeat in the war of 1994. Thereafter, reforms were gradually revoked. Saleh amended the unity constitution by dismantling institutions of joint

---

[2] Personal communication with chief negotiators, 22 March 2012, London.

[3] "الرئيس اليمني: ثورات الربيع العربي لوثة وتخريب", www.bbc.co.uk/arabic/middleeast/2012/02/120213_yemen_saleh.shtml.

[4] Several jihadis, some of whom had fought the Soviet army in Afghanistan during the 1980s, were incorporated into various security units (Boucek 2010: 12).

[5] Quoting Daniel Brumberg and others, Phillips (2008: 34) notes that state-initiated political openings can be instrumental in perpetuating authoritarian regimes.

[6] Here Wedeen theorizes an argument made earlier by the International Crisis Group (2002: 14).

governance and granting himself increasing authority to rule by decree (Day 2010: 65). In 2009, all political parties agreed to postpone parliamentary elections to initiate a dialogue on reforms of the electoral and constitutional framework that had hitherto mainly served the GPC's own interests. Instead of promoting dialogue, a few months before the uprising the ruling party suggested amendments to the constitution that would abolish presidential term limits and thus enable Saleh to seek another term after the end of his present one in 2013. Promises made by him in 2010 to implement administrative and economic reforms to tackle growing poverty and declining oil and water resources were not kept (Phillips 2011: 41). The following year, Muhammad al-Dhurafi, then assistant deputy minster at the Ministry of Finance, claimed that 'since the beginning of the 1970s... no new hospitals were built in San'a other than private ones. This violates the principles of a nation that is concerned with the well-being of its citizens. The level of unemployment and poverty probably exceeds that of African nations... Saleh's palace is only 200 meters away from the traffic light junction that is filled with beggars of all ages. It cannot be said that he is ignorant of the situation'.[7]

A 'stabilisation' project initiated by the 'Friends of Yemen' in 2010 attempted to salvage a regime that had lost its legitimacy amongst the population, but took into account neither political grievances nor Saleh's history of broken promises. Modelled on simultaneous revolts in North Africa, the uprising against Saleh's regime a year later brought those grievances into sharp focus. What was more, intra-elite divisions and rivalries within the powerful Hashid confederation from which the political elite was recruited had already become apparent during the 2006 presidential elections and Saleh's war in the northern province of Sa'da (2004–2010). These power struggles reverberated in the uprising and even manifested themselves in violent clashes between republican guards commanded by Saleh's son Ahmad and Hashid militia in the spring of 2011. In the elections, Hamid al-Ahmar, a wealthy businessmen whose father was the paramount shaykh of Hashid and founder of al-Islah, Yemen's first 'Islamist' party, supported Saleh's rival candidate.[8] In those years, tensions between the Ahmars and members of Saleh's family about the monopolisation of economic assets took on a political dimension.

[7] 'Yemen: The stolen revolution?' YouTube (http://www.presstv.ir), 14 September 2011.
[8] Al-Islah was founded in 1990 as a counterweight to the Yemeni Socialist Party. Divided internally, it is made up of tribal leaders, businessmen, hard-line Salafi groups, and religious moderates such as Nobel Laureate Tawakkul Karman.

According to one of the president's loyalists, 'Saleh encouraged and supported the Ahmars' entrepreneurial activities in order to keep them away
from politics. He did not realise that Hamid was accumulating money in
order to satisfy his political ambitions in the future'.

In 2009, Saleh was more occupied with outmanoeuvring his rivals than
with the new threat arising from the merging of the Yemeni and Saudi
branches of al-Qaeda (Al-Qaeda in the Arabian Peninsula – AQAP). The
military campaign in Sa'da, ostensibly to weaken the charismatic new
Zaydi-Shi'i leadership that had emerged in response to aggressive Salafi
missionary activity, turned in its later phase into a theatre for humiliating
Saleh's key rival, General 'Ali Muhsin al-Ahmar.[9] The general, one of the
biggest landowners in the country who commanded the First Armoured
Division (FAD) until December 2012 and was a prominent member of the
regime's inner circle, opposed Saleh's grooming of his eldest son Ahmad
as successor. King 'Abdullah and Prince Nayif of Saudi Arabia, who had
long been weary of President Saleh, contemplated replacing him with
the general. Subsequently, Saleh had the General's brigades moved away
from the capital and established new security organizations headed by
his nephews who he believed would back his son. One of the reasons
for rekindling the Sa'da war in August 2009 was to expose the general's
poor performance on the battlefield, thus undermining his credibility.
Whenever the general appeared on the point of success, Saleh halted
military operations.[10]

Renewed warfare might also have forced Hamid al-Ahmar to abandon his plan to organize nationwide anti-regime demonstrations to fetter
Saleh's power.[11] Such protests would have been inappropriate at a time
the regime claimed to defend national unity. At that time, Hamid tried
to convince 'Ali Muhsin to join the opposition.[12] However, the general
defected only after he surmised the regime might unravel after the killing
of over forty protesters on 18 March 2011. He exploited the uprising to
launch his opposition to Saleh and to take revenge; by assuming prominent roles as sponsors and protectors of the protesters, he and Hamid
were able to claim the moral high ground.

---

9   'Ali Muhsin, who hails from a humble background in Sanhan, is not related to the
    shaykhly al-Ahmar family that belongs to a section of Hashid called al-'Usaymat. The
    Zaydi-Shi'is are a moderate branch of the Twelver-Shi'a.
10 Army commander Hamid al-Qusaybi, cited by a government official requesting
    anonymity.
11 Wikileaks Sanaa 00001617 002 OF 003.
12 Ibid.

The Uprising: A View from Within

Inspired by the fall of Ben 'Ali's regime, on 15 January 2011, students and unemployed graduates in Ta'izz and San'a took to the streets in support of the Tunisians, calling for an end to corruption and for economic and democratic reforms in their own country.[13] Protests quickly spread to other parts of the country, including Aden where demonstrations in favour of south Yemen's renewed separation from the north had taken place since 2007. In response, Saleh proposed constitutional amendments limiting the number of presidential terms – a move that left protesters unconvinced. In an attempt to stop the movement from gaining momentum, a few days later activist and subsequent Nobel Peace Prize winner Tawakkul Karman, who was leading some of the student protests, was accused of organizing illegal demonstrations and was detained along with dozens of other activists.

At an emergency parliamentary session on 2 February, Saleh announced that he would not 'extend [his] mandate' and that he disapproved of 'hereditary rule'.[14] However, the next day ('Day of Rage'), following calls by the Joint Meeting Parties (JMP – the opposition main coalition) for 'million-man marches' all over the country, 10,000 people gathered at San'a University.[15] Like in several North African countries, protesters shouted slogans demanding 'the end of the regime'. Demonstrations continued until Mubarak's resignation on 11 February. Thousands of people went to the streets to celebrate the fall of a second Arab dictator, seeing it as a sign that Saleh might be next. That night, hundreds of security forces and armed thugs attacked the protesters with knives and sticks, while police arrested dozens.[16] A week thereafter, a group of students set up tents outside the gate of San'a University and vowed not to leave the area. Day by day more people joined, until the place was transformed into a 'tent-city' with thousands of inhabitants: Change

---

[13] Demonstrations may also have been linked to the long history of labour strikes and protests that began in the South and later extended to the North. In 2008, strikes by port workers, teachers, labourers, and professors took place in cities throughout Yemen. In 2011, demands for employment, increased wages, and better work conditions reinvigorated this labour movement.

[14] *Time*, 2 February 2012. This is an allusion to the accusation made by many Yemenis that Saleh wanted his son Ahmad to assume power after him.

[15] The JMP, founded in 2002, is a coalition of six opposition parties dominated by the Islah party, seconded by the Socialist Party that used to be the ruling party of the PDRY.

[16] http://www.hrw.org/news/2011/02/11/yemen-pro-government-forces-attack-demonstrators.

Square was born.[17] With time, the 'tent city' covered more than four kilometres strung across the road. Its inhabitants came from different social and regional backgrounds, including Islamists, socialists, liberals, artists, judges, academics, women, children, the elderly, the unemployed... all sharing food and qat.[18] From one entrance, a sign read 'Welcome to the land of liberty'. However, in Change Square and other squares around the country, Yemenis were not newly discovering the power of acting as a public (see Tripp, Chapter 6 in this volume). By virtue of its tradition of civic activism (Carapico 1998), party politics and its daily qat sessions often involving large numbers of people and intense political deliberation, Yemen's public sphere has never been depoliticized, nor could it be entirely controlled by security agents (Wedeen 2008). On the one hand, collective political activism at the square constituted continuity with other forms of citizen participation (yet in more potent form). On the other hand, it promoted novel forms of national solidarities that might change the terms of Yemeni citizens' political subjectivities and interaction in the future.

At the square, social boundaries related to gender, class, and region were transcended to some degree. Existing gender moralities and local legal codes were challenged. San'ani women, who traditionally must neither be out at night nor talk to unrelated men (except in places such as universities and offices), slept in (women-only) tents and chewed qat with men.[19] Self-identified tribesmen shared tents with opposing tribesmen with whom for years they had been locked into cycles of revenge killings, agreeing on peaceful relations and instructing their tribes not to revenge their deaths in case they were killed by security forces during the uprising.[20] Networking, awareness-raising activities, debates, seminars, and art exhibitions constituted democratic practice more inclusive than, say, at qat chews. Literacy classes were held and more than twenty newspapers were produced and distributed by both professional and 'citizen journalists'. Prior to the uprising, these activities targeted above all urban elite or civil society groups, building the foundation of an

---

[17] Many 'squares' were created in various cities throughout Yemen. By virtue of the location of our field research, and the fact that many of the protesters and activists from other cities congregated in San'a, we focus on events there.

[18] Qat is a mild stimulant chewed by adults.

[19] Qat chews are usually gendered.

[20] 'Un tribalisme civilisé', *La Voix du Yémen*, 27 April 2011. http://www.lavoixduyemen .com/2011/04/27/un-tribalisme-civilise/239.

inclusive nationwide grass-roots movement that was partially blocked owing to events following 18 March.

18 March – A Turning Point in the Movement?

On 18 March, after Friday prayers, snipers fired on pro-democracy protesters at Change Square, causing many deaths. Several government officials resigned in protest. 'Friday of Dignity', as it was referred to later, was the bloodiest and most violent day witnessed by peaceful protesters in San'a, and a turning point in the uprising, changing the scene on the ground, the players, the decision-makers, and the movement's direction. Activists held the government responsible, but Saleh denied his forces were behind the shooting and court proceedings have been suspended. Saleh declared a state of emergency, imposed a curfew on 'armed men in all cities'[21] and fired his entire cabinet. The most important consequence of the shooting was the announcement by General 'Ali Muhsin and several senior army commanders of their support for the 'revolution' and the deployment of army units to 'protect' the protestors.[22] FAD soldiers surrounded the square and replaced the civilian security. However, the general did not officially resign, nor was he dismissed from the army. Nor did he remove Saleh's portrait from his office – in fact, he added another one later on. At the square, his joining of the protests was controversial. Some protesters, who felt vulnerable after the killings, hailed him and his soldiers as heroes who had vowed to make the square a sanctuary for peaceful demonstrators. Others took a pragmatic view arguing that the FAD's defection created a balance between army factions and offered protesters more bargaining power. However, others suspected that the general besieged the square as a form of protection for his units from possible attacks by the Republican Guards. Some also thought 'Ali Muhsin, who has always been a shadowy figure in Yemeni politics (Phillips 2008: 52), was playing a double game, implying that he wanted to settle scores with Saleh and pursue his own interests rather than support the youth's demands.[23] Some of those who contested the general's presence at the square, considering him to be part of the regime

---

[21] "Yemen unrest: 'Dozens killed' as gunmen target rally", *BBC News*, 18 March 2011. http://www.bbc.co.uk/news/world-middle-east-12783585.

[22] Ibid.

[23] Interview with Hamza al-Kamali, 'Independent Media Centre', Change Square, 20 March 2011.

and a political player seeking to maintain the status quo, left the square. They were also concerned about a possible military coup by the general. According to Hamza Al-Kamali, a young protestor, 'how can a man who has a bloody past and is responsible for the death of thousands of people, be moved by the death of only fifty-two? This is surely his way of getting on the winning team and to save himself'. Indeed, sympathizers of the Southern Movement[24] and the Zaydi-Shi'i revivalist movement (Huthis) disapproved of the general's announcement on the grounds that he had participated in the war of 1994 that led to the defeat of southern forces and was in charge of the military campaign in Sa'da.

Similar discussions took place in the southern provinces, which by the time the nationwide uprising began had already witnessed four years of mass opposition to the Saleh regime. When the protests spread to several cities, many amongst the Southern Movement believed that there was a real opportunity for change and put aside their calls for secession, hoping that a new regime would mean justice for the South. However, after 'Ali Muhsin embraced the protest movement, they became disillusioned; subsequently, calls for 'an end to northern occupation' and separation intensified.

Another implication of his joining was the gradual militarisation of the square. Despite the commitment to peaceful resistance, since the arrival of the FAD, the line between soldiers and protesters became more blurred. Soldiers were seen entering tents with their Kalashnikovs, something that was forbidden at the outset of the 'revolution'. Occasionally, they changed their uniforms for civilian clothes. At the square, 'Ali Muhsin recruited unemployed young men – often under eighteen – for the FAD and Islah-affiliated militias.

In a newspaper interview, Yahya al-Dhib, the first soldier who defected from Saleh's army prior to 'Ali Muhsin and the FAD, spoke of the negative effect of the general's control over the square, especially because he had been recruiting civilians to fight in his army. He also explained how he was threatened after refusing orders from 'Ali Muhsin to use violence against attackers. 'They told me that if you want your salary, you have to hold the weapon and kill whoever assaults the protesters', adding 'they will make us kill each other and they will not care how many of us die'.[25]

---

24 The Southern Movement emerged as a result of discontent in the southern provinces after 1994. Earlier demands for equal citizenship rights and jobs have culminated in calls for the reinstatement of the PDRY (see Day 2010).
25 'Faces from Yemen's revolution: Yahia al-Dheeb', *Yemen Times*, 10 October 2011.

In fact, in September and October 2011, attacks by security forces on protesters soon evolved into clashes between them and the FAD.

Post-18 March: 'Establishment' Actors Consolidate their Power in Change Square

Echoing Filiu (2011 57), Tripp (Chapter 6 in this volume) highlights the 'leaderless' nature of the uprisings of 2011. However, in Yemen's Change Square there were powerful actors who aspired to control the protest movement and did not shy away from the use of force. In spite of declaring their opposition to Saleh, those men – all members of the regime – began to exercise authority over the space that had been previously reclaimed by protesters as part of 'a counter-hegemonic project of resistance' (ibid.). As a self-styled leader of the opposition against Saleh, 'Ali Muhsin became a paradoxical figure who maintained his government salary after his defection. His joining also consolidated the power of his close affiliate, the Islah party that after the 'Friday of Dignity' came to play a crucial role in determining the protest movement's direction. At the square, this raised questions as to whether the uprising was an independent movement led by 'youth' – as it has often been portrayed – or whether it was dominated by the most powerful opposition party, al-Islah. Thanks to its access to mosques and party-affiliated NGOs, al-Islah has a large following. The large presence of unemployed youth at the square has also helped al-Islah and 'Ali Muhsin to 'buy' loyalties through money and food distribution.

Al-Islah's attempt at controlling the square and Hamid Al-Ahmar's intention to use his constituency to gain power caused resentment, especially amongst the younger generation who does not hold memberships of officially recognised political parties, nor close ties or affiliations ('independents').[26] Those who had spearheaded the protest movement and felt empowered were disillusioned. As one of the student protesters who had been amongst those who began the sit-in in front of San'a University in February 2011 noted, 'our tents were not as nice as they are now, we did not have enough food, and we were not as organized, but we were in control'. Although lacking experience and funding, they were successful in forming coalitions with other groups. For example, the Coordination Council for the Yemeni Revolution for Change (CCYRC), an umbrella coalition intended to bring together independent groups in squares across

---

[26] Some have been active in politics on an independent basis or in NGOs.

Yemen, was made up of about seventy groups nationwide. Grass-roots groups emerged whose numbers steadily increased, taking on different tasks: medical, security, financial, provision of services, and the establishment of media task forces. However, once well-organized and well-funded members of the JMP (mainly Islahis) joined the movement, they began infiltrating the organizing committee that was in control of security and planning activities. At first, 'independent' youth welcomed them because organizing and coordinating the movement was a priority. Yet, eventually, Islahi hardliners who had assumed the leadership of many of the major groups consolidated their power and monopolised decisions. In an arena where emphasis was placed on freedom and change, the organizing committee began censoring information and confiscating private property.

Thus, after 18 March, with the support of the FAD, al-Islah grew stronger and slowly began monopolising the square's platform – the centre of media broadcasting and live coverage – and decision-making processes.[27] Consequently, independent groups became marginalized, unable to express their own opinions – their choices were to stay quiet, to suffer abuse, or to leave the square. The Islah party and the independent youth were caught in a tug of war, with leading activists chanting, 'No partisan politics, no political parties. Our revolution is a Youth Revolution'.

Independent groups repudiated accusations that they were controlled by either al-Islah or more generally the JMP. They often used these two terms interchangeably, highlighting the hegemony of al-Islah over other parties (of the JMP) as exemplified by their control over political decision-making. Many argued, since the other JMP parties remained in the coalition even after many abuses were committed against activists, that they were complicit in the crimes. As one protester asked, 'while it is al-Islah hardliners who commit the crimes, why are the other parties still partners in the coalition even though they are also targets?'

Islah's control over the square often led independent activists to defy its decisions in order to demonstrate that it does not control 'the street'. Feeling excluded and resentful, on various occasions they and others organized their own marches without the approval of the organizing committee – only to experience violence from Islahi hardliners and 'Ali Muhsin's soldiers. Following protesters' complaints about the organizing committee's policies, its members were replaced, but maltreatment of protesters did not stop.

---

[27] Controlling the square, of course, means controlling the outgoing messages.

After Saleh's speech about inappropriate mixing of men and women protesters, a cross-gender march was planned in protest at his remarks. The organizing committee was concerned to 'prove' that women did not fraternize with men at the square. Some of those who marched jointly that day were beaten by committee members and FAD soldiers – those who had vowed to protect the protesters. Defying the committee's orders, on another occasion independent protesters marched to (the then Vice President) 'Abd-Rabbu Mansur Hadi's house and were met with batons and gun shots in the air, and some were detained once again. Al-Islah's and 'Ali Muhsin's authority manifested itself not least in the prisons run by them – the clichéd hallmark of Foucault's disciplined subject – where recalcitrant youth were taken. The rationale given for operating private jails at the square (and new ones established by 'Ali Muhsin, found in various public institutions) was to 'detain thugs who attacked peaceful protesters'. The organizing committee often detained independent protesters on the false premise that they were 'thugs', and soon these prisons became populated with people who had been too vocal against the decisions of either al-Islah or 'Ali Muhsin. Protesters were to defy state power, but not theirs. Human rights organizations were not allowed to visit the prisoners who claimed to have been repeatedly beaten. 'There are many methods they use to impose their decisions, such as [offering] food in return for loyalty, making accusations that someone is a government spy, or detaining people as happened to me' said Nasir al-'Ujaybi, an independent protester and member of the CCYRC. Independent protesters and groups opposed to al-Islah's or 'Ali Muhsin's practices in the square were also faced with smear campaigns via Facebook and the Suhayl television channel owned by Hamid al-Ahmar.

Although the JMP – especially al-Islah – was criticised by 'independents' over these violations, it was able to deny responsibility because of the clever distance it created between them and other groups in the square. For example, the organizing committee did not officially carry al-Islah's name, and many of its members were not affiliated to the party. However, a closer look into the group's composition reveals that the decision-makers were members of al-Islah and often received direct orders from top party leaders. Similarly, many other groups who claimed to be independent were in fact affiliated to the party. This has allowed them to control the square and simultaneously evade responsibility when the organizing committee is accused of violations, giving it the opportunity to play both sides.

Moreover, some leading Islah civil society members remained quiet even while abuse occurred, often questioning the truth behind such accusations. Amongst them was Tawakkul Karman, chairwoman of the NGO 'Women Journalists without Chains' who had already organized protests several years before the uprising began. Jointly with other members of civil society groups, she demonstrated weekly in favour of the right to freedom of expression and an end to corruption. Karman, who prefers to be known as a youth activist rather than a member of al-Islah's advisory council, exemplifies the double game played by her party; members of the party – including 'Ali Muhsin, who has ties to it – secured leading roles in both camps. In the early days of the 'revolution', Karman's decisions often varied from the politics of her party. Occasionally, she was at odds with its leadership, most notably on 11 May 2011, when she decided to march without the approval of the organizing committee. Thereafter, however, Karman's political decisions were in line with Islah's. For example, in a BBC interview after Saleh's signing of the transition agreement, she declared her opposition to the initiative and the forthcoming election. 'If there is only one consensus candidate where is the people's choice then?' she asked. 'This is a conspiracy against the Yemeni people, and against the revolution. It means nothing to us, and has nothing to do with us. We reject it wholeheartedly'.[28] Her party, however, asked its members and followers to take part in the election. A month before the election, Karman publicly declared her loyalty to the political process and encouraged people to vote, stating on the day of the election, 'this [election] is the successful product of the people's struggle'.[29] In response to a post on Facebook where a man wondered about her change of mind regarding the election, suggesting that her and her party's main goal was to gain seats in the new government, Karman responded 'if we look at the statistics of the martyrs and the wounded, we see that the largest share goes to the Islah party. You cannot find a single martyr from the Huthis [adherents of the Zaydi revivalist movement] and very few from the armed Southern Movement. They cry about the wounded and the martyrs but left them [protesters associated with al-Islah] alone to fight 'Ali 'Abdullah Saleh's regime'.[30]

By highlighting Islah's sacrifices and dismissing those made by others who had fought Saleh's regime, Karman made claims in the name of her party to the ownership of the 'revolution', and underscored rivalries and fault lines within the opposition, which has become more sharply

---

[28] http://youtu.be/VVD_OiDiJaY. Karman had herself planned to contest the elections.
[29] http://youtu.be/omQeVZ7TBB8.
[30] Her statement was met with indignation amongst members of the Southern Movement and the Huthis whose uprising claimed as many victims as Syria's between March 2011 and June 2012, most of them non-combatants.

polarised. In Change Square, members of the Islah party tried to burn tents set up by the Southern Movement (Hirak). After 18 March peaceful coexistence amongst Islahis and Huthis gradually gave way to collision, reflecting tensions and armed conflict between them in the northern provinces. These different sides are clearly demarcated by the slogans and posters that decorate their tents, dividing the square into a northern and southern part, with independent groups in the central area often mockingly calling the square 'north and south Beirut'. In June 2012, Islah hardliners for the first time chanted 'No to Huthis, our revolution is the revolution of the Ikhwan (Muslim Brothers)'. Thus, Islah indicated its unwillingness to eschew partisan politics, but none the less subscribed to political dialogue. Its general secretary, 'Abd al-Wahhab al-Anisi, was a member of an 'outreach committee' that discussed the Huthis' participation in the national dialogue with their leadership in Sa'da in February 2012.

Islah's double game continued even after the signing of the power-sharing agreement. As part of the JMP, Islah signed it and joined the transitional government (as will be discussed), but by May 2012, its members were still at the square shouting revolutionary slogans against the agreement. This led many younger members of al-Islah and other parties to leave them, sometimes joining new groups such as al-Watan ('Homeland'), made up of emerging youth leaders and businessmen; the Justice and Development party, headed by Muhammad Abu Luhum, a former GPC member; and the Yemeni Labour Party, the first party created by and for a stigmatised group who is attributed to East African descent and often referred to by the derogatory term 'al-Akhdam'. The first Salafi-affiliated al-Rashad party was also established. Moreover, because it joined the new government, al-Islah sought ascendancy within the JMP, which is unlikely to remain a united opposition against the new president. As for the GPC, at the time of this writing, several of its members wish to reform the party and envisage a coalition with the Yemeni Socialist Party (YSP) and the Huthis against al-Islah.

A Negotiated Transition

The Yemeni uprising alarmed both the Saudi and American governments because of its potential for stirring up revolts in neighbouring Gulf countries, for backtracking on and jeopardising U.S. counterterrorism policy and, after 'Ali Muhsin's defection, for descending into violence. During the early phase of the uprising, U.S. and EU officials were already discouraging Yemeni activists from continuing their protests.[31] In April, efforts were made to contain 'the revolution' by ousting the man at the regime's apex without altering its fundamental structure. To this end, an agreement was drafted in consultation with Saleh's advisor 'Abd al-Karim al-Iryani and others. It was Saleh's idea to involve the GCC, and subsequently the draft agreement was adopted by the secretary general of the GCC, 'Abd al-Latif al-Zayani. Like other GGC countries, at that time Saudi Arabia was opposed to Saleh's departure and played no role in the drafting of the agreement. (Qatar made a few minor amendments but later withdrew from the mediation process.) According to one political observer, 'there was a fatwa from Riyadh [that is, an endorsement of the initiative], but it was a GCC initiative without the GCC'. The agreement, which during its initial phase was not based on negotiations between the GPC and JMP, was presented to Saudi Arabia only a few hours before the signing ceremony. Calculating that it might not win fresh elections, Islah was hesitant at first but decided to support the agreement because it wanted to see Saleh squeezed out of office. What came to be known as the 'GCC initiative' centred on the formation of a government under the leadership of an opposition candidate and on demands that demonstrations end and public spaces be evacuated.[32] Following his resignation, the president was to be granted immunity from prosecution, a measure rejected by human rights groups and 'revolutionary youth' who insisted that he be held accountable for the killing of protesters.[33] The draft agreement is pursuant to several basic principles such as the preservation of Yemen's unity, security, and stability; the fulfilment of the Yemeni people's aspiration for change and reform; and a transfer of power based on national consensus. It stipulates that a national unity government will be formed with equal representation from the GPC and the opposition parties, and that the vice president will become the legitimate president thirty days after the agreement. Terms such as 'democracy', 'national dialogue', 'women', and 'youth' do not appear in the initial GCC document of April.

After Ansar al-Shari'a (Partisans of Shari'a), an affiliate of AQAP, had gained control of two cities in southern Yemen and had come close to Aden and the Arabian Sea in July 2011, the United States insisted on an

---

[31] *New Yorker*, 11 April 2011.
[32] http://www.yobserver.com, 23 April 2011.
[33] 'Yemen: Deadly attacks follow Saleh immunity pact', Human Rights Watch, 28 April 2011.

immediate transition of power. Political analysts suspect that Saleh, keen to raise fears that the militants would expand their operations were he to step down, allowed the militants some leverage. However, the United States, which still supported Saleh's regime even when it had become the main threat to national stability, seem to have interpreted their territorial gains as demonstrating the regime's inability to protect their interests in a country of geostrategic importance.[34]

Although Saleh had agreed to the GCC proposal, he declined to sign the agreement for several months – presumably, he resented the prospect that his rivals would celebrate his resignation as their victory and feared that power might fall into their hands. Consequently, he pledged to step down on behalf of the youth movement rather than the JMP (Filiu 2011: 68). In November 2011, Saleh was persuaded by UN envoy Jamal Benomar to sign the second agreement. Saleh wanted neither to suffer Qaddafi's fate nor have his assets frozen. The November agreement, which unlike the first one, was based on UN-led negotiations between Saleh and the opposition, reflects the UN's concern that the political process be participatory and inclusive. It calls for early presidential elections within ninety days and the formation of a government of national unity, stipulating that the first phase of the transition period shall end with the inauguration of the new president (this has been completed). The second phase is to last for two years – which includes the time of this writing – and is to end with the holding of general elections in accordance with a new constitution. The agreement – essentially a compromise between elites – places emphasis on human rights and good governance. It calls for the establishment of a committee on military affairs for achieving security and stability and a conference for national dialogue focussing on changes to the constitution and national reconciliation. It is to include all political actors, amongst them 'revolutionary youth', the Southern Movement, the Huthis, civil society, and women representatives. After the signing of the agreement, different members of the Security Council 'volunteered' to take on complementary advisory roles: Russia dealing with the national dialogue committee, France with constitutional reform, the United States with restructuring the army, and Britain – in liaison with EU partners – with the security and justice sector.

---

[34] For some time, Saleh's strategy had worked: in 2010, the United States spent $176 million on training and other military assistance (*Washington Post*, 16 May 2012), and King 'Abdullah granted him $700 million (*New York Times*, 17 March 2012).

A presidential election was held on February 21, 2012. 'Abd-Rabbu Mansur Hadi, a consensus figure, was the only candidate.[35] Ordinary Yemenis hoped that the election – in reality a referendum and a symbolic act sealing Saleh's exit from power – would end the 'paralysis' (a term they often used) of previous months. The new Prime Minister Muhammad Basindwa, tasked to form a government of national unity, was nominated by the opposition. Half of the coalition government is composed of members of the GPC that is still headed by the former president. He has become the éminence grise who has not ceased interfering in government affairs. Key portfolios such as foreign affairs and defence are still in the hands of his party. Like Hadi, the minister of defence General Muhammad Nasir Ahmad 'Ali hails from Abyan province (southern Yemen) and moved to the YAR in 1986. One of the shortcomings of the GCC agreement is that key members of the political elite, some of whom have attempted to stifle the political process, have not been asked to leave the country temporarily, in spite of agreeing with this proposal (the GCC objected). The power struggle within the elite – beginning before and during the uprising – has been carried into the new, post-Saleh era. Even though its members belong to various political parties, their conflict is driven by interest rather than ideology.

In addition to constitutional legality, Hadi enjoys the backing of the 'international community' and of 'Ali Muhsin, and has started to dismantle some of the old regime's pillars and to assert his authority. (This has been one of the 'revolutionary youth's' demands.) However, he has yet to demonstrate his ability to build a broad base of support within Yemeni society. In an effort to reduce southerners' alienation from the central government and indeed from himself (since he helped to defeat southern forces in 1994), he replaced Aden's governor and police chief as well as the commander of the southern region, Mahdi Maqwala, who stands accused of having collaborated with AQAP-affiliated elements in order to make the region ungovernable and of having illegally appropriated land in the south for personal gains. Hadi also replaced the governors of five provinces and nearly twenty military commanders who were loyal to

---

35 Hadi, trained at Sandhurst and in Egypt and Russia, rose in the military ranks of the PDRY. Following clashes within the ruling party in 1986, Hadi – along with his battalions – fled to the North joining 'Ali Nasir Muhammad (former PDRY prime minister) and became one of Saleh's advisors. Having dealt the southern separatist forces a decisive blow in the war of 1994, Hadi was given the defence portfolio and vice presidency. His appointment also allowed Saleh to rebut accusations that his government was dominated by the (northern) victors.

Saleh. He began to establish his own power base and – during the early months of his rule – to redress the balance between North and South in the military and security institutions. However, more recently, sustained recruitment of army and security personnel from Abyan and Shabwa has raised suspicion that he will build another, different patronage system rather than a supra-regional professional army. Former PDRY governor of Abyan Muhammad 'Ali Ahmad has returned from his exile in Britain and now supports Hadi against another PDRY veteran politician, 'Ali Salim al-Bidh, who advocates Yemen's renewed partition. Some of the governors Hadi appointed hail from the provinces they govern, amongst them those in charge of Abyan, Aden, and Ta'izz. This policy, which might help to heal divisions, constitutes a delicate balancing act because regional affiliation in the distribution of power has been a contentious issue for centuries. However, his more recent appointment of several Islahi governors in the northern provinces (in September 2012), which reflects the strong influence of the Islah party on his government, has exacerbated the violence there.

Some of Saleh's relatives and loyalists who were dismissed from their posts were defiant and even mutinous. Saleh's half-brother Muhammad Saleh al-Ahmar laid siege to San'a airport, forcing its closure after threatening to shoot down planes.[36] The transfer of the Third Brigade – an advanced military unit of the Republican Guard stationed on a mountain overlooking the presidential palace – from Saleh's nephew Tariq to 'Abd al-Rahman al-Halili, a friend of 'Ali Muhsin, carried more than symbolic weight; the brigade included about 200 tanks and was in charge of protecting the capital from all directions.[37] Several months after his inauguration, Hadi had not removed any high profile allies of 'Ali Muhsin. The officer corps was still Sanhani[38] and a number of Saleh's loyalists remained in their posts. Rather than calling off the military parade for the twenty-second anniversary of Yemen's unification after the murder of ninety-six cadets who had been rehearsing for the event the previous day, Hadi had it moved from Sab'in Square (where parades took place during Saleh's era) to the Aviation Academy located in a part of the city

[36] *Agence France-Presse*, 3 May 2012. Subsequently in June, the UN Security Council approved a resolution threatening non-military sanctions against anyone who obstructs the implementation of the GCC initiative and its mechanism (*Washington Post*, 12 June 2012).
[37] Ibid.
[38] Members of Hashid's sub-section Sanhan from which most of the regime's inner circle was recruited (see note 9).

controlled by 'Ali Muhsin,[39] thus preventing this provocative act from undermining his authority.

The dismissal of Saleh's nephews left his son Ahmad more vulnerable. Given the bold steps Hadi has taken, since 2013 his political survival has no longer depended on maintaining a balance of power between Saleh's relatives on the one hand and 'Ali Muhsin (who maintained his independent power base until December 2012) on the other hand. By June 2012, Hadi had gained considerable popular support even amongst some 'revolutionary youth' who had argued that the GCC agreement had 'hijacked the revolution'. The reshuffle pursued by Hadi may yet provoke a coup by remnants of Saleh's inner circle who resent losing power and suspect that the dismissal of their peers will strengthen their rivals' position; or by opposition figures who seek power and are concerned that men linked to the South's old political elite encroach on their status. Some key political brokers might be inclined to hinder substantial changes to the status quo unless their interests are well served. They may be disinclined to acquiesce in the dialogue's Technical Committee's recommendation to Hadi to return all properties and funds appropriated, as a kind of booty, after the war of 1994. 'Ali Muhsin, who has protected Hadi since 1986 and has declared his loyalty to him, might well abstain from obstructing the unification of the army and be content with taking up the position he held in the old regime prior to the discord between him and Saleh. Tribal leaders have been mediating between them trying to minimise the rift. Several leaders of the Hashid and Bakil confederations, amongst others, feel alienated by Hadi's personal style and by the number of southerners who have been appointed to key positions in the government and the army. They complain that Saleh was more readily available for personal consultation. Political rumours and speculation abound; this has led some government officials to recall President Ibrahim al-Hamdi's fate whose rule came to a sudden end after he ousted several important tribal leaders from their posts.[40] A number of attempts on politicians' lives, amongst them Yasin Nu'man, leader of the Socialist party, and Minister of Defence Muhammad Nasir Ahmad 'Ali (third attempt on 11 September 2012) invoked fearful memories amongst Yemenis.[41]

[39] Al-Quds al-'Arabi, 23 May 2012.
[40] Al-Hamdi ruled from 1974–1977.
[41] Between mid-2011 and November 2012, at least fifty-five military and security officials had been killed (Associated Press, 7 November 2012).

Hadi's Challenges

Three months after Hadi's inauguration, Jamal Benomar noted that the transition was taking place 'against a backdrop of serious security concerns, an unprecedented humanitarian crisis and many unresolved conflicts'.[42] Hadi's credibility will depend in part on his ability to rescue the collapsing economy, to create jobs, and to restore political stability so that the national dialogue can be brought to fruition.[43] Unlike his predecessors, he cannot rely on the 1962 revolution as a source of legitimacy, and his record does not help – during the period he served as vice president, living conditions were only fractionally better than those experienced under the ousted Hamid al-Din dynasty.

One of Saleh's burdensome legacies is the re-energised AQAP. Outfits such as Ansar al-Shari'a have failed to benefit from the turmoil in Arab countries – except in Yemen. Hadi is concerned to prove that he is capable of establishing a government that will have sovereignty over its territory and of fighting AQAP. His first statement following his election emphasized his willingness to do so. In March 2012, Ansar al-Shari'a took control of a district in Shabwa (on Yemen's south-eastern coastline) where the country's largest liquid natural gas plant operates, and of al-Briga, where Yemen's major oil refinery is located.[44] By June, Ansar al-Shari'a was driven out of southern cities such as Jaar and Zinjibar.[45] The recapture of cities in Abyan – Hadi's home province – is, of course, symbolically significant.

In 2011, divisions within the army brought the country to the brink of civil war. They have continued to stifle the political process. Therefore, one of Hadi's greatest challenges is to reorganize and unite the army under a single command. As a first step, Hadi established a new military unit composed of elements from the military police, the Central Security Forces, the Republican Guard, and the First Armoured Division. This move has helped eliminate the capital's division of several zones of rival control.[46] By helping to revamp the army, the United States is likely to gain more leverage over the Yemeni leadership and to orient it

[42] http://www.un.org/apps/news/printnews.asp?nid=42109.
[43] There is up to 70 per cent unemployment amongst Yemen's youth (*Financial Times*, 27 March 2012). A month after his election, Hadi announced the creation of 60,000 new jobs, raising the salaries of civil servants and medical treatment for those wounded in the uprising (*Yemen Times*, 25 March 2012).
[44] Al-Sharq al-Awsat, 13 March 2012.
[45] Reuters, 9 June 2012.
[46] Ginny Hill, 'Yemen's presidential gambit', *Foreign Policy*, 16 May 2012.

more strongly towards counterterrorism operations. The United States envisages 'developing interoperable and integrated approaches' in liaison with GCC countries.[47] Given Saudi Arabia's incompetent army and its disgruntlement at losing an ally, Hosni Mubarak, whose forces might have contributed to fighting its enemies in future conflicts, such a vision is of great significance, indicating that the United States is already re-thinking the Middle East's military structure within the framework of the US-GCC strategic alliance. The Saudi-owned Al-Sharq al-Awsat (15 May 2012) noted that 'Yemen is considered the geo-strategic extension of the GCC countries' security'. Al-Hayat (3 August 2012) went as far as to suggest that Yemen was likely to join the regional and international alliance against Iran.

The United States has taken advantage of the turmoil to increase its influence and the scope of its military operations in Yemen. It has increased the number of CIA operatives and Special Forces, has taken over the former Soviet air force base in al-Anad, and begun to send military aircraft to Yemen. Fourteen out of thirty-one drone attacks carried out in Yemen since 2002 have occurred in 2012, and Yemeni troops fighting in the south receive direct help from U.S. forces.[48] However, the United States's counterterrorism policy might undermine the caretaker government that in order to gain legitimacy needs to be perceived as independent by Yemeni citizens. As for Yemen's powerful northern neighbour, the obstruction of democracy and independence in Yemen will remain part of its foreign policy agenda. Unwilling to tolerate the emergence of an alternative leadership from the youth 'revolutionary movement', it has acquiesced in Hadi's presidency. Against the backdrop of Yemen's fragile economy and volatile political situation, Saudi Arabia is likely to maintain and even enlarge its patronage network there. Hadi, who will depend on Saudi Arabian largesse, will not be able to prevent it from meddling in Yemen's affairs. A GCC-sponsored conference held in Riyadh in January 2013 by Hadrami-born politicians and merchants calling for a GCC-affiliated independent Hadramaut has renewed fears amongst Yemenis that Saudi Arabia might still seek to annex it in order to gain access to the Indian Ocean.

Hadi is aware that failure of the national dialogue might lead to renewed violence and to Yemen's fragmentation. The political stalemate

47 Gerald Feierstein cited in http://yemen24news.blogspot.com/2012/02.
48 *Economist*, 12 May 2012; *Washington Times*, 17 May 2012; *Los Angeles Times*, 21 June 2012. *The Long War Journal* (13 June 2012) reports forty air strikes since 2002.

during Saleh's rule was linked partly to the fact that the 'responsible national dialogue...among the full political spectrum' (Phillips 2011: 41) he had called for never took place. As noted by the UN envoy to Yemen, 'the success or failure of the national dialogue is likely to make or break Yemen's transition'.[49] In March 2012, a preliminary meeting took place in Potsdam to explore the possibility of an inclusive dialogue. In May, Hadi formed a committee charged with contacting different political representatives; above all, those not yet represented in the political process, such as the Huthis and followers of 'Ali al-Bidh.[50] In June, talks were held in Cairo with southern leaders, amongst them 'Ali Nasir Muhammad and Haydar al-'Attas. Attempting to discourage the southern provinces from seeking secession, one of the dialogue's central goals is regional détente. Questions about sovereignty – centralised union or decentralised federation – will have to be tackled, and Yemenis will have to decide whether to choose a presidential or parliamentary system of governance. A federal constitutional system would allow those provinces that are no longer under the government's control to be incorporated. The outcome of the dialogue will feed into the constitution-making process that is to conclude in 2013.

Conclusion

Compared to the other uprisings dealt with in this volume, that in Yemen is unprecedented. A prominent member of the governing elite, but with no dynastic ties to the former leader and who came to power via a deal rather than a coup, has begun to unseat members of the old regime.[51] Saleh has been the only ousted leader granted immunity from prosecution and remains in charge of the former ruling party. Until well into the twenty-first century, Saleh used to label his adversaries 'enemies of the revolution', thus linking his rule to the 1962 revolution and claiming that it had come to fruition in him. Cognisant of the dramatic events of 2011–12, many of his fellow citizens might feel that revolution in their country is indeed a long-term project. Did Hadi, by ordering that parts of

---

[49] See note 42.
[50] Because of the GCC agreement's provision to include only members of established political parties in the new government, significant groups such as the Huthis were given neither cabinet posts nor governorships. Thus, an opportunity was missed to integrate them into the political process and to weaken their role as a militia.
[51] Note in this context that Hadi became a member by default – he was an opportunist rather than a regime loyalist.

Change Square be cleared, declare it complete? Several months thereafter, there were still many tents left in the square; for some time, Karman even moved her family and secretary to hers.[52]

The negotiation of the power-sharing agreement as well as the forthcoming national dialogue constitute democratic practice even while institutionalized; procedural democracy – a key demand of the protesters – is unlikely to be established any time soon. The impetus towards political change came from the protesters, but it was the joint effort of Yemeni politicians, foreign powers, and the UN who brought about Saleh's resignation. According to one Yemeni analyst, 'the protesters were the spark but not the fire'. In accordance with the transition agreement, power has passed between elites to the exclusion of the 'revolutionary youth'. The agreement constitutes a fragile equilibrium of sorts. It is hoped that it will not come under strain like that between the GPC and YSP in the early 1990s that ended in armed confrontation. The regime has been reframed but not undone, thanks partly to the split within Hashid. 'Ali Muhsin's desertion made Saleh vulnerable but also safeguarded the stake of the Sanhanis – not least because he also prevented Hamid al-Ahmar from monopolising the revolutionary stage.

Irrespective of what the 'revolution' may or may not have achieved,[53] the effects of public-sphere joint activism are likely to be lasting and productive of new political subjectivities. As political analyst 'Abd al-Ghani al-Iryani declared enthusiastically, 'the election provided a political opening – a shift of power from the tribal north to a democratic centre. Yemeni subjects have become Yemeni citizens'.[54] However, at Change Square, people's sense of empowerment alternated with disappointment. As it was put by a businessman whose young nephew was still going to the square in May 2012, 'in the future he will insist on his right to demonstrate. He has learnt to distinguish between people who want real change and those who want power, and that "the street" can change things. He first felt empowered and then disillusioned, but that doesn't matter'.

Protesters' demands for democratic reform have been overshadowed by a power struggle within the elite that climaxed in 2011 and might yet haunt the new government. The militarisation of Change Square

---

52 The Organizing Committee of the Youth Revolution decided to dismantle the tents in April 2013, a month after the start of the National Dialogue.
53 Space does not permit us to examine whether indeed another "revolution" has occurred.
54 Interview, 2 May 2012.

undermined the experience of solidarity, which was starting to transcend familiar divide-and-rule strategies. Self-styled 'revolutionary' leaders purporting to protect the lives of the protesters and to provide guidance also exercised censorship, intimidating and even imprisoning those who disagreed with their policies. Moreover, the initially peaceful protest movement was marred by tensions and clashes amongst the regime's opponents. *Whether* or not the national dialogue, with its emphasis on reconciliation, will be able to deflect such tensions is for the future to tell.

Postscript

After several months of political stalemate, on 19 December 2012, President Hadi issued a decree dealing with the restructuring of the army, thus starting to implement one of the principal points of the transition agreement. With the restructuring of the security forces still outstanding, the elite Republican Guard and the First Armoured Division have been amalgamated with the Strategic Reserve Force, one of the five newly established military branches. The Republican Guard is now under President Hadi's control and its former commander, Saleh's son Ahmad, will take up an ambassadorship in the UAE. General 'Ali Muhsin has been appointed presidential advisor on security affairs.

The National Dialogue Conference (NDC) began on 18 March 2013, the anniversary of the 'Friday of Dignity'. It includes 565 delegates from across Yemen's political and social spectrum, among them members of new political movements and historically marginalised groups. Women constitute 30 per cent of the representative body. The dialogue is wider in scope than those conducted in Bahrain in 2011 and 2013, and promotes discussion of issues of substance rather than their agendas. By mid-2013 it was expected that an agreement regarding the introduction of a federal system would soon be reached (few, among them Islah, have not endorsed it). Nine separate committees, some led by women, have been discussing specific issues. By June 2013, they had visited 18 governorates in an attempt to reach out to non-delegates, and made more than 100 recommendations to the Plenary. A newly created ND Consensus Committee is to reconcile those recommendations and to aid reaching consensus.

The issue of the South remains the most contentious one. In his speech to the UN Security Council on 11 June 2013, Jamal Benomar noted that without a consensual settlement of the 'Southern question' the foundations of a new constitution could not be developed. Several representatives of southern political groups are taking part in the NDC, among them Lutfi Shatarah and Muhammad 'Ali Ahmad, but many remain outside. A significant number of recommendations ("twenty points") made to President Hadi by the ND's Technical Committee address grievances and human rights violations in the South. According to a new presidential decree, issued in January 2013, two committees composed of lawyers and military personnel are to solve outstanding issues such as land appropriation in the South since the war of 1994. Proposals on the status of the South are likely to be debated within the context of discussion of a new system of governance. The UN envoy also noted that the Yemeni government has yet to establish a Commission of Inquiry into the events of 2011 or to adopt a law on transitional justice.

Critics (among them independent youth) dispute that a new inclusive politics is emerging, and object to what they consider interference in local decisions by foreign bodies. They argue that participants' daily stipends of around $100 alienate them from the rest of the population (40 per cent live on less than $2 a day). Against the background of the threat of UN sanctions, key players or their representatives at the NDC may hesitate risking their fortunes by seeking to undermine the transition process. Despite some Yemenis' reservations, for the time being the NDC would seem the only workable mechanism for resolving differences peacefully.

14

Libya in Transition

From Jamahiriya *to* Jumhūriyyah*?*

Karim Mezran

Abstract

The case of Libya in the so-called Arab Spring has been widely debated and repeatedly marked by uncertainties and complexities. To point out the main features of the Libyan case, this chapter analyses the causes and the socio-economic drivers and forces at play in the Libyan revolution, the role played by outside powers, both Western and Arab, before, during and after the international military intervention, and finally the challenges and prospects for a successful political transition, pluralistic transformation and consolidation in Libya. The Libyan revolution will have a profound impact on local and international politics. Many local counterweights to central authority emerged during and after the war in the form of local councils and militias whose membership was based on cities, families and tribes. Indeed, the first important effect of the revolution on the country is the rediscovery of local ties at the subregional level (local and tribal). In addition to that, new values, based on pluralism and participation in the political life of the country, have emerged. Whether the older allegiances will merge with the new values and produce a vibrant and democratic republic or will clash and return to a dictatorship is the point of the struggle ahead.

---

* *Jamahiriya* is a term coined by Muammar Qaddafi to identify Libya under his ruling, usually translated as 'state of the masses'. *Jumhūriyyah* is the world for 'republic' in the Arabic language.

Introduction

The case of Libya in the so-called Arab uprisings has been widely debated and repeatedly marked by uncertainties and complexities. Libya was the first case in which the international community applied the United Nations doctrine of the 'responsibility to protect', showing determination to safeguard civilians, only to discover a few months later that, in reality, the intervention had been instrumental in executing a regime change. Libya was the third country, following Tunisia and Egypt, to protest against a dictatorial regime in the 2011 North African uprisings, but was also the first in which peaceful demonstrations soon turned into an armed insurgency and a civil war because of the harsh repression perpetrated by the regime against the protesters. Libya was the only country where the political organ of the revolution was headed mostly by defectors – former members of the regime – and the first example, followed later by Syria, where the rebels fighting against human rights abuses ended up committing human rights abuses themselves.[1]

In order to point out the main features of the Libyan case, this chapter will analyse: the causes and the socio-economic drivers and forces at play in the Libyan revolution; the role played by outside powers, both Western and Arab, before, during, and after the international military intervention; and, finally, the challenges and prospects for a successful political transition, pluralistic transformation, and consolidation in Libya.

Causes and Socio-Economic Drivers at Play in the Libyan Revolution

Three main variables explain the 2011 Libyan revolution: 1) the failure of the Libyan rentier state as an economic system to guarantee full employment and modernisation of the economy; 2) the underdevelopment of the eastern region of Cyrenaica and its marginalization from the centres of economic and political power; and 3) the domino effect of the Tunisian and Egyptian revolts.

Qaddafi's capricious and repressive rule will only be touched on in this chapter, as it is not considered per se as the main driver behind the 2011 uprising. On the contrary, this paper will analyse extensively the failure of the Libyan *rentier state* to equally redistribute wealth in the country,

---

[1] Amnesty International, *The Battle for Libya: Killings, Disappearances and Torture*, 2011, p. 70.

creating pockets of discontent in the east and determining structural economic and political deficiencies in the *Jamahiriya*. Moreover, while, on the one hand, the domino effect of the protests in Tunisia and Egypt played a key role in the outbreak of the protests in Libya, on the other hand, the UN-authorized military intervention was crucial in guaranteeing the success of the rebels in the conflict. This second aspect will be analysed in the second section of this study.

Libya is a rentier state.[2] As such, the Libyan economy relies for a substantial part of its income on external rent derived from oil.[3] The rent was redistributed by the state to the people in order to co-opt social forces and guarantee the survival of the regime, making in this way Libya an *allocative* or *distributive* state.[4] According to Vandewalle, distributive states may appear more capable of resisting economic and political challenges.[5] Because they do not need to extract resources from their citizens through taxation in order to fund the functioning of the state, distributive states demand their people accept a trade-off between relatively high standards of living and low political and civil freedoms – a trade-off that the Libyan people seemed to have accepted. However, Libya's rulers pursued policies that were politically expedient and economically ruinous that disenfranchised the citizens and, eventually, produced widespread popular discontent.[6]

Although the regime funded generous welfare programmes guaranteeing relatively higher standards of living to the population compared to other Middle Eastern and North African countries, the regime failed to modernise the economy and create the new jobs needed to employ the burgeoning youth population.[7] At the onset of the 2011 revolt, the unemployment rate was around 30 per cent, affecting mostly the youth and

---

[2] H. Beblawi, 'The Rentier State in the Arab World' in G. Luciani (ed.), *The Arab State* (Berkeley: University of California Press, 1990).

[3] According to World Bank data, in 1998 fuel exports as a percentage of merchandise exports in Libya was 92.6 per cent (URL: data.worldbank.org/indicator/TX.VAL.FUEL.ZS.UN).

[4] G. Luciani, 'Allocation vs. Production States' in G. Luciani (ed.), *The Arab State* (Berkeley: University of California Press, 1990), p. 73; D. Vandewalle, *Libya since independence. Oil and state-building* (London: Cornell University Press, 1998), p. 7.

[5] Vandewalle, *Libya since independence*, p. 7.

[6] M. Villa, 'Un caso poco studiato di rentier state' in K. Mezran and A. Varvelli (eds.), *Libia. Fine o rinascita di una nazione?* (Rome: Donzelli Editore, 2012).

[7] Looking at the 2009 per capita GDP of Libya ($9,957), Tunisia ($4,169), Algeria ($4,022), Morocco ($2,828) and Egypt ($2,371) this aspect is striking (World Bank Data, [http://data.worldbank.org/indicator/NY.GDP.PCAP.CD]).

women.[8] Few economic reforms had been attempted in the first decade of the twenty-first century: the modernisation of infrastructures and the transition from a socialist to a market economy were expected to create new jobs as well as small- and medium-size enterprises, reducing the dependence of Libya from the cyclical dynamics of oil prices.[9] However, the privatisation, liberalisation, diversification and modernisation of the Libyan economy were completed only partially and only in certain economic sectors (mainly banking and communications). Moreover, these reforms were not paralleled by substantial improvements in the Libyan education system. This inevitably produced frustration amongst the population, particularly amongst the youth of Cyrenaica who took to the streets in 2011.

Cyrenaica was the centre of the opposition to Muammer Qaddafi's rule since his rise to power in 1969 when Qaddafi marginalized the local tribes whom he viewed as supporters of the Sanusi monarchy (1951–1969). Cyrenaica possesses 80 per cent of Libya's oil reserves, but was steadily impoverished and rendered politically irrelevant. Cyrenaica has also traditionally represented the core of the Islamist opposition to the regime, including the Libyan branch of the Muslim Brotherhood and militant cells that sprang up in the 1970s and 1980s. These groups existed primarily in and around the eastern cities of Benghazi, Derna, and Ajdabia.[10] In reaction to this opposition, the regime exerted a harsh repression and discriminated against the region in the repartition of oil revenues. A strong opposition with an Islamist face was nurtured in Cyrenaica until it exploded in 2011 on the wave of the demonstrations in Egypt and Tunisia.

The influence of the Tunisian and Egyptian revolts on Libya should not be underestimated. The success achieved by the protesters in Tunisia and Egypt encouraged Libyans to take to the streets on 15 and 16 February 2011. Apparently, the trigger was the arrest of Fathi Terbil Salwa, a young lawyer and human rights activist who represented the families

---

[8] International Labour Organization, DWT for North Africa, Cairo Office, Libya Country Page, URL: www.ilo.org/public/english/region/afpro/cairo/countries/libya.htm. See also CIA, The World Factbook, URL: www.cia.gov/library/publications/the-world-factbook/geos/ly.html.

[9] A. Varvelli, 'Libia. Vere riforme oltre la retorica?' *ISPI Analysis*, 17 (2010), URL: www.ispionline.it/it/documents/Analysis_17_2010.pdf.

[10] A. Pargeter, 'Localism and radicalization in North Africa: Local factors and the development of political Islam in Morocco, Tunisia and Libya', *International Affairs*, 85: 5 (2009), 1031–1044.

of the 1,200 detainees massacred by the regime at Abu Salim prison in 1996. On 17 February 2011, a 'Day of Rage' was organized by the National Conference for the Libyan Opposition,[11] an organization based in London since 2005 that brought together different political opposition groups.[12] Social networks such as Facebook and Twitter helped spread the word and brought people to the streets. The army responded by shooting at the demonstrators, causing fourteen casualties in Benghazi and ten and six in Bayda and Derna, respectively.[13] On 18 February 2011, the protesters occupied a military base in Bayda where the local police joined the demonstrators against regime forces.[14] The same happened in Derna where the rebels set fire to a police station while the army joined the demonstrators.[15]

In contrast to Egypt and Tunisia, the army did not act as a neutral buffer between the protesters and the regime. Comprising an estimated 25,000 ground troops, with additional reserves of 25,000, the army was kept weak and divided under Qaddafi's rule in order to prevent it from challenging the colonel. The army was not a professional army and had a reputation for being corrupt.[16]

By contrast, Qaddafi's special security forces were far stronger than the regular army, being dominated by the leader's family and tribe along with those allied tribes (such as the Magarha) that remained loyal to the regime throughout the war, defending him to the last.[17] Since the beginning of the uprising there has been a group of Libyans, mainly around the cities of Bani Walid, Sirte, and Tripoli, that chose to side with the regime.

---

[11] 'Gaddafi Ready for Libya's Day of Rage', *Asharq Alawsat*, 9 February 2011.

[12] Headed by Ibrahim Sahad, member of the National Front for the Salvation of Libya (NFSL), this umbrella group rose out of a national opposition conference held in June 2005 in London. The conference brought together a number of opposition groups including the NFSL, the Libyan Constitutional Union and the Libyan League for Human Rights, as well as several individuals. At its conclusion, the conference issued a statement laying out its objectives, in particular the demand that Qaddafi step down in order for a constitutional government to be established. Despite this attempt to unify the opposition, divisions have persisted and the group remained of marginal significance (International Crisis Group, '*Popular Protest in North Africa and the Middle East (V): Making Sense of Libya*', Middle East/North Africa Report N°107, 6 June 2011).

[13] 'Anti-government protesters killed in Libyan clash', *USA Today*, 17 February 2011.

[14] 'Libya Protests: Massacres Reported as Gaddafi Imposes New Blackout', *The Guardian*, 18 February 2011.

[15] *The New York Times*, 'Map of the Rebellion in Libya, Day by Day', 20 February 2011 (URL: www.nytimes.com/interactive/2011/02/25/world/middleeast/map-of-how-the-protests-unfolded-in-libya.html).

[16] International Crisis Group, *Making Sense of Libya*.

[17] *Ibid.*

Unlike Tunisia and Egypt, the confrontation between the protest movement and Qaddafi's regime quickly became a violent life-or-death struggle that rapidly turned into a civil war. The peaceful and spontaneous demonstrations on 15 and 16 February 2011 soon turned into an armed insurgency. The protests in Benghazi were initiated by a small group of peaceful lawyers and university professors who had sustained the cause of freedom and human rights even during Qaddafi's regime.[18] However, they were soon marginalized while other social and political forces more organized and grounded in the social fabric of the country took the lead in the revolution.

On 21 February 2011, defectors from the army, the government, and the diplomatic corps joined the rebels' cause. Amongst them were: Mustafa Abdel Jalil, then minister of justice and later president of the National Transitional Council (NTC); Abdul Fattah Younis, then minister of the interior who became commander in chief of the rebel army and whose assassination on 24 July 2011 signalled the high level of political infighting amongst the rebels; Mahmoud Jibril, then head of the National Economic Development Board who was prime minister of the NTC until 24 October 2011 when he resigned following the killing of Qaddafi and the declaration of liberation of the country; and a few Libyan ambassadors amongst whom were Abd al-Rahman Shalgam (UN), Ali Suleiman Aujali (United States) and Hafed Ghaddour (Italy).

The defections were justified on the base of the violence committed by the regime against the demonstrators. However, this happened at a time when the only evidence against the regime was offered by Al-Jazeera, the Qatari TV channel owned by Emir al-Thani whose involvement in the events of the Arab uprisings has not always been very clear. Some events and facts reported by the TV network were bloated out of proportion. For instance, on 22 February 2011, Al Jazeera English reported that warplanes were being used to bomb protesters in Tripoli.[19] The news had been denied by the Russian military intelligence that was monitoring the Libyan skies with their satellites since the beginning of the unrest in the country,[20] as well as by Libyan citizens in Tripoli.[21] Furthermore, inflammatory

---

[18] W. Lacher, 'Families, tribes and cities in the Libyan revolution', *Middle East Policy*, Vol. XVIII, No. 4, Winter (2011): 140–154.

[19] 'Fresh violence rages in Libya', *Al Jazeera English*, 22 February 2011 (URL: www .aljazeera.com/news/africa/2011/02/201122261251456133.html).

[20] *Russia Today*, video posted on YouTube on 7 March 2011 (URL: www.youtube.com/ watch?v=sHqlVgQGSMk).

[21] Interviews of the author with Libyan citizens living in Tripoli the day after the purported bombing of the city confirm the falsity of this news.

news regarding the existence of mass graves in Tripoli was reported by Al Jazeera, showing a video that went viral on the Internet on 22 February 2011.[22] However, the video only showed one of the graveyards of Tripoli and not mass graves as confirmed by journalists who had the chance to visit the site.[23] Nevertheless, the sensationalism of these news and many others legitimised the defectors who abandoned the regime and became the head of the political organ of the revolution, the National Transitional Council, which they established with the support of some expatriates. Meanwhile, many local councils and militias sprung up both in the east and the west of the country, some under the influence of Islamist groups.

At the beginning of the revolt, the Islamists opted for a low-profile strategy, even if rumours suggested that a group of well-armed Islamists was responsible for storming a military arms depot and a nearby port in the city of Derna, seizing numerous weapons and army vehicles after killing four soldiers, between 16 and 18 February 2011.[24] Officially, the Islamists only entered the scene with the liberation of Tripoli on 18 August 2011, and with the arrival in the capital of Abdel Hakim Belhaj, leader of the Tripoli Military Council. Belhaj, in the 1990s, was the head of the Libyan Islamic Fighting Group (LIFG), a militant Islamist movement allied with al-Qaeda. He was subjected with his wife to extraordinary rendition, in 2004, in an operation initiated by British intelligence officers, as shown by documents recently discovered in Tripoli.[25] With the help of British MI6, Belhaj and his wife, Fatima Bouchar, were detained in Bangkok in a U.S.-run detention facility where they were tortured before being rendered to Libya.[26]

During the revolt, hundreds of millions of dollars were funnelled to the opposition through the few channels Qatar had cultivated with expatriates such as Belhaj and Ali Sallabi.[27] The latter is an Islamic scholar and

[22] The footage was recorded and distributed by supporters of the website OneDayOn Earth.com (URL: www.youtube.com/watch?v=cj17F5GaEsc).

[23] Interview of the author with Vincenzo Nigro, correspondent from Libya for the newspaper *Il Sole 24 Ore*, Rome, 14 May 2012.

[24] 'Libyan Islamists seize arms, take hostages', *The Sidney Morning Herald* (AFP), 21 February 2011 (URL: www.news.smh.com.au/breaking-news-world/libyan-islamists-seize-arms-take-hostages-20110221-1b19c.html).

[25] I. Cobain, 'Special report: Rendition ordeal that raises new questions about secret trials', *The Guardian*, 8 April 2012 (URL: www.guardian.co.uk/world/2012/apr/08/special-report-britain-rendition-libya).

[26] *Ibid.*

[27] 'Qatar Wields an Outsize Influence in Arab Politics', *The New York Times*, 14 November 2011 (URL: www.nytimes.com/2011/11/15/world/middleeast/qatar-presses-decisive-shift-in-arab-politics.html?pagewanted=all). Interviews of the author with Ali Sallabi and Abdelhakim Belhaj, Tripoli, 29 May 2012.

populist orator instrumental in leading the mass uprising and channelling assistance from Qatar to the 17 February brigade led by his brother Ismail Sallabi and to other Islamist groups.[28] Differently from the other militias, the Islamist brigades established close ties with the NTC that, having never led the uprising militarily, could not manage to establish effectively in much of the country, particularly in the west.[29]

As Benghazi became the centre of the political power of the revolution through the establishment of the NTC, new centres of power emerged in the west, challenging the legitimacy and the role of both the rebel army and the NTC. Local rebellions and ad hoc military groupings used both military means and negotiations to achieve what has been defined as the 'piecemeal' liberation of Libya.[30] The NTC established control over the capital immediately after the declaration of liberation on 24 October 2011. An interim government, headed by Prime Minister Abdurrahim El-Keib, was appointed on 22 November 2011. Throughout its tenure, the government tried unsuccessfully to address the issue of the struggle between the centre (NTC) and the periphery (local councils and militias).

Two brigades proved particularly resistant to the centralisation attempts by the NTC: the Western Military Council (WMC), whose leadership was dominated by former National Army officers from the city of Zintan, and the Misrata Military Council. The WMC was established during the Nafusa Mountains campaign, a series of battles fought between pro-Qaddafi forces and rebels that proved of critical importance owing to the proximity of the Nafusa Mountains, an opposition pocket in Tripolitania, to the capital of Tripoli.[31] The WMC was meant to coordinate the efforts by the militias emerged in the area. It claimed to control 140 military councils and given the dominance of ex-army officers in its leadership, it proved to be extremely well organized and disciplined. The appointment of Osama al-Juwaili, commander of the WMC, as defence minister of the interim government, was meant to solidify his formation, which was responsible for capturing Saif-al Islam Qaddafi, within the current government initiative.

Following a completely different path, the Misrata Military Council grew out of small cells of civilians formed to resist the attacks of regime

[28] International Crisis Group, 'Holding Libya Together: Security Challenges after Qadhafi', Middle East/North Africa Report N°115, 14 December (2011), p. 21.
[29] J. Pack and B. Barfi, In War's Wake: The Struggle for Post-Qadhafi Libya, The Washington Institute for Near East Policy, Policy Focus N. 118 (2012).
[30] International Crisis Group, Holding Libya Together.
[31] Pack and Barfi, In War's Wake, p. 5.

forces. It lacked military structure and leadership, but gained experience on the ground. The council is a loose coalition without a centralised command structure that depended on local financing to fund its fight against the regime.[32] The Misrata Military Council was responsible for capturing Muammar Qaddafi. The treatment reserved to the former Libyan leader from this military formation demonstrated its independent streak vis-à-vis the National Transitional Council. The appointment of the Misratan, Yussef al-Mangush, as army chief of staff was supposed to bring some calm amongst the militias in this region, but this did not seem to be the case.[33] Indeed, as some analysts pointed out, the militias benefitted from impeding a return to security and economic growth as such developments would most likely lead to their political marginalization.[34]

In addition to the militias, Islamists have emerged as leading players in post-Qaddafi Libya. The Muslim Brotherhood formed a political party, the Justice and Construction Party (*al 'adala wa al bina*), on 3 March 2011, led by Mohammed Swan. The party portrays itself as a moderate force, following the example of its counterparts in Egypt and Tunisia.[35] It rejected the invitation to join Ali Sallabi's party, the National Gathering for Freedom, Justice and Development. Domestic and international legitimacy along with the expansion of public consensus and control of the party members seem to be the determinants of the Libyan Muslim Brotherhood's behaviour in the current transitional period.[36] Another party belonging to the Islamist grouping has been formed by Abdelhakim Belhaj, '*al Watan*', with the purpose of unifying the Islamists of the country.[37] It must be noticed that all the Islamist movements in Libya, in one way or another, have a point of reference in the figure of Ali Sallabi who seems to be acting more as a general guide for the whole group then as a political leader of his own party.

One aspect needs to be clarified at this point of the analysis. The rebels during the revolution were organized on the basis of either local (cities and tribes) or militant Islamist formations. Amongst them were former army members and militant Islamists but also civilians, youths,

---

[32] *Ibid.*
[33] Pack and Barfi, *In War's Wake.*
[34] *Ibid.*
[35] O. Ashour, 'Libya's Muslim Brotherhood faces the future', *The Middle East Channel*, Foreign Policy, 9 March 2012 (URL: www.mideast.foreignpolicy.com/posts/2012/03/09/libya_s_muslim_brotherhood_faces_the_future).
[36] *Ibid.*
[37] Interview of the author with Abdelhakim Belhaj, Tripoli, 29 May 2012.

and women who joined the fight against the regime and who expected to apply their commitment to new democratic and development processes in today's Libya.[38] In particular, during the revolt, women dominated the second front, raising money for munitions and smuggling bullets past checkpoints. They took care of wounded fighters in improvised hospitals and spied on government troops, relaying their movements to the rebels. These women were determined to leverage their wartime activism and sacrifices into increased clout, demanding a greater role in the nascent political system.[39] After all, values such as pluralism and political participation were at the core of the National Transitional Council's agenda for post-Qaddafi Libya. Today, the Libyan people demand that these values translate into political practice.

The UN-Authorized Military Intervention and the Role of Outside Powers

The Libyan case is unique within the Arab uprisings of 2011 also because of the international military intervention. At first, the revolt seemed unstoppable, but after the initial shock, loyalist forces showed their determination to repress harshly the insurgents. The resolve of the regime and the brutality of its initial reaction determined the decision of Western powers – notably France, the United Kingdom, and the United States – to side with the rebels and advocate foreign military intervention.[40]

This decision, at first, seemed in sharp contradiction with the efforts, in the first decade of the twenty-first century, towards reconciliation made by the international community that had fully rehabilitated Qaddafi after more than a decade of isolation. Indeed, in the 1980s, Libya had been ostracised from the international arena because of the involvement of the Libyan government in acts of terrorism. Following the U.S. bombing of Tripoli in 1986 and the terrorist attacks of Lockerbie and Ténére, in 1988 and 1989, Qaddafi – facing the worsening of UN and U.S. sanctions – found himself isolated and, therefore, forced to take a more

---

[38] Report of the Secretary-General on the United Nations Support Mission in Libya, 1 March 2012 (URL: www.daccess-dds-ny.un.org/doc/UNDOC/GEN/N12/244/73/PDF/N1224473.pdf?OpenElement).

[39] J. Hammer, 'Women, the Libyan rebellion's secret weapon', *Smithsonian Magazine*, April 2012 (URL: www.smithsonianmag.com/people-places/Women-The-Libyan-Rebellions-Secret-Weapon.html).

[40] 'Libyan Opposition Warns of Bloodbath, Calls for Intervention', *Bloomberg*, 19 February 2011.

conciliatory stance towards the West if he wanted to survive. However, the breakthrough came only in 1997 when the newly elected British prime minister, Tony Blair, determined to find a solution to the Lockerbie case, obtained the handover of Abdelbaset Ali Mohmed al-Megrahi, one of the Lockerbie attempters. In 1999, the UN suspended the economic sanctions allowing Libya to re-emerge from the isolation to which it had been relegated. In 2003, the UN sanctions were completely removed to reward the Libyan government for its collaboration in the trials of the aforementioned terrorist attacks and for the support offered to George Bush's America in the 'war against terror' after the 9/11 terrorist attacks. In 2006, Libya was removed from the U.S. list of 'rogue states'. But tensions persisted and they clearly emerged in 2009 when the Libyan leader gave a long and, for many, embarrassing speech at the UN General Assembly attacking the UN system and the West for their roles in the Iraq War and in Palestine. Nevertheless economic, financial, and strategic interests prevailed until 2011 when the West saw its chance to get rid of the idiosyncratic leader once for all.[41]

France was the driving force behind this move. A week after the outbreak of the revolt, the French president, Nicolas Sarkozy, demanded the departure of Qaddafi, denounced the repeated and systematic violence of the regime against the demonstrators, and called for an investigation by the International Criminal Court.[42] From that moment it became politically very difficult for any other European country to advocate a negotiated solution to the conflict. It also made it impossible for any country to offer political asylum to the Libyan leader. This action prevented any initiative in favour of the Libyan regime by Italy and its pro-Qaddafi prime minister, Silvio Berlusconi. The embarrassment shown by Berlusconi in the first days of the Libyan revolution and few speeches of the Italian Foreign Minister, Franco Frattini, clearly showed their concern about Italy's stance in the Libyan uprising. Berlusconi declared: 'We are worried for what is happening in the region . . . the situation is evolving and I do not dare to disturb anyone'.[43] He was echoed by Frattini who stated: 'I hope that in Libya a national reconciliation is started that will lead

[41] K. Mezran, 2012, 'La rivolta', in *Libia. Fine o rinascita di una nazione?* For a detailed reconstruction of the events, see also: D. Vandewalle, *A History of Modern Libya* (Cambridge: Cambridge University Press, 2006); R. B. St. John, *Libya from Colony to Independence* (Oxford: Oneworld, 2008).
[42] 'France Claims the Departure of Mu'ammar Gaddafi', *All Voices*, 25 February 2011.
[43] 'Berlusconi: Preoccupato ma non voglio disturbare Gheddafi', *Rai News 24*, 19 February 2011.

towards a Libyan Constitution as suggested by Saif al-Islam Qadhafi'.[44] The Italian foreign minister also affirmed: 'we should not give the wrong impression as if we want to interfere or export our democracy. We have to help and sustain a peaceful reconciliation: this is the way to go'.[45]

Nevertheless, following the meeting of the Council of Europe, on 21 February 2011, Italy aligned with the Franco-British duet. Indeed, the UK supported Sarkozy's demand for Qaddafi's departure since the very beginning. Consequently, on 28 February 2011, the European Union announced a package of sanctions against Qaddafi's family and his inner circle.[46]

The Franco-British initiative then moved to the UN arena where the duet presented a draft of resolution 1973 demanding the immediate cease-fire and the imposition of a no-fly zone over Libya. The UN had already adopted resolution 1970 that requested the referral of Qaddafi to the ICC and the imposition of an arms embargo while calling for the freezing of the assets owned by Qaddafi's clan and forbidding Qaddafi, his family, and his collaborators to leave the country. This resolution came after the UN high commissioner for human rights, Navy Pillay, had demanded an investigation into the violent repression perpetrated by the regime against protestors.[47]

The Franco-British diplomatic action succeeded in obtaining the support of President Obama, in part thanks to the support given by a resuscitated Arab League and the Islamic Conference.[48] At the time, Qaddafi's troops were marching towards Benghazi, forcing the international community to act with speed and resolve in order to avoid a bloodbath. The UN Security Council invoked the principle of 'responsibility to protect' and, having obtained the abstention of China and Russia, the council adopted resolution 1973 on 17 March 2011. That same night, Operation Odyssey Dawn was launched with the U.S. military leading the

---

44 'L'ira della UE contro la Farnesina: Non può difendere un dittatore', *La Repubblica*, 22 February 2011.

45 *Ibid.*

46 'Hague: Gaddafi must go', *BBC News*, 27 February 2011.

47 'Navy Pillay chiede un'inchiesta internazionale sulle violenze libiche e la giustizia per le vittime', UNRIC (URL: www.unric.org/it/attualita/27326-navy-pillay-chiede-uninchiesta-internazionale-sulle-violenze-libiche-e-la-giustizia-per-le-vittime-).

48 Boffey, Black, MacAskill, Townsend, and Helm, 'Tutti contro Gheddafi', *Internazionale*, 25 March 2011; 'Libia. Ban, Egitto e Lega Araba stanno con Onu e comunità internazionale', *Adnkronos*, 21 March 2011; 'Libya No-Fly Zone a UN decision, Says Hillary Clinton', *BBC News*, 9 March 2011.

coalition initially also comprising France, the United Kingdom, Italy, and Canada.[49]

The military intervention created tensions between Italy and France. The Italian government resented the interference of France in what it considered a country of special relevance to Italy and demanded the mission be brought within the NATO framework. The following week, Operation Odyssey Dawn passed under NATO command and was renamed Operation Unified Protector. The support of the international community was sufficient to give the Libyan rebels confidence for an easy victory. This caused a lack of interest from the part of the rebels in the mediation efforts coming from the African Union, Turkey, Venezuela, and the UN.

NATO's intervention in what had already become a civil war saved the anti-Qaddafi side from immediate defeat. Although the declared rationale of the intervention was to protect civilians, leading Western governments supporting NATO's campaign made no secret of the fact that their ultimate goal was regime change. Civilians suffered heavily in the war that created high numbers of civilian casualties and refugees.[50] When it became clear that air power alone was not enough to topple the regime, France and the UK sent military advisors to guide airstrikes and work with the rebels.[51] France was the first country to recognise the NTC as the legitimate Libyan government on 10 March 2011, followed by Qatar on 28 March 2011.

While France was key in pushing Western powers to intervene in Libya, Qatar actively secured the Arab League's cover that enabled the UN Security Council to adopt resolution 1973. Doha played many important roles during the crisis: financing, arming, and training the Libyan fighters; offering assistance, in particular to the Islamists; and dispatching Western-trained advisers to the rebels.[52] Having recently made major investments in Libya, Qatar's involvement was probably spurred by economic and geostrategic interests. Qatar is the world's largest exporter of liquefied natural gas and it sees Libya as a gateway to Mediterranean markets. By adopting this interventionist policy, Qatar gained increased

---

[49] 'Coalition Launches Operation Odyssey Dawn', *American Forces Press Service*, U.S. Department of Defence, Washington, 19 March 2011.

[50] International Crisis Group, *Making Sense of Libya*.

[51] 'Britain's Secret War', *BBC News Africa*, 19 January 2012 (URL: www.bbc.co.uk/news/world-africa-16624401).

[52] Pack and Barfi, *In War's Wake*.

prominence in the regional arena and an advantage in its competition for influence with Saudi Arabia.[53]

Because of multiple military commitments elsewhere and resource challenges, the United States opted for a limited support role in Libya.[54] Indeed, since the beginning of the military operation, started on 19 March 2011, President Obama sought NATO's agreement to take over command and control of the operation in order to integrate the militaries of allies and partners.[55] Given that many NATO countries, such as Italy, France, the United Kingdom, Belgium, Canada, Denmark, the Netherlands, Norway, Spain, and the United States were already contributing to the intervention, NATO was the logical choice to assume command.[56] On 27 March 2011, NATO took command of the operation. The United States was left to 'lead from behind'.[57] Indeed, the limited operational capabilities of some NATO states, strained by cuts in defence spending, led Washington to continue to participate in military operations in Libya even if only by gathering and analysing intelligence, refuelling NATO and partner aircraft, and contributing other high-end military capabilities, such as electronic jamming.[58]

The Libyan intervention also exposed issues of political unity and cohesiveness amongst European countries, reflected in the hesitant action of the European Union. At the outbreak of the revolt, following the 1970 UN Security Council Resolution, the EU adopted restrictive measures against Muammar Qaddafi, his family, and members of his regime such as a visa ban and a freeze of their assets.[59] The twenty-seven member states seemed aligned with the diplomatic activity promoted by France and the UK in the international arena but, in fact, deep divisions ran amongst them, as demonstrated by Germany's decision to abstain from the vote on UNSC resolution 1973, for instance, but also by the French unilateral recognition of the TNC as the sole legitimate representative

53 *Ibid.*
54 R. B. St. John, *A Transatlantic Perspective on the Future of Libya*, Mediterranean Paper Series, the German Marshall Fund of the United States, May 2012, p. 13.
55 I. H. Daalder and J. G. Stavridis, 'NATO's Victory in Libya: The Right Way to Run an Intervention,' *Foreign Affairs*, Vol. 91, No. 2 (March/April 2012).
56 *Ibid.*
57 R. Lizza, 'The Consequentialist', *The New Yorker*, 2 May 2011 (URL: www.newyorker .com/reporting/2011/05/02/110502fa_fact_lizza?currentPage=10).
58 Daalder and Stavridis, '*NATO's Victory in Libya*'.
59 'Libya: EU imposes arms embargo and targeted sanctions', Europa Press Release, 28 February 2011 (URL: www.europa.eu/rapid/pressReleasesAction.do?reference= PRES/11/41&type=HTML).

of the Libyan people on 11 March 2011.[60] The unilateral actions or inactions of the member states mainly account for the EU's incoherent response in Libya,[61] and consequently, they resulted in a sort of paralysis of EU action in the country.

At the time of this writing, following the liberation, foreign powers involved in the war support different factions, often in conflict with each other. In particular, French companies, supported by the French government, sustain groups close to the circle of the former Prime Minister Mahmoud Jibril while Italian ENI support the oil establishment and in particular, the Libyan oil minister, Abdulrahman Ben Yazza. Qatar is strongly supporting the Islamist factions and lobbying extensively for other members of the government in order to open up to its investments. Moreover, rumours circulate in Tripoli of activities carried on by Turkish and Korean business associations that support economically different candidates in the forthcoming elections.[62] These independent actions do not help the Libyan government to establish its control, but rather deepen the internal fragmentation of the country. The United States, largely absent from post-conflict Libya, is the only exception to this intermingling of policies. A more active role by the United States will assist in consolidating the authority of the Libyan government.

Challenges and Prospects

The General National Congress (GNC), the elected body that emerged from the 7 July 2012 elections, faces major challenges: establishing the legitimacy of interim-governing institutions; rebuilding state institutions and the economy while integrating the militias in a unified police and military force; securing borders and collecting weapons to avoid arms proliferation; dealing with perpetrators of human rights abuses without triggering further tensions and reprisals among the population; all this while keeping the country united.[63]

Establishing the Legitimacy of New Institutions
The legitimacy, representativeness, and effectiveness of the interim government and of the NTC were widely questioned. The authority of the

---

[60] N. Koenig, '*The EU and the Libyan Crisis: In quest of coherence?*' IAI Working Papers, 11,19, July 2011.

[61] *Ibid.*

[62] Interviews of the author with members of the interim government in Tripoli, May 2012.

[63] International Crisis Group, *Holding Libya Together*.

NTC and the interim government, appointed by the former, were disputed. Membership in the NTC was granted in a relatively opaque ad hoc fashion, through negotiations conducted by its chairman, Abdel Jalil. Cities' representatives on the NTC were normally decided by local councils in consultation with elders, militia leaders, and other prominent personalities although the exact process in each city was unclear. This created a gap between the people and the political organ of the revolution.[64] While the NTC and the rebel army were focussed on the conquest of the western region of Libya, leaders of local militias and councils organized the liberated cities to rebuild normal life and resisted attempts by the NTC to centralise power. The NTC did not prove particularly capable in responding to day-to-day governance issues in the areas of defence, policing, and vital service delivery such as health care or garbage collection.[65]

Moreover, the NTC could not even claim a leading role in the revolution because the liberation of the western region was conducted at the local level by militias from western cities such as Zintan and Misrata. In the eyes of many Libyans, the members of the militias and local councils were the heroes. They filled a leadership vacuum at the beginning of the revolution, demonstrating their ability to mobilize resources faster than the NTC, possession of superior local connections and information, along with control of heavy weaponry. Hence, their leadership is strong and hard to challenge. The elections scheduled for 7 July 2012 may offer a way to do so as a body will be elected to draft a new constitution and appoint a new government. This may then solve the legitimacy problem of the governing institutions.

Rebuilding State Institutions and Integrating the Militias

Libyans have an opportunity to transform their political, economic, and cultural life. As UN special rapporteur on human rights, Richard Falk, pointed out: 'In this respect, it could turn out to be helpful that Gaddafi *was* the Libyan state, and left no institutional infrastructure behind following his departure. [However] It may prove to be a mission impossible to engage in state-building without a state'.[66] The current interim authorities have inherited inefficient government bureaucracies that struggle to assess the country's needs. Building new functioning institutions from scratch will be a long and difficult process.

[64] *Ibid.*
[65] *Ibid.*
[66] R. Falk, 'Libya after Gaddafi: A dangerous precedent?' *Al Jazeera*, 22 October 2011.

Nevertheless, two factors may rescue Libya and enable reconstruction: oil and a relatively small population. An important test will be how effectively the new leadership manages the economy. The NTC, conscious of the potential of the Libyan rentier state, tried to rebuild the economy by reviving oil production and exports. In March 2012, oil production was 1.4 million barrels per day – equivalent to the level of 1.6 million barrels per day in 2010 before the conflict began.[67] Moreover, it will be crucial to insulate the national wealth of the country from foreign corporate predators, while creating new jobs in sectors other than hydrocarbons.[68]

However, the efforts towards rebuilding institutions responsible for the management of the state and the economy might prove meaningless if these attempts do not go hand in hand with the integration of the militias in a unified national police and military force. This might be the most difficult challenge facing the Libyan authorities, particularly in the western region where each brigade developed its own chain of command, military culture, and narrative of revolution largely independent from the government and the national army.[69] This aspect was partially tackled by the NTC through the creation of a 'Mobilization Committee' intended to reintegrate militia fighters and a 'Commission of Warrior Affairs', including the Ministries of Defence, Interior, Finance, and Labour, which is developing a strategy for DDR (Disarmament, Demobilization, and Reintegration). This is critical because political transition could be undermined by failure to strengthen the public's perception of security, an essential condition for civic engagement, as well as for socio-economic activity.[70]

Securing Borders and Collecting Weapons

Illegal migration is another major challenge facing the new Libyan government, as the incident at the Algerian gas plant in Amenas demonstrated in January 2013. In order to support the government in addressing normative and operational needs, at the beginning of 2012, the UN border security and management coordination group – established within the framework of the UN Support Mission to Libya (UNSMIL) – set up a subgroup, currently chaired by UNSMIL and comprising the Interior and

---

[67] A. Varvelli, M. Zupi, and S. Hassan, *La Libia dopo Gheddafi*, Osservatorio di Politica Internazionale, n.52, March–April 2012.
[68] Falk, *Libya after Gaddafi*.
[69] International Crisis Group, *Holding Libya Together*.
[70] Report of the Secretary General on the United Nations Support Mission in Libya, 1 March 2012.

Defence Ministries, the Office of the United Nations High Commissioner for Refugees (UNHCR), the International Organization for Migration (IOM) and the European Union (EU).[71] The EU is currently undertaking a needs assessment mission for border management that will make recommendations to the EU to help Libya ensure secure and efficient border management.[72] Meanwhile, UNSMIL and the United Nations Mine Action Service are helping the Ministry of Defence and some brigades to explore a programme for the registration of weapons and for ammunition storage and management. To this end, the Ministry of Defence has established a task force with UNSMIL and bilateral partners including the African Union.[73]

The necessity of help in securing borders has become even more pressing in the light of recent events in Mali. Spillover from the Libyan crisis into the security dimension of the Sahara and Sahel region was evident in the Tuareg rebellion and the following coup d'etat in March 2012. Following the end of hostilities in Libya, the Tuareg, who fought with Qaddafi, returned to the north of Mali from where they led a rebellion against the Malian authorities. The Libyan crisis has created instability in the region; therefore, action in securing borders and collecting weapons will be paramount in stabilising the wider region as well as Libya itself.

Human Rights Abuses

The transfer of prisoners from the Libyan civil war to the custody of the Ministry of Justice continues to be a major challenge – UNSMIL estimates place the number at 5,000– 6,000. Revolutionary brigades continue to carry out arrests and interrogation of alleged former regime supporters at undisclosed locations as well as known detention centres where conditions remain mostly poor. Alleged acts of severe torture and ill-treatment by the brigades, including deaths in custody, are continuously reported, particularly in Tripoli, Misrata, Zintan, and Gheryan. A fact-finding and reconciliation commission to investigate human rights violations since 1969 and provide compensation to victims has been set up to deal with past and current abuses. However, it will be crucial that this

---

[71] *Ibid.*

[72] 'EU launches a needs assessment mission for border management in Libya', European Union External Action Service (URL: www.eeas.europa.eu/libya/docs/2012_lybia_border_management_en.pdf).

[73] Report of the Secretary-General on the United Nations Support Mission in Libya, 1 March 2012.

commission does not turn into a witch-hunt that might further hamper the reconstruction.

Libyan Identity and National Unity

It is worth stressing that Libya is a product of colonialism as much as of the Ottoman Empire and its aftermath. It was officially united in 1929 by the Italians, although two separate administrations, each one with its own governor, were maintained throughout the Italian colonisation that initially followed the indirect rule system and the division already institutionalized during the Ottoman rule. Indeed, in the East, the Italian colonisers negotiated with the Sanussia to whom they offered the de facto control of the territory, whereas in the West, the Italians relied on the collaboration of traditional leaders and notables to control the region.[74] However, this system of rule was interrupted by the rise to power of the fascist dictatorship in Italy that resulted in a harsh military occupation of Libya and in the reunification of the 'two colonies' of Tripolitania and Cyrenaica, even if regionalism remained a determinant feature in the Italian colonial policy.[75]

Following the Second World War and the British and French adminis-trations, respectively, in the North and in the South of the country, inde-pendence and the rise to power of the Sanussi monarchy in 1951 did not solve the deep division that has run through Libya since Ottoman times.[76] On the contrary, it further deepened them through a federal system that gave wide autonomy to the provinces while the Sanussia favoured Cyre-naica over Tripolitania.[77] The 1969 coup led by Muammar Qaddafi had its seeds in the corruption of the monarchy and in its policies meant to favour Cyrenaica while, initially, the coup was supported by some groups within society – in particular, the youth and the urban population – it lost legitimacy very quickly. With its emphasis on transnational values such as Arab nationalism and anti-colonialism, the coup further weakened the fragile sense of Libyan identity.

---

[74] A. Baldinetti, 'La formazione dello Stato e la costruzione dell'identità nazionale' in K. Mezran and A. Varveli (eds.) *Libia. Fine o rinascita di una nazione?*. See also: A. Baldinetti, *The Origins of the Libyan Nation. Colonial Legacy, Exile and the Emergence of a New-Nation State* (London-New York: Routledge, 2010).

[75] Baldinetti, 'La formazione dello Stato e la costruzione dell'identità nazionale', p. 8.

[76] R. B. St John, *Libyan Myths and realities*, Report for the Royal Danish Defense College, August 2011 (URL: forsvaret.dk/FAK/Publikationer/Research%20Papers/Documents/Libyan_Myths_and_Realities.pdf).

[77] Baldinetti, 'La formazione dello Stato e la costruzione dell'identità nazionale', p. 15.

Paradoxically, hatred of Colonel Qaddafi and his regime would become a unifying factor amongst the Libyan people in the forty-two years of reign of the colonel. Indeed, this factor was key in uniting the people against the regime during the 2011 revolution. A Western diplomat attending the liberation ceremony of the country declared: 'Toppling Gaddafi was the unifying force. Now that he's gone, will they be able to hold it together?'[78]

In fact, now that Qaddafi is gone, Libyans have to face his bitter legacy: a country torn apart by war. In such contexts, local clashes could easily turn into national confrontations because of the many different groups and interests involved: 'These are the kinds of conflicts that have so often devastated postcolonial states, and they can last for many years'.[79] In a state lacking civil-society institutions and strong central governance, connecting the 'periphery' to the 'centre' is the only way to avoid the partition of the country.[80]

The question of the unity of Libya is pivotal. From the provinces of the east to the many local councils in the west and the south, centrifugal forces are pushing for the establishment of a political system that would give significant powers to local entities. These forces pay only lip service to the Libyan state; most of their claims in support of national unity hide separatist tendencies. Examining the existence of a 'Libyan Nation' and a 'Libyan identity' are beyond the scope of this chapter, but it is important to recognise that if the current and future Libyan governments do not embark on serious nation-building activities, Libya could split up. The way the revolution was conducted, fragmented, and decentralized reflected the lack of national institutions and cohesive national identity. This is the main challenge for the GNC: to create a Libyan national identity that will keep the country united while not ignoring the demands of the local councils and institutions.

Conclusion

The Libyan revolution will have a profound impact on local and international politics. Many local counterweights to central authority emerged during and after the war in the form of local councils and militias whose membership was based on cities, families, and tribes. The first important effect of the revolution on the country is the rediscovery of local ties at

---

[78] 'Libya declares liberation with an Islamic tone', *The Washington Post*, 24 October 2011.
[79] T. Barkawi, 'Peace may be war in post-war Libya', Al Jazeera, 21 October 2011.
[80] Pack and Barfi, *In War's Wake*.

the subregional level (local and tribal) rather than at the regional one (Tripolitania, Cyrenaica, and Fezzan). Towns and cities were as important as tribes to mobilize the people in the revolutionary struggle through the formation of local transitional councils (political mobilization) and revolutionary brigades (military organization).[81]

New peripheral centres of power emerged vis-à-vis the central government based in Tripoli and they will be reluctant to give up their authority. However, this does not necessarily mean that the country will be partitioned. On 6 March 2012, members of Cyrenaican tribes gathered in Benghazi to declare Cyrenaica a semi-autonomous region. Although on 6 March 2012 the participants at the Barqa Conference claimed the right to speak for their region, the initiative for self-administration and federalism triggered furious reactions in the region itself, making the push unlikely to succeed.[82]

A solution to contain these centrifugal forces might be found in the administrative decentralisation to which the interim government of Prime Minister el-Keib was committed.[83] Whether this issue will be tackled in the same way by the newly elected government of Ali Zidan remains to be seen.

At the international level, the revolution marked the entrance of new actors into the Libyan scenario, notably Qatar, France, and the United Kingdom. Nevertheless, according to el-Keib and then Ali Zidan, Libya aims at being friends with anyone willing to help rebuild the country and overcome forty-two years of dictatorship: 'We want to be a positive force in this world in a small way based on our size', he stated.[84] The message was clearly directed at ex-allies of the Qaddafi regime, such as Russia and Italy, but also to old allies and rivals in the North African region. However, it remains to be seen how in practice the new government of Ali Zidan will act and what alliances will be formed with neighbouring states.

Meanwhile, a deep reassessment of values and ideologies is taking place. Qaddafi's relationship to the great debates of Arab politics in the

---

[81] W. Lacher, 'Families, tribes and cities in the Libyan revolution', in *Middle East Policy*, Vol. XVIII, No. 4, Winter 2011.

[82] W. Lacher, 'Is Autonomy for Northeastern Libya Realistic?' *Sada Journal*, 21 March 2012.

[83] Carnegie Endowment for International Peace, Libyan Prime Minister Abdel-Rahim El Keib, 9 March 2012, Washington, DC (http://carnegieendowment.org/2012/03/09/libyan-prime-minister-abdel-rahim-el-keib).

[84] *Ibid.*

twentieth century was tempestuous.[85] In the aftermath of the 1969 coup, he declared himself the heir to Gamal Abdel Nasser's Arab nationalism, modernization, and anti-colonialism. However, at the end of the 1980s, when he realized that these ideologies were no longer capable of guaranteeing the survival of his regime against regional and international hostility, he abandoned Arab nationalism for a new pan-African adventure. Through diplomatic and economic tools, he strengthened his position in the African continent as well as in the international arena. Qaddafi changed course frequently – modernisation was abandoned at the beginning of the 1970s for a socialist economy that was discarded in the twenty-first century in favour of partial liberal reforms. However, his anti-colonialism was never really discarded. Indeed, until recently, the ex-leader used anti-colonialism as a flag to foster sentiments of unity amongst the Libyan people. On his first official visit to Italy in 2009, Qaddafi arrived with a picture of Omar al-Mukhtar, leader of the anti-colonialist struggle against the Italians in the 1910s and 1920s, pinned on his chest. The Libyan TV and the media put a lot of emphasis on this fact reiterating the success of the Libyan leader in forcing the ex-colonial power to present its excuses for the 'crimes' committed at the time of colonialism.

However, this is the past. The leaders of the 2011 revolution subscribe to very different ideological paradigms. They requested and embraced foreign military intervention to topple the regime and now seem more than willing to reward their Western supporters with economic and political advantages. Anti-colonialism and pan-Africanism have been abandoned in favour of a new focus on the Libyan nation and the Maghreb. In particular, efforts are going to be exerted in elaborating a new vision for the Libyan nation as well as for the strengthening of a Libyan identity that would be representative of the people and not of the idiosyncrasies of its leader. National identity and the national interest are the two main topics on the agenda of the new assembly elected in July 2012.

The Islamist factor might prove to be a new binding force. From what has emerged so far, the Libyan Islamists reject the use of violence, share a love for the Libyan nation, and have a political platform that opposes

---

[85] On this aspect, see: Y. Ronen, *Qaddafi's Libya in World Politics* (London: Rienner Publishers, 2008); M. J. Deeb, *Libya's Foreign Policy in North Africa* (Boulder, CO: Westview Press 1991); R. Lemarchand, *The Green and the Black: Qadhafi's policies in Africa* (Bloomington: Indiana University Press, 1988); A. Alunni, 'L'Africa di Gheddafi tra ideologia e pragmatismo', in K. Mezran and A. Varvelli, (eds.), *Libia. Fine o rinascita di una nazione?*

federalism, supports an international peaceful role – except for the condemnation of Israel – aims at good relations with the United States, and favours economic liberalism.[86] Whether this programme will be maintained remains to be seen but their commitment is certain, expressed at all levels, to the unity of Libya and against any form of federalism or separation.

What is going on in Libya at the time of this writing is a struggle for power rather than an ideological clash. From a conceptual point of view, there are no significant differences amongst the stances presented. Nobody in Libya calls himself/herself a secularist nor defines himself/herself or his party as Islamist. From a quick look at the platforms of the parties that competed in the 2012 elections, one can see that there is a wide sharing of ideas and visions. Where they differ is in the personalities of their leaders, their history, and personal behaviours. The hope for Libya is that this clash of personalities will be set aside for the good of the country in order to find a compromise that will allow new institutions to work effectively, thus creating a stable and democratic Libya.

[86] Interviews of the author with Ali Sallabi and Abdelhakim Belhaj, Tripoli, 29 May 2012.

15

Bahrain's Uprising

Domestic Implications and Regional and International Perspectives

Kristian Coates Ulrichsen

Abstract

This chapter explores the domestic, regional, and international implications of the uprising in Bahrain. It demonstrates how the revolutionary protests at the Pearl Roundabout that began on 14 February 2011 fit into a longer pattern of recurrent opposition to the ruling Al-Khalifa family. Nevertheless, the February 14 movement was distinct from previous bouts of protest both in its size and its initial cross-sectarian mobilisation. The chapter begins by describing the reasons behind the emergence of this burgeoning social movement as well as the regime's measures to contain and suppress it. Subsequent sections examine the reconfiguration and fragmentation of Bahrain's political landscape as extremist groups have undercut the moderate middle ground, the continuing impasse between a regime unwilling to make substantive concessions and an enraged opposition movement, and the complex interplay between domestic and regional counter-revolutionary processes and their consequences for Bahrain's international credibility.

The uprising in Bahrain that began on 14 February 2011 has been contained, but not resolved. Although the immediate period of danger to the position of the ruling Al-Khalifa family has passed, positions on all sides have hardened, and there is little prospect of a political settlement to Bahrain's deep-rooted social and economic inequalities. As the Bahraini government has failed to offer meaningful concessions to political reform, it has splintered and radicalised an opposition unsure what to do next, but also undermined its own constituency of support amongst the kingdom's Sunni communities. These trajectories have set in motion a radical reconfiguring of the island's political landscape in ways that do not augur well for longer-term prospects for reconciliation and recovery.

This chapter examines the regional and international dimensions of Bahrain's aborted revolution. It describes how the pro-democracy movement that erupted in early 2011 became entrapped in the crosshairs of regional and international geopolitics. This ensured that the burgeoning social movement in support of peaceful political reform was violently crushed as Bahrain's international partners opted to look the other way. Yet, this came at a very high price economically and politically, and it shattered social cohesion in a country polarised as never before. Moreover, it shredded the image of 'Business-Friendly Bahrain' that had formed the cornerstone of the country's economic diversification and development programmes. Bahrain's unhappy experience has implications for the ruling families of the other Gulf Cooperation Council (GCC) states as they also struggle to adapt to greater participatory pressures and societal demands for political freedoms.

Several major points emerge from the analysis. One is the speed with which a cross-sectarian movement developed to seriously challenge the pillars of Al-Khalifa rule. Another is that the magnitude of the threat to the status quo exposed the lack of substance in the political concessions offered by the regime in response. These indicated that core issues relating to the balance and distribution of power were simply not on the table for discussion. Neither was there any suggestion that ruling elites were prepared to open themselves up for high-level accountability for the abuses that occurred. This extended to the hard-hitting report of the Bahrain Independent Commission of Inquiry (BICI) as well as the national dialogue convened over the summer of 2011. As a result, the political opposition has fragmented as power and influence has shifted to radical voices on all sides of the spectrum that have undercut the moderate middle ground. The spectacle of a ruling family resisting the calls for reform from a large number of its citizens has consequences for regime security in the other Gulf monarchies, particularly Saudi Arabia, as well as for Bahrain's international partners. Finally, the trajectory of events in Bahrain highlights the interplay between the domestic and regional counter-revolutionary processes designed to minimise and contain the threat to regimes posed by the 'Arab Spring'.

The first section of this chapter describes the uprising in Bahrain. It demonstrates how the current unrest forms part of a cycle of recurrent periods of contestation and predates the Arab Spring revolutions in Tunisia and Egypt. The second section examines how the range of governmental and opposition responses have redrawn the political landscape within the country. The third section explores the regional and international dimensions to the uprising and contextualises it within an upsurge of sectarian rhetoric directed against Iran. This upsurge occurred as GCC governments sought to externalise the roots of unrest and discredit oppositional elements within their own societies. It is within this context that the overly ambitious plans for a Gulf Union must be assessed. It also highlights the differing reactions from Bahrain's external partners and from international civil society organizations. The conclusion asks whether the crushing of the pro-democracy movement holds significant lessons for the prospects for peaceful political reform in any of the other Gulf monarchies predicated on a genuine sharing of power and control.

Revolution at the Pearl Roundabout

Bahrain has a long history of popular opposition to the Al-Khalifa dynasty rooted in policies of unequal and selective development. Periodic outbreaks of major social unrest have alternated with periods of détente in cycles dating back to the 1920s. Sustained and organized campaigns for more rights occurred at regular intervals in 1921–23, 1934–35, 1938, 1947–48, 1953–56, 1965, and 1975, with the 1950s being notable for the creation of a non-sectarian social movement that openly challenged the ruler, Sheikh Salman bin Hamad Al-Khalifa, and his longstanding British advisor, Sir Charles Belgrave.[1] Feelings of popular anger against British policy towards Egypt and the Suez Crisis in 1956, and, subsequently, the appeal of Arab nationalism and socialism provided a platform around which disparate groups could coalesce. However, after 1979, the Islamic Revolution in Iran – and alleged Iranian involvement in an attempted coup attempt in Bahrain in 1981 – cast a shadow over such cross-sectarian mobilization.[2] In the 1990s, the longest sustained period of pressure on the Bahraini government culminated in an uprising between 1994 and 1999. Once again, that protest pitted advocates of political and

---

[1] J. E. Peterson, 'The nature of succession in the Gulf', *Middle East Journal*, 55 (2001), 587–88
[2] H. T. Alhasan, 'The role of Iran in the failed coup of 1981: The IFLB in Bahrain', *Middle East Journal*, 65 (2011), 603.

economic reform against a ruling family determined to maintain the status quo and avoid diluting its power.[3]

The longstanding ruler of Bahrain, Sheikh Isa bin Salman Al-Khalifa, died unexpectedly in March 1999, and was succeeded as Emir by his son, Hamad bin Isa. Similar to the case in neighbouring Qatar, the process of generational change of leadership was followed by a programme of tentative political reform. A series of constitutional reforms were launched in November 2000 that promised much, but ultimately delivered little of substance. In 2001, the draconian 1974 State Security Law that had provided cover for the suppression of political opposition and massive human rights violations (under the charge of a British national until 1998) was scrapped. Constitutional changes were laid out in a National Action Charter that was overwhelmingly approved by 98 per cent of Bahrainis in a referendum on 14 February 2001. This paved the way for the return of an elected assembly in 2002, twenty-seven years after the suspension of the previous short-lived (two years) parliamentary experiment in 1975. Also as part of the reforms, Bahrain became a constitutional monarchy, with the emir taking the title of king.[4]

However, the initial promise of a unicameral elected legislature was subsequently diluted by the addition of an upper house of royal appointees. Low confidence in the sincerity of the political opening also led to a range of political societies, spanning the ideological and religious spectrum, boycotting the 2002 election. Although most societies participated in the 2006 and 2010 elections, the former was marred by allegations of systematic fraud and gerrymandering while the latter followed a heavy-handed clampdown on opposition and human rights activists.[5] During the run-up to the 2010 election, accounts of arbitrary detention of opposition and human rights activists, and allegations of torture, seemed to herald a return to the repressive ways of the regime's murky past. Meanwhile, socio-economic discontent was bubbling up, propelled by high levels of unemployment, the inability of economic diversification to generate sufficient jobs or economic opportunities for

[3] M. Fakhro, 'The uprising in Bahrain: An assessment' in G. Sick and L. Potter (eds.), *The Persian Gulf at the millennium: Essays in politics, economy, security, and religion* (London: Routledge, 1997), pp. 167–68.

[4] A. Ehteshami and S. Wright, 'Political change in the Arab oil monarchies: From liberalization to enfranchisement', *International Affairs*, 83 (2007), 919.

[5] N. Quilliam, 'Political reform in Bahrain: The turning tide' in A. Ehteshami and S. Wright (eds.), *Reform in the Middle East oil monarchies* (Reading: Ithaca Press, 2008), pp. 92–93.

Bahraini youth, and popular anger at perceived corruption at the heart of government.[6]

Feelings in Bahrain were therefore running high even before the revolutions in Tunisia and Egypt rocked the Arab world. It was in this context of rising tension that Bahraini organizers planned a day of protest on 14 February 2011. The date was symbolic as it marked the tenth anniversary of the referendum that had approved the National Action Charter in 2001. It also followed in the wake of the popular uprisings that swept away the Ben Ali and Mubarak regimes in Tunisia and Egypt. The inspirational sight of largely non-violent demonstrations defying political suppression and refusing to submit to the security regimes that had kept authoritarian leaders in power for decades was transformative. Cafes in Manama that usually showed Lebanese music videos were instead filled with images from Tahrir Square in Cairo that transfixed their audience, as elsewhere throughout the region. Emboldened protesters voiced their demands ahead of the 14 February day of protest for greater political freedom and equality for all Bahrainis. These protesters targeted the regime's policies of fomenting sectarian division to inhibit the emergence of any popular cross-community opposition movement.[7]

Although initially small in scale and predominantly confined to Shia villages outside Manama, the demonstrations gathered momentum after Bahraini police killed two protesters on 14 and 15 February. They also migrated to the heart of the capital's Pearl Roundabout, close to the flagship Bahrain Financial Harbour. Ominously for the regime, the demonstrations quickly assumed popular overtones as Sunnis and Shia alike gathered in unprecedented numbers and chanted slogans such as 'No Shia, no Sunnis, only Bahrainis'. By the evening of 16 February, tens of thousands of overwhelmingly young Bahrainis were camped in Pearl Roundabout and shouting 'Down, down Khalifa!' This was aimed at the prime minister of forty-one years, Sheikh Khalifa bin Salman Al-Khalifa, rather than at the regime itself, but the dramatic cross-sectarian escalation directly threatened their grip on power and domestic legitimacy. The regime responded violently, as security forces stormed the roundabout in the middle of the night and opened fire on demonstrators.[8]

---

[6] C. Davidson and K. Coates Ulrichsen, 'Bahrain on the Edge' *Open Democracy*, 19 October 2010.

[7] M. Lynch, *The Arab uprising: The unfinished revolutions of the new Middle East* (New York: Public Affairs, 2012), pp. 109–10.

[8] K. Coates Ulrichsen, 'Bahrain: Evolution or Revolution?' *Open Democracy*, 1 March 2011.

As the protests moved into a new post-clampdown phase, the regime reacted by sponsoring counterdemonstrations to try to fracture the social movement confronting them. Thousands of pro-government supporters gathered at the Al-Fateh Mosque in Juffair on 21 February (and again on 2 March 2011) to declare their support for the regime. They formed The Gathering of National Unity (TGONU), consisting of a loose umbrella grouping of loyalist Sunni communities spanning a spectrum from Salafist, Muslim Brotherhood, tribal, and urban communities loyal to the regime. In response, an estimated 200,000 Bahraini citizens (one in three of all Bahraini citizens) participated in a pro-democracy march to the Pearl Roundabout on 25 February, as two massive columns of protesters converged on the roundabout to demand the resignation of the prime minister, Khalifa bin Salman. This protest represented a level of societal mobilization unprecedented in any of the Arab Spring movements before or since.[9]

With the position of the ruling family clearly in jeopardy, negotiations between the regime's leading modernising figure, the crown prince, Salman bin Hamad Al-Khalifa, and the largest opposition political society, Al-Wefaq, commenced in March. Despite coming close to an agreement based around a set of agreed political reforms (the 'seven principles'), the talks broke down when Al-Wefaq refused to enter a formal dialogue unless the government agreed to a new constitutional arrangement. Accordingly, the offer of talks was withdrawn, and on 14 March the GCC sent in its Peninsula Shield Force to help restore stability in Bahrain. This consisted of 1,000 men of the Saudi Arabian National Guard and a contingent of 500 military police from the United Arab Emirates. The troops provided the essential backbone while the Bahrain Defence Force pursued and arrested thousands of people across the country in a prolonged campaign of political repression and retribution.[10]

A state of national emergency was declared the following day, 15 March, that lasted until 1 June 2011. There followed a brutal crackdown as the Bahraini government mercilessly pursued all forms of dissent, detaining doctors and lawyers merely for treating or representing detainees, suspending opposition political societies and arresting their leaders, and detaining a founder of Bahrain's major independent newspaper *Al-Wasat*, who subsequently died in custody. Up to 2,000 mostly Shia

---

[9] Lynch, Arab uprising, p. 110.
[10] Anon., 'Saudi Arabian forces bring a temporary halt to Bahrain's unrest, but opposition remains firm', *Gulf States Newsletter*, 35/897, 25 March 2011.

public-sector and 2,400 private-sector workers were dismissed from their positions for 'absenteeism' during the demonstrations. Widespread tactics of intimidation also included the destruction of Shia shrines and posters showing prominent Shia leaders with nooses around their necks. Meanwhile, a relentless propaganda campaign was unleashed on Bahrain TV and through the state media, portraying dissidents as 'traitors' and inciting violence against them. Targets included the captain of the national football team, Ala'a Hubail, previously a national hero after guiding Bahrain to the brink of qualification for the 2010 World Cup.[11]

Simultaneously, the Bahrain National Guard embarked on a hasty recruitment drive in Pakistan to augment its limited manpower with non-Bahraini personnel with fewer qualms about opening fire on civilian protesters. Although Bahraini Shias were already barred from holding senior-level positions in the Bahrain Defence Force and the police, this move reinforced the sense of exclusivity and partiality in the security services.[12] Meanwhile, the bulldozing of the Pearl Roundabout, with its iconic monument to Gulf unity, on 18 March represented a crude attempt to destroy the symbolic heart of the protest movement. With this act, the authorities hoped to prevent it from becoming an anti-regime equivalent of Cairo's Tahrir Square. However, it highlighted the darkly ironical nature of the emerging counter-revolution, as the Pearl Monument had been erected in 1982 to mark the creation of the GCC. Its six pillars represented each of the GCC members, yet it was destroyed just days after the entry of those Gulf forces into the kingdom.[13]

Martial law was lifted on 1 June 2011, and shortly thereafter, the king convened a national dialogue and created an ostensibly independent investigation into the springtime unrest. Through these initiatives, the government hoped to begin a process of reconciliation with the opposition. However, flawed implementation widened the chasm between the Al-Khalifa and their opponents by casting serious doubt on the credibility of the commitment to reform. This also revealed deepening divisions within the ruling family as a hard-line faction emerged around the increasingly powerful bin Ahmed brothers – Khalid bin Ahmed Al-Khalifa, the

---

[11] K. D'Almeida, 'Bahrain: McCarthyism in Manama?' *IPS News*, 27 April 2011.

[12] J. Gengler, 'The (sectarian) politics of public-sector employment in Bahrain' *Religion and Politics in Bahrain*, 27 May 2012, available online at http://bahrainipolitics.blogspot.co.uk/2012/05/sectarian-politics-of-public-sector.html (last accessed 5 June 2012).

[13] Ben Farmer, 'Bahrain authorities destroy Pearl Roundabout' *The Daily Telegraph*, 18 March 2011.

head of the Royal Court, and Khalifa bin Ahmed Al-Khalifa, the chief of the Bahrain Defence Force.[14]

A Shifting Political Landscape

The national dialogue convened on 2 July and ran until 30 July 2011. It began under a cloud following the 22 June decision of the National Safety Court to sentence thirteen prominent opposition figures to varying terms of imprisonment. The majority were committed to non-violent protest and many had participated in the political opening that followed the ending of the previous period of internal unrest in 1999. In addition to amounting to 'a who's who of the predominantly Shia opposition', they included the head of the secular-leftist Wa'ad political society, Ibrahim Sharif. Their imprisonment illustrated the glove-fisted nature of the regime's approach, jailing some of its opponents while simultaneously reaching out to others.[15]

From the start, the national dialogue lacked credibility. Despite winning up to 45 per cent of the vote in the October 2010 parliamentary election, the major opposition group Al-Wefaq was only granted 5 out of 300 delegates. This was consistent with the overall composition of the dialogue, in which delegates representing all Bahraini opposition societies only constituted 11.67 per cent of the total. The remaining participants overwhelmingly favoured keeping the regime in its current form. Moreover, core opposition demands, for redrawing electoral boundaries, greater proportional representation, and creating an elected government were not on the agenda. Neither was any discussion permitted of the nature or extent of the ruling family's power. This led one Al-Wefaq ex-MP, Jasim Hussain, to describe the meetings as 'more of a social event than a political dialogue'.[16]

Al-Wefaq withdrew from the national dialogue halfway through, its own judgement to participate being called into question by its critics. The dialogue continued, and concluded with a series of recommendations, including one that the prime minister (rather than the king) would appoint the government. As the long-serving prime minister (in office since 1971)

---

[14] Patrick Cockburn, 'Power struggle deepens divisions among Bahraini royal family' *The Independent*, 27 September 2011.

[15] Anon., 'Bahrain security court sentences eight prominent Shia activists to life' *Gulf States Newsletter*, 35/903, 24 June 2011.

[16] Anon., 'Bahrain's national dialogue continues despite walk-out by main opposition' *Gulf States Newsletter*, 35/905, 22 July 2011.

represented one of the key obstacles to reform, this hardly constituted a political concession. Nor did the dialogue come to an agreement over the electoral boundaries, another major opposition grievance. Far from drawing a line under the unrest, the flawed process reinforced existing divisions and demonstrated very clearly that critical issues of political contention were simply not up for debate.[17]

The national dialogue partially overlapped with the Bahrain Independent Commission of Inquiry (BICI). This was established by King Hamad on 29 June to 'enquire into the incidents' in February and March and their consequences. Its chair was Egyptian Professor Cherif Bassiouni, who led the UN Security Council commission that investigated war crimes in the former Yugoslavia in the 1990s. Similar to the national dialogue, the commission quickly ran into difficulty. This stemmed from a series of interviews given by Bassiouni that appeared to prejudge its outcome and exonerate officials of any responsibility for human rights violations. These comments drew a furious reaction from Bahraini human rights groups and opposition figures, who pointed to statements made by members of the Al-Khalifa family praising and (in some cases) egging on the security forces.[18]

Doubtless chastened by the hostility to his remarks, Bassiouni surprised most observers with the hard-hitting content of his report when it was published on 23 November. In a televised speech in front of the king, Bassiouni stated that the authorities had used torture and excessive force during its crackdown on protesters. He pinpointed a culture of non-accountability amongst the security services operating during the state of emergency, and accused unnamed officials of disobeying laws designed to safeguard human rights. Most notably of all, he argued that many of the protests did not fall outside the rights of citizens to participate in, and that he had not found evidence of any link to Iranian involvement, contradicting regime narratives that ascribed them to external intervention rather than domestic grievances. The 513-page report painted a detailed picture of abuses of power by the Bahraini security forces and elements of the regime, most damagingly in its finding of 'systematic practice of physical and psychological mistreatment, which in many cases amounted to torture'.[19]

[17] K. Coates Ulrichsen, 'Dark clouds over Bahrain' *Foreign Policy*, 6 September 2011.
[18] Anon., 'Bahrain commission chief's comments raise questions over impartiality of inquiry' *Gulf States Newsletter*, 35/907, 2 September 2011.
[19] 'Report of the Bahrain Independent Commission of Inquiry' available online at http://www.bici.org.bh/, 23 November 2011, p. 298 (last accessed 3 June 2012).

In response, the king pledged to initiate reforms, and established a national commission to oversee their implementation. Yet, the measures taken (at the time of this writing in June 2012) left unaddressed many of the roots of Bahrain's political and economic inequalities. Furthermore, they took place against the backdrop of continuing clashes and daily low-level violence between protesters and security forces. Specific measures included the revocation of arrest powers from the National Security Apparatus, legislative amendments that expanded the definition of torture and lifted time limits for the prosecution of cases, pledges to rebuild Shia houses of worship destroyed by the regime during the crackdown, and the announced construction of more than 3,000 social housing units. They also included the reinstatement of workers dismissed on grounds of political expression and the dismissal of charges against 343 individuals accused of the same charges.[20]

Yet, while the measures did open up new pathways of redress for individual victims of abuse, they also highlight one of the major shortcomings dampening expectations of (and prospects for) deeper reform. This is that the changes rectified specific (or high-profile) instances of abuse, instead of constituting deep reforms to structures of political and economic power. Thus, recruiting foreign police leaders (John Yates and John Timoney) to re-train Bahrain's security services played well in London and Washington, but left unresolved the structural exclusion of large numbers of Bahraini citizens from an organization many perceive as exclusionary and deeply partial. In consequence, a hard-hitting report from Amnesty International in April 2012 concluded that 'hardly any efforts have been made to implement recommendations relating to national reconciliation, ending discrimination against the Shi'a community, especially in the security and armed forces and ending incitement to hatred in the government-controlled media'.[21]

Perhaps most damagingly, the culture of impunity identified by Bassiouni within the security services has yet to result in any high-level accountability. In early 2012, a trial began of five police officers – none of them Bahrainis – charged with involvement in the death of a blogger while in their custody on 9 April 2011, which was attributed (implausibly) at the time to 'complications from sickle cell anaemia'. Yet it stretches

[20] K. Coates Ulrichsen and E. Fakhro, 'Post-BICI Bahrain: Between reform and stagnation' *Open Democracy*, 19 January 2012.
[21] Amnesty International, 'Flawed reforms: Bahrain fails to achieve justice for protestors' April 2012, p. 54.

credibility to suggest that the scale and ferocity of the crackdown may solely be ascribed to the actions of (ostensibly renegade) junior personnel. To be credible, accountability cannot be narrowly limited to those who actively carried out abuses. It must include those who ordered and orchestrated the crackdown, and follow the chain of command upward, as events did not unfold in a total vacuum. This has not yet happened, nor is there any meaningful sign it might yet do so.

The result has been the empowerment of radical voices across the political spectrum and the marginalization of Bahrain's political middle ground. The emergence of radicalised splinter groups means it is no longer possible to speak of a 'regime-opposition' dichotomy. Elements of the opposition are growing more violent while extreme loyalist groups calling on the regime to crush the opposition once and for all have also intensified. Together, these trends are redrawing the political landscape of Bahrain by weakening the moderate wings of the government and the opposition whose leadership is vital to building support for political reform and reconciliation.

Of particular interest is the splintering of the Sunni community that hitherto provided the backbone of support for the Al-Khalifa regime. This has fragmented as the initial Gathering of National Unity has largely broken up, although in truth, it always identified itself as a 'soft opposition' with reform demands of its own. In its place, rival factions and individual groups have become increasingly vocal critics of government policy and started to make political demands of their own. Partially borne out of frustration at the government's seeming inability to resolve the issue, groups of vigilante squads have started to take local enforcement of law and order into their own hands.[22] Meanwhile, the resignation of Al-Wefaq Members of Parliament from the National Assembly opened the door for Sunni political societies, led by the Muslim Brotherhood (*Al-Menbar*) and Salafi (*Al-Assala*) groups, to articulate oppositional positions without fear of being 'tainted' by cooperation with the Shia-led political opposition. They have been joined by a reactionary mobilization of young Sunni loyalists (*Sahwat al-Fateh*) who seek to reclaim the counter-revolutionary movement from TGONU.[23] This multiplication of political opposition societies calls to mind the processes in Saudi Arabia, described by Madawi

---

[22] J. Gengler, 'Bahrai's Sunni awakening' *Middle East Research and Information Project*, 17 January 2012., available online at http://www.merip.org/mero/mero011712 (last accessed 4 June 2012).

[23] H. T. Alhasan, 'Bahrain: Split over proposed GCC union, and chronic failure of Sunni groups to mobilize' *Open Democracy*, 29 May 2012.

Al-Rasheed in this book, which are designed to dilute the opposition into segmented fractions less likely to coalesce against the government.

Although the government can no longer rally the 'Sunni street' behind it, the same can be said of the predominantly Shia opposition. Al-Wefaq and the established political societies have been damaged by their failure to show substantive results from their decision to engage the regime. They have been outflanked by the shadowy 'February 14' youth movement that emerged at the time of the Pearl uprising in 2011. Little is known about 'February 14': a recent article described them as 'a confederation of loosely organized networks... faceless, secretive, and anonymous', consisting of 'thousands of supporters [who] have abandoned the failed leadership of the country's better established, but listless, political opposition'.[24]

It is likely that it is 'February 14' that constitutes the vanguard of the protesters who confront the security services daily. However, it is unclear whether those who subscribe to its ideology necessarily organize themselves through coordinated networks. Rather, their effectiveness comes from the sporadic, uncoordinated, and unpredictable nature of their tactics. Moreover, despite attempted surveillance by the security forces, they retain a capacity to mobilize and coordinate massive demonstrations at short notice, as evidenced in their organization of a march of more than 100,000 people on 9 March 2012. This was their powerful response to a throwaway remark by King Hamad bin Isa that the protesters only represented a tiny minority of Bahraini citizens.[25] However, their decentralised nature makes it more difficult for the government to reach out to them, or to prevent individual acts of violence, such as a bombing in the village of Al-Eker on 9 April 2012 that injured seven policemen.[26]

Bahrain's shifting political landscape holds significant lessons for both the domestic legitimacy of the ruling family and for its regional and international partners. The speed with which the initial demonstrations for political reform escalated into calls for regime change amongst a significant segment of the demonstrators testifies to the low threshold of confidence in the regime's ability to reform itself. Calls for regime change were once the preserve of extremists such as the splinter *Haq* movement, yet they have migrated dangerously close to the mainstream

---

[24] T. C. Jones and A. Shehabi, 'Bahrain's revolutionaries' *Foreign Policy*, 2 January 2012.
[25] Anon., 'Bahrain protestors demand reforms in huge opposition rally' *USA Today*, 9 March 2012.
[26] H. Toumi, 'Bahrain probes bombing that injured seven' *Gulf News*, 10 April 2012.

opposition. Having witnessed the previous cycle of revolt (1994–99) and political opening (2001–10) end with the crushing repression in 2011, Bahraini opposition activists will be loath to give the government the benefit of the doubt in future reform initiatives. Nor is it clear that there exists a powerful advocate of reform within the ruling family or the government. The crown prince, Salman bin Hamad Al-Khalifa, has been marginalized, as power has shifted to the hard-liners clustered around the bin Ahmed brothers to the right of the prime minister himself, while reforming institutions such as the Economic Development Board (EDB) have effectively been closed down.[27]

Regional and International Implications

The fate of the EDB provides succour to sceptics of the GCC states' recent emergence as powerful regional actors. It seems to confirm that reforms will only be skin deep at best, and, in Bahrain's 'worst-case scenario' will, if necessary, be sacrificed for the sake of regime survival. Until recently, the slogan 'Business-Friendly Bahrain', which formed the pillar of the EDB and its 'Bahrain 2030' vision of economic diversification, could be found adorning black taxis in London, and was stamped into visitors' passports alongside their entry visa – no longer. Critics of the Gulf States, as well as proponents of incremental reform within them, will be questioning whether they, too, would choose survival over reform if forced to do so.

This has more than mere 'what if' interest. It strikes at the heart of the ambitious 'state-branding' models of engagement that have repositioned the GCC states in the changing global order. Along with Qatar and the United Arab Emirates, Bahrain competed for business on the lucrative MICE (meetings, incentives, conferences, and exhibitions) circuit. This reached its apotheosis with the awarding of the 2022 FIFA World Cup to Qatar on 2 December 2010 – only two weeks before the self-immolation of Mohammed Bouazizi triggered the Arab Spring chain of events. Although less high profile, Bahrain acquired a stream of high-profile events, including the annual Formula One Grand Prix, and regional security conferences such as the Manama Dialogue and the Bahrain Global Forum.

Such events bring international prestige as well as money. The Manama Dialogue brought senior American politicians such as Hillary

---

[27] Anon., 'Formula One leaves Bahrain anything but "UniFied"' *Gulf States Newsletter,* 36/922, 26 April 2012.

Clinton and Robert Gates to Bahrain to reaffirm U.S. commitment to regional (and Bahraini) security. On her visit in December 2010, just two months before the uprising at the Pearl Roundabout, Secretary of State Clinton told her hosts that 'I am very impressed by the progress that Bahrain is making on all fronts – economically, politically, socially. There is a very comprehensive vision of where the people and the Government of Bahrain are headed'.[28] Meanwhile, a 2008 study by the Bahraini sovereign wealth fund, *Mumtalakat*, estimated the value of the Formula One race at $600 million, through its knock-on effects on the tourist and travel sectors. This, it concluded, was the equivalent to adding 2.7 percentage points to GDP, and, for the race's major sponsor, the struggling national carrier, Gulf Air, it was a vital commercial lifeline.[29]

Although the Bahrain Grand Prix went ahead in April 2012 after its cancellation in 2011, it took place against the backdrop of a week of relentlessly critical media coverage. Sports journalists ostensibly in Bahrain to cover the motor racing performed the tasks of news editors whose own visas to enter the country were declined. The death of one protester and running battles between demonstrators and the security services dominated the reporting of the weekend. This exposed as hollow the government's efforts to promote the Grand Prix as signalling Bahrain's return to normality following the uprising, as evidenced by its choice of the 'UniFied' slogan for the race weekend.[30]

The unhappy weekend served to underline Bahrain's persistent troubles. Yet, they also brought its regional and international dimensions into sharper focus, as the criticism from international civil society and foreign journalists contrasted with the relatively muted statements from Bahrain's external partners, including the UK. Aside from largely meaningless statements urging all parties to commit to a generic reform process, there has been little follow-up from foreign governments to ensure implementation and/or monitoring of the declaratory commitments to reform. This became clear in a speech made by Secretary Clinton to the National Democratic Institute in Washington, DC on 8 November 2011, which highlighted the multiple dimensions shaping U.S. policy towards the upheaval in the Arab world. Arguing that 'it would be

---

[28] 'Townterview hosted by Bahrain TV' transcript of interview with Hillary Clinton, available at http://www.state.gov/secretary/rm/2010/12/152355.htm (last accessed 4 June 2012).

[29] J. Kinninmont, 'Bahrain's Formula One for failure' *Foreign Policy*, 19 April 2012.

[30] Anon, 'Formula One leaves Bahrain anything but "UniFied"' *Gulf States Newsletter*, 36/922, 26 April 2012

foolish to take a one-size-fits-all approach', Clinton went on to state that 'Our choices also reflect other interests in the region with a real impact on Americans' lives – including our fight against al-Qaeda; defense of our allies; and a secure supply of energy . . . There will be times when not all of our interests align . . . That is our challenge in a country like Bahrain'.[31]

At a time of rising international tension with Iran over its disputed nuclear programme, the United States is unlikely to abandon a key regional ally and the host of its Fifth Fleet. This provides succour to hard-liners within the regime who oppose far-reaching reforms, even if some of them, most notably the minister of defence, have suggested (bizarrely) that the uprising was 'by all means a conspiracy involving Iran with the support of the United States'. Indeed, Khalifa bin Ahmed (mentioned earlier in his guise as head of the Bahrain Defence Force) went on to add, in his interview to Egypt's *Al-Ahram* newspaper on 6 July 2011, that 'More important than talking about the differences between the US and Iran' are 'their shared interests in various matters that take aim at the Arab welfare'. His sentiments were repeated by other Bahraini officials and media outlets, which appeared to genuinely believe that U.S. policy was aimed at undermining the Sunni rulers of the Gulf based on an apparent ideological affinity towards Shi'ism.[32]

However odd these feelings may seem, in light of the longstanding U.S. security posture in the Gulf, they tapped into a deeper streak of rising sectarian rhetoric, as ruling elites across the GCC struggled to respond to the new regional zeitgeist. Immediately after the Bahraini uprising in February–March 2011, a plethora of participatory pressures and demands for reform hit the Gulf rulers at their most vulnerable point. These include petitions in the United Arab Emirates (UAE) and Saudi Arabia signed by prominent intellectuals and activists, weekly demonstrations and episodes of violence in Saudi Arabia's restive Eastern Province, deadly clashes between protesters and demonstrators in normally placid Oman, and escalating public protests in Kuwait directed against the unpopular prime minister there.[33]

These calls for inclusion were met with repressive countermeasures. In both Saudi Arabia and the UAE, petitioners were arrested and detained

31 K. deYoung, 'In Arab Spring speech, Clinton defends U.S. stance on Syria, Bahrain' *Washington Post*, 8 November 2011.
32 J. Gengler, 'The other side of radicalization in Bahrain' *Foreign Policy*, 15 July 2011.
33 K. Coates Ulrichsen, 'Gulf States: Studious silence falls on the Arab Spring' *Open Democracy*, 12 April 2011.

for long periods, with the latter also closing down branches of international think tanks and research institutes that had set up their regional branches in Abu Dhabi or Dubai.[34] The closures, which affected the Gulf Research Centre and the National Democratic Institute in Dubai, and the Konrad Adenauer Foundation and Gallup International in Abu Dhabi, dealt damaging blows to the international branding strategy that had brought them to the UAE in the first place.[35] Meanwhile, limited political reforms were enacted in Oman that did not address the extreme concentration of power around the sultan. In Kuwait, it took the unprecedented storming of parliament in November 2011 to precipitate an enforced change of prime minister, against the wishes of the emir.[36]

Yet, in response to these pressures, and despite the grassroots calls for change focussing not on regime change, but on a more equitable distribution of political power, officials in the GCC turned to an old tactic of blaming Iran for meddling in their internal affairs. This externalised the roots of dissent and deflected them from any possible domestic grievances. Thus, in addition to the Bahraini foreign minister's claim that 'We have never seen such a sustained campaign from Iran on Bahrain and the Gulf as we've seen in the past two months', the foreign minister of the UAE bluntly warned Iran 'to respect the unity and sovereignty of Gulf countries'.[37] This tactic served two purposes: first, it enabled the (Sunni) regimes to de-legitimise any (Shia-led) opposition activity or demand for reform by conflating the issues of Shia loyalties and Iranian manipulation into one amorphous threat. Second, by portraying demonstrators as disloyal and/or potential extremists, the regimes played a classic divide-and-rule card by hindering the emergence of a unifying cross-sectarian opposition. Both tactics were heavily used in Bahrain and elsewhere in the Gulf in 2011.[38]

The GCC therefore closed ranks to defend its member states against the internal demands of its citizenry as much as the external threat from Iran. After surprising his fellow rulers with an unexpected call for Jordan

---

[34] C. Davidson, 'The making of a police state' *Foreign Policy*, 14 April 2011.

[35] V. Nereim, 'Gallup and think tank leave Abu Dhabi' *The National*, 29 March 2012; P. Kannan, 'Dubai office of US-funded National Democratic Institute shut down' *The National*, 1 April 2012; S. L. Meyers, 'Emirates detain pair from U.S.-backed group' *New York Times*, 5 April 2012.

[36] K. Smith Diwan, 'Kuwait's constitutional showdown' *Foreign Policy*, 17 November 2011.

[37] Anon., 'UAE calls on Iran to "respect" Gulf neighbours' *Saudi Gazette*, 21 April 2011.

[38] Coates Ulrichsen, Studious Silence.

and Morocco to join the 'club of monarchs', King Abdullah of Saudi Arabia expressed a desire to deepen the union at the annual GCC summit in December 2011. This was fleshed out in greater detail in a speech by the Saudi foreign minister, Saud al-Faisal, on 28 April 2012. He called on the GCC states to move towards 'a phase of union with full integration of key affairs to give greater impetus and strength' to the organization.[39] In the days prior to the convening of an unprecedented mid-year 'consultative summit' in Riyadh on 14 May 2012, rumours of union escalated, with Bahrain's prime minister one of its most enthusiastic advocates, declaring that 'the great dream of the peoples of the region is to see the day when the borders disappear with a union that creates one Gulf'.[40]

Yet, in the event, nothing of significance was achieved at the meeting, which was noticeably not attended by the rulers of Oman and the UAE. It ended with Saud al-Faisal announcing that the participants had agreed to further study King Abdullah's proposal to transition the GCC into a union, and to submit recommendations to the annual summit in December 2012.[41] The great divergence of expectation from reality was remarkable as Saudi policy-making normally prioritises the avoidance of losing face over public statements of expected outcomes. It underscored the difficulty of getting all six member states to agree on a common vision beyond that of confronting Iran, and also reflected the smaller states' fears that any eventual union would inevitably be dominated by Saudi Arabia.[42]

Conclusion: Bahrain and the Gulf – Evolution or Revolution?

Developments in Bahrain therefore have a significance that far transcends the kingdom's shoreline. Its dwindling oil reserves mean that Bahrain functions as a bellwether for charting the speed of the winds of change in the Gulf, as well as the challenges of transitioning to a post-oil future. And, as previously described, the country is caught between powerful geopolitical cross-currents that give domestic developments a regional and international dimension.

---

[39] A. Hammond, 'Wary of Iran, Saudis seek progress on Gulf union' *Reuters*, 30 April 2012.

[40] A. Hammond and A. McDowall, 'Gulf leaders expected to announce unity plan' *Reuters*, 13 May 2012.

[41] Anon., 'Summit fails to agree on Gulf union' *Gulf States Newsletter*, 36/824, 24 May 2012.

[42] D. Roberts, 'The Gulf union that never was', http://www.rusi.org, 17 May 2012 (last accessed 3 June 2012).

The Saudi incursion into Bahrain in 2011 and its desire to create a Gulf Union stems from acknowledgement that it has the most to lose from prolonged or major instability in its eastern neighbour. From an ideological perspective, the ruling Al-Saud family in Riyadh has demonstrated twice – in the 1990s uprising and again in 2011 – that it is prepared to use force if necessary to support a fellow ruling dynasty in the Gulf. In addition to exercising political and security influence over Bahrain, Saudi Arabia wields economic leverage as well, through the sharing of the Abu Safah oilfield, which provides the majority of Bahrain's fast-depleting oil reserves and revenues.[43]

This notwithstanding, the ideational damage to ruling families throughout the Gulf, were one of their number to be forced into major concessions to popular opinion, or indeed ousted from power, is magnified in Saudi Arabia's case. This arises from the fact that Bahrain lies off the coast of its oil-rich Eastern Province with its large Shia minority. Like their Bahraini counterparts, Shias in Saudi Arabia have long complained of systematic discrimination and marginalization at the hands of state authorities. Deep frustration at the politics of uneven development caused a week of major unrest in 1979 centred on the oasis town of Qatif.[44] Worryingly for Saudi officials, Qatif has again been at the epicentre of persistent anti-government protests over the past year, replete with declarations of support for their Bahraini brethren across the water.[45]

Bahrain now finds itself poised at a profound juncture. It can either move towards deep and lasting changes to the structure and balance of power between state and society, or the regime will have to continue to rely on the use of force against an increasingly determined segment of its citizenry. The challenge facing the government is compounded by memories of the previous cycle of repression followed by partial promises of reform in the 1990s. The longer that the old guard remains untouched by high-level calls to account for the abuses of power committed over the past year, the harder it will be to convince sceptics of the government's good faith to engage. Calls to violence, by opposition and regime hardliners alike, make any solution more difficult, absent a decisive shift in influence towards moderate elements on all sides.

---

[43] R. Mills, 'Pioneering Bahrain finds itself reliant on Saudi largesse' *The National*, 1 May 2012.

[44] T. C. Jones, 'Rebellion on the Saudi periphery: Modernity, marginalisation, and the Shi'a uprising of 1979' *International Journal of Middle East Studies*, 38 (2006), 213.

[45] Anon., 'Saudi Shi'ites protest, support Bahrain brethren' *Reuters*, 16 March 2011.

This has implications for the other Gulf States, should they experience an upsurge in protest in the future. Their commercial and geostrategic importance means the West will neither abandon its Gulf partners nor necessarily make a stand on humanitarian grounds. Although this places Western commercial and institutional partners in a difficult position, caught between their core regional allies and mounting concern at the erosion of human rights and narrowing of political space, the consequence for Gulf polities are momentous. Officials throughout the region will be observing how cracking down so hard has saved the Al-Khalifa, at least for now. But their survival has come at a very high price economically and politically, and shattered social cohesion in a polarised country. With a ruling family seemingly trying to swim against the tide of the Arab Spring and reliant on foreign protection as the ultimate guarantor of regime security, ruling elites elsewhere will be absorbing the lessons from the Al-Khalifa's crushing of opposition at the expense of their domestic and international credibility.

PART IV

REGIONAL AND INTERNATIONAL IMPLICATIONS

16

Saudi Internal Dilemmas and Regional Responses to the Arab Uprisings

Madawi Al-Rasheed

Abstract

This chapter argues that Saudi Arabia's responses to the Arab uprisings of 2011–12 have been dictated by its internal political and social dilemmas. The Saudi leadership is most concerned with maintaining the status quo and it has used various strategies as the revolts spread. At home, economic rewards, coupled with renewed religious discourse about obedience to rulers and heavy security measures, ensured the silencing of protest, at least among the Sunni majority. However, these measures failed to contain the Shia protest in the Eastern Province. Abroad, the regime deployed three strategies: containment of the revolts in Tunisia, Egypt, and Libya; counterrevolution in Bahrain and Yemen; and support for the revolution in Syria. This chapter highlights the connections between internal Saudi dilemmas and the mixed responses to the Arab uprisings.

Saudi Arabia remains an authoritarian state without political participation or democratic institutions. Its internal political and social dilemmas have dictated its responses to the Arab uprisings of 2010–12. Unlike other monarchies in the region, the Saudi leadership has not engaged in serious political reform or encouraged open debate about the uprisings.[1] On the contrary, severe restrictions on freedom of expression

---

[1] After demonstrations gathered momentum, Jordan and Morocco introduced political reforms in anticipation of a domino effect. Moroccan reform proved to be more progressive than in Jordan. In the Gulf, Qatar promised national elections by 2013 and Oman launched a campaign against corruption. See Paul Silverstein, 'Weighing Morocco's New

and assembly were imposed and a wave of new intimidation began.[2] Arguably, Saudi Arabia is most concerned with maintaining the status quo. When revolts spread from North Africa to the Arabian Peninsula, the Saudi rulers resorted to multiple strategies. At home, economic rewards, coupled with renewed religious discourse about obedience to rulers and heavy security measures, ensured the silencing of protest – at least amongst the Sunni majority. However, these measures failed to contain the Shia protest in the Eastern Province.[3]

Throughout 2011–12, the Saudi regime seemed to have entered a new phase of confrontation with the Shia minority of the Eastern Province while carefully suppressing low-level mobilization amongst the Sunni majority. The first bolder confrontation with the Shia, which at the time of this writing has led to Saudi security forces killing sixteen young Shia activists following demonstrations in Qatif and Awamiyya, attracted media attention and scholarly analysis for obvious reasons, the most important of which is the region's connection to Bahrain and the presence of the largest oil fields in the area. However, the mobilization amongst the Sunni majority remained low key and failed to attract any significant reporting, simply because this is still limited in scope, magnitude, and demands.

Abroad, the regime deployed three strategies: containment of the revolts in Tunisia, Egypt, and Libya; counter-revolution in Bahrain and Yemen; and support for revolution in Syria.[4] This chapter highlights the

---

Constitution', Merip online report, 5 July 2011, www.merip.org/mero/mero070511; Curtis Ryan, 'Reform Retreats Amid Jordan's Political Storms', Merip online Report, 10 June 2011, www.merip.org/mero/mero061005; Kristian Coates Ulrichsen, 'Qatar and the Arab Spring', *Open Democracy*, 12 April 2011; and David Roberts, 'The Arab World's Unlikely Leader: Embracing Qatar's Expanding Role in the Region', Project on Middle East Democracy, 13 March 2012.

[2] Amnesty International, *Annual Report, Saudi Arabia*, London: Amnesty International, 2011. In 2011–12, security forces shot several Shia activists. The last death was reported on 11 February 2012. See 'New Clashes in Saudi Arabia Leave "Protester" Dead', BBC, 11 February 2012, available at www.bbc.co.uk/news/world-middle-east-16995286.

[3] Madawi Al-Rasheed, 'No Saudi Spring: Anatomy of a Failed Revolution', *Boston Review*, March/April 2012 and Toby Matthiesen, 'A "Saudi Spring?": The Shia Protest Movement in the Eastern Province 2011–12', *Middle East Journal*, 2012, vol. 66, no. 4, pp. 628–59.

[4] Although this chapter relies on an analysis of the official Saudi position vis-à-vis the Arab uprisings, there remains an unofficial, less-exposed field where Saudi Arabia operates, especially in its patronage and sponsorship of Arab non-governmental actors. Whereas open state-to-state relations can be accessed in the public sphere, state-to-non-state actors or transnational connections between non-state actors themselves are more opaque.

connections between internal Saudi dilemmas and the mixed responses to the Arab uprisings.

Revolutions, Internal Dynamics, and Regional Players

Sidney Tarrow defines revolutions as collective contentious action mounting a challenge against elites, authorities, and other social, political, and religious groups. They often involve the collision of human agency and structural processes.[5] Jack Goldstone summarizes the conditions necessary for the success of such action:

For a revolution to succeed, a number of factors have to come together. The government must appear so irremediably unjust or inept that it is widely viewed as a threat to the country's future; elites (especially in the military) must be alienated from the state and no longer willing to defend it; a broad-based section of the population . . . must mobilise; and international powers must either refuse to step in to defend the government or constrain it from using maximum force to defend itself.[6]

Goldstone does not include the role of regional players, who during a revolution may operate as clients of international powers. This was so obvious during the 2011 Arab uprisings that its importance cannot be ignored. In fact, regional client states of the international powers (Saudi Arabia, Qatar, the UAE), regional powers in a conflict relationship with

---

This chapter will only deal with the officially documented Saudi responses to the Arab uprisings. It will not engage with rumours and allegations regarding the second type of regional connections, namely those between the Saudi regime and non-state actors such as old and newly founded Arab political parties, ex-Arab regime circles (for example, in Egypt), and civil society organizations (for example, secular and Salafi groups that operate in other Arab countries with ideological and religious connections to Saudi Arabia), or arming rebels in the ongoing Syrian uprising. Equally, the chapter will not explore transnational connections between Saudi non-state groups and other non-governmental organizations in the Arab region, such as independent charities, religious centres, donations, and media support. For analysis of transnational connections, see Madawi Al-Rasheed, 'Localizing the Transnational and Transnationalizing the Local', in Madawi Al-Rasheed (ed.), *Transnational Connections and the Arab Gulf*, London: Routledge, 2005, pp. 1–18. On Saudi connections, see Madawi Al-Rasheed (ed.), *Kingdom without Borders: Saudi Arabia's Political, Religious and Media Frontiers*, London: Hurst, 2008.

[5] Sidney Tarrow, *Power in Movement: Social Movements and Contentious Politics*, Cambridge: Cambridge University Press, 1998, p. 1.

[6] Jack A. Goldstone, 'Understanding the Revolutions of 2011', *Foreign Affairs*, 90, 3, 2011: 8–16, at p. 9.

the main international powers (Iran), and relatively autonomous regional powers (Turkey) played important roles in the events that swept the Arab region. States, such as Saudi Arabia, Qatar, Iran, and Turkey – those most likely to be affected by revolution in neighbouring countries – were active players.

Regional powers have much to lose in such a situation. Geographical proximity, economic relations, a possible domino effect, loss of influence over regional allies, competition with neighbouring powers, aspirations for regional leadership, the burden of refugees and exiles, loss of border controls, arms smuggling, and military infiltration during an armed uprising are but a few of the concerns that may push regional powers to act in their national interest at such a time.

This chapter highlights Saudi Arabia's responses, reactions, and interventions during the Arab revolts, which caught the leadership by surprise. Turkey,[7] Iran,[8] and Qatar[9] did not expect to be directly affected. Saudi Arabia, however, had internal reasons to fear the 'contagion' of the Arab Spring, especially after the protests that started in Bahrain in February 2011.[10] The Shia in the Eastern Province staged demonstrations, demanded equality, and stood in solidarity with their co-religionists in Bahrain.

---

[7] Turkey appears to be a prosperous stable democracy with old institutions and a constitution. Its main concern had so far been the Kurdish question, which, in addition to trouble on the Iraqi Kurdish borders, may come to haunt it in Syria. See 'Turkey and Syria: One Problem with a Neighbour', *The Economist*, 20 August 2011.

[8] Iran had its revolution in 1979, and is unlikely to experience a second wave. The Green Movement staged serious demonstrations in 2009, and may well do this again in the future. But according to many analysts, this movement is a corrective impulse from within the Islamic revolutionary framework that currently dominates Iranian politics. The Green Movement's concern with human rights, transparency, and limitations on the authority of the Supreme Leader is understood as a post-Islamist dissent within Iranian Islamism that seeks greater freedoms and less compulsion in religion and politics. Asef Bayat offers a nuanced analysis of the post-Islamism phase in contemporary Iran. See Asef Bayat, *Making Islam Democratic: Social Movements and the Post-Islamist Turn*, Stanford: Stanford University Press, 2007. According to Hamid Dabashi, the Green Movement is driven by an Iranian cosmopolitan agenda. For further details, see Hamid Dabashi, *Iran, The Green Movement and the USA: The Fox and the Paradox*, London: Zed Books, 2010.

[9] Qatar is currently immune from the domino effect of the Arab uprisings. It has played a major role both at the level of media and international forums to promote the Muslim Brotherhood as an alternative to the secular Arab dictatorships. Its leadership proposed national elections in 2013. See Steven Wright, 'Qatar', in Christopher Davidson (ed.), *Power and Politics in the Persian Gulf Monarchies*, London: Hurst, 2012, pp. 113–33.

[10] F. Gregory Gause, III, *Saudi Arabia in the New Middle East*, Report 63, New York: Council on Foreign Relations, 2011.

This local 'revolt' has attracted academic analysis and will not be fully explored in this chapter.[11] Suffice it to say that unlike predictions that the Shia revolt would spread to Sunni majority areas, it has failed to do so. In fact, one may argue that the Shia uprising in the Eastern Province was advantageous to the regime in the way it pacified an agitated Sunni majority because the regime capitalised on this revolt and linked it to Iranian conspiracy. In fact, the regime may have had a serious vested interest in keeping the Shia revolt ongoing as long as it was circled and contained in specific areas of two Shia cities, Qatif and Awamiyya. Contrary to all predictions, the Shia rebellion served regime interests in the way the Sunni majority started backing the regime against a minority with whom they had never had sympathy or support. The regime played on hollow legitimacy narratives that it is the guardian of Sunni interests against an Iranian Shia conspiracy that was unfolding in Bahrain and Qatif. Salafi circles and even Saudi liberal constituencies backed the regime in its security operations in the Eastern Province and the regime emerged triumphant as defender of the pious Sunni realm.

Sunni Saudis called for demonstrations on 11 March, dubbed the Day of Rage; although this did not materialize,[12] Saudi Arabia witnessed more demonstrations and mobilization than it had known since the labour protest of the 1950s. Agitation, debate, and controversies intensified the regime's fears about future protest. The nervous leadership, a long-time advocate of stability and security, acted quickly to prevent a full-scale revolt, although this was unlikely.

Saudi Internal Challenges

On the eve of the Arab uprisings, Saudi Arabia lacked the organizational potential of youth, women's, and labour movements, although it had a youth bulge comparable to that in other Arab countries. Civil society is restricted and political parties are banned. Most importantly, Saudi Arabia lacked what Charles Tripp calls 'publics' – the convergence of groups, ideological trends, classes, and sects with a common vision and desire for change – while nevertheless experiencing the economic grievances, corruption, nepotism, and oppression prevalent in other parts

[11] One of the most relevant analyses is Toby Matthiesen, 'A "Saudi Spring?": The Shia Protest Movement in the Eastern Province 2011–12', *Middle East Journal*, 2012, vol. 66, no. 4, pp. 628–59.

[12] Madawi Al-Rasheed, 'Arabie saoudite: demain, la tempete?' *Politique Internationale*, 132, Summer 2011, pp. 195–222.

of the Arab world. These reasons for protest were not, however, sufficient to precipitate the formation of 'publics' and a consequent broad-based revolt. The Saudi publics were segmented as a result of sectarianism (the Sunni-Shia divide, men-women divide, tribal and regional differences, in addition to class hierarchies).

The structure of the Saudi regime differed considerably from that of secular Arab authoritarianism. First, its oil resources allowed it to absorb economic hardship, whereas the Arab republics could not. Second, the Saudi experience of civil disobedience and peaceful protest cannot be compared to that in places such as Tunisia and Egypt. Even though there were protest movements in the 1950s and 1960s, which were mainly a reflection of Arab ideological imports such as anti-imperialism, Arabism, and communism,[13] the only indigenous Saudi opposition came from militant Islamists, such as the Ikhwan rebellion of 1927,[14] Juhayman's movement in 1979,[15] and Jihadi violence in 2003.[16] The peaceful Tunisian and Egyptian uprisings demonstrated different mobilization strategies, which the Shia minority of the Eastern Province had tried in the early 1980s but which had failed.[17] Shia protests, including the mobilization in March 2011, had been suppressed because they reflected Shia grievances and demands rather than generating the nationwide collective action that defines revolutions. The Sunni areas remained loyal despite their economic and political grievances, with only minor and small-scale demonstrations focussed on specific demands.

Despite the 2003 oil boom, the Saudi leadership faced clear internal challenges. Tensions at both leadership and society levels were exacerbated by the turmoil in the wider Arab region, even if an imminent revolution was unlikely. Politically, Saudi Arabia, like much of the region, faced the crisis with an old, inert leadership. The king, crown prince,

---

[13] Robert Vitalis, *America's Kingdom: Mythmaking on the Saudi Oil Frontier*, Stanford: Stanford University Press, 2007.

[14] On the 1927 Ikhwan rebellion, see John Habib, *Ibn Saud's Warriors of Islam: The Ikhwan of Najd and their Role in the Creation of the Saudi Kingdom, 1910–1930*, Leiden: Brill, 1987.

[15] On Juhayman's revolt in Mecca, see Thomas Hegghammer and Stephane Lacroix, 'Rejectionist Islamism in Saudi Arabia: The Story of Juhayman al-Utaybi Revisited', *International Journal of Middle East Studies*, 93, 1, 2007, pp. 103–22.

[16] On the Jihadi trend after 9/11, see Madawi Al-Rasheed, *Contesting the Saudi State: Islamic Voices from a New Generation*, Cambridge: Cambridge University Press, 2007, pp. 134–74.

[17] On the Saudi Shia uprising in 1979, see Fuad Ibrahim, *The Shi'is of Saudi Arabia*, London: Saqi, 2006.

and interior minister all had health problems, for which they regularly sought treatment abroad. Before departing for New York in November 2011, King Abdullah appointed his son Mitab as commander of the Saudi National Guard, a position he himself had occupied since 1962.[18]

Crown Prince Sultan had been suffering from cancer since 2004, undergoing treatment and convalescence abroad. Several senior princes regularly travelled to Morocco to meet him, which the Saudi media portrayed as normal procedure. Sultan promoted his son Khalid in the Ministry of Defence, and when he died in October 2011, Khalid became deputy defence minister and Prince Nayif, the interior minister, became crown prince while remaining interior minister, thus gaining multiple powers in the Council of Ministers. The Interior Ministry has extensive powers, and controls all religious, judicial, and security matters inside Saudi Arabia. But Nayif too has health problems, for which he sought treatment abroad in March 2012. Following the death of Sultan, governor of Riyadh, Prince Salman was made minister of defence and his deputy Prince Satam became governor of Riyadh.

In 2007, King Abdullah established the Committee of Allegiance to deal with succession issues, but it was not mobilized throughout 2011– 12, when the king and crown prince were ill.[19] It did not even meet to discuss the office of crown prince when Sultan died. Abdullah simply made new appointments to the committee, bringing in two junior princes and ignoring its theoretical role in the event of the sudden death or prolonged illness of the king or crown prince. When Abdullah dies, Nayif's son, Muhammad (currently, minister of interior) and Salman, crown prince at the time of writing this chapter, will undoubtedly consolidate their control over key government positions, while junior relatives will continue in minor posts such as education, tourism, sports, culture, and heritage. The senior princes, all in their eighties, have groomed their sons to replace them.

At the time of writing in June 2013, the king's son, Mitab ibn Abdullah (commander of the Saudi National Guard) was elevated to the rank of minister. Deputy defence minister Khalid ibn Sultan was dismissed. Muhammad ibn Nayif was promoted to minister of interior and Saud ibn Nayif was promoted to become governor of the Eastern Province. The

[18] Eleanor Gillespie (ed.), *Politics, Succession and Risk in Saudi Arabia*, Gulf States Newsletter Special Report, January 2010.
[19] On the Committee of Allegiance, see Madawi Al-Rasheed, *A History of Saudi Arabia*, 2nd edition, Cambridge: Cambridge University Press, 2010, pp. 257–61.

shuffle in portfolios that followed the death of both Sultan and Nayif excluded Talal ibn Abd al-Aziz, known for his dissenting politics and calls for constitutional monarchy.[20] Talal resigned from the Committee of Allegiance after Nayif became crown prince and started giving interviews to Arab and international media, urging the king to adopt a reformist agenda, national elections, and more representative government.[21] He noted that Saudi Arabia is vulnerable to the uprising fever sweeping the region. He remarked that he remains bound by his oath of allegiance to his brother Abdullah, but that after the king's death, he may revisit his position, implying that he may not feel obliged to give the oath to Nayif, the current crown prince and Talal's junior. Since Nayif's death, Talal has not reiterated his subtle threats.

Talal has long appeared to be restless, and has continued to warn of dissent and chaos if the current policy of excluding other princes and society from the decision-making process continues. His media protest remains marginal as he has no real power base to challenge Nayif, when the latter was alive, and Nayif's son who became minister of interior. Talal criticised Nayif in the media but without naming him. Talal's son al-Walid remains an important financial player and media tycoon who can make a serious impact on the local stock market. During the upheavals in Egypt and the closure of its stock market, he reportedly injected funds, preventing a collapse of real estate investments.[22] His new pan-Arab news channel, al-Arab, is scheduled to broadcast from Bahrain in 2014. Although it is promoted as an alternative to al-Arabiyya and al-Jazeera, al-Arab is likely to be a soft power in a future leadership contest. However, it is unlikely that al-Walid or his father will play a leading political role after Abdullah dies. Talal remains a disenchanted senior prince whose recent tweets and web page continue to feed rumours about the struggle within the ruling family over senior office.[23]

Factionalism remains a serious challenge, and is likely to intensify. The Arab uprisings broke when Saudi princes were expressing conflicting

[20] In the 1960s, Talal was known for his involvement in the Free Princes movement. For more details, see Al-Rasheed, *A History of Saudi Arabia*, pp. 102–10.

[21] Asma Alsharif, 'Senior Saudi Prince Resigns from Allegiance Council', 16 November 2011, see www.reuters.com/article/2011/11/16/us-saudi-prince-idUSTRE7AF1XP20111116.

[22] 'Land deal seen boosting Egypt's property stocks at http://arabia.msn.com/business/market/af/2011/june/6513332/land-deal-seen-boosting-egypt.aspx.

[23] Prince Talal's web page: www.princetalal.net/new/index.php. On Twitter, see @TalalAbdulaziz.

messages about the country's future. There are now multiple centres of power within the ruling group, but two discernible factions are currently in competition; one is believed to be led by Abdullah and the other by Nayif's successors, each comprising a wide circle of senior and junior princes. Abdullah, who is in his late eighties, seems hardly capable of running the daily affairs of the state, although he continues to appear in public. Around Abdullah there is a circle of princes who may be apprehensive about the Nayif dynasty. After his death this is now comprised of his hawkish sons and is becoming even more powerful. Nayif's sons have never expressed support for national elections or some sort of constitutional monarchy. Both Talal and ex-director of intelligence services, Turki al-Faisal, have called for public participation in decision-making. Talal warned of years of upheaval if King Abdullah does not achieve political reform before his death.

During the uprisings, Talal started interacting with his followers on Twitter. His use of this new social media, in which his son invested $300 million,[24] surprised many Saudis and prompted some young activists to send comments accusing him and his family of plundering the country's wealth and confiscating both national resources and private land. Talal has responded that he does not own land in Saudi Arabia apart from his house in Riyadh. He had previously pointed out that junior princes receive a mere 750 Saudi riyals in monthly salaries, do not own their own property, and are often in debt. Talal's voice appeals to politically marginalized members of the royal family, amongst them several women.

These women include Talal's outspoken daughter Sara; his daughter-in-law Amira, the wife of al-Walid; Loulwa, a daughter of King Faisal, appointed as member of the Consultative Council in 2013; and Basma, a businesswoman and daughter of King Saud. Basma, a regular commentator in the Saudi press, has appeared on satellite television, discussing corruption and women's rights. In interviews with the BBC Arabic Service and Iranian Arabic satellite television, she talked about Islamic unity and internal reform in Saudi Arabia. The British media have dubbed her the dissident princess from Acton, a reference to her house in a London suburb.[25]

---

[24] Mark Sweeney, 'Twitter Stake Bought by Saudi Billionaire', *The Guardian*, 19 December 2011.
[25] Cahal Milmo, 'The Acton Princess Calling for Reform in Saudi Arabia', *The Independent*, 3 January 2012.

None of these critical royal voices openly questions the legitimacy or performance of senior princes. In fact, they highlight the credentials of their fathers, brothers, and uncles; their criticism is often aimed at *al-batana*, a group of state advisors, bureaucrats, and technocrats who allegedly mismanage or plunder resources. It absorbs criticism of the government and shelters more senior princes from tough questioning in the public sphere. Marginalized royals are often critical of religious radicalism, with respect to both terrorism and *fatwa*s barring the emancipation of women. They always congratulate the king for his social reforms, especially his recent cosmetic changes such as promising women participation in municipal elections and the Consultative Council, and allowing them to work in lingerie shops and perhaps in the future as vigilantes under the authority of the Committee for the Promotion of Virtue and Prohibition of Vice.[26] In 2013, the king appointed thirty women to the Consultative Council, two of whom are princesses.

The Quest for Political Reform

Since the Arab uprisings broke out, Saudi Arabia has experienced bottom-up pressure for political reform. In February 2011, two petitions calling for political change were posted online. The regime moved quickly to censor the sites, but many young activists and reformers associated with previous political mobilization signed these.

The first petition, *Ilan watani lil-islah* (The declaration for national reform), demanded a constitutional monarchy.[27] The authors, together with forty young activists, helped circulate it online. While retaining their commitment to a national agenda, they envisaged a federal system that would free the provinces from the interior ministry's centralized control. They feared that in light of the Egyptian revolution, the hard line Sunni Islamist opposition – both that based in London and its new counterpart in Saudi Arabia, such as the Salafi Omma Party – would hijack the state's agenda and dominate the Saudi street after Abdullah's death.[28] The signatories included both liberal and moderate Islamists such as Muhammad Said al-Tayib, Ali al-Damini, Abd al-Aziz al-Qasim,

---

[26] Madawi Al-Rasheed, 'The Meaning of Rights for Women', *World Today*, February 2012.

[27] The petition and the names of signatories are at www.saudireform.com/?p=petintion, accessed 20 April 2011.

[28] Communication with activist Ahmad Adnan, April 2011.

and Muhammad al-Ahmari as well as Shia activists such as Tawfiq al-Saif and Jaafar al-Shayib. Female human rights activists and academics such as Wajiha al-Howider, Fawziyya al-Bishr, and Fawziyya al-Ouyoni were also signatories. The petition can be described as a liberal document expressed within a moderate Islamic framework.

The petition demanded urgent political, economic, social, and judicial reforms, including the rule of law, the protection of civil and human rights, political participation, equitable economic development, eradication of poverty and corruption, and an elected national assembly. It called for a written constitution, independent civil society, and elected provincial governments. These demands were not new, but reflected dissatisfaction with the existing government-appointed human rights association. Regional autonomy was especially important after corruption and mismanagement of development projects led to flooding and deaths in several Saudi cities, such as Jeddah in January 2011.[29]

A second petition, *Nahwa dawlat al-huquq wa al-muassasat* (Towards a state of rights and institutions), expressed commitment to Islamic principles. It asked for an elected national assembly, separation between the offices of king and prime minister, and an end to corruption. It demanded freedom of speech, independent associations, release of all political prisoners, and unrestricted travel for activists. It had a clear Islamist tone, avoiding terms such as democracy, regional government, and constitutional monarchy and highlighting the importance of equitable distribution of wealth, political participation, and representation. Sahwi Islamist shaykh Salman al-Owdah endorsed it. It attracted thousands of signatories, reflecting a growing Islamist trend grounded in both Islamism and human rights discourses.[30]

Sahwa is a term that refers to the complex contemporary Islamist movement in Saudi Arabia that emerged as a solid trend following the 1990 Gulf War when outspoken members contested the Saudi decision to invite American troops to defend Saudi Arabia against the Iraqi invasion. It consists of Muslim Brotherhood supporters, Salafi-Ikhwani activists known as the Sururis, and other fringe Islamists who adopted strategies ranging from violent confrontation to peaceful activism against the Saudi regime throughout the last two decades.[31] Famous leaders of this diverse

---

[29] 'Saudi Scrambles Rescue Teams for Jeddah', *Agence France Press*, 26 January 2011.
[30] The petition is posted at http://dawlaty.com/services.html, accessed on 20 April 2011.
[31] Madawi Al-Rasheed, *Contesting the Saudi State: Islamic Voices from a New Generation*, Cambridge: Cambridge University Press, 2007; Stephane Lacroix, *Awakening Islam: The*

group were imprisoned in the 1990s and most of them were released by 2000. They have remained quiet, but with the Arab Spring and the success of the Muslim Brotherhood in Egypt and Tunisia, they reappeared again with a new political discourse and strategies. They celebrated the Arab Spring and praised the peaceful mobilization that overthrew Arab dictators. So far, they have not called openly for demonstrations in Saudi Arabia. In fact, they opposed the 11 March call for demonstrations, which led to these calls remaining unheeded.

Both petitions represented moderate political demands. They did not call for the overthrow of the regime, but pointed to serious shortcomings and disappointments. There were no demonstrations like those seen in Egypt. The authors ensured that the external opposition, for example the Shia Khalas movement and the Movement for Islamic Reform in Arabia, were not openly involved in their preparation. It was clear that the petitioners refrained from taking a radical stance to avoid arrest.[32] Petitioners invoked reform agendas from 2003–05 and pledged allegiance to the king. Most were either well-known veterans of reform such as Nasserite Muhammad Said al-Tayib, Islamist Abdullah al-Hamid, or new young 'netizens',[33] who played an important role in disseminating the petitions. Although the Saudi press ignored them, they were circulated on Facebook and Twitter.

There is obvious frustration and disappointment with King Abdullah, who so far has failed to implement demands from the previous petitions. Reformers from across the political spectrum were worried about the future given the king's age and the uncertainty of the succession. Abdullah has developed a quasi-liberal entourage, which has been instrumental in shaping his image as a great reformer. Many fear that Nayif's security-based approach to government inherited by his son will end their influence and increase repression. In most closed political systems, the existing functionaries are gradually removed from office to make room for the new ruler's circle.

The severest denunciation of Nayif and his son came from a new unofficial organization, Jamiat al-Huquq al-Madaniyya wa al-Siyasiyya (Association for Civil and Political Rights in Saudi Arabia: HASM).[34]

Politics of Religious Dissent in Contemporary Saudi Arabia, Cambridge, MA: Harvard University Press, 2011.

32 Personal communication with Saudi activists, March 2011.

33 The term 'netizens' is coined here to refer to citizens who are active on the Internet, especially for the purpose of engaging in social and political discussion.

34 HASM communiqués and reports are posted on the association's web page. See www .acpra.info/news.php?action=list&cat_id=12.

Its co-founder, Buraydah-based Muhammad al-Bjadi, was detained in March 2011 after being accused of encouraging female relatives of political prisoners to stage demonstrations. In March 2012, he went on hunger strike. HASM accuses the regime of arresting al-Bjadi after he exposed details of the death under torture of a Yemeni immigrant and demanded that Nayif be tried for human rights abuses.

HASM confirms its allegiance to Abdullah, seen as a reformist, while denouncing his brother as a conservative security apparatchik, whose policing practices violate human rights and Islamic law. While several HASM activists are imprisoned, the movement's leaders remained free to mobilize, at least online until 2013 when it was banned. Islamist veteran Abdullah al-Hamid, who spent several years in prison and was regularly interrogated, backs HASM. At the time of writing, founders of HASM, al-Qahtani, al-Rushudi and al-Hamid were sentenced to more than 10 years in prison.

Nayif is now dead but his dynasty has its surviving loyalists. His son, newly appointed minister of the interior, Muhammad commands a large security apparatus and religious groups controlling religious education, the Committee for the Promotion of Virtue and Prohibition of Vice, the judiciary, and other Wahhabi religious and jurisprudential establishments. In Western capitals and amongst sections of Saudi society, Muhammad is believed to be a strategic player in Saudi and international security, given his involvement in the War on Terror and his pacification of al-Qaida operatives following 11 September 2001. At the beginning of the Arab uprisings, Nayif emphasized the state's Salafi character, a fact that his son is destined to celebrate in an attempt to appease Islamists. This message must be understood within the context of the uprisings, especially in Tunisia and Egypt, where the Muslim Brotherhood established itself as a viable alternative to dictatorships. As the post-Arab Spring governments appear more Islamic, Nayif needed to stress Saudi Arabia's Salafi credentials in contrast with the Brotherhood's current mix of democracy and Islam. His successor is destined to continue to adopt multiple strategies, convincing the West that he is indispensible for security and intelligence purposes and maintain the image of Saudi Arabia as the only legitimate Islamic state in the region, very much like his father used to do in order to maintain Salafi loyalty.

Traditional Salafi–Wahhabi loyalists share Nayif's denunciation of the Shia; their alleged backer, Iran; and the Muslim Brotherhood, seen by traditional Wahhabis as religiously lax and politically divisive (*hizb*). Some loyal Salafis are keen to renew their allegiance to a political power that promises to control the Shia, of whose creed they remain suspicious, and their relatively moderate competitors such as the Brotherhood. Although Nayif ensured that Salafis who criticize him are detained, he tended to accommodate their social conservatism. One of the strategies used to suppress the Shia revolt in the Eastern Province is the propagation of anti-Shia Wahhabi sectarianism.[35] Furthermore, traditional Wahhabi discourse is deployed to demonize the Saudi Muslim Brotherhood and the Sururis, two organized groups belonging to the Sahwis.[36]

The political, religious, and ideological schisms within Saudi Arabia on the eve of the uprisings were thus between the king's loyalists who praise his gender reforms and Nayif's hard line Salafi followers who see those reforms as a distortion of the country's Islamic identity. When Abdullah allowed mixed sexes in his new science university (KAUST), a member of the Council of Senior Ulama, Saad al-Shithri, was critical of both the gender mixing and of the university's curriculum, which the council had not approved. He was sacked from the council and demonized in the official press as a hard line dissident.[37]

In September 2011, the king announced that women would be allowed to participate in municipal elections and would be appointed to the Consultative Council, within a Sharia framework.[38] He declared that religious scholars had been consulted regarding these decisions. Ex-head of the judiciary Shaykh Salih al-Lohaydan announced that not all members of the Council of Senior Ulama were aware of these reforms, hinting that not all senior *ulama* approved them. He later issued a statement against women visiting King Abdullah's Janadiriyya heritage festival in February 2012, whose organizers had encouraged singing and dancing. He dismissed the idea that the festival was like the Eid celebrations, in which women participate. Many Saudis thought that al-Lohaydan's opinion encouraged a group of *muhtasibin* (voluntary vigilantes) to force their way into the festival. The king had sacked the head of the Committee for the Promotion of Virtue and Prohibition of Vice, Abd al-Aziz al-Humayin, after excessive policing and surveillance of the population was reported in

---

35 Madawi Al-Rasheed, 'Sectarianism as Counter-Revolution: Saudi Responses to the Arab Spring', *Studies in Ethnicity and Nationalism*, 11, 3, 2011, pp. 513–25.

36 The Islamist field in Saudi Arabia is complex. It includes a mixture of politically active Salafis, Sururis (a mix between Salafis and Muslim Brotherhood), and other fringe movements. For more details, see Madawi Al-Rasheed, *Contesting the Saudi State: Islamic Voices from a New Generation*, Cambridge: Cambridge University Press, 2007.

37 An *al-Watan* journalist, Jamal Khashoggi, wrote a severe critique of al-Shithri. See Jamal Khashoggi, 'al-Sheikh al-shithri wa qanat al-majd', *al-Watan*, 29 September 2009.

38 'Women in Saudi Arabia to Vote and Run in Elections', BBC, 25 September 2011.

the press. Rumours circulated that al-Humayin had been sacked because he objected to the harsh treatment that women were subjected to when they demonstrated in front of the Interior Ministry. He was replaced with a more moderate religious scholar, Abd al-Latif al-Sheikh, who had been Prince Salman's advisor. Although the council itself remains loyal to the king and crown prince, the loyalty of individual members cannot be taken for granted.

The increasing polarization between liberal and hard line Islamists peaked over the case of Hamza Kashgari. Kashgari is a twenty-three-year-old journalist at *al-Bilad* electronic newspaper who tweeted on the Prophet's birthday on 6 February 2012 and wrote doubtful statements about god on his blog page.[39] He belonged to a new religious discussion group in Jeddah, that held regular meetings in Jusoor, a privately owned library and coffee shop. The Committee for the Promotion of Virtue and Prohibition of Vice raided it under the pretext of investigating mixing between the sexes amongst visitors who were attending a lecture by Abdullah Hamiddin, a writer and commentator in *al-Hayat*, a naturalized Yemeni and descendent of the exiled ruling Hamiddin family.[40] His ideas for 'reconstructing religion', articulated in his book *Harmonious Being*, are thought to have inspired the formation of the Jusoor reading group.

However, it seems that the raid was prompted by discussions and lectures regarded by the religious committee as subversive. Islamists considered Kashgari's tweets offensive, and called for his trial as an apostate flooded Twitter while groups of activists filed complaints at local courts. Many religious scholars and activists accused him of being influenced by the Jusoor group, especially Hamiddin's ideas. The king ordered his arrest, but Kashgari had already fled to Malaysia. Malaysian police arrested him at the airport and sent him back to Riyadh.[41] Although

[39] Kashgari's case attracted international attention after calls for his beheading on Twitter escalated the tension. See Amnesty International, 'Man Might Face Death Penalty for Tweets: Hamza Kashgari', 13 February 2012, www.amnesty.org/en/library/asset/MDE23/002/2012/en/3d97adea-6c10-4b82-976d-fobfd926776f/mde230022012en.html.

[40] Abdullah Hamiddin, *al-Kaynouna al-mutanaghima* (Harmonious Being), Dubai: Madarek, 2nd edition, 2012. See also oral lecture on Internet, www.4shared.com/music/3JIBTA8G/. (July 2011). See interview on Idhaat, al-Arabiyya 20 April, http://www.alarabiya.net/programs/2012/04/20/209027.html This reflects that certain media and their media outlets endorse and patronize these social and intellectual trends, thus giving them greater exposure in the Saudi-dominated public sphere, while other Saudi princes promote more conformist radical intellectual and religious opinions.

[41] 'Malaysia Deports Saudi Journalist Hamza Kashgari', BBC, 12 February 2012, www.bbc.co.uk/news/world-asia-17001900.

Kashgari recanted and wrote a long apology, he will almost certainly be tried and will undergo some kind of punishment, unless the king pardons him. After this, radical Islamists felt empowered and tried, unsuccessfully, to file complaints against other controversial writers, including political scientist and novelist Turki al-Hamad and Abdullah Hamiddin. Since March 2012, the discussion group associated with this revisionist youth debating group moved to the private house of young lawyer Walid Abu al-Khair who named it Somood (Resistance).[42]

Official Saudi policy revolves around patronising opposition groups and intellectual, political, and religious trends, thus contributing to the consolidation of a segmented Saudi public, which cannot unite to challenge the rule of the Al-Saud. Osama Bin Laden once enjoyed official patronage and Saudi princes occasionally pursue this policy with naturalised Saudi subjects. If such personalities reach high celebrity status and threaten Saudi hegemony, they can be dismissed as foreign agitators, and have their nationality revoked. Both Bin Laden and Hamiddin were Yemenis who became naturalised Saudis. The latter became the target of intense debate, most of which denounced him as a naturalised Zaydi foreigner, who undermines the authenticity of Saudi religious purity. In my discussions with Hamiddin, it transpired that he feels threatened especially by religious preachers such as Ghamdi Sanad al-Kodhr.[43] The Kashgari case prompted Saudi youths, belonging to Islamists and liberal trends to issue petitions calling for greater respect of the principles of Islam in the case of the former, and more tolerance, and freedom of religion and diversity in the case of the latter. Such petitions mirror earlier statements in February 2011 and even the wave of petition in the 1990s and 2004.

New communication technology such as Facebook and Twitter played an important role in the Arab uprisings,[44] and are intensifying debates in Saudi Arabia. They are also increasing the polarization between those who want greater openness in the social sphere and those who would like it more restricted. Liberals and Islamists attack each other on Twitter

---

[42] Walid Abu al-Khair, 'Our Steadfast Pursuit of a Freer Saudi Arabia', *Washington Post*, 20 April 2012.

[43] London, 10 May 2012. See also Carool Kersten, 'Dissonace or Harmony? Critical Muslim Thinking in Saudi Arabia', at http://caroolkersten.blogspot.co.uk/2012/04/dissonance-or-harmony-critical-muslim.html.

[44] See Marc Lynch, *The Arab Uprising; the Unfinished Revolutions of the New Middle East*, New York: Public Affairs, 2012; and Jeffrey Alexander, *Performative Revolution in Egypt: The Power of Cultural Power*, London: Bloomsbury, 2011.

hashtags. Shaykh Nasir al-Omar,[45] ex-member of the Council of Senior Ulama, for example, told the government to return to the right path of Islam and apply the apostasy punishment – beheading – to people such as Kashgari. He said that the bargain between the state and religious scholars depended on applying Sharia and upholding the principles of Islam. He reminded the government that scholars had helped to defeat violent Jihadis and prevent the Arab Spring from reaching Saudi Arabia by telling the youth to obey their rulers. This was a reference to Mufti Abd al-Aziz Al-Sheikh's *fatwa* prohibiting demonstrations and peaceful disobedience during the Egyptian uprising. Al-Omar warned that if the government does not respect Islam and eradicate debauchery and apostasy, then the *ulama* would withdraw their allegiance, and might even mobilize people against the government. Al-Omar is famous for denouncing Prince Faisal, the minister of education and the king's son-in law, for permitting mixing between the sexes in educational forums. He has also issued several religious opinions against the Shia. Kashgari's case is still unresolved and he remains in custody.

The aging Saudi leadership stands to profit from the social and religious polarization, which delays and may hinder the emergence of a unifying national polity. The uprisings created a heightened sense of expectation amongst Saudi activists across the board. Unlike loyal Salafis, Sahwis appreciate the recent success of Islamist parties across North Africa and in Kuwait. Liberals, however, hesitate to take any action that might undermine the government and increase the Islamists' popularity. These divisions are fuelled by the rivalry between Abdullah and Nayif and their sponsorship of opposing social, intellectual, and religious factions. Liberals fear that the demise of the Al-Saud would strengthen the likes of al-Omar and destroy the limited opportunities they had enjoyed under Abdullah. Many think that Nayif would promote his religious loyalists at their expense. Although Shia activists continue to demonstrate, many fear that the weakening of the Saudi regime may strengthen the Wahhabi trend. At the time of this writing, security forces had killed several Shia activists during demonstrations in Qatif and put many others on wanted lists. The official Saudi media continue to refer to Shia demonstrators as criminals and thugs, mobilized by Iran to undermine national security.

---

[45] For further details, see Abd al-Aziz al-Khodr, *al-Saudiyya sirat dawla wa mujtama* [Saudi Arabia: Biography of state and society], Beirut: Arab Network for Research and Publishing, 2010, pp. 168–70.

The religious radicals criticize the king's minor social reforms, and would probably appreciate greater control over liberal factions.

A divided royal circle deploys religious and political activists in an equally divided society. Despite timid attempts at unified national politics, severe disagreement remains over the nature and direction of reforms. The younger generation is mobilizing over common grievances. These minor protests will have a cumulative impact, eventually undermining absolute monarchical rule, corruption, repression, nepotism, and inequality. But in the short term, Saudi "publics" remain divided, and the regime can claim the role of arbiter. Even though new communication technology proved to be a useful tool in the Arab uprisings by unifying diverse publics, the same technology is dividing Saudi publics and delaying national mobilization across well-entrenched divisions, with sectarian discourse, tribal chauvinism, and ideological schism assuming greater prevalence over unity. Official responses to the uprisings echo internal turmoil, confirming that foreign policy often reflects local dynamics.

Saudi Responses to the Uprisings: Containment, Counter-Revolution, and Revolution

Saudi Arabia initially condemned the revolts and their transformative character, and supported the Tunisian and Egyptian regimes. Its official *ulama* called the demonstrations *fitna* (dissent), invoking a long Sunni heritage that prohibits peaceful protest and civil disobedience. The official press highlighted the sometimes bloody chaos of these revolutions and the resulting uncertain future.

Official Saudi *ulama* condemned Mohammed Bouazizi when he set himself alight on 4 January 2011, sparking widespread revolt in Tunisia.[46] Saudi Arabia offered refuge to President Zine El Abidine Ben Ali on 14 January, and ignored calls for his repatriation. Saud al-Faisal justified this by invoking Arab hospitality. Although Tunisia was important to Saudi Arabia for the security and intelligence links that Nayif had established, it was hardly central to Saudi influence in North Africa. The victory of Rashid al-Ghannouchi's Islamist al-Nahda Party will nevertheless have dismayed the Saudi leadership. Ghannouchi had previously been denied entry to Saudi Arabia, and remained aloof from its leadership during his

---

[46] 'Tunisian Suicide Protestor Mohammed Bou Azizi Dies', BBC, 5 January 2011, www .bbc.co.uk/news/world-africa-12120228.

years in exile. During the uprisings, his daughter Soumaya attacked Saudi Arabia's authoritarian rule and its hosting of Ben Ali.[47] After his election victory, Ghannouchi denounced the hypocrisy prevalent in countries such as Saudi Arabia while explaining his Islamic programme, which so far has not made it compulsory to enforce Islamic law. He said that Tunisian women who wear the veil do so voluntarily, while explaining that in countries where veiling is compulsory, women take the first opportunity to remove it, a subtle reference to Saudi Arabia.

Saudi Arabia was amongst the few Arab countries that did not congratulate the Tunisian transitional government after the revolution. Prime Minister Hamadi Jibali did not visit Saudi Arabia until February 2012.[48] Moderate Tunisian Islamism presented a real challenge, given that Saudi Islamists, especially the Sahwis, expressed their joy at al-Nahda's success, labelling it an Islamic awakening in a country where official secularism had failed to weaken society's commitment to Islamic ideals. The official Saudi press offered a platform for Tunisian secularists and activists, and highlighted restrictions on personal liberties since the revolution, reporting vigorously on Islamists chasing unveiled women from Tunisian university campuses. In contrast, al-Jazeera promoted the moderate Islamism of the Muslim Brotherhood and its branches in countries such as Tunisia, Libya, and Egypt. Ironically, the pan-Arab Saudi media, for example *al-Arabiyya*, *al-Sharq al-Awsat*, and *al-Hayat*, were critical of such developments while remaining silent on human rights abuses in Saudi Arabia. The Saudi press promoted the idea that personal freedoms, allegedly guaranteed under the rule of the deposed dictators and promised by surviving ones such as the Saudi monarchy, are the first casualty when Islamists win elections.[49]

Saudi Arabia did not offer sanctuary to deposed Egyptian president Hosni Mubarak, although the regime would probably have liked to do so. Hosting Mubarak would have enraged activists in Egypt and antagonised international players such as the United States, who seemed to have

---

[47] Soumaya Ghannoushi, 'Egypt Haunts Saudi Arabia Again', *The Guardian*, 11 June 2011.

[48] 'Tunisian PM due in Riyadh on 2 Day Visit', *Saudi Gazette*, 28 February 2012, http://www.saudigazette.com.sa/index.cfm?method=home.regcon&contentID=20120218117810.

[49] This view is also common amongst some journalists in the West. See John Bradley, *After the Arab Spring: How Islamists Hijacked the Middle East Revolts*, New York: Palgrave, 2012.

accepted his departure. After Mubarak stepped down on 12 February 2011, Saudi Arabia promised the Egyptian armed forces aid worth £4 billion.[50] During Mubarak's initial exile in Sharm al-Sheikh, unsubstantiated rumours circulated that the Saudis were plotting his escape. The first round of elections resulted, as expected, in victory for the Muslim Brotherhood and, unexpectedly, for the newly founded Salafi Nour Party. Sociologist and civil society activist Saad al-Din Ibrahim suspected that the Salafi candidates received funds from Saudi Arabia and that Qatari money went to the Muslim Brotherhood.[51] Although it is difficult to prove this, Saudi Arabia may have sponsored Salafis in Egypt to counter the Muslim Brotherhood. It is more certain that the Saudi regime backed the Supreme Council for Armed Forces (SCAF) financially, to ensure that Islamists of all shades remain balanced by the Egyptian military forces.

Saudi Arabia can no longer count on Egypt's backing in the Arab region. The new openness in the Egyptian public sphere, including the media, has ended the silence over the country's previous subservience to the Saudi agenda. In particular, ONTV, owned by Najib Sawiris, a Copt who founded the al-Ahrar Party, regularly discusses alleged Saudi 'backwardness' and sponsorship of radical Salafis. Demonstrations in front of the Saudi embassy in support of Egyptians in Saudi prisons became regular after the revolution. In 2011, Saudi Arabia banned two Saudi activists, Muhammad Said al-Tayib, a Nasserite, and the Islamist shaykh Salamn al-Awdah, both supporters of the uprising, from travelling to Egypt.

Saudi Arabia had rewarded the Mubarak regime for silencing criticism of Saudi Arabia and for long-term intelligence and diplomatic cooperation, and had enjoyed Egypt's support against Iran. More than a million Egyptians work in Saudi Arabia, and while it has been willing to expel a large expatriate community, such as Yemeni immigrants in 1990 during the Gulf War, the regime would hesitate to repeat this because of the changing regional context. As long as Egypt remains economically weak and politically unstable, Saudi Arabia and other Gulf states could

---

[50] '$4 Billion Saudi Aid for Egypt', *Arab News*, 19 May 2011, www.arabnews.com/saudiarabia/article420017.ece In March 2012, the Egyptian finance minister declared that his ministry had not received any cheques from Saudi Arabia, thus negating Saudi foreign minister Saud al-Faisal's claims that Saudi Arabia had transferred funds to Egypt. See 'Egyptian Finance Minister Replies to Saud al-Faisal: Cheques Haven't Arrived and Your Talk is Diplomacy', *al-Quds al-Arabi*, 2 March 2012.
[51] 'Mufakir masri bariz yatahim Qatar wa al-saoudiyya bi dhakh malayyin', *Arab Times*, 17 December 2011.

displace it from regional forums while retaining it in a symbolic capacity for times of regional crisis. But Saudi Arabia needs Egypt as much as Egypt needs Saudi Arabia, especially with the prospect of a confrontation with Iran. Notwithstanding Saudi fears of the Muslim Brotherhood, the regime will try to contain the outcome of the Egyptian revolt through subsidies, backdoor diplomacy, and cooperation with the military and intelligence services. Egypt's relationship with Crown Prince Nayif, who previously accused the Egyptian Ikhwan exiles of radicalizing Saudi youth and triggering the wave of terrorism that hit the country after 9/11, remains fragile.[52] Muslim Brotherhood cadres have made it clear that the organization does not aim to export the Egyptian revolt to the GCC countries and would honour Gulf investments made before the revolution.[53] The Egyptian courts will investigate only suspicious investments made under Mubarak's regime.[54] Saudi Arabia remains nervous of any rapprochement between the Egyptian Muslim Brotherhood and Iran. Containing the revolution serves Saudi interests, as it cannot tolerate an Islamically inspired democracy in one of the largest Sunni Arab countries without fearing ideological contamination. Currently, the most effective weapon against such developments inside Saudi Arabia is the promotion of a radical indigenous and quietist Salafi trend that denounces alleged Ikhwani religious laxity, corrupt creed, and political pragmatism, while prohibiting peaceful protest.

On the Libyan uprising, Saudi Arabia initially remained silent. Libya was not an immediate threat to Saudi Arabia, and the uprising promised to remove an arch enemy. While Qatar, the UAE, and Jordan nominally participated in the heavy NATO bombing that brought down Muammar al-Qaddafi's regime, Saudi Arabia only offered verbal backing. The participation of Gulf states ensured that the Libyan revolt could be easily contained, and Qaddafi's downfall could only serve Saudi interests. Saudi Arabia had another, more menacing, uprising to deal with nearer home: Yemen.[55]

---

[52] Nayif's accusations against the Muslim Brotherhood are discussed in Madawi Al-Rasheed, *Contesting the Saudi State*, p. 77.

[53] Sultan al-Qassimi, 'The Brotherhood and Gulf Security', *Egypt Independent*, 23 February 2012.

[54] Relations between the UAE and the Egyptian Muslim Brotherhood deteriorated in March 2012 when Brotherhood ideologue Shaykh Qaradawi denounced the UAE for expelling Syrians who protested against Bashar al-Assad and after the chief of the police force said that the Brotherhood, together with Iran, represents a real danger to the Arab Gulf.

[55] See Chapter 13 in this volume.

Saudi Arabia had long considered Yemen a security threat, and had interfered in its local politics since the 1930s.[56] In addition to direct intervention and subsidies to tribal chiefs and activists, Saudi Arabia was cooperating militarily with the Yemeni regime. It had participated in bombing the Zaydi Huthis in Saada in 2009, in support of President Ali Abdullah Saleh. It also sponsored Salafi institutions in the heartland of Zaydism, creating internal tension.[57] From 2005, Saudi Arabia succeeded in expelling al-Qaida operatives, compounding Yemeni problems with militant Islamism. In January 2011, when Yemenis took to Taghiir Square in Sana'a to overthrow Saleh, Saudi Arabia was alarmed, and immediately attempted to control the revolt. Under the umbrella of the GCC, Saudi Arabia designed the Yemeni Accord, which guaranteed Saleh immunity in return for a transfer of power to the vice president, Abd Rabu Mansour Hadi. Saleh delayed signing.[58] He was given medical treatment in Saudi Arabia after an assassination attempt in Sana'a, and remained there for a while, before returning to Sana'a en route to the United States for further treatment.

Although the Yemeni uprising was too complex for the Saudis to micro-manage, demonstrators were aware of Saudi interventions supporting old Yemeni tribal groups, veteran activists, and Saleh regime military figures. On one occasion they chanted 'al-Yaman mush il-Bahrain' (Yemen is not Bahrain), clearly denouncing Saudi interference and reminding the Saudi leadership that Yemen would not be as easy to dominate as Bahrain. At the time of this writing, it seems that Saudi Arabia succeeded in preventing the worst – mainly, an unpredictable and hostile political climate. Hadi was elected president in February 2012, but the previous Yemeni regime remains partly intact. In addition to the troubled border area between the two countries, the al-Qaida threat, and the Huthis in the north, Saudi Arabia wanted to maintain its influence in Yemen by promoting a counter-revolution disguised as negotiation.

It is only in Bahrain that Saudi Arabia pursued military intervention rather than negotiation, also for it own internal reasons.[59] Saudi Arabia was determined to preserve monarchies in the GCC states and score a victory over Iran in Bahrain. On 14 February 2011, protestors marched

---

[56] Gregory Gause III, *Saudi–Yemeni Relations: Domestic Structures and Foreign Influence*, New York: Columbia University Press, 1990.

[57] Laurent Bonnefoy, 'Salafism in Yemen: A "Saudisation?"' in Al-Rasheed (ed.), *Kingdom without Borders*, pp. 245–62.

[58] Gabriele vom Bruck, 'When Will Yemen's Night End?' *Le Monde Diplomatique*, July 2011.

[59] See Chapter 15 in this volume.

to Pearl Square in Manama, where security forces struggled to control the situation.[60] The GCC states forged a policy to thwart the revolt and support the Sunni Al-Khalifa rulers. This swift response confirmed Saudi Arabia as a counter-revolutionary force in the region. The Bahrain government continues to cement its GCC connections, and aspires to a quick confederation of Gulf states. During the 2011 GCC summit, King Abdullah announced that they should move from cooperation to union, and Bahrain agreed enthusiastically. In contrast, in February 2012, Kuwaiti speaker of parliament Ahmad al-Sadoun expressed doubt over union with countries that have an excess of political prisoners, a reference to Saudi Arabia.[61]

The ruler of Bahrain, Hamad Al-Khalifa, continues to claim that the revolt was driven by an Iranian conspiracy to undermine Sunni rule, a line that appeals to the Saudi regime. Yet, a Bahraini report found no clear evidence of direct Iranian involvement in the Bahraini uprising.[62] According to the report, Saudi troops moved to Bahrain to protect government buildings, but there was little evidence that they helped suppress the revolt. However, mainly because of its desire to preserve monarchical rule in the Arabian Peninsula and fear of a pro-Iranian regime on its eastern borders, Saudi Arabia continued to regard the Bahraini uprising as an Iranian-backed sectarian rebellion. Although the situation remains volatile, Saudi Arabia's counter-revolution allowed it to claim a victory over Iran in this small Gulf island.

Saudi Arabia embraced the Syrian revolt. As it became a long, violent confrontation between the security forces and the rebels, the Saudi king broke his silence in July 2011 and gave a speech indicating some solidarity with the Syrian people.[63] Saudi Arabia agreed to the sending of Arab League observers to Syria, but the delegation failed to stop the bloodshed. The Syria portfolio moved to the UN Security Council, which also failed to end the crisis. Russia and China blocked a resolution calling for Bashar al-Assad to step down.

Officially, Saudi Arabia, which had close relations with Bashar and his father, initially hesitated in its response to its *ulama*'s calls for arming the Syria Free Army, recognizing the Syrian National Council, or supporting

---

[60] Bill Law, 'Bahrain Protest Prompts Global Concerns', 15 February 2011, www.bbc.co .uk/news/world-middle-east-12471243.

[61] 'Kuwait Parliament Speaker Says GCC Union Unlikely', al-Arabiyya, 21 February 2012, www.alarabiya.net/articles/2012/02/21/196034.html.

[62] Report of the Bahrain Independent Commission of Enquiry, 10 December 2011, www. bici.org.bh/BICIreportEN.pdf.

[63] 'Danger in Syria', at http://arabnews.com/opinion/editorial/article485528.ece.

calls for *jihad* in Syria. But the recent tension with Iran prompted the Saudis to push for sanctions on the Syrian regime as a prelude to ousting Bashar and depriving Iran of its most important ally. Saudi Arabia withdrew its ambassador from Syria and in February 2012 took a strong position against Bashar: Saud al-Faisal declared support for arming the Syrian rebels after the Friends of the Syrian People conference, attended by sixty countries, was held in Tunis in February 2012.[64] Saudi Arabia walked out of the conference on hearing a Tunisian suggestion for ending the crisis by negotiation, offering Bashar a safe exit and forming a transitional government. By the end of February 2012, it was clear that Saudi Arabia was arming the rebels, despite a lack of international consensus.[65]

Although the Saudi regime saw in the demise of the Assad dynasty an end to *pax syriana*, its support for the revolution stems from three practical concerns. First, problems with the Saudi Shia and the ongoing revolt in Qatif are attributed to Iranian intervention and close historical links between the Shia and the Syrian regime.[66] Second, the Saudi regime parades its religious credentials by showing support for Sunni Syrians against what is sees as a heretical Alawi regime. Third, it desires a pro-Saudi-Syrian regime that will erode Iranian influence in both Damascus and Beirut, where Saudi influence waned after Saad Hariri lost the premiership. The more the Saudi Shia look defiant and ready to challenge the regime, and the more the Sunni majority feel agitated by delayed reforms and promises, the more the Saudi government wants to pursue aggressive regional policies against a 'Shia Safavid enemy' and its local Arab allies. In June 2013, it became clear that the Syrian crisis has become a fully-fledged platform for regional rivalry between Saudi Arabia and Iran. Saudi Arabia awaits the collapse of the Syrian regime but remains apprehensive about the prospect of an alternative radical Islamist trend

---

[64] 'Saudi Delegation Pulls Out of "Friends of Syrian People" Delegation in Tunis Citing Inactivity', al-Arabiyya, 24 February 2012, http://english.alarabiya.net/articles/2012/02/24/196751.html.

[65] Jonathan Schanzer, 'Saudi Arabia is Arming the Syrian Opposition', *Foreign Policy*, 27 February 2012. However, Saudi arming of the Syrian rebels remains controversial. The main worry of the American administration is related to the experience of the Afghan *jihad*, where Saudi involvement in sponsoring Jihadi fighters was linked to the rise of global *jihad*. Marc Lynch provides a counter-argument against military intervention in Syria: see Marc Lynch, *Pressure not War: A Pragmatic and Principled Policy Towards Syria*, Policy Brief, Centre for New American Security, February 2012.

[66] From the 1980s, important Shia opposition figures established themselves in Syria where the Assad regime turned a blind eye to their activities. For further details, see Ibrahim, *The Shi'is of Saudi Arabia*.

establishing Muslim government in Syria that may not be loyal to the Saudi leadership.

Conclusion

Saudi Arabia has witnessed intense debates, and real and virtual protest amongst both the minority Shia and the Sunni majority, to which the aging leadership has responded by fighting for security and survival. At the time of writing this chapter, intense debates amongst old political and religious activists, together with fragmented and polarised protests and mobilization on the ground amongst women, employees in the government and private sector, students and unemployed youth, have remained confined to specific demands. These dissenting voices have not consolidated into what John Chalcraft describes in this volume as 'unruly contentious action'.[67] The Arab uprisings have added to the regime's internal burdens and encouraged Saudis to voice daring criticism of the regime, while a small minority demonstrate on the ground.

However, vast numbers of activist youths seem to have migrated to virtual forums, where we find calls for reform and even the overthrow of the Al-Saud. Even though Saudis had serious grievances, this alone was not enough to trigger 'unruly contentious action', leading to a revolution. The leadership continues to divide the public along regional, sectarian, gender, ideological, and political lines in order to prevent these from crystallising into a unified national trend with the common goal of thwarting the Saudi domination. Those who cross these divides are immediately repressed, accused of undermining security, and pursuing foreign agendas.

Apart from the Shia minority, the population remains quiescent, with agitation fermenting under the surface, manifested in petitions, demonstrations, and intense controversies over various social and political issues. In the aftermath of the Arab uprisings, Saudis seem to be engaged in internal warfare, which can only benefit the leadership. They have redirected their protest inward, becoming more daring in exposing administrative mismanagement, corruption, and shortcomings of a broadly defined *al-batana*, which has absorbed some of the anger and frustration, leaving the leadership in the role of neutral arbiter when in reality it is responsible for most of the divisions and shortcomings.

[67] See Chapter 7 in this volume.

Saudi Arabia responded to the uprisings according to the interest of the ruling family, which privileges security and the status quo over change and democratization, both at home and abroad. The leadership therefore pursued a mixed strategy. The revolts in North Africa were viewed as spawning chaos and dissent that could erode Saudi influence. Those in Bahrain and Yemen were seen as a threat to Saudi supremacy, while the revolt in Syria was considered an opportunity to score internal and regional goals.

It is ironic that as a state claiming to rule according to Islamic principles, Saudi Arabia fears the rise to power of Islamists – both at home and in neighbouring countries. Two regional Islamist trends worry the Saudi leadership: the Muslim Brotherhood and the Salafis, who have decided to engage in politics through elections and democratic institutions. Saudi legitimacy is based on an appropriation of Islamic symbols such as claims that 'our constitution is the Quran' and the application of Sharia. Countries where secular dictators have been deposed are now adopting moderate Islamic slogans, too. Their newly elected parliaments have Islamist majorities drawn from both the Brotherhood and the Salafis. The Saudi leadership is losing its unique Islamic credentials, and is eager to contain the uprisings in such a way as to remain the sole Islamic model in the region. The possibility of neighbouring states combining Islamist politics with democracy threatens this model and hence seriously alarms the Saudi state.

The real danger facing Saudi Arabia in the aftermath of the Arab uprisings remains internal. At the level of leadership, a young generation of senior princes are eager to fix their position at the top level of government. At the time of this writing, Muhammad ibn Nayif has secured his position as minister of interior and his brother Saud as governor of the Eastern Province, while Salman remains crown prince, equally eager to place his own sons in vital jobs. King Abdullah seems to remain as a revered figurehead, unable to run state affairs because of his old age, but his son Mitab commands the Saudi National Guard. Any open contestation amongst the second-generation princes threatens the stability of the regime. As long as the politically marginalized princes accept financial rewards without political positions and remain quiet, the regime can absorb them. Prince Talal may be a nuisance as a result of his media interviews, but he does not seriously represent a challenge to the regime given that his support base lacks a serious military foundation. So far, the Nayif dynasty has control over security and the regional governorship of the oil-rich province, while Abdullah's son is in charge of the National

Guard. It is difficult to see other senior or junior princes challenging their powerful brothers and their sons.

At the social level, mobilization amongst the Sunni majority is taking new forms with small demonstrations in support of political prisoners taking place almost weekly. Saudi Islamists may in the future abandon their truce with the regime and declare their dissatisfaction with its policies in ways other than virtual protest. So far, however, they have not openly confronted the regime that seems to have absorbed their dissent by convincing them that it is the great defender of their interest against the rebellious Shia in the Eastern province and their alleged Iranian backers. Most Saudi Islamists are now occupied with the Syrian uprisings, awaiting the destruction of the Assad regime and its ally, Lebanese Hezbollah after it has openly participated in suppressing the rebellion. Sectarian politics seems to have diverted Saudi Islamist attention from engagement with local politics.

17

Israel, Palestine, and the Arab Uprisings

Avi Shlaim

Abstract

This chapter examines the reaction of the Israeli political-military elite to the Arab spring. Israel has always presented itself as an island of democracy in a sea of authoritarianism. One would have therefore expected Israel to welcome the pro-democracy movements that began to sweep through the region in early 2011. In fact, the reaction has been negative at all levels of Israeli society. Two main factors are put forward to explain this negative reaction. The first factor has to do with the politics of identity. Israelis think that their values and their culture make them part of Europe and they have no desire to become part of the Middle East. The second factor is the fear that the transition from dictatorship to democracy will generate instability and undermine Israel's security. The article focuses more specifically on the impact of the Arab Spring on the Israeli-Palestinian conflict. It shows how turmoil around its borders has led Israel to stiffen further its terms for a settlement with the Palestinians. It concludes that the Arab Spring has widened the gulf between Israel and its Arab neighbours and deepened its conflict with the Palestinians.

Throughout the Arab lands, from the Atlantic to the Persian Gulf, popular, pro-democracy movements burst into the public space as 2010 turned into 2011. These distinct national movements quickly acquired collective pan-Arab labels such as the Arab Spring, the Arab Awakening, the Arab Uprisings, and the Arab Revolution. None of these labels is perfect, but between them, they convey the magnitude of the change. An Arab Revolution is not too strong a term to apply to this phenomenon, provided one distinguishes between a revolutionary process and a revolutionary outcome. A truly revolutionary outcome has not yet been achieved in any of the countries involved. But whatever the final outcome, 2011 will almost certainly be regarded by future generations as a major watershed in the modern history of the Middle East. The wheels of history have started to turn; they cannot be turned back.

Following a hesitant start, the wave of protest spread from country to country with tremendous force with people coming together, breaking the barrier of fear, defying the dictators, claiming their rights, and taking their destiny into their own hands. The popular uprising that toppled the dictatorship of Zine El Abidine Ben Ali in Tunisia, in mid-January 2011, sent a message of hope that continued to reverberate throughout the rest of the Arab world. Hosni Mubarak of Egypt was the second Arab dictator to be forced from power by pressure from below. Ali Abdullah Saleh, the president of Yemen, was compelled to step down after thirty-three years in power. In Libya, the rebels gained control of the entire country, overthrowing the regime of Muammar Gaddafi and killing the dictator. Bashar al-Assad of Syria responded to the calls for freedom with savage brutality, sparking a bitter and protracted – but so far, inconclusive – struggle for power. In Bahrain, popular protest was suppressed by brute force following a Saudi military intervention. In other Gulf countries, the protest was more muted. The vast revenues from oil enabled the Gulf emirates to defuse some of the economic, if not the political, drivers of the revolution. And Saudi Arabia, the country with the biggest financial resources, became the fulcrum of the regional counter-revolution.

The Place of Palestine in the Arab Uprisings

Conditions vary from country to country, but a common thread runs through popular protests in the entire region: the demand for economic opportunity, social justice, human rights, political reform and, above all, national dignity. This agenda is primarily, but not exclusively, domestic. Although the popular rebellions are rooted in local grievances related to decades of political, economic, and social stagnation, they have major implications for every aspect of the international relations of the region, not least of all the Palestine-Israel conflict.[1] Foreign-policy issues

---

[1] Khaled Elgindi and Salman Shaikh, 'The Impact on the Peace Process: Peacemaker or Peacebreaker?' in Kenneth M. Pollack et al., *The Arab Awakening: America and the Transformation of the Middle East* (Washington, DC: Brookings Institution Press, 2011), p. 47.

intermingle with domestic issues in the rebels' agenda in complex and manifold ways. National dignity, for example, encompasses both the right of the people to choose their own governments and freedom from manipulation and control by foreign powers. Popular protests in the Arab lands are not primarily anti-American or anti-Israeli, but they are these things as well. Palestine has been a central issue in inter-Arab politics since the foundation of the Arab League in 1945. Consequently, the place of Palestine in the rebellion that is sweeping slowly through the Arab world is of particular interest. In the Western coverage of what is most commonly referred to as the Arab Spring, the Israeli-Palestinian conflict has received very little attention. The conventional wisdom in the West is that the protesters are focussed not on Israel or Palestine, but on conditions in their own countries.

It has long been an article of faith of Israel's partisans in the West that Palestine is a peripheral issue, deliberately inflated by corrupt Arab dictators to deflect attention from the dire conditions at home. In accordance with this article of faith, the protests in the Arab streets are said to be directed not against America or Israel, but against the despotism of the local rulers. One friend of Israel who views the turmoil in this light is Josef Joffe, publisher-editor of *Die Zeit*, the weekly German newspaper. In Joffe's view, the Arab uprisings have finally exploded the 'shoddy theory' that Palestine was a 'core regional issue' when in fact, it was nothing but a 'distraction' by the region's dictators.[2]

Reem Abou-El-Fadl, a Middle East expert at Oxford University, has forcefully rebutted this claim by focussing on Egypt, the principal Arab player in the Israel-Palestine arena. There is a long history in the Arab world, she notes, of popular solidarity with the Palestinians and the 2011 uprisings began to transmit this solidarity to the official level. Anti-Zionism and Palestine solidarity, Dr Abou-El-Fadl argues, was an important but largely overlooked element in the uprising that brought down President Hosni Mubarak. She traces popular support for the Palestinian cause and opposition to the normalizing of relations with Israel to Anwar Sadat's peace initiatives of the late 1970s and shows how the anti-Mubarak movement that took off in the mid-2000s built on networks that were already in place. Although the trigger of the revolution in January 2011, and the focus of the first eighteen days, was domestic

[2] Josef Joffe, 'The Arab Spring and the Palestine Distraction', *Wall Street Journal*, 26 April 2011.

change, her article shows in detail how domestic and foreign policy issues, especially Israel and Palestine, were inextricably intertwined. Side by side with domestic grievances against the Mubarak regime – poverty and growing inequality, corruption and authoritarianism – there was concern for national security and dignity, as well as hostility to Israel as a common threat to all Arabs.[3] One of the main grievances against Mubarak was his collaboration with Israel and the United States in imposing the savage siege of one-and-a-half million Palestinians in Gaza.

In other Arab countries too, although to a lesser extent than in Egypt, pro-Palestinian sentiments and pro-Palestinian slogans featured in the street protests against the regimes. For ordinary people in the Arab world, Palestine is not just a political issue, it is an identity issue. Palestine is sometimes so deeply internalized that it ends up as an integral part of people's collective identity as Arabs. What makes Algerians, Tunisians, Syrians, and Saudis Arabs is, at least in part, the Palestine question. Disappointment with the conservative as well as the radical Arab regimes for their failure to match words with deeds in support of the Palestinian cause is thus a natural addition to the long litany of popular grievances against them.

Palestine was relevant to the Arab protesters who took to the streets in the early months of 2011 at three distinct levels. In the first place, sympathy and support for the Palestinian cause was a common feature of the popular demonstrations as clearly manifested in the waiving of Palestinian flags and scarves, in their slogans, and in the pronouncements of their spokesmen. Secondly, some of the inspiration for the Arab revolutions came directly from the Palestinian experience during the first and second intifadas. The part played by Hamas in driving the Israelis out of the Gaza Strip provided a particularly striking example of successful Islamic resistance to Zionist occupation and oppression. Last but not least, is the enduring significance of Palestine at the symbolic level. Palestine has always been of huge importance in the ideological struggle of the Arab nationalists against Western imperialism and against the State of Israel, which they regard as an outpost of Western imperialism in the region. Today the Palestinians are engaged in what is possibly the last anti-colonial struggle in the world. In the minds of the masses,

---

[3] Reem Abou-El-Fadl, 'The Road to Jerusalem through Tahrir Square: Anti-Zionism and Palestine in the 2011 Egyptian Revolution', *Journal of Palestine Studies*, Volume XLI, Number 2, Winter 2012. See also John Chalcraft's Chapter 7 in this volume.

national dignity is thus inextricably linked to justice for the Palestinians. The Palestine cause remains suffused in symbolism that transcends the narrow borders of its patrimony.[4]

Popular revolutions across the Arab world gave the Palestinians a new sense of hope. The stagnant old Arab regimes enabled Israel to preserve the status quo in the Palestinian territories. Regime change in the Arab world emboldened the Palestinians to take to the streets and to challenge the status quo. In Tunisia and Egypt, the old regimes were brought down by peaceful means. This reinforced the belief in the Palestinian camp in the efficacy of non-violent resistance. In Palestine, the Arab Spring took the form of demonstrations by non-affiliated youth groups in Ramallah and in Gaza, accompanied by calls for greater freedom, accountability, political reform, and national dignity. National dignity meant ending the subservience to Israel and the United States and a more robust defence of Palestinian national rights.

A second major demand directed by the young demonstrators at both Fatah and Hamas was to set aside their differences and work together for the common good. Both parties had low levels of support in the regions they controlled – Fatah in the West Bank and Hamas in Gaza. Both parties were regarded as having failed to advance an effective strategy for national liberation. Consequently, both parties came under strong pressure from civil society to stop cultivating their own interests and to do something about the central national problem: ending the occupation. The upshot was a historic reconciliation accord between Fatah and Hamas, signed in Cairo on 4 May 2011, vowing common cause against the Israeli occupation. The common goal was a fully independent Palestinian state along the 1967 borders with Jerusalem as the capital. Mistrust and rivalry between Fatah and Hamas cannot, of course, be eliminated by the stroke of a pen. But their adoption of a two-state solution is a significant development. The difference is that Hamas persists in its refusal to recognise Israel officially.

A third development, to which the Arab uprisings contributed, was the shift towards Palestinian unilateralism. The most dramatic manifestation of this shift was the Palestinian application, in September 2011, for full membership of the United Nations. The purpose of this bid, as President Mahmoud Abbas told the General Assembly, was not to delegitimise Israel but to gain legitimacy for a Palestinian state. Israel, he

4 Edward W. Said, *The Question of Palestine* (New York: Vintage Books, 1980).

pointed out, had persistently refused to accept negotiations based on UN resolutions and international legality and pressed ahead with settlement expansion in the Palestinian occupied territories. Israel and America strongly opposed this bid, denouncing it as an act of unilateralism and insisting on a return to negotiations. Abbas indeed chose a unilateral route but, as two Israeli scholars persuasively argued, he was using unilateralism in a surprisingly new and peaceful way to achieve different objectives. The objective was not to undercut negotiations, but rather to enter negotiations from a slightly more balanced position. In the past, the huge power differential between Israel and the Palestinians had precluded meaningful negotiations. 'Israeli unilateralism, in other words, has driven the Palestinians to choose the unilateral path; the only difference is that Abbas's new unilateralism aimed at creating the necessary conditions for advancing a fair peace agreement, whereas the objective of Israel's unilateral acts in the West Bank and East Jerusalem has been to destroy it'.[5]

Israel and the Status Quo

In Israel and the United States, the dawn of Arab democracy was initially perceived as more of a problem than a prospect. On the face of it, this response is rather surprising in as much as both countries pride themselves on being proponents and promoters of democracy. Israel has always presented itself to the outside world as an island of democracy in a sea of authoritarianism. America's post-war leadership of the Free World was based not just on power but also on ideology, on being a beacon of liberty, democracy, and the rule of law. The U.S. invasion of Iraq in 2003, for example, was justified in the name of helping the Iraqi people to rid themselves of an evil tyranny, of enabling them to replace it with a parliamentary democracy, and of turning Iraq into a model for the rest of the Arab world.

Israel's commitment to democracy helps to account for the exceptionally high level of international sympathy and support it has enjoyed since its birth in 1948. It is the foundation of the special relationship between the United States and Israel. During the Cold War there was much talk of Israel as a strategic asset, a strong and reliable partner in checking

---

[5] Neve Gordon and Yinon Cohen, 'Western interests, Israeli unilateralism, and the two-state solution', *Journal of Palestine Studies*, XLI:3, Spring 2012, p. 16.

Soviet advances in the region. But the special relationship rested much more heavily on shared values than on common strategic interests. Consequently, when the Soviet Union disintegrated and the Cold War ended, the special relationship endured.

The attack on the twin towers, on 11 September 2001, brought the two countries closer together in the ill-conceived and ill-starred Global War on Terror. Islamic militants replaced the old Soviet Union as the main threat to U.S. security and Israel joined the United States in waging a protracted war against them. The notion of a 'clash of civilizations', propagated by Harvard professor Samuel Huntington, was superficial in the extreme, but it caught the public's imagination. Israel once again took its place by America's side in this imaginary divide between the West and the rest. The clash was supposed to be about values and both allies extolled one value above all others: democracy. Yet, when democratic revolution began to sweep through the Arab lands, the reaction in Israel and America was ambivalent at best. Why?

In the case of Israel, the short answer is that regional stability is seen as dependent on dictators, whereas democracy is associated with uncertainty, chaos, and the rise to power of extremist parties bent on the destruction of their state. For Israeli policy-makers, Arab democracy is not a philosophical or ethical question but a practical one. These policy-makers are the guardians of Israel's security and in their view security requires stability around the borders of their state and stability is best served by dictators, not by liberal democrats, still less by Islamists.

The longer answer has to do with ideology, sentiments, and national identity. The great majority of Israelis simply do not want to be part of the Middle East and have therefore no interest in promoting democracy in the region. Distrust and disdain for Arabs long preceded the emergence of the State of Israel. The founding fathers of the state shared a strong pro-Western orientation and a sense of alienation from their Arab environment. For Ze'ev Jabotinsky, the spiritual father of the Israeli Right, the essential characteristics of the Arab East were psychological passivity, social and cultural stagnation, and political despotism. David Ben-Gurion, leader of the Labour Party and Israel's first prime minister, laid similar stress on the distinction between 'us' and 'them'. 'We live in the twentieth century, they in the fifteenth', he said in one speech. 'We have created a modern society . . . in the midst of a medieval world'. He often remarked that Israel was located in the Middle East by an accident of geography, despite its values and culture that made it part of the West. 'Israel is not a Middle Eastern state, it is a Western state', he insisted.[6] This worldview translated into a geostrategic conception in which the Jewish state was permanently locked into an alliance with the West against the 'backward' East.[7]

Benjamin Netanyahu, Israel's prime minister since 2009, has never tried to conceal his distrust and disdain towards Arabs in general and Palestinians in particular. Netanyahu views Israel's relations with the Arab world as one of permanent conflict, as a never-ending struggle between the forces of light and the forces of darkness. In his 1993 book, *A Place among the Nations: Israel and the World*, his image of the Arabs is consistently and comprehensively negative. Nor does it admit any possibility of diversity or change. The book does not contain a single positive reference to the Arabs, their history, or their culture. Arab regimes are portrayed as ready practitioners of violence against the citizens of their own countries, and across their borders: 'Violence is ubiquitous in the political life of all the Arab countries. It is the primary method of dealing with opponents, both foreign and domestic, both Arab and non-Arab'.[8]

In addition, Netanyahu claimed that 'international terrorism is the quintessential Middle East export' and that 'its techniques everywhere are those of the Arab regimes and organizations that invented it'.[9] Netanyahu was critical of the West for its indulgence towards Arab autocrats and for failing to uphold democracy as a universal value. Underlying this critique was the assumption that change could only come from the outside. The possibility that Arab people would rise up and claim their democratic rights, without any reference to the West, presumably did not occur to him.

Consequently, the outbreak of the democratic revolution in the Arab lands came as an unpleasant surprise for Netanyahu. He had always maintained that peace and security depended on an Arab shift to democracy. Echoing the 'Democratic Peace Theory' propounded by liberal Western political scientists, he often pointed out to foreign journalists that 'democracies don't fight each other'. In the past, he used to argue against relinquishing territory to undemocratic countries because they are untrustworthy. Yet when the shift towards democracy got underway, he was

---

[6] Quoted in Zaki Shalom, *David Ben-Gurion, the State of Israel and the Arab World, 1949–1956* (Brighton: Sussex Academic Press, 2002), p. 6.

[7] Avi Shlaim, 'Israel between East and West, 1948–1956', *International Journal of Middle Eastern Studies*, 36:4, November 2004.

[8] Benjamin Netanyahu, *A Place among the Nations: Israel and the World* (London: Bantam, 1993), p. 103.

[9] Ibid., p. 102.

panic stricken. Evidently, the talk about the virtues of democracy was just empty rhetoric, a convenient cover for diplomatic intransigence. In his double-speak on Arab democracy, Netanyahu was not a lone voice but a faithful representative of the Israeli establishment.

In truth, Netanyahu always supported the status quo; he believed that the status quo was sustainable, and he was arrogant enough to think that it was the job of the United States and of the Arab dictators to sustain it. To his countrymen, Netanyahu described the popular upheavals in the Arab world as 'a political and security earthquake which we have not seen the end of'. He urged them to prepare for 'any outcome' and vowed to 'reinforce the might of the state of Israel'.[10] In the face of this upheaval, he also proclaimed his firm intention to maintain Israeli military presence along the Jordan River in any future arrangement involving the Palestinians. In short, Netanyahu is doggedly determined to defend the status quo and to perpetuate the occupation of Arab land even if the Arabs embrace democracy. Like his colleagues on the Israeli Right, he reads the Egyptian revolution as a warning against territorial compromises, even if part of a comprehensive peace agreement.

Netanyahu's reaction to the Fatah-Hamas unity accord of 4 May 2011 was particularly revealing. He warned Mahmoud Abbas, the Palestinian president, before the signing of the accord that he had to choose between Hamas and peace. Abbas retorted that it was the Israeli government that had to choose – between settlements and peace. Once the agreement was signed, Netanyahu immediately condemned it as 'a tremendous blow to peace and a great victory for terrorism'. This instant rejection of Palestinian unity was symptomatic of a more general inability to come to terms with political change in the region. One consequence of the Arab Spring was the empowerment of people and the Fatah-Hamas unity accord was just one example of that. Netanyahu, however, wanted to retain the ability to dictate to the Palestinians who would govern them, what sort of a state they would have, and on what borders. A more enlightened leader might have welcomed the moves towards democracy and unity in the Palestinian camp and used them as stepping stones towards a peace settlement. With Netanyahu in command on the Israeli side, a constructive approach of this kind was out of the question.

Netanyahu's real mentor was not Ze'ev Jabotinsky but Yitzhak Shamir, who, with a two-year break, was prime minister from 1983

---

[10] Sam Coates, 'Hague tells "belligerent" Israelis to soften line', *The Times*, 9 February 2011.

to 1992. Back in the 1920s, Jabotinsky promulgated the 'Iron Wall' strategy – dealing with the Arabs from a position of unassailable military strength. Jabotinsky's analysis, however, incorporated a theory of change. He posited that once the Palestine Arabs despaired of defeating the Jews on the battlefield, the moderates will come to the fore and that will be the time to negotiate with them about their status and rights in Palestine.[11] Shamir, on the other hand, regarded the Arabs as an implacably hostile enemy and he denied any possibility of change in their attitude towards the Zionist project. His favourite saying was 'the Arabs are still the same Arabs, and the sea is still the same sea'. Shamir turned political inaction into a policy and political stalemate into a goal. At the Madrid peace conference in October 1991, Shamir faced Arab and Palestinian delegations who were not just ready but impatient to negotiate peace agreements with Israel. Shamir, however, stubbornly clung to the thesis that whatever their representatives might say in public, in their hearts all the Arabs would always refuse to accept Israel as a permanent entity in the Middle East. Shamir's spokesman in Madrid was Benjamin Netanyahu. A British journalist gave the following account of the conference:

The Israelis possessed the best organized, most efficient, least flustered, public relations team at the conference, with Mr Netanyahu, its intellectual bruiser, rushing before the CNN cameras every other minute. But for all its military élan, the Israeli PR machine has without question lost the battle for hearts and minds to the Palestinians this week. Its principal problem was that a million glib sound bites from Mr Netanyahu could not efface the image of Yitzhak Shamir, scowling in repose and truculent in action, a visual epitome of the policy he represents.[12]

Twenty years on, with the Likud once again in power and Benjamin Netanyahu at the helm, Israel's policy is essentially what it was in the Shamir era. It is completely fixated on the regional status quo. It asserts, again against overwhelming evidence to the contrary, that the Arabs are rejectionists at heart; it doubts that a genuine change is possible in the Arab world; it denies that the Palestinians are a suitable partner for peace; and it persists in settlement expansion on the West Bank in flagrant violation of international law and in dogged defiance of international public opinion. Twenty years on, all Netanyahu has to offer in defence of this indefensible policy is sound bites. His most famous sound bite is: 'We live in a tough neighbourhood'. This observation is undoubtedly

[11] Avi Shlaim, *The Iron Wall: Israel and the Arab World* (New York: W. W. Norton, 2000), pp. 12–16.

[12] Michael Sheridan, *The Independent*, 2 November 1991.

true, but it overlooks the part that the Jewish state has played making the Middle East such a tough neighbourhood.

Ehud Barak, the minister of defence in the Likud-led coalition government, is Israel's most decorated soldier and one of its most incompetent politicians. Barak effectively destroyed the Labour Party and the peace camp by propagating the myth that there is no Palestinian partner for peace following the failure of the Camp David summit of July 2000 for which he himself was largely responsible. A former chief of staff, Barak is the proverbial soldier who can only view Arabs through the sights of a gun. He approaches negotiations with Arab leaders as the extension of war by other means; his method is peace by ultimatum. Like Netanyahu, Barak underlined the security threats rather than the democratic potential of the popular uprisings in the region.

The Arab struggle for democracy also translated in Barak's reactionary mind into an opportunity to extract more cash from the gullible Uncle Sam. The United States already supports Israel, a small country with a population of 7.9 million people, to the tune of $3 billion a year. For just an extra $20 billion from U.S. taxpayers, Barak offered stability against the Arab democratic threat. To his way of thinking, regional stability can be achieved by channelling more state-of-the-art U.S. hardware to Israel: more fighter planes, attack helicopters, missile boats, tanks, and artillery. In an interview with the *Wall Street Journal*, Barak outlined the thinking behind his plan. 'The issue of qualitative military aid for Israel becomes more essential for us, and I believe also more essential for you', he said. 'It might be wise to invest another $20 billion to upgrade the security of Israel for the next generation or so...a strong, responsible Israel can become a stabilizer in such a turbulent region'.[13]

Stability in the eyes of Israel's political and military elite is procured by working with dictators whereas democracy is associated with uncertainty and high risks. The dreams of the young Arab revolutionaries and reformers are the stuff of nightmares for Israel's strategic planners. Distrust of Arab democracy was a key theme in the deliberations of the conference of the Interdisciplinary Center in Herzliya, Israel's most prominent annual policy gathering. Major General Amos Gilad set the tone and he stated his position with blinding frankness: 'In the Arab world, there is no room for democracy', he told a nodding audience. 'This is the truth. We prefer stability'.[14]

---

[13] *Wall Street Journal*, 8 March 2011.
[14] Matthew Duss, 'Letter From Herzliya, Neocon Woodstock', *The Nation*, 14 February 2011.

Moshe Arens, a Likud hard-liner and former minister of defence, is another exponent of the received wisdom. 'Peace you make with dictators', he said matter-of-factly. Only a tyrant, Arens explained, can deliver two essentials of any peace deal with Israel: a promise to terminate the conflict and a guarantee of security, with no armed attacks from his territory.[15] This argument is supported by Israel's experience with President Anwar Sadat of Egypt and King Hussein of Jordan, but it is not supported by its experience with the Palestinians. Here the main problem is not the absence of a strongman to enforce a peace agreement, but the Zionist colonial project on Palestinian land. Even if the argument was valid, it is rather ironic, coming from Israel of all countries. On the one hand, Israel expects U.S. support on the grounds that it is a democracy but, on the other hand, it urges the United States to continue to back Arab dictators so as not to open the gate for the advance of democracy.

Israel and the Old Order in Egypt

Egypt, the epicentre of the peaceful revolution, exposed the internal contradiction, not to say hypocrisy, of Israel's stand on democracy. The Egyptian revolution is not primarily about Israel; it is about freedom, justice, jobs, and dignity. The first and most insistent demand of the demonstrators in Tahrir Square was the departure of Hosni Mubarak, the corrupt and authoritarian president who ruled Egypt for the previous thirty years. As the 82-year old tyrant was fighting for political survival, two of America's regional allies urged the United States to support him: Saudi Arabia and Israel. The Saudis wanted a dignified exit for Mubarak so as to ensure a peaceful transition. The Israelis made frantic calls to the White House, urging President Obama to support Mubarak all the way on the grounds that he was indispensable to regional order and that any alternative could only be worse. They also lobbied European capitals to adopt a more supportive approach to the Mubarak regime.

Despite all of Mubarak's many faults, or possibly because of them, the Israeli elite greatly appreciated him. For Defence Minister Moshe Arens, he was the dream strategic partner who ticked all the boxes and met all of Israel's needs. For thirty years, Mubarak remained a permanent fixture in the rugged landscape of this tough neighbourhood. Under his leadership, Egypt remained the cornerstone of the U.S.-Israeli order in the region. And he himself performed an undignified and unpopular but lucrative

---

[15] Jonathan Freedland, 'When Egypt shakes, it should be no surprise that Israel trembles', *The Guardian*, 2 February 2011.

part as the subcontractor for U.S. and Israeli security interests in his own country and in the Arab world.

In 1978, Anwar Sadat concluded the Camp David Accords and the following year he signed a peace treaty with Israel. At Camp David, Israel recognized the 'legitimate rights of the Palestinian people and their just requirements' but it later reneged on this commitment and continued to colonize the Palestinian-occupied territories. The number of Jewish settlers on the West Bank and East Jerusalem increased from 10,000 in 1978 to nearly 650,000 in 2011.[16] In Arab eyes, the peace treaty constituted a separate bilateral deal with Israel and a betrayal of the Palestinians, and Egypt was therefore drummed out of the Arab League. In Israeli eyes, on the other hand, the peace treaty was a major strategic gain because it removed the largest and the most powerful Arab country from the ranks of the confrontation states. The Arabs no longer had a military option against Israel, but Israel had an enhanced military option against them. In 1981, Sadat was assassinated by a young Islamic officer and Hosni Mubarak succeeded him. One of the first things Mubarak did on assuming the presidency was to send a message to the Israelis to assure them that he would honour the peace treaty and all the subsequent understandings that had been reached between their two countries. For the next thirty years, Mubarak served as the faithful enforcer of the unloved treaty.

The peace treaty with Egypt enabled Israel to reduce its defence budget from nearly thirty to only eight per cent of its GDP. But it also allowed it to attack any of its other neighbours with impunity. Since 1982, Israel has invaded Lebanon twice; carried out a series of large-scale military campaigns against the Palestinians, culminating in the savage onslaught on Gaza in December 2008; launched bombing raids against nuclear facilities in Iraq and Syria; and sent hit teams to assassinate Palestinian militants in Jordan and the UAE. These acts of aggression provoked widespread popular anger against Israel, but Mubarak and his generals simply sat on their hands. An annual U.S. subsidy of $1.3 billion to the Egyptian army helped to keep it in line.

Mubarak understood that by pleasing the Israelis, he would win U.S. approval and aid. He won many plaudits for the constructive role he was supposed to have played in advancing the U.S.-sponsored peace process between Israel and the Palestinians. In practice, however, the

---

[16] Harriet Sherwood, 'Palestinians see hopes for state fade as settlers' numbers jump', *The Guardian*, 27 July 2012.

'go-nowhere' peace process only served to frustrate the Palestinian hopes of statehood, to entrench the occupation, and to shield Israel from international criticism. It also fuelled further opposition to Mubarak inside Egypt. Mubarak collaborated with Israel in imposing the illegal blockade of the Gaza Strip and in its campaign to overthrow its democratically elected Hamas government. He personified the old order that enabled Israel to pursue its aggressive colonial project on the West Bank at the expense of the Palestinians. No wonder Israel's leaders were sad to see him go.

Undermining Palestinian Unity

The Mubarak regime and the Bush administration were Israel's secret allies in a conspiracy to subvert Palestinian democracy. Before the Arab uprisings, Palestine was, with the possible exception of Lebanon, the only genuine democracy in the Arab world. This achievement was all the more remarkable given the adverse conditions surrounding its birth. The Palestinians developed a democratic political system while living under one of the most prolonged and brutal military occupations of modern times. In January 2006, free and fair elections were held in the West Bank and the Gaza Strip and the clear winner was Hamas, the Islamic resistance movement, the main rival of Fatah, the secular, mainstream ruling party. Numerous international observers, including former U.S. President Jimmy Carter, confirmed that the elections had been both peaceful and orderly. Hamas won a clear majority (74 out of 132 seats) in the Palestinian Legislative Council and it proceeded to form a government. Israel refused to recognize the new government; the United States and European Union followed its example. Israel also withheld tax revenues while its Western allies suspended direct aid to the Hamas-led Palestinian Authority (PA). Their commitment to democracy apparently had its limits. They were in favour of democracy in theory, but not when the people voted for the wrong party. Worse was to follow: what Noam Chomsky called deterring democracy.[17]

With Saudi help, the warring Palestinian factions managed to reconcile their differences. On 8 February 2007, Fatah and Hamas signed an agreement in Mecca to stop the clashes between their forces in Gaza and to form a government of national unity. They agreed to a system of power-sharing, with independents taking the key posts of finance,

[17] Noam Chomsky, *Deterring Democracy* (New York: Verso, 1991).

foreign affairs, and the interior. Israel and the United States did not like this government either and secretly plotted with Fatah strongman Muhammad Dahlan to undermine it. They hoped to reverse the results of the parliamentary election by encouraging Fatah to stage a coup in order to recapture power. Hamas pre-empted a Fatah coup with a violent seizure of power in Gaza in 7–14 June 2007.[18] From this point onwards, the Palestinian national movement has been fractured, with Fatah ruling the West Bank and Hamas ruling the Gaza Strip.

Details of the plot are contained in 'the Palestine Papers', the cache of 1,600 diplomatic documents of the Israel-PA negotiations leaked to Al Jazeera and *The Guardian*.[19] The papers include the minutes of two meetings of a high-level and ultra-secret quadripartite 'Gaza Security Committee'. Israel, the United States, Egypt, and the PA were represented on this committee whose aim was to undermine the national unity government. The meeting on 11 March 2007 established the 'quadripartite forum' and laid down the 'rules of engagement', above all, the absolute imperative of secrecy. The minutes also noted that 'The forum is backed by the highest political echelons of each government represented'. The actions of the forum were to be directed against the common enemy – Hamas.

A second meeting was held on 3 April 2007. It discussed the political situation in Gaza and the need to disrupt the flow of weapons through the tunnels between Egypt and Gaza. Lieutenant General Keith Dayton, the head of the U.S. team, observed that 'The purpose of these efforts is to prevent Hamas from using the NUG [National Unity Government] as a means of gaining more powers and building up more arms'. Dayton's more immediate purpose was to prepare Fatah for military confrontation with Hamas. Egypt played an important part in safeguarding Israeli security. The head of the Israeli team, Major General Amos Gilad, was fulsome in his praise for his Egyptian colleagues. 'I always believed in the abilities of the Egyptian Intelligence service', he said. 'It keeps order and security among 70 millions – 20 millions in one city – this is a great achievement, for which you deserve a medal. It is the best asset for the middle east'.[20] Major General Gilad was therefore not too pleased when the pro-democracy uprising in Egypt threatened this asset.

18 David Rose, 'The Gaza Bombshell', *Vanity Fair*, April 2008.
19 Clayton E. Swisher, *The Palestine Papers: The End of the Road?* (London: Hesperus Press, 2011).
20 Ali Abunimah, *The Electronic Intifada*, 'The Palestine Papers and the "Gaza coup"', 27 January 2011, http://electronicintifada.net/content/palestine-papers-and-gaza-coup/9200. All the Palestine Papers documents can be viewed at: http://www.ajtransparency.com/en/search_english.

Israeli Responses to the Arab Uprisings

The Arab revolution did not resonate positively with the Israeli public, either – with a few exceptions, one of the most notable being Israel's own social protest movement. This movement, which made its dramatic appearance on the scene in the summer of 2011, was influenced by the example of the Arab awakening. The agenda of the demonstrators in Tel Aviv's leafy Rothschild Boulevard was strikingly similar to that of their Arab counterparts. On both sides of the Arab-Israeli divide, the demonstrators demanded jobs, housing, economic opportunity, and social justice. And on both sides the protests sprang from the same source: the failure of the neoliberal model of development. Yet the Israeli demonstrators deliberately downplayed the element of solidarity with the protest movements beyond their borders. They did so for fear of being denounced as unpatriotic in what is an increasingly ethnocentric, chauvinistic, and racist society.

The young Israeli liberals and leftists in the vanguard of the 14 July movement were given a rare chance to reach out to the whole region on another matter of common concern: a settlement of the Israeli-Palestinian conflict. A major concern of the Israeli protesters is the price of the occupation for their own society inside the Green Line – the pre-1967 border. They know only too well that the staggering subsidies that support the settlers in the occupied territories mean there is less money for housing, education, and welfare in Israel. Many of the activists who helped to launch the social protest movement in Tel Aviv are also active in the peace camp that calls for an end to the occupation and a two-state solution. But here again they made a tactical decision to avoid any appearance of siding with the enemy and to focus on just one set of issues in order to maximise their impact at home.

In the country at large, the general mood is one of gloom and doom and fear of the unknown. The hopes evoked by the Arab Spring around the world are shared by only a tiny minority of Israelis. There is a widespread suspicion that the real leaders of the Arab uprisings are not the young idealists who appear before the television cameras, but Islamic extremists dedicated to the annihilation of the Jewish state. Muslims are constantly painted with a broad brush of suspicion and distrust. Behind ordinary citizens demanding a better life, the commentators warn, stands a new Islamist order. Despite much evidence to the contrary, Israelis cling to the reductionist notion that political Islam is incompatible with democracy and that Arabs are culturally inclined towards authoritarianism. What the uprisings actually suggest is that ordinary Arabs, like ordinary people anywhere else in the world, want freedom, liberty, social justice, human rights, and human dignity. Israeli pundits, however, are not convinced that events are moving in that direction. They persist in purveying all the same old stereotypes of sinister Islamists waiting in the wings and plotting democracy of the 'one man, one vote, on time' variety. The end result of the Arab awakening, they predict, will not be democracy as understood in the West but an Islamic theocracy more intolerant and more vicious than the secular autocracies it is struggling to replace.

In foreign policy, the Israeli public tends to follow its leaders and in relation to political change in the Arab world, Prime Minister Netanyahu has given a particularly strong lead. Netanyahu himself epitomises both the arrogance of power and the pessimism of the Israeli Right. He and his fellow hard-liners tend to interpret recent events as confirmation of their view that they live in a tough and unpredictable neighbourhood, with Islamic radicalism lurking behind every corner. These same events also reinforce their reluctance to contemplate any territorial concessions for the sake of peace with the Palestinians. For Netanyahu's government, the Arab Spring evokes only dangers and his response is to consolidate Israel's control over the West Bank by expanding settlements, increase the defence budget, enhance Israel's military power, hunker down, and prepare to ride out the gathering storm. In short, his response is 'Fortress Israel'. In a speech to the Knesset, on 23 November 2011, Netanyahu blasted Western politicians who support the Arab Spring and accused the Arab world of 'moving not forward, but backward'. He himself, he reminded his audience, had forecast that the Arab Spring would turn into an 'Islamic, anti-Western, anti-liberal, anti-Israeli and anti-democratic wave'. Time had proved him right, he claimed. But the wisdom of the people in the Arab street is that the occupation of Palestine has been the toughest and most destabilizing reality in the neighbourhood for the last forty-five years.

Netanyahu's public statements reflect the views of Israel's powerful defence establishment. Within the defence establishment, a broad consensus quickly crystallised around the notion that Arab Spring posed nothing but dangers to Israel's security. Nothing good was expected to come out of the changes taking place in the Arab world. 'In the best case', said Major General Yoav Galant, 'we will see military leaders who lean on force like their predecessors. In the less positive case, we will see a coalition come to power that includes radical Islamists; and in the worst case, we may get a full-scale Islamist rule'.[21] Major General Eyal Eisenberg,

---

[21] The Begin-Sadat Center for Strategic Studies, *BESA Bulletin*, No. 27, September 2011.

Israeli Defense Force (IDF) Home Front command chief, went further in suggesting that the recent revolutions in the Arab world increased the likelihood of a regional war in the Middle East, with the possibility of weapons of mass destruction being used. 'It looks like the Arab Spring, but it can also be a radical Islamic winter', he said in a speech at the Institute for National Security Studies in Tel Aviv in September 2011.[22] The IDF chiefs asked for an increase in the defence budget, arguing that Arab regime changes create instability and growing security threats to Israel. In short, the Arab Spring had the effect of pushing Israel deeper into a 'bunker mentality', in the face of events it perceived as existential threats rather than as circumstances that have been created partly by itself, especially by continuing to build illegal settlements in the West Bank and East Jerusalem.[23]

The Rise of the Muslim Brotherhood

Israel's leaders viewed with especially deep misgivings the rise to power of the Muslim Brotherhood in Egypt following the fall of Mubarak. Spokesmen for the Muslim Brotherhood repeatedly insisted from the start that this was not an Islamic Revolution but an Egyptian revolution that belonged to all Egyptians. They also promised to honour all of Egypt's international obligations, to uphold the peace treaty with Israel, and to preserve the strategic partnership with the United States. In September 2011, the Brotherhood won a majority in parliament after free and fair elections. In June 2012 the Brotherhood's candidate, Mohamed Morsi, won the presidential elections by a narrow margin. Nevertheless, his victory represented a historic achievement for the Islamic movement and a defining moment in the Arab uprisings. Morsi was the first democratically elected president of Egypt and the first civilian to hold the post. He represents the moderate and modernist core of the Muslim Brotherhood that renounced violence decades ago. Immediately following his election, Morsi reiterated his party's commitment to democratic values, to the peace treaty with Israel, and to cooperation with the United States. Israelis, however, remained sceptical. The government issued a terse statement, saying it 'appreciates the democratic process in Egypt and respects its outcome'. More representative of national opinion, however, was

---

[22] Ynet, 5 September 2011: http://www.ynetnews.com/articles/0,7340,L-4118220,00.html.

[23] Menachem Klein, 'Is the Arab Spring Israel's Winter?' *Palestine-Israel Journal*, Volume 18, Number 1, 2012.

Yediot Aharonot, Israel's largest circulation newspaper. The newspaper expressed alarm at what it called 'darkness in Egypt' – a reference to one of the biblical ten plagues.

The security implications of the upheaval in Egypt top the list of Israeli concerns. Here the worse-case scenario is that Hosni Mubarak's Islamic successors will renounce the peace treaty with Israel after they have secured their hold on power. This would knock out the strategic bedrock of Israel's dominant position in the area; it would entail high risks, great economic costs, and a complete recasting of the country's defence doctrine. It may also imperil Israel's only other peace treaty, the one with Jordan. But the peace treaty serves Egyptian as well as Israeli interests and so far, no one in a position of influence has called for its abrogation. SCAF, the Supreme Council of the Armed Forces that rules Egypt during the transition to democracy, has given repeated assurances that it would continue to honour all of Egypt's international obligations, including the peace treaty with Israel. It is likely to retain its dominant influence in national security and foreign policy even as it yields more and more power to the civilian government in the domestic sphere. And it will strongly resist any attempt to abrogate the treaty, not least because of the damage such a move would entail for relations with the United States. For the Muslim Brotherhood, the peace with Israel is certainly a sensitive issue. But it has been moving steadily from ideology to pragmatism in for-eign affairs and it is unlikely to propose any abrupt departure from the pattern of low-key but peaceful relations that served Egypt well for more than three decades. Abrogation of the 1979 treaty would return Egypt to the state of war that cost it thousands of lives, jeopardise the U.S. subsidy to the army, and severely strain its hopelessly weak economy. Surveys show that more than 70 per cent of Egyptians registered their preference for maintaining the agreement with Israel.[24]

Under pressure from its pro-Palestinian constituency, however, a Brotherhood-led government is likely to adopt a much more critical stand towards Israel than the Mubarak regime. In fact, relations between the two countries began to deteriorate before the rise to power of the Islamists. In August 2011, Egyptian and Israeli forces clashed in Sinai following a terrorist attack launched from Egypt into southern Israel, killing six and wounding twenty-five Israelis. On 9 September, angered by the military government's feeble response, crowds broke into the Israeli embassy in Cairo and set it on fire. The decision of the Egyptian

[24] Fawaz Gerges, 'Out of the shadows', *New Statesman*, 28 November 2011.

authorities to stop the export of natural gas at preferential rates to Israel came as another blow to Tel Aviv and underlined both the tensions and the transformation in relations between the two countries. What has all along been a 'cold peace' – a peace between governments, but not between peoples – is likely to become a frozen peace. The empowerment of the Egyptian public, and its strong identification with the suffering people of Palestine, are bound to translate eventually into a more restrictive inter-pretation of the 1979 treaty at the official level. After all, the treaty does not require Egypt to collaborate with Israel in thwarting the Palestinian aspiration to independence and statehood, or in the suppression of Pales-tinian democracy, or in the cruel siege of Gaza, or indeed in any of the shameful policies that generate so much anger towards Israel throughout the Arab and Islamic world and beyond.

Even a modest change of mood is enough to feed Israel's imperial paranoia. As a result of its own failure to anticipate or to adapt to seismic changes that are taking place, and owing to the poor advice it has given its Western allies for dealing with them, Israel is likely to suffer the erosion of the privileged position it has enjoyed for so long as America's guru and guide to the affairs of the region. With its influence in Washington on the wane, Israel may come to feel not just isolated in the region, but abandoned by its Western allies. Before long it will also come to see itself as the victim of Islamic encirclement with Hezbollah from the north, Hamas from the west, and the Muslim Brotherhood from the south. Added to that there is the growing fear of what one member of the Israeli government called the 'poisonous crescent', consisting of Iran, Iraq, Turkey, Syria, and Lebanon. What is utterly missing from this bleak Israeli mindset is any understanding of the part that they themselves have played in generating so much hostility all around them.

Conclusion

The democratic revolution that is sweeping through the Arab world today undoubtedly involves risks and uncertainties for Israel, but it also presents a historic opportunity – to make peace with the people of the region in which they live. A more sober analysis the Arab uprisings points to its potential to serve as a new foundation for peacemaking with the Palestinians and the rest of the Arab world. The best blueprint for peace with the Palestinians are President Clinton's 'parameters' of December 2000: an independent Palestinian state over the whole of Gaza and 94–96 per cent of the West Bank with a capital in East Jerusalem. There is

also the Saudi peace plan that was endorsed by all twenty-two members of
the Arab League at their Beirut summit in March 2002. This plan offers
Israel peace and normalization with all twenty-two members in return
for withdrawal from all occupied Arab land and the establishment of
an independent Palestinian state on the West Bank and Gaza. No Israeli
government ever found the Saudi initiative interesting enough even to
discuss it.

The same siege mentality underlies Israel's foreign policy today. No significant political leader has reached out to the revolutionaries to express
sympathy for their aspirations or support for their democratic project.
Israel's current leaders are afraid of the winds of change, they are jittery
about the transition from authoritarianism to democracy, and they are
therefore unable to seize the opportunity. Indeed, Israel today represents
the antithesis to political reform and political change in the region. By
remaining so rigidly wedded to the status quo, Israel's leaders are in
fact helping to turn the Arab awakening against them. Their response to
the transition is understandably cautious and calculating, but it is also
myopic. In the past, they used to cite the Arab democratic deficit as a reason against ending the occupation. Now they seem to be saying that the
advent of democracy in the Arab world, and the uncertainty that accom-
panies it, point to the same conclusion. Deep down, the real problem
is that Israelis do not want to be part of the region. With characteristic
tactlessness, Ehud Barak coined the phrase 'a villa in the jungle' and,
more recently, 'an oasis fortress in the desert', to describe the relationship
between Israel and its neighbourhood.[25]

Accustomed as they are to doing business with dictators, Israel's leaders have difficulty in imagining any other kind of relationship with the
neighbouring Arab countries. Dealing with open societies is a much more
challenging task than cutting deals with autocrats and their cronies. One
can dictate to dictators but not to democracies. Ehud Barak admitted as
much. 'Those leaderships', Barak noted, 'as much as they were unaccepted
by their peoples, they were very responsible on regional stability . . . they
are much more comfortable [to us] than the peoples or the streets in
the same countries'.[26] The style is grotesquely clumsy but the meaning
is unmistakeable and it is profoundly reactionary. Yet, at this critical
juncture, comfort ought not to be the controlling consideration in Israel's
response to the Arab Spring. The stakes are simply too great.

[25] Aluf Benn, 'Israel is Blind to the Arab Revolutions', *The Guardian*, 23 March 2011.
[26] Ibid.

Throughout the Greater Middle East, the tectonic plates are shifting, the old order is crumbing under the weight of its own failures, and radical new thinking is needed from all the players, not least from Israel. In the long run, the Arab dictatorships, like dictatorships anywhere else in the world, are doomed. A new political culture is evolving in the region, a constructive culture of focussing on the real social, economic, and political problems and of working for the common good. In this new setting, the military despots and the family mafias are rapidly losing control over their societies. They are part of the problem, not part of the solution. It is not the absolute rulers, clinging to their power and privileges, but the people who are protesting in the Arab streets who represent the wave of the future. The old status quo is simply not sustainable. Unless Israel makes a sustained effort to become part of the Middle East, and unless it learns to work with the new political forces that are slowly but steadily coming to the fore in the politics of the region, it runs the risk of ending up on the wrong side of history.

18

Turkey and Iran in the Era of the Arab Uprisings

Mohammed Ayoob

Abstract

This chapter argues that the Arab uprisings will constitute a long, drawn-out process that will leave the major Arab powers, with the partial exception of Saudi Arabia, preoccupied with issues of domestic order for years, if not decades. Major Arab countries such as Egypt will, therefore, be unable to play any major role in the regional politics of the Middle East. This will create the space for the two major non-Arab powers, Turkey and Iran, which already possess considerable hard and soft power, to dominate the political landscape in the region. Consequently, in the short to medium term, the course of regional politics will be determined by the policies adopted by Ankara and Tehran and the bilateral relations between them. It acknowledges that currently there are visible strains in the Turkey-Iran relationship, caused principally by their opposing stands on Syria. However, it concludes that policy makers in Turkey and Iran will not allow their relationship to deteriorate to the point of open conflict because they share several common interests that include, in addition to a booming trade in oil and gas, protecting the integrity of Iraq, curbing Israel's aggressive proclivities, and minimizing the intervention of non-regional powers in the Middle East.

The 'Arab uprisings' seem to have become the defining characteristic of the 'new' Middle East emerging from decades' long authoritarian and repressive rule. However, one should be cautious about inflating the importance of the democratic uprisings in several Arab countries in shaping the future contours of the Middle East. This caution applies especially to exaggerating both the prospects of democracy, particularly the unhindered linear transition to representative rule, in the Arab world and the role of major Arab powers in determining political outcomes in the Middle East in short and medium terms.

The major reason for this caution is the fact that the transition to democracy in the Arab world is very much a work in progress that after initial successes in Tunisia, Egypt, and Libya, seems to have ground to a halt. The counter-revolution succeeded in Bahrain thanks to the military might of Saudi Arabia, which is firmly opposed to any political opening in its backyard and is not averse to sending its troops to crush democratic stirrings on the Arab shores of the Persian Gulf.[1] Furthermore, Syria appears to have descended into civil war with Saudi Arabia, paradoxically, leading the 'democratic' charge against the Assad regime.

Iran, which did not engineer but certainly sympathized with the uprising in Bahrain, has stood solidly behind the authoritarian Assad regime in Syria. The geopolitical rivalry between Iran and Saudi Arabia has dictated the actions of both countries towards democratic uprisings far more than normative concerns or ideological affinity.[2]

Arab Immobilizm

Even where the old regimes have been overthrown, the success of the democratic movements cannot be taken for granted and the democratic wave is far from irreversible. Egypt, the most important Arab country that has undergone regime change, demonstrates the validity of this assertion given the recent attempts by SCAF (Supreme Council of the Armed Forces) to thwart the transfer of power to the elected representatives of the Egyptian people by disbanding the parliament and seriously circumscribing the powers of the elected president. Such actions guarantee a long period of instability and uncertainty in the Arab Spring countries, thus ensuring that most of the energies of Arab governments, whether authoritarian, democratic, or in between, will be concentrated on tackling domestic issues for the next few years if not decades. The only major Arab country likely to engage in active diplomacy is Saudi Arabia both because of its enormous oil wealth and because its regime feels threatened by a nexus of

---

[1] Mehran Kamrava, 'The Arab Spring and the Saudi-Led Counterrevolution', *Orbis*, Winter 2012, pp. 96–104.

[2] Mohammed Ayoob, 'The New Cold War in the Middle East', *National Interest*, 16 January 2013, accessed at http://nationalinterest.org/commentary/the-new-cold-war-the-middle-east-7974?page=2#.UPbVJF2gw8c.email

external and internal forces that requires an active foreign policy to curb the growth of Iranian influence in the region. However, Saudi Arabia's inherent vulnerabilities and in-built contradictions in its foreign policy are likely to limit its regional appeal and hobble its diplomacy.[3]

Egypt, the traditional leader of the Arab world, will remain politically introverted for a long time, thus detracting from its capacity to influence regional affairs. Despite more political openness and a public face of civilian rule, it is unlikely that the fundamental power structure in Egypt or its foreign-policy orientation will undergo radical transformation except in the very long run, if and when civilian forces are able to chip away at the military's domination of the country's political and economic life. It is worth noting in this context that it took six decades for Turkey to assert a reasonable amount of civilian control over its military, and that the process is still far from complete. Therefore, it is unlikely that the Egyptian revolution will have a major impact on the political and strategic landscape in the Middle East in the short and medium terms.

The other traditional major centre of Arab power, Iraq, is located centrally in the Middle East connecting the Fertile Crescent to the Persian Gulf. However, Iraq's power was drastically depleted and its influence dramatically curtailed beginning with the Gulf War of 1991. Iraq's decline became a full-blown reality following the invasion by the United States in 2003. Since then it has been mired in the domestic mess created by the invasion, the attendant destruction of its state institutions and governing capacity, and the sectarian basis of its politics. Furthermore, the invasion has decimated it militarily as well as drastically reduced its capacity to influence regional events diplomatically. In fact, it has become more an object of influence – by Iran, Turkey, Saudi Arabia, and the United States – rather than an autonomous centre of power with the capacity to influence regional events.

The basic conclusion one draws from the events surrounding the Arab uprisings is that the Arab world in general and major Arab powers in particular, with the possible and partial exception of Saudi Arabia, will not be in a position to greatly affect regional outcomes for the next couple of decades. This leaves the three non-Arab powers – Israel, Turkey, and Iran – as major regional players and they bring different strengths and weaknesses to the table.

---

[3] For a very insightful analysis of the vulnerabilities of the Saudi regime, see Madawi Al-Rasheed, 'Yes, It Could Happen Here: Why Saudi Arabia Is Ripe for Revolution', *Foreign Policy-Middle East Channel*, 28 February 2011, accessed at http://mideast.foreignpolicy .com/posts/2011/02/28/yes_it_could_happen_here. See also Chapter 16 in this volume.

The Regional Influentials

Israel's major strength is its military capacity – conventional and nuclear – underwritten by the United States. So far, it has been a strategic objective of the United States to ensure Israeli conventional military dominance and nuclear exceptionalism in the Middle East. This has encouraged Israel to engage in policies of continued occupation and colonization of Palestinian territories. It has also allowed Israel to destroy with impunity Iraqi and Syrian nuclear facilities and seriously threaten Iran over the latter's nuclear enrichment programme with the aim of dragging Washington into a war with Tehran.[4]

However, despite its military power, the vast majority of the region's population considers Israel as being *in* the Middle East but not *of* the Middle East because of the settler-colonial origins of the Jewish state. This perception is augmented by Israel's demonstrated capacity to draw on America's unquestioning support for its policies, including those perceived in the region as expansionist and aggressive, based on the Israeli lobby's enormous domestic clout in the United States.[5] Israel, therefore, suffers from a huge legitimacy deficit in the Middle East and is considered an extension of Western power in the midst of the Middle East.

Furthermore, democratic upheavals and transitions in the Arab world have significantly eroded Israel's room for manoeuvre as popularly elected governments sensitive to public opinion, while not breaking treaties, are likely to be more hostile towards Israel than their autocratic predecessors. This conclusion is augmented by the fact that, as Robert Malley points out, '[T]he question of Palestine still resonates more deeply than any other [in Arab countries], and it's going to be very hard for any aspiring political leader in these countries to try to gain political capital by normalization or by advocating peace with Israel'.[6] Furthermore, the impact of the Arab uprisings on the Palestinian population in the context of a failed peace process is likely to lead to further non-violent and possibly violent challenges to the Israeli occupation and colonization, thus focussing greater international attention on the issue of Palestinian self-determination. This will make it more difficult for Israel to divert

---

[4] Mohammed Ayoob, 'Why Israel Really Advocates War on Iran', *CNN World*, accessed at http://globalpublicsquare.blogs.cnn.com/2012/03/13/why-israel-really-advocates-war-on-iran/?iref=allsearch.

[5] John J. Mearsheimer and Stephen M. Walt, *The Israel Lobby and U.S. Foreign Policy*, Farrar, Straus and Giroux, New York, 2007.

[6] Robert Malley, Karim Sadjadpour, Omer Taspinar, 'Symposium: Israel, Turkey and Iran in the Changing Arab World' *Middle East Policy* 19(1), Uprisings 2012, p. 3.

attention to other issues such as Iran's nuclear enrichment programme. All in all, despite America's unstinting support, Israel's political position in the region is likely to weaken further especially as the United States begins to disengage from the Middle East in the wake of disastrous interventions in Iraq and Afghanistan.

The Pivotal Powers – Turkey and Iran

The constellation of internal and external factors – domestic transitions in the Arab world and strategic realignments in the region – have paved the way for the emergence of the two major non-Arab powers in the Middle East, Turkey and Iran, as the pivotal powers in the region. Both are likely to influence the future of the region to a far greater extent than any of the Arab states or Israel.

The rise of Iran and Turkey is the result of a combination of hard and soft power and the increasing dexterity with which Ankara and Tehran have been able to maximize these assets in particular situations. Latest World Bank figures show that Turkey has risen to the fifteenth position amongst world economies in the past few years based on total gross domestic product (GDP) calculated on the basis of purchasing power parity (PPP). Iran is ranked in the eighteenth position based on the same calculation.[7] Turkey's GDP grew by 8.5 per cent in 2011 and by 9.2 per cent in 2010, making it one of the fastest-growing economies in the world.[8] Iran is currently the world's fourth-largest producer and third-largest exporter of oil.[9] It is also the world's second-largest producer of natural gas and the leading producer in the Middle East, where 40 per cent of the world's gas reserves are located.[10] Iran's oil and natural gas reserves make it a very important player in the energy market, now and well into the future, when natural gas is expected to play a more prominent role as a source of energy. Additionally, both Turkey and Iran possess respectable military capabilities, although Iran faces great difficulty in acquiring sophisticated weapons and suffers from a lack of spare parts for imported weaponry because of military and economic sanctions imposed by the United States since the 1979 revolution.

---

[7] http://siteresources.worldbank.org/DATASTATISTICS/Resources/GDP_PPP.pdf.

[8] http://data.worldbank.org/indicator/NY.GDP.MKTP.KD.ZG.

[9] Data provided by U.S. Energy Information Administration and accessed at http://www
      .eia.gov/countries/index.cfm?topL=exp.

[10] Data provided by U.S. Energy Information Administration and accessed at http://www
      .eia.doe.gov/oiaf/ieo/nat_gas.html.

Turkey's soft power is based on its successful political model that has combined Islamic societal values with those of a secular state and has asserted civilian supremacy over the military. This is a model that many in the Arab world would like to emulate. Iran's soft power is considerably less than that of Turkey and its image suffered a great deal as a result of the crackdown on popular protests following the controversial presidential elections of 2009. Iran's image has also taken a beating recently because of its support to the Assad regime in Syria, which is faced by a domestic political revolt. Iran's economic performance has also been uninspiring thanks in part to Western sanctions and in part to the mismanagement of the Iranian regime. Had Iran not possessed huge energy resources and had the price of oil not stayed relatively high in the past couple of years, the country would have been in dire economic straits. Nonetheless, its resistance against Western, especially American, hegemony as well as its opposition to Israel's regional hegemony has endeared Iran greatly to the Arab publics.[11]

Iran's defiance of the Western powers on the uranium enrichment issue and its willingness to pay a high price for such defiance has also garnered great sympathy for it amongst Arabs used to seeing their governments afraid of standing up for their national rights and submitting meekly to Western demands. According to the latest annual poll conducted in 2011 by the University of Maryland in six Arab countries, 64 per cent of the respondents declared that Iran has the right to develop its nuclear programme. This was a significant increase from the 53 per cent who had expressed a similar opinion in 2009.[12] Coming as it did in the midst of ever more stringent sanctions being imposed on Iran for continuing to enrich uranium, a part of the increase could well be attributed to the Arabs' perception of unfair treatment meted out to Iran as compared to Israel, which has never been held to account for its substantial nuclear arsenal.

The Iranian and Turkish stock in the Middle East rose further as a result of the shift in the strategic and political balance in the region in their favour that began in the early years of this century as a result of domestic, regional, and global factors. The U.S. and allied invasions of Afghanistan and Iraq in 2001 and 2003 (respectively) dramatically changed the balance of forces in the eastern part of the Middle East by

---

[11] For details of this argument, see Mohammed Ayoob, 'Beyond the Democratic Wave: A Turko-Persian Future?' *Middle East Policy* 18(2), Summer 2011, pp. 113–14.

[12] http://newsdesk.umd.edu/pdf/2011/telhamipoll2011.pdf.

removing Iran's two major regional adversaries – the Taliban and the Ba'ath party – from power in Afghanistan and Iraq. These coincided with a major shift in the balance of political forces within Turkey, as the AKP (*Adalet ve Kalkınma Partisi* or Justice and Development Party) came to power in 2002. The international implications of this event began to become clear with the refusal of the Turkish parliament in 2003 to provide U.S. troops passage into northern Iraq to open a second front against the Saddam regime. The parliament's decision mirrored deep-seated opposition amongst the Turkish public – in an increasingly democratic Turkey – against the U.S. invasion of Iraq.

The first three years of this century were crucial for the Middle East; events in those years radically changed Iran's security environment and Turkey's foreign-policy orientation. While Tehran was greatly concerned about the presence of U.S. troops on both its flanks in Iraq and Afghanistan, fearing a pincer movement, Iranian ruling circles quickly realized that the United States was stuck, not in one quagmire, but two. They also realized that Iran was a key player in both of these theatres and that it would be extremely difficult for the United States to disengage from either Iraq or Afghanistan in the absence of Iran's cooperation or at least consent.

The aftermath of the invasions of Afghanistan and Iraq made it very clear that Iran was indispensable to the construction of a stable and legitimate security structure in the Persian Gulf and beyond. The debilitation of the Iraqi state and the near-total decimation of Iraqi power following the U.S. invasion reinforced Iran's position as the pre-eminent, if not yet the predominant, power in the eastern half of the Middle East.[13]

At the same time, the election results of 2002 demonstrated the coming of age of a post-Kemalist democratic Turkey increasingly comfortable with its Muslim identity. In time, this would have ramifications for Turkish foreign policy as well with the AKP becoming actively engaged in the Arab world and with Iran for strategic and economic reasons. Cultural and religious affinities with the Arab world also contributed to this reorientation of Turkish policy, as did Israel's predatory behaviour in occupied Palestine that culminated in the brutal attack on Gaza in December 2008. Consequently, as Turkey's relations improved with its Arab neighbours and with Iran, they deteriorated with Israel. Matters

---

[13] Mohammed Ayoob, 'American Policy toward the Persian Gulf: Strategies, Effectiveness, and Consequences', in Mehran Kamrava ed., *The International Politics of the Persian Gulf* (Syracuse, NY: University of Syracuse Press, 2011), pp. 120–43.

came to a head with the Israeli raid on the Turkish relief ship, the Mavi Marmara, that left nine Turks dead and eventually led to the expulsion of the Israeli ambassador from Ankara. This incident showed that Turkey was willing and able to undertake foreign policies even when they came into conflict with U S. preferences.[14]

This shift amounted more to balancing Turkey's relations between the West and the East rather than to jettisoning the West in favour of the East.[15] Nonetheless, it created a furore in certain policy-making and opinion circles in the United States and Europe that saw it as Turkey's betrayal of its Kemalist ideals, as well as of its relations with the West that had stood the country in good stead for more than half a century. Turkey's new policy orientation was dubbed 'neo-Ottomanism', a term loaded with pejorative connotations.[16] Nonetheless, the new balancing act performed by the Turkish government left it well placed to influence the course of events resulting from the Arab uprisings while at the same time leaving it open to the impact of the turmoil.

The rise to power of the AKP also signalled a subtle shift in Turkish policy towards both Iraqi Kurdistan and Turkey's own Kurdish population that bodes well for Turkish-Kurdish reconciliation. The latter has stuttered, both because of the PKK's revived terrorist campaign and because of a short-sighted ultra-nationalist backlash that has put the AKP government on the defensive and forced it to take a hard line with Kurdish nationalists.[17] However, it has paid handsome dividends in terms of Turkey's vastly improved relations with the autonomous government of Iraqi Kurdistan that has brought Turkey both economic and strategic dividends. Turkey has even gained support from the Kurdistan Regional

---

[14] Mohammed Ayoob, 'Turkey's Stance on Israel will Reverberate in Washington', *The Guardian*, 12 September 2011, accessed at www.guardian.co.uk/commentisfree/2011/sep/12/turkey-israel-reverberates-washington?INTCMP=SRCH.

[15] Mohammed Ayoob, 'Turkey's Balancing Act', *Project Syndicate*, 9 January 2012, accessed at http://www.project-syndicate.org/commentary/ayoob1/English.

[16] The term 'neo-Ottoman' used in a pejorative sense especially to refer to Turkish foreign minister Davutoglu's conception of his country's foreign policy even found its way into multiple cables sent by the U.S. embassy in Ankara to the State Department. See Robert Mackay, 'Reaction to Leak of U.S. Diplomatic Cables, Day 2,' in *The Lede*, 29 November 2010, accessed on *The New York Times* website at http://thelede.blogs.nytimes.com/2010/11/29/updates-on-the-global-reaction-to-leaked-u-s-cables/?scp=1&sq=neo-ottoman&st=cse. Also, see 'The Davutoglu Effect' *The Economist*, 21 October 2010, accessed at http://www.economist.com/node/17276420.

[17] Mohammed Ayoob, 'Turkey's Kurdish Conundrum', *Foreign Policy-Middle East Channel*, 9 November 2011, accessed at http://mideast.foreignpolicy.com/posts/2011/11/09/turkeys_kurdish_conundrum.

Government for Turkey's opposition to the Iraqi government's treatment of domestic opponents. A convergence of interests between Erbil and Ankara seems to be evolving vis-à-vis the high-handed policies of the Shia-dominated Iraqi government that is closely allied with Iran.[18]

Improved relations with Iraqi Kurdistan were part of Turkey's regional strategy of 'zero problems with neighbours', best articulated by Foreign Minister Ahmet Davutoglu.[19] This policy was also in evidence in Turkey's steadily improving relations with Syria, with whom Turkey shares a long land border, but with whom relations had been tense, if not hostile, for the past several decades. Although both Turkey and Syria benefited economically from this relationship, its significance went beyond economics. Given Syria's close relationship with Iran, the improvement in Turkish-Syrian relations also had a positive impact on Turkey's relations with the Islamic Republic. However, the events of 2011 and 2012, especially the uprising in Syria against the Assad regime, have complicated matters for Ankara as well as for Tehran.

Turkish and Iranian Responses to the Arab Uprisings

In the initial phases of the Arab uprisings, both Turkey and Iran welcomed the democratic uprisings against authoritarian rulers but for different reasons. For Turkey, the Arab uprisings meant the reaffirmation of its own success in democratic consolidation, especially the curtailment of the military's power in the political sphere. Several Arab movements for democracy openly declared that Turkey provided the model they would like to emulate, thus raising Turkey's stature further in the eyes of the Arab publics. Prime Minister Erdoğan was treated like a rock star when he visited Egypt, Libya, and Tunisia soon after the overthrow of authoritarian rule and Turkish leaders were happy that their country was being seen as a role model.[20]

---

[18] 'Barzani, Erdogan Find Common Ground against Maliki Government', *Today's Zaman*, 20 April 2012, accessed at http://www.todayszaman.com/news-278110-barzani-erdogan-find-common-ground-against-maliki-government.html.

[19] For a vision statement of Turkey's current foreign policy, see the article by current foreign minister and author of the 'zero problems with neighbors' policy Ahmet Davutoglu, 'Turkey's Foreign Policy Vision: An Assessment of 2007', *Insight Turkey*, Vol. 10, No. 1, 2008, pp. 77–96. For an intelligent and balanced critique of this policy, see Ziya Onis, 'Multiple Faces of the "New" Turkish Foreign Policy: Underlying Dynamics and Critique', *Insight Turkey*, Vol. 13, No. 1, 2011, pp. 47–65.

[20] Anthony Shadid, 'In Riddle of Mideast Upheaval, Turkey Offers Itself as an Answer', *New York Times*, 26 September 2011, accessed at www.nytimes.com/2011/09/27/world/

Similarly, Iran welcomed the overthrow of pro-Western Arab dictators in Egypt and Tunisia and celebrated the Arab revolutions as an extension of its own Islamic revolution. Moreover, in the words of one analyst,

[Supreme Leader] Khamenei's view has always been that the more democracy there is in the Middle East . . . the better it is for Iran. He's seen over the last decade or so that, when democratic elections have taken place, in Lebanon they empowered Hezbollah, in Palestine they empowered Hamas, in Iraq they empowered Shiite Islamists. So . . . when the uprisings began in the Arab world, Khamenei felt fairly confident that this was going to be in line with Iran's interest, not America's.[21]

Paradoxically, as the democratic contagion spread, the upheavals and civil conflicts accompanying the Arab uprisings put several of the gains made by Turkey and Iran in jeopardy and also strained relations between Ankara and Tehran. This was the result of two factors: the unpredictable nature of the Arab uprisings and equally unpredictable outcomes of such upheavals; and the intrusion of geostrategic interests that complicated the cost-benefit analysis made both in Ankara and in Tehran.

Libya and Bahrain tested Turkey's ideological commitment to the goal of democratization (ideology triumphed in the case of Libya but remained dormant in the case of Bahrain) and Syria posed the same problem for Iran (in this case, geostrategy trumped every other consideration). Syria also posed a major challenge for Turkey as Ankara had invested a great deal economically and politically in the past few years in improving relations with the Assad regime. Furthermore, Syria also threatened to unravel the recently burgeoning relations between Turkey and Iran. The democratic upsurge in Syria forced Turkey to choose sides both to remain true to the democratic principles by which the AKP government swore and because the Assad regime constantly reneged on its promises to Ankara that it would seek a peaceful resolution to the conflict through dialogue with the opposition.[22] Instead, the regime launched a policy of brutal suppression of peaceful protesters that contributed to militarizing the Syrian revolt. Turkey became the principal refuge for civilians fleeing regime repression as well as the launching pad of increasingly effective attacks on regime

europe/in-mideast-riddle-turkey-offers-itself-as-an-answer.html?scp=3&sq=erdogan%20in%20cairo&st=cse.

[21] Robert Malley, Karim Sadjadpour, and Omer Taspinar, 'Symposium: Israel, Turkey and Iran in the Changing Arab World', *Middle East Policy* 19(1), Uprisings 2012, p. 6.

[22] Sebnem Arsu, 'Turkish Premier Urges Assad to Quit in Syria', *New York Times*, 22 November 2011, accessed at http://www.nytimes.com/2011/11/23/world/middleeast/turkish-leader-says-syrian-president-should-quit.html?_r=1.

targets by the rebel Syrian Free Army. The Syrian civilian opposition also
established its headquarters in Turkey with the connivance of the Turkish
government.

Consequently, Tehran and Ankara ended up on opposite sides of the
Syrian divide. Iran could not afford to let the Assad regime, its principal
Arab ally and the main conduit for its financial and military support to
the Lebanese Hezbollah, be overthrown by a motley opposition whose
future political orientation was uncertain and that could turn out to be
hostile to Iran. Turkey's initial hesitation on Syria quickly gave way to
support, both moral and material, for the opposition. This made Turkey
the opposition's prime centre of operations against the Assad regime as
well as the spearhead of the international campaign to change the regime
in Syria.

Three factors seem to have affected Turkey's decision regarding Syria.
First, Ankara could not be seen to be ambivalent on the Syrian issue
once the regime started brutally suppressing the opposition and killing
civilians. Turkey was flooded with refugees and the AKP government's
own legitimacy rested on its democratic credentials. Second, Ankara calculated that the Assad regime would fall sooner or later and did not
want to alienate the future rulers of Syria given Turkey's geostrategic
and economic interests there. Third, Turkey found the Syrian uprising a
convenient medium through which to show the United States that it was
on the same side as the Western powers on issues related to the Arab
uprisings and that stories of Ankara cozying up to Tehran were highly
inflated. The convergence of Turkish and Western interests on Syria was
particularly useful for the former given the deterioration in Turkey's relations with Israel and the negative impact of this development on Turkey's
relations with the United States.

Iran had its own compulsions regarding Syria, not least the Hezbollah
connection. Furthermore, Syria had been Iran's primary Arab ally since
the Iranian Revolution, standing firm behind Iran even when almost all
other Arab powers supported Iraq during the Iraq-Iran War of 1980–88.
Although the overthrow of Saddam Hussein opened up major opportunities for Iran to gain influence in Iraq, continuing uncertainties in that
country, including prospects of renewed sectarian conflict and the unstable nature of the Shia-dominated governments in Baghdad, make Syria a
strategic asset for Iran that it cannot readily sacrifice.

Also, any form of foreign intervention, especially of the Western-Arab
variety that toppled the Libyan regime, is anathema to Iran because
it is likely to set a precedent that could one day be used against the
Iranian regime. Moreover, while Iran was not particularly invested in the

Qaddafi regime, especially after the latter joined the Western camp in 2003, it is heavily invested in the Assad regime militarily, diplomatically, and economically. The fact that Saudi Arabia and its GCC partners, especially Qatar, are taking the lead role in demanding Assad's removal from power makes the Iranians even more suspicious of the reasons behind the demand for regime change in Syria. Such calls have also squarely placed the Syrian issue at the centre of the cold war between Iran and Saudi Arabia over primacy in the Persian Gulf.[23]

The Turkish decision to station a North Atlantic Treaty Organization (NATO) anti-missile defence facility in Malatya in south-eastern Turkey has added to tensions with Iran because the Iranians perceive the facility, with some justification, to be aimed against their country. According to Iranian authorities, NATO's system is designed to neutralize Iran's deterrent capacity vis-à-vis Israel, thereby increasing the likelihood of an Israeli or U.S. strike against Iranian nuclear facilities. Iranian military officials went so far as to warn Turkey that Iran would make the Malatya facility its first target in retaliation for a U.S. or Israeli strike on Iran's nuclear facilities. Although Iranian foreign ministry officials have been quick to deny such assertions, the message does sound threatening to Turkish ears, especially in light of reports of decentralized decision-making in Iran, including defence matters.[24] However, these tensions did not deter Prime Minister Erdoğan from assuring Iranian leaders during his visit to Tehran in March 2012 that the data collected by the Malatya facility will not be shared with Israel and that 'If NATO does not comply with Turkey's conditions, we can ask them to dismantle the system'.[25]

Turkey has been a consistent supporter of Iran's right to enrich uranium for peaceful purposes and in March 2012 Prime Minister Erdoğan stated categorically that 'No one has the right to impose anything on anyone with regards to nuclear energy, provided that it is for peaceful purposes'.[26] He went further by stating that the West should be fair

---

[23] Mohammed Ayoob, 'The Arab Spring: Its Geostrategic Significance', *Middle East Policy*, Vol. 19, No. 3 (Fall 2012), pp. 89–97.

[24] 'Davutoglu Tells Salehi Concerned over Latest Iranian Threats to Turkey', *Today's Zaman*, 30 November 2011, accessed at www.todayszaman.com/newsDetail_getNewsById.action?newsId=264443.

[25] 'Erdogan, in Iran, Says NATO Radar Could Be Dismantled If Needed', *Today's Zaman*, 30 March 2012, accessed at www.todayszaman.com/news-275856-erdogan-in-iran-says-nato-radar-could-be-dsmantled-if-needed.html.

[26] 'Turkey Offers Help with Iranian Nuke Talks, Refutes "Imposition"', *Today's Zaman*, 28 March 2012, accessed at http://www.todayszaman.com/news-275694-turkey-offers-help-with-iranian-nuke-talks-refutes-imposition.html.

and treat everyone equally on the issue of nuclear energy, reiterating his criticism of Western silence regarding Israeli possession of nuclear weapons. 'This should be accounted for as well. Otherwise we have to question why they are not acting with honesty and fairness', he said.[27] Similarly, Turkish President Abdullah Gül has declared that '[W]e are categorically opposed to the presence of weapons of mass destruction in our region. Attempts to develop or acquire WMDs might well trigger a regional arms race, leading to further instability and threatening international peace and security. That is why we have always called for the establishment of a WMD-free zone in the Middle East, including both Iran and Israel'.[28] At the same time, however, Turkey announced its decision to cut its import of Iranian oil by 20 per cent in order to appease the United States and to prevent sanctions being imposed on it.[29] This is an indication of the extent of America's pressure on Turkey to cut off relations with Iran and Turkey's attempt to continue to balance its relations with Iran with its relationship with the United States.

However, the decision to cut oil imports from Iran does not change Turkey's position on Iran's right to enrich uranium for peaceful purposes. This is in line with Turkey's attempt with Brazil in 2010 to find a solution to the dispute on Iran's nuclear enrichment. Although this attempt failed because of U.S. opposition to the nuclear swap deal negotiated by Turkey and Brazil, it had a positive impact in terms of Turkey's image in Iran. This image was further augmented by Turkey's vote in the UN Security Council on 9 June 2010, opposing the imposition of further sanctions against Iran. This vote was partially a reaction to the P5+1's[30] rejection of the uranium swap deal negotiated by Turkey and Brazil. However, in large part it reflected Ankara's desire not to alienate Iran, which it considers a very important neighbour and economic partner. Economic relations have played a major role in promoting Turkish-Iranian relations. According to the latest statements by Turkish and Iranian leaders, the two

---

[27] 'Erdogan, in Iran, Says NATO Radar Could Be Dismantled If Needed', *Today's Zaman*, 30 March 2012, accessed at www.todayszaman.com/news-275856-erdogan-in-iran-says-nato-radar-could-be-dismantled-if-needed.html.

[28] Abdullah Gul, 'Turkey's New Course', *Today's Zaman*, 22 May 2012, accessed at www.todayszaman.com/news-281079-turkeys-new-course-by-abdullah-gul*.html.

[29] 'Turkey to Reduce Iranian Oil Imports by 20 per cent Under Pressure from US', *Washington Post*, 30 March 2012, accessed at www.washingtonpost.com/world/middle_east/turkey-to-reduce-iranian-oil-imports-by-20-percent-under-pressure-from-us/2012/03/30/gIQACrV4kS_story.html.

[30] The five permanent members of the UN Security Council plus Germany.

countries aim to increase their bilateral trade from $16 billion annually to $35 billion by 2015.[31]

The good neighbourliness and restraint on issues that divide Iran and Turkey that had helped Turkish-Iranian relations blossom in recent years has been severely tested by the Syrian uprising. It has also come under strain on the issue of Iran's support to the Shia-dominated government in Iraq headed by Nuri al-Maliki that has increasingly alienated the Sunni and Kurdish minorities and brought the country once again to the verge of civil war.[32] Erdoğan and Maliki also engaged in a war of words in April 2012. Maliki characterized Turkey as a 'hostile state' engaged in 'unjustified interferences in Iraqi internal affairs', and 'still...dreaming [of] controlling the region'. When asked to comment on Maliki's statement, Erdoğan said, 'If we respond to him, we give him the opportunity to show off there. There is no need to allow him to gain prestige'.[33]

Conclusion

However, there are indications that Ankara and Tehran are aware of the dangers of letting their differences over Iraq and Syria draw them into a confrontation that neither side desires. Ahmet Davutoglu has reiterated recently that differences over Syria would not be allowed to undermine relations between Iran and Turkey. According to him, 'There is common ground between Turkey and Iran. We will not let a regional balance based on Turkish-Iranian rivalry to emerge...There could be those who want a new cold war but both Turkey and Iran know history well enough to not let this happen'.[34]

Iraq can actually become the prime arena for cooperation between Iran and Turkey since the two countries share a common interest in avoiding the disintegration of Iraq amongst other things because it could lead to

---

[31] 'Erdogan Meets Iran's Ahmadinejad in Tehran', *Today's Zaman*, 29 March 2012, accessed at www.todayszaman.com/news-275742-erdogan-meets-irans-ahmadinejad-in-tehran.html.

[32] Mohammed Ayoob, 'Only Iran Can Save Iraq', *CNN Opinion*, 28 December 2011, accessed at www.cnn.com/2011/12/28/opinion/ayoob-iran-iraq-sectarian-strife/index.html?iref=allsearch.

[33] Gozde Nur Donat, 'Erdogan Says Turks, Iraqis Still Brothers, despite Maliki's Enmity', *Today's Zaman*, 22 April 2012, accessed at http://www.todayszaman.com/news-278271-erdogan-says-turks-iraqis-still-brothers-despite-malikis-enmity.html.

[34] 'Erdogan, in Iran, Says NATO Radar Could Be Dismantled If Needed', *Today's Zaman*, 30 March 2012, accessed at http://www.todayszaman.com/news-275856-erdogan-in-iran-says-nato-radar-could-be-dismantled-if-needed.html.

the creation of an independent Kurdish state that is anathema to both. An Iraq divided on sectarian and ethnic lines can easily become the source of region-wide instability, threatening the Balkanization of the Middle East, a prospect that alarms both Ankara and Tehran. The Turkish and Iranian leaderships are aware of their common interest in Iraq, with Iran conceding primacy for all practical purposes to Turkey in northern Iraq and Turkey conceding primacy to Iran in the Shia-dominated south.

In the final analysis, therefore, it is unlikely that differences between the two countries over Syria and Iraq will bring Iran and Turkey into direct confrontation or seriously imperil their long-term relations. As one analyst concludes, '[A]lthough divergent interests in the Syrian conflict pull Turkey and Iran in opposite directions, their mutual interest in maintaining cordial relations will likely prevent the Syrian issue from precipitating a major split... [S]o far, Turkey and Iran's opposing interests in Syria have only led to heated rhetoric [which] indicates that Ankara and Tehran value their cooperative rivalry even as the ongoing turmoil in Syria polarizes their interests'.[35] It is, however, true that their sparring with each other – especially over Syria – weakens the influence of both countries in the rest of the Middle East. This is all the more reason that Tehran and Ankara make a concerted effort to return their bilateral relationship to an even keel.

It would be wrong to interpret the current disagreement between Turkey and Iran over Syria as an extension of the Ottoman-Safavid rivalry or as a struggle for primacy in the Fertile Crescent. Both Iran and Turkey realize that they need each other economically as well as to keep foreign intervention in the Middle East to a minimum. Moreover, they also realize that their spheres of interest in the Middle East are largely distinct with Iran primarily concerned with the Persian Gulf and Turkey with the eastern Mediterranean. It is only in Syria and Iraq, where their interests overlap, that they could potentially collide; but even here friction is likely to be contained. Although Syria is important to Iran, it is less so than Iraq; Iran may in the final analysis come to terms with a post-Assad regime as long as such a regime is not unduly anti-Iranian and as long as Turkey concedes Iranian primacy in terms of influence in Iraq outside Iraqi Kurdistan.

---

[35] Giorgio Cafiero, 'Will Syria Cause a Divorce Between Iran and Turkey?' *Jaddaliya*, 11 July 2012, http://www.jadaliyya.com/pages/index/6401/will-syria-cause-a-divorce-between-iran-and-turkey.

Although the Arab uprisings may have introduced complications in Iran-Turkey relations, they have not affected Iran and Turkey's pre-eminence in the Middle East. The future of the region is likely to be determined more by what happens in Ankara and Tehran than by what happens in any other capital in the region. The course of Middle East politics will also depend on the bilateral relationship between Iran and Turkey, especially their ability to insulate their overall relationship from areas of potential friction. This is likely to be a complex task, but not an impossible one given the potential for creative diplomacy in both Ankara and Tehran.

19

U.S. Policy and the Arab Revolutions of 2011

William B. Quandt

Abstract

The response of the Obama administration to the various manifestations of the Arab Spring reflected a long-standing tension in American foreign policy between hard strategic interests and values such as human rights and support for democracy. The easiest case was Tunisia, where Obama quickly sided with the protesters calling for the ouster of President Ben Ali. The Egyptian case was more challenging, but the United States also had more clout because of its close relationship with the Egyptian military. The U.S.-preferred outcome of a soft transition to intelligence chief Omar Suleiman was unrealistic and damaged Obama's credibility in the eyes of the revolutionaries, but before long his administration was adjusting to the new realities, including the likely dominant role of the Muslim Brotherhood. All of the remaining cases – Libya, Yemen, Bahrain and Syria – posed dilemmas for U.S. policy makers. No grand strategy emerged, and Obama revealed himself as a cautious, generally pragmatic politician who is very attentive to the currents of domestic public opinion.

There is a certain irony in the fact that the Arab 'revolutions' erupted in 2011 on President Barack Obama's watch. Had they done so a few years earlier, President George W. Bush and his cheerleaders for the 'democracy agenda' would quite likely have embraced them – and taken credit for them as well – at least until their Islamist tone had become manifest. But Obama's cool, realist stance towards the Middle East had been forged in opposition to the Iraq war and its forceful experiment in regime change and in imposed democratization, as well its many other excesses, rhetorical and real. Obama had opposed the war in Iraq, had spoken of engaging with regimes such as Iran and Syria, and was putting the Israeli-Palestinian peace process ahead of democracy promotion in his strategy towards the region.

The Arab revolutions of 2011 were not the first challenge to his initial approach to the region. Within months of his election, he had to confront the reality of Benjamin Netanyahu's election as Israel's prime minister, and it did not take long for him to realize that this was very bad news for his hopes for energizing the 'peace process'. Shortly thereafter, Iranians went to the polls in what turned out to be a hotly contested, and very controversial, election that saw the defeat of the moderate 'Green' movement. Mahmoud Ahmedinejad's re-election in these circumstances seemed to make any rapprochement with Iran a distant prospect.

But these challenges to Obama's initial expectations were soon overshadowed by the tidal wave of change that began in Tunis in December 2010, sweeping away the Ben Ali regime in January 2011; then on to Egypt and the downfall of Hosni Mubarak in February; and finally to Muammer Qaddafi's ouster and death in October, followed a few weeks later by the abdication of Ali Abdullah Saleh in Yemen. All in all, it was quite a year when compared with the seemingly frozen political landscape of the Middle East in previous decades. And in addition to these 'successful' ousters of long-entrenched leaders, there have also been sustained uprisings against the Assad regime in Syria, against the Sunni-minority monarchy in Bahrain, as well as smaller protest movements and demands for reform in Morocco, Jordan, Algeria, and elsewhere. In short, the region is ripe for change, and change is always difficult for U.S. foreign policy to deal with. It requires deep knowledge to understand what is happening; it requires sound strategic leadership to get one's bearings; it requires a very skilled team of decision-makers to fashion and explain new policies. The worst guides for what to do in uncertain times are likely to be the most vocal pontificators – in the press, in the think tanks, in Congress – for public discussion of nearly all policy issues today, domestic and foreign, is little more than partisan bickering, all part of games of self-promotion and fierce competition. The fact that 2012 was an American presidential election year was not unrelated to this atmosphere.

So, facing unprecedented and bewildering change in a crucial region of the world, along with intense partisan opposition at home, how has Obama coped with the challenge of the Arab Spring? The answer, in my view, is not very well.[1] But it would not have been easy for a more astute and self-confident foreign-policy team and a more experienced president to have done much better. It is instructive to look at the major cases and examine the record.

Tunisia was not much of a test. It is clear from cables released by Wikileaks that by 2009–10, the U.S. Ambassador in Tunisia was reporting in detail that Tunisia should no longer be considered a reliable ally of the United States, that the regime was deeply corrupt, and that there was growing opposition to Ben Ali's dictatorial rule.[2] The leaked cables became public in early December 2010, just before the uprisings triggered by Mohammed Bouazizi's self-immolation began. U.S. policy makers who kept an eye on Tunisia – and there were not many of them – were perhaps surprised by the way events unfolded, but they were not alarmed or shocked. Thus, the United States fairly quickly rallied behind the new order and has generally been supportive of the 'revolution'. Hillary Clinton visited Tunisia and uttered nice words. Ennahda leader Rashid Ghannouchi travelled to Washington in December 2011 where he praised the Obama Administration, and for now Tunisia is regularly placed on the 'most likely to succeed' side of the ledger in commentary about democracy in the Arab world – a judgement with which I concur.

Egypt was a much tougher case, and Obama and his team were not very sure footed in dealing with it.[3] Mubarak, for all his flaws, had been a solid American ally. He had cooperated on Gulf security, had kept the peace with Israel, and had provided unmentionable services to the United States in the War on Terror. The relationship between the Pentagon and the Egyptian military was particularly strong. George W. Bush had pushed gently for reform and democratization, but when the Muslim Brotherhood showed their strength in the 2005

[1] For a relatively sympathetic assessment of Obama's policies towards the Arab uprisings, see Marc Lynch, *The Arab Uprising: The Unfinished Revolutions of the New Middle East*, New York: Public Affairs, 2012, especially ch. 9. For a more critical perspective, see Fawaz A. Gerges, *Obama and the Middle East: The End of America's Moment?* New York: Palgrave Macmillan, 2012, pp. 233–47.
[2] http://wikileaks.foreignpolicy.com/posts/2011/01/13/wikileaks_and_the_tunisia_protests; also, http://www.guardian.co.uk/world/us-embassy-cables-documents/217138 for the actual text of some of the crucial cables.
[3] A detailed narrative of the Egyptian Revolution of 2011 can be found in Ashraf Khalil, *Liberation Square: Inside the Egyptian Revolution and the Rebirth of a Nation*, New York: St. Martin's Press, 2011.

parliamentary elections, Washington tamped down its ardour for democratic reform.[4]

Cairo was an early stop for Obama in his outreach to the Muslim world and his major speech there in June 2009 contained some implied criticism of Mubarak – who was not in the audience nor was he mentioned in it – but there was certainly no sign that Washington was reassessing the relationship.[5] That said, all Egypt-watchers in the United States were aware that a change of some sort was on the horizon. Mubarak was ageing, rumours of his son's succession were rife, and the favourite Cairene guessing game in establishment circles was to speculate about the 'après Mubarak'.[6] When, who, and what difference would it make? I have been visiting Cairo each year for the past twenty years, and some version of this conversation was standard fare since at least the mid-1990s.

25 January 2011 – the beginning of the Tahrir Revolution – was a surprise to most Americans, but, after Tunisia, not a shock. It was mostly peaceful, focussed on a clear national demand, was not primarily about Israel or the United States, and many Americans watched – for the first time relying on live Al-Jazeera English TV – with admiration as Egyptians from all backgrounds stood up for dignity and democracy. Mubarak's wooden, paternalistic performances won him no friends, and within days, officials in Washington were trying to ensure a 'soft transition'. Exactly what this would mean was not clear, but for some in the Central Intelligence Agency (CIA) and at the State Department, it seemed to mean insuring that power would end up in the hands of Intelligence Chief Omar Suleiman (whom Mubarak had just named vice president) and that the army should not shoot the protesters, so that it could emerge as a powerbroker in the post-Mubarak era.

During the eighteen days of the revolution – and then over succeeding months – U.S. policy was generally reactive, usually lagging behind the rapidly changing reality on the ground. The key channel of communication between the two countries, as the crisis unfolded, was the link between the Pentagon and the Supreme Council of the Armed Forces (SCAF). On the diplomatic side, the secretary of state and the White

---

[4] On U.S.-Egyptian relations, see Jason Brownlee, *Democracy Prevention: The Politics of the U.S.-Egyptian Alliance*, New York: Cambridge, 2012, especially chs. 1 and 2.
[5] For the text of the speech, see http://www.whitehouse.gov/blog/NewBeginning.
[6] Brownlee, ch. 3.

House seemed to believe that 'Mubarakism without Mubarak' might be an option. Omar Suleiman was known and respected, and had the added advantage of being favoured by the Israelis. The fact that many in Washington thought he might be acceptable to the protesters in Tahrir shows how out of touch with Egyptian opinion they really were.

By early February, Secretary Clinton had the idea of sending Frank Wisner, a former ambassador to Egypt and a very able diplomat, to Cairo to deliver a message to Mubarak and the army. It seems as if he was given instructions to urge Mubarak to step down and to announce that his son would not be a candidate to succeed him. Wisner also urged that force not be used against unarmed protesters. At this point, a number of observers were making a rather 'legalistic' argument that Mubarak should stay on until the end of his term in the fall so that the constitution could be amended and that new parliamentary and presidential elections could be held in an orderly way.[7] Wisner seems to have adopted this view, and Secretary Clinton publicly endorsed it as well. To say the least, this was not a view that was welcome in Tahrir. But in any case, events made it an irrelevant option, as the crowds demanded the departure of Mubarak and Suleiman, and the army took their side. Obama saw this coming before his aides did and he quickly signalled his support for the new order.[8] The Pentagon then conveyed his supportive views to the SCAF, and as a result, the United States ended up – barely – on the side of the revolution.

In trying to fashion a policy towards Egypt, Obama faced both the intrinsic difficulty of trying to balance interests and values in conditions of uncertainty, a daunting prospect in the best of circumstances, and the dysfunctionality of the U.S. political system when it comes to the formulation of foreign policy. The president, of course, is the ultimate decision-maker, but other parts of the bureaucracy – especially the State Department, the Pentagon, and the CIA – have large interests in Egypt. In addition, public opinion was aroused by the Egyptian uprising and pundits were aggressively holding forth in the media and before Congress with recommendations of what to do. The Republican Party seemed determined to see Obama fail in virtually all of his policy challenges, which meant that he was subject to criticism from Republicans both for abandoning an ally and for being slow to embrace democracy. When a

[7] For example, http://www.nytimes.com/2011/02/04/opinion/o4masoud.html by Harvard professor, Tarek Masoud.
[8] Khalil, op. cit., p. 260.

president and his inner circle have a clear strategy, they are able to navigate these currents, but the greater the uncertainty and urgency, the more likely it is that policy will be influenced by the cross currents that are now commonplace in the polarized reality of contemporary America.

U.S. policy during the crucial days of the Egyptian revolution did not look very agile or well informed. But it is hard, in the midst of upheaval, to see clearly, and it would not have been without some costs to abandon a long-time ally or to turn a deaf ear to the Saudis and Israelis who were in a state of near panic. Finally, as much as the revolution seemed to be all about ending dictatorship and allowing a pluralistic democracy to flourish, a cautious policy-maker might be excused for wondering about whether the 'new Egypt' of the 'Facebook-eyeen' would be all that new, or whether we might see a more familiar Egypt in which the military and the Muslim Brotherhood would be the two major actors, not the secular liberals. Such an Egypt, especially if the Muslim Brotherhood played a major role, would almost certainly take its distance from the United States on a number of important issues, especially involving Israel and the Palestinians.

Despite the rocky start in dealing with the Egyptian revolution, Obama and his team have done fairly well in coming to terms with the untidy realities of the new Egypt. The remarkable legislative victory of the Islamists in late 2011 did not lead to panic in Washington. Instead, within a short period, a delegation of Muslim Brotherhood parliamentarians was making the rounds of the think tanks, Congressional offices, and even the State Department.[9]

Given all the uncertainties, one might have assumed that the United States would have expressed support for the new order, wished the Egyptian people well as they rebuilt their institutions of governance, offered general promises of support as Egypt got its economy up and running, and otherwise adopted a somewhat detached stance. But this aloof posture would run counter to the enthusiastic pro-democracy views of frustrated neoconservatives and well-meaning liberal interventionists – and perhaps also counter to a tendency of U.S. policy-makers to think that they must speak out on every issue, even when silence might be a more prudent course. Whereas 'democracy promotion' may seem high-minded and constructive to most Americans, from the viewpoint of Egypt's new rulers – the SCAF and the powerful Muslim Brotherhood – it looked

---

[9] http://www.thedailybeast.com/articles/2012/04/05/egypt-s-muslim-brotherhood-woos-washington.html

very much like foreign interference, and was firmly rebuffed. The new U.S. ambassador was very nearly declared persona non grata for offering funds to Egyptian pro-democracy groups.[10]

Before the United States was really able to digest what had happened in Egypt, it had to confront four other manifestations of the Arab Spring – in Libya, Yemen, Syria, and Bahrain. If anyone thought – based on Tunisia and Egypt – that the United States could develop a 'one size fits all' policy, these four cases showed that each one would have to be dealt with in terms of a specific mix of interests, costs, and perceived values.

Libya was the most difficult and costly. Qaddafi was an easy leader to despise, but in the mid-2000s he had given up his nuclear capability, had re-established diplomatic relations with the United States, and had cooperated in the War on Terror. Secretary of State Condoleezza Rice, about whom he had an odd obsession, had even visited him in Tripoli, where he entertained her with a song of his own composition praising her as a daughter of Africa. Everyone knew he was odd, but he no longer seemed very dangerous – except, perhaps, to his own people.

Obama's initial response to the uprising in eastern Libya was more restrained and cautious than that of his British and French allies. Almost immediately, domestic American politics came into play. Why wasn't Obama doing more to help the brave protesters in Cyrenaica? All the old examples of Rwanda and Somalia were dragged out, cases where a Democratic President had stood by and allowed massacres to take place. Already thinking about the president's foreign policy credentials going into his re-election campaign, his advisers helped to persuade him to intervene, but not too visibly and not too assertively. Part of the caution came from the Pentagon, where outgoing Secretary of Defense Robert Gates' parting words were still fresh: 'In my opinion, any future Secretary who advises the President to again send a big American land army into Asia or into the Middle East or Africa should have his head examined'.[11]

The compromise position adopted by the Obama team was to seek regime change in Libya, but not à la George W. Bush. Instead, the United States would 'lead from behind', as some wag termed the policy – waiting for the Arab League and the UN to frame the issue as humanitarian

---

[10] This issue of U.S. NGOs promoting democracy flared up in early 2012 and became a major issue when a number of Americans were ordered not to leave the country and to stand trial for possible violation of Egyptian law for their activism. See http://www.huffingtonpost.com/2012/02/07/egypt-ngo-crackdown_n_1260780.html.

[11] http://www.nytimes.com/2011/02/26/world/26gates.html

intervention to save civilian lives by establishing a no-fly zone. The United States left the ostensible military leadership role to North Atlantic Treaty Organization (NATO), especially French and British planes, and added its own lethal and efficient contribution in the form of intelligence, command and control, and drones – this latter apparently being the new preferred instrument of U.S. foreign policy. The 'no-fly zone' quickly morphed into a quick reaction force from the air, and, over time, Qaddafi's forces were ground down, enabling the Libyan rebels to win crucial battles in Misrata and the western mountains, and then finally in Tripoli itself.

Qaddafi and his immediate entourage disappeared, but he was later captured and killed in a grisly act of revenge, indicating that a post-Qaddafi Libya was likely to be a troubled and turbulent place for some time to come. But at least the outside intervention had been limited – lots of sorties, but few boots on the ground – and there was no real fear of an Iraq-style commitment. By the time Qaddafi was gone, the heat had gone out of the U.S. domestic debate. Some of the Republicans seemed to resent what appeared to be a successful outcome for Obama and claimed, with hindsight, that the United States should have stayed out of the whole affair, since post-Qaddafi Libya might turn Islamist. On the other hand, curmudgeonly John McCain grumbled that the United States should have done more, that leading from behind was cowardly. Most Americans seemed glad it was over, that the cost had been limited, and that there had been no American casualties. For most Americans, Libya was not of great strategic importance, so there was little real concern for what might come next.

Of considerably more strategic significance – and much more complex – was Syria. As usual, Obama showed caution at the outset. After all, the United States had been dealing with the Assads – father and son – for four decades, often with a sense of pragmatism, if not real warmth. This pattern had been broken under George W. Bush, when regime-change enthusiasts wanted to put Syria in the crosshairs, but Obama had explicitly campaigned on the basis of wanting to 'engage' with regimes like Syria and Iran and to revive the Arab-Israeli peace process. Over considerable opposition in Congress, he sent an ambassador back to Damascus in early 2011.

But as Assad dealt more and more brutally with his opposition in spring 2011, the Obama administration found it impossible to maintain a policy of engagement with the regime. At the same time, there was no appetite for military intervention. The Libyan model did not seem very relevant to the facts on the ground in Syria. Instead, diplomatic pressure and sanctions were all that Washington could suggest. No one showed much confidence in the possibility of encouraging a negotiated transition, as called for by Kofi Annan, the representative of the United Nations, and his successor Lakhdar Brahimi. And so the conflict went on drifting to civil war. Ironically, Syria's crisis came just as U.S. troops were making their final departure from Iraq. There were few, if any, calls for those troops to turn towards Syria for their next engagement. Obama seemed of two minds – he called on Assad to leave power, but also ruled out taking forceful measures apart from sanctions. To those Republicans and Democrats who urged some form of military intervention, at least in the form of arms to the opposition, Obama turned a deaf ear – at least until the summer of 2013 when he finally decided to supply arms to the opposition, though it is unclear if the U.S. would provide advanced weapons. In short, the United States seemed to have few ideas and little influence when it came to Syria.

A brief word about Yemen is necessary. Apart from a few specialists on terrorism and a few Pentagon planners, most Americans would have a hard time finding Yemen on a map or recounting any relevant facts about its past or present. So, when the uprising against Saleh began in spring 2011, and showed remarkable staying power, it attracted far less attention in the U.S. media than the other manifestations of the Arab Spring. Even when Tawakkul Karman won the Nobel Peace prize in October 2011 for her remarkable role in the protests, Yemen remained a far-off mystery. Some pundits anguished over Al-Qaida in the Arabian Peninsula, and some Pentagon planners seemed to be eager to increase drone attacks against this remnant of the terrorist franchise. And the United States did seem to lend support to the Saudi and Gulf Cooperation Council (GCC) effort to persuade Saleh to give up power. But the overall impression was that for most people in Washington, Yemen was a confusing and distant problem, one probably best left to the ministrations of the GCC and the few people in the Department of Defense and CIA who had clever ideas that did not involve high visibility or cost. The most senior U.S. official with a sustained role in managing relations with Yemen was John Brennan, who then counterterrorism adviser to Obama.

It would be a mistake to overlook Bahrain. Here, the values and interests of the United States came into a direct clash – and interests won out. Even enthusiasts for pro-democracy intervention were worried that Iran might be playing a role behind the largely Shia uprising. And once Saudi Arabia decided to act, the United States was not prepared to second guess its moves. Only late in 2011, once the Bassiouni report was released, with its clear condemnation of the Bahraini leadership for its abuses, did the United States lend it weight to calls for reform.[12]

So, what can we conclude from all this? First, Obama and his team are generally cautious, pragmatic in their approach, balancing values and interests, and wanting very much to avoid another engagement like Iraq. In this sense, they are by temperament and outlook quite different from George W. Bush, Dick Cheney, Donald Rumsfeld, and the neo-cons. But their caution often means that they seem to be lagging behind, unsure of how to proceed and reactive more than strategic.[13] There are few people in the upper reaches of the administration who have real expertise on the Middle East region – certainly not at the National Security Council and not very many in the State Department. And the level of the surrounding public debate, in the world of think tanks, Congress, and the media, is often even worse. Foreign policy discussion has become deeply polarized and politicized.

As Obama headed into his re-election campaign, he seemed determined to avoid big, costly mistakes. Some see merit in a new policy of 'offshore balancing' – a policy much touted by academics from the realist school such as Harvard's Stephen Walt[14] – which has the virtues of costing less than dreams of imperium, provides some 'spare capacity' for contingencies that may arise, and accepts the reality that the United States is simply not very good when it tries to assert itself as a global hegemon, when it tries to 'nation build', or when it tries to export democracy.

Yet, it would be a mistake to read into this picture a return to U.S. isolationism. The United States is too engaged with the world for that, and is too big, too large a part of the world economy, and too powerful to be a passive observer while an important part of the world such as the Middle East is going through unprecedented change. And although U.S. influence is limited, it is not negligible. So, what I hope to see,

---

[12] http://www.bici.org.bh/BICIreportEN.pdf
[13] Obama's major speech on the Arab Spring phenomenon was given on 19 May 2011. See http://www.whitehouse.gov/the-press-office/2011/05/19/remarks-president-middle-east-and-north-africa. Unfortunately, he also addressed the controversial issue of how Israel and the Palestinians should settle their differences over a future border between their two states. Because the Israeli government reacted very negatively, it was that part of the speech that got the most attention. See also Lynch, op. cit, pp. 193–94.
[14] http://walt.foreignpolicy.com/posts/2011/11/02/offshore_balancing_an_idea_whose_time_has_come

especially now that Obama has been re-elected, is a serious rethinking of U.S. priorities in the region along the following lines:

First, bring in a new team of advisers who actually know something about the Middle East region.

Second, get serious about supporting the new democracies in smart ways – economic aid, trade, investment, technology, education – all of which the United States is relatively good at – and work closely with Turkey, Egypt, Tunisia, Morocco, and others who are seriously trying to reform and democratize.

Third, do not give up on Israeli-Palestinian peace, and do not give Israel a blank cheque, especially on Iran or settlement building.

Fourth, if and when a new regime comes to power in Syria, try to explore the possibility of an Israeli-Syrian peace agreement. All the ingredients for this are there and were nearly agreed upon in previous years.

Fifth, cool off the hysteria about Iran, lean on the Israelis not to undertake pre-emptive military action, and look for openings on the Iranian side. Patience is not much of a policy, but the alternatives are all worse.

Finally, understand that the Arab Spring, as exciting and dramatic as it is, will play itself out over many years and in many different configurations. Americans should try to help where possible, but not try to control the process.

The Arab Spring phenomenon has the great virtue of bearing the 'made in the Arab world' label, not 'made in America'. The United States should wish the Arabs well as they reshape their ossified political institutions, but it should largely remain on the sidelines at this point. Part of the excitement of watching the Arab Spring unfold has been to see the pride that ordinary people show in standing up for themselves. They will let outside actors know when and how they can be helpful as they try to undo the legacy of decades of stagnation.

20

Europe and the Arab Uprisings

The Irrelevant Power?

Federica Bicchi[*]

Abstract

The European response to the Arab uprisings has been fundamentally conservative, reflecting the attitude of European policy makers towards change in the Mediterranean, but also greatly limiting the potential relevance of Europe in political developments post–Arab Spring. The Arab Spring caught Europe not only by surprise but also in a bad moment, given the deep economic and social crisis that has engulfed it and the unfinished transformations triggered by the Lisbon Treaty. With pressing domestic concerns and little available political leadership, the Europeans have resorted to their traditional pattern of reacting to events. But the set of policy initiatives put forward has not succeeded in shaking off the impression that Europe, and its conservative attitude, is part of the problem rather than part of the solution.

Introduction

The European response to the Arab uprisings has been fundamentally conservative, reflecting the attitude of European policy-makers towards change in the Mediterranean, but also greatly limiting Europe's relevance in political developments post-Arab Spring. As a pro-status quo actor,

[*] I would like to thank the following people for commenting on this chapter: Tobias Schumacher, Stephan Stetter, Sven Biscop, Jean-Pierre Cassarino, Francesco Cavatorta, Benoit Challand, Raffaella Del Sarto, Fawaz Gerges, Patrick Holden, Peter Seeberg, Nathalie Tocci, Benedetta Voltolini, and an anonymous reviewer. Any remaining mistakes are my sole responsibility.

Europe did not push for change in the Mediterranean,[1] and finds itself in the post-Arab Spring context in the difficult position of having to adapt to change, rather than being able to participate in it and contribute to shaping the future of the area. This chapter will show how the Arab uprisings have transformed only marginally the substance of five decades of European foreign policy. Although Europe, in its various guises, is often the only international actor that has consistently engaged on the ground in the area, its conservative attitude and its increasingly short-term approach threatens to make it irrelevant in a volatile context.

The Arab uprisings caught Europe not only by surprise, but also in a bad moment. Countries belonging to the Euro-area were hit by an economic crisis that soon became a political and social crisis, too. Moreover, thanks to the Lisbon Treaty entering into force (in December 2009), the European Union (EU) was witnessing the birth of its newest actor, the European External Action Service (EEAS).[2] With pressing domestic concerns on their agendas, and a new instrument for speaking with one voice about foreign policy still in the making, the European countries struggled to come up with a policy response that met the challenge. They repeated the usual patterns of EU foreign policy-making towards its Mediterranean neighbours, thus reacting to events and depending on the limited available leadership. They did, eventually, formulate a set of policy initiatives, but they have not succeeded in shaking off the impression that Europe, and its conservative attitude, is part of the problem, rather than part of the solution.

When Mohamed Bouazizi set himself on fire in December 2010, the economic situation was negative on both sides of the Mediterranean. Countries in Europe and in the Southern and Eastern Mediterranean were locked in the attempt to re-think economic growth and the role of the state in the aftermath of the 2008 sub-prime crisis imported from the United States. On the Northern shore, hopes of a fast recovery were fading. Greece and Ireland had just agreed to draconian austerity plans, with the intervention of the EU and the International Monetary Fund (IMF), while the financial and fiscal crisis was fast highlighting the weaknesses of Italy, Portugal, Spain and, therefore, the entire Euro-area. This led

---

[1] For evidence of how the Europeans (and more generally, Western countries) avoided promoting human rights and democracy when it endangered stability, see Hollis (2012), Pace (2009), Tocci and Cassarino (2011), and contributions in Alcaro and Haubrich-Seco (2012).

[2] Duke (2012), Van Vooren (2011).

not only to 'less time for the neighbourhood'[3] but also to a more limited capacity to see 'through the fog created by the uncertainty of the future' (Kirzner, 1997). On the Southern shore, Arab countries lingered in the relatively positive but very inequitable growth trend that characterised the previous decade,[4] while also affected by the slack demand in the EU for Southern Mediterranean industrial exports and by the spill-over effects of reforms adopted on the Northern shore. Having spent the previous decade pressing for more integration of economies across the Mediterranean, Europe was not in a position to lead economic development in its neighbourhood.

The political scene in Europe was mixed. Although public opinion was mesmerised by the dedication with which Arabs fought for freedom, bread, and social justice, the European collective mechanisms for foreign policy-making were stumbling. The Lisbon Treaty led to the creation of the EEAS, to support the work of the High Representative of the Union for Foreign Affairs and Security Policy, thus encompassing both the Common Foreign and Security Policy (CFSP) and the Common Security and Defence Policy (CSDP).[5] The EEAS is composed of officials drawn from the European Commission and the Council Secretariat, as well as of seconded diplomats from member states' ministries of Foreign Affairs. It complements with a political vision the work done on international trade and aid by the European Commission. The establishment of the EEAS did not mark the leap forward in EU foreign policy many were hoping for. On the contrary, the nature of the new actor's creation meant it could not call the shots in the short run. It was rumoured that the institutional device was meant to resemble the Dutch Ministry of Foreign Affairs and not to grow to rival bigger diplomatic actors. The choice of the relatively low-profile Catherine Ashton to head the EEAS was also seen to intentionally leave room for national politicians to retain a say in foreign policy. Despite these premises, Ashton managed to appoint most of the EEAS' key posts by December 2010, but there was still much left to do.

In this political fragmentation, the Europeans repeated their usual pattern in Euro-Mediterranean relations, combined with an aversion to deep change in their neighbourhood. They reacted to events, and their response depended both on the available leadership and on the policy categories

---

[3] Whitman and Juncos (2012), p. 148.
[4] Cf. Kadri, Chapter 4 in this volume, and Paciello (2011).
[5] On the EEAS, see Van Vooren (2011) and Duke (2012).

applied within Europe (but in a socially 'light' version). The European reaction was initially very slow. Zine El Abdine Ben Ali had to flee from Tunisia before European leaders were prepared to admit that something significant was occurring. They were then forced to focus quickly and learn how to respond to the unfolding crises. But the little political leadership that was forthcoming had a vested interest in the status quo. In the case of Tunisia and, to a large extent, also Egypt, the main actors formulating the responses have been the EEAS and, in particular, the European Commission, two actors with a lot of expertise, especially in economic affairs, but little political clout to go against the conservative attitude of European member states. The EU motto 'more for more', which is meant to embody the European commitment to provide more cooperation for more democratic reforms, should not obscure the fact that the Europeans have not really changed their approach to economic development and international trade, as well as their protectionist view of migration, while avoiding provision of the social and economic benefits that generally accompany neoliberal economic policies within Europe.[6]

In the case of Libya, intra-European cooperation floundered on fundamental differences; France and the UK, with their political and military strengths, imposed a very different pace to the European response, springing on the opportunity to be seen as fencing off the spectre of humanitarian disaster in Libya. But the difficulties encountered in mounting the operation and in achieving a degree of success cautioned Western countries against an intervention in Syria.

This chapter examines the pattern of European foreign policy towards its Southern neighbours over the last five decades. It then provides an overview of the European response(s) to the Arab uprisings, highlighting how it continued this policy and provided no change in substance, leading to the conclusion that this course of action is making Europe largely irrelevant in the context of the post-Arab Spring.

The Pattern of European Foreign Policy towards the Mediterranean Countries: The Reactive Power

It is a long-standing feature of the EU to be slow in crises (e.g., de Schoutheete, 1997, p. 42) and, if crises are 'in slow motion', at times not to respond at all. Historically, the capacity of the Europeans to focus

---

[6] For an overview of the academic debate, see Pace and Cavatorta (2012).

on their Southern neighbours and formulate a new foreign policy initiative has depended on two conditions (Bicchi, 2007). First, the Europeans act together when a window of opportunity opens, namely when policy-makers perceive a worsening of the political and/or security situation on the ground that has the potential to affect the situation in Europe, too. Second, the Europeans put forward a response to a crisis when a policy entrepreneur (or, even better, a *political* entrepreneur) is ready to capitalise on the occasion and inject a new vision, as well as new instruments to implement it.

First, the Europeans have reacted to perceived challenges from the Southern shore in three periods of activism, namely the early 1970s, the early 1990s, and the early 2000s. These periods were all characterised by a heightened perception of challenges emanating from the Southern shore, which constituted a window of opportunity to (re)formulate a European response. In the early 1970s, the challenge came from a combination of terrorism spilling over from the Arab-Israeli conflict and turbulent economic relations. The early 1970s marked the beginning of modern terrorism (Engene, 2004) and in Europe, this trend was led by a dramatic increase in terrorism driven by Arab-Israeli hostilities. It escalated to the point when it became a major security issue, as at the Olympic Games in Munich in September 1972. The economy was the second aspect of European security to become progressively sensitive, culminating with the oil shock in 1973. In a long wave of nationalisations lasting from 1956 to the early 1970s, Arab states nationalised European-owned firms in all the productive sectors. These two elements sparked a debate about relations with Mediterranean countries and paved the way to the launching of the Global Mediterranean Policy in 1972 and the Euro-Arab Dialogue in 1974. These were the first two innovative initiatives towards the Southern neighbourhood ever undertaken by the Europeans after decolonisation.

Similarly, in the early 1990s, a new political issue focussed the attention of European policy-makers, namely migration (Brochmann and Hammer, 1999). Southern European states, traditionally countries of emigration, turned instead into destination countries, with social, economic, and political repercussions (King et al., 2000). Moreover, in the rest of Europe, immigrants from former communist countries and refugees from the former Yugoslavia contributed to increase the numbers and complicate the problem. This created a window of opportunity that led to the adoption of the Euro-Mediterranean Partnership (EMP) in 1995 (generally known as the 'Barcelona process' and later re-labelled Union for the Mediterranean [UfM]) (Adler et al., 2006). Migration remained an open issue for a long time, and coupled with the lessons of the EMP, terrorism after 9/11, and a broad trend towards bilateralism, prompted the Europeans to launch the European Neighbourhood Policy (ENP) in 2004 (Smith, 2005, Del Sarto and Schumacher, 2005). The 'Barcelona process' and the ENP have been the two main building blocks of the EU's policy towards the Mediterranean countries since then.

Second, the most successful initiatives were led by member states, whereas initiatives led by European institutions such as the European Commission were much less politically significant. Both the Global Mediterranean Policy and the Euro-Arab Dialogue were the outcome of a very active French leadership, which convinced the other member states of the benefits of providing a single frame for relations with Southern non-members. Similarly, the EMP, although a predominantly Spanish endeavour, was supported by France and Italy – the three Southern European countries being also central in the inclusion of the Mediterranean in the ENP. A member state without a window of opportunity is not sufficient: when France under Nicolas Sarkozy managed to convince partners to transform the EMP and launch the UfM in 2008, the outcome was a complete flop and the virtual end of region-building in the Mediterranean (Bicchi and Gillespie, 2011). Similarly, when there is a window of opportunity, but the only policy entrepreneur is a European institution, the outcome is less politically salient. This was the case when the European Commission was able to launch the Renovated Mediterranean Policy in 1990, the only outcome being that more funds were allocated to the Mediterranean non-members in a slightly more innovative way. This situation resembles closely the current lack of political innovation in the European response to the Arab uprisings, which is left to the European Commission and to the EEAS.

Therefore, traditionally, the Europeans have addressed the Arab countries when the consequences of crises in the South threatened to affect the North of the Mediterranean, and their response has been more innovative when at least one member state was keen to impress political momentum to the initiative. The policies that have been so formulated have all tended to centre on a mix of economic and political aspects, with social (and geopolitical) aspects always in the shade. The economics of trade, codified in the trade agreements between the Europeans and single Mediterranean countries, has been central to Euro-Mediterranean relations (Hoekman and Djankov, 1996, Radwan and Reiffers, 2005, Pierros et al., 1999). It has tended to reflect the prevailing consensus of the time.

In the 1970s, when economic development was seen as dependent on economies of scale, the Europeans granted free access to the European Common Market to industrial goods produced in Southern Mediterranean countries, in order to increase the potential scale of their markets (Tovias, 1977). In the 1990s, when the leitmotif was liberalisation and competition, the Europeans have negotiated with their Southern partners the gradual opening of their markets to industrial goods produced in the EU, in order to spark economic development in the Arab countries through shock therapy (Aghrout and Alexander, 1997).

Either way, the Europeans, by largely excluding agricultural goods from trade, have remained in a relatively comfortable position as the burden of adjustment has fallen on Arab economies. The financial assistance provided, while important, has never addressed the full economic and social costs of adjustment (Holden, 2008). The political side of the story has been consistent. Although the Europeans would have preferred less autocratic neighbours (and Northern Europeans particularly so), the overall consensus has been pragmatic long before Barack Obama codified this approach.[7] If the same leaders had been elected to pursue the same foreign policies and on top of it, they cooperated more amongst themselves, the Europeans would have been satisfied. Instead, when elections threatened to affect the foreign attitude of a country, such as in Algeria in 1991 or in Palestine in 2006, the Europeans backtracked on their stated objectives of democracy promotion.

The Arab uprisings have thus presented a challenge to the well-established pattern of Euro-Mediterranean relations, in which the Europeans have consistently been able to respond by protecting their interests more than supporting progressive change. But this challenge, as we are going to see, has largely gone unmet.

Europe's Response to the Arab Uprisings: 'More for more' or More of the Same?

The Europeans' response(s) to the Arab uprisings was in line with the previous decades. It was reactive (and particularly so at the beginning) and reflected the priorities of the policy entrepreneurs who capitalised on the window of opportunity as it opened.

At first, there was widespread confusion and no real response. In fact, amid popular enthusiasm for progressive developments in various Arab

---

[7] See Chapter 19 by William Quandt in this volume.

countries, not all member states were immediately supportive of the uprisings. France and Italy found it difficult to let go of old-time allies. The
complicity of France with autocrats was particularly visible, leading to
the dismissal of the minister of Foreign Affairs, Michèle Alliot-Maire,
who had benefited from paid hospitality in Tunisia during the early days
of the uprisings and had offered Tunisia the 'savoir-faire' of French security forces in crowd control just days before Ben Ali fled the country.[8]
Italy kept a low profile, despite longstanding arms' deals with North
African countries, with the UAE, and with Saudi Arabia (an issue that
was also pertinent for France, Spain, and the United Kingdom).[9] But the
stakes were raised in February 2011 when immigrants started arriving
on Italian shores. Migration later became one of Muammar Qaddafi's
weapons, as he threatened to stop policing the border and instead send
refugees across the Mediterranean. This prompted the Italian government
to call for a more united European voice, while simultaneously diluting
the European positive response to the Arab uprisings[10] (and raising the
possibility of Italian police forces operating directly on Tunisian soil).[11]

The first collective, EU official acknowledgement that something significant was happening came only on 10 January 2011, and it was ambiguous. Catherine Ashton and Stefan Füle[12] stated that negotiations on the
'advanced status' of Tunisia[13] would continue, although with a greater
emphasis on human rights and fundamental freedoms. Given that human
rights were – in theory – part and parcel of the EU-Tunisia Free Trade
Agreement, in force since 1998, this was condemned as a lame response.
But the EU waited for Ben Ali to leave the country before 'paying tribute

---

[8] See 'The first European casualty of the Arab uprisings', *The Economist*, 28 February
2011. See also the debate in the French Parliament at http://www.assemblee-nationale
.fr/13/cri/2010-2011/20110091.asp#P145_18310.

[9] See SIPRI Yearbook 2011, Oxford University Press, as well as 'Le esportazioni
di armi italiane nel 2010', Archivio Disarmo. http://www.archiviodisarmo.it/siti/sito_
archiviodisarmo/upload/documenti/93632_Bertozzi_rel2011ad.pdf.

[10] See 'Mediterranean EU states block stronger action on Tunisia', *EU Observer*, 14 January 2011.

[11] 'Emergenza sbarchi: scontro UE-Maroni', *La Repubblica*, 13 February 2011. www.
repubblica.it/cronaca/2011/02/13/news/maroni_emergenza-12402756/. The emergency
in the Southern island of Lampedusa was addressed also by a joint Frontex-Italy operation, name-coded Hermes 2011, with an initial budget of €2 million, later extended and
expanded.

[12] European Commissioner for Enlargement and Neighbourhood Policy.

[13] The EU and Tunisia had been negotiating how to further relations since the entry into
force of the free trade area for industrial goods between the two actors in 2008.

to the courage and determination of the Tunisian people'[14] and freezing the assets of Ben Ali, his wife,[15] and, shortly afterwards, of his entourage.[16] In the case of Egypt, the EU improved its record slightly: Ashton was a bit swifter (although not bold)[17] and European countries a little more united.[18] In Bahrain, Algeria, Yemen, and Iraq, however, the EU remained 'a distant player',[19] while calling for national dialogue in Jordan and Morocco.

The EU seemed to be on a learning curve. As uprisings in Libya steadily veered towards civil war, the EU was more vocal and more precise in its statements. But then the EU became stuck on the most divisive issues in Europe: namely, the use of force for humanitarian intervention and the recognition of new political actors.

In a political move aimed at regaining a leading role in the area, Sarkozy was the first to recognise unilaterally and with no previous consultations (even with his own ministry of Foreign Affairs) the National Transitional Council in Libya, taking all European partners by surprise. To find a similar lack of intra-European solidarity on recognition, we need to go back to Hans Dietrich Genscher's decision to recognise Croatia and Slovenia in 1991 and, similarly, to the Balkan crises, it bode badly for intra-European cooperation. In the Libyan event, only selected EU member states followed the French and British leaders in supporting the second UN Resolution on Libya (UNSC Res. 1973), which paved the way to military action. Just eleven out of twenty-seven EU countries participated in the NATO-led intervention, which relied heavily on Italian intelligence and U.S. technology, and which France and the UK had apparently practiced in a military exercise shortly before it took place (Bishara, 2012, p. 172). Countries who were unconvinced of the intervention's benefits included not only Germany (historically, reluctant to use force beyond

[14] Foreign Affairs Council, Conclusions, 31 January 2011.
[15] Council Decision 2011/72/CFSP, in *Official Journal of the EU*, L 28/62, 2 February 2011.
[16] On the EU response in the case of Tunisia and Libya, see also M. Pinfari, 'Tunisia and Libya' in J. Peters, ed., *The European Union and the Arab Spring* (Lexington Books, 2012), pp. 33–48.
[17] Statement by the EU High Representative C. Ashton on the events in Egypt, 27 January 2011, A 032/1.
[18] Foreign Affairs Council, Conclusions, 31 January 2011. On the EU response in the case of Egypt, see also M. Pace 'Egypt' in in J. Peters, ed., *The European Union and the Arab Spring*.
[19] Timo Behr, 'The European Union's Mediterranean Policies after the Arab Spring', *Amsterdam Law Forum*, vol. 4, n. 2, p. 79.

its borders), but also others such as Poland. Still, following the political leadership of France and the United Kingdom, the Libyan operation was carried out from March-October 2011.[20]

Europeans' unity on Libya was restored (and only up to a point) on low politics, namely the attempt to coordinate evacuations of European citizens and post-conflict humanitarian assistance, including a military mission (EUFOR) to support it. EUFOR was supported strongly by France, Italy, and the UK and less so by countries such as Germany, Sweden, and Finland. It did, however, also raise several issues about coordination with the UN Office for Coordination of Humanitarian Affairs (OCHA) and about the safety of personnel deployed. It never became operational, thus increasing the perceived incoherence of Europe's response to the Libyan crisis (Schumacher, 2013).

The experience in Libya cautioned the Europeans against early and military involvement in an Arab country undergoing the consequences of popular uprisings. When similar conditions occurred in Syria, the EU suspended years of frustrating cooperative efforts in the framework of the European Neighbourhood Policy in May 2011, and then called for Bashar Assad to 'step aside'[21] in March 2012, a call often repeated since.[22] The EU also introduced and progressively strengthened a sophisticated and unprecedented set of economic sanctions. Sanctions targeted individuals, belonging to the Assad family and more generally the Syrian elite supporting the regime, as well as entities and bodies such as investment funds and their assets. They also aimed at embargoing specific imports from Syria – such as oil – as well as exports to Syria – such as arms, technologies for the construction of oil and energy plants, and software and equipment for monitoring communications. Sanctions also banned trade in precious metals and diamonds with Syrian public bodies and access to EU airports for cargo flights operated by Syrian carriers.[23]

Alongside the tightening of the sanctions' regime against Syria, the EU reverted to what it does best under the leadership of EU institutions (in this case the EEAS and, most importantly, the European Commission): offer financial and technical aid and manage its economic border with the other Arab countries. These initiatives took two forms: emergency measures and an attempt at rewriting the EU foreign policy guidelines for

---

[20] On Libya, see also Koenig (2011) and Schumacher (2013).
[21] European Council Conclusions, Brussels, 2 March 2012.
[22] See, e.g., Joint Communication, 'Delivering on a new European Neighbourhood Policy', Brussels, 15.V.2012, JOIN(2012) 14 final, SWD(2012) 110–124 final.
[23] For further analysis, see Blockmans (2012), Schumacher (2013), and Seeberg (2012).

relations with the Southern neighbours. The pattern was the usual one, but the leadership provided by the EEAS and the European Commission did not deliver significant political innovations.

Emergency measures were adopted in the case of Tunisia, also in response to the Libyan crisis. The first meeting between Ashton and the Tunisian transitional government took place on 14 February,[24] but Ashton offered a meagre €17 million in immediate aid that was unrepresentative of the needs of the Tunisian government at the time. The EU later nearly doubled the foreseen financial aid for Tunisia for 2011 (which was €80 million), to just under €160 million. It also added a further €80.5 million for humanitarian assistance (mostly on Tunisian soil) in the context of the Libyan crisis.[25] These measures were accompanied by a much higher amount of soft loans by the European Investment Bank, which approved a €1.87 billion loan to Tunisia on 3 March 2011.[26]

The extent to which these resources could make a difference is, however, questionable. Production stoppage and damage to physical properties during the first weeks of riots in Tunisia cost the equivalent of €1.6 billion,[27] and this was before taking into account the downturn in 2011 owing to loss of foreign direct investments (estimated at −35 per cent),[28] the vertical drop in tourism's revenues (estimated at −40 per cent) and the disruption in production for both internal consumption and export.[29] The estimates of the IMF in April 2011 forecasted the financing needs of oil-importing Middle East and North Africa (MENA) countries at $90 billion for 2012 alone.[30] It took the whole set of most advanced countries, gathered in the G8 in May 2011, together with the World Bank and the International Monetary Fund, to start talking

---

[24] 'Remarks by the High Representative/Vice President Catherine Ashton at the end of her visit to Tunisia', Tunis, European Commission Press Release, 14 February 2011.

[25] EuropeAid, 'Neighbourhood: Working for the Southern Mediterranean, EU Support for Tunisia'. http://ec.europa.eu/europeaid/where/neighbourhood/documents/tunisia_eu_support_for_tunisia_en.pdf.

[26] The discussion with Egypt came instead at a much later stage, at the request of Egyptian authorities.

[27] A. Galal, J. L. Reiffers, *Towards a New Med Region: Achieving Fundamental Transitions*, FEMISE Report on the Euro-Mediterranean Partnership, 2011, p. 17.

[28] Ibidem.

[29] Document de travail conjoint des services, 'Mise en oeuvre de la Politique Européenne de Voisinage en Tunisie, Progrès réalisés en 2011 et actions à mettre en oeuvre', Brussels, 15 May 2012, SWD (2012), 123 final.

[30] 'Middle East and North Africa: Historic Transitions under Strain', IMF Regional Economic Outlook Update, 20 April 2012. www.imf.org/external/pubs/ft/reo/2012/mcd/eng/pdf/mena-update0412.pdf.

figures. Pledges (but not commitments) for Egypt and Tunisia reached
$20 billion, potentially doubling with the contribution of Arab countries
and other governments.[31] But, regardless of size, Western aid and soft
loans came with strings attached. On a smaller scale, aid pointed strongly
in the direction of tightening controls on migration, an issue single member states also were quick to take up.[32] On a broader scale, the issue was
raised of what type of socio-economic development Western countries
were envisaging for the area.

The type of socio-economic development EU leaders had in mind
became clearer with three communications that constituted the second
step in the EU response to the crisis: namely, the attempt at rewriting the
EU foreign policy guidelines for relations with the Southern neighbours.
In the first one, 'A Partnership for Democracy and Shared Prosperity
with the Southern Mediterranean',[33] published in March 2011, the EEAS
and the European Commission presented an 'incentive-based approach'.
It was summarised in the motto 'more for more', indicating that more
reforms would be repaid with more cooperation and greater support from
the EU. Ashton summarised the issues at stake in the communication as
the '3-Ms': money, mobility, and market access. This approach, heralded
as a 'fundamental step change in the EU's relationship' with those partners that commit themselves to reforms,[34] offered 'mobility partnership'
to ease legal migration, an increase in funds, and more market access
through the negotiation of 'Deep and Comprehensive Free Trade Areas',
including, for instance, 'regulatory convergence'.[35] The document was
followed by another communication, 'A New Response to a Changing
Neighbourhood', issued in May 2011.[36] It elaborated further on the previous one and it stressed again conditionality as a cornerstone of EU foreign
policy: 'Increased EU support to its neighbours is conditional'.[37] The third

---

[31] See 'G8 pledges $20 billion to foster Arab Spring', *Reuters*, 27 May 2011. www.reuters
.com/article/2011/05/27/us-g-idUSTRE74P00320110527.

[32] Italy was particularly active on this front. See Y. Maccanico, 'The EU's self-interested
response to unrest in North Africa', *Statewatch*, n. 165. www.statewatch.org/analyses/
no-165-eu-north-africa.pdf.

[33] Joint Communication to the European Council, the European Parliament, the Council,
the European Economic and Social Committee, and the Committee of the Regions,
Brussels, 8 March 2011, COM(2011)200 final.

[34] Idem, p. 5.

[35] Idem, p. 9.

[36] Joint Communication to the European Council, the European Parliament, the Council,
the European Economic and Social Committee and the Committee of the Regions,
Brussels, 25 May 2011, COM (2011) 303 final.

[37] Idem, p. 3.

one launched a programme entitled SPRING (Support for Partnership, Reforms and Inclusive Growth) in September 2011, aimed at supporting democratic transitions, economic growth, and institution building.

There is nothing really new in these communications, and especially in the principles they embody. While additional funds are important (and for specific cases, very important) and the discussion about mobility partnerships is interesting, the main tools of the EU are still trade and limited aid, coupled with conditionality, which remain fundamentally biased in favour of the EU. Conditionality is the traditional EU instrument for linking trade and aid to political developments and as such, it has received substantial scholarly attention.[38] Its role is reconfirmed in the post-Arab Spring context. The role of trade is well exemplified by the EU approach to regulatory convergence. Agreements on Conformity Assessment and Acceptance of Industrial Products (ACAAs), which the EU aims to conclude with all Southern partners in order to foster free trade and economic development, are a 'specific type of mutual recognition agreement based on the alignment of the legislative system and infrastructure of the country concerned with those of the European Community'.[39] The aim of 'mutual recognition by alignment on the EU law' in Mediterranean non-members has been an objective of the European Commission for a long time.

Similarly, sustainable economic development, which is now taken as a synonym of equitable development,[40] remains a challenge more than a policy. The EU has consistently relied on the mantra that economic liberalisation would contribute to political liberalisation. However, there is increasing evidence that political elites have managed to benefit from EU-induced privatisations[41] and affect political developments *a contrario*, by exacerbating social tensions. The EU tried to be the soft side of the so-called Washington consensus, but it could not change its main tenets, nor its consequences. This should not come too much as a surprise, as the European Commission started a sustainability impact assessment of the Euro-Mediterranean Free Trade area as early as 1999. Results delivered

---

[38] See, e.g., Balfour (2012) and Smith (1998).

[39] The European Community is the legal entity on which the EU Single Market is based. Taken from http://ec.europa.eu/enterprise/policies/single-market-goods/ international-aspects/acaa-neighbouring-countries/index_en.htm, accessed on 31 October 2012.

[40] In the past, it was instead a synonym for environment-friendly practices. See the assessments of Euro-Mediterranean relations made by the Mediterranean Commission for Sustainable Development (Blue Plan studies) and Friends of the Earth Middle East.

[41] See, e.g., contributions in Galal and Reiffers (2010), Costa-Font (2012), Roccu (forthcoming) as well as Kadri, Chapter 4 in this volume.

in 2005 and in 2007 mirrored a number of confidential studies carried out by the Commission. They all highlighted not only the very negative impact in the short run on manufacturing sectors in Arab countries, but also its 'significantly adverse' social effects (including on the Millennium Goals of poverty reduction) in the absence of mitigating policies by Mediterranean governments.[42] It is true that Mediterranean countries have little alternative to liberalisation under the aegis of the EU, but this only enhances the responsibilities of the EU in terms of its role vis à vis Arab societies post-Arab Spring.

The more interesting innovations concern the socio-political aspects of Arab transitions. There is a new emphasis in supporting civil society, including political actors. This is a first for the EU, although some member states, such as Germany, have long been in this line of business. The support was expressed in the adoption of a Civil Society Facility and of a European Endowment for Democracy, which will open new budgetary lines devoted not only to NGOs, but also to political parties, trade unions, and non-officially sanctioned NGOs. This is a potentially interesting development, which however partly replicates the efforts of the European Instrument for Democracy and Human Rights (EIDHR) and further complicates tracking of funds.[43] Moreover, funds have been increased for the programme Erasmus Mundus, which allows exchanges of students and academic staff across the Mediterranean.[44] Finally, there is an increased attention to marginalized areas and unemployed people.[45] All these ideas, however, will need to withstand the test of implementation, and funds will need to be committed and disbursed so as to contribute to the proclaimed aims. Most importantly, this new emphasis on socio-political dynamics has yet to become central in the overall architecture of Euro-Mediterranean relations.

Rather than a 'more for more' approach, Europe has thus opted for a 'more of the same' approach, in which the EU is in charge of

---

[42] *Final Report of the SIA-EMFTA Project*, November 2007, p. 46. The assessments and the Commission's reply are available at: http://ec.europa.eu/trade/analysis/sustainability-impact-assessments/assessments/.

[43] The European Endowment for Democracy was formally set up in June 2012, but encountered further difficulties before becoming operational.

[44] 'The European Commission boosts the number of Erasmus Mundus scholarships for South Mediterranean students', Brussels, 27 September 2011. http://europa.eu/rapid/press-release_MEMO-11-637-en.htm.

[45] E.g., 'Programme d'Appui au Développement des Zones Défavorisées, Fiche Action pour la Tunisie', worth €20 million and funded by the European Commission. See more at http://ec.europa.eu/europeaid/documents/aap/2011/af_aap-spe_2011_tun.pdf.

protecting a conservative vision for the Southern neighbourhood beyond the demise of the 'Arab Presidents for life' (Owen, 2012), maintaining rather than reversing the order of European priorities (Cassarino, 2012) and re-packaging old concepts in 'new bottles' (Colombo and Tocci, 2012, Mustapha, 2012). In fact, it could even be argued that the EU is offering 'less of the same', as region building, which used to be a cornerstone of Europe's foreign policy, has disappeared from the political spectrum of the EU (Bicchi and Gillespie 2011). The shift from the EMP to the UfM has greatly diminished the relevance of regional gatherings, which the EU is unable to relaunch in a Mediterranean context that seems more fragmented than ever. While at the beginning of the crisis in Libya there were attempts at coordinating responses with Turkey and the Arab League, little came out of them and only NATO seems at times to be relevant in the scenarios about Syria.

Conclusion: The Irrelevant Power?

Europe's response to the Arab uprisings has been limited and inspired by a conservative, rather than progressive, attitude to Euro-Mediterranean relations. While rejoicing for the 'cathartic moment'[46] shaking the Arab world, European policy-makers have also been fretting about its consequences. The consolidated benefits of the EU's policy towards the Southern neighbours have thus been at the core of the EU's response to the changing context, which has centred on trade and conditionality, accompanied by increased aid. Reacting to the ongoing changes on the Southern shore, Europe has relied on the leadership of France and the UK for military issues in Libya, and on the European Commission and the EEAS for economic issues in the rest of the region. The political scene remains largely unexplored, as member states are not taking the lead on a new dialogue with the newly elected regimes, or making use of regional frameworks of cooperation for fostering a political vision of Euro-Mediterranean relations.

This pattern is more suited to defend the status quo than to participate in the future making of the region, and this can only contribute to the progressive irrelevance of Europe in developments in its Southern neighbourhood. The lukewarm support given to democracy-promotion policies in the past already showed how the Europeans were not willing to push for real change in the area. Several smaller initiatives flagged in

[46] See Fawaz Gerges's Introduction in this volume.

the early months of the post-Arab Spring period are potentially interesting and might contribute to the consolidation of the transition in Arab countries. A key aspect will be implementation, which should be effective, transparent, and thoroughly scrutinised, to make the EU accountable and coherent in its rhetorical discourse on supporting transition in the Arab world.[47] When addressing human rights and democracy, the EU has a track record of avoiding tough choices and opting for uncontroversial issues when it comes to implementation (Bicchi, 2010). However, if the Europeans' focus remains inward-facing, devoted to economic priorities and fending off 'illegal' migrants, the contribution of Europe to the consolidation process post-Arab Spring will in any case remain limited.

To what extent this is a bad thing is open to discussion. On the one hand, this attitude leaves broad margins of freedom to the Arab peoples to decide their own future, which hopefully will deliver the end of neo- and postcolonialism. The responsibility and, ultimately, the freedom to choose and found democratic practices belong (and should belong) to Arab citizens alone. For a very long time the Europeans have interfered with the local practices in the Middle East and North Africa, contributing to making this one of the most penetrated areas in the world (Brown, 1984, p. 5), characterised by the 'on-going struggle for regional autonomy from external control' (Hinnebusch, 2003, p. 4). If the Arab uprisings are to usher the end of postcolonialism (Dabashi, 2012), this should be the hour of the Arab world, not of Europe.

On the other hand, Europe – and more generally, Western countries – can and should accompany, support, and anchor transitions to democracy, especially in a context of economic crisis. Europe, in particular, has a long-standing tradition of acting as a credible anchor for democracy, as it has shown during the 'third wave' of democratization (cf. Huntington, 1991). In the 1980s, when Greece, Spain, and Portugal (at the time labelled 'Mediterranean' rather than 'Southern European') transitioned to democracy, member states of the then-European Communities were quick and consistent in recognising the benefits of democratization and in offering membership as a mid-term perspective for democratizers. Similarly, in the 1990s, when communist regimes fell in Central and Eastern European countries, the EU acted for a long period as the main reference point for economic and political transitions, ultimately enlarging to include ten new members. Even in the most dramatic case of the

---

[47] On rhetorical entrapment, see Schimmelfennig (2001).

Balkans, the Europeans have been able to stabilise the truce (but not to stop genocide and war).

As the Arab uprisings turn into a long power struggle, the issue of what role the Europeans play and what 'political messages' they bring forward (Perthes, 2011, p. 75, Schumacher, 2011) has become more important than ever. Not only is EU membership not a viable instrument, but doubts are also cast on the utility of traditional EU mechanisms of influence, such as conditionality and socialisation, in a context characterised by the reinvention of categories of citizenship and by unresolved nationalism. Socio-economic development remains, on the contrary, a paramount priority in the Arab world, thus highlighting the importance of the EU as an economic bloc, but not necessarily the appropriateness of its approach. As the Europeans 'listen' to changes in their Southern neighbourhood, they might do so as part of a process of communicative exchange (cf. Börzel and Risse, 2009) in which they not only aim to persuade and influence, but also learn, adapt, and redefine their interests – even at a time when the Euro-crisis continues to dictate political priorities at home.

21

Conclusion

Rebellious Citizens and Resilient Authoritarians

Valerie Bunce

Abstract

Why are analysts so surprised by cross-national waves of popular mobilizations against authoritarian rulers? This chapter compares three such waves – the collapse of communism in the Soviet Union and Eastern Europe, the colour revolutions in postcommunist Europe and Eurasia, and the Arab uprisings – and develops two complementary lines of explanation. One is the inherent difficulty of making such predictions because of the ability of some short-term events to convert individualized private anger into large-scale public actions. While compelling, this explanation needs to be supplanted with a second one: the tendency of analysts to exaggerate the strength and the durability of authoritarian regimes and rulers.

Waves of Popular Upheavals

Over the last quarter of a century, there have been three cross-national waves of popular mobilizations against authoritarian rulers. The first was in 1989 (more strictly speaking, 1987–1991), when citizens in one regime after another in what was then called the Soviet Union and Eastern Europe rose up in large numbers to demand that their communist rulers leave power.[1] The second was the colour revolutions in

---

[1] Gale Stokes, *The Walls Came Tumbling Down: The Collapse of Communism in Eastern Europe* (Oxford: Oxford University Press, 1993) and Valerie Bunce, *Subversive Institutions: The Design and the Destruction of Socialism and the State* (Cambridge: Cambridge University Press, 1999).

post-communist Europe and Eurasia from 1998–2008.[2] In this wave, citizens in collaboration with civil society groups and opposition parties in nine competitive authoritarian regimes in the region – Armenia, Azerbaijan, Belarus, Croatia, Georgia, Kyrgyzstan, Serbia, Slovakia, and Ukraine – carried out unprecedented and extraordinarily ambitious electoral challenges to authoritarian incumbents or their anointed successors. When the losers in most of these contests refused to admit defeat, citizens mounted large-scale post-election demonstrations that in many instances forced a transfer of political power to the opposition. The final wave, which is ongoing, is the subject of this volume. Once again, large-scale demonstrations broke out in a series of countries within the same region – in this case, the Middle East and North Africa (MENA).[3] Like the other waves, these popular uprisings settled quickly on the radical goal of removing authoritarian incumbents from power.

Despite the contrast between street-based and electoral-based mobilizations, the types of authoritarian regimes in which these popular challenges took place, and the willingness and ability of incumbent regimes to use force to defend the status quo, these three rounds of popular challenges to authoritarian rulers featured nonetheless some striking similarities. For example, each one targeted leadership change, each one was propelled by what Charles Tripp terms in Chapter 6 in this volume the 'denigration and exclusion of the public' and the rapid 'evaporation' of the public's 'awe of the state', and each one demonstrated that innovative repertoires of protest could travel across state boundaries. In addition, all three waves featured an uneven geography. Not every country in each of the regions joined the wave, and, if joining, not every outbreak of popular mobilizations produced a turnover in leadership, let alone a subsequent transition to a new regime, whether authoritarian, democratic, or a mixture of the two.

Surprise, Surprise[4]

It is a final similarity that serves as the focus of this chapter. Each of these waves caught most specialists in authoritarian regimes – in general

---

[2] Valerie Bunce and Sharon Wolchik, *Defeating Authoritarian Leaders in Post-communist States* (Cambridge: Cambridge University Press, 2011).

[3] Marc Lynch, *The Arab Uprising: The Unfinished Revolutions of the New Middle East* (New York: Public Affairs/Perseus, 2012).

[4] Nancy Bermeo, 'Surprise, Surprise: Lessons from 1989 and 1991'. In Nancy Bermeo, ed., *Liberalization and Democratization in the Soviet Union and Eastern Europe* (Baltimore: Johns Hopkins University Press, 1992), pp. 3–17.

and in the specific countries that hosted these developments – by surprise. Indeed, three surprises presented themselves: the initial eruption of
large-scale protests in the region (as in, say, Tunisia in 2010), the success of so many of these efforts in removing authoritarian leaders from
office, and the ability of the precedent set by this 'early riser' to spread –
and so quickly – to other states in the region. Here, one is reminded of
Robert Kaplan's depiction of the Tunisian uprising as 'one small revolution' that would remain geographically contained – an observation
that was published (unfortunately for him) several days before Egyptian
citizens began their occupation of Tahrir Square.[5] Similarly, on a more
personal note, this author, like virtually all specialists in Eastern Europe
during the communist era, did not anticipate that East Germany would
experience large-scale protests in the late summer and early fall of 1989.
In fact, a working group of academics and policy-makers – organized
by the U.S. Department of State in the late spring of 1989 to discuss
the implications of the Gorbachev reforms and the roundtables between
regime and opposition in Poland and Hungary – brought its business to
a close when those roundtables ended, only to be quickly re-convened
when East Germany broke out in revolution.

Why have scholars been so surprised by these waves of anti-regime
mobilizations? The answer is not that we were naïve about the problems
that these various authoritarian regimes faced. Marc Lynch's observations about the 'crumbling foundations of the Arab order' echoed the
characterizations scholars had repeatedly offered earlier of both communist regimes in Eastern Europe prior to 1989 and the post-communist
competitive authoritarian regimes that in many cases succeeded them.[6]
It was also not, as Charles Tripp and John Chalcraft document for the
MENA (Chapters 6 and 7 in this volume, respectively), that publics in
these countries supported their regimes and refrained from protest, or that
analysts were unaware of the existence of restive citizens and histories of
anti-regime mobilizations – although, as Chalcraft reminds us, the societal
side of Arab authoritarianism was in fact overlooked, which was not, in
fact, the case for research on Eastern European communism in particular.
Instead, as I will argue in this chapter, there were two other reasons. The
first is that large-scale public unrest in authoritarian regimes is virtually
impossible to predict because it is prompted by short-term events that

---

[5] 'One Small Revolution.' *New York Times*, 23 January 2011, p. 11.
[6] Lynch, *The Arab Uprising*, p. 1. For the earlier two waves, see Bunce, *Subversive Institutions* and Bunce and Wolchik, *Defeating Authoritarian Leaders*, chs. 3–7.

unexpectedly redraw the informational landscape of mass politics. The second explanation, which addresses some of the limitations of the first one, shifts our attention from the behaviour of ordinary citizens to the operation of authoritarian regimes.[7] Here, I argue that scholars would have been less surprised by such uprisings, including their ability to travel among states, if they had not spent so much time identifying the sources of regime resilience and paid more attention to the limitations built into the authoritarian political project. Thus, while it is always difficult to anticipate eruptions of popular protests in authoritarian regimes, it is especially so when the basis for prediction is so heavily invested in the political status quo.

The Inherent Limits of Prediction

The fluidity and the complexity of the social world make it far easier for social scientists to explain what has already happened than to predict what will happen. This distinction is particularly clear-cut in the case of popular revolts in authoritarian political settings because the dependent variable of interest is both a rare event and one that generates a radical departure from the past. Social scientists, however, have nonetheless shown an ability to adapt quickly to these circumstances by then generating competing explanations of 'big change'. It is precisely this contrast between explanation and prediction that Alexis de Tocqueville captured in his characterization of the French revolution as an event that was unforeseen, yet in retrospect so overdetermined.

One theory that takes 'the element of surprise' in large-scale popular upheavals as its point of departure – and that is also addressed by Roger Owen in Chapter 11 in this volume – is Timur Kuran's.[8] Kuran argues, building on Lenin (which provides a nice bridge amongst the waves of interest in this study), that revolutions are responses to events that 'spark' dramatic changes in mass behaviour, but that cannot be foreseen as a result of the nature of authoritarian politics. Because of

---

[7] Jack Goldstone, 'Bringing Regimes Back In: Variations in the Arab Revolutions and Revolts'. Paper presented at the Workshop on Contentious Politics, Democratization, and Political Change: A Comparative Perspective, The Hebrew University of Jerusalem, 21–23 May 2012.

[8] 'Now Out of Never: The Element of Surprise in the East European Revolution of 1989'. *World Politics* 44, 1 (October 1991): 7–48. For an extension of this argument, see Susanne Lohmann, 'The Dynamics of Informational Cascades: The Monday Demonstrations in Leipzig, East Germany, 1989–91'. *World Politics* 47 (October 1994): 42–101.

repression and the premium it understandably places on conformity as a necessary condition for personal survival as well as success, authoritarian regimes draw a sharp distinction between the private and the public preferences of ordinary citizens, as well as others, such as members of the ruling coalition. As a result, individuals in such regime settings hide any hostility they may feel towards the regime and display supportive or at least acquiescent public behaviours. Thus, in addition to the familiar constraints on collective action that operate in most political settings, there are additional ones in authoritarian regimes. These include few public or political venues to express concerns, fears of severe reprisals if such sentiments are expressed (with punishment also extending to families, friends, and even communities), and, as Kuran particularly emphasizes, a lack of knowledge on the part of individuals in these systems about the true sentiments of their fellow citizens.

False preferences, therefore, are endemic in these regimes, and they lead to atomization and demobilization. As a result, citizens are deprived of the coordinative resources they need to confront the regime en masse. However, 'sparks' (which was the name, in fact, of one of the most influential Bolshevik publications) occur at unpredictable times and in unexpected places, and they are distinguished by their ability to reveal important information about the true preferences of a large number of other citizens. If this new (and more accurate) information circulates widely and quickly, it can produce 'information cascades' that serve as the basis for large-scale mobilizations against the regime.

It is precisely this dynamic that we saw, for example, in the cases of the self-immolation of a street vendor in Tunisia in late 2010 and in Serbia a decade earlier when the contrast between the official presidential election results and those circulated by the opposition confirmed electoral fraud and produced a rapid mobilization of citizens throughout the country that converged in a matter of a few days on the capital. As a result, Milosevic suffered the same fate as Ben Ali. Similarly, in East Germany in 1989, some relatively modest actions by a few iconoclasts on a central square prompted many others to monitor this behaviour and eventually to join these individuals in progressively large numbers. The end result was large-scale demonstrations that led to the end of the incumbent regime and, for that matter, the end of communism and the East German state. A final example of what has also been termed 'triggers' comes from Poland in 1980 when large increases in the price of basic foodstuffs produced initially some scattered protests that then congealed quickly into not just sizeable demonstrations, but also the formation of

Solidarity.[9] Because the Soviets did not respond by invading Poland and because of the sheer size of this movement, its cross-class composition, and its remarkable success in bringing in one-quarter of the members of the Polish communist party into its ranks, the rise of Solidarity constituted the first stage in what became nine years later the end of communist party hegemony in Eastern Europe and the Soviet Union.

What is important about these sparks is not just that they can take many forms, as our examples suggest, but also that they are, in part because of their variety and their sudden and significant impact, unpredictable events. What they share is their success in transforming private into public and actionable preferences. Thus, as Kuran argues, the key constraint on protest in authoritarian regimes is the absence of information – a problem that disappears as a result of these triggers. Also implied in the Kuran framework is another argument. Because publics in these systems are in the dark, so necessarily must be those who analyze them. Thus, neither can be faulted for failing to anticipate the eruption of large-scale protests in authoritarian regimes.

The Limits of Informational Limitations

Kuran's explanation has a great deal of merit. This is particularly the case, if we focus on two aspects of surprise in these waves; that is, the eruption of large-scale protests in the 'early risers' and the subsequent spread to neighbouring countries of similar challenges to authoritarian rulers. For example, focussing on the second issue, cross-national diffusion, we can argue that the successful removal of an authoritarian leader from one country in a region composed of authoritarian regimes provides regime opponents in neighbouring countries with two vital sources of information that encourage emulation. One is the heightened optimism that grows out of the fact that collective action against the regime has demonstrated that it can succeed in removing authoritarian leaders from office, and the other is the provision of a portable ensemble of targeted public actions that can achieve that objective.

While Kuran's insights are valuable, they nonetheless leave some important questions unanswered. First, to return to the issue of diffusion:

[9] Philipp Kuntz and Mark R. Thompson, 2009. 'More than just the Final Straw: Stolen Elections as Revolutionary Triggers', *Comparative Politics*, 41 (April): 253–272 and Joshua A. Tucker, 'Enough! Electoral Fraud Collective Action Problems and Post-Communist Coloured Revolutions', *Perspectives on Politics* 5 (September 2007): 535–551.

if information is so critical and if the MENA wave, more than the others, profited from a relatively levelled informational playing field as a result of the impact of social media and the Al-Jazeera effect, then what explains the contrasting participation rates of the MENA countries in this wave?[10] Put differently: there must have been other important factors in play that facilitated the movement of contentious politics to some countries, but not others.

Second, popular uprisings in authoritarian regimes do not by any means always travel, even if they break out in regions composed primarily of authoritarian regimes and if they succeed in their mission. A case in point is the successful challenge to the Ferdinand Marcos regime in the Philippines in 1986. Although there were some successful challenges to authoritarian rule in southeast and east Asia after the breakthrough in the Philippines, such as in South Korea, Taiwan, and Indonesia, none of these events exhibited the same repertoire. Indeed, the transition from authoritarianism in Taiwan was an elite-centred process similar to what had taken place in Spain after Franco died and in Poland and Hungary in 1989. Thus, while one could argue that optimism might have travelled, the innovative toolkit developed by the Filipino opposition to challenge Marcos did not. And it is the transfer of a specific innovation amongst sites that distinguishes a diffusion dynamic from other mechanisms that produced spatially clustered change. Although there are many factors that could account for the contrast between diffusion and its absence, one logical candidate would be the presence of similarities amongst states within the region because of, say, a common language, history, religion and/or political-economic system. These commonalities could explain, for instance, why the MENA and the communist region were particularly prone to hosting waves – both in the recent cases of interest here, but also earlier, such as with the cross-national clustering of public upheavals from 1953–1956 in Eastern Europe or a similar pattern exhibited in the MENA with respect to popular reactions to neoliberal policies in the 1970s and 1980s. Such commonalities, it could be argued, were less of function of information than of the fact that they encouraged citizens in other countries to draw parallels between their own situations and those present in the trailblazing cases.[11]

---

[10] For a cautious reading of the impact of social media, see Marc Lynch, 'After Egypt: The Limits and Promise of Online Challenges to the Authoritarian Arab State', *Perspectives on Politics*, 9, no. 2 (June 2011): 301–310.

[11] David Patel, Valerie Bunce, and Sharon Wolchik, 'Fizzles and Fireworks: A Comparative Perspective on the Diffusion of Popular Protests in the Middle East and North Africa'.

This line of argument, however, introduces a new wrinkle. Diffusion is always double.[12] Similar regime contexts should mean that their leaders, watching these dangerous precedents closely, would be quick to draw lessons and take pre-emptive actions. Although one can suggest that such lessons might take some time to develop, this claim is not persuasive, given the facts that the threats involved were existential; leaders in these regions were practiced in 'protest-proofing' and waves did, after all, take shape in at least six countries. These points, in turn, call into question the ability of Kuran to explain not just diffusion, but also the success of the 'later risers'.

In fact, the success of the protests in these three waves poses some more problems for Kuran's theory. He seems to imply that authoritarian leaders fell because of the sheer size of the movements. Because so many citizens were able to reveal their true preferences and take corresponding actions, the regime was doomed. This assumption, moreover, appears in some of the other chapters in this volume in the sense that the distinction between the eruption of large-scale mobilizations versus the question of their impact on the tenure of leaders is not problematized. Students of contentious politics, for instance, would respond by arguing that many factors, in fact, play a role in successful protests (and, for that matter, in the size of the movements) – for example, whether challengers to the status quo develop creative and effective ensembles of protest repertoires; whether their frames trump those offered by the regime; whether brokers appear; whether the regime is able to maintain its coalition and dampen protest by, for instance, exercising its coercive powers, introducing reforms, or, as in Yemen and Syria, combining the two; and a host of other factors that are associated with the largely silent antagonist in Kuran's study – the regime.[13]

Finally, the history of protests in these countries and others cast some doubt on an explanation that gives sparks so much responsibility for providing the information citizens need to mobilize. At least some of

Paper presented at annual POMEPS conference, 'The Arab Uprisings in Comparative Perspective', George Washington University, 20–21 May 2011.

[12] See Donatella della Porta and Sidney Tarrow, 'Double Diffusion: The Co-Evolution of Police and Protest Behavior with an Application to Transnational Contention'. Unpublished manuscript, 2010.

[13] Sidney Tarrow, *The Dynamics of Contention* (Cambridge: Cambridge University Press, 1998) and Sidney Tarrow, *The New Transnational Activism* (Cambridge: Cambridge University Press, 2005). In addition, see Kurt Weyland, 'The Arab Spring: Why the Surprising Similarities with the Revolutions of 1848?' *Perspectives on Politics* 10 (December 2012): 917–934.

the uprisings in these three waves – and especially those that took place early in the dynamic – were preceded by a number of dress rehearsals. This was, for example, the case for Poland, Hungary, Yugoslavia, and Czechoslovakia in the 1989 dynamic; for Serbia and to a lesser extent Ukraine and Georgia in the colour revolutions; and for Tunisia, Egypt, Bahrain, Jordan, Syria, and Yemen in the Arab uprisings.[14] Moreover, as already noted, there were precedents for earlier 'micro-waves' in these regions, and these included a sharing of protest repertoires, such as with the Qab'at movement in Jordan and Kefaya in Egypt and the growing coordination in the last years of communism amongst the Czech, Hungarian, and Polish oppositions. Also illuminating is the fact that every colour revolution in post-communist Europe and Eurasia that succeeded in toppling authoritarian leaders or their anointed successors – in contrast to those that failed to do so – was preceded by opposition victories in local elections.

We can, of course, insert these examples of prior mobilizations and instances of cross-state contagion effects and coordination into Kuran's framework (but giving history as well as the ripening of oppositions more due) by arguing that the 'failed revolts' and the local-level successes of the past had the effect of circulating a great deal of information about 'true' preferences before, not just because of, the triggering event. In fact, the Egyptian example offers evidence of both contributors to information. First, there was a clear pattern of rising demonstrations and especially strikes in Egypt (but also in other countries in the region) prior to the Tunisian developments.[15] At the same time, encouraged by the Tunisian precedent, opposition leaders in Egypt ran experiments in various localities to test how receptive citizens were to criticisms of the Mubarak regime and how willing they were to vocalize their anger.[16] Rather than retrofit Kuran's theory to accommodate past protests, however, we should

---

[14] See, for example, Lynch, *The Arab Uprising*, pp. 44–46; Rabab El-Mahdi, 'Enough: Egypt's Quest for Democracy'. *Comparative Political Studies* 42 (February 2009): 1011–1039; Grzegorz Ekiert, *The State Against Society: Political Crises and their Aftermath in East Central Europe* (Princeton: Princeton University Press, 1996); and Bunce and Wolchik, *Defeating Authoritarian Leaders*, chs. 2–7.

[15] Solidarity Center, AFL-CIO, 'Justice for All: The Struggle for Workers' Rights in Egypt: A Report by the Solidarity Center'. February 2010. Available at http://www.solidaritycenter.org/files/pubs_egypt_wr.pdf; Marsha Pripstein Posusney, *Labor and the State in Egypt: Workers, Unions and Economic Restructuring, 1952 to 1996* (New York: Columbia University Press, 1997).

[16] David Kirkpatrick, 'Wired and Shrewd, Young Egyptians Guide Revolt'. *New York Times*, 9 February 2011. www.nytimes.com/2011/102/10/world/middleeast/10youth .html.

recognize a more general point that also appears in the chapters in this volume by Charles Tripp (Chapter 6), John Chalcraft (Chapter 7), and Roger Owen (Chapter 11). Seemingly sudden developments often, if not always, have deeper roots. Sparks become precisely that when there is kindling. And the presence of kindling suggests not simply that the evolution of regime-society interactions matter in addition to short-term events and perhaps give the latter more causal impact, but also that the powerful effects of these events and the consequences of their ability to build on the past mean that the outbreak of large-scale protests can be – or at least should be – anticipated. Although their timing is always hard to foresee, of course, the possibility that they could take place should not be dismissed out of hand.

This conclusion is particularly warranted in light of Acemoglu and Robinson's rational choice account of the origins and dynamics of democracy and dictatorship – an account that arrives at conclusions that are quite similar to what students of revolution have long argued.[17] Put succinctly: popular protests are the Achilles heel of authoritarian regimes. Although many such regimes are successful in deterring or repressing such upheavals, the French, American, Russian, Chinese, Yugoslav, Cuban, Vietnamese, and Iranian revolutions indicate they often fail in these endeavours.[18] Moreover, speaking to a few of these cases, along with a host of others, Daniel Slater has observed that: 'Democratic revolutions are far from "an everyday occurrence." However, they occur more frequently than a purely rational choice account of democratic mobilizations seems capable of allowing.'[19] Indeed, the same critique could be levelled at historical-institutional accounts. Largely as a result of their preoccupation with long-term trends (but only some of them), their predilection for path dependence, and their assumption that change occurs slowly, rather than spasmodically, such studies also, before the fact, under-predict revolutionary change.

It is precisely at this point that we need to confront the numbers represented in the three waves that serve as the empirical backdrop of this chapter. In 1989, all nine countries that made up the Soviet Union

---

[17] Daron Acemoglu and James Robinson, *Economic Origins of Dictatorship and Democracy* (Cambridge: Cambridge University Press, 2005).

[18] On the strategies authoritarian regimes use to protect themselves, see Karrie Koesel and Valerie Bunce, 'Diffusion-Proofing: Russian and Chinese Responses to Waves of Popular Challenges to Authoritarian Rulers'. *Perspectives on Politics*, forthcoming, September, 2013.

[19] Daniel Slater, *Ordering Power: Contentious Politics and Authoritarian Leviathans in Southeast Asia* (Cambridge: Cambridge University Press, 2010).

and Eastern Europe joined the dynamic (a number that would nearly triple were we to unpack the federations of the Soviet Union, Yugoslavia, and Czechoslovakia and count up mobilizations by republic); in post-communist Europe and Eurasia, there have been fifteen significant mobilizations against authoritarian rulers or their anointed successors before, during, and after elections from 1990–2012 (expanding the idea of the colour revolutions to include the Russian demonstrations in late 2011 and early 2012); and in the MENA there were six such major uprisings (Bahrain, Egypt, Libya, Syria, Tunisia, and Yemen). This leaves us with a conservative estimate of thirty 'surprises' over the past quarter of a century – which is an undeniably large number, albeit one that is less impressive if we use as our denominator not the number of authoritarian regimes in the world, but rather the combined total of years that authoritarian regimes have been in place. At the same time, thirty underestimates the frequency of these purportedly exceptional events because it excludes popular uprisings in countries in other parts of the world that did not become waves – for example, in east and southeast Asia (the Philippines, South Korea, and Indonesia) and sub-Saharan Africa (for example, the Ivory Coast, Ethiopia, and Togo). What we find, in short, is a very high incidence of sparks.

It is somewhat easier to explain why students of communism failed to anticipate the mobilizations of 1987–1990, and, just as importantly, the success of these efforts. For example, these were authoritarian regimes that were anchored by ideology, extraordinary institutional penetration of the party-state, isolation from the international system, and the Soviet role as both a regional hegemon and a Super Power. Moreover, scholars had at that time few historical precedents for 1989 upon which to draw, aside from the wave of uprisings in support of democratic change throughout Europe in 1848. Less understandable is the case of specialists in the MENA, who had the precedents of both 1989 and the colour revolutions at their disposal, as well as the Palestinian intifada and the Lebanese protests in 2005 that were inspired in part by the Orange Revolution in Ukraine that had taken place the previous year. Here, I would hypothesize that these scholars, like their counterparts who specialize in other parts of the world, were stuck in their area study silos. Just as they presumed that the past in these countries contained the most important clues to the future (but it seems only some aspects of the past), so they knew very little about either 1989 or the colour revolutions. Because of the remove afforded by geography and the passage of time, moreover, it was likely easy for them to see 1989 – which is more comparable to the

Arab uprisings than the colour revolutions because of the role of mass protest – as both unique and inevitable.

At the same time, the global wave of democratization since the mid-1970s had prompted a number of specialists on the MENA to focus on the issue of democratization during the 1990s.[20] However, because their region continued to be a holdout to this global dynamic (and thereby cast some doubt on whether the global wave was accurately named) and because of the biases in the study of democratization of assuming its inevitability, as Lisa Anderson has observed in Chapter 2 in this volume, scholars working in this region understandably shifted their attention by the turn of the century to the topic of the durability of authoritarianism.[21] This shift, moreover, resonated with the growing interest in this subject in political science as the payoffs of studying democratization and demo-cratic transitions began to wane and as rational choice approaches to the study of politics became more popular. This trend was particularly well-represented amongst students of authoritarianism who had the lux-ury, in contrast to their counterparts working on more pluralist orders, of restricting their focus to a handful of political leaders and carrying out their studies without the complications introduced by having a wealth of information about politics on the ground and within the palace. Here, it is worth remembering that in his influential book, *The Third Wave*, Samuel Huntington argued that it was unlikely that the Soviet Union and Eastern Europe would join the transition trend because these regimes had succeeded in combining ideology and organization and were thus able to avoid the problem, as argued in his earlier work, that participation would be in a position to outpace institutionalization.[22] This prediction reminds

[20] For an insightful discussion of this flirtation with democracy amongst MENA specialists, see Lisa Anderson, 'Searching Where the Light Shines: Studying Democratization in the Middle East', *Annual Review of Political Science* 9 (2006), 189–214.
[21] Marsha Pripstein Posusney, 'Enduring Authoritarianism: Middle East Lessons for Com-parative Theory', *Comparative Politics* 36: 2 (January 2004), 127–138; Kenneth Perkins, *A History of Modern Tunisia* (Cambridge: Cambridge University Press, 2004); Ellen Lust-Okar, 'Divided They Rule: The Management and Manipulation of Political Oppo-sition'. *Comparative Politics* 36: 2 (January 2004), 159–179; Stephen King, *The New Authoritarianism in the Middle East and North Africa* (Bloomington: Indiana Univer-sity Press, 2009); Jason Brownlee, 'Low Tide After the Third Wave: Exploring Politics Under Authoritarianism'. *Comparative Politics* 34:4 (July 2002), 477–498; and Eva Bellin, 'The Robustness of Authoritarianism in the Middle East'. *Comparative Politics*, 36: 2 (January 2004), 138–157.
[22] Samuel Huntington. *The Third Wave: Democratization in the Late Twentieth Century* (Norman: University of Oklahoma Press, 1992).

us that 1989 was neither as unique nor as inevitable as many analysts have assumed.

All of these arguments lead to two related conclusions. One is that there were some reasons to anticipate the possibility of these waves of protest, and the other is that a persuasive explanation of these waves counsels us to look beyond Kuran and his focus on the information deficits of mass publics. The next section of this chapter will address both issues by arguing that we need to factor authoritarian regimes into our explanations of what happened. Thus, we need to recognize not just the roots of their resilience, which was the focus of many studies on the eve of these events, but also the sources and extent of their vulnerabilities.

Clever Leaders

As already noted, the many deficiencies of these regimes were well-chronicled by scholars who worked on them. However, they tended to be discounted in the rush to identify sources of authoritarian resilience. This was in part because anger is one thing and the ability to mount ambitious popular challenges to authoritarian rulers quite another – as theorists of social movements and of revolutions have emphasized. Popular protests, in short, were assumed to have stringent requirements. In addition, specialists tended to believe that the rot would work slowly through the system, leading not to popular upheavals, largely because of the regime's coercive powers and the constraints on popular protest, but rather to one of several scenarios: the introduction of piecemeal reforms and/or incremental change arising from, say, generational turnover and the accumulation of pressures for change. To borrow from Michael Jones-Correa, the crises of these systems were likely to be slow moving.[23] A third reason was the obvious fact of authoritarian resilience, even in the face of global pressures for democratic change and other challenges. Indeed, much emphasis was placed on the ways in which these challenges invested in authoritarianism by forcing these regimes to make modifications and by giving them opportunities, in the cases of attempted coups and popular protests, to demonstrate their survival skills.

As a result, the key research question, especially in the study of the MENA in the decade preceding the Arab uprisings, became one

---

[23] See, for example, Lynch, *The Arab Uprising* and Bruce Rutherford, *Egypt after Mubarak: Liberalism, Islam and Democracy in the Arab World* (Princeton: Princeton University Press, 2008).

of accounting for the durability of authoritarian leaders and authoritarian regimes. Once that became the question, then not surprisingly, answers were quickly forthcoming. For example, scholars wrote about such topics as the effectiveness of coup-proofing, the use of nationalist rhetoric to mobilize popular support while demobilizing and dividing the opposition, and the construction of alliances with powerful states, such as the role of the United States in co-constituting the Mubarak regime in Egypt.[24] In the case of the communist world, a social compact was introduced in the aftermath of the turbulent 1950s and 1960s that included state-guaranteed jobs, more consumer goods, low and steady prices for basic social and consumer items, reduced repression, and fewer demands on publics to demonstrate their ideological fervour in exchange for popular compliance with the regime.[25]

Although such a strategy was largely unavailable to authoritarian regimes in more recent times because of the diffusion of neoliberal reforms, the Saudis and others in the MENA who enjoy substantial resource rents have been able to incorporate elements of this deal – for instance, by expanding state jobs and the number of bureaucratic agencies, as well as, in the wake of the Arab uprisings, transferring significant sums of money to their citizens and embarking on an ambitious house-building spree.[26] Finally, these authoritarian regimes, like most others, enhanced their powers by projecting an image of invincibility.[27] As Andreas Schedler has observed for authoritarian regimes: 'If opposition parties are the private detectives of elite fissures,[then] governments are the official propagandists of elite unity'.[28]

---

[24] James Quinlivan, 'Coup-Proofing: Its Practice and Consequences in the Middle East'. *International Security* 24: 2 (Fall 1999), 131–165; Valere P. Gagnon, *The Myth of Ethnic War: Serbia and Croatia in the 1990s* (Ithaca: Cornell University Press, 2004); Jason Brownlee, *Democracy Prevention: The Politics of the U.S. Egyptian Alliance* (Cambridge: Cambridge University Press, 2012).

[25] Valerie Bunce, *Leadership Succession and Policy Innovation in Communist and Capitalist Countries* (Princeton: Princeton University Press, 1981) and Valerie Bunce, 'The Empire Strikes Back: The Evolution of the Eastern Bloc from a Soviet Asset to a Soviet Liability'. *International Organization*, 39 (Winter, 1984–1985): 1–46.

[26] See, for example, Steffen Hertog, *Brokers and Bureaucrats: Oil and the State in Saudi Arabia* (Ithaca: Cornell University Press, 2010); Gregory Gause III, 'Rageless in Riyadh: Why Al Saud Dynasty Will Remain'. *Foreign Policy*, 16 March 2011; and Neal McFarquhar, 'In Saudi Arabia, Royal Funds Buy Peace for Now', *New York Times*, 8 June 2011.

[27] Beatrix Magaloni, *Voting for Autocracy: Hegemonic Party Survival and its Demise in Mexico* (Cambridge: Cambridge University Press, 2006).

[28] Andreas Schedler, *The Politics of Uncertainty: Sustaining and Subverting Electoral Authoritarianism*, Unpublished manuscript, April 2012, p. 42.

The logic of a united and powerful front is inescapable. It encourages publics, as Wael Ghonim has argued, for example, in his memoir of the Egyptian uprising, to develop an '... exaggerated perception of the regime's strength'.[29] If there is no credible alternative to the regime, then publics – along with regime allies – have little choice but to comply because in doing so they escape danger and position themselves, where possible, to reap some rents. It was precisely this calculus that was endangered, for example, by the rise of Solidarity in Poland. Choice meant that the communist party's monopoly had been deregulated. This in turn meant that the party had a competitor, and that citizens were in a position to imagine a different future.

What stands out in many studies conducted of authoritarian rule during the last decades of communism and especially during the decade leading up to the Arab upheavals, therefore, is a common theme: the ability of leaders to engage in exceptionally clever 'regime-craft'. This is an argument that is also central in the study of contemporary China.[30] The academic investment in authoritarian resilience, therefore, was sizeable. It was in part for this reason and the temptation to repurpose their knowledge, along with an overestimation of the prerequisites for democracy, that scholars of communism tended, once the regimes they knew so well departed from the scene, to under-predict the rise of democratic experiments in their region and especially the ability of so many of them to endure.

Whether that pattern will be repeated by specialists in the MENA remains to be seen. On the one hand, there are, of course, reasons to doubt democratic change in the MENA, especially in those countries that lack the well-established state boundaries and the strong sense of a common national identity that exist in Egypt and Tunisia; have militaries that are used to wielding domestic power; face enormous social and economic problems; or, like Yemen and Libya, have experienced extraordinary levels of disorder during and after the removal of an exceptionally long-serving leader from power.[31] With these important limitations on the democratic project recognized, however, it is instructive to note that

---

[29] Wael Ghonim, *Revolution 2.0: The Power of the People is Greater than the People of Power: A Memoir* (New York: Houghton-Mifflin, 2012), p. 133.

[30] See, for example, Teresa Wright, *Accepting Authoritarianism: State-Society Relations in China's Reform Era* (Stanford: Stanford University Press, 2010).

[31] See the chapters in this volume by Lisa Anderson (Chapter 2); Gabriele vom Bruck, Atiaf Alwazir, and Benjamin Wiacek (Chapter 13); Karim Mezran (Chapter 14); Roger Owen (Chapter 11); and Rami Zurayk and Anne Gough (Chapter 5).

many countries in the former communist world that became democratic orders after 1989 (immediately or within fifteen years) lacked in fact any democratic tradition and faced at the same time the daunting and simultaneous tasks of building a capitalist economy while constructing democracy and a new state. Some of these countries, moreover, had experienced significant ethnic conflict. The surprising ability of democracy to prevail in these contexts reflected a number of factors, including divisions amongst authoritarians that led to the triumph of democracy largely by default and decisions by former communists and nationalists to support democratic change because it was more in their interest than the alternatives. These arguments have some relevance to those presented by Fawaz Gerges in Chapter 1 in this volume.

The Costs of Success

There is no doubt that authoritarian leaders have been vigilant and that they have developed a creative set of policies and institutions that preempt challenges to their rules and extend their powers. At the same time, however, we have learned and now need to learn again that these strategies did not have the shelf life that many expected. This is because there were important aspects of authoritarian rule that these arguments overlooked. One is the mounting costs, rather than the presumed benefits, associated with iterative confrontations between authoritarian regimes and their opponents.[32]

It has often been suggested in the aftermath of waves (such as by specialists in communist politics) that repeated rounds of popular protests are associated with a greater likelihood of eventual success. This is usually attributed to two factors: the ripening of oppositions and the implication drawn from these jousts that the regime must have some inherent weaknesses to have hosted such repeated challenges. However, there is another interpretation that focusses on learning, and that places interactions between regime and opposition at the centre of the political dynamic. It can be argued that, having succeeded at putting down protests a number of times, the regime becomes complacent; less compelled to monitor its environment and less able to notice changes that had taken place in that environment; and increasingly reliant, as a consequence, on what could be termed the 'same old, same old' diagnoses of their powers and the strategies most likely to protect, if not maximize those powers. In this

---

[32] *The Arab Uprising*, p. 65.

sense, the more experienced the regime has been with the management of protests, the less able it is to deal effectively with them. This is particularly the case because of reputation and the way that it locks regimes into a particular location on the political spectrum.[33]

By contrast, oppositions and their allies are, because of repeated failures, encouraged to innovate as a means of survival, to build institutional capacity and popular support, and, therefore, present themselves as viable alternatives to the regime.[34] In this sense, iterative interactions between regime and opposition can produce in more contentious political environments divergent learning trends that at some point can favour the opposition. This is one reason why, for example, one often sees regimes responding in what can be only seen as stupid ways to popular protests, despite the fact that they are so practiced (as, say, Mubarak, Saleh, and Milosevic were) in these areas and why, moreover, waves of popular protests usually begin in those countries where anti-regime mobilizations have a long history. This also explains an example used earlier. When protests broke out in protest-prone Poland in 1980, the first secretary, Edward Gierek, thought so little of the development that he went on vacation, only to return home and lose his job.

We can also add regime allies to this argument. If it is true, as Daniel Slater has argued, that unruly citizens in authoritarian regimes can encourage key players in the system to coalesce with the regime because of a shared fear of unrest and that this decision can lead in turn to an extension of the state's 'infrastructural grip' and a firming of the coalitional and institutional foundations for durable authoritarianism, then it is also plausible that continued protests are likely to have the effect of unravelling the deal and short-circuiting institutional development.[35] This is because protests indicate to regime allies that the regime is unable to uphold its end of the bargain, and that the taxes they have paid to join the coalition are too high in view of their meagre benefits. Thus, the premium placed on political stability can encourage key actors not just to join, but also to exit from the regime's coalition. At the same time, a

---

[33] See Aleksandar Matovski, 'Public Opinion and Russia's Post-communist Political Development'. Paper presented at the Annual Meeting of the American Political Science Association, 1–4 September 2011.

[34] The impact of contentious politics on the power and the future of authoritarian regimes has been explored by Daniel Slater, *Ordering Power*, and by Vince Boudreau, *Resisting Dictatorship: Repression and Protest in Southeast Asia* (Cambridge: Cambridge University Press, 2004).

[35] *Ordering Power*, pp. 34–36.

point can come when it is better for regime allies to be future-oriented – that is, to assume that the regime will be replaced and to begin siding with likely winners, thereby contributing to a self-fulfilling prophecy – than to remain stuck in the past by staying within the coalition and resisting flirtations with defection. It is precisely these types of recalculations amongst long-time supporters of the regime that we are beginning to see in the Syrian upheaval.

Unintended Consequences

A second problem is that the arguments that grew out of the desire to explain authoritarian resilience ignored an obvious fact of political life, one that is particularly relevant to authoritarian regimes. Politics and policies all have unintended consequences, especially when they suffer from unusually poor information. For example, while it was rational with respect to the goals of legitimating their rule at home and abroad and also fragmenting and co-opting the opposition for authoritarian leaders in the post-communist region to hold competitive elections, it was precisely these political opportunities that under certain circumstances oppositions were able to exploit to their own advantage. The same can be said, more generally, about the issue of stealing elections – a classic example of the earlier point about 'sparks'. Winning handily while purportedly tolerating opposition might look like having your cake and eating it too, but it creates serious problems when the margins of victory strain credulity (as was the case, for instance, with Ben Ali) and when victory comes at the cost of providing ample evidence that the elections were stolen. The latter was not just the lesson of the colour revolutions, but also, for example, of the Egyptian elections in late 2010 and the Iranian presidential elections that took place the previous year. Although neither the Iranian nor the Egyptian contests produced, like most of the colour revolutions, an opposition victory, they did prime publics for mobilizations against the regime.

   To provide another example: Gorbachev looked creative and clever in 1986 and early 1987 when he introduced economic reforms and glasnost, encouraged the rise of popular fronts in support of his reform project, and through a series of speeches and new policies built bridges not just to the West, but also to oppositions and party reformers in Eastern Europe. These actions were seen at the time as policies that were popular with important segments of the public, divided his opponents, and addressed important problems while efficiently buttressing his power as the first secretary. Five years later, however, it was clear – given nationalist mobilizations throughout the Soviet Union, the attempted coup d'état in August 1991, the dissolution of the Soviet state at the end of that year, and Gorbachev's loss of a job because of the departure of the state he led, together with the dissolution of communist party hegemony in Eastern Europe – that there were significant costs associated with the very same policies that had been earlier characterized as being unusually sophisticated because they were attentive to both power and policy.

We can also highlight several recent examples from the MENA. Saudi Arabia acted quickly to contain the damage done by the protests in Tunisia by providing an easy exit for Ben Ali and his family. In doing so, however, Saudi actions ensured that the protests would succeed in their objective – quickly and with little violence – and thereby enhance the external appeal for regime opponents elsewhere of the Tunisian precedent. Actions intended to contain diffusion, therefore, contributed to it – although the Saudis were admittedly, as Madawi Al-Rasheed argues in her contribution to this volume in Chapter 16, between the proverbial rock and a hard place when confronting the MENA wave. It was precisely such difficult decisions, moreover, that the Soviet Union repeatedly faced when confronting the eruption of popular protests in Eastern Europe during communism. While, as often noted, regional powers benefit from the significant resources at their disposal to buttress domestic stability by promoting regional stability, they can also, as is less often recognized, pay a high price for linking the two, especially when citizens in the regional neighbourhood mount large-scale demonstrations that show an ability to spread across borders.[36] Thus, the Saudi regime could very well be more vulnerable than its formidable resources would lead us to expect.

Finally, when Russian politics was not competitive, it made sense in terms of the allocation of political and economic resources for the Putin regime to stagger presidential, parliamentary, and local elections. Also logical in that context was the decision to change the constitution in ways that made it easier for Putin to extend his rule, despite a two-term limit. However, the self-serving logic of these actions began to crumble in 2011 when Putin began to lose his image of invincibility. For example, staggered elections extended the group and geographical reach, as well as the momentum of protests. Moreover, in such circumstances, the opposition is more able to concentrate its efforts and do so sequentially rather than face the daunting project in terms of money and manpower

---

[36] See Bunce, 'The Empire Strikes Back'.

of conducting nationwide and simultaneous campaigns in a country that has eleven time zones. In addition, the possibility that Putin could rule for twelve more years, following his election in March 2012, after having already served eight (and perhaps twelve, if we take into account the role of Medvedev as his puppet), has increased significantly the stakes associated with his return to power. This, plus the cavalier way in which then-President Medvedev passed the mantle back to Putin in mid-2011 in anticipation of the March 2012 presidential election, has had the effect of encouraging popular resistance not just at the level of ordinary citizens, but also (in part because United Russia, the ruling party, suffered a significant loss of seats in December 2011) within the parliament as well.

Uncertainty

The discussion thus far leads us to a more fundamental point about authoritarian politics. As Andreas Schedler has argued in an unpublished book manuscript, analysts of authoritarian regimes have failed to give proper consideration to the impact of uncertainty on how and how well these rulers and regimes function.[37] In particular, authoritarian rulers face two kinds of uncertainty. The first is about their tenure in office. Aside from the monarchies and China's current experiment with a regularized succession process, authoritarian regimes typically lack mechanisms for leadership succession or expose themselves to regular and competitive elections, albeit on a highly favourable playing field. What is striking about succession in these regimes is, first, the lack of institutionalization of the executive office. Such a situation invites challenges and reminds us, as well as them, of how provisional incumbency is. Second, authoritarian regimes often produce exceptionally long tenures – as both the Soviet Union and Eastern European, along with the MENA, regimes demonstrate.[38] Here, it is striking how similar the MENA looked in this regard in 2010–present to the Soviet Union and Eastern Europe in 1989. As previously argued, long tenure can stand in the way of authoritarian learning. Although it can discourage and demobilize regime opponents, it can also lead incumbent leaders, as we saw, for example, in both Tunisia and Egypt, to become too confident of their powers and too attached to

---

[37] *The Politics of Uncertainty: Sustaining and Subverting Electoral Authoritarianism*, Unpublished manuscript, April 2012.
[38] See, for example, Roger Owen, *The Rise and Fall of Arab Presidents for Life* (Cambridge, MA: Harvard University Press, 2012).

the political strategies they used in the past to protect and extend their powers.

Finally, succession is associated with protests. This is most obviously the case with respect to the coloured revolutions where authoritarian incumbents or their anointed successors walked the difficult line between assuring that the elections were won, but then providing publics in the process with the issue of electoral fraud as a trigger for mass protest, and running clean elections, but then risking defeat. However, it is also the case that succession periods correlated in the Soviet Union and Eastern Europe during communism with protest cycles, and the same was true in Mexico the last few decades of *Partido Revolucionario Institucional* hegemony.[39] Finally, there is evidence that protests in Egypt, Libya, and Yemen were influenced by popular anger about actions leaders were taking to pass on power to their sons. These actions, at the same time, created fissures within two sets of key regime allies: the military and the security apparatus.

The other aspect of uncertainty in authoritarian regimes is the information problem – an issue that is also highlighted by Lisa Anderson in Chapter 2 in this volume. This issue takes us back to Kuran, but with the twist that the focus this time is on elites, not publics. Authoritarian leaders, as Schedler has argued, are very uncertain about the facts on the ground, whether inside or outside the palace. Thus, precisely because of the nature of rule in these regimes and the ways they are founded and in turn propagate bad information, their leaders are in unusually poor positions to predict how long they will remain in power and the kinds of challenges they face. At the same time, they are forced to make decisions, many of which have the purpose of defending and extending their power, in the dark or at least the twilight. Informational uncertainty explains, for example, why there are risks attached to virtually all their actions, and why these actions are prone to unintended consequences, along with why, as a result of poor feedback, these policies are so hard to amend after they are taken in ways that would seem to better suit their purposes. The information problem also accounts for some other common characteristics of authoritarian regimes, such as why their surveillance costs escalate along with the number of state jobs and bureaucratic agencies. Authoritarian leaders, therefore, are desperate for information and

---

[39] See Bunce, *Leadership Succession* and Guillermo Trejo, *Popular Movements in Autocracies: Religion, Repression, and Indigenous Collective Action in Mexico* (New York: Cambridge University Press, 2012).

control, the latter because they want it for its own sake and because they think that it will counteract their information deficits. Their reach always exceeds their grasp. Miscalculation is always a possibility.

Authoritarian leaders have dealt with their information deficits in several ways, all of which generate costs and fail to solve the problem. They can assume that it does not exist; engage in faux democratization in the hopes of getting some of the benefits of pluralism, placating publics and dividing oppositions, but without taking on the vulnerabilities associated with a genuinely open society (as with Gorbachev); or increase surveillance. If the cost of the first strategy is arrogance, isolation, and overreach (as with, for instance, the spectacular property grabs of Ben Ali's wife in Tunisia), the cost of the second is expanding opportunities for citizens to mobilize, elites to defect, and alternatives to present themselves. The cost of the third is to generate even more incentives for people around and below the leader to adopt false preferences and for the system to prioritize the blockage of negative information in particular. In all three cases, however, the information problem at best remains and at worse increases.

The information problem that lies at the heart of authoritarian rule has two implications. One is that bargaining between authoritarian regimes and their societies is best understood as a dynamic wherein poorly informed publics who undertake substantial risks if they reveal their private preferences face off against regimes that, while having coercive resources, are nonetheless burdened by the insecurity of their tenure and their own informational deficits. The other is that the vulnerabilities of authoritarian rulers enhance the prospects not just for elite defections, but also for popular upheavals – and combinations of the two in various sequences. As a result: 'The risks of rulers are the opportunities of their opponents'.[40] In this way, we have come full circle – in two ways. Kuran's information problem is not restricted to publics. At the same time, if our discussion of the sources of popular rebellion led us to a discussion of the regimes, the analysis of the latter leads us back to publics.

Conclusion

Why have scholars been repeatedly surprised by waves of large-scale popular uprisings against authoritarian rulers? The purpose of this chapter has been to use this question in order to reflect on the questions of why

---

[40] Schedler, *The Politics of Uncertainty*, p. 167.

people rebel and how authoritarian regimes operate. As we discovered with respect to the first issue, Kuran's idea of sparks and thus the unpredictability of popular upheavals in authoritarian political settings has considerable merit, whether we focus on the events of 1989, the colour revolutions, or the Arab revolts. These waves of anti-regime mobilizations did seem to follow quickly from events that were at once mundane and powerful, especially if we focus attention on the earlier risers in each of these waves. Moreover, the idea of the spread of information as the driver in such processes rang true. At the same time, however, it is hard to explain from this vantage point why the environment was so receptive to such mobilizations, why so many of them succeeded in deposing authoritarian incumbents, and why such waves materialized. Moreover, the sheer number of these mobilizations, coupled with ample evidence that these regimes had serious problems, including in many cases long histories of popular protests, calls into question the claims that sparks are inherently unpredictable and they are distinguished by their ability to circulate a significant amount of new information.

These issues led us to focus on a second topic: the nature of the authoritarian political project. Here, students of authoritarianism, whether addressing the communist, post-communist, or MENA variations, did themselves a disservice by defining their object of study as authoritarian resilience and thereby overlooking or at least minimizing the many limitations on the leaders of these regimes to manage their political environments effectively. Such leaders are burdened in particular not just by their uncertain tenure in office, but also, ironically, by poor information. In this sense, authoritarian politics can be seen as the interaction between poorly informed publics, as Kuran has noted, and, less often recognized as a core feature of these regimes, poorly informed leaders. Whereas publics have anger, numbers, and the potential to coalesce around a common cause on their side in this game, authoritarian leaders draw strength from their ambitions and their coercive resources. Upheavals seem to occur when the playing field evens out; that is, when authoritarians are still burdened by information deficits and fickle allies and when publics are able to surmount their information deficits and thereby capitalize on their resources.

Selected Bibliography

Abdallah, Ahmad. 2009 *The Student Movement and National Politics in Egypt, 1923–1973*. Cairo: American University in Cairo Press.

Abdelrahman, Maha. 2009. '"With the Islamists? – Sometimes. With the State? – Never!" Cooperation between the Left and Islamists in Egypt'. *British Journal of Middle Eastern Studies*, 36, 1 (April), pp. 37–54.

Adler, E., Bicchi, F., Crawford, B., and Del Sarto, R. 2006. *The Convergence of Civilizations: Constructing a Mediterranean Region*. Toronto: University of Toronto Press.

Afary, Janet. 2009. *Sexual Politics in Modern Iran*. Cambridge: Cambridge University Press.

Aghrout, A. and Alexander, M. S. 1997. 'The Euro-Mediterranean New Strategy and the Maghreb Countries'. *European Foreign Affairs Review*, 2, 307–328.

Al-Aswany, Alaa. 2010. *Why Don't the Egyptians Rise Up?* Cairo: Dar al-Shuruq.

Al-Aswany, Alaa. 2011. *On the State of Egypt: What Caused the Revolution*. Trans. by Jonathan Wright. Edinburgh: Canongate.

Alcaro, R. and Haubrich-Seco, M. (eds.). 2012. *Re-thinking Western Policies in Light of the Arab Uprising*. Rome: Edizioni Nuova Cultura/IAI.

Alesina, A. and Rodrik, D. 1994. 'Distributive Politics and Economic Growth', *Quarterly Journal of Economics*, 109, 2, pp. 465–490.

Alexander, Anne. 2009. 'Egypt's Strike Wave: Lessons in Leadership', Research Briefing, ESRC Non-Governmental Public Action Programme.

Alexander, Anne. 2011. 'The Growing Soul of Egypt's Democratic Revolution'. *International Socialist Journal*, 131 (June), online at http://www.isj.org.uk/index.php4?id=741&issue=131 (accessed 24 June 2013).

Alexander, Jeffrey. 2011. *Performative Revolution in Egypt: The Power of Cultural Power*. London: Bloomsbury.

Alford, C. Fred. 2000. 'What Would It Matter if Everything Foucault Said about Prison Were Wrong? "Discipline and Punish" after Twenty Years', *Theory and Society*, 29, 1, pp. 125–146.

Al-Kadri, J. Mayer and Butkevicius, A. 2002. 'Dynamic Products in World Exports', United Nations Conference on Trade and Development, Discussion Paper 159, May.

al-Khodr, Abd al-Aziz. 2010. *al-Saudiyya sirat dawla wa mujtama*. Beirut: Arab Network for Research and Publishing.

Al-Rasheed, Madawi. 2005. 'Localizing the Transnational and Trasnationalizing the Local', in Madawi Al-Rasheed (ed.), *Transnational Connections and the Arab Gulf*. London: Routledge, pp. 1–18.

Al-Rasheed, Madawi. 2007. *Contesting the Saudi State: Islamic Voices from a New Generation*. Cambridge: Cambridge University Press.

Al-Rasheed, Madawi (ed.). 2008. *Kingdom without Borders: Saudi Arabia's Political, Religious and Media Frontiers*. London: Hurst.

Al-Rasheed, Madawi. 2010. *A History of Saudi Arabia*, 2nd edition. Cambridge: Cambridge University Press.

Al-Rasheed, Madawi. 2011a. 'Arabie saoudite: demain, la tempete?' *Politique Internationale*, 132 (Summer), pp. 199–222.

Al-Rasheed, Madawi. 2011b. 'Sectarianism as Counter-Revolution: Saudi Responses to the Arab Spring', *Studies in Ethnicity and Nationalism*, 11, 3, pp. 513–525.

Al-Rasheed, Madawi. 2012a. 'The Meaning of Rights for Women', *World Today*, February.

Al-Rasheed, Madawi. 2012b. 'No Saudi Spring: Anatomy of a Failed Revolution', *Boston Review*, March/April.

Alunni, A. 2012. 'L'Africa di Gheddafi tra ideologia e pragmatismo', in K. Mezran and A. Varvelli (eds.), *Libia. Fine o rinascita di una nazione?* Rome: Donzelli Editore, pp. 137–156.

Amin, Ash. 2008. 'Collective Culture and Urban Public Space', *City*, 12, 1, pp. 5–16.

Amnesty International. 2011a. *Annual Report, Saudi Arabia*, London: Amnesty International.

Amnesty International. 2011b. *The Battle for Libya: Killings, Disappearances and Torture*. London: Amnesty International.

Amnesty International. 2012. *Egypt: A Year after "Virginity Tests", Women Victims of Army Violence Still Seek Justice*. London: Amnesty International.

Anderson, Benedict. 2006. *Imagined Communities*. Revised edition. London: Verso.

Aschauer, D. A. 1989. 'Is Public Expenditure Productive?' *Journal of Monetary Economics*, 23, 2, pp. 177–200.

Ashour, O. 2012. 'Libya's Muslim Brotherhood Faces the Future', *The Middle East Channel, Foreign Policy*, March 9.

Badran, Margo. 1995. *Feminists, Islam, and Nation: Gender and the Making of Modern Egypt*. Princeton, NJ: Princeton University Press.

Baldinetti, A. 2010. *The Origins of the Libyan Nation: Colonial Legacy, Exile and the Emergence of a New Nation-State*. London and New York: Routledge.

Baldinetti, A. 2012. 'La formazione dello Stato e la costruzione dell'identità nazionale', in K. Mezran and A. Varvelli (eds.), *Libia. Fine o rinascita di una nazione*. Rome: Donzelli Editore, pp. 3–20.

Balfour, R. 2012. 'EU Conditionality after the Arab Spring', 16 *Papers IEMed*.

Barany, Z. 2011. 'The Role of the Military', *Journal of Democracy*, 22, 4 (October), pp. 28–39.

Barnett, Clive and Low, Murray (eds.). 2004. *Spaces of Democracy: Geographical Perspectives on Citizenship, Participation and Representation*. London: Sage Publications.

Baron, Beth. 1994. *The Women's Awakening in Egypt: Culture, Society and the Press*. New Haven, CT: Yale University Press.

Bashir, Muhammad Jamal. 2011. *The Book of the Ultras*. Cairo: Dar Dawwin.

Bassiouni, Mustafa and Omar, S. 2007. *Banners of the Strike in the Skies of Egypt: A New Labour Movement in 2007*. Cairo: Center for Socialist Studies.

Bayat, Asef. 1997. *Street Politics: Poor People's Movements in Iran*. New York: Columbia University Press.

Bayat, Asef. 2007. *Making Islam Democratic: Social Movements and the Post-Islamist Turn*. Stanford, CA: Stanford University Press.

Bayat, Asef. 2010. *Life as Politics: How Ordinary People Change the Middle East*. Stanford, CA: Stanford University Press.

Beblawi, H. 1990. 'The Rentier State in the Arab World', in G. Luciani (ed.), *The Arab State*. Berkeley: University of California Press, pp. 85–98.

Beinin, Joel. 1994. 'Will the Real Egyptian Working Class Please Stand Up?' in Zachary Lockman (ed.), *Workers and Working Classes in the Middle East: Struggles, Histories, Historiographies*. Albany: State University of New York Press, pp. 247–270.

Beinin, Joel. 2009. 'Workers' Struggles under "Socialism" and Neoliberalism', in Rabab El-Mahdi and Phil Marfleet (eds.), *Egypt: The Moment of Change*. London: Zed Books, pp. 68–86.

Beinin, Joel. 2011. 'A Workers' Social Movement on the Margin of the Global Neoliberal Order, Egypt 2004–2009', in Joel Beinin and Frédéric Vairel (eds.), *Social Movements, Mobilization, and Contestation in the Middle East and North Africa*. Stanford, CA: Stanford University Press, pp. 181–201.

Beinin, Joel and Hamalawy, Hossam. 2007. 'Strikes in Egypt Spread from Center of Gravity', *Middle East Report Online*, May. Online at http://www.merip.org/mero/mero050907 (accessed 15 February 2010).

Bellin, E. 2002. *Stalled Democracy*. New York: Cornell University Press.

Bellin, E. 2012. 'Reconsidering the Robustness of Authoritarianism in the Middle East', *Comparative Politics* (January), pp. 127–149.

Bicchi, F. 2007. *European Foreign Policy Making toward the Mediterranean*. New York and Basingstoke: Palgrave Macmillan.

Bicchi, F. 2010. 'Dilemmas of Implementation: EU Democracy Assistance in the Mediterranean', *Democratization*, 17, pp. 976–996.

Bicchi, F. and Gillespie, R. 2011. 'The Union for the Mediterranean or the Changing Euro-Mediterranean Relations'. Special issue. *Mediterranean Politics*, 16, 1.

Biscop, S. 2012. 'Mediterranean Mayhem: Lessons for European Crisis Management', in S. Biscop, R. Balfour and M. Emerson (eds.), *An Arab Springboard for EU Foreign Policy?* Egmont Paper 54. Brussels: Academia Press.

Bishara, M. 2012. *The Invisible Arab: The Promise and Peril of the Arab Revolution*. New York: Nation Books.

Blockmans, S. 2012. 'Preparing for a Post-Assad Syria: What Role for the European Union?' *CEPS Commentaries*.

Bonnefoy, Laurent. 2008. 'Salafism in Yemen: A "Saudisation?"' in Madawi Al-Rasheed (ed.), *Kingdom without Borders: Saudi Arabia's Political, Religious and Media Frontiers*. London: Hurst, pp. 245–262.

Börzel, T. A. and Risse, T. 2009. 'The Transformative Power of Europe: The European Union and the Diffusion of Ideas', *FG Working Papers. Research College 'The Transformative Power of Europe'*. Berlin: Free University of Berlin.

Boucek, C. 2010. 'Yemen: Avoiding a Downward Spiral', in C. Boucek and M. Ottaway (eds.), *Yemen on the Brink*. Washington, DC: Carnegie Endowment for International Peace, pp. 1–27.

Bourdieu, Pierre. 1993. *Language and Symbolic Power*. Ed. and Intro by John B. Thompson. Trans. by Gina Raymond and Matthew Adamson. Cambridge: Polity Press.

Bradley, John. 2012. *After the Arab Spring: How Islamists Hijacked the Middle East Revolts*. New York: Palgrave.

Brochmann, G. and Hammer, T. 1999. *Mechanisms of Immigration Control: A Comparative Analysis of European Regulation Policies*. Oxford and New York: Berg.

Browers, Michaelle L. 2009. *Political Ideology in the Arab World: Accommodation and Transformation*. Cambridge: Cambridge University Press.

Brown, C. L. 1984. *International Politics and the Middle East. Old Rules, Dangerous Game*. London, I. B. Tauris.

Butler, Judith. 2011. 'Bodies in Alliance and the Politics of the Street', Lecture in Venice, 7 September, European Institute for Progressive Cultural Policies. Online at http://www.eipcp.net/transversal/1011/butler/en (accessed 4 June 2012).

Calvert, John. 2010. *Sayyid Qutb and the Origins of Radical Islamism*. London: Hurst and Company.

Camau, M. and Geisser, V. 2003. *Le syndrome autoritaire, Politique en Tunisie de Bourghiba à Ben Ali*, Paris: Presses de Sciences-Po.

Carapico, S. 1998. *Civil Society in Yemen: The Political Economy of Activism in Modern Arabia*. Cambridge: Cambridge University Press.

Cassandra. 1995. "The Impending Crisis in Egypt", *The Middle East Journal*, 49 (Winter), pp. 9–27.

Cassarino, J. P. 2012. 'Reversing the Hierarchy of Priorities in EU-Mediterranean Relations', in J. Peters (ed.), *The European Union and the Arab Spring: Promoting Democracy and Human Rights in the Middle East*. New York: Lexington Books, pp. 1–16.

Chalcraft, John. 2005. 'Pluralising Capital, Challenging Eurocentrism: Toward Post-Marxist Historiography', *Radical History Review*, 91, pp. 13–39.

Chalcraft, John. 2009. *Invisible Cage: Syrian Migrant Workers in Lebanon*. Stanford, CA: Stanford University Press.

Chalcraft, John. 2011. 'Labour Protest and Hegemony in Egypt and the Arabian Peninsula', in Alf Nilsen and Sara Motta (eds.), *Social Movements in the Postcolonial*. Houndmills: Palgrave Macmillan, pp. 35–59.

Chalcraft, John. 2012. 'Horizontalism in the Egyptian Revolutionary Process'. *Middle East Report*, 262 (Spring), pp. 6–11.

Chalcraft, John and Noorani, Yaseen (eds.). 2007. *Counterhegemony in the Colony and Postcolony*. Houndmills: Palgrave Macmillan.

Chatterjee, Partha. 2001. 'On Civil and Political Societies in Post-Colonial Democracies', in S. Kaviraj and Sunil Khilnani (eds.), *Civil Society: History and Possibilities*. Cambridge: Cambridge University Press, pp. 165–178.

Colombo, S. and Tocci, N. 2012. 'The EU Response to the Arab Uprising: Old Wine in New Bottles?' in R. Alcaro and M. Haubrich-Seco (eds.), *Re-thinking Western Policies in Light of the Arab Uprising*. Rome: Edizioni Nuova Cultura/IAI, pp. 71–97.

Costa-Font, J. (ed.). 2012. *Europe and the Mediterranean Economy*. London and New York: Routledge.

Daalder, I. H. and Stavridis, J. G. 2012. 'NATO's Victory in Libya: The Right Way to Run an Intervention', *Foreign Affairs*, 91, 2 (March/April), pp. 2–7.

Dabashi, H. 2012. *The Arab Spring: The End of Postcolonialism*. London and New York: Palgrave and Zed Books.

Dabashi, Hamid. 2010. *Iran, the Green Movement and the USA: The Fox and the Paradox*. London: Zed Books.

D'Arcus, Bruce. 2004. 'Dissent, Public Space and the Politics of Citizenship: Riots and the "Outside Agitator"', *Space and Polity*, 8, 3, pp. 358–361.

Day, S. 2010. 'The Political Challenge of Yemen's Southern Movement', in C. Boucek and M. Ottaway (eds.), *Yemen on the Brink*. Washington, DC: Carnegie Endowment for International Peace, pp. 61–74.

De Schoutheete, P. 1997. 'The Creation of the Common Foreign and Security Policy', in E. Regelsberger, P. De Schoutheete and W. Wessels (eds.), *Foreign Policy of the European Union. From EPC to CFSP and Beyond*. Boulder, CO and London: Lyne Rienner Publishers.

De Smet, Brecht. 2012. 'The Prince and the Pharaoh: The Collaborative Project of Egyptian Workers and Their Intellectuals in the Face of Revolution'. Unpublished PhD Dissertation, University of Utrecht.

Deeb, M. J. 1991. *Libya's Foreign Policy in North Africa*. Boulder, CO: Westview Press.

Del Sarto, R. and Schumacher, T. 2005. 'From EMP to ENP: What's at Stake with the European Neighbourhood Policy towards the Southern Mediterranean?' *European Foreign Affairs Review*, 10, pp. 17–38.

Droz-Vincent, P. 2007. 'From Political to Economic Actors, the Transforming Role of Middle Eastern Armies', in O. Schlumberger (ed.), *Debating Arab Authoritarianism*. Stanford, CA: Stanford University Press, pp. 195–211.

Droz-Vincent, P. 2011a 'Authoritarianism, Revolutions, Armies and Arab Regime Transitions', *The International Spectator*, 46, 2 (June), pp. 5–21.

Droz-Vincent, P. 2011b. 'A Return of Armies to the Forefront of Arab Politics?' Working Paper 11/21, Rome, Istituto Affari Internazionali, July.

Duboc, Marie. 2011. 'Egyptian Leftist Intellectuals' Activism from the Margins: Overcoming the Mobilization/Demobilization Dichotomy', in Joel Beinin and Frédéric Vairel (eds.), *Social Movements, Mobilization, and Contestation in the Middle East and North Africa*. Stanford, CA: Stanford University Press, pp. 61–82.

Duke, S. 2012. 'The European External Action Service: Antidote against Incoherence?' *European Foreign Affairs Review*, 17, pp. 45–68.

Eken, S., Helbling, T. and Mazarei, A. 1997. *Fiscal Policy and Growth in the Middle East and North Africa Region*. London: International Monetary Fund.

El-Erian, M. A, Bisat, A. and Helbling, T. 1997. *Growth, Investment, and Saving in the Arab Economies*. London: International Monetary Fund.

El-Erian, M. A. and Fennell, S. 1997. *The Economy of the Middle East and North Africa in 1997*. London: International Monetary Fund.

El-Erian, M. A., Fennell S., Eken, S. and Chaffour, J. P. 1998. *Growth and Stability in the Middle East and North Africa*. London: International Monetary Fund.

El-Mahdi, Rabab. 2009. 'The Democracy Movement: Cycles of Protest', in Rabab El-Mahdi and Phil Marfleet (eds.), *Egypt: The Moment of Change*. London: Zed Books, pp. 87–102.

El-Mahdi, Rabab and Marfleet, Phil (eds.). 2009. *Egypt: The Moment of Change*. London: Zed Books.

El-Tahawi, Mona. 2012. 'Why Do They Hate Us?' *Foreign Policy* (May–June). Online at http://www.foreignpolicy.com/articles/2012/04/23/why_do_they_hate_us

Elyachar, Julia. 2005. *Markets of Dispossession: NGOs, Economic Development, and the State in Cairo*. Durham, NC: Duke University Press.

Engene, J. O. 2004. *Terrorism in Western Europe: Explaining the Trends since 1950*. Cheltenham and Northampton, MA: Edward Elgar.

Everhart, S. S. and Sumlinski, M. A. 2001. *Trends in Private Investment in Developing Countries, Statistics for 1970–2000 and the Impact on Private Investment of Corruption and the Quality of Public Investment*. International Finance Corporation. Washington, D.C.

Fahmi, Wael Salah. 2009. 'Bloggers' Street Movement and the Right to the City: (Re)claiming Cairo's Real and Virtual "Spaces of Freedom"', *Environment and Urbanization*, 21, 1 (April), pp. 89–107.

Faraj, Muhammad Abd al-Salam. 1980. *Holy War: The Neglected Obligation*. Cairo: Publications of the Islamic Movement in Egypt.

Fasano, U. and Wang, Q. 2001. *Fiscal Expenditure Policy and Non-Oil Economic Growth: Evidence from GCC Countries*. London: International Monetary Fund.

Filiu, Jean-Pierre. 2011. *The Arab Revolution: Ten Lessons from the Democratic Uprising*. London: Hurst.

Foucault, Michel. 1991. *Discipline and Punish: The Birth of the Prison*. London: Penguin.

Galal, A. and Reiffers, J. L. (eds.), 2010. *The Euro-Mediterranean Partnership at Crossroads: FEMISE Report 2010*. FEMISE. Marseille.

Gause III, F. Gregory. 2011. *Saudi Arabia in the New Middle East*, Report 63. New York: Council on Foreign Relations.

Gause III, Gregory. 1990. *Saudi-Yemeni Relations: Domestic Structures and Foreign Influence*. New York: Columbia University Press.

Gerges, A. Fawaz. 2011. 'Out of the Shadows'. New Statesman.

Gerges, A. Fawaz. 2012. Obama and the Middle East: The End of America's Moment? New York: Palgrave Macmillan.

Gerges, A. Fawaz. 2013 'The Islamic Moment: From Islamic State to Civil Islam?' Political Science Quarterly, Vol. 128, No. 3.

Ghanim, David. 2011. *Iraq's Dysfunctional Democracy*. Santa Barbara, CA: Praeger.

Gheissari, Ali. 1998. *Iranian Intellectuals in the Twentieth Century*. Austin: University of Texas Press

Ghonim, Wael. 2012. *Revolution 2.0: The Power of the People Is Greater Than the People in Power*. London: Harper Collins.

Gillespie, Eleanor (ed.). 2010. *Politics, Succession and Risk in Saudi Arabia*. Gulf States Newsletter Special Report, January.

Goldstone, Jack A. 2011. 'Understanding the Revolutions of 2011', *Foreign Affairs*, 90, 3, 8–16.

Grossman, G. M. and Helpman, E. 1990. 'Comparative Advantage and Long-Run Growth', *American Economic Review*, 80, 4, pp. 796–815.

Guazzone, L. and Pioppi, D. (eds.). 2012. *The Arab State and Neo-Liberal Globalization*, 2nd edition. Reading: Ithaca Press.

Guha, Ranajit. 1998. *Dominance without Hegemony: History and Power in Colonial India*. Cambridge, MA: Harvard University Press.

Gunning, Jeroen. 2012. 'Seeing the Egyptian "Revolution" through Social Movement Glasses: Networks, Frames, Protest Cycles and Structural Changes'. Unpublished paper delivered at BRISMES Annual Conference, LSE, London, 26–28 March.

Habermas, Jürgen. 1996. *Between Facts and Norms*. Trans. William Rehg. Cambridge, MA: MIT Press.

Habib, John, *Ibn Saud's Warriors of Islam: The Ikhwan of Najd and their Role in the Creation of the Saudi Kingdom, 1910–1930*, Leiden: Brill, 1987.

Halpern, M. 1963. *The Politics of Social Change in the Middle East and North Africa*. Princeton, NJ: Princeton University Press.

Hamiddin, Abdullah. 2012. *al-kaynouna al-mutanaghima* (Harmonious Being), 2nd edition. Dubai: Madarek.

Hammer, J. 2012. 'Women, the Libyan Rebellion's Secret Weapon', *Smithsonian Magazine*, April.

Hardt, Michael and Antonio Negri. 2011. 'Arabs Are Democracy's New Pioneers'. *The Guardian*. 24 February. Online at http://www.guardian.co.uk/commentisfree/2011/feb/24/arabs-democracy-latin-america (accessed 24 June 2013).

Hegghammer, Thomas and Lacroix, Stephane. 2007. 'Rejectionist Islamism in Saudi Arabia: The Story of Juhayman al-Utaybi Revisited', *International Journal of Middle East Studies*, 93, 1, pp. 103–122.

Heydemann, S. 2000. *War, Institutions, and Social Change in the Middle East*. Berkeley: University of California Press.

Hind, Dan. 2010. *The Return of the Public*. London: Verso.

Hinnebusch, R. 2003. *The International Politics of the Middle East*. Manchester: Manchester University Press.

Hoekman, B. M. and Djankov, S. 1996. 'The European Union's Mediterranean Free Trade Initiative'. *The World Economy*, 19, 4, pp. 387–406.

Holden, P. 2008. 'Development through Integration? EU Aid Reform and the Evolution of Mediterranean Aid Policy', *Journal of International Development*, 20, pp. 230–244.

Hollis, R. 2012. 'No Friend of Democratization: Europe's Role in the Genesis of the "Arab Spring"', *International Affairs*, 88, pp. 81–94.

Huntington, S. 1957. *The Soldier and the State: The Theory and Politics of Civil-Military Relations*. Cambridge, MA: Harvard University Press.

Huntington, S. P. 1991. *The Third Wave: Democratization in the Late Twentieth Century*. Norman: University of Oklahoma Press.

Hurewitz, J. 1969. *Middle East Politics, the Military Dimension*. New York: Praeger.

Ibrahim, Fuad. 2006. *The Shi'is of Saudi Arabia*. London: Saqi.

Idle, Nadia and Nunns, Alex. 2011. *Tweets from Tahrir*. Doha: Bloomsbury Qatar Foundation Publishing.

International Crisis Group. 2002. *Yemen: Beyond the Myth of a Failed State*. Middle East Report No. TK, Amman and Brussels.

International Crisis Group. 2011. *Holding Libya Together: Security Challenges after Qadhafi*. Middle East/North Africa Report 115, 14 December.

International Crisis Group. 2011. *Popular Protest in the Middle East and North Africa (V): Making Sense of Libya*. Middle East/North Africa Report 107, 6 June.

International Crisis Group. 2011. *Popular Protest in the Middle East and North Africa (VI): The Syrian People's Slow-Motion Revolution*, Middle East/North Africa Report 108, 6 July.

International Crisis Group. 2011. *Popular Protest in the Middle East and North Africa (VII): The Syrian Regime's Slow-Motion Suicide*. Middle East/North Africa Report 109, 13 July.

Ismail, Salwa. 2006. *Political Life in Cairo's New Quarters: Encountering the Everyday State*. Minneapolis: Minnesota University Press.

Ismail, Salwa. 2011. 'The Syrian Uprising: Imagining and Performing the Nation', *Studies in Ethnicity and Nationalism*, 11, 3, pp. 538–549.

Jones, C. I. 1995. 'Time Series Tests of Endogenous Growth Models', *Quarterly Journal of Economics*, 110, 2, pp. 485–517.

Kamrava, M. 2000. 'Military Professionalization and Civil-Military Relations in the Middle East', *Political Science Quarterly*, 115, 1, pp. 67–92.

Kandiyoti, Deniz (ed.). 1991. *Women, Islam and the State*. Philadelphia: Temple University Press.

Keddie, Nikki R. 2007. *Women in the Middle East: Past and Present*. Princeton, NJ: Princeton University Press.

Ketchley, Neil. 2012. 'The People and the Army Are One Hand! A Micro-Sociology of Fraternisation in the Egyptian Revolution'. Paper presented at BRISMES Annual Conference, 26–28 March.

Khalil, Karima. 2011. *Messages from Tahrir*. Cairo: American University in Cairo Press.

King, R., Lazaridis, G., and Tsardanidis, C. 2000. *Eldorado or Fortress? Migration in Southern Europe*. London and New York: Macmillan and St. Martin's Press.

Kirzner, I. M. 1997. *How Markets Work: Disequilibrium, Entrepreneurship and Discovery*. London: The Institute of Economic Affairs.

Knight, Alan. 2007. 'Hegemony, Counterhegemony and the Mexican Revolution', in John Chalcraft and Yaseen Noorani (eds.), *Counterhegemony in the Colony and Postcolony*. Houndmills: Palgrave Macmillan, pp. 23–48.

Koenig, N. 2011. 'The EU and the Libyan Crisis: In Quest of Coherence?' IAI Working Papers 11, 19 July, Rome.

Lacher, W. 2011. 'Families, Tribes and Cities in the Libyan Revolution', *Middle East Policy*, 18, 4 (Winter), pp. 140–154.

Lacher, W. 2012. 'Is Autonomy for Northeastern Libya Realistic?' *Sada Journal*, 21 March.

Lefèbvre, Henri. 2000. *The Production of Space*. Trans. D. Nicolson-Smith. Oxford: Blackwell Publishers.

Lemarchand, R. 1988. *The Green and the Black: Qadhafi's Policies in Africa*. Bloomington: Indiana University Press.

Lockman, Zachary. 1994. 'Introduction', in *Workers and Working Classes in the Middle East: Struggles, Histories, Historiographies*. Albany: State University of New York Press, pp. xi–xxxi.

Low, Setha and Smith, Neil (eds.). 2006. *The Politics of Public Space*. London: Routledge.

Lucas, R. E. 1988. 'On the Mechanics of Economics Development', *Journal of Monetary Economics*, 22, 1, pp. 3–42.

Luciani, G. 1990. 'Allocation vs. Production States', in G. Luciani (ed.), *The Arab State*. Berkeley: University of California Press, pp. 65–84.

Lynch, Marc. 2012a. *Pressure, Not War: A Pragmatic and Principled Policy Towards Syria*. Policy Brief, Centre for New American Security, February.

Lynch, Marc. 2012b. *The Arab Uprising: The Unfinished Revolutions of the New Middle East*. New York: Public Affairs.

Makram-Ebeid, Dina. 2010. '"We Are Like Father and Son": Neo-Liberalism and Everyday Production Relations at the Egyptian Iron and Steel Plant in Helwan'. Unpublished paper given at MESA Annual Conference, San Diego.

Matynia, Elzbieta. 2009. *Performative Democracy*. Boulder, CO: Paradigm Publishers.

Mehrez, Samia (ed.). 2012. *Translating Egypt's Revolution*. Cairo: American University in Cairo Press.

Mernissi, Fatima. 1991. *Women in Islam: An Historical and Theological Enquiry*. Trans. Mary Jo Lakeland. Oxford: Blackwell.

Mezran, K. 2012. 'La rivolta', in K. Mezran and A. Varvelli (eds.), *Libia. Fine o rinascita di una nazione?* Rome: Donzelli Editore, pp. 157–176.

Mezran, K. and Varvelli, A. 2012. *Libia. Fine o rinascita di una nazione?* Rome: Donzelli Editore.

Mir Hosseini, Ziba. 1999. *Islam and Gender: The Religious Debate in Contemporary Iran*. Princeton, NJ: Princeton University Press.

Mir Hosseini, Ziba. 2000. *Marriage on Trial: A Study of Islamic Family Law.* London: I. B. Tauris.

Mossallam, Alia. 2012. "These Are Liberated Territories – Everyday Resistance in Egypt", in Larbi Sadiki (ed.), *Democratic Transition in the Middle East: Unmaking Power.* London: Routledge, pp. 124–152.

Munib, Abd al-Mun'im. 2010. *The Renunciation of the Holy Warriors: The Hidden Story of the Renunciation of Holy War and the Islamic Group in and out of Prison.* Cairo: Madbuli.

Mustapha, Y. 2012. 'Donors' Responses to Arab Uprisings: Old Medicine in New Bottles?' *IDS Bulletin*, 43, pp. 99-109.

Naguib, Sameh. 2009. 'Islamism(s) Old and New', in Rabab El- Mahdi and Phil Marfleet (eds.), *Egypt: The Moment of Change.* London: Zed Books, pp. 103–119.

Najmabadi, Afsaneh. 1991. 'Hazards of Modernity: Women, State and Ideology in Contemporary Iran', in Deniz Kandiyoti (ed.), *Women, Islam and the State.* Philadelphia: Temple University Press, pp. 48–76.

Owen, R. 1987. 'Arab Armies Today', Paper presented for the BRISMES conference at Exeter University, July.

Owen, R. 2012. *The Rise and Fall of Arab Presidents for Life.* Cambridge, MA and London: Harvard University Press.

Özcan, K. M. and Özcan, Y. Z. 2005. 'Determinants of Private Savings in the Middle East and North Africa', in N. A. Colton and S. Neaime (eds.), *Money and Finance in the Middle East Missed Opportunities or Future Prospects, Vol. 6.* Bingley: Emerald Group Limited, pp. 95–113.

Pace, M. 2009. 'Paradoxes and Contradictions in EU Democracy Promotion in the Mediterranean: The Limits of EU Normative Power', *Democratization*, 16, pp. 39–58.

Pace, M. and Cavatorta, F. 2012. 'The Arab Uprisings in Theoretical Perspective – An Introduction', *Mediterranean Politics*, 17, pp. 125–138.

Paciello, M. C. 2011. *La Primavera Araba: sfide e opportunita' economiche e sociali.* Rome: CNEL/IAI.

Pack, J. and Barfi, B. 2012. *In War's Wake: The Struggle for Post-Qadhafi Libya,* Policy Focus 118, The Washington Institute for Near East Policy.

Page, J. 1998. 'From Boom to Bust and Back? The Crisis of Growth in the Middle East and North Africa' in N. Shafik, ed., Prospects for Middle Eastern and North African Economies – From Boom to Bust and Back? London: Macmillan Press, pp. 133–158.

Pargeter, A. 2009. 'Localism and Radicalization in North Africa: Local Factors and the Development of Political Islam in Morocco, Tunisia and Libya', *International Affairs*, 85, 5, pp. 1031–1044.

Perlmutter, A. 1977. *The Military and Politics in Modern Times.* New Haven, CT: Yale University Press.

Perthes, V. 2011. 'Europe and the Arab Spring', *Survival*, 53, pp. 73–84.

Phillips, S. 2008. *Yemen's Democratic Experiment in Regional Perspective: Patronage and Pluralized Authoritarianism.* New York: Palgrave Macmillan.

Phillips, S. 2011. *Yemen and the Politics of Permanent Crisis.* London: International Institute for Strategic Studies.

Picard, E. 1993. 'State and Society in the Arab World: Towards a New Role for the Security Services?' in B. Korany, P. Noble and R. Brynen (eds.), *The Many Faces of National Security in the Arab World*. London: Macmillan, pp. 258–274.

Pierros, F., Meunier, J. and Abrams, S. 1999. *Bridges and Barriers: The European Union's Mediterranean Policy, 1961–1998*. Aldershot: Ashgate.

Posusney, M. Pripstein and Angrist, M. (eds.). 2005. *Authoritarianism in the Middle East: Regimes and Resistance*. Reading: Ithaca Press.

Posusney, Marsha. P. 1993. 'The Moral Economy of Labor Protest in Egypt', *World Politics*, 46, 1, pp. 83–120.

Radwan, S. and Reiffers, J. L. (eds.). 2005. *FEMISE Report. The Euro-Mediterranean Partnership, 10 Years after Barcelona: Achievements and Perspectives*. FEMISE. Marseille.

Report of the Secretary-General on the United Nations' Support Mission in Libya, 1 March 2012.

Roberts, David. 2012. 'The Arab World's Unlikely Leader: Embracing Qatar's Expanding Role in the Region', Project on Middle East Democracy, 13 March.

Romer, P. M. 1986. 'Increasing Returns and Long-Run Growth', *Journal of Political Economy*, 94, 5, pp. 1002–1037.

Ronen, Y. 2008. *Qaddafi's Libya in World Politics*. London: Rienner Publishers.

Rosefsky-Wickham, Carrie. 2002. *Mobilizing Islam: Religion, Activism and Political Change in Egypt*. New York: Columbia University Press.

Rosefsky-Wickham, Carrie. 2011. 'The Muslim Brotherhood after Mubarak', *Foreign Affairs*, 3 February. Online at http://www.foreignaffairs.com/articles/67348/carrie-rosefsky-wickham/the-muslim-brotherhood-after-mubarak#

Rubin, Barry. 2002. *Islamic Fundamentalism in Egyptian Politics*. Updated Edition. Houndmills: Palgrave Macmillan.

Ryan, Curtis. 2011. 'Reform Retreats amid Jordan's Political Storms', Merip Online Report, 10 June. Online at http://www.merip.org/mero/mero061005

Sala-I-Martin, X. and Artadi, E. V. 2002. 'Economic Growth and Investment in the Arab World', Discussion Paper No. 0203–08, Columbia University, New York.

Sayigh, Y. 2011. 'Agencies of Coercion: Armies and Internal Security Forces', *International Journal of Middle East Studies*, 43, 3, pp. 403–405.

Sayigh, Y. 2012. 'Above the State: The Officers' Republic in Egypt', Beirut, Carnegie Middle East Center, The Carnegie Papers, August.

Schimmelfennig, F. 2001. 'The Community Trap: Liberal Norms, Rhetorical Action, and the Eastern Enlargement of the European Union', *International Organization*, 55, pp. 47–80.

Schlumberger, O. (ed.). 2007. *Debating Arab Authoritarianism*. Stanford, CA: Stanford University Press.

Schumacher, T. 2011. 'The EU and the Arab Spring: Between Spectatorship and Actorness', *Insight Turkey*, 13, pp. 107–119.

Schumacher, T. Forthcoming. 'The EU and Democracy Promotion: Readjusting to the Arab Spring', in L. Sadiki (ed.), *The Routledge Handbook on the Arab Spring*. London: Routledge.

Scott, Rachel. 2012. 'What Might the Muslim Brotherhood Do with Al-Azhar? Religious Authority in Egypt', *Die Welt des Islam*, 52, pp. 131–165.

Seeberg, P. 2012. 'Syria and the EU. The crisis in Syria and the international sanctions with a focus on Syrian-EU relations'. *Working Paper Center for Mellemoststudier.*

Sewell, William. H. 1993. 'Towards a Post-Materialist Rhetoric for Labour History', in L. Berlanstein (ed.), *Rethinking Labour History*. Urbana: University of Illinois Press, pp. 15–38.

Shari`ati, Ali. n.d. *Fatima Is Fatima*. Tehran: The Shari`ati Foundation.

Silverstein, Paul. 2011. 'Weighing Morocco's New Constitution', Merip Online Report, 5 July. Online at http://www.merip.org/mero/mero070511

Singerman, Diane. 1995. *Avenues of Participation: Family, Politics, and Networks in Urban Quarters of Cairo*. Princeton, NJ: Princeton University Press.

Smith, K. E. 1998. 'The Use of Political Conditionality in the EU's Relations with Third Countries: How Effective?' *European Foreign Affairs Review*, 3, pp. 253–274.

Smith, K. E. 2005. 'The Outsiders: The Neighbourhood Policy', *International Affairs*, 81, 4, pp. 757–773.

Solow, R. M. 1956. 'A Contribution of the Theory to Economic Growth', *Quarterly Journal of Economics*, 70, 1, pp. 65–94.

Springborg, R. and Henry, C. 2011. 'Army Guys', *The American Interest*, May–June.

St. John, R. B. 2008. *Libya from Colony to Independence*. Oxford: Oneworld.

St. John, R. B. 2011. *Libyan Myths and Realities*, Report for the Royal Danish Defense College, August.

St. John, R. B. 2012. *A Transatlantic Perspective on the Future of Libya*, Mediterranean Paper Series, the German Marshall Fund of the United States, May.

Tarrow, Sidney. 1998. *Power in Movement: Social Movements and Contentious Politics*. Cambridge: Cambridge University Press.

Tocci, N. and Cassarino, J. P. 2011. 'Rethinking the EU's Mediterranean policies Post-1/11', Rome: IAI Working Papers, 11–06.

Topol, Sarah. 2012. 'Feminism, Brotherhood Style', *Foreign Policy* (April). Online at http://www.foreignpolicy.com/articles/2012/04/23/Feminism_Brotherhood_Style

Tovias, A. 1977. *Tariff Preferences in Mediterranean Diplomacy*. London: Macmillan.

Traboulsi, Fawwaz. 2009. 'Public Spheres and Urban Space: A Critical Comparative Approach', in Seteney Shami (ed.), *Publics, Politics and Participation – Locating the Public Sphere in the Middle East and North Africa*. New York: Social Science Research Council, pp. 45–63.

Tripp, Charles. 2007. *A History of Iraq*. Cambridge: Cambridge University Press.

Ulrichsen, Kristian Coates. 2011. 'Qatar and the Arab Spring', *Open Democracy*, 12 April.

Van Vooren, B. 2011. 'A Legal-Institutional Perspective on the European External Action Service', *Common Market Law Review*, 48, pp. 475–502.

Vandewalle, D. 1998. *Libya since Independence: Oil and State-Building*. London: Cornell University Press.

Vandewalle, D. 2006. *A History of Modern Libya*. Cambridge: Cambridge University Press.

Varvelli, A. 2010. 'Libia. Vere riforme oltre la retorica?' *ISPI Analysis*, 17.

Varvelli, A., Zupi, M. and Hassan, S. 2012. *La Libia dopo Gheddafi*, Osservatorio di Politica Internazionale, n. 52 – March–April.

Villa, M. 2012. 'Un caso poco studiato di rentier state', in K. Mezran and A. Varvelli (eds.), *Libia. Fine o rinascita di una nazione?* Rome: Donzelli Editore, pp. 61–82.

Vitalis, Robert. 2007. *America's Kingdom: Mythmaking on the Saudi Oil Frontier*. Stanford, CA: Stanford University Press.

vom Bruck, Gabriele. 2011. 'When Will Yemen's Night End?' *Le Monde Diplomatique*, July.

Walton, J. and Seddon, D. 1994. *Free Markets and Food Riots: The Politics of Global Adjustment*. Oxford: Blackwell.

Ware, L. B. 1985. 'The Role of the Military in the Post-Bourguiba Era', *The Middle East Journal*, 39, 1 (Winter), pp. 27–47.

Wedeen, L. 2008. *Peripheral Visions: Publics, Power, and Performance in Yemen*. Chicago: Chicago University Press.

Whitman, R. G. and Jurcos, A. E. 2012. 'The Arab Spring, the Eurozone Crisis and the Neighbourhood: A Region in Flux', *Journal of Common Market Studies*, 50, pp. 147–151.

Williams, Raymond. 1983. *Keywords*. New York: Oxford University Press.

Wingenbach, Edward C 2011. *Institutionalising Agonistic Democracy: Post-Foundationalism and Political Liberalism*. Farnham: Ashgate Publishing.

Wright, Steven. 2012. 'Qatar', in Christopher Davidson (ed.), *Power and Politics in the Persian Gulf Monarchies*. London: Hurst, pp. 113–133.

Zahid, Muhammed and Michael Medley. 2006. 'Muslim Brotherhood in Egypt and Sudan', *Review of African Political Economy*, 33, 110 (September), pp. 693–708.

Zubaida, Sami. 2003. *Law and Power in the Islamic World*. London: I. B. Tauris.

Zubaida, Sami. 2009. *Islam, the People and the State*, 3rd edition. London: I. B. Tauris.

Zubaida, Sami. 2011. *Beyond Islam: A New Understanding of the Middle East*. London: I. B. Tauris.

Index